Corporate Responsibility

THE UNIVERSITY OF

Corporate Responsibility

SECOND EDITION

MICHAEL BLOWFIELD

ALAN MURRAY

OXFORD
UNIVERSITY PRESS

OXFORD

UNIVERSITY PRESS

Great Clarendon Street, Oxford OX2 6DP

Oxford University Press is a department of the University of Oxford.
It furthers the University's objective of excellence in research, scholarship,
and education by publishing worldwide in

Oxford New York

Auckland Cape Town Dar es Salaam Hong Kong Karachi
Kuala Lumpur Madrid Melbourne Mexico City Nairobi
New Delhi Shanghai Taipei Toronto

With offices in

Argentina Austria Brazil Chile Czech Republic France Greece
Guatemala Hungary Italy Japan Poland Portugal Singapore
South Korea Switzerland Thailand Turkey Ukraine Vietnam

Oxford is a registered trade mark of Oxford University Press
in the UK and in certain other countries

Published in the United States
by Oxford University Press Inc., New York

© Oxford University Press 2011

British Library Cataloguing in Publication Data

Data available

Library of Congress Cataloging in Publication Data

Typeset by Techset Composition Ltd, Salisbury, UK
Printed in Italy on acid-free paper by L.E.G.O. S.p.A.

ISBN 978–0–19–958107–8

10 9 8 7 6 5 4 3

■ PREFACE

The subject of 'corporate responsibility' is at a stage at which it needs a text that introduces the key ideas and practices in the field, and places them in wider contexts. As we finish this fully revised Second Edition, the news media is filled with acts of corporate responsibility: from Foxconn in China to BP in the Gulf of Mexico to the Trafigura court case in the Netherlands to the inquiries into Goldman Sachs' financial dealings in the USA. By the time this book is published there will be new stories of both negligence and innovation. What links the old and the new is that they are all the result of how business' role in society is defined, negotiated and managed. That is the domain of corporate responsibility, and explaining that domain is the purpose of this book.

The book is intended for students and tutors of corporate responsibility at both undergraduate and graduate levels, although it is also relevant to other disciplines that are concerned with the role of business in modern society. The text provides a strong framework for studying corporate responsibility, which links a wealth of theoretical analysis with more practitioner-oriented materials. Its 14 chapters are divided into three broad themes: the origins and meaning of corporate responsibility; how it is being managed and implemented; its impact to date and likely future directions. Under these themes, we examine such topics as: the social and historical context of corporate responsibility, and its business case; key areas of management practice, including stakeholder engagement, partnership, ethical supply chains, social auditing, and corporate governance; the role of responsible investment, as well as that of government and civil society.

We provide an international dimension in that the theories and examples are drawn from around the world. We provide a critical perspective in that we do not advocate any particular ideas about corporate responsibility; preferring instead to compare and contrast a host of differing perspectives. Our aim above all is to assist in building an understanding of the potential and limitations of the private sector in areas of extra-financial performance.

Michael Blowfield
Alan Murray

ACKNOWLEDGEMENTS

This book reflects our experiences as academics, practitioners, and consultants working in the field of corporate responsibility for companies, civil societies, and government organizations. I am grateful to the many friends and colleagues who have knowingly, or unknowingly, contributed to that experience. I am grateful also to the Smith School of Enterprise and the Environment at the University of Oxford for granting me the time to revise the second edition. It would be unfair to single out anyone in particular, but this in no way diminishes my accumulated gratitude over the years, and I trust that those involved will understand why the only people mentioned by name are John MacLean, Catherine, Ieuan, Lucy, and Terry.

MEB

I would like to acknowledge the work of the Centre for Social and Environmental Accounting Research at the University of St Andrews—particularly the efforts of Rob and Sue Gray, and all of the researchers who have attended the annual summer schools over the last decade or so, whose scholarship and rigour has helped to develop and inform my views and opinions. I would also like to acknowledge the love of Kathryn, Rosie, Ellie, and Florence in supporting me in this endeavour.

AM

We are grateful to the anonymous reviewers whose comments have added immensely to the text, and to Cary Krosinsky, William Frederick, the Center for Corporate Citizenship at Boston College, CANOPUS, and the Ethical Trading Initiative, each of which has granted permission to use some of their materials. Crown copyright is reproduced under Class License Number C20060110631 with the permission of OPSI and the Queen's printer for Scotland.

■ NEW TO THIS EDITION

- A new chapter on small and medium sized enterprises has been included to highlight this area of increasing importance.

- Increased coverage of social enterprise has been provided throughout the text.

- A dedicated chapter on developing economies has been added to this edition of the book.

- Longer end-of-chapter case studies have been incorporated in addition to the 'snap-shot cases' within the text of each chapter, to provide material for extended seminar discussions or assignments.

- The Online Resource Centre has been updated and expanded; this now includes a number of film trailers related to corporate responsibility.

■ CONTENTS

■ LIST OF FIGURES

■ LIST OF BOXES

LIST OF CASE STUDIES

■ LIST OF SNAPSHOTS

■ LIST OF ABBREVIATIONS

ACCA	Association of Chartered Certified Accountants
BAU	business-as-usual
BCCI	Bank of Credit and Commerce International
BITC	Business in the Community
BSE	bovine spongiform encephalopathy
BSR	Business for Social Responsibility
CCAB	Consultative Committee of Accountancy Bodies
CEO	chief executive officer
CERES	Coalition for Environmentally Responsible Economies
CFA	chartered financial analyst
CPI	University of Cambridge Programme for Industry
CSEAR	Centre for Social and Environmental Accounting Research
CSP	corporate social performance
CSR	corporate social responsibility
EAI	Enhanced Analytics Initiative
EBITDA	earnings before interest, taxes, depreciation, and amortization
EIL	Environmental Impairment Liability Centre for Competence
EIRIS	Ethical Investment Research Service
EPA	Environmental Protection Agency
EPZ	export processing zone
ESG	environmental, social, and governance
ETF	Exchange Traded Fund
ETI	Ethical Trading Initiative
EU	European Union
EurepGAP	European Retailers Group Guidelines on Good Agricultural Practice
EuroSIF	European Sustainable and Responsible Investment Forum
FDI	foreign direct investment
FLA	Fair Labor Association
FRC	Financial Reporting Council
FSC	Forest Stewardship Council
GAAP	Generally Accepted Accounting Principles
GEMI	Global Environmental Management Initiative
GRI	Global Reporting Initiative
IBLF	International Business Leaders' Forum
ILO	International Labour Organization
IMF	infant milk formula
IPCC	United Nations Intergovernmental Panel on Climate Change
ISC	Institutional Shareholders' Committee

ISO	International Organization for Standardization
LEAF	Linking Environment and Farming
LSE	London Stock Exchange
MDG	Millennium Development Goal
MFA	Multi-fibre Agreement
MIC	methyl isocyanate
MIMCO	Mattel Independent Monitoring Council for Global Manufacturing Principles
MSC	Marine Stewardship Council
NGO	non-government organization
NPV	Net present value
OECD	Organisation for Economic Co-operation and Development
OFR	Operating and Financial Review
ONS	Office for National Statistics
PETA	People for the Ethical Treatment of Animals
PPP	public–private sector partnership
PRI	United Nations Principles for Responsible Investing
RAN	Rainforest Action Network
ROSPA	Roundtable on Sustainable Palm Oil
SAI	Social Accountability International
SCP	sustainable consumption and production
SIF	Social Investment Forum
SME	small and medium-sized enterprise
SRI	socially responsible investing/investment
SSE	social stock exchange
UN	United Nations
UNCED	United Nations Conference on Environment and Development
UNEP	United Nations Environment Programme
UNFCC	United Nations Framework Convention on Climate Change
UNGC	United Nations Global Compact
UNRISD	United Nations Research Institute for Social Development
VBLI	Vietnam Business Links Initiative
WBCSD	Word Business Council for Sustainable Development
WCED	World Commission on Economic Development
WEF	World Economic Forum
WMO	World Meteorological Organization
WRAP	Worldwide Responsible Apparel Production
WRI	World Resources Institute
WTO	World Trade Organization

■ HOW TO USE THIS BOOK

Chapter overview

In this chapter, we introduce the idea of corporate responsibility: its conc
and why it is a significant part of the business agenda. In particular, we w

- set out the context within which contemporary corporate responsi
  flourished;
- examine the different perspectives on and definitions of corporate

Chapter overview

Each chapter opens with an overview that provides a route map through the material and summarizes the goals of the chapter.

Main topics

Main topic boxes

Each chapter has a list of the main topics it covers, acting as a helpful signpost of what you can expect to learn.

■ Key terms

Business and society   Legal responsib

Business ethics and values   Economic respo

Corporate philanthropy   Sustainability

Key terms and concepts

Key terms are presented in boxes at the start of each chapter; they are also defined in the glossary at the end of the book. As a new feature for this second edition, 'key concept' boxes introduce and discuss seminal concepts within the chapters.

■ Online resources

- Case study of a multinational company's worker welfare scandal: the consequences for the company
- Teaching notes on the chapter's main case study
- More detailed overview of business ethics and political theory
- Films, books, and other resources
- Links to other web-based resources

Online resource box

Each chapter contains a helpful list of the resources available on the Online Resource Centre to support the topics discussed.

Snapshot cases

The book is packed with case examples designed to place the content of the chapter into a practical context. The snapshot cases are followed by quick questions.

SNAPSHOT 1.1

147 'species' of corporate responsibility

'*Explorers discover at least 147 species of CSR*': so was headed an article i about a 2005 Ashridge Business School study of corporate responsibility research in Denmark, the study identified seven main areas of corporate which were then divided into 31 classes of activity, as follows.

Area 1 Leadership, vision, and values

(a) Defining and setting the corporate purpose, values, and vision

(b) Translating this into policies and procedures

Discussion points

These points, dispersed throughout the chapters, invite you to reflect on the various aspects of corporate responsibility.

■ **Discussion points**

Surveys of executives and the public repeatedly show that business is distru of society.

- Why do you think there is a high degree of distrust?
- Is corporate responsibility a good way to restore business' reputation?
- How would you factor distrust into a company's business plan?

End-of-chapter case study

A longer case study at the end of each chapter provides an opportunity to apply what you have learnt and analyze further examples; these are followed by extended questions to promote deeper thinking.

CASE STUDY 1

What are the limits to responsibility? The case of pharmaceuticals

Some industries seem to have a responsibility advantage just because o instance, it is much easier to imagine a responsible pharmaceutical comp firm. Like other segments of the health sector, the pharmaceutical indust ethical investors because of the social good that its products bring. Many of the industry because of the good they can do. On top of this, the industry is back, and has long donated drugs to poor countries to treat tropical diseases sis, river blindness, and leprosy.

Yet pharmaceutical companies are also highly controversial. While J

Further reading

An annotated list of recommended reading on each subject will help guide you through the literature and provide sources of information for writing essays and researching projects.

FURTHER READING

Take your learning further: Online Resource Centre www.oxfor murray2e/

VISIT THE WEBSITE
for links to useful sources of further information

Visit the Online Resource Centre which accompanies this book chapter.

Students: explore web links and further reading suggestions. K developments by undertaking web exercises.

Lecturers: you will find additional case studies, including one or

■ HOW TO USE THE ONLINE
RESOURCE CENTRE

www.oxfordtextbooks.co.uk/orc/blowfield_murray2e/

For students

Find out more about what companies are doing to reduce total greenhouse gas emissions:

- The Climate Group - http://theclimategroup.org
- Carbon Trust - www.carbontrust.co.uk
- International Emissions Trading Association - www.ieta.org

Web exercises
The internet can be a powerful research tool and is a popular medium for today's students. These readymade online activities are designed to help further your knowledge and understanding of corporate responsibility topics in an interactive way. For each chapter, you're asked to find out information and answer questions based on web links to relevant articles and websites.

Here are some films that deal with issues relevant to corporate responsibility manag We have only listed films that are publicly available, and you will note that more are of corporations than praise them. However, major companies such as BP have priv film archives that may contain films about their corporate responsibility programmes policies: it is worth trying to get access if you can.

An Inconvenient Truth – Al Gore's documentary about climate change.

Suggested films
A list of suggested films is provided to reinforce your learning and act as a great practical exercise to see what you have learnt put into practice.

UK Combined Code on Corporate Governance - www.frc.org.uk/documents /pagemanager/frc/Combined%20Code%20June%202006.pdf

Public Interest Disclosure Act - www.hmso.gov.uk/acts/acts1998/19980023.htm

Department of Trade and Industry Guide to Public Interest Disclosure Act - www.dti.gov.uk/employment/employment-legislation/employment-guidance /page16186.html

Annotated web links
Links to relevant websites direct you towards valuable sources of information, as well as professional associations.

Look at the bibliography at the end of the book and you will see the wealth of publishe material relevant to corporate responsibility. Some of that material is readily available some can be difficult to get hold of. Here is a list of 100 corporate responsibility book should be available from high street bookstores or online.

[A - C] [D - F] [G - I] [J - L] [M - O] [P - R] [S - U] [V - Z]

1. ANDRIOF, J and MCINTOSH, M., 2001. Perspectives on corporate citizenship

Further reading and email listservs
A list of recommended reading on each subject will help guide you through the literature providing additional information for writing essays, preparing for exams and for researching projects.

Readers wanting additional company-specific case studies have various sources they can turn to. **Companies** producing CSR or sustainability reports offer a wealth of material on their websites. **Case Place** <www.caseplace.org> specializes in case studies related to corporate responsibility and sustainability. The **Center for Corporate Citizenship** at Boston College offers a variety of reports suitable for case studies <www.bccc.net> Some books also contain a variety of case study material, including the following:

CRANE, A. and MATTEN, D., 2007. Business ethics: managing corporate citizenship and

Additional case study sources
A suite of case study sources allow you to do further reading and improve your knowledge of this subject area.

For registered adopters of the book

Images from the book

The images from the textbook have been uploaded to the Online Resource Centre and can be added to your lecture materials or virtual learning environment.

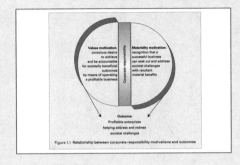

Additional case study material

A suite of additional cases have been provided, to help you prepare for each term's teaching. One 1,000-word case study has been provided per chapter, complete with essay and discussion questions. The authors have also included an online bank of 'old favourites': shorter cases taken from the first edition.

CASE STUDY 4: THE STATE OF CORPORATE RESPONSIBILITY IN DIFF COUNTRIES

Introduction for teachers

The rise of corporate responsibility as an international phenomenon has gen discussion about the degree to which corporate responsibility can, should, an between countries and regions (Chapter 6). This case study provides a snap

Trailers of films that illustrate corporate responsibility issues

These trailers, which include The Corporation and Enron, bring corporate responsibility to life in a visual and lively way. They are accompanied by teaching notes to provide a complete seminar package.

Essay questions

The authors have provided further essay questions to support your teaching.

ESSAY 1:

Every month, Ethical Corporation, a magazine for corporate responsibility pro summarises what companies and brands are doing in the area of corporate r Students should obtain a copy of the magazine, and examine the News Brief Environment Digest, Brand Watch, and similar sections in order to write an e a class debate on one or more of the following:

1.   Present evidence for and against the proposition that corporate res

Part 1

The meaning and origins of corporate responsibility

Introducing corporate responsibility

Chapter overview

In this chapter, we introduce the idea of corporate responsibility: its concerns, its meanings, and why it is a significant part of the business agenda. In particular, we will:

- set out the context within which contemporary corporate responsibility has flourished;

- examine the different perspectives on and definitions of corporate responsibility;

- discuss the values that companies are being asked to uphold;

- look at the main issues with which contemporary corporate responsibility is wrestling.

Main topics

■ Key terms

Business and society

Business ethics and values

Corporate philanthropy

Legal responsibility

Economic responsibility

Sustainability

■ Online resources

- Case study of a multinational company's worker welfare scandal: the problem and the consequences for the company
- Teaching notes on the chapter's main case study
- More detailed overview of business ethics and political theory
- Films, books, and other resources
- Links to other web-based resources

Why corporate responsibility?

In 2005, *The Economist* published a series of articles castigating corporate responsibility and the folly of managers who thought it would benefit their companies. Corporate responsibility conscious managers were accused of taking their eye off of shareholder interests. Accusations were made that corporate responsibility and bad governance went hand in hand. In an accompanying survey, the Economist Intelligence Unit found only 35 per cent of managers felt corporate responsibility was a priority.

Fast forward to 2008, and *The Economist* again runs a feature on corporate responsibility. But this time the tone is different. Now it says 96 per cent of managers believe corporate responsibility offers value for money, and 56 per cent of managers surveyed by the Economist Intelligence Unit say it is a high priority. Three years after its original dismissal, *The Economist* now professes that few big companies can ignore corporate responsibility.

The Economist was far from the first to find that a growing body of company managers were increasingly interested in corporate responsibility, but its was a mainstream voice; proof that corporate responsibility was well advanced on its journey from margins to mainstream. It echoed the message from KPMG's biennial survey of corporate responsibility reporting worldwide, and what McKinsey & Co's CEO, Ian Davis, called the need for business to recast its role in society.[1] Were they witnessing a genuine change in the world of business, and if so, what was happening and why?

We live in a world in which the richest 20 per cent of people possess 86 per cent of gross national product, in which one country accounts for 23 per cent of worldwide energy consumption, and in which the USA and Europe account for 65 per cent of annual wealth creation.[2] We live in a world where emerging economies such as India and China are outperforming developed economies in many respects, not least during the first major financial crisis of the new millennium.

In this world, prosperity is measured in terms of economic growth, made possible through greater productivity and production. With the drive for growth comes greater demand for natural resources and the quest for lower cost production in what was once called the Third World. Economic growth has historically been associated with increased energy usage, but now the major sources of energy are not only scarcer, but are a culprit in climate change. Business has been blamed for its contribution to climate change, but has been praised also for helping find a solution. Tackling global warming is the latest example of the importance attached to the new economy of ideas, creativity, and innovation, within which a prerequisite for being competitive is being able to participate in a virtual global network, and which brings with it new patterns of employment, social interaction, and investment, as well as new threats to national and personal security.

This shifting world brings prosperity for some and change for many. New economic powerhouses are emerging, although the distribution of wealth within, and between, countries is often highly unequal. The capacity not only to manufacture, but also to research and develop, is being dispersed more widely around the world, even if the vast majority of patents still originate in a handful of established industrial economies, such as Japan, the USA, and Germany. Out of this, different levels of conflict arise, such as those between the affluent and the poor, between short-run gains and long-term success, between senior managers and the rest of a company's stakeholders, and between the interests of companies and nations.[3]

In the midst of this world, business is being ascribed roles and a significance that had never previously been imagined. The private sector creates wealth, generates employment, utilizes natural resources, and attracts investment at unprecedented levels. Consumption plays a pivotal role in our social lives and in our personal identities. Brands have a significance that is not dissimilar to that of religion and ideology in previous eras. Companies play important roles in public policy, not least in countries where the standard of governance is low, or in situations in which international governance mechanisms are inadequate.

In today's world, the absence of the private sector seems unimagineable. Despite the financial collapse of 2008–2009, alternatives to a free market economy are scarce and have little popular support. Individual companies can collapse and whole industries allowed to wither on the vine, but governments around the world have stepped in to save business—from investment banking to manufacturing—from its own failings. Allowing widespread business failure is unthinkable, because we seem increasingly less able to imagine an alternative to the free enterprise economy. In parts of the world such as Eastern Europe, the free market is welcomed as an alternative to totalitarian government, but elsewhere there are qualms about how powerful business should be, and how best and how far to moderate its behaviour to strike a balance between social benefits and pain.

People in business are often vexed that private enterprise's contribution to society is not better understood. Nonetheless, company behaviour is often a cause for concern, firms are being subjected to new levels of transparency, whether in terms of the demands that the largest stock markets make for greater disclosure and changes to corporate governance, or in terms of public outcry on issues as diverse as environmental pollution, consumer rights, child labour, corruption, and support for military regimes. Adverse disclosure threatens shareholder confidence, brand reputation, production stability, employee trust, and other corporate assets, both tangible and intangible.

What is more, the conditions that leave companies open to charges of irresponsibility, when looked at differently, can become business opportunities. Public opinion is becoming less tolerant of corporate excess and malfeasance, but there are also increasing expectations that business will come up with solutions to some of the twenty-first century's main social and environmental challenges, such as water accessibility, global warming, and affordable health care. These are the twin hemispheres that corporate responsibility is charged to embrace: on the one hand, it must deal with what Baker (2005) calls 'capitalism's Achilles heel', within which capital, poverty, and inequality are intertwined; on the other, it must promote capitalism as a solution to the key social and environmental issues of the age.

■ Discussion points

Surveys of executives and the public repeatedly show that business is distrusted as a member of society.

- Why do you think there is a high degree of distrust?
- Is corporate responsibility a good way to restore business' reputation?
- How would you factor distrust into a company's business plan?

Definitions of corporate responsibility

The above is the context within which corporate responsibility has come to the fore—but what does the term itself actually mean? There never has been a straightforward answer to this, and growing interest in the field—whether from companies, governments, the general public, academics, or civil society organizations—has only served to extend the array of definitions.

Long before there was a name for corporate responsibility, there were ideas about what it meant for business to make a positive contribution to the rest of society. Owen, Rowntree, and Lever were among the many individuals who utilized company assets to improve the conditions of nineteenth-century workers. Throughout the twentieth century, companies such as Norsk Hydro would take responsibility for social conditions in their, often isolated, company towns; many logging, mining, plantation, and oil operations throughout the world set up housing schools, clinics, and other social amenities. Just as importantly, many more were criticized for failing to take on such responsibilities.[4]

The positive and the negative impacts that business had on society generated public, political, and academic debate. While it was quite clear that business sought a profit from providing goods and services in response to society's demands, it was much less obvious what constraints should be put on its activities and who should impose them. Was all profit legitimate? Was all profit legitimate, provided that the company stayed within the law? What was a fair distribution of the wealth business created between shareholders, employees, and wider society? Should companies give part of their wealth back to the communities within which they operated? Could markets be relied upon to set a fair price, whether for labour, products, or natural resources? Could governments reliably decide what was in the public interest?

Questions such as these gave rise to different notions of corporate responsibility. The field called 'corporate social responsibility' (CSR) began with a focus on the role of business leaders: particularly, on how they managed their companies with a view to society and how they gave back to their local communities. In the 1950s, the focus of CSR shifted to the behaviour of companies rather than that of individuals. This generated a fair degree of academic debate about what companies should be responsible for; it also spawned the concepts of 'corporate social responsiveness' and then 'corporate social performance', which, in the 1980s, put less stress on the philosophical meaning of responsibility and more on the act of being responsible.

Other terms were introduced. 'Corporate sustainability', for example, was used in the 1990s to emphasize how environmental concerns were increasingly an area in which companies were expected to exhibit responsibility. More recently still, 'corporate citizenship' (originally used to refer to the types of corporate philanthropy common in the USA) has been used as a development of CSR that emphasizes the role of business as a citizen in global society and its function in delivering the citizenship rights of individuals.[5]

Changes in the focus of corporate responsibility inevitably affect the way it is defined. For Davis (1973), corporate responsibility begins where the law ends. In other words, it is about what companies do to make a positive contribution to society above and beyond that which constitutes their legal obligations. This simple parameter gets to the heart of much of the debate about corporate responsibility in recent years, i.e. the desirability and effectiveness of market-based solutions to social and environmental challenges, and, in particular, their voluntary and self-regulatory nature.

The different definitions of corporate responsibility shown in Box 1.1 share in common the belief that companies have a responsibility for the public good—but they emphasize different elements of this. The definitions used by Starbucks and Chiquita, for

Box 1.1 Definitions of corporate responsibility

A responsible company is one that listens to its stakeholders and responds with honesty to their concerns.

Starbucks, CSR Report, 2004

CSR commits us to operate in a socially responsible way everywhere we do business, fairly balancing the needs and concerns of our various stakeholders—all those who impact, are impacted by, or have a legitimate interest in the Company's actions and performance.

Chiquita, **www.chiquita.com**, accessed 24 March 2004

CSR [is] the proposition that companies are responsible not only for maximising profits, but also for recognising the needs of such stakeholders as employees, customers, demographic groups and even the regions they serve.

PricewaterhouseCoopers, **www.pwcglobal.com**, accessed 24 March 2004

CSR requires companies to acknowledge that they should be publicly accountable not only for their financial performance but also for their social and environmental record.

Confederation of British Industry, 2001

[CSR is] a concept whereby companies integrate social and environmental concerns in their business operations and in their interactions with their stakeholders on a voluntary basis.

European Commission, Directorate General for Employment and Social Affairs

[Corporate responsibility is the] responsibility of an organization for the impacts of its decisions and activities on society and the environment, through transparent and ethical behaviour that (a) contributes to sustainable development, health and the welfare of society; (b) takes into account the expectations of stakeholders; (c) is in compliance with applicable law and consistent with international norms of behaviour; and (d) is integrated through the organization and practiced in its relationships.

Draft of ISO 26000, International Guidance Standard
on Social Responsibility, 4 September 2009

example, highlight that responsibility is gauged by how companies listen and respond to stakeholders' concerns. PricewaterhouseCoopers' definition sets out the kinds of stakeholder groups to whom companies are responsible. It also stresses that responsibility involves balancing profit maximization and stakeholders' needs. The Confederation of British Industry's definition sheds light on what some of the responsibilities to stakeholders are, while that of the European Commission stresses that actions under the corporate responsibility umbrella are voluntary in nature. Finally, the ISO 26000 draft, the most recent of these definitions, refers to what companies are responsible for, reiterates the importance of stakeholder involvement and accountability, and adds that responsibility should be integrated into organizational practices.

These broad definitions reflect claims about the values that companies wish to uphold, such as honesty, fairness, and integrity, and these may be set out in standards or codes of practice (see Box 1.2). The values can be quite diverse, and Paine et al. (2005) have tried to categorize them, differentiating, for example, between management's responsibility to investors (fiduciary responsibilities), respecting human rights (dignity principle), and a duty to honour commitments (reliability principle).

Box 1.2 **Published standards of corporate responsibility**

The following is a selection of standards, guidelines, and declarations that set out some of the rights that companies are being asked to uphold.

Agenda 21

A far-reaching plan of action for governments, companies, and civil society to address human impacts on society.
www.un.org/esa/sustdev/documents/agenda21

Beijing Declaration

An international United Nations declaration on the rights of women.
www.un.org/womenwatch/daw/beijing/platform

CERES principles

A ten-point code of corporate environmental conduct, for use as an environmental mission statement or ethic.
www.ceres.org/coalitionandcompanies

Global Reporting Initiative

A framework for reporting on social, environmental, and economic performance.
www.globalreporting.org

Marine Stewardship Council

Standards for sustainable fishing and seafood traceability.
www.msc.org

Organisation for Economic Co-operation and Development (OECD) guidelines for multinational enterprises

Government recommendations on responsible business conduct.
www.oecd.org

Principles for Responsible Investment

Principles on environmental, social, and corporate governance issues pertaining to investors.
www.unpri.org/principles

Social Accountability 8000

Workplace standard against which to assure worker rights and welfare.
www.sa-intl.org

Wolfsberg Anti-Money Laundering Principles

Principles for private banks to counter money laundering.
www.wolfsberg-principles.com

There are also companies and individuals that define corporate responsibility in terms of its commercial benefits, emphasizing the instrumental value (the business case) acts of responsibility can bring. Windsor (2001) says that the degree and types of responsibility that individual companies have are a factor of the wealth and power of the company, so that a multinational corporation will have different responsibilities to those of a small or medium-sized enterprise. Equally, separate industries have distinctive social and environmental impacts, so that, for example, good performance in cosmetics will look quite different from that in transportation. Indeed, according to Werther and Chandler (2006), there are so many variables that it is impossible to prescribe what mix of responsibilities any company faces: companies should not look for universal definitions, but should instead build their strategies around the perspectives of their stakeholders (even though that term is itself subject to multiple interpretations—see Chapter 9).

Corporate governance

In the US tradition of corporate responsibility which shaped much of the thinking in the field until fairly recently, corporate governance was not given much consideration. However, as corporate responsibility theory has stopped being the preserve of academe, other thinkers—notably those in socially responsible investing (see Chapter 10)—have argued it needs to be part of corporate responsibility's scope. Hence, the Certified Financial Analyst Institute's material refers to corporate responsibility as ESG—environmental, social and governance—as do fund managers such as Henderson Global Investment.

A valid criticism of corporate responsibility practice is that companies have not taken more seriously the governance dimension, and that it played no discernible part in identifying or addressing the various crises of governance affecting Western markets in the early and late 2000s (see Chapter 13). We explore the evolution of corporate governance and how it relates to corporate responsibility more widely in Chapter 7, and would tend to agree that governance is an important (if underdeveloped) aspect of the business-society relationship. Insofar as governance is the primary responsibility of boards, and the board's role, as defined by John Harvey Jones (1988), is to 'create tomorrow's company out of today's', corporate responsibility would seem to offer useful frameworks for board-level governance. However, corporate responsibility is also part of the reconstruction of governance: something that is connected to globalization (see Chapter 5), and social accounting (see Chapter 8), and is evident for instance in phenomena such as civil governance when companies are affected as much by the beliefs and actions of groups such as online protest communities, as they are by the interests of investors that conventional governance is intended to protect.

A framework for understanding corporate responsibility

Snapshot 1.1 demonstrates the wide variety of corporate responsibility activities presently being practised by companies. Furthermore, observers such as academics have a multitude of perspectives on the meaning of corporate responsibility (see Chapter 2). Given this array, it is not surprising that no single definition adequately captures the range of issues, policies, processes, and initiatives covered in this book. As we will explore in the coming chapters, the notion of stakeholders, the way issues become recognized, and the role of values are all important elements of corporate responsibility today.

SNAPSHOT 1.1

147 'species' of corporate responsibility

'*Explorers discover at least 147 species of CSR*': so was headed an article in *Ethical Performance* about a 2005 Ashridge Business School study of corporate responsibility activities. Based on research in Denmark, the study identified seven main areas of corporate responsibility activity, which were then divided into 31 classes of activity, as follows.

Area 1 Leadership, vision, and values

(a) Defining and setting the corporate purpose, values, and vision

(b) Translating this into policies and procedures

(c) Putting it into practice, including empowering and embedding

(d) Ethical leadership and championing

Area 2 Marketplace activities

(a) Responsible customer relations, including marketing and advertising

(b) Product responsibility

(c) Using corporate responsibility product labelling

(d) Ethical competition

(e) Making markets work for all

Area 3 Workforce activities

(a) Employee communication and representation

(b) Ensuring employability and skills development

(c) Diversity and equality

(d) Responsible/fair remuneration

(e) Work–life balance

(f) Health, safety, and well-being

(g) Responsible restructuring

Area 4 Supply chain activities

(a) Being a fair customer

(b) Driving social and environmental standards through the supply chain

(c) Promoting social and economic inclusion via the supply chain

Area 5 Stakeholder engagement

(a) Mapping key stakeholders and their main concerns

(b) Stakeholder consultation

(c) Responding to and managing stakeholders

(d) Transparent reporting and communication

Area 6 Community activities

(a) Financial donations

(b) Volunteering employee time

(c) Giving gifts in kind

(d) Being a good neighbour

Area 7 Environmental activities

(a) Resource and energy use

(b) Pollution and waste management

(c) Environmental product responsibility

(d) Transport planning

(Sources: *Ethical Performance*, 2006c; Ashridge Centre for Business and Society, 2005)

Quick questions

It is sometimes argued that companies are asked to take on too many different types of responsibility and that there are too many corporate responsibility initiatives.

1 Should companies be allowed to choose which issues to address?

2 Which of the above activity areas do you think are most important for companies to tackle?

3 How can companies set about prioritizing the areas of activity in which they should get involved?

Likewise, the tensions that arise because of competing interests, priorities, and goals affect what corporate responsibility means in practice.

However, rather than try to adopt and defend a particular definition, in this book, we use corporate responsibility as an umbrella term that captures the variety of ways in which business' relationship with society is being defined, managed, and acted upon. Therefore, for us corporate responsibility comprises (a) the responsibilities of business in the context of wider society, (b) how those responsibilities are defined and negotiated, and (c) how they are managed and organized. The chapters of this book emphasize one or other of these dimensions, highlighting where the various observers and practitioners share common ground, and where they disagree.

Readers will see soon enough that we do not pretend that there is a unifying vision of corporate responsibility. However, there are two broad motivations for companies to treat corporate responsibility as a management issue: (a) because companies, like people, have values that guide their interactions with other society members (values motivation), and (b) because to succeed companies need to manage their relationship with wider society (materiality motivation) (see Figure 1.1). We tackle these ways of thinking in the following sections.

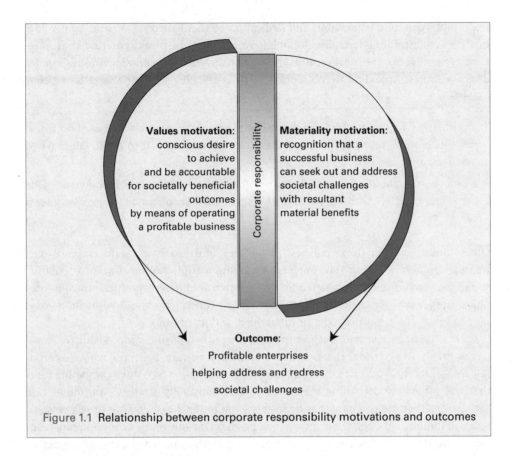

Values motivation: conscious desire to achieve and be accountable for societally beneficial outcomes by means of operating a profitable business

Corporate responsibility

Materiality motivation: recognition that a successful business can seek out and address societal challenges with resultant material benefits

Outcome:
Profitable enterprises
helping address and redress
societal challenges

Figure 1.1 Relationship between corporate responsibility motivations and outcomes

---

■ Discussion points

Historically, many companies interpret corporate responsibility as 'giving back to their communities' through philanthropy and community affairs, yet in the following sections we show that today other types of responsibility are considered more important.

- Why do you think 'giving back' is increasingly less acceptable as a definition of corporate responsibility?

- When some executives say their companies do not give back to communities because they have 'already given', what do they mean?

- Why do you think there is a stronger tradition of corporate philanthropy in the USA than in Europe?

Values motivation

When executives talk about corporate responsibility, many stress the importance of their companies' values. Sam Palmisano, IBM's CEO, describes his company's values as innovation that matters for the world as well as the company, trust and personal responsibility in all relationships, and dedication to client success.[6] Nestlé's core values include favouring long-term development over short-term profit, entering into long-term commitments and relationships, being fair and honest, and showing respect for diverse cultures. According to Waddock (2001), at the core of what she calls *'corporate citizenship'* are:

1   a company's adoption of policies, procedures, and processes that are based on integrity (i.e. honesty to oneself and to others), and which allow it to build values-based practices; and

2   a company's capacity to perceive and evaluate the long-term consequences of its behaviour, and its willingness to make short-term sacrifices to realize long-term gains.

Others flesh out what those policies, procedures, and processes might embrace (e.g. transparency, empowering stakeholders, managing a triple bottom line of economic, social, and environmental value added, etc.), offering different political and philosophical frameworks for understanding what ethical constructs should be included (e.g. human liberty, social justice, communitarianism, a duty of care).[7]

There is debate about who decides the values to which business should adhere: companies themselves or the societies within which they operate. For those who see corporate responsibility as a choice that business makes, companies face three competing cases that will ultimately determine their corporate responsibility strategy: the moral case (obligations that the company has to society); the rational case (taking proactive steps that will minimize the restrictions society imposes on business); the economic case (adding financial value to the company by preserving its legitimacy with its stakeholders).[8] For others, however, companies do not choose to practice corporate responsibility; rather, it is an integral part of the free enterprise system, and the issues and problems at the heart of corporate responsibility are:

> a natural consequence of the industrialized quest for profits [and] represent the raw edge of business values rubbing against the social values of human communities and the ecosystems that sustain those communities.
>
> *(Frederick, 2006, p 59)*

Underlying these different vantage points is a common acceptance that a legal construct such as a corporation can have values, and that notions of ethics, justice, responsibility, and obligation rooted in human experience can be meaningfully adapted to guide corporate behaviour. As we discuss in Chapter 2, these are debatable assumptions, and an important question is whether corporate responsibility practice today makes companies sufficiently accountable for adhering to society's values in the same way that people are held to account, or whether it, de facto, allows companies to pick and choose those things for which they want to be responsible in a way that would seem preposterous if the choices were to be made by individuals.

Business ethics

Not surprisingly, this pushes us in the direction of the field called 'business ethics', which refers to ethical systems applied in the context of profit-oriented organizations. Some will argue that business ethics should be treated as the overarching framework within which corporate responsibility theories and practices are devised and implemented. For example, under a theory of environmental ethics, humanity may have a duty of care to the planet, and hence corporate responsibility practices should be guided by that duty. If we were concerned only with views on what ideologies should inform corporate behaviour, we might treat corporate responsibility and business ethics as synonymous. However, our interest is something broader, that embraces theory, management practice, and the societal context within which business exists. Just as neither politics nor religion can be entirely explained by reference to theoretical principles, neither can corporate responsibility.

There are many fascinating introductions to business ethics, and we are not going to attempt to duplicate them here. Some of these are concerned with the behaviour of individuals as members of the company and wider society, but others concentrate on business as an institution and how a company integrates values, such as honesty, trust, integrity, respect, and fairness, into its policies, practices, and decision making. This can involve ensuring that employees abide by the law and are not left in a position in which, in order to achieve one set of targets (e.g. earnings), they are necessarily encouraged to bend or break the law. It can also involve going beyond legal requirements and adhering

---

■ Key concepts: Business ethics

Business ethics is a sub-set of corporate responsibility offering a crucial analytical tool for understanding, conceptualizing, and legitimizing whether the actions and behaviour of companies is *morally* right or wrong. The field comprises two broad areas: (a) normative business ethics with its roots in theoretical philosophy, and a focus on understanding what is moral or immoral in a particular situation; and (b) descriptive business ethics rooted in a wider range of disciplines (e.g. psychology, organizational behaviour, anthropology), and a focus on ethical decisions, how they are made, and what influences the process and outcomes (Visser et al. 2007).

One could argue that business ethics underpins the entire field of corporate responsibility theory and practice, but while it is important (and is supported by a vast number of publications), it is not the only lens through which corporate responsibility is being viewed. The influential idea of a 'business case' for corporate responsibility (see Chapter 6) largely relies on societal consensus to set out a moral case which is then addressed by harnessing the capacities of business. Or, if one takes the example of stakeholder theory (see Chapter 9), while it can be used to help understand what is moral or not for business, ethics is not an intrinsic element of it, and it can be (and often is) used just to analyze corporate self-interest. Therefore, even if almost every action involving human-beings has an ethical dimension at some level, it can be too regressive and unhelpful to resort to first principles in each discussion of corporate responsibility.

to company, industry, or professional codes of conduct, such as those that have long been adopted in the medical, military, and legal professions.

It might be argued that, before business management can be considered a mature profession, it too needs to develop comprehensive and relevant codes of ethics. Khurana (2007) claims that business schools were originally intended to educate managers in how to lead socially responsible institutions, but that these 'higher aims' were sacrificed to a focus on profit maximization so that managers today are simply the hired hands of investors. Certainly, there is now a resurgence of interest in business ethics, both in companies and business schools, as a result of the corporate corruption scandals of the late 1990s and 2000s. The changing nature of business also presents new ethical challenges in order to resolve issues arising from operating globally and within multiple cultural norms, from new industries such as biotechnology and information technology, and from increasing public scrutiny of business behaviour. Some companies and industries have invested in internal mechanisms to manage the ethical dimensions of their operations, such as the medical company Baxter International's overarching set of bioethics principles, and defence and aircraft manufacturer Raytheon's appointment of a corporate director for ethics compliance and ethics officers in its major business segments.

There are, however, two readily identifiable difficulties with how companies currently implement business ethics. First, there are many examples of even companies with strong ethical policies and processes being found in breach of the law. This was the case with Boeing, which, despite its extensive ethical guidelines on procurement, corruption, and marketing, used confidential materials stolen from rival Lockheed Martin to win nearly $2 billion-worth of defence procurement contracts with the US government in 1998, an action that later led the company to be suspended from bidding for defence contracts.[9]

The second difficulty is that company codes and guidelines, as Davies (1997) points out, mostly take the form of usable algorithms that are intended to guide managers through ethically contentious situations, rather than help them to develop a coherent ethical theory that will inform overall business practice. Consequently, ethics is often described as something that is necessary to achieve business imperatives such as profitability, growth, and shareholder value, rather than as something that is at the heart of business behaviour and a prime determinant of what that behaviour should be, especially if there is conflict between instrumental and moral imperatives.

This may seem odd given that much of business ethics seeks to apply ethical theory to the business context. Thus, we find a variety of texts seeking to adapt the ideas of Aristotle, Kant, Mill, Locke, Heidegger, and others to the needs of business.[10] Scherer & Palazzo (2007) argue that companies should not expect to act in accordance with a specific ethical theory, but rather in line with Habermas' view of contemporary ethics, they should adopt the values that emerge from an informed and inclusive negotiation with different sections of society. In what has been characterized as part of a distinct European as opposed to American school of business ethics, companies are seen as uniquely placed organizations in relation to issues with distinct ethical dimensions. For example, Crane and Matten (2004) focus on three core themes that influence the ethical dimension to business behaviour—globalization, sustainability, and citizenship—and, in doing so, refer as much to sociology, political economy, and international relations as they do to philosophy. They highlight, for example, how the Rhenish model of capitalism, found in Italy, Germany, Spain, France, and elsewhere, creates different expectations and challenges to those of the Anglo-Saxon model that is typical of the UK and USA. They also describe how factors such as age, gender, national identity and culture, level of education, personal integrity, and moral imagination all affect individuals' ethical decisions. And they make clear that the concerns of business ethics are affected by the role, capacity, and responsibilities of government and other social institutions.

The Online Resource Centre (www.oxfordtextbooks.co.uk/orc/blowfield_murray2e) contains a more detailed overview of business ethics in relation to corporate responsibility. But what the new European school of business ethics highlights is that ethics itself is a social construct; not an absolute value that business should adopt or be judged against, but something that companies as institutions or collectives of individuals both shape and are shaped by. It is insufficient to apply values to business. Rather, values should be seen as an element of what business needs to be cognizant of in building its societal relationships.

Materiality motivation—managing business and society

Central to this European school of business ethics is the idea that the relationship between business and society is subject to continual renegotiation. This counters a criticism of some other forms of business ethics which encourage the idea that responsibility is an end state, or a goal to be strived for, rather than a way of thinking about the role of business in wider society. According to Jonkers, it is confusing to managers to portray responsibility as something that can be accomplished, rather:

> [Corporate responsibility] is a 'sensitising concept': a term that draws attention to a complex range of issues and elements that are all related to the position and function of the business enterprise in contemporary society.
>
> *(2005, p 20)*

There is a strong and growing belief that corporate responsibility means something different in the USA than in most of Europe because of the different social contracts business is a part of in these regions. Ideas such as the sensitizing concept help discussions of corporate responsibility steer clear of national relativism, but we should still be aware that in countries such as the USA and the UK where the welfare state is relatively weak, the responsibilities of corporations will be different than in Denmark and Germany where government provides greater worker protection and social security. However, we should also stay clear of convenient stereotypes, and recognize, for example, that in the USA in areas such as consumer protection the opportunities for legal recourse are far greater than in most of the world.

There is a long tradition of business and society as an area of academic study and public policy, but its primary concern has been how to regulate and motivate business so as to contribute more to the public good. Thus, for example, governments have passed legislation on issues from working hours, to maternity leave and equal pay, so as to

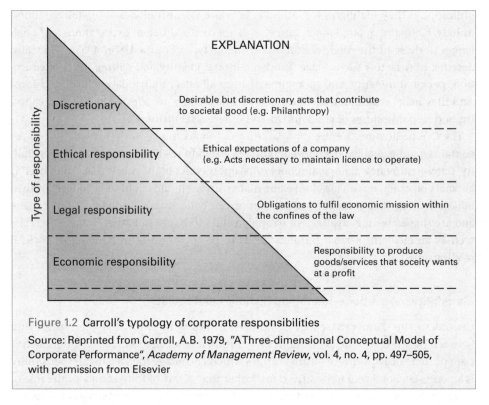

Figure 1.2 Carroll's typology of corporate responsibilities

Source: Reprinted from Carroll, A.B. 1979, "A Three-dimensional Conceptual Model of Corporate Performance", *Academy of Management Review*, vol. 4, no. 4, pp. 497–505, with permission from Elsevier

enhance workers' well-being. Business and government are depicted as having separate concerns: the former, to do with creating wealth; the latter, to do with social cohesion and security, which has often required intervening in the world of business through both regulation and redistribution.

Since the 1950s, it has become clear that this idea of separate sectors with discrete responsibilities is confusing and, moreover, that different societies around the world have very specific, and often complex, expectations of the role that business should play, which go well beyond paying taxes and abiding by the law. These became apparent in the flurry of literature in the 1960s and 1970s, which provided the theoretical context for contemporary corporate responsibility (see Chapter 2). In 1979, Carroll offered what is perhaps the most widely cited framework for understanding the different aspects of social responsibility that had emerged (see Figure 1.2). He identified four types of responsibility under which the various actions taken to manage business' relationship with society should fall, and we examine these individually now.

Economic responsibility

Economic responsibility refers to the fundamental responsibility of business to produce goods and services that society wants, and which it sells at a profit. Many eminent theorists and business leaders would argue that this is the limit of a company's responsibilities, and to attempt any more is at best folly, and at worst a misuse of owners' capital (see Snapshot 1.2). They argue that under the free enterprise system, creating jobs, shareholder value, and goods and services—and doing this in a law-abiding manner—are all inherent ways in which business contributes to society. Managers as agents of the company's owners do not need to worry about the different outcomes because ultimately the company's value will reflect its utility. Indeed, as soon as managers do anything more than focus on profit they risk creating an enterprise with multiple objective functions that ends up having no clear accountability or definition of good performance.[11]

As we will see in other chapters of this book, there are various counter-arguments to this view. But the idea that companies have a purpose other than simply to make money—that, at the very least, they should consider not only profitability, but also the way in which profits are made—is central to understanding corporate responsibility in terms of business' relationship to society. Indeed, where you stand on this argument can significantly influence what you see as the value of corporate responsibility (see Box 1.3).

Box 1.3 **How the value of corporate responsibility depends on your viewpoint**

If your starting point is this . . .	Then the value of corporate responsibility to you is likely to be this . . .
Capitalism is fundamentally wrong	Corporate responsibility has little if anything to offer you, although it might help you to criticize capitalism.
Free markets are self-regulating and successful companies inherently contribute to the social good	Corporate responsibility has nothing to offer you, and may appear a threat to your beliefs.
Some forms of capitalism are worse than others	Corporate responsibility theory offers some insight: see for instance Reich, 2007 and Vogel, 2005.
Free market capitalism is essentially good but needs controlling or moderating	Corporate responsibility theory has a lot to offer in areas from strategy to social accounting.
There are business models within the capitalist framework that offer particular social and environmental benefits	Certain aspects under the corporate responsibility help you understand and manage these models, such as fairtrade, social enterprise, and socially responsible investment.
Responsible behaviour is a driver for business success	Corporate responsibility can provide a framework for identifying behaviour that will deliver value to the financial bottom-line.
Companies can choose to behave more or less ethically	Business ethics as a subset of corporate responsibility can help to understand and manage ethical behaviour.
Individuals within companies can be unethical	Individual ethics in the workplace is a subset of corporate responsibility.

Legal responsibility

Legal responsibility refers to the obligation of business to fulfil its economic mission within the confines of the law. Most people who believe corporate responsibility is synonymous with economic responsibility would add the caveat that companies must abide by the law. Equally, those who think corporate responsibility is much more than profit maximization, would accept that companies need to be lawful, at least insofar as the laws are legitimate and just. Local, national, and international law sets out the rules by which corporations play, and, over time, has prescribed what companies can and can not do with regards to areas such as employment, environmental protection, corruption, human rights, and product safety. One only needs to think of pornography, arms sales, and narcotics to realize how the law defines what is legitimate business activity; one need only consider corporate law to appreciate how it spells out the purpose of the company.

But there are also good reasons for saying that corporate responsibility is concerned with more than legal compliance, and forceful arguments have been made that corporate responsibility refers to the actions companies take beyond what is legally required of them. In other words, corporate responsibility as a field is about voluntary not mandatory actions. The distinction between voluntary and compulsory behaviour may be useful for demarcating a particular subset of corporate responsibility theory and practice. Legislation is not comprehensive, and is often the final resort to address a major issue when neither societal norms nor other means of resolution prove adequate. This means that the law by itself will never define everything that society expects companies to take responsibility for. Moreover, companies can have significant influence on what is passed as law, and spend large sums of money persuading law-makers about how to apply their powers. For example, in the 2009 debate over health care reform in the USA, pharmaceutical companies spent over $80 million on lobbying. Indeed, company wealth can be used to influence the meaning of acceptable or unacceptable influence, while some companies as part of their corporate responsibility strategies have said they will simply not engage in political debate.

The deployment of company wealth to influence politicians has been linked to wider debates about the diminishing power of government. Globalization, including the increased international flows of capital, goods, and services (see Chapter 2) has in some respects increased the scope of corporate influence. Headlines along the lines of 'Tesco: Richer than Peru', raise fears about unfettered corporate power, and the lack of regulation, especially once one looks beyond national borders. Such information should be treated with caution. For example, to say a company is richer than a country is a bit like saying a short person standing up is taller than a fat person lying down: it is not an accurate, or even a useful comparison.

Despite arguments that if governments are too harsh on companies, business will invest elsewhere, by some measures governments have become stricter on business. For instance, the European Union's Pollution Prevention and Control Directive raises the bar on controlling industrial pollution; the EU fined Microsoft €899 million because of anti-competitive practices; in 2009 the USA Department of Justice forced Pfizer to pay

$2.3 billion for illegally promoting unapproved drugs; and in the same year the world's richest countries promised regulatory reform of banking. Nonetheless, fears that business wields too much power are widespread and not totally without foundation. For example, in 2006 the British government refused to enforce anti-corruption laws against BAE, the defence company, following what were later described as 'blatant threats'; and Total successfully prevented a case about human rights abuse in Burma from going to court in Belgium.

But, even if it is true that governments find it harder to regulate business than in the past, it is a mistake to ignore the very real power that legislation has. The Alien Torts Claims Act 1789, for example, despite being a US law, has been used to make companies legally accountable for their behaviour overseas and laws modelled on the US Foreign Corrupt Practices Act 1977 are starting to find their way onto statute books in other countries. There is also a complex body of international law for issues such as labour rights, slavery, economic rights, and the environment, which, despite being incomplete, unwieldy, and poorly enforced, nonetheless offers the basis for regulating business in the coming years.

However, legal requirements that vary greatly from country to country present (depending on one's perspective) a problem or an opportunity for business. For example, the work week in China is 44 hours, in France it is 35, and in South Korea it is over 50: will companies choose to invest where the legal work week is longest? Is it immoral for investors to refuse to relocate to a country where environmental management costs are low due to weak environmental laws? If it is legal in Indonesia to use lead paint, why should a retailer there insist its suppliers use more expensive non-toxic ones? Time and again in the contemporary world, corporations are finding themselves held to account not for abiding by the laws in a particular country of operation, but for upholding the non-legislated norms and values of globally dispersed groups and individuals.

Similar developments are taking place in the corporate governance field. Both Harvard University's Kennedy School and the environmental non-government organization (NGO), CERES, for example, have, in different ways, put governance to the fore of their work on corporate responsibility. Companies such as Walt Disney, IBM, and Intel include corporate governance as part of their corporate responsibility reports, while pressure groups such as the Interfaith Center on Corporate Responsibility see aspects of governance, such as executive compensation, the independence and inclusivity of boards of directors, and transparency and accountability to shareholders and other stakeholders, as important parts of the corporate responsibility agenda. Transparency and disclosure are recurring themes in debates about good governance and corporate responsibility more broadly.

Another area where the legal requirements of one region are being spread into other countries is corruption. Business has long been criticized from different parts of the ideological spectrum for using bribery and corruption to influence policy, win contracts, and otherwise distort both the functioning of free markets and the political process. Transparency International, an international NGO that lobbies against corrupt practices, defines corruption as the abuse of entrusted power for private gain. Although often portrayed as a victimless crime, corruption has been associated with low wages, unsafe counterfeit products, and hazardous living and working conditions. It is also blamed for undermining democracy and sound governance, stifling private sector growth, and encouraging inefficient business management (because winning contracts comes down to influence rather than competency).

Industries such as mining, construction, and defence have been especially criticized for paying commissions to win business, not least in countries with limited transparency and accountability. Although in advanced democracies industries from banking, to pharmaceuticals, to football, have all been implicated in corruption scandals, nonetheless, the traditional targets have been at the forefront of corporate responsibility initiatives in this area, including the Extractive Industries Transparency Initiative, which enables the public to compare company payments with declared government revenues from oil, gas, and mining. Combating corruption has also been added to the principles of the United Nations' Global Compact, but, despite these developments, some still downplay its importance, either because it is held to be culturally acceptable in some parts of the world, or because of fears that, by getting too strict with certain governments, companies will lose business to less scrupulous competitors.

Ethical responsibility

Ethical responsibility refers to the responsibilities of companies that go beyond legal compliance, and which are not determined through economic calculations. For some people, this is the most interesting part of corporate responsibility because it is asking what companies can do beyond what is demanded by regulation and economic rationality. Sometimes, companies preempt tougher legislation (e.g. the chemical industry's Responsible Care standard) believing that voluntary agreements will be easier to manage, and perhaps less stringent. But ethical responsibility is not always so pragmatically motivated. In the 1980s, The Body Shop gave a significant boost to campaigners who since the publication of Harrison's *Animal Machines* in 1964 had wanted the testing of cosmetics on animals outlawed. Today, campaign groups such as People for the Ethical Treatment of Animals (PETA) are successful in getting companies such as McDonald's to improve animal welfare.

The environment is one area where companies in the past relied on government to say what was permissible, but which in the face of global challenges from climate change to water availability to deforestation they are, at least to some degree, willing to go beyond legal compliance. This is part of a trend commencing in the 1980s when the effectiveness of command-and-control regulatory solutions started to be questioned, and both companies and regulators began to accept that preventing pollution could be a more effective way forward than simply punishing it. Environmental issues found their way into marketing strategies, and industries focused on environmental technologies and services emerged. In the 1990s, environmental management standards such as BS 7750, the EU Eco-Management and Audit System (EMAS), and the ISO 14000 series provided new ways for companies to understand and manage their environmental impacts. Companies began to realize that, in certain situations, improved environmental performance could have a positive impact on the financial bottom line. In what came to be called the 'greening revolution', the business–environment relationship became, for some companies, less costly problem than a strategic opportunity.[15]

The greening revolution was accompanied by a shift in government attitude, notably in Europe, where the legal responsibility of producers for their products began to cover more of the product life cycle, so that factors such as disposal and recycling had to be considered in product design, manufacturing, and marketing. 'Cradle to grave' thinking has become part of designer philosophy in industries ranging from electrical goods, to footwear, to automotives. Major chemical companies have invested heavily in developing more environmentally beneficial substitutes for harmful materials. At the same time, new industries, such as biotechnology, have presented new environmental challenges (e.g. the perceived environmental consequences of genetically modified organisms) and established industries, such as energy, have generated new debates by investing in renewable energy at the same time as they remain dependent on environmentally damaging carbon-based fuels.

With its emphasis on financial and environmental benefits, the greening revolution marked a significant step forward in corporate responsibility and one that most corporate responsibility theorists failed to predict. The term 'eco-efficiency' has become widely used, highlighting that there need not be a trade-off between business and environmental performance. As McDonough and Braungart (2002) point out, however, there is a significant difference between being eco-efficient and eco-effective: it is the distinction between being *less bad* and consciously striving to do *more good*. If the greening revolution helped companies to think about making their products less harmful, ecoeffectiveness (what has been called 'beyond greening') requires companies to rethink their technologies, their products, and their whole vision of the contribution that business makes to society.

The importance of beyond greening has grown as sustainability has become a major public concern. Sustainability—the ability to sustain a high quality of life for current and future generations—requires companies to rethink what they produce and how they do so. It also involves society rethinking what it wants from commercial enterprise: a question that is capturing widespread attention, as the potentially catastrophic consequences of global climate change become more widely believed.

Although 'sustainability' is still used in some corporate responsibility literature to refer to an eco-efficiency agenda, in its fullest sense, it refers to something that cannot be captured only by reference to an environmental or a business rationale.[16] The triple bottom line was developed to address this by encouraging companies to think in terms of adding economic, social, and environmental value.[17] This provides the framework for some companies' sustainability reports, but merging these three dimensions of value in a way that shows the company's relationship to sustainable development has proved difficult and there is a marked tendency to treat each topic in isolation.

The distinction between doing less harm compared to doing more good is evident too amongst entrepreneurs whose motivation for going into business is measured by their social or environmental success. In the 1950s, faith-based and other organizations began responding to their members' concerns about unequal distribution of the wealth created by trade by establishing alternative trade organizations. Oxfam Trading, Traidcraft, and others invested in building the capacity of producers in poor countries, and sold their handicrafts and other products in Western markets. Later, beginning in the Netherlands, fairtrade labelling organizations were formed, guaranteeing to the consumer that certified producers and traders, in commodities such as coffee, tea, and cocoa, met specified fairtrade standards that include a minimum price to growers that exceeds the cost of production, and payment of a social development premium. Today, companies such as Starbucks, Virgin Atlantic, and J Sainsbury offer fairtrade-certified products.

The same principle of harnessing the power of the markets for the benefit of the poor is found in initiatives popularized under the headings 'bottom of the pyramid' and 'corporate social opportunity'.[18] A well-known example of this is the microfinance model, originally developed in Bangladesh, but now found throughout the world. Microfinance provides poor people with financial capital without the need for collateral, helping them to avoid high usury charges and providing them with a safe place to keep their money. Initially, it was promoted by non-government and aid organizations, but more recently, major banks such as Citigroup and Deutsche Bank have started to offer microfinance services. A variety of models have evolved, such as the pioneering Grameen Bank, BRI in Indonesia with 30 million savers, and ProCredit with banks throughout Eastern Europe (see Chapter 10).

Discretionary responsibilities

Discretionary responsibilities are ones, such as philanthropy, which a company can assume even if there are no clear-cut societal expectations. As noted, for some, corporate responsibility is what lies beyond the law and an important area of discretionary responsibility has been the idea of 'giving back' to society through philanthropic donations. Business leaders such as Carnegie, Rowntree, and Ford gave back large amounts of their individual wealth to establish foundations or to invest in favoured projects. Companies such as Hitachi, ExxonMobil, and Tata, often encouraged by tax regimes, gave as much as 5 per cent of their pre-tax income to the arts, community development, education, and other valued causes. Even though it no longer defines corporate responsibility, philanthropy remains important, as the multi-billion-dollar endowments by Bill Gates and Warren Buffet show. In the USA, where 2,600 companies have charitable foundations, corporate giving rose 14 per cent in 2005 to $8.4 billion, equivalent to $685 per employee. That same year, the UK's 500 largest business donors contributed £1.07 billion in cash and kind, a rise of 15 per cent.

In the 1990s, companies increasingly began to take a more strategic view of philanthropy, seeking out causes that were aligned with their business goals. For example, AT&T's foundation used its funding of education projects to win the ear of government policy advisers and this gave it an inside track in subsequent policy making about the information superhighway. Companies such as Taiwan's King Car Food, and Japan's Sony and Toyota, have shown this to be a worldwide trend and the US Conference Board

(2006) reckons nearly half of companies align their community investment programmes with business objectives.

This has led some companies to adopt cause-related or affinity marketing, under which companies invest in social causes that complement their brands. But companies are wary of criticism that anything they do to give back is perceived as a public relations exercise and have sought to emphasize the win–win nature of investing in communities, while also taking a more critical view of staff volunteering and product gifting. Company-backed initiatives, such as the Partnership for Quality Medical Product Donation and the London Benchmarking Group, have helped focus attention on what constitutes good practice and the impact that philanthropy can have.

■ Discussion points

We have set out two ways of thinking about corporate responsibility: company values and the business–society relationship.

- Which of these do you find most useful as a way of starting to think about the meaning of 'corporate responsibility'?
- Which of these do you think would resonate most with business managers?
- Do you think the type and size of a company and its industry affect how it approaches corporate responsibility?

Limitations of corporate responsibility frameworks

There are now more sophisticated frameworks for comprehending corporate responsibility than that of Carroll (1979), as we explore in Chapter 6, and some of these put much greater emphasis on the process of managing the relationship with wider society. Interestingly, although Carroll denied that his was a hierarchical framework under which some types of responsibility were more important than others, many of these subsequent theories have perpetuated and expanded on the idea that there are qualitatively different tiers of responsibility. This, in turn, has encouraged the idea that companies undergo different evolutionary stages within which their responsibilities and the nature of their relationship with other elements of society discernibly change (see Box 1.4).

Demonstrating that these transitions are beneficial either to business or society is an important part of the debate about corporate responsibility, as we discuss in Chapters 6 and 13. Transitions comprise new issues business is having to address (e.g. climate change and shifts to a low carbon economy), and also new concepts (e.g. responsibility to stakeholders). But when thinking about such changes, one should be as alert to the responsibilities that are seldom mentioned as one is to the ones highlighted in corporate responsibility reports or at conferences. Moreover, one should be prepared to ask why issue A has been included whereas issue B has not. For example, companies such as IBM and Barclays celebrate their commitment to corporate responsibility, but do not include the closing of their company pension schemes or its consequences for workers as a responsibility issue. Likewise, accounting firms such as KPMG and PWC provide corporate responsibility consulting services, but are not especially vociferous on corporate taxation as a dimension to corporate responsibility.

Issues such as tax and pensions draw attention to the importance of long-term corporate performance. In considering how companies negotiate their responsibilities to society, an important test is whether they use their power and resources for the long-term benefit of society, even if there are short-term costs to the company. In its 2005 *Citizenship Report*, multinational conglomerate GE stressed that good citizenship has a more positive and enduring purpose than tackling the ills of the moment: it is about delivering high performance with high integrity over a sustained period of time, so as to create benefits for the long-term health of society and the enterprise. Commentators on business and society have pointed to a number of situations in which private enterprise is most at odds with society's interests, such as when monopolies replace competitive markets, or when companies get so powerful that they unduly influence public policy. These threats exist today, but to these has been added a situation in which the short-term interests of investors prevent companies from taking a long-term view of either the enterprise's, or society's, well-being.

It is interesting to note that economist Milton Friedman, who made probably the most forceful statement that companies are responsible only to shareholders (see Snapshot 1.2), introduced his theory of corporate responsibility at a time when investors were more inclined to hold shares for the longer term. Nowadays, notably in the Anglo-Saxon model that has become the norm against which other business systems are examined, many of his unspoken assumptions about what underpins the business–society relationship no longer hold, because investors look for higher and speedier returns, employees are more mobile, and senior managers are rewarded for pushing up the price of shares and increasing productivity, regardless of the human cost.

It is these types of change that some feel corporate responsibility should redress, either by putting limits on what is acceptable behaviour in the short run, or by encouraging companies to pay more attention to long-term performance. As one group of managers within the World Business Council for Sustainable Development has concluded, corporate responsibility (specifically sustainability) becomes a logical element of profit maximization as soon as one insists that shareholder value equates with long-term shareholder value.[19] The reality for many companies, however, is that they have to straddle the demands of both the short and the long terms. In the words of an oil industry CEO who had to contend with pressure from both the financial markets and civil society:

> On the one hand, you've got Wall Street squeezing you harder and harder for shorter and shorter term performance. On the other hand, you have a broader constituent base that wants more than financial results ... Most CEOs will tell you, 'This is damn hard work'.[20]

SNAPSHOT 1.2

What responsibilities do companies have?

The only social responsibility a law-abiding business has is to maximize profits for its shareholders.

This, in short, is economist Milton Friedman's theory of free market corporate responsibility. It is a controversial viewpoint among corporate responsibility theorists because it appears to say that what's good for investors is good for everyone. That is a difficult position to defend because profit maximization can drive companies to bend or break the law to the point of self-destruction (e.g. Enron and Arthur Andersen). But Friedman isn't saying that everything is justified by the share price: he believes that government sets the rules of the game, and companies have to operate within them. An important question, therefore, is whether governments do a good job at regulating business behaviour; and the answer to that might be very different in today's globalized economy than it was when many companies primarily operated within national boundaries.

Another important question is what do we mean by shareholder. In the 1960s, it was common for individuals and institutions to hold shares for many years, and people's wealth was closely related to the long-term well-being of the firm. That has changed with the emergence of day-traders, the high turnover in shares even amongst institutional investors, the emphasis put on publicly traded companies' quarterly earnings, and the way success is defined by private equity firms. The shareholder is not the long-term owner that he or she once was.

Even amongst libertarian entrepreneurs, who would typically favour markets over governments as arbiters of the social good, Friedman's view of the firm has been criticized as outdated. For example, John Mackey, CEO of US retailer Whole Foods and a self-proclaimed libertarian, has said: '*The enlightened corporation should try to create value for* all *of its constituencies.*' In a dialogue with Friedman, he argued that shareholders are one group with an interest in the company and that they want the firm to maximize profits. According to Mackey, it is too narrow to say that shareholder interests are paramount: the entrepreneur defines the company's purpose and if he says from the outset that part of that purpose is, for example, to give a stated percentage of net profits to philanthropy, then subsequent investors have no right to dispute that—they know what they are buying into.

(Sources: *Rethinking the Social Responsibility of Business*, **www.reason.org**, accessed 17 May 2006; *Wall Street Journal*, 2005; Friedman, 1962)

Quick questions

Corporate responsibility is often depicted as a 'left wing' intervention to disrupt market capitalism, yet people on 'the right' also disagree about its value and importance.

1 What changes have taken place in society since the 1960s that might make Friedman's notion of corporate responsibility outdated?

2 How convincing is Mackey's argument that profits are not the purpose, but a means to realizing social and environmental ends?

3 Which companies would you hold up as examples of Friedman's view of the responsible company? Which ones represent Mackey's view?

Box 1.4 **Prominent areas of corporate responsibility activity today**

Business ethics	Human rights
Legal compliance	Worker rights and welfare
Philanthropy and community investment	Market relations
Environmental management	Corruption
Sustainability	Corporate governance
Animal rights	

CASE STUDY 1

What are the limits to responsibility? The case of pharmaceuticals

Some industries seem to have a responsibility advantage just because of what they do. For instance, it is much easier to imagine a responsible pharmaceutical company than a tobacco firm. Like other segments of the health sector, the pharmaceutical industry is popular among ethical investors because of the social good that its products bring. Many of its employees enter the industry because of the good they can do. On top of this, the industry is renowned for giving back, and has long donated drugs to poor countries to treat tropical diseases such as elephantiasis, river blindness, and leprosy.

Yet pharmaceutical companies are also highly controversial. While Johnson & Johnson enhanced its reputation when it swiftly removed contaminated Tylenol-brand capsules from the shelves in the early 1980s, other firms have fought expensive and damaging legal campaigns to do with similar pain-relief products. Merck, for example, faced thousands of personal-injury lawsuits brought by people who claimed its Vioxx-brand had caused heart attacks or strokes. The company promised to fight every suit, but between 2007 and 2009 agreed to settlements worth over $5 billion. In 2009, Pfizer, a competitor, had to pay a $2.3 billion fine for promoting a similar drug, Bextra, for unapproved uses.

Around the world, the pharmaceutical salesforce has been criticized for persuading doctors to prescribe inappropriate or ineffective drugs, while prestigious medical journals such as the New England Journal of Medicine have spoken out about the way the pharmaceutical industry can undermine the integrity of research. Companies have been accused of over-zealously protecting their patents, and for focusing on developing drugs for the rich rather than the poor. In 1998, a consortium of drug companies filed suit against the South African government, naming Nelson Mandela as a defendant. The case revolved around the companies' attempt to block the distribution of generic drugs used in treating HIV/AIDS; drugs that 39 major companies had patented, but which were 98 per cent cheaper in their generic form. The industry said it was simply protecting its intellectual property rights, but it came under repeated assault for price fixing and for denying the poor access to medicine.

In the same year, a Canadian drug maker applied to manufacture a generic form of the popular anti-depressant, Paxil. With its original patent about to expire, GlaxoSmithKline (GSK), the drug's original inventor, filed four patent infringement lawsuits that effectively stopped the generic drug entering the US market.

The drug industry dropped the case in South Africa in 2001 and GSK was among the companies that proceeded to sell HIV/AIDS treatments at heavily discounted prices in developing countries. Jean-Pierre Garnier, GSK CEO, famously stated that he did not want to head a company that catered only to the rich and said that the company's primary objective must always be public health. Since then, other pharmaceutical companies such as Abbott Laboratories have backed initiatives to make HIV/AIDS treatments available and affordable in developing countries, and have become less aggressive in restricting generic brands.

However, elsewhere the industry is still portrayed as very defensive. The Paxil case was continued and 46 US states accused the company of filing frivolous patent infringement lawsuits that drove up the cost of medicine for the poor. Again, GSK was accused of denying access to the most needy in order to maximize its profits. It settled the suit with a $14 million payment to the states in 2006, but admitted no wrongdoing. More recently, pharmaceutical firms contributed some of the $380 million spent in 2008-2009 by the healthcare sector on lobbying US politicians about health care reform.

Yet the industry claims it is only participating in a democratic process where it is in a unique position to educate politicians. Furthermore, without the profits it generates in wealthier markets, it says it would be unable to develop the drugs that people are crying out for, from cancer treatments to combating Alzheimer's disease, to defeating malaria. And while one judge has ordered a former executive of a drug company to write a book to teach others about his firm's anti-competitive practices, there are still well-respected companies in the industry such as Novo Nordisk which has the corporate purpose of curing diabetes.

(Sources: Smith, 2003; Barmann, 2006; McGreal, 2009; Rockoff & Kendall, 2009; Loftus, 2009; Singer, 2009)

Questions

1 Headlines about miracle cures from swine flu to erectile dysfunction show the thirst modern society has for ever improved drugs. But the furore over drug costs, lobbying, and biased research is evidence that many are deeply suspicious about how the pharmaceutical industry behaves.

    a What are the advantages and disadvantages of making the private sector responsible for this aspect of health care?

    b Do you think the profit-motive of pharmaceutical companies helps or harms their ethical mission?

    c What are the main corporate responsibility issues that the pharmaceutical industry needs to address?

2 Health care is typically depicted as a human right, something that puts pharmaceutical companies in a very different position to most industries.

    a Is GlaxoSmithKline justified in making drugs available on a not-for-profit basis in Africa, but not in the USA?

    b Why do you think various pharmaceutical companies have agreed to provide drugs at lower costs in developing countries?

    c Would it be responsible for a pharmaceutical company to use profits from a drug used in cosmetic surgery to provide lower cost cancer treatments to poor communities?

SUMMARY

Corporate responsibility is the newest 'old' thing in business management. What we mean by 'corporate responsibility' is constantly changing as society itself evolves, affecting our expectations of business and the way in which its relationship with society is handled. The discussion about what corporate responsibility means can be entered into from several doors. We can think of the company as an entity with its own values, or at least as a vessel that has to accommodate the competing values and moral principles of different people. We can also think of it as a member of society that has to uphold certain duties and obligations in order to be a good citizen.

Each doorway has its advantages and disadvantages from an analytical standpoint, but it would be a mistake to conclude that corporate responsibility is diminished because there is no universal definition or overarching theory. Instead, what these different perspectives reveal are a multitude of ways in which business impacts upon, and is affected by, the rest of society and hence a multiplicity of reasons why companies might want to manage that relationship. They will do this differently, depending on such variables as the type of company, the moment in history, the nature of the industry, and the geopolitical context. Similar variables will also determine the benefits of addressing the relationship. But the constant and central concern of corporate responsibility is how the relationship between business and wider society is defined and acted upon, whether by business as a whole, through collective action, or by single corporate actors.

FURTHER READING

**VISIT THE
WEBSITE**
for links to useful
sources of further
information

Take your learning further: Online Resource Centre **www.oxfordtextbooks.co.uk/orc/blowfield_ murray2e/**

Visit the Online Resource Centre which accompanies this book to enrich your understanding of this chapter.

Students: explore web links and further reading suggestions. Keep up to date with the latest developments by undertaking web exercises.

Lecturers: you will find additional case studies, including one on the topic of Labour rights and wrongs—producing apparel for export in Indonesia (taken from 1st edition), for use in class or assessment. Show your students trailers from films related to Corporate Responsibility, and use images from the book in your PowerPoint slides.

- Barrett, R, 1998, *Liberating the Corporate Soul: Building a Visionary Organization*, Boston, MA: Butterworth-Heinemann.

  An interesting approach to blending and aligning personal and organizational values.

- Crane, A and Matten, D, 2004, *Business Ethics*, Oxford: Oxford University Press.

  Comprehensive introduction to business ethics, with an interesting focus on the company as a member of society.

- Davis, I, 2005, 'Ian Davis on business and society', *The Economist*, 26 May, online at **www.economist.com**.

  Provocative take on the need to rethink the role of business, from the head of McKinsey's management consultancy.

- Frederick, WC, 2006, *Corporation Be Good!: The Story of Corporate Social Responsibility*, Indianapolis, IN: Dog Ear Publishing.

  Several decades of corporate responsibility thinking collected together by an American academic.

- Jenkins, RO, Pearson, R and Seyfang, G (eds), 2002, *Corporate Responsibility and Labour Rights: Codes of Conduct in the Global Economy*, London: Earthscan.

  Good collection of articles on issues to do with voluntary codes of labour conduct in supply chains.

- Roddick, A, 2000, *Business as Unusual*, London: Thorsons.

  The Body Shop founder's take on her own experiences of creating a successful company rooted in ethical principles.

- Vogel, D, 2005, *The Market for Virtue: the Potential and Limits of Corporate Social Responsibility*, Washington, D.C: Brookings Institution Press.

  Concise overview of the main drivers and hurdles affecting corporate responsibility today.

ENDNOTES

[1] Davis, 2005.

[2] Mattar, 2001.

[3] Starbuck, 2005.

[4] May et al., 2007.

[5] For overviews of CSR, see Carroll, 1999; Birch, 2001; Basu and Palazzo, 2005. For a discussion of corporate social responsiveness and performance, see Wartick and Cochran, 1985. Bennett et al., 1999, contains essays on the progress of corporate sustainability. Wood and Logsdon, 2001, 2002 and Moon et al., 2005, Moon et al., 2008 provide different viewpoints on corporate citizenship.

[6] Hemp and Stewart, 2004.

[7] See, e.g. Birch, 2001; Woods and Logsdon, 2001; Dion, 2001.

[8] Werther and Chandler, 2006.

[9] Anderson, 2003; 2005.

[10] See, e.g. Sorell and Hendry, 1994; Chryssides and Kaler, 1993; Donaldson and Dunfee, 1999; Ladkin, 2006.

[11] Jensen and Meckling, 1976. For a fuller discussion, see Chapter 8.

[12] www.npr.org/templates/story/story.php?storyId=106899074, accessed 5 October 2009.

[13] www.guardian.co.uk/business/2007/apr/15/supermarkets.uknews, accessed 5 October 2009.

[14] www.news.bbc.co.uk/1/hi/business/7339231.stm, accessed 5 October 2009.

[15] Freeman et al., 2000; Schaltegger et al., 2003.

[16] Renn, 1995, cited in Schaltegger et al., 2003.

[17] Elkington, 1998.

[18] Prahalad, 2005; Grayson and Hodges, 2004.

[19] WBCSB, 2006.

[20] Blowfield and Googins, 2007, p22.

2

The origins of corporate responsibility

Chapter overview

In this chapter, we set out the theoretical and historical origins of modern-day corporate responsibility. In particular, we will:

- plot the evolution of the modern corporation and its relevance for the business–society relationship;

- explore how corporate responsibility has evolved from the Industrial Revolution to the current era of globalization;

- trace the development of theories of corporate responsibility.

Main topics

■ Key terms

Capitalism	Licence to operate
Corporate philanthropy	Limited liability
Industrial Revolution	New Deal
Welfare state	Social contract
Globalization	

■ Online resources

- A history of globalization and accompanying references

- Exercises and discussion topics for students

- Fordlandia—case study of corporate responsibility in the 1930s

- Links to other web-based resources

- Additional reading

Introduction

In 1909, George Cadbury found himself in court because the company bearing his name had been buying cocoa produced by slaves in Africa.[1] In 2000, the company found itself accused once more of the same offence. These incidents demonstrate that issues such as slavery do not go away. More to the point, when corporate behaviour clashes with people's sense of justice and permissibility, companies are held responsible: even if there is no legal liability, and despite the absence or presence of shareholder interest.

The issues that matter, why they come to the fore, and what a company does to address them vary: according to the company, the industry, the location, and the time. Cadbury's response in 1909 was very different to what it was in 2000 (see Case Study 2), even if slavery was always more likely to be more of an issue for the chocolate manufacturer compared to its Birmingham neighbour, the car-maker Rover, which in 2000, faced with bankruptcy and allegations of pension fund fraud, had its own corporate responsibility headaches to deal with.

Corporate responsibility is constant yet variable and dynamic. In this chapter, we examine how society has consistently held expectations of business that go beyond the narrow sphere of wealth creation. We begin by exploring the relationship of business has had with society during different historical periods, and in different countries. Then we examine how various theories of corporate responsibility have emerged to help understand and manage that relationship.

What the following sections reveal is that private enterprise has always been the subject of public scrutiny. What we mean by 'corporate responsibility' today has been influenced enormously by our economic systems, the evolution of the modern corporation, and the emergence of theories of corporate responsibility itself. This chapter is a discussion of that heritage.

The *Cadbury* case is a useful starting point for putting corporate responsibility in context. The issues in 1909 were, in many ways, the same as those today. First, companies were then, and are now, felt by many to have a duty to uphold certain human rights, even when there is no legal liability. Second, companies that purchase commodities or manufactured goods are held to have influence over, and responsibility for, the behaviour of their producers. These principles were apparent in the 1909 court case and are central to areas of modern corporate responsibility, such as ethical trade.

Echoes of the Cadbury experience can be heard throughout this chapter as we explore the origins of corporate responsibility. The company's experiences are not unique: stick a pin anywhere in the timeline of corporate evolution and the issues of what a company should be responsible for, who decides, and where accountability lies are recurring themes. Responses can vary, as do the levels of trust in corporations (see Figure 2.1), but what this chapter shows is that the issues of corporate responsibility and the role of commercial endeavour in society are constants throughout human history.

Three eras of responsibility

The Cadbury experience straddles three historical periods, during which the nature of business' relationship with society has changed significantly:

1 the Industrial Revolution;
2 the mid-twentieth-century welfare state;
3 the globalization era.

Each period has raised new issues about what business should be responsible for, but, as we will see, many of the issues remain relevant from one era to the next.

The Industrial Revolution

Throughout much of Europe, the biggest change in human demographics and human working life came with the Industrial Revolution, as the poor from the countryside headed towards the cities in search of work. In the UK, the first industrial power, between

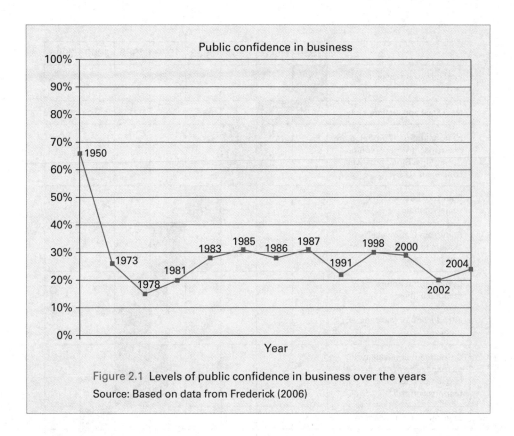

Figure 2.1 Levels of public confidence in business over the years
Source: Based on data from Frederick (2006)

1801 and 1871, the proportion of the population engaged in manufacturing increased from one fifth to nearly two-thirds.[2]

But this massive increase in urban living brought with it problems of overcrowding and disease. Children were employed in sweeping chimneys, domestic service, and manufacturing, as depicted in the popular novels of Dickens and Kingsley. Factories and mines were responsible for a large number of injuries and fatalities. Slave labour on the African and American continents produced many of the raw materials that industrialization required. In some industries, women became important components of the workforce, not out of choice, but due to poverty.

Industrialization provoked civil unrest. From the late 1770s, there were numerous popular, frequently violent, protests aimed at resisting industrialization or improving the lives of those affected by it. Information about human exploitation spurred various reform movements, such as Wilberforce's anti-slavery society, while the UK's first Factory Acts were passed in 1819 and laws to control conditions in mines were passed in 1842.

In addition to government intervention, it was around this time that writers such as Carlyle and Arnold began to suggest how heads of industry might behave, marking the start of the era of Victorian philanthropy. Robert Owen had already set up his mills at New Lanark and was an instigator of the early Factory Acts. He strove to establish a new

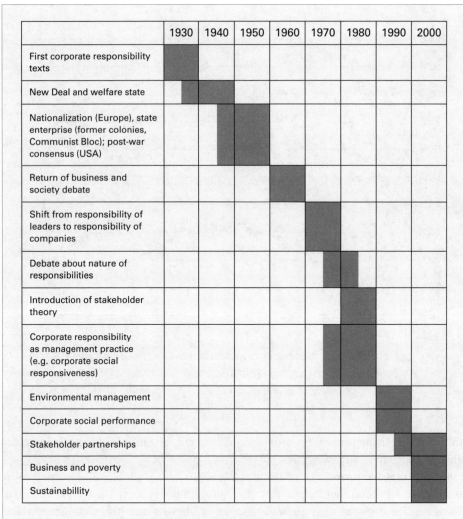

	1930	1940	1950	1960	1970	1980	1990	2000
First corporate responsibility texts	■							
New Deal and welfare state	■	■						
Nationalization (Europe), state enterprise (former colonies, Communist Bloc); post-war consensus (USA)		■	■					
Return of business and society debate				■				
Shift from responsibility of leaders to responsibility of companies					■			
Debate about nature of responsibilities					■	■		
Introduction of stakeholder theory						■		
Corporate responsibility as management practice (e.g. corporate social responsiveness)					■	■		
Environmental management							■	
Corporate social performance							■	
Stakeholder partnerships							■	■
Business and poverty								■
Sustainabillity								■

Figure 2.2 **Timeline of corporate responsibility**

model of industrial development in Scotland and the USA, based on the belief that a man's character was formed by his surroundings, and the conditions under which he worked and lived. This vision was developed later in the century by the likes of Cadbury and Rowntree, who established villages at Bourneville and New Earswick respectively, within which their workers could live in supportive communities with open spaces, shops, and schools in easy reach.

Carnegie—who famously said that the wealthy should consider their wealth to be trust funds that they should use for the good of the community—pursued a different form of benevolence using his fortune from steel to embark on a philanthropic quest that saw him donate some $350 million to charitable and other philanthropic causes, including the building of libraries, the establishment of educational trusts, and contributions towards creating such iconic buildings as the Carnegie Hall in New York and the Peace Palace in The Hague.

Each industrial economy has its own history of industrialization, and we only have to look at the different timelines of the abolition of slavery in the UK, the USA, and Belgium, for example, to see that change happened at different speeds and in different ways. And some countries' toleration of slavery overseas when it had been outlawed at home is but one example of how standards of business behaviour were affected by location. Similar aspects of industrialization have arisen again today with the emergence of new industrial powers. For example, in countries such as China, the massive influx of rural people into urban areas is one trend that has redefined notions of corporate responsibility, as have aspects of economic growth and overseas investment that appear to be at the expense of human and environmental well-being (see Chapter 5).

The evolution and rise of the modern corporation

In the mind's eye, the first Industrial Revolution in Europe and the USA conjures up images of technological innovation: steam engines, mills, belching factory chimneys, and the like. But this was as much an institutional revolution as an industrial one. Worklife changed, governed by clocks and machines rather than seasons. But the idea of business itself changed as well. As important as technology was institutional innovation, not least the emergence of the 'limited liability company' and changes in the meaning of 'incorporation'. These legal constructs were to have a profound effect on the business-society relationship: not only on where liability fell, but what the rights and responsibilities of the company were. Today, the meaning of 'business' is either taken for granted, or the subject of typically polarized arguments over whether it is a good or a bad thing. But in capitalism's early days, the advantages and disadvantages of different types of company were widely debated. Limited liability was a major factor that allowed the modern corporation to emerge: the construct by which shareholders in a company are not liable for its debts beyond the nominal value of their shares. The economist, Adam Smith, disliked this idea and favoured partnerships over corporations, because he felt that separating the owner from direct control of the company opens the way for professional managers to pursue their own self-interest.[3] But, despite the fact that the limited liability company is only one of several forms of commercial enterprise, it has nonetheless come to dominate the modern business world.

Limited liability encourages entrepreneurship, but has also been singled out as the root cause of problems in the business–society relationship. It has made possible the emergence of multinational corporations, the power of which Korten (1995) views as a threat to society and Henderson (2004) sees as an asset. It also creates the tension between shareholders and corporate officials that is central to arguments about where a company's responsibilities lie. For some, such as Friedman (1962) and Novak (1982), the primacy given to shareholder interests is the genius of capitalism; for others, such as Mitchell (2001) and Ellsworth (2002), it is the reason why managers focus on short-term results and therefore restricts their freedom to serve the interests of others in society. Thus, limited liability is central to the roles that companies play in creating jobs, paying taxes, and generating wealth, but also to aspects of corporate behaviour such as downsizing, bankruptcy, and who has claim to the company's assets. We discuss these issues in other chapters, not least in the context of the socially responsible investment movement, which seeks to change the investor–company relationship (see Chapter 10).

The Twentieth-Century—a more mature capitalism

From corporate to government responsibility

By the early twentieth century, changes in the legal definition of the firm led to a huge increase in the number of mergers and corporations came to be seen by some as huge, impersonal monoliths that were beginning to exert political pressure as never before, leading to public calls for greater regulation and supervision (see Snapshot 2.1). Private enterprise had flourished in the late nineteenth century until the period prior to World War I. Yes, it could be highly exploitative of people and nature. Yes, it was often the bed-fellow of imperialism and militarism. Yes, it frequently relied on monopoly and oligopoly to the point where John D Rockefeller, who famously stated that 'competition is a sin', owned wealth equivalent to nearly two per cent of US GDP (Bill Gates is worth 0.65 per cent).[4] Capitalism took various forms and had many facets, making it difficult to generalize. But for all its weaknesses and failings, capitalist free enterprise and with it global free trade flourished before World War I, corporate power grew and private self-interest was promoted as serving the public good. This triumphalism faded after the war, and momentum increased for greater equality and a rethinking of the social order following the leadership failures that had left eight million dead on battlefields around the world, and the image of the capitalist as war profiteer depicted in Shaw's play, 'Major Barbara', was commonplace. The International Labour Organization, founded in 1919 as part of the League of Nations, brought together government, business, and trade unions, and explicitly recognized the dangers of an unjust political or economic order. Business leaders were forced to consider the impact their activities were having on wider society and some engaged in movements such as 'New Capitalism'[5] promoting the idea that business should voluntarily take steps to portray itself and its activities as beneficial to society at large.

But such ideas gained limited traction, partly because of the greater struggle between managers and organized labour that was a feature of the post-war period, and also because economic growth (particularly increases in share value in some countries) encouraged a belief that markets could be the ultimate guarantors of the public good. This came to a head with the Great Depression, when corporate greed was blamed as one of the possible causes of the 1929 Wall Street Crash that left millions destitute in the USA, with ramifications throughout the world's economy. It was time to rein in corporate and shareholder excess, and where possible government stepped in to rescue the economy. In Germany, the National Socialist Party struck alliances with big business to align private enterprise with the national good. In the US, President Franklin D Roosevelt initiated the 'New Deal', a series of measures that were, in part, designed to limit the power of corporations. If the 1920s' view of corporate managers is encapsulated in the phrase of General Motors' President, Alfred Sloan, '*The business of business is business*', Roosevelt's view can be seen in the quote: '*We consider too much the good luck of the early bird, and not enough the bad luck of the early worm.*' Despite the very different fortunes of countries such as Germany, USA, and Japan, the idea of social welfare as a safety net for when capitalism wobbled or fell remained a platform of the social order for the rest of the twentieth century, at least in wealthier nations. Countries from Argentina to Indonesia governments have continued to step in to tackle market failure, and the interventions by major economic powers around the world to save the finance industry in 2008 show that in the world of *real politik* free markets are not trusted to serve the public good.

SNAPSHOT 2.1

Is big business desirable, inevitable or irredeemable?

Ever since the nineteenth century the size of companies has grown and grown. When people think about corporate responsibility, they often think about the giant, multinational companies and conglomerates that dominate industries from Information and Communication Technologies to Retail to Pharmaceuticals. Most private sector workers may work for small firms, but it is large business that attracts attention. Unilever, Tata, BHP Billiton, and Samsung are a handful of the many multinational companies that put corporate responsibility on their websites' front pages. But are these companies too big to be responsible members of society?

Thomas Quinn called such companies '*Monster Business*'. The monster business was the inevitable end result of business evolution where companies evolved from small enterprising firms to large ones, then into giant corporations, and finally into monsters. Monster companies not only stifle competition—something that has led to antitrust laws around the world —but also affect social and political institutions, and even pose a menace to the democratic way of life.

Although he was writing during the 1930s' Depression, his views find echoes in corporate responsibility discussions today. For example, he pointed to big-banker trustees who control voting at the dominant corporations, representing what he called '*the highest degree of concentrated economic power in our history*'. Reflecting recent criticisms about board responsibility, he claimed that directors were responsible for setting '*wholly arbitrary, self-serving judgments, compensation and recognition awards*'. He also blamed corporate officials for paying themselves excessive salaries, bonuses, pensions, and stock options, and went on to explain why monster business was inherently anti-social.

Quinn was no radical outsider: certainly not the 1930s equivalent of Naomi Klein or Joel Bakan. He was a star executive at that quintessential 'monster business', General Electric; the man who established that company's refrigerator division. In the economic and social upheaval of his time, his views were part of the cauldron of public debate. Now, when executives are typically portrayed as conservatives, his cry to limit the size of business is in marked contrast to right-wing thinkers such as Rand and Hayek who treated a company's growth within the free market as the best way to increase shareholder value, lower prices, and serve the general good.

Quinn's views are more aligned with the political left, but even here things are not clear cut. Canadian economist, JK Galbraith, did not necessarily favour big business, but saw its growth as inevitable as perfect competition disappeared beneath its shadow. He agreed with Quinn that by itself, this would have undesirable outcomes across society. However, we should not worry about this because the interests of capital and management, he argued, would be counterbalanced by trade unions and other organized groups. It was what he called this *'countervailing power'* that would keep monster business honest and continuing to serve the public good.

(Sources: Galbraith 1952; Quinn, 1962; Rand 1966)

Quick questions

1 Does the fact that parts of what Quinn observed still resonate today suggest that 'the problem' of big business is nothing new and is something that society adequately controls through conventional political processes?

2 Do you agree with Galbraith that the power of 'business' can be controlled by 'countervailing powers'?

3 Is Rand right to argue that controls on the size of business such as antitrust laws stifle innovation, success, and economic rewards?

Post World War II

Business emerged from World War II with a mixed reputation. Companies such as Mitsubishi and Mercedes had been part of their nations' war machines, while firms from IBM to Coke were to spend years cleansing themselves of associations with fascism. But business had played a key part in winning the war, whether it be through unprecedented levels of production or fast-track innovation. Where the war had hit hardest, there was exhaustion and an appetite for change. In the UK, the post-war Labour government put in place a system of welfare safety nets. It also acted on its belief in state-owned industry by nationalizing major industries such as coal, railways, steel, gas distribution, and power generation. The idea that business best served the public good if it was state-controlled took hold in much of Western Europe and, of course, in the Eastern Bloc of Communist countries, in which private enterprise was outlawed. It also characterized the role of business in newly independent countries such as Indonesia and India which saw the nationalization of industry as essential to the long-held dream of independence.

In West Germany and Italy, new models of governance were put in place to ensure that workers, as well as shareholders, had a say in how companies were run. In the USA, a seemingly spontaneous interplay between business and society emerged, similar to what chaos theory would later term 'complex adaptive systems', but which, at the time, was seen as a debate over how much of its power business would cede to wider society.[6]

These different approaches to managing the role of business in society all marked a significant change in thinking from that of the days when it was assumed that business best benefited others by being left largely to its own devices. The welfare state was primarily concerned with a more equitable distribution of the benefits of economic prosperity. Distribution was the responsibility of government and the primary role of business was to create jobs, obey the law, and pay taxes. The concerns of the welfare state, however, such as health care, living wages, and education, influence what we think of as 'corporate responsibility' today. Equally, national governments' renewed interest in human rights in the aftermath of the war gave rise to such agreements as the United Nations' Universal Declaration of Human Rights, which is now referenced in important corporate responsibility initiatives.

It is easy to idealize the post-World War II contract between business and government. In the former colonies, new governments lacked the expertise or wealth to deliver the comprehensive safety nets enjoyed in wealthier countries. Companies such as Zambia Consolidated Copper Mines found themselves directly involved in community development. Equally, prosperity brought with it new social concerns. In the early 1950s in both the UK and USA, smog claimed the lives of many citizens, with serious instances in London, New York, and Los Angeles. Pollution became a political issue, resulting in the passing of the US Air Pollution Control Act in 1955 and the UK Clean Air Act in 1956. A year later, Scripps Oceanographic Institute scientists were surprised to discover rising carbon dioxide levels in the world's oceans.

In 1962, Carson's *Silent Spring* was published, detailing the effect of man-made pesticides, and, throughout the decade, scientific discovery into the effects of leaded petroleum, water pollution, and chemical seepage served to make increasing numbers of people aware of the connection between environmental degradation and corporate activity. In the following decades, regular instances of corporate malfeasance, such as the Love Canal, Bhopal, Chernobyl, and the *Exxon Valdez*, served to reinforce this connection.

Non-government environmental groups, such as Greenpeace (founded in 1971), began advocating for change outside the mainstream political process. In terms of organization and strategy, they set the agenda for a much broader range of rights-focused activists, such as those protecting the interests of workers, indigenous people, animals, children, bonded labour, etc.—the advocacy groups that play an important in contemporary corporate responsibility today.

The women's rights movement also became more visible in the 1970s and, among other things, raised issues of equality in the workplace. One aspect of this was equal treatment in terms of remuneration and working conditions, and another was equality of opportunity. The movement worldwide has had an enormous impact in a relatively short space of time, most notably in the area of legislation (e.g. maternity rights, equal pay). In terms of corporate responsibility, the women's rights movement established the basic principle that companies shall not discriminate against women. Similar principles have been applied in relation to age, ethnicity, race, disability, and sexual orientation, and, in the USA especially, racial discrimination has been a significant part of the corporate responsibility agenda.

■ **Discussion points**

There are expectations across the political spectrum that big business has the power and responsibility to benefit society. There are also fears across the spectrum that big business is a 'monster'.

- Does 'big business' have different responsibilities to those of other types of business?
- How does limited liability influence how companies view their relationships with society?
- Find examples, at the national and provincial levels, of ways in which company law makes companies responsible to stakeholders other than shareholders.

The globalization era

Business' relationship with society has changed again with globalization, the phenomenon that has affected social, political, economic, and business life since the 1980s. Globalization is often portrayed as a new era, bringing changes that are as momentous as those of the Industrial Revolution. It is certainly an era during which business' place in society is being transformed and, for that reason alone, it is important that we understand its meaning and consequences.

But we can go further than this. Writers such as Wood et al. (2006), Pedersen and Huniche (2006), and Crane and Matten (2004) tie corporate responsibility to the social, political, and environmental challenges of globalization. In fact, to some degree, its success may influence the direction of globalization overall.[7] This is because globalization is associated, on the one hand, with a limited set of global governance mechanisms and weakened national governments, and on the other, with unprecedented private sector wealth, power, and impact. Corporate responsibility has thus become an important means for addressing what Stiglitz (2002) sees as the fundamental problem with contemporary globalization—a system of global governance without global government.

However, there is a lot of confusion about what is meant by globalization. In corporate responsibility literature, the term is often used in its narrowest sense to mean the world-wide flows of data, capital, goods and services. Indeed, some aspects of globalization highlighted by certain corporate observers were already features of previous eras. For example, globalization critic Naomi Klein (1999) talks about global colonization by brands—what she calls '*McDonaldization*'—and a wider process as part of which Western norms and values wipe out diversity and local cultures. Yet generations earlier in his travels between South Africa, England, and India, Mahatma Gandhi would have found it as easy to buy a packet of Players cigarettes as we would find it to buy a Big Mac today.

Many economists use globalization to mean the global spread of liberal economic ideas, notably the creation of a global market built on free trade. This kind of liberal globalization is essentially the realization of the economic relations explained by economists such as Smith, Ricardo, or Marx, and the socio-economic system described by Mises and Hayek. Some political economists, on the other hand, argue that we should think more broadly than just economics: that we should see globalization as a social condition that also includes politics, culture, ethics, ecology, and all of the other facets that affect human life. What separates globalization today from any previous historical period is that a combination of technological innovation, policy shifts, power relations, and values has meant that physical space and time have become much less important determinants of economic and social activity, and of social identity. Alluding to Fukuyama's (1989) idea that globalization marks the end of history, Virilio (2000) concludes that globalization is really the end of geography.

Understandably, the economic dimension to globalization is attractive to many in business, but it is worthwhile understanding political economists' perspective, what has been called 'globalization as deterritorialization'.[8] In our business lives, we witness many symptoms of globalization, such as the offshoring of jobs, rapid growth in international trade, and international capital flows. Deterritorialization theorists say that all of this reflects more fundamental changes in our social condition (e.g. new social orders transcending traditional political and geographical boundaries; powerful companies and other organizations not strongly linked to a specific place; intense, rapid interaction between groups allowing events in one region to trigger reactions anywhere in the world), and is part of a growing consciousness of our interconnectedness and interdependence.[9] This is important for companies to understand because on the one hand they are often criticized for exerting excessive power in this new global order, and on the other they can fall victims to it such as when people connected through cyberspace form an alliance to hold a company to account for its behaviour. This is what the chocolate industry experienced when journalists found slave labour on cocoa farms in West Africa (see Case Study 2), or what Monsanto still experiences because of some people's objections to genetically modified organisms. Moreover, while not all such alliances survive for long, some do as Nestlé will vouch after three decades of fighting allegations about its infant milk formula.

Business in the modern globalization era is fundamental to understanding contemporary corporate responsibility, and we discuss it in far more depth in Chapter 4. It accounts for many of the issues companies are being held responsible for, the growth in wealth, poverty and inequality that has accompanied unprecedented private sector activity, and the recognition of the values and materiality dimensions of issues such as global poverty and sustainability that business is being asked to address. It also accounts for the changing nature of corporate governance, investment, public scrutiny, and social expectation that affect companies' licence to operate and the very definition of success. However, before we flesh out these statements, let us explore the evolution of corporate responsibility theory that shapes some of our thinking today.

Theories of corporate responsibility

The preceding sections describe the historical landscape that has influenced corporate responsibility theory and practice. It feels at times that there is an archaeological quest to discover the earliest instance of corporate responsibility, with examples reported as long ago as Mesopotamian and Roman times.[10] If by theory we mean something that is written down, corporate responsibility theory is relatively new; but if we mean the ideas

SNAPSHOT 2.2

Royal Dutch Shell Group and global protesters

In the development of the 'global company', the energy sector has probably led the way by virtue of its need to search for reserves worldwide. Shell is a major sector player and has a massive impact on the economies of the 135 countries it operates in.

In the 1990s, two Shell subsidiaries were caught up in events that undermined the company's reputation, causing it to alter long-held approaches to business practice and find new strategies to regain lost trust. In Nigeria, where the company had been extracting oil in the Niger River Delta since 1956, local populations were increasingly agitated by what they saw as the high social and environmental costs, and slender rewards, of oil production.

The Ogoni People, in particular, under the leadership of Ken Saro-Wiwa, staged public protests that were met with extreme force by the Nigerian government forces, leading to the deaths of demonstrators and accusations that Shell was complicit in the killings. Saro-Wiwa was eventually arrested and executed for allegedly killing pro-government tribal leaders. His death provoked an international outcry and, despite assertions by Shell that it was not in any way involved, the impression lingered that it had a case to answer.

A continent away, Shell was also facing criticism for wanting to scrap its Brent Spar oil storage platform in the deep Atlantic: something that environmental groups saw as a dangerous precedent. Greenpeace mobilized a number of popular campaigns to raise awareness among the public. In the UK and Germany, people began picketing Shell petrol stations and mounting anti-Shell campaigns, and the firm Pensions Investments Research Consultants (PIRC) warned investors of the possible negative fallout.

Despite denials by Shell of its involvement in the Saro-Wiwa affair and the subsequent findings that Brent Spar was not carrying toxic waste, the company was under pressure to respond to the concerns being expressed by many stakeholder groups, including its shareholders. It employed the consultancy company, SustainAbility, to review its policies on reporting and it was not long before the company was rebranded with the slogan 'People, Planet, Profits', echoing the 'triple bottom line' philosophy of the consultancy's founder, John Elkington. Yet its investment in being responsible was only partially successful, and in 2009 it agreed to pay US$15.5 million to settle a legal action brought in the USA because of its alleged collaboration in Saro-Wiwa's death. According to lawyer, Anthony DiCaprio, the settlement would 'encourage companies to seriously consider the social and environmental impact their operations may have on a community or face the possibility of a suit.'

(Sources: Mirvis, 2000; **www.pirc.co.uk**—accessed 30 July 2005; www.guardian.co.uk—accessed 20 September 2009)

Quick Questions

1 Are companies more susceptible now than in the past to accusations of unfair collaboration with national governments?

2 How can corporations guard against allegations of complicity in government actions against indigenous peoples?

3 What other examples can you think of where companies have had trouble protecting their reputations against community and NGO attacks?

that underpin business practice, then any enterprise at any moment in history has had to establish what Donaldson and Dunfee (1999) call its 'licence to operate' because without the support of those in power or the wider public it cannot prosper. The different histories and cultures of corporate responsibility are a fascinating area of enquiry, but for purely practical reasons the following discussion of corporate responsibility theory's evolution takes as its starting point business in the West.

■ Key concepts: Licence to operate

Licence to operate refers to the public's acceptance of a company's impact on wider society. It is an idea rooted in philosophers' such as Hobbes and Locke's theories of the social contract that exists between a government and the people. Just as in a democracy the electorate can grant and remove a government's permission to govern, so a company's constituents (e.g. consumers, investors, customers, communities) grant tacit or explicit approval to companies to conduct their business.

The right to extract profit from commercial activities is one part of the licence to operate, but the company's constituents can dictate what is a legitimate profit-seeking activity. For example, human trafficking might be profitable but the criminal networks that are involved cannot claim to have a licence to operate. The tobacco industry is an example of where companies have had their licence to operate severely restricted, not least because of their role in hiding the connection between smoking and cancer. An alternative energy company such as Vestas can claim to have a strong licence to operate because of the positive relationship it seems to have with tackling climate change, whereas a company such as EDF may have to invest more in building its licence because of its association with coal-fired and nuclear power.

There are numerous ways companies can strengthen their licence including stakeholder engagement, transparency, and corporate responsibility reporting. Such approaches may help companies build better relations with their constituents, but they should not regard the licence as irrevocable as it will be under continual scrutiny and reevaluation.

Evolution of corporate responsibility theory

Before corporate responsibility had a name, philosophy and theology was already informing the thinking of entrepreneurs. Carnegie's *Gospel of Wealth* (1889) sets out the duties wealthy capitalists have to society. The Lever Brothers, the Clarks, and the Cadburys were not only successful industrialists but also Quakers who found it contrary to their faith to ignore worker well-being, or to leave people's fates to the market. They differed from Carnegie in their belief that responsibility was not just about how one used one's wealth, but how that wealth was created in the first place. Early academic writers on corporate responsibility such as Berle and Means (1932) focused on the responsibilities of the individual business leader rather than the company, reflecting a widely held view in the USA that success and responsibility go hand in hand. Davis called this the 'Iron Law of Responsibility' which states that the social responsibilities of business leaders need to be commensurate with their social power[11] (Figure 2.2).

Davis (1973) was, however, also one of the first corporate responsibility theorists to argue that social responsibility was more than the acts of individuals; that corporate responsibility should refer to the company as an institution. The shift in focus from the individual to the company led to a new discussion of responsibilities. Some saw corporate responsibility as a way of utilizing company resources towards broad social ends rather than to serve only narrow private interests.[12] In addition to linking responsibility to power, Davis himself held that the social responsibility of business demanded that companies should be open to public input and scrutiny; that social costs and benefits should be factored into their business decisions and also priced into products, and that, where it has the necessary competencies, the company as a citizen should be involved in social affairs.[13] He also noted that there might be long-term economic gain from behaving responsibly.

All of these issues are relevant to corporate responsibility today. So too are some of the dilemmas raised: should companies take actions beyond what is legally required? (See Chapter 1) Should a company's assets be used for purposes other than maximizing shareholder value (see Chapter 13)? Are the fiduciary duties of executives and directors too narrowly defined (see Chapter 7). However, since the 1990s, the theory and practice of corporate responsibility has evolved more rapidly than ever before, raising questions and possibilities that Davis could not have imagined. Corporate responsibility in the 1990s and beyond dominates most of the discussion in this book; but it is interesting and worthwhile to look at its earlier forms because Davis and his peers spurred thinking about how companies could demonstrate their contribution to social goals such as economic justice, stability, and freedom,[14] and the ways in which this can be accomplished, asking three questions that are still as pertinent today:

1 How can business be responsible?

2 For what is it responsible?

3 To whom is it responsible?

It is to these questions that we now turn.

Defining the responsible enterprise

How can business be responsible?

Identifying the enterprise as the focus of corporate responsibility led theorists to question when and how companies should exhibit responsibility. Manne and Wallich (1972) said that corporate responsibility refers to actions for which the company is under no legal compulsion. If corporate responsibility begins where the law ends, however, what does this mean? Manne claimed that true corporate responsibility expenditure, as well as being voluntary, was that which:

1 generates marginal returns less than those available from alternative courses of action;

2 is an actual corporate expenditure, not a conduit for individual largesse.[15]

This raises two interesting questions: first, should corporate responsibility be limited to what companies do to generate a profit; second, should companies be denied moral credit for actions taken for commercial reasons? The Committee for Economic Development, comprising US corporate leaders, identified three concentric circles of responsibility that blurred Manne's distinctions:

1 creating products, jobs, economic growth;

2 sensitivity to changing social values;

3 emerging responsibilities such as poverty and urban blight.[16]

These circles embrace both core business activity and how the company manages its relationship with society more widely, but, again, the emphasis is on voluntary actions and in no case is the company required to be accountable for failing to carry out these responsibilities.

Debates about voluntary versus mandatory approaches to corporate responsibility continue to this day. They are further complicated because companies may feel they have to take particular actions even without legal compulsion (e.g. because of civil society pressure—see Chapter 9). We explore these issues elsewhere and so, for now, limit ourselves to flagging voluntarism as a recurring theme in this book.

■ Discussion points

George Soros, American financial speculator, stock investor, philanthropist, and political activist, has said: '*We can have a market economy, but we cannot have a market society.*'[17]

* What distinction is he making between 'economy' and 'society'?

* Does corporate responsibility help the market economy to become a market society?

* Describe how a company from the former Eastern Bloc might use corporate responsibility to establish its licence to operate in the European Union.

For what is business responsible?

Defining corporate responsibility as voluntary action does little to explain for what business should take responsibility. In Chapter 1, we set out various perspectives on this, including Carroll's (1979) multidimensional model of corporate responsibility, which has proved one of the most widely referenced frameworks because it makes clear important principles and spheres of responsibility (i.e. economic, legal, ethical, and discretionary responsibilities—see Figure 1.2). Its strength is that it draws together different types of responsibility that had tended to be treated as mutually exclusive or otherwise problematic. It does this by identifying separate categories and any action that falls under one category or another can be considered part of corporate responsibility. But this, in itself, can cause problems: for example, does a company accept responsibility for any issue that fits into one of the categories? If not, how does it prioritize its response? Equally, how does the company go about deciding what is ethical, or what discretionary actions it should take?[18] Consequently, at least as important as what companies are responsible for is how those responsibilities are defined.

Corporate responsibility, as already noted, is dynamic, and changes according to time, industry and location. Much of academic corporate responsibility theory originates from the USA, and therefore reflects social conditions that are different even in similarly advanced capitalist economies. For example, an American employee often has the legal status of 'at-will employment' meaning that worker and employee can break their relationship without liability to either party. In Europe, a worker may have a three-month notice period before their relationship with the company ends: in the USA, as anyone who watches American TV knows, a worker can walk out the same day, taking their box of personal effects with them. Therefore, in Europe severance pay and dismissal may not be spelled out as a corporate responsibility because the responsibilities are set out in legal statute: in the USA, on the other hand, corporate responsibility might offer a counterbalance to relatively limited legal protections.

The nature of the American free enterprise system—its financial and governance systems, its culture, its education and labour systems, the institution of the firm, etc.—is unique, and different in important ways from that in Europe and elsewhere.[19] This may account for the differences in corporate responsibility between the USA and elsewhere, with the USA adopting what has been called 'explicit' corporate responsibility (i.e. the company carries out certain activities with the explicit intent of serving social interests), and Europe concentrating on 'implicit' corporate responsibility (i.e. business is one of many institutions that are expected to serve the social good, and must conform with the social consensus about its role).[20] It may also explain why business in the USA has been what Drucker (1946) called 'the representative institution', responsible for representing and upholding American society's basic values and beliefs; whereas in Europe, for example, companies have been viewed more as supplicants to the social good.

The Atlantic Ocean is not the only corporate responsibility fault line: claims about the geographical distinctions in what companies are responsible for have been made about India, Japan, China, Brazil, and Africa and Asia in general. We will touch on these differences, as well as dissimilarities in responsibility between industries in later chapters. But it is important to consider some of the consequences of thinking in terms of disparities in responsibilities. It may be that an area of behaviour has to be spelled out as an explicit responsibility in one region, but not in another because of different laws. But to what extent can something be acceptable in one country and not in another? If violence on the factory floor is commonplace in one country, should a French multinational such as Carrefour accept that behaviour amongst its suppliers when it would not be able to do so in France?

This is the area of ethical relativism. There may be good reasons to define the responsibilities of corporations in the context of where they are being applied, but there is also a risk of turning a blind eye to unacceptable actions on the grounds that something is a cultural convention. For example, when abuse of workers in global supply chains first hit the headlines in the late 1980s, companies and politicians argued that European consumers had no right to dictate what was tolerable in developing countries. Relativism is a topic of much discussion in business ethics,[21] reflecting wider philosophical debates about whether or not morals are universal or culturally contingent; and if they are not applicable everywhere, are there value systems originating in one part of the world that are universalizable to all parts in much the same way that the economic system we know as capitalism, originating in Europe, has been introduced throughout much of the world.

Underpinning these debates are quite different philosophical traditions (see Online Resource Centre for a more detailed overview). For example, justice under the Utilitarian school is defined quite differently than it is by non-consequentialists such as Kant. The former believe justice is whatever benefits the majority; the latter that justice is not a popularity contest, and the good of the many cannot be achieved at the expense of the few. These are contradictory schools of thought. Likewise Aristotle's belief in absolute values is at odds with Habermas's notion of discourse ethics two millennia later whereby values are the result of public consensus. This is not a book on business ethics, and therefore we are not going to unpack how different ethical schools influence ideas of responsibility. That is not to dismiss them as unimportant: on the contrary, business ethics is a vital subset of corporate responsibility with its own body of literature—Oxford University's Bodleian library alone has 216 business ethics titles.

There are various management studies texts on how to incorporate the ideas of Mill, Aristotle, Jesus, Kant, and others, and there are many books offering ethical advice to the individual manager. But rather than repeat much of what has already been written, our focus is on filling two gaps that affect the defining of corporate responsibility. First, instead of studying what companies ought to do, we want to emphasize what they actually do and why they make some of the choices they make. Second, mirroring Davis' accomplishment in moving the wider debate about corporate responsibility from the role of the individual to the role of the company, we want to explore how companies as entities manage their responsibilities. In doing this, we are not only going beyond the scope of conventional business ethics, we are building a bridge between what Scherer and Palazo (2007) call positivist and deliberative corporate responsibility, the former concentrating on actual business practice without much reflection on the wider context that affects what companies do and do not do, the latter concerned primarily with theories of responsibility, and not how these are actually enacted.

To whom is business responsible?

For economist Milton Friedman, it was straightforward that companies were responsible to the law and their investors, and nobody else. Some still defend this position, some say it was never accurate, and some say that it may have been right once but not any longer (see Chapter 1). Investors' interests may conflict with those of wider society, especially when they want rapid or high yield returns on their capital. Irrespective of business' behaviour, the law is never a comprehensive code, and for every Bernie Madoff or Ernest Saunders who goes to jail there is a Dick Fuld or Phoenix Four who oversee their companies' collapse with seeming impunity despite public outrage. Moreover, legal responsibilities differ from jurisdiction to jurisdiction, and multinational companies can to a degree choose which laws they like or not by relocating their operations. There may be no legal distinction between someone who invests for the short run and one who does so for longer, but their interests and what they would like the company to do may be quite different.

According to IBM CEO, Sam Palmisano, the biggest shift in recent business history is that from shareholder to stakeholder companies.[22] The idea that business has responsibility to a variety of stakeholders has been an important element of corporate responsibility theory, at least since Preston and Post's 1975 book on how host environments affect corporate behaviour. As we explore in Chapters 6 and 9, stakeholder theory suggests a way of explaining with whom and why corporations should engage. It is based on the notion that many people (and groups of people) have a stake in any corporation and that, in order for a company to achieve its objectives effectively, it must consider them all, not only the shareholders to whom corporations have long discharged accountability. In this regard it is not only distinct from previous ideas of the responsibility of companies, but echoes the discourse ethics of Habermas (see above) and the idea that duties and responsibilities are fluid, defined as part of a social consensus that itself depends on the populous' free and informed participation in democratic processes.

Stakeholder theory promises a way in which companies can learn what is needed to establish and maintain the aforementioned 'licence to operate', i.e. the idea that business requires the approval of others in society in order to function effectively. It provides a potentially stronger rationale than Carroll's framework for choosing certain courses of action by implying that a company should do whatever is necessary to maintain its legitimacy, but that it is under no obligation to go further than that.

The licence to operate is central to legitimacy theory and posits that an organization can only continue to exist if its core values are aligned with the core values of the society in which it operates. The fate of accounting firm Arthur Andersen, in the wake of the Enron scandal, brought this into stark relief when the company's integrity was so badly damaged that it went out of business. Legitimacy theory offers a method of managing stakeholders in the face of various threats, through, for example, educating them about the company's intentions, changing their perceptions of events, diverting their attention, and altering their expectations.[23] Such strategies are evident in the actions taken by Shell in response to Brent Spar, or the treatment of the Ogoni people in Nigeria (see Snapshot 2.2).

Important though theories such as those described above are in their own right, one of their major contributions is that they have made management practice part of corporate responsibility enquiry. Early corporate responsibility theory was primarily concerned with the normative behaviour of companies, but, since the 1970s, there has been at least equal emphasis given to corporate responsibility as management practice.[24] For example, Ackerman and Bauer's (1976) theory of 'corporate social responsiveness' put the emphasis on what companies *can* do to respond to societal expectations (i.e. capacity), in contrast to more theoretical ideas of what they *should* do. Social responsiveness shunned the idea of philosophy in favour of a managerial approach and, in many ways, helped corporate responsibility to get out of academia and into day-to-day business. By the 1990s, managerial approaches to corporate responsibility were evolving rapidly and measurement had become an integral part of this, summed up in MacGillivray and Zadek's phrase: '*If you want it to count, count it.*'[25]

We take a closer look at corporate responsibility as management practice in Chapter 6 and later chapters. But we would not pretend that responsiveness to society is an unproblematic way of resolving what business should take responsibility for; on the contrary, as later discussions of stakeholder theory reveal (see Chapter 9), it can leave companies without clear moral guidance of the kind promised by ethical theory.

■ Discussion points

A number of companies publicize the amounts they donate to philanthropic causes. Indeed, it is one of the measures used by some rating agencies when scoring corporate responsibility points.

- To what extent does philanthropic donation act as a measure of corporate responsibility?
- What arguments can you put forward against using this criterion as a measure of corporate responsibility?
- Using other companies as benchmarks, present a case to the board for adopting a particular philanthropic strategy.

CASE STUDY 2

Corporate responsibility in different eras: Cadbury

In 1909, the *London Evening Standard* accused the confectionary company Cadbury of knowingly profiting from the widespread use of slaves on cocoa plantations in the Portuguese colony of São Tomé. The public was shocked: the company was not only one of the most famous brands in the British Empire, but also an exemplar of compassionate capitalism founded in the Quaker religious tradition.

Cadbury sued the *Evening Standard* for libel. The company won the case, but over the course of the trial, Charles Cadbury, joint head of the firm and a figurehead of virtuous capitalism, was forced to admit that he not only knew slaves were being used, but actually regarded it as essential to his company's prosperity. Despite the court's ruling in Cadbury's favour, it lost in the court of public opinion, and the reputation of the firm was damaged.

A century later, in 2000, the company found itself once again accused of buying slave-farmed cocoa beans from West Africa in a media assault by the full spectrum of the British press, from the *Daily Mirror* to the *Financial Times*. Acting with others in the industry, Cadbury (by then Cadbury Schweppes) denied the allegations. In contrast with the 1909 case, this time the industry condemned the use of slavery outright, but to no avail, because it was unable to prove that it really knew what was happening on cocoa farms. The human rights advocates seemed to know little more: their early allegations of slavery soon switched to ones about child labour as it became apparent that slavery was not prevalent on cocoa farms. But that did not matter: these groups held the moral high ground and the industry could do nothing to displace them.

The news headlines could not have come at a worse time, appearing on the front pages in the run up to Easter, a peak time for chocolate sales. Schoolchildren around Britain wrote in to

Cadbury saying they would not be buying Easter eggs that year. In the USA, two congressmen persuaded the industry to sign up to the Harkin-Engel Protocol, an industry-wide certification standard to eliminate the worst forms of child labour. Cadbury had once again lost in the court of public opinion. The company's share price was not hurt but its reputation was. The question was whether it needed to take action, and if so what?

Across the industry, companies pondered whether to be defensive and protect their reputations, or to become more proactive and see if there was a value-adding dimension to the cocoa labour problem. Cadbury supported a 2002 study by the International Institute of Tropical Agriculture to investigate the extent of child labour and forced labour. It also joined the International Cocoa Initiative, a partnership of business, NGO, and government representatives committed to getting rid of unacceptable labour practices in cocoa production. In 2006 it asked consultants to map out what sustainable production would mean for the company.

These activities helped the company realize that it had lost touch with its supply base. Not only was it blind to human rights issues in the supply chain, it was ignorant of the production issues affecting the millions of small independent farmers it depended on. If anything, the risk of being out of touch was greater now than in 2000. In 2005, Cadbury had acquired Green & Black's, the organic chocolate company with a loyal ethical consumer base. This was one of Cadbury's fastest growing business areas, a brand built on product quality and ethical credibility. Any criticism of the Cadbury supply chain now would damage Green & Black's reputation as well.

But another problem came to light as Cadbury started to reacquaint itself with its supply base: for various farmers were growing less cocoa, and if the situation continued Cadbury risked not having enough beans to meet demand. Cadbury-commissioned academic research had shown that the average production for smallholder cocoa farmers in Ghana had dropped to just 40 per cent of potential yield, and that cocoa farming was becoming less and less appealing to the next generation of farmers despite rising prices. In January 2008, Cadbury launched its £44 million Cocoa Partnership 'to secure the economic, social and environmental sustainability of around a million cocoa farmers and their communities in Ghana, India, Indonesia and the Caribbean.' Furthermore, in 2009 Cadbury announced that all cocoa used in its top-selling Dairy Milk brand would be sourced from Fairtrade certified farms with the hope that farmers would benefit from the stable prices and community investment Fairtrade promises.

(Sources: original research; Du Cann, 1993; IITA and ILO 2002; Satre, 2005; Institute for Development Studies; **www.cadbury.com/ourresponsibilities/cadburycocoapartnership/Pages/mappingsustainableproduction.aspx**—accessed 21 September 2009; **www.cadbury.com/ourresponsibilities/cadburycocoapartnership/Pages/cadburycocoapartnership.aspx**—accessed 21 September 2009)

Questions

1 The events of 1909 and 2000 had few major commercial ramifications for Cadbury and until the 2010 takeover by Kraft, the company was a long-time member of the Fortune Global 500 list of leading businesses. In fact, Cadbury Schweppes won the 2004 UK 'Most Admired Company' award presented by Nottingham Business School.

  a Did the company overreact by stopping its sourcing of 'slave-produced' cocoa?

  b Why did the company feel the need to act at all?

  c Is it not the role of government to regulate how industries are run and to prevent these practices from recurring?

2 Cadbury faced similar issues in 1909 and 2000, and in both cases had to mount a defence of its reputation and practices.

   a Are companies more responsible today than they were in the past?

   b Are Cadbury's responsibilities different today than they were in the early twentieth century?

   c Why do you think companies' responsibilities have changed in the last hundred years?

3 In corporate responsibility theory, a distinction is sometimes made between actions taken to reduce risks such as protecting reputation, and those taken to add value such as using ethical values to promote a brand.

   a Which of Cadbury's actions do you think were done to protect its reputation?

   b Why do you think Cadbury purchased Green & Black's?

   c How would you persuade senior management to support the Cocoa Partnership?

SUMMARY

Corporate responsibility did not spring out of nowhere. What we think of as the responsibilities of business and how these get acted upon reflect some of the main debates about social justice going far back in time. Nowhere is this more apparent than in theories about how private enterprise impacts upon economic well-being and how the economy itself relates to society. In this chapter, we have discussed how different types of economy affect what we mean by 'justice' and 'well-being'. We have also compared different theories of how business and free markets can best contribute to the good of society in capitalist societies. What emerges is a set of questions on issues such as the relationship between private self-interest and the public good, and how the rewards of enterprise are distributed—things that lie at the heart of contemporary corporate responsibility.

Tackling these questions has occupied politicians, academics, company managers, and community leaders since the earliest days of capitalism. We have explored how corporate responsibility theory developed as one way of finding answers about what business should be responsible for and to whom. We have also examined the way in which different approaches to thinking about responsibility can lead to quite different conclusions about what companies should be responsible for.

The origins of corporate responsibility are not, however, only to be found in theory. The evolution of modern business, and, in particular, the emergence of limited liability and the corporation, have all affected business' relationship with society and expectations about companies' responsibilities. Equally, the specific aspects of business activity that society addresses have, paradoxically, both changed and remained constant over time. What the exploration of aspects of corporate responsibility over three eras does show, however, is how the role of business in resolving these issues has changed. In fact, the unintended consequence of the market liberalization that was central to economic globalization is that business is being expected, as never before, to take action to rectify perceived weaknesses in markets on issues such as social justice and sustainability. It is how globalization has affected corporate responsibility in developing countries to which we turn in the next chapter.

FURTHER READING

**VISIT THE
WEBSITE**
for links to useful
sources of further
information

Take your learning further: Online Resource Centre **www.oxfordtextbooks.co.uk/orc/blowfield_
murray2e/**

Visit the Online Resource Centre which accompanies this book to enrich your understanding of this
chapter.

Students: explore web links and further reading suggestions. Keep up to date with the latest
developments by undertaking web exercises.

Lecturers: you will find additional case studies, including one on the topic of Fordlandia—Henry Ford's
jungle city of responsibility, for use in class or assessment. Show your students trailers from films
related to Corporate Responsibility, and use images from the book in your PowerPoint slides.

Historical context

- Bakan, J, 2004, *The Corporation: The Pathological Pursuit of Profit and Power*, New York, NY: Free
  Press.
  Readable and provocative critique of the dominance of corporations.

- Kenneally, T, 1983, *Schindler's Ark*, Sevenoaks, Coronet.
  *Novel based on the true story of a businessman's struggle to do good in Nazi Germany. The
  Spielberg film adaptation is Schindler's List.*

- Nace, T, 2003, *Gangs of America: The Rise of Corporate Power and the Disabling of Democracy*, San
  Francisco, CA: Berrett-Koehler.
  Lively account of the dangers of modern business by one-time entrepreneur.

- Thompson, EP, 1963, *The Making of the English Working Class*, London: Victor Gollancz.
  *Comprehensive study of workers, working conditions, and worker protest in nineteenth-century
  England.*

Theoretical context

- Carroll, AB, 1999, 'Corporate social responsibility: evolution of a definitional construct', *Business
  and Society*, 38(3), pp 268–95.
  Widely cited overview of corporate responsibility theory.

- Drucker, PF, 1946, *Concept of the Corporation*, New York, NY: The John Day Company.
  Early work by leading management thinker on the nature of the corporation.

- Kelly, M, 2001, *The Divine Right of Capital: Dethroning the Corporate Aristocracy*, San Francisco,
  CA: Berrett-Koehler.
  Insightful and contentious discussion of the nature and role of business.

- Marx, K, 1865, *Value, Price, and Profit: An Introduction to the Theory of Capitalism*, abridged by P
  Zarembka, 2000, Amsterdam and New York, NY: JAI/Elsevier Science, online at ourworld.
  compuserve.com.
  Marx's own attempt to make basic Marxist theory accessible—the first 'Marx for Dummies'?

ENDNOTES

[1] Du Cann, 1993.

[2] Kennedy, 1987; Evans, 1983.

[3] Carney, 1998, p 662.

[4] McQuaid, 1977.

[5] Fortune undated. http://money.cnn.com/galleries/2007/fortune/0702/gallery.richestamericans.fortune/index.html, accessed 11 September 2009.

[6] Frederick, 2006.

[7] See, e.g. Demirag, 2005; Blowfield, 2005a.

[8] The term comes from Scholte, 2000, but a similar conceptualization of globalization has been set out by many theorists (e.g. Gray, Mittelman, Held) and has evolved from early work on interdependence, such as Giddens, 1990, and Robertson, 1992.

[9] Steger, 2003.

[10] Asongu, 2007.

[11] Cited in Carroll, 1999, p 271.

[12] Frederick, 1960, cited in Carroll, 1999, p 271.

[13] Birch, 2003, pp 7–8.

[14] See the discussion of the work on corporate social performance by Anshen and Johnson in Birch, 2003.

[15] Cited in Carroll, 1999, p 276.

[16] Cited in Carroll, 1999, p 278.

[17] Soros, undated.

[18] Carroll is not unaware of these types of question and revisited his model in Schwartz and Carroll, 2003.

[19] Matten and Moon, 2008.

[20] ibid.

[21] See Donaldson, 2003; Beauchamp et al. 2008.

[22] Blowfield, 2007.

[23] Lindblom, 1994.

[24] Tinker, 1985; see also: Sethi, 1975; Wartick and Cochran, 1985.

[25] MacGillivray and Zadek, 1995; see also Gray, 1996.

3

Sustainable development

Chapter overview

In this chapter, we grapple with the concept of 'sustainable development', tracking its rising importance in the business context, as global warming and climate change are recognized as business issues. In particular, we will:

- consider what is meant by the term 'sustainable development';

- examine the evolution of sustainability;

- assess the scientific evidence about climate change;

- identify the challenges that sustainable development poses for 'business as usual';

- review research into new models of sustainable business;

- examine the capital market implications of sustainable development.

Main topics

■ Key terms

Brundtland Commission

Climate change

Financing sustainability

Global warming

Sustainable development

■ Online resources

- Suggested additional materials on sustainability-related issues
- Exercises and discussion topics for students
- Emerging sustainability initiatives
- Links to other web-based resources

Introduction

Scientific findings all point to the fact that the resources available to the human species on this planet are being consumed at a rate which is not sustainable. Rising oil prices and the push for greener fuels has led to both the clearance of some pristine rainforests to make way for new crops to meet this demand, and the conversion of agricultural land to produce biofuels for power stations is another trend which potentially reduces the food producing capacity within any given country. Evidence also suggests that we are approaching the point where the daily rate of oil extraction reaches its maximum, after which point production fails to keep up with demand. The exact time at which we reach this point of 'peak-oil', as it is called, ranges from a pessimistic one to five years, and an optimistic 15 to 20 years. Basic economics tells us that when demand exceeds supply prices go up, and high oil prices are already being blamed for worsening the effects of the major recession in 2008. Of equal significance is the recent scientific evidence of the human links with climate change which conclude that '...The wealth of attribution studies … shows that there is an increasingly remote possibility that climate change is dominated by natural rather than anthropogenic factors.'[1] These findings, which will be augmented with additional evidence later in the chapter point to a pressing need to respond to the challenges presented by climate change and sustainable development.

Meanings of 'sustainability' and 'sustainable development'

A brief examination of how these terms are defined by various organizations offers a bewildering series of options to researchers and students of the subject. For example, for BP sustainability means *'the capacity to endure as a group'*;[2] for Shell, *'…helping to meet the world's growing energy needs in economically, environmentally and socially responsible ways'*;[3] for AMEC, *'Managing our triple bottom line, interactions with people, environmental responsibilities and how we make profit'*.[4] Indeed, it is unsurprising that each corporation will have its own way of interpreting what these terms mean in relation to its own commercial activities. As such, each company can identify particular challenges and explain how they are being met effectively, to give assurance to stakeholders and investors alike.

The questions that we wish to address in this chapter, however, relate not to how each company defines the concept in terms of its ability to achieve its own aims, but to a more critical examination of how commercial development activity, necessary to support life in communities around the globe, can continue without depleting natural resources to a degree that jeopardizes the ability of future generations to support themselves. To understand the degree to which this is possible, we must first establish for ourselves what the term means, and to that end, we look at the background to the emergence of 'sustainable development' as a concept and the imperatives that led to the definition that was initially ascribed to it. This is because, for many, issues of sustainability lies at the theoretical heart of corporate responsibility: if we ruin our biosphere, as scientific evidence suggests we are in the process of so doing, then all other corporate initiatives whether responsible or not, become somewhat meaningless.

The UN World Commission on Economic Development

It is now approaching 25 years since the World Commission on Economic Development (WCED), more commonly known as the 'Brundtland Commission' deliberated on, inter alia, *'environmental strategies for achieving sustainable development by the year 2000 and beyond'*. Having sat for almost three years, the Commission finally agreed a definition of 'sustainable development', which, although intended more as a challenge to governments, is widely referred to in debates about the role of business.

How effective and sufficient has been the progress that has been made since the Brundtland Report was published is a matter of debate. The authors may well be further alarmed by the escalation of the threat to the environment posed by the effect of industrial activity on climate change. Yet in order to appreciate fully the difficulty of linking corporate activity to notions of sustainable development, it is useful to review the processes that led up to the Report's publication.

> ■ **Key concepts: Sustainability**
>
> Sustainability refers to the ability of a company to continue indefinitely by making a zero impact on environmental resources. That way, future generations will also benefit from the goods and services provided and from the employment offered.

The Commission was established by the United Nations in 1983, as the result of a process that can be traced back to the 1960s, at which time environmental concerns became the focus of various pressure groups. Carson's *Silent Spring* (1962) had raised popular consciousness about the dangers of excessive pesticide use, and some progress had been made in improving air and water quality in industrialized areas through 'Clean Air' Acts and similar laws. By the early 1970s, non-government organizations (NGOs), such as Friends of the Earth and Greenpeace, had been established in response to the perceived dangers posed to the planet by such phenomena as nuclear testing and the flooding of vast areas caused by dam building.

The calls for a UN conference on the environment originated from the Swedish ambassador to the UN, however, who was particularly concerned with the effects of 'acid rain' and the general acidification of the water systems in Scandinavia. By the time the conference took place in Stockholm in 1972, the issue of pollution had been widened to include the problems being experienced by developing countries. In 1971, a UN-sponsored meeting of experts in pollution in Founex, Switzerland, had, for the first time, made the explicit connection between industrial development—a perceived desire of developing nations—and environmental degradation, which was seen as the price the nation had to pay. Indeed, environmental protection was seen as one of the limiting factors to development.[5] But, in what some saw as a rather contradictory compromise, this meeting concluded that *'there is no inherent contradiction between environment and development, and that these two concerns should be mutually supportive'*.[6]

This conundrum of whether environmental issues can be tackled without jeopardizing economic growth remains central to sustainable development debates today. For example, the 2007 Stern Review for the UK government argued that not only was there not a contradiction, but that tackling climate change was a prerequisite for long-term prosperity. Certainly, the debate was not settled at Stockholm, but, in many ways, the conference was of greater international significance than is often reported. It involved the participation of not only more than a hundred countries, but of over 400 intergovernmental and NGOs. It ended with the *Stockholm Declaration on Human Environment* and the *Action Plan for the Human Environment*.[7] In sum, it not only raised the environment to national consciousness, but also placed it firmly on the international agenda.[8] Indeed, within 20 years of the end of the conference, over a hundred countries had a government department dealing with the environment. Also, the principles of the sovereign right to exploit national resources and the responsibility for transboundary pollution became explicit, and were subsequently ratified in international agreements such as the UN Framework Convention on Climate Change (see 'Climate change and global warming', p 63). It also led to the establishment of the United Nations Environment Program (UNEP) a year later.[9]

In addition, throughout the 1970s, there was continuing concern about a number of issues that impacted on notions of justice and fairness. The oil supply crisis in 1973 caused oil prices to rise to their highest ever levels (after inflation adjustment). While the debt of developing countries was already rising, this enormous rise in oil prices brought debt to crisis levels, not only because of the increased costs of oil (from which some developing nations benefited), but because lending institutions awash with oil money encouraged such countries to take on more debt than they could afford—something that has only started to be resolved in recent years, with debt relief programmes. Equally, a number of projects designed to aid prosperity in the developing world, particularly huge hydroelectric schemes involving dam building and population relocation, were criticized for their adverse social and environmental ramifications.

In 1982, a special session of UNEP's governing council was convened to discuss Stockholm, 'ten years on'. It was here that it was decided that something far more radical and wide-ranging was needed to look much further forward. It was felt that, while the world economy had grown considerably, the least developed countries had made little ground and that, in fact, many had seen a fall in per-capita production during the 1980s.[10] It was at this point that the UN convened the World Commission on Environment and Development under Gro Harlem Brundtland,[11] 'at a time of unprecedented growth in pressures on the global environment, with grave predictions about the human future becoming commonplace'. Its aim was to build a future that would be 'more prosperous, more just, and more secure', resting on ecologically sound policies and practices. Even at the outset, however, there was an overwhelming conviction that, in order to attain this goal, 'significant changes in current approaches', would have to be confronted, which would involve changes in individual attitudes and lifestyles, and, more crucially, 'changes in certain critical policies . . . and the nature of co-operation between governments, business, science and people'.[12]

The significantly different approach that this Commission took was to try to conceptualize the relationship between the environment and development, in light of the continuing disparity between levels of prosperity in the Northern and Southern Hemispheres, and the sentiments expressed at Founex in 1971. During its sitting, which lasted two and a half years, a number of unprecedented events occurred: the famine in Ethiopia, which led to the death of over a million people, was broadcast to the West in graphic detail. It led to the 'Band Aid' concerts in London and Philadelphia, transmitted on television non-stop for over 16 hours. The role of the government of Ethiopia, in terms of its willingness and ability to help it own peoples, was questioned amid accusations of corruption and ineptitude.[13]

Additionally, Joe Farman discovered the 'hole' in the ozone layer over Antarctica. The importance of this discovery was not fully understood at the time and was met with some scepticism, because US monitoring satellites did it not immediately corroborate the discovery. Once the monitoring parameters were adjusted to access the data, however, and the phenomena was confirmed, the implications began to impact on policymakers.

As these events unfolded, another tragedy struck: this time, in Bhopal, India, in 1984. In what has become an iconic study of corporate responsibility or irresponsibility, Union Carbide, which had established a site in Bhopal in 1969 to manufacture pesticides, initially imported one of the key ingredients, methyl isocyanate (MIC), before developing its onsite manufacturing facility in 1979. It seems clear from subsequent investigations that the level of maintenance was seriously short of the required standards. In November 1984, a leak of MIC caused the deaths of some 20,000 people. The health of over 120,000 remains affected by the effects of the gas and the site is still not considered safe.[14]

In late April 1986, a nuclear reactor at Chernobyl in the USSR (now Ukraine) exploded and 30 people were killed at the scene. Again, lack of maintenance was cited as the main cause and, like Bhopal, the legacy remains.[15] The developed world did not escape either: in November 1986, agricultural chemicals and solvents leaked into the River Rhine following a chemical spill that was the result of a fire at a factory operated by Sandoz, a pharmaceutical conglomerate, in Basel, Switzerland. The Swiss government failed to act quickly enough to contain the spill, and, as a result, the drinking water of millions of people was affected and fishing stocks were seriously depleted.

The WCED definition of sustainable development

Some of these events are acknowledged as having had an impact on the Commission[16] and what emerged was a vision for a sustainable future that was dependent on some fundamental changes to what, in the West, had become an accepted way of life, with standards of living measured in terms of capital accumulation, levels of technological application, travel options, etc. In this vision, the environment was to be placed at the centre of strategic decision making. Rather than being seen as a limiting factor in the cause of continued development, the environment was to be seen as an *'aspect of policy'* if growth was to be sustained.[17] It also articulated notions of justice and fairness to the peoples of the developing world, in terms of fair shares of the world's resources and redistribution of wealth to improve the standards of living of the world's worst off.

> Humanity has the ability to make development sustainable—to ensure that it meets the needs of the present generation without compromising the ability of future generations to meet their own needs. The concept of sustainable development does imply limits—not absolute limits, but limitations imposed by the present state of technology and social organization on environmental resources and by the ability of the biosphere to absorb the effect of human activities.
>
> *(WCED, 1987, p 8)*

This definition of sustainable development—*'meeting the needs of the present generation without compromising the ability of future generations to meet their own needs'*, as it is commonly paraphrased—carries with it a number of implications and, equally, a number of challenges to the business world. This definition requires companies to act in *'three time zones'*:

1 dealing with liabilities arising from a time at which it was acceptable to externalize part of a company's costs onto the environment, people, or future generations;

2 meeting the increased expectations of today's citizens and consumers that the company will be a responsible citizen;

3 taking account of the interests and rights of future generations.[18]

In the next sections, we look at this definition, which may, at first glance, seem relatively straightforward, and consider the implications within each part of it. First, we look at the implications of the needs of this generation ('intra-generational' equity) and the needs of this generation, together with those of the next generation ('inter-generational' equity).

Intra-generational equity and inter-generational equity

If we break down the definition and look at its component parts, we begin to unravel the complexity of the idea and to understand why it poses such a potential challenge to present commercial activity. *'Development that meets the needs of the present generation'* suggests fair distributions across the present population of the world, in terms of quality of life, measured, perhaps, by comparative standards of living or benefits from sharing the resources of the planet. There is some evidence that this is not happening at the present time. If we reflect on living standards in terms of Western developed societies and think of the comforts that the majority of the population enjoy, we can still observe that there are levels of inequality many find unacceptable and which, in extreme cases, have resulted in civil unrest.[18] If we then reflect on the developing world, we need little reminding that poverty and famine still blight many peoples of the world. For example, few of over 50 per cent of Africa's 812 million people have access to safe drinking water.[19] It can be argued, therefore, that we are not achieving the first of the tenets of sustainable development and, if that is the case and we are not meeting the needs of the present generation, it is logical to ask if the next generation will fare any better.[20]

The challenge that this offers business is how commercial activity can be organized to address the needs of the peoples of the world, when the theory of the firm suggests that the overriding imperative is to maximize shareholder wealth.[21] We discuss the business case for adopting some of the strategies for sustainability elsewhere (see Chapter 6), but most of that case involves identifying opportunities for business, whether in terms of market niche, efficiencies, or in terms of tackling issues of risk and reputation. Putting environmental or social issues at the heart of business strategy is a more challenging proposition and, if these strategies seriously seek to address social justice issues, then the challenges become even more profound.

Eco-justice and eco-efficiency

Wrapped up in this definition are notions of 'eco-justice' and 'eco-efficiency'. By 'ecojustice', we mean that there is some fairness applied to the distribution of benefits that accrue from the development of the world's resources. To read the history of various

European nations' colonial past, for example, is to read how single countries sought to exploit the resources of many other countries without considering the needs of the indigenous peoples. Robins (2006) draws parallels between the companies that led the colonial charge and today's multinationals. He is not alone in believing that commercial exploitation continues to ignore the needs of local communities, and that, often, the profits from such activities are expatriated from the host country, to benefit shareholders and investors who are far removed from the theatres of activity.

Eco-justice is often interpreted as laying the blame at business' door for impacts that may not have been anticipated at the time, or which may not even be substantiated by the evidence. Even when legal decisions, such as those against GE over the Hudson River or those in the case of the *Exxon Valdez*, show that companies are culpable, pointing fingers of blame may not motivate companies to be environmentally responsible. 'Eco-efficiency', on the other hand, is a concept that has an appeal to the commercially minded. The idea that one should 'get more from less' is the sort of challenge to which a company can rise and there is ample evidence that industrial processes are becoming more efficient. As noted in Chapter 6, in discussion of the business case, it is in this area that we see most innovation. There are good commercial reasons for this, but there are also drivers from outside the economic sphere. Most of these stem from an increasing recognition that industrial activity poses specific threats to the world's environmental health.

It is, however, important not to conflate notions of eco-efficiency with those of sustainable development. Eco-efficiency may well become the goal of each commercial entity, but, in itself, this might not prevent overall world resources from becoming depleted. So far, we have reviewed the development and challenges of sustainable development in terms of the Brundtland Commission's remit; we now move on to look at what has now been identified as the greatest threat to modern society—climate change.

■ **Discussion points**

In the 1970s and 1980s, there were many dire predictions of ecological collapse that did not materialize, and many natural systems have proved to be less fragile and faster to mend than once thought.

- What ecosystem services was it feared that were being irresolvably degraded in that era?
- Does the fact some predictions were not borne out undermine or strengthen current arguments about climate change and other aspects of sustainable development?
- Which industries have most to win, or lose, from adopting a 'business as usual' attitude to sustainable development?

Climate change and global warming

Sizeable sections of today's business community believe that climate change is a phenomenon that has to be tackled. According to Stephen Schwarzman, head of private equity firm the Blackstone Group: *'Businesses have to do things to address* [climate change]. *It's not a green issue, it's not a red issue. It's the issue.'*[22] It is well beyond the scope of this book to discuss the science, or even the business implications, of climate change in any depth: there are all manner of questions relating to the types of response required, their cost, and their timing that have yet to be answered. But the future of corporate responsibility is likely to be greatly affected by the way in which business and government respond. For some, climate change is the most crucial scientific question of the twenty-first century, and the 'winning side' might shape economic, political, and technological development for years, even centuries, to come.[23] Although, like many aspects of corporate responsibility, responses to climate change have typically been treated as involving trade-offs in terms of profitability and competitiveness, economists such as Stern (2009) are now treating it as the pro-growth strategy of the future.

The notion that the planet has a finite capability to absorb or to process the results of human (industrial) activity is the underlying theory of sustainable development, yet, even in the mid 1980s, the scientific basis for concern was only just emerging. Indeed, between 1940 and 1970, as the mean worldwide temperature cooled by 0.2°C, so interest in the phenomena of 'greenhouse' effects waned from what had previously been little more than a passing interest. Following the first World Climate Conference in Geneva in 1979—a predominantly scientific gathering, sponsored by the World Meteorological Organization (WMO)—a call was put out to governments to *'foresee and prevent potential man-made changes in climate'.*[24] The first serious concerns were raised in 1985, when UNEP and WMO jointly organized a scientific conference in Villach, Austria. Here, predictions were made of the possibility of global temperature rises that would be greater than those in all history and of consequent sea level rises of over 1 metre by 2050.[25] In addition, two years later, UNEP published a further report, *Environmental Perspectives to the Year 2000 and Beyond*, which provided a framework within which to operationalize the findings of the Brundtland Commission, and which led the UN General Assembly to convene its Conference on Environment and Development (UNCED), widely known as the 'Earth Summit', held in Rio in June 1992.

Before the Earth Summit, the UN had begun to frame a document for ratification at Rio. The UN Framework Convention on Climate Change (UNFCCC) was adopted by the UN in 1992 and became open for member-country signature at Rio. By June 1993, it had received 166 signatures. It has since been ratified by 189 states and by the European Union as a bloc.[26] But the scepticism held in some quarters on the science of climate change is clear in the wording of the original document, under which a precautionary approach is urged *'in the absence of scientific certainty'*. A tension was developing within governments between appearing to support calls for a cut in emissions, on the one hand, and the political imperative of doing nothing to threaten economic growth within their own economies, on the other.

In response to this political impasse, in 1997, the UNFCCC held a summit in Kyoto to try to bind countries into a legally binding Protocol aimed at reducing greenhouse gas emissions. The Kyoto Protocol, as it became known, which came into force in

2005, was to be remembered as much for those who refused to ratify the agreement as for the measures that were proposed. Notably, the USA would not sign, for fear of harming its own economic growth prospects, and this stance was also adopted by Australia, Japan, China, South Korea, and India.[27] This position became entrenched by these countries with the formation of the Asia–Pacific Partnership on Clean Development and Climate, also known as 'AP6'. This non-treaty pact was designed to allow foreign, environment and energy ministers from partner countries to collaborate to develop technology designed to reduce emissions. Unlike the Kyoto Protocol, which imposes limits on emissions, this agreement allowed the member countries to set their own goals.[28]

Yet, while all of this political activity was going on, more and more conclusive evidence was emerging about the inevitability and immediacy of the threats from global warming and climate change. Throughout 2005 and 2006, there was news, on a regular basis, of new scientific evidence of the likely effects of climate change. Centres of research, such as the Hadley Centre operated by the UK Meteorological Office and the Tyndall Centre for Climate Change Research, have each published numerous reports on the subject and countless articles have been published in scientific journals such as *Science* and *Nature*. In 2007, scientists on the UN Intergovernmental Panel on Climate Change (IPCC), in their 4th Assessment Report (4AR) gave their strongest statement yet that not only is global warming happening, but that it is primarily as a result of human activity.[29]

While some in business have long taken climate change seriously, some industries (notably, coal, oil, and gas companies associated with high carbon dioxide emissions), have backed climate change sceptics, not least with funding. Since BP broke ranks with the Global Climate Coalition (an oil-industry group that had sought to discredit climate change science) in 1997, however, the business community as a whole has become split: sometimes castigated, as in ExxonMobil's backing of the American Enterprise Institute's offer of prize money to scientists able to refute the IPCC's 'findings',[30] and sometimes lauded, as in Wal-Mart's commitment to taking nonrenewable energy off its shelves.[31]

In each successive IPCC assessment the range of scientific methods of enquiry has increased and techniques refined to make predictions on issues such as sea level rises and arctic ice melt more robust. However climate science is complex and some of the methods used to make these predictions use proxies which, while fully accepted and understood by this scientific community, seem disconnected from the subject, and bizarre, to some outside. Looking at tree rings, for example, led to a controversy when email discussions among scientists, primarily from the University of East Anglia's Climatic Research Unit, were hacked into and published. The emails referred to were informal discussions among scientists but the language used, where they referred to using tree rings to derive proxy temperature records as a 'trick', came back to haunt them. In context, the word 'trick' seems to be no more than an informal way of summarizing a 'clever method', but out of context can be taken to suggest some dishonest sleight of hand.

However, scientists studying climate change in Centres around the world are increasingly collaborating to compare trends. In a recent review paper Stott et al. (2010)[32]

SNAPSHOT 3.1

Aviation and climate change

Most of us who read this book will have benefited from cheap air travel, whether for holiday travel or business trips. Flights from Europe to the USA are frequently on offer for under £400 and from Europe to the Far East and Australasia often at little over £500. Few would have not been left wondering on the one hand, how some airline companies can offer flights so cheaply, and on the other, perhaps tinged with guilt, how this activity contributes to global warming. Indeed, whilst the EU total greenhouse gas emissions fell by 3 per cent between 1990 and 2006, emissions from international aviation increased by almost 100 per cent.[1] It may be surprising to learn that it was only in 2009 that aviation was included in the EU Emissions Trading Scheme (ETS); before that it was excluded on the basis that the scheme focused on national boundaries, and aviation was thought to be outside the scope of the scheme.

[1]http://ec.europa.eu/environment/climat/aviation/index_en.htm.

Quick questions

1 What is the purpose of an ETS?

2 How can an ETS lead to reduced overall emissions

3 Is it possible to have a sustainable airline industry at the present scale?

reviewed the IPCC data from a regional perspective to 'reflect a growing interest in understanding the regional effects of climate change, which can differ markedly across the globe' (p 1). The review included evidence of effects felt in Antarctica, excluded from the 4AR, as well as further evidence, gathered since 4AR, attributing a much wider range of climate change to human activity. Their conclusions support the underlying thesis that human activity is exerting 'external force' on the climate in terms of regional temperatures, oceanic changes, etc. However, as is common in many scientific texts, they conclude with a caveat:

To better assess the pace of change, and to understand more about the regional changes to which societies need to adapt, we will need to refine our understanding of the effects of external forcing and internal variability. (p 1)

These findings, conducted by scientists from four continents, are likely to feed into the next IPCC Report (the 5th Assessment) which is due to be published in 2013.

The complex science of climate change which is discussed in the above paper is often contrasted with the rather stark statistics released on annual temperatures released by other agencies. According to NASA scientists, for example, 2009 was the second warmest year in the USA since 1880, just behind 2005, and together with a cluster at almost the same temperature, in 2002, 2003, 2006 and 2007, makes the first decade of the 21st Century the warmest on record.[33] These findings pose issues not just for policymakers, but for business leaders as well.

■ **Discussion points**

Climate change is a very important and high-profile aspect of sustainable development, but it is not the only one.

- About which other aspects of sustainable development is it important for business to be thinking?
- Are there contradictions and dichotomies between some of these various aspects?
- Which of these aspects are beyond the concerns of corporate responsibility at the present time?

The challenge to business

We opened this chapter with examples of how three businesses defined sustainability in the context of their own business operations. To our knowledge, the only business that has openly acknowledged that it is not environmentally sustainable, and that has taken positive steps to correct this, is Interface Inc., the global floor coverings company (see Case Study 3, below). Indeed, the weight of evidence suggests that organizations operating under the traditional business model operate within a framework where externalizing costs is seen as good practice. Equally, investors require returns on their investment and returns are obtained by growing the profits of the business. The challenge is that growth of the business has invariably meant increasing resource usage, which both depletes the earth's stock of resources and leads to increased emissions.

Traditionally, the government might have controlled growth through regulation, but in the Western model of neo-liberal capitalism, command-and-control regulation has gone out of favour. Governments might consider initiatives such as insuring risk, taxation, or schemes of emissions trading, but business is, largely, left to manage these challenges itself—something to which some companies have started to draw politicians' attention, through initiatives such as the European Corporate Leaders Group on Climate Change. Furthermore, it can be argued that business has been proactive in initiatives aimed at avoiding regulation, by either demonstrating that it is behaving responsibly,[34] or sponsoring activities that attempt to play down some of the perceived threats of climate change and other environmental issues[35] (Snapshot 3.1).

As with the business case for adopting a corporate responsibility agenda (see Chapter 6), however, many perceive that these challenges are bound together with opportunities to engage with new technologies, and with new approaches to deliver alternative products and processes. To the fore in this endeavour is the World Business Council for Sustainable Development (WBCSD), stressing that the opportunities to open new markets, develop new businesses, and access new revenue streams mean that companies should not shirk the challenges that sustainable development presents. New initiatives, involving business leaders, are encouraging those most closely involved in the business debate to offer solutions to these challenges. Indeed, in a publication by the Tomorrow's Leaders Group of the WBCSD, when considering the *'role of business in tomorrow's society'*, there are a number of objectives for business going forward. These include developing new businesses and new technologies, setting global benchmarks and new strategies, and offering greater opportunity to larger sections of world communities.[36]

The Tomorrow's Leaders Group accepts what, for some, remains a contentious idea: that sustainability can be achieved without compromising economic growth. As noted earlier, the Stern Review goes further and argues that stabilizing climate change is actually essential for economic growth. There are attractive features to sustainability-led growth (e.g. the opportunities for technological innovation and new markets), but, as Stern also recognizes, government may well have to steer business in new directions and towards adopting new business models.

New models of sustainable business

In light of the challenges that sustainable development poses for business, researchers have been working to develop enterprise models that take account of the parameters of sustainable development. Some have looked at the capitalist business model to see if it can be adapted to meet these challenges; others have sought to develop new models. Writing on the theory behind such new models, Birkin (2000) calls for managers to adopt a different ontology,[37] recognizing the '*inter-connectedness*' of corporate decision making. This may be seen as a development of, or an alternative to, the '*systems thinking*', offered by Gray (2002a) as his explanation of a similar phenomenon: that of reductionism, under which the focus is on a specific aspect of a system, rather than on the system itself[38] (Snapshot 3.2).

What both authors call for is a recognition that concentration on specific issues may not be helpful if sustainability is the goal and that wider consequences of specific actions need a much more considered response. Birkin developed his thesis by arguing for the consideration of '*relationships*' within models of business and, in particular, of the relationships among resource flows, resource flow impacts, stakeholder analysis, and carrying capacity assessments.[39] In developing this model of sustainable business, Birkin suggests that only by examining the interaction among these elements will managers fully appreciate the impacts of their actions and the necessary changes that have to be faced to become sustainable. Others have suggested a fundamentally different approach to this form of modelling, by thinking outside the conventional financial model. Traditionally, the 'bottom line' refers to the profit that a company makes in financial terms; 'capital' means financial capital to most people. But if we think of capital in wider terms that encompass the different aspects of resource application, then we can develop different business models. Forum for the Future, the sustainable development NGO, believes that a sustainable future can be achieved, but that:

> We are facing a sustainability crisis because we're consuming our stocks of natural, human and social capital faster than they are being produced. Unless we control the rate of this consumption, we can't sustain these vital stocks in the long-term . . . but for this to happen, it is the responsibility of every organization, business or otherwise, to manage these capital assets sustainably.[40]

Taking this idea of different kinds of capital, some researchers have constructed new models of business that they employ to decide, ex ante, whether or not a business is sustainable. Pioneering work in this field has been conducted with BP, and by Bebbington (2001a) and Baxter et al. (2004), who, in developing a sustainability assessment model, have advanced the notions of 'full cost accounting' and offer additional possibilities in terms of investment appraisal.[41] Briefly, a sustainability assessment model is applied to assess the social, economic, resource, and environmental impacts of a project over its life cycle, and then to reduce these impacts into a cash–value measurement. These data are then used in the project investment appraisal. This model tracks the internal and external effects of the proposed investment, and allows a much more rounded appraisal to be made than that of traditional accounting techniques such as net present value or internal rate of return, which focus purely on financial issues.

■ Discussion points

One of the most controversial areas is whether economic growth and sustainable development are compatible.

- Is the Stern Review right to say that sustainable development is essential for economic growth?
- Is it possible to run a business that will grow within the limits of the earth's ecosystem?
- Is it possible to grow a business while shrinking its environmental footprint?

Capital markets and sustainable development

Despite these initiatives to find new models of sustainable business, there are those who believe that the most fundamental challenge to sustainable practices is that posed by the way in which capital markets reward and punish participants. Although the tension between sustainability and the capital market has been acknowledged for some time, the debate was widened in the 1990s with the work of Stephan Schmidheiny, *Changing Course* (1992), and Schmidheiny with Federico Zorraquin, *Financing Change* (1996). Both of these authors are industrialists who depend upon the capital market system for their business success, yet have tackled problematic questions regarding the role that capital market activity might play in either helping or hindering the development of sustainable practices.

Elsewhere in this book, we look at some of the mechanisms that govern the ways in which companies operate (see Chapter 6), and equally at the notion of responsible investing which considers social and environmental impacts on a par with financial returns (see Chapter 10). But it might be useful to review briefly the mechanisms of the capital market system, to illustrate the dilemmas that they reveal.

First and foremost, capital markets transfer funds from those who save to those who wish to apply these funds to means of producing goods or services. In this process is

SNAPSHOT 3.2

Individual freedom and the common good

The western model of liberal democracy is based on a number of rights which attach to individuals, and a limitation on the role of the state to interfere with an individual as (s)he exercises their rights. In this economic model there is an over-riding right for an individual to make economic decisions to maximize his/her own wealth, and that the state should not intervene, except to prevent injustice. The right to trade and own property is intertwined in this philosophy and these assumptions are largely taken for granted in our daily lives.

The problem arises when actions, in aggregate, pose a threat to the way of life of all of us, in the long term. Over-use of resources, as demonstrated below, poses a threat to the way we do business and live our lives, especially if we use more resources than the world can provide in a sustainable context.

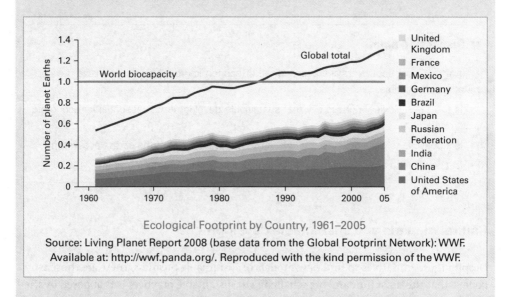

Ecological Footprint by Country, 1961–2005

Source: Living Planet Report 2008 (base data from the Global Footprint Network): WWF. Available at: http://wwf.panda.org/. Reproduced with the kind permission of the WWF.

Quick questions

1 How do we reconcile private notions of freedom with wider responsibilities to humankind?

2 Who should take responsibility for limiting our use of resources?

3 What can we do, as individuals, to make a difference?

achieved a separation of ownership from control (see Chapter 7). In traditional business models, this equation is not seen as problematic: savers expect a return on their savings by way of an annual dividend, or by a capital gain when they sell the shares, or both. Businesses aim to operate at a level that gives a return in excess of this 'cost of capital' and which allows them to invest in new projects, as well as giving a return to shareholders. The problem, in relation to the connection between capital market investment practices and sustainable development, arises in the way in which companies are rewarded, or punished, by the market and the way in which financial intermediaries are rewarded for their expertise in investment.

Signals to the market

It is acknowledged in the finance literature that markets respond to 'signals'. These signals are interpreted from information about company activity that is obtained from diverse sources. For example, if a company is thought to be underperforming, a good signal to the market might be an announcement of a change in top management; reducing declared dividends is seen as a bad signal. These signals are interpreted by financial analysts in terms of potential future cash flows and are reflected in patterns of investment, or disinvestment. They contribute to some of the changes that we witness in share price movements over time. Traditionally, the information that tends to move share prices is normally financial, relating to earnings forecasts, dividend policy, investment policy, etc. Indeed, the nature of the investments that a company makes in the course of its operations is central to the way in which the future performance of a company may be assessed. These strategies are disclosed in the course of both formal and informal discussions with analysts, and the concern here is that the fear of communicating the wrong signal may act to inhibit companies from undertaking innovative or experimental investments, which may be necessary if a sustainable development agenda is to be adopted.[42]

Schmidheiny and Zorraquin (1996) list several 'worrying' assumptions about sustainable development that might convey the wrong signal to markets. They include the facts that:

- there is a common perception that sustainability requires longer-term investments, where pay-back times might not fall in the 'good signal' time span;
- a concerted effort to innovate may reduce present earnings;
- for global companies, investment in sustainable development initiatives in developing countries bring with it additional high risk premiums; and
- accounting and reporting systems do not adequately reflect risks and opportunities.

(p 8)

Another issue that companies try to avoid signalling to the market is the threat of regulation. The idea that governments are about to intervene in a particular sector creates uncertainty, which is interpreted as a bad signal. This helps to explain why companies combine to form strong associations aimed at helping to persuade governments that there is no need to regulate. If they can demonstrate that they are handling thorny issues, the hope is that governments will accept that industry is capable of regulating itself. The WBCSD is one such organization, boasting a large number of major corporations worldwide within its membership. The Global Reporting Initiative is another example and adoption of its guidelines (see Chapters 8 and 9) has been used to demonstrate that serious efforts are being made to address previously perceived reporting imperfections. These examples and countless others, at professional, industrial, national, or supranational levels, are all designed to counter the possibility of the adverse market effect of announcements of regulation.

Those in favour of a more regulated approach, however, remain sceptical of the motives behind this lobbying process. Their argument is that if regulation only represents the lowest level of acceptable behaviour beyond which it is so deemed illegal; and that as corporate responsibility programmes are supposed to go beyond this point in any case, what is the issue with regulation?

As judged by markets, however, operating to the minimum standards allowed by law is usually seen as a positive signal. It also gives rise to the acronyms that are taken as a guide to much commercial activity in the area of environmental management systems, such as 'BATNEEC' and 'CATNIP'.[43]

The question is, what will it take for the market to reward behaviour that goes beyond regulation, even if that involves expenditure that might have an adverse impact on short-term earnings? At what stage, for example, might markets see initiatives such as switching away from biomass back to coal in the production of electricity as a bad signal?[44]

■ Discussion points

The accountancy profession is seen by some as an essential element in encouraging companies to tackle sustainable development.

- What can the accountancy profession bring to sustainable development that will help companies to change their business models, enabling them to operate with less of an environmental impact?
- To what extent does the accountancy profession lock companies into outdated business models?
- What can it do to remove the barriers to client change?

Rewarding financial intermediaries

Since the financial crisis in 2008–9 which led to national governments 'bailing out' many global financial institutions, the award of bonuses to employees by banks has become a discussion about corporate responsibility in itself. Those involved in the investment process as financial intermediaries work within a bonus system, which can represent a large percentage of an individual's salary and which, collectively in the City of London in 2006, amounted to some £8 billion,[45] a figure equivalent to the GDP of some developing countries. As the depth of the financial crisis began to emerge and allegations of imprudent trading products and practices emerged, focus turned to those senior executives in the banks at the point of collapse. In a move that further enraged the public, many of those who were accused of being involved in the bad practice that led to the collapse left their posts on very generous terms, a move which seemed to many to epitomize the problems that brought about the problem in the first place. The global recession which followed the financial meltdown meant that bonuses in 2008 and 2009 were lower than previously, but 2010 saw a return to a figure in the region of £6 billion, though some high profile CEOs of banks declined to take their bonuses.[46]

Bonuses are made on trading shares and other financial instruments, and depend on increases in returns fuelled by quarterly earning announcements. Equally, company success is judged by the same announcements, and the value of the shares, which in aggregate represents the overall value of the company feed into company compensation and bonus structures.

One can only speculate whether all those involved in a system of bonuses measured in three monthly cycles would favour strategies designed to produce short-term gains rather than long-term sustainable growth but, intuitively, there would seems to be grounds for scepticism. Although climate change is grabbing investors' attention, overall there is limited evidence for concluding that capital market activity will change in response to what some see as the demands of sustainable development. As Chuck Prince, former Citigroup CEO, has put it: *'The investment community has no sense of social responsibility. And when I say "no sense," I can't use smaller words than that.'*[47]

In Joel Barkan's documentary film (2004), *The Corporation*, a Wall Street trader, Carlton Brown, enthuses over the profits made from trading in gold on 11 September 2001, as the twin towers turned to dust. When discussing the possibility of disease affecting the population numbers of pigs, Brown talks of the opportunities that the news presents: *'It's almost ludicrous not to jump on board.'* Other interviewees talk of the market as *'amoral'*, suggesting that issues of morality and ethics should have been negotiated before the trading process began—that is, that it is not the trader's job to think about morality. These are important questions that are not fully acknowledged by market participants. There is nothing in corporate governance guidelines that gives companies any direction or reassurance should they consider any such strategy and shareholder return remains the main driver of market activity.

There are, however, attempts to engage analysts in considering social and environmental impacts. A 2006 survey of analysts found no innate hostility to sustainability, but a dearth of tools with which to incorporate the issue into assessments.[48] The CFA has recently included governance in its exams for the first time and some approaches pioneered by the socially responsible investment community are starting to be noticed by the investment mainstream (see Chapter 10). The Enhanced Analytics Initiative, the UN Principles for Responsible Investment, the London Accord, and the Marathon Club, which all have the backing of major financial institutions, are working in different ways to get financial intermediaries to take sustainability seriously. The Institute of Chartered Accountants in England and Wales in association with the WWF has also launched the Finance Innovation Laboratory, a broad multi-stakeholder initiative that aims to activate solutions for change in financial systems. These emergent trends are discussed further in Chapter 10.

■ **Discussion points**

Some believe that business can only go so far in addressing sustainable development without the support of other members of society.

- Do markets incentivize short-term and continued-cost externalization of the kind cited as a threat to sustainable development?
- Are consumers motivated as much by encouraging good performance in sustainability as they are by punishing poor performance?
- Would NGOs be likely to criticize a company more or less if it were to take on sustainable development issues?

CASE STUDY 3

Interface Inc.

From modest beginnings in 1973, Interface has risen in stature to become one of the world's leading manufacturers of floor coverings selling products in 110 countries, sales approaching $1 billion, and over 3,000 employees. What singles out Interface from other companies in an industry which typically relies on petrochemicals in the manufacturing process, is its commitment to become environmentally neutral. Until 1994, like its competitors, Interface used an accepted business model to grow the company, complying with laws and regulations as required.

However, in 1994, the founder of the company and then CEO, Ray Anderson, was asked to make a presentation on the company's environmental plans. In preparation for this he was given a copy of Paul Hawken's book, *The Ecology of Commerce*. The effect, in Anderson's words, was like 'a spear to the chest'. From that point Anderson determined to change the way the company interacted with nature, and set about its journey to conquer 'Mount Sustainability'.

The Interface journey toward sustainability has marked a considerable shift in both the way the company operates and designs its products. The company was faced with the considerable challenge of reimagining its business model, and then redesigning all of its processes, as well as moving away from its dependency on petrochemicals. It developed a vision to become 'the first company that, by its deeds, shows the entire industrial world what sustainability is in all its dimensions: people, process, product, place and profits—by 2020.'

The journey is characterized by addressing 'the seven fronts of mount sustainability:

1 Eliminate waste
2 Benign emissions
3 Renewable energy
4 Closing the loop
5 Resource efficient transportation

6 Sensitizing stakeholders

7 Redesign commerce

Each of these approaches is developed and explained with practical advice on how to approach the challenges offered.

Equally, the company was open to taking advice and guidance from a number of partners to help it achieve its aims, including the World Resources Institute, Forum for the Future, the US Environmental Protection Agency, and The National Minority Supplier Development Council. It also has an 'Eco Dream Team' comprising leading thinkers, architects, and engineers to maintain the momentum. Far from costing money, Interface sees its move to a sustainable business model as a positive benefit. As Ray Anderson puts it:

> Costs are down, not up, dispelling a myth and exposing the false choice between the economy and the environment, products are the best they have ever been, because sustainable design has provided an unexpected wellspring of innovation, people are galvanized around a shared higher purpose, better people are applying, the best people are staying and working with a purpose, the goodwill in the marketplace generated by our focus on sustainability far exceeds that which any amount of advertising or marketing expenditure could have generated–this company believes it has found a better way to a bigger and more legitimate profit–a better business model.

(Source: original research; **www.interfaceglobal.com**)

Questions

1 Sustainable development is often seen as an insurmountable objective for many companies.

   a How might a company approach this challenge, and where might it look for help?

   b How can companies involve NGOs in this process?

   c To what extent does collaboration pose a threat to a company's competitive advantage, and how should that threat be managed?

2 Sustainable Development, in the Brundtland definition, encompasses notions of social justice across and between generations.

   a How can notions of social justice be assimilated into the neo-classical theory of the firm which places the emphasis on maximising shareholder wealth?

   b What responsibilities do transnational corporations have to their employees in different locations?

   c To what extent is product re-engineering a viable strategy to address sustainability?

3 Interface embarked on a 25 year journey towards 'mission zero', where it will eliminate any negative impact on the environment.

   a What other sectors might follow this example?

   b What are the major obstacles to achieving this mission for other companies?

   c How important is it to have top-level support for this kind of initiative?

SUMMARY

This chapter began and ended with looking at how companies portray their activities in terms of sustainability. In between, we examined how concepts of sustainable development emerged and were defined, how that definition conceals subtle notions of equity and fairness, and how these notions present challenges to the 'business as usual' model of corporate behaviour. Although there are broadly accepted definitions of sustainable development, individual companies still choose to define the concept in their own ways. As will be discussed in relation to the impact of corporate responsibility (see Chapter 13), companies are, at best, only starting to understand that they must take responsibility for some of their most significant sustainability consequences. This is evident in the sustainability reports that many companies are producing and, as we have illustrated, some companies approach this task by redefining sustainable development in ways that can be addressed while leaving out the issues that present the greatest challenges. This also relates to the accountability framework within which reporting sits (see Chapter 8).

If, initially, such reports were dismissed as a public relations exercise, the seriousness with which issues such as climate change and sustainable energy are being taken by both governments and the private sector strongly suggests that sustainability will become an increasingly important part of the business agenda. In some ways, this makes getting the management and reporting frameworks right even more important. As Fred Pearce wrote in the *New Scientist*: '*Climate change is the most crucial scientific question of the twenty-first century. The winning side will shape economic, political and technological development for years, even centuries.*'[49] This and other aspects of sustainable development, such as demographic change, may also be among the most crucial business questions and with equally significant prizes at stake. Although questions remain about the exact science of climate change (as they do in relation to most areas of scientific enquiry), there is an overwhelming consensus—and one that is increasingly endorsed by business—that it poses a real risk and is related to human activity.[50] As the different dimensions of sustainable development become more apparent in everyday life, so people will turn to major institutions to take a lead in controlling harmful emissions. Business is clearly one such institution and its role is likely to become more prominent, not least because the conventional command-and-control regulatory model of government is being tested by the social and political realities of globalization.

VISIT THE WEBSITE
for links to useful sources of further information

FURTHER READING

Take your learning further: Online Resource Centre **www.oxfordtextbooks.co.uk/orc/blowfield_murray2e/**

Visit the Online Resource Centre which accompanies this book to enrich your understanding of this chapter.

Students: explore web links and further reading suggestions. Keep up to date with the latest developments by undertaking web exercises.

Lecturers: you will find additional case studies, including one on the topic of Wal-Mart—the greening of the world's largest retailer (expanded version of first edition CS 12.3), for use in class or assessment. Show your students trailers from films related to Corporate Responsibility, and use images from the book in your PowerPoint slides.

- Anderson, RC, 1998, *Mid-Course Correction: Toward a Sustainable Enterprise : The Interface Model*, Atlanta, Ga.: Peregrinzilla Press.

  Theoretical analysis of the significance of environmental management and sustainability to corporations.

- Elkington, J, 1998, *Cannibals With Forks: The Triple Bottom Line of 21st Century Business*, Gabriola Island, BC/Stony Creek, CT: New Society Publishers.

  Influential introduction to the case for considering social, economic, and environmental added value.

- Gore, A, 2006, *An Inconvenient Truth*, London: Bloomsbury Publishing.

  The book accompanying the Oscar-winning film about the importance of climate change.

- Hawken, P, 1993, *The Ecology of Commerce: A Declaration of Sustainability*, New York, NY: Harper Business.

  Arguments for the importance of sustainability to business.

- Henriques, A and Richardson, JA, 2004, *The Triple Bottom Line: Does It All Add Up? Assessing the Sustainability of Business and CSR*, London: Earthscan.

  Critical analysis of triple bottom-line theory and practice.

- Schmidheiny, S and Zorraquin, F, 1996, *Financing Change: The Financial Community, Eco-Efficiency, and Sustainable Development*, Cambridge, MA: MIT Press.

  Influential early book by two business leaders on the role of the finance industry in sustainability.

ENDNOTES

[1] Stott et al., 2010.

[2] BP Sustainability Report 2008 available at www.bp.com

[3] Shell's Sustainability Report, 2008, available at www.shell.com.

[4] www.amec.com.

[5] Grubb et al., 1993.

[6] Tobin, 1997; Engfeldt, 2002.

[7] www.unep.org

[8] It also signified a triumph for the efforts of an individual who was to rise to considerable prominence in the UN environmental initiatives. Maurice Strong was appointed Secretary-General of the Stockholm Conference, because it was felt that he had the necessary connections to get both the developing and developed nations to cooperate. There is also evidence that it was Strong's personal intervention that led to China's participation.

[9] The headquarters of UNEP is in Nairobi and its first Executive Director was Strong.

[10] Tolba and El-Kholy, 1992.

[11] Again, Strong was one of the Commissioners.

[12] WCED, 1987, p 356.

[13] Since then and despite massive amounts of aid raised in the West for the starving of Africa, famines still occur and continuing allegations of malpractice are laid at the feet of host governments.

[14] There are many websites that chronicle the sad tale of Bhopal and the tragedy surrounding those affected.

[15] Incidences of thyroid cancer in children of up to 15 years old increased tenfold between 1986 and 1997, and it is feared that about 2,500 people have died as the direct consequence of the radiation leak.

[16] Tolba and El-Kholy, 1992.

[17] Grubb et al., 1993.

[18] *The Times*, 4 November 2005, reported that: '*The poor suburbs of Paris were set ablaze in the worst of eight consecutive nights of rioting, with 500 cars torched and a gym and primary school razed.*' The report continued: '*Unemployment among French men aged 15 to 24 has risen from 15 per cent four years ago to more than 22 per cent. It is thought to be as high as 30–40 per cent among young second- and third-generation immigrants in poorer high-rise suburbs.*'

[19] UNEP, see www.unep.org.

[20] See, e.g., Gray, 1992; Hawken, 1993; Welford, 1995; Daly, 1996; Tobin, 1997; Elkington, 1998; Birkin, 2000; Gray and Bebbington, 2000; Suranyi, 2000; Bebbington, 2001b; Epstein and Roy, 2001; Gray, 2002b; Gray and Collison, 2003; Bebbington et al.; 2004; Gray, 2006b.

[21] See; e.g. Jensen and Meckling, 1976.

[22] *Financial Times*, 27 February 2007.

[23] Pearce, 2005.

[24] WMO, 1979.

[25] UNEP, 1987.

[26] See www.unfccc.int/kyoto_protocol.

[27] The alignment in policy between the government of a country and the economic desires of its most significant corporations is nothing new, but, because the size of some commercial enterprises now dwarfs the GDP of many small nations, the issue has attracted widespread popular interest in the last few years.

[28] At the time of writing, a new US stance on climate change has just been announced at the 2007 G8 government meeting.

[29] IPCC, 2007.

[30] We deliberately put the notion of IPCC findings in inverted commas because IPCC does not conduit research: rather, it synthesises the findings of the global research community.

[31] See www.walmartfacts.com.

[32] Stott et al., 2010.

[33] www.forumforthefuture.org.

[34] See, e.g., www.csr.org.

[35] See, e.g., www.exxonsecrets.org.

[36] See, e.g., Vigar, 2006.

[37] 'Ontology' refers to our perception of reality, the way in which we 'view the world'. Instead of seeing the world as a myriad of discrete issues, each to be managed on its own, Birkin, 2000, calls for managers to adopt an '*ontology of interconnected events*', within which the consequence of one action will have an effect on others.

[38] This concept is discussed in more detail in Chapter 8, along with the roots of social and environmental accounting.

[39] Birkin, 2000, pp 303–4.

[40] www.employeebenefits.co.uk/item/9561.

[41] For further information on full cost accounting, see Bebbington, 2001b.

[42] See, e.g. Murray et al., 2006.

[43] BATNEEC: 'Best Available Technology Not Entailing Excessive Cost'; CATNIP: 'Currently Available Technology Not Involving Prosecution'.

[44] See *The Guardian*, 13 September 2006.

[45] *The Guardian*, 20 November 2006.

[46] www.worldbank.org

[47] Blowfield and Googins, 2007, p 23.

[48] Hummels, GJA and Wood, D. 2005, *Knowing the Price, but also the Value? Financial Analysts on Social, Ethical and Environmental Information.* Neyenrode Business Universiteit and Boston College.

[49] environment.newscientist.com—accessed 7 February 2007.

[50] For those who remain sceptical, a very accessible summary of the latest science and predictions is available in Al Gore's book and film, *An Inconvenient Truth*, 2006, in addition to the sources already cited in this chapter.

4

Corporate responsibility in developing economies

Chapter overview

In this chapter, we discuss the role of business in developing economies, and whether and how business can be an agent of poverty reduction.[1] In particular, we will:

- review the role of business in social and economic development;

- what it means for business to be an agent of development;

- examine under what circumstances business takes on a developmental role;

- explore the limitations of business as a force for development.

Main topics

■ Key terms

International development	Bottom of the pyramid
Poverty	Fairtrade
Business as development agent	Microfinance

■ Online resources

* Additional case study on private sector alternatives to weak governance
* Facts and figures on global poverty
* Teaching notes on chapter case study
* Exercises and discussion topics for students
* Additional reading and web-based resources

Introduction

Since the mid-2000s, there has been a flurry of activity around the role of business in advancing social and economic development in what are variously called emerging or developing economies. There are diverse arguments for putting business and development towards the top of theoretical and practical corporate responsibility agendas. Companies have great wealth; by some measures greater than that of many poor nations. Companies have a significant, sometimes negative, impact on developing economies. Governments cannot always be trusted to deliver the social and economic benefits the poor and marginalized have a right to expect. Business activity is essential to economic growth. Certain types of enterprise are well suited to meeting the needs of the poor. The gap between rich and poor is a threat to political and economic stability. It is, according to philosophers such as Singer (1972), morally indefensible to allow suffering on the grounds that it happens in far off places, and as part of this ethical debate, it could be argued companies have a responsibility not just for the harms they produce but equally the ones they fail to prevent.

Typically in considering these perspectives, the emphasis is on the role of multinational companies, and sometimes one can forget that many developing economies have a vibrant private sector, especially at the level of small and medium-sized enterprises, and often located in the informal rather than formal economy. We examine corporate responsibility in the context of small and medium-sized companies in Chapter 11, but their role in developing economies should not be overlooked as some of the examples in this chapter remind us.

Nonetheless, much more is known about the responsibilities and practices of larger companies, but as we shall see there are many views about when, where, and how they should act in developing economies. A company's relationship to poverty is a major determinant of how it behaves in this environment (e.g. whether it is a cause or victim of poverty), and understanding this relationship is very useful in assessing what a company can and should be doing. As the following sections reveal, it is possible to build a framework for understanding what can and cannot be expected of business in the development context.

Development agent or development tool?

The array of viewpoints on why business is important to the prosperity of developing countries and vice versa have given rise to quite different ideas about what business should be doing and why. Liberal economists argue that companies exist to create value for shareholders, subject to legal constraints (see Chapter 2), and by so doing they are a positive force for development: creating jobs, supplying goods and services, and helping to fund necessary social institutions. This thinking underpinned the so-called 'Washington Consensus', the set of private-sector oriented policies that countries around the world had to adopt if they were to receive assistance from the major international financial institutions in the 1980s and 1990s. The Consensus in its pure form has gone out of fashion, but echoes of it can be heard in discussions about growth-driven development, and in particular the view that as sustainable poverty alleviation depends on economic growth, then business as the primary creator of wealth has a central role to play.

But this gives rise to another question: should business be regarded as a development agent, consciously striving to deliver and moreover be held to account for developmental outcomes? Or should it be considered a development tool, no more responsible for positive or negative outcomes than a hammer is for a carpenter's thumb? When business acts as a development tool, the outcomes can be positive—creating jobs, generating wealth, meeting people's needs through the provision of goods and services. Two studies of Unilever's impact on the poor, and its economic footprint in Indonesia and South Africa respectively show the complex economic outcomes that can result from a multinational producing and marketing goods in developing countries.[2]

However, the question is not simply whether business has an impact on poverty, but whether or not it can and should be accountable for causing, preventing, and alleviating poverty. For instance, the development tool might create jobs, but business as development agent takes responsibility for the number of jobs it creates, their location, and the quality. The development tool might make products available in poor countries, but the development agent makes products suited to the needs of and accessible to poor segments of the population. And whereas the business-as-usual approach to development emerges from managerial calculations related to costs, returns and competition, business as a development agent is also motivated by stakeholder concerns, pressures, and demands.

In this chapter, our main interest is private enterprise as development agent: something that not only affects poverty, but is the subject of conscious actions undertaken because of poverty. The agent can be a company, an industry, an inter-company alliance, a multi-sector partnership, or any other entity where the actions of the private sector are influenced by an awareness of poverty. Our main focus will be on company actions (e.g. by management or investors), but we will also explore how others such as international development agencies have influenced the private sector.

A brief history of business as development agent

There is nothing new about companies being development agents. From the Dutch East India Company in Indonesia to the British South Africa company in 1920s' Zambia, private companies have administered vast territories, and performed parallel governmental and commercial functions. The expectations of companies may shift over time, but what these examples and other histories[3] highlight is that while definitions of responsibility change, the idea of companies having responsibility towards society remains constant. Yet despite the evidence that the responsibilities of corporations alter, corporate responsibility theory has failed to produce a substantive theory of change. The analysis other disciplines bring to business' relationship with society are not widely used in corporate responsibility theory.[4] For instance, there is a considerable body of scholarship about business and international development, concerning areas such as corporate imperialism, and influence over newly independent post-colonial states,[5] but it has not significantly influenced discussion about corporate responsibility and poverty.

There are exceptions such as Ruggie (2003) who draws on Polanyi's theory of embedded and disembedded economies to explain general shifts in the nature of the business-society relationship: '[Corporate responsibility] *may be seen as a voluntary effort to realign the efficiency of markets with the shared value and purposes that societies demand, and that markets themselves require to survive and thrive.*' (cited in Nelson, 2007, p 58) But more typically, the responsibilities of companies are presented as ahistorical. Shifts over time are treated as normative, and there is little attempt to explain why, for instance, the radical agendas of the 1930s have been replaced with something much less ambitious in recent times.[6] In other words, the definition of corporate responsibilities is treated as something divorced from the social, political, and historical context of the locations where business is operating. The consequences of this become apparent when we consider the shifting nature of development as a concept.

■ Discussion points

International development is increasingly emphasized as an important aspect of corporate responsibility:

- Why are social and environmental issues associated with international development important for business?
- Should companies be held to account for the harms they fail to prevent as much as for the ones they cause?
- What can national governments do to encourage companies to be more proactive as development agents?

Theories of development

In the literature on business and development, it is common to concentrate on the type of things companies are doing, and why they add value to society and the bottom line. However, the potential trap of focusing on a business rationale is that the scope of companies' responsibilities comes to be defined from within the framework of

---

■ Key concepts: International development

International development refers to efforts to improve standards of living in the poorer countries of the world. It is not a new idea: one of the justifications for colonialism, particularly in its later years, was that it would bring about economic growth and better social conditions. But international development as an idea really took off in the post-colonial era as it became clear that independence alone was not going to end the low levels of health, education, household income, infrastructure development, and other features that seemed characteristics of what are variously called less developed countries, emerging economies, and developing nations.

Since the 1960s, international development has been a distinct aspect of social and economic reform, typically referring to the efforts of wealthier countries to help poor ones. Most rich countries have specific government departments dedicated to funding and promoting international development. Often these were set up to deal with emergency aid (e.g. famine relief), but their remit was soon extended to address such emergencies through longer term development activities based on the principle that if you give someone a fish they will eat for a day, but if you teach them how to fish they will eat forever.

However, international development is not the preserve of donor governments, and indeed there is considerable frustration that so few rich countries have lived up to their agreement in principle to commit 0.7 per cent of GDP to development spending. Oxfam (short for Oxford

Famine Relief) was one of the first of what is now an enormous number of development-oriented NGOs with offices around the world. Some of the largest NGOs such as BRAC in Bangladesh were founded in developing countries, but there are also numerous development consultancies such as the USA's 'beltway bandits', so called for their location around Washington DC where some of the most significant development funding decisions are made.

In earlier development paradigms such as those of Frank and Wallerstein, the condition of poor countries was held to be a direct consequence of the wealth of others. Today, however, mainstream international development practice has discarded such structural considerations, and development's core aim is to establish the conditions whereby a country is ready to compete in a capitalist world economy. Business' unique position in that economy is the main reason why in recent years attention has been paid to business as a development agent, and how, for instance, it can contribute to measures of that development, exemplified for instance in the targets of the Millennium Development Goals.

management theory, rather than that of development. Yet what we have labelled the development agent role can be constructed quite differently depending how we think about development. For example, Utting (2007) discusses the relationship between corporate responsibility and an equality/equity approach to development. If such an approach were used to inform business strategy, then the responsibilities of business would include aspects of social protection, rights, empowerment, and redistribution.

Different models of development have been favoured over time ranging from Streeten's theory of basic human needs to Rostow's take-off model to Sen's work on welfare economics. Each model has its implications for what business might do. However, contemporary corporate responsibility theory in general does not openly acknowledge these different models. Instead, for the most part it adheres to, and tacitly accepts, what Rodrik (1997) calls the augmented Washington Consensus, a model that dominates current development theory.

Current approaches to corporate responsibility as management practice are stronger in some areas than others. For example, for all the widespread adoption of core labour rights into the responsibility discourse, meaningful interventions have proved difficult, especially on issues such as freedom of association, and the rights of women. Moreover, the role of business looks different again if one emphasizes the rights-based, empowerment, redistributive or neo-liberal elements of development agendas.[7] However, the distinct responses demanded by such differing ideas of development are often blurred in business-poverty discussions, something that can lead to unwarranted criticism and praise of the private sector's role.[8]

International agencies such as the United Nations Conference on Trade and Development (UNCTAD), the United Nations Development Programme (UNDP), the World Trade Organization (WTO), the World Bank, and the Organisation for Economic Co-operation and Development (OECD) have set out various ways business can help alleviate poverty.[9] For example, the International Labour Organization (ILO) highlights low wages and vulnerable employment as causes of poverty, OECD stresses the consequences of short-termism amongst multinational corporations, and their abuse of political and economic muscle, while UNCTAD concentrates on the importance of backward linkages, and embedding companies into local economies. The United Nations Industrial Development Organization (UNIDO) distinguishes between the substantive dimension to corporate responsibility (i.e. the particular issues that get addressed), and the process dimension (the ways business goes about addressing these issues, and identifying the boundaries of accountability) (Nelson, 2007). Various international organizations emphasize the importance of this process dimension as a determinant of the effectiveness of poverty interventions, including support for the self-organization of the poor at community level or workers in factories, a cognizance of local conditions, and cross-sector coordination.[10]

However, there is a mismatch between this kind of aspirational development agenda and what companies are actually doing as development agents. The array of substantive issues being addressed is incomplete, but is nonetheless more comprehensive than that of process ones which may not be included at all.[11] Various questions arise from this observation. Is it the case that business has an ad hoc poverty agenda, and if so how has that come about, and what are the likely outcomes? Can business be more effectively integrated into established agendas, and what would this take? Or is it that business is already part of an alternative poverty agenda, and what are the implications of this? We will explore these questions in the coming sections.

■ Discussion points

Theorists such as Easterly claim government aid to developing countries is a failure, and that the private sector offers a better alternative for economic growth.

• Why do you think the private sector was previously overlooked in some development theories?

• What are the strengths of companies in tackling development issues?

• Are there aspects of development where a private sector response is inappropriate?

SNAPSHOT 4.1

Merrill Lynch and conservation in Ulu Masen

In March 2008, investment firm Merrill Lynch announced it would invest US$9 million in protecting endangered forest in the Indonesia province of Aceh. In return it would get 500,000 carbon credits worth $2 million a year for four years plus an option to buy a further $1 million. The money will be invested in building the capacity of villagers to reduce their dependency on the forest by growing coffee, cocoa, or oil palm. The carbon credits can be sold or used to offset Merrill Lynch's own emissions as part of the growing system of greenhouse gas emissions trading.

The credits meet the standards of the Climate, Community and Biodiversity Alliance, the members of which include large environmental groups such as Conservation International, The Nature Conservancy, and the Rainforest Alliance that also validate the credits of companies such as BP, Intel, and SC Johnson. But unlike those companies which are primarily interested in offsetting their own emissions, Merrill Lynch is investing in a model of what it calls 'carbon farming' where an economic value is attached to the societal value of storing carbon by planting or conserving trees. Under the original Kyoto Protocol, it was not permitted to balance emissions with carbon credits generated from forest protection, but that seems likely to change when the protocol expires in 2012, recognizing that deforestation is a significant contributor to human-related carbon emissions. If that happens, credits that can currently only be traded on unregulated markets, could be traded on the more lucrative, regulated markets in Europe and Japan (and which are being considered in the US and Australia).

In some ways this is a very conventional development model because the money from Merrill Lynch will largely go to the Acehnese government to fund both alternative livelihood and forest conservation activities in Ulu Masen. It is similar in some ways to initiatives such as Plan Vivo where investors get credits for funds invested in conserving forests in Mexico, Mozambique, and Uganda, Fundo Bioclimatico in Mexico, or the work of Canopy Capital in Guyana which is paying towards the protection of the forest, in return for a share of the rights to its ecosystem services should these one day have a marketable economic value. Although they are different in detail (and are all largely untested), they represent part of a new trend in valuing the assets of poor regions, and rewarding the poor as environmental stewards. They raise all manner of issues about equity, implementation, rights, sovereignty, and distribution of benefits, and perhaps beg the question whether business is acting as a solution to poverty, or the poor are solving a problem for business. But they are indicative of the new ways business is being portrayed as a development agent, and a source of innovation in tackling societal concerns.

(Sources: Efstathiou, 2008; Gunther, 2008; Wright, 2007)

Quick Questions

1 What is the business case for Merrill Lynch's investment?

2 What are the possible outcomes in development terms?

3 Is business better placed than government to conserve forests?

The business-poverty framework

Irrespective of whether we consider business to be a development tool or a development agent, to have a bit-part or the starring role in tackling poverty, we need to understand that there are multiple facets to the business-poverty relationship. One might argue, in line with Kramer and Kania's (2006) model that corporate responsibility is either defensive (protecting a company's reputation) or offensive (burnishing the company's reputation), but from society's perspective, such a two-dimensional model does not capture the variety of ways that business affects or is affected by poverty. To do this we need to give equal consideration to three dimensions: business as a cause of poverty, its victim, and a solution (see Figure 4.1).

There is also a fourth dimension that is not explored here, but that is worth noting, i.e. that business can be indifferent to poverty, seeing it as neither a threat nor an opportunity, but simply as something that is not factored into decisions. Thus, for instance, decisions about investment are not typically based on their impact on poverty, but what will bring the best return on investment. Sometimes poverty might be appraised as an

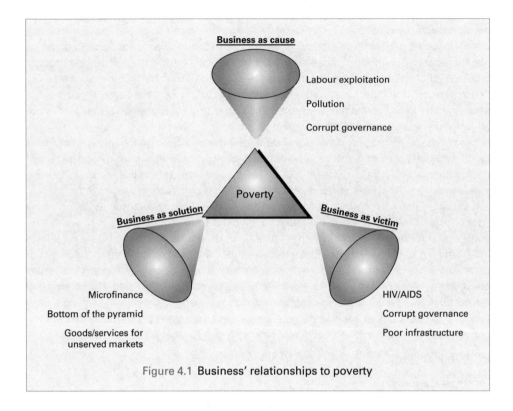

Figure 4.1 Business' relationships to poverty

opportunity in those deliberations (e.g. low labour costs), or it might be a barrier (e.g. weak infrastructure), but in many instances (perhaps in the majority of investment decisions) poverty is not a consideration, and business positions itself as a bystander.

Business as a cause of poverty

In the free market system, an inefficient company has the potential to cause poverty if it fails to generate wealth, create jobs, and provide goods and services (i.e. when it fails as a development tool). However, it is the way seemingly efficient companies can cause or exacerbate poverty that is our interest here. At one level, some argue that the very functioning of international markets may exacerbate poverty, although for reasons too complex to do justice to here. Equally, business and government in developed economies have been accused of protecting parts of their markets from developing economy competition, and also for denying developing economies the kind of protections some feel are essential for economic development.[12]

Advocates of free markets having a singularly important role in economic development, make the case that business cannot cause poverty if it acts rationally because the market is the most effective way of determining price and allocating resources. Even if one accepts this, power asymmetries that favour certain business actors mean that there are wide disparities in how the proceeds of trade are distributed, and that poor producers in particular (e.g. marginal smallholder farmers) can find themselves selling their produce for even less than the cost of production.[13] Similarly, the power some brand-owners hold as gatekeepers to lucrative consumer markets means that some manufacturers have limited bargaining power regarding price or specification, making labour one of the few areas where management can influence profitability. Hence, low wages, long hours, and other abusive labour practices are the norm in places where low-skilled labour is plentiful, the opportunity cost of relocation is low, and law enforcement is lenient.[14]

In the long-run, developing economy labour markets may obey the laws of liberal economics, and if so wages will rise with the overall upgrading of a country's economy. But in the short term, wages at less than the cost of survival and reproduction put enormous burdens not only on individual workers, but also their families and social networks. For example, in a sample of factories in China producing for Wal-Mart, the hourly wage is less than the legal minimum, and overtime hours exceed the legal maximum.[15] Only by working excessive overtime can they achieve earnings approximating a living wage. Rural to urban migrants often face particularly difficult conditions in terms of stagnating real wages and having to pay for health care and education.[16]

Sudden injections of wealth, and unequal distribution, can have long-term consequences. For example, the promotion of cocoa production in parts of Sulawesi, Indonesia, in the 1990s together with weak enforcement of traditional land rights, allowed certain migrant ethnic groups to prosper using land alienated from the indigenous population.[17] Other impacts of private sector activity are also experienced differently by different sections of the population. For example, labour markets are gendered institutions that impact differently on women than men, not least because of the former's need to balance productive and reproductive responsibilities. Poverty as experienced by women is not just a matter of unequal wages, but also relates to issues such as childcare, maternity leave, and care of the elderly, aspects that are often neglected in the corporate responsibility initiatives of companies that either do not understand or are not concerned about the connections between reproductive work or care and both business and societal sustainability.[18]

These are examples of the substantive dimension to business' relationship to poverty, and there are more facts and figures on the Online Resource Centre. But we should not forget what we earlier called the process dimension including, for example, the issue of empowerment. Poverty is often associated with disenfranchisement, marginalization, and the lack of capacity or opportunity to advocate for one's own interests. Freedom of association and collective bargaining are amongst the rights business has been accused of interfering with, the absence of which can perpetuate poverty. Companies can also affect the process of poverty alleviation by paying low wages, or avoiding or evading taxes, thereby denying governments essential resources that potentially could be used to invest in the poor.[19] And short-term contracts with suppliers may ultimately limit the opportunity to build up the capacity of poor producers and their communities.[20]

There are other areas where business relates to poverty, if not as the direct cause, then at least as the apparent beneficiary. The poverty that is behind child labour, forced labour, and labour trafficking is something that has benefited business in some circumstances. In an indirect way, business is held responsible for these types of poverty, not just because it is seen as a beneficiary of the global economic system within which such poverty exists, but because it is associated with the changing patterns of governance that are characteristics of that system.

Bad (i.e. corrupt) and weak (i.e. ineffective) government is one cause of poverty, and business has variously supported, tolerated, and resisted such practices. Corporate ambivalence in this regard can be seen from the positions taken by the private sector during the apartheid era in South Africa where parts of the business community both supported and undermined the government.[21] Generalizations, however, are difficult to make.

While good public governance is generally accepted as essential to alleviating poverty, it remains to be seen if that is true of the alternative models of governance that business is part of. Companies have played a part in the process of deregulation, and the subsequent emergence of an international regulatory system that is highly skewed toward the protection of capital and non-human corporate assets.[22] For Ruggie (2003), companies must help redress the imbalances of the global governance system, and 'the key governance question before us' is how much burden companies, and in particular the kind of voluntary efforts associated with corporate responsibility management, should bear. Wrapped inside that question are issues of regulatory capture by the private sector, and how well self-regulation and voluntary regulation protect the interests of the poor.

The specific relationships between business and poverty are important to understand because they affect how companies behave as development agents. For example, the relocation of factories in contexts of deregulation can have serious impacts in terms of lost employment and downward pressures on wages and working conditions in former host countries. The lifting in 2005 of the Multi-fibre Agreement (MFA), which had helped developing countries build up export-oriented garment industries, threatened to have negative consequences for workers, communities and local and national economies, as competition from China forced factories to close in several countries. This prompted the formation of the private sector-led MFA Forum that proposed solutions for garment industries in countries such as Bangladesh and Lesotho. Another dimension of the business-poverty nexus, namely the bias of markets against the poor, in terms of both the difficulties small producers have in accessing international markets, and the unequal distribution of value along the trading chain, is addressed by fairtrade. Elements of the fairtrade model, which involves the payment of a premium price to small producers and the organization of producers into associations, are finding their way into large companies trading practices such as Starbucks' Coffee and Farmer equity (CAFE) Practices.[23]

To date, when business has been accused of causing poverty, if it has not denied the charge (as has typically been the case with regard to disinvestment, relocation, and corporate tax avoidance and evasion), it has for the most part sought to protect its reputation, notably by adopting new regulatory systems such as company, industry or multi-stakeholder codes of conduct that promise some form of social accountability. The most significant approach in the development context is the use of multi-stakeholder or non-governmental systems of regulation involving multiple actors in new roles and relationships, and new processes of standard-setting, monitoring, benchmarking and enforcement. Examples include the Fair Wear Foundation (FWF), the Ethical Trading Initiative (ETI) and the Fair Labor Association (FLA).

SNAPSHOT 4.2

Fairtrade: an approach to market redistribution

Fairtrade is concerned with the bias of markets against the poor, in terms of both the difficulties small producers have in accessing international markets, and the unequal distribution of value along the trading chain. Although it initially grew as part of a network of alternative trade producers, buyers, processors, and retailers, the term fairtrade today is mostly associated with a product labelling initiative that ensures a place for the products of marginalized producers in developed economy markets. While there is tension within the fairtrade movement between those who see it as a tool for radically modifying the dominant economic model for the benefit of the poor, and those who see it as an entry point for products from developing economies,[24] fairtrade labelled products today succeed because they respect the many of the rules, norms, behavioural expectations, and cultural assumptions of the wealthiest markets. As Leigh Taylor (2005) observes, the challenge for fairtrade is to be in the market but not of it.

Distinguishing features of fairtrade include a focus on the products of small-scale, often family-based producers (although over time fairtrade buyers have also sourced from plantations and commercial farms); and the organization of producers into politically independent, democratic associations such as cooperatives. Fairtrade buyers agree to enter into long-term contracts (more than one harvest cycle) with these organizations, and to pay farmers at least the minimum price that Fairtrade Labelling Organisation International has calculated represents a fair return. Buyers also agree to pre-finance farmers so they can avoid falling into debt, to pay for producer certification, and to pay a portion of all sales to producer organizations as a social premium to help empower and develop the producer community.

Poverty, from a fairtrade perspective, is therefore not only a factor of financial wealth, but also of impersonal, commoditized relationships, power asymmetries within trading chains, lack of institutional capacity amongst poor producers, and the disadvantageous decisions producers make in consequence. Fairtrade challenges liberal economic assumptions that markets are impersonal and fair, and turns trade into a more personal relationship between grower, buyer, retailer, and consumer that requires a managed distribution of value-added is distributed along the chain (Leigh Taylor, 2005). While this model is coming under pressure as mainstream demand for fairtrade products from processors and retailers increases, it is also noticeable that features of the fairtrade system (e.g. long-term contracts, capacity building, and buyer-producer trust) are finding their way into larger companies' trading practices such as Starbucks' Coffee and Farmer Equity (CAFE) Practices (Macdonald, 2007).

(Sources: Macdonald, 2007; Nicholls & Opal, 2005; Leigh Taylor, 2005)

Quick Questions

1 What weaknesses in conventional trading systems does fairtrade address?

2 Why are consumers attracted to fairtrade?

3 Would the use of fairtrade certified products help defend a multinational brand from accusations that it is a cause of poverty?

Business as poverty's victim

One only needs to look at the facets of poverty set out in the Millennium Development Goals (MDGs) to see how business can be a victim of poverty. The goals are indicators of human development, and failure to achieve them is indicative of the insufficiencies that can hamper business in developing economies. For example, the fact that half the world lives on less than two dollars a day, and 1.1 billion people live in 'extreme poverty'—less than a dollar a day—shows how much greater the market for goods and services could be if only people had more income. The number of children who do not finish primary school is a warning of how difficult it can be for companies to fill even relatively low-skilled positions. Women are less likely to get education, more likely to work at home, and less likely to obtain full-time salaried positions, and gender inequality and disem-powerment can harm companies that need educated and independent workers and consumers.

Goals 4, 5, and 6 of the MDGs concern health (child mortality, maternal health, and major diseases such as HIV/AIDS respectively), and high morbidity, failing health care systems, malnutrition, and disabling or terminal diseases can all harm business. Companies such as SABMiller in South Africa have invested in programmes to prevent AIDS and provide anti-retroviral drugs because of the attrition the disease was causing amongst experienced personnel. Wall (2007) shows how in Kazakhstan, oil companies are having to compensate for the declining quality of state health care provision.

Weak public governance and the failure of government as development agents are underlying themes of the MDGs. They are equally factors in business being a victim of poverty. Though not explicit in the goals themselves, the idea that the private sector can compensate for weak government is evident in crucial agreements and policies surrounding the MDGs. For example, the 2002 Monterrey Consensus which announced US support for the MDGs, bound the MDG implementation process to the mainstream neo-liberal strategic and policy framework.[25] According to Saith (2006), one of the problems with the MDGs is that they are silent on certain important dimensions of global poverty. Rising inequality, for example, is something that poses particular threats for business. This situation creates all manner of uncertainties that risk averse companies might rather not face such as mass migration, conflict over natural resources, and political unrest. Moreover, it should not be forgotten, that an earlier era of economic globalization in the 1900s came to a halt because of a political backlash against globalization's distributional effects.[26]

There are innumerable examples of companies addressing issues which could affect their long-term prospects, particularly in relation to education. Mining companies in Africa, such as Anglo American, have had to engage seriously with the issue of HIV/AIDS. In addition to investing in human capital, companies respond to other weaknesses in their value chain. The Forest Stewardship Council (FSC), for example, has enabled companies to reduce reputational and supply risks arising from weak governance of forest resources.[27] Recently, Cadbury launched its Cocoa Partnership to address the risk of long-term shortages of cocoa should the lack of investment by farmers continue. And one of the UN Global Compact's aims is to increase business' commitment to reaching the MDGs.

■ **Discussion points**

Evidence of poverty negatively affecting business prospects has attracted many companies to consider corporate responsibility as a management approach.

- Is it more important for companies to tackle issues where they cause poverty or where they are its victims?
- What are some of the main areas where business can justify its investment in tackling poverty on the grounds it would otherwise be a victim?
- How are small and medium-sized enterprises in developing countries affected by poverty?

Business as solution

Increasing attention is being paid to the idea of business as a solution to poverty. This is not simply a restatement of the centrality of business to the capitalist economy as the source of employment, goods and services, and wealth. Rather, it is the belief that business can consciously invest in ways that are simultaneously commercially viable and beneficial to the poor. This relates to and overlaps with ideas of social entrepreneurship, a concept with many definitions, but where typically business methods are employed for social development ends (see Chapter 11). In contrast, Hammond, Hart, and Prahalad in their influential work on the 'fortune at the bottom of the pyramid' (BOP) emphasize that there are genuine commercial, market-based opportunities to be had by targeting the poor.[28] They argue that whereas the richest 0.8 billion people represent a largely saturated, and over-served market, and despite there being significant opportunities to serve the 1.5 billion emerging middle class, the greatest unexplored opportunity is the five trillion dollar market of four billion people who individually or as households have low incomes, but as a group account for a significant percentage of national income and expenditure.

While these figures are controversial given the varying income thresholds that have been suggested,[29] the insight that the poor control considerable wealth is important because it suggests that what is considered the untapped purchasing power at the BOP provides an opportunity for companies to profit by selling to these unserved or underserved markets.

If that was the extent of the BOP model's proposition, it would have little direct relevance to the idea that business can be a development agent because all it would imply is that the poor represent a rational, if overlooked, business opportunity. However, bottom of the pyramid advocates say that by meeting the needs of the poor, business can increase their productivity and incomes, and be an engine of empowerment, not least by allowing them to enter into the formal economy. In other words, by selling to the poor, companies can help eradicate poverty. Prahalad (2005), in particular, emphasizes the role multinationals can play in this by allowing the poor to benefit from both the quality of their products and the efficiencies of their systems.

A large number of companies invest in building the capacity of local entrepreneurs, for example, in response to government policy such as the Black Economic Empowerment (BEE) programme in South Africa or as a result of business initiatives such as Business Action for Africa), and creating markets for their produce. Organizations such as Market for Change, and the Shell Foundation are building on this by helping link small businesses with buyers. In a different way, the consultancy Accenture is giving the private sector in developing economies access to management and technological expertise through its Accenture Development Partnerships programme.

Microfinance is perhaps the most widespread example of business providing a solution to the problems of the poor. Put simply, it is a system that enables poor people without conventional collateral to access loans at affordable rates of interest, making them less dependent on traditional moneylenders, and providing them with a form of savings, insurance, and investment. In recent years, several commercial banks have offered microfinance services including Citigroup, Deutsche Bank, and ABN Amro. There are a number of examples such as ICICI Prudential, Hindustan Lever Limited (HLL), and Grameen Phone where the infrastructure developed for microfinance has been used to develop other services such as retail and distribution.

A major criticism of the BOP theory is that it places too much emphasis on integrating the poor into consumer markets and treating the poor as consumers, when in fact they might be better served if they had better jobs or access to markets as producers.[30] It is inaccurate to say that BOP theory entirely ignores the role of the poor as producers. Indeed, organizations such as the Shell Foundation (e.g. through their collaboration with the retailer Marks & Spencer to promote flower growing groups on the Agulhas Plain, South Africa—Case Study 11), and others involved in Business Action for Africa are focused on the production opportunities for the poor, and especially the promotion of entrepreneurship.

However, within BOP theory and practice the role of the poor as consumers is very important. Many companies that identify with the BOP approach emphasize precisely this aspect. Companies such as Coca Cola and Procter & Gamble have invested in making their products available to the poor, and organizations such as KickStart (capital equipment), Freeplay Foundation (sustainable energy), and Aravind (healthcare) specialize in serving poor communities. Vodafone is amongst the telecommunication companies that has recognized the need of migrant workers to remit money home, and has launched its mobile phone-based M-Pesa remittance system in Kenya, and is exploring a system for international remittances with Citigroup. Companies as diverse as Philips, Intel, Infosys, and Godrej have also developed new products tailored to the needs of poor communities.

To understand the theory behind this 'consumerist' dimension of BOP, one needs to consider the situation facing many poor people. Not only do they have low incomes: (a) they have significant unmet needs; (b) they are typically part of an informal or subsistence economy (the ILO estimates that 70 per cent of the workforce in developing economies is in the informal sector); (c) they are part of high cost micro-economic systems where they pay more for goods and services (e.g. water is more expensive in a Nairobi slum than in central New York); (d) they are often 'prisoners' of local monopolies (e.g. moneylenders); and (e) they lack access to quality products. Therefore, according to Prahalad, if companies compete to serve the poor, the upshot will be lower living costs (e.g. because interest rates will fall), increased productivity (e.g. because if medicines are more affordable, people will be healthier), and new employment opportunities (e.g. from selling the products).

One of the issues in relation to this model as a conscious approach to tackling poverty is the degree to which, having identified the opportunity, the market alone will deliver developmental benefits. The difference between certain proponents and critics of BOP is to a degree a moral one, with the former reluctant to make choices about what the poor should have access to, and the latter arguing that high spending by some poor people on tobacco, alcohol, and gambling suggest they do not always make 'wise' purchasing decisions. This tension is evident in case studies of the BOP,[31] but if we are thinking of business as a development agent, then it is important to distinguish between companies that serve the poor, and ones that factor poverty alleviation outcomes into their decisions and strategies. This is not straightforward. For example, at first glance it may seem that HLL supply of shampoo to rural women is less beneficial than Aravind's provision of low cost cataract surgery, yet this conclusion ignores the increase to rural women's incomes arising from new opportunities to sell shampoo and other household items. However, in the business-poverty context, the key point is that financial performance ultimately should be less important an indicator than social outcomes.

This is not to say that companies should approach poverty as a social enterprise where profits are unimportant,[32] although successful examples of targeting the poor such as Aravind, HealthStore Foundation, and the Grameen Bank have been run on a not-for-profit basis, or involve some form of subsidy or alternative funding. However, to be profitable can require unconventional business models, not only in terms of understanding the market, or designing products, but equally in the collaborations that are required. There are various examples of companies collaborating with NGOs to identify needs, and deliver products: these include Telenor and Grameen's collaboration to create Grameen Phone, ICICI Prudential's with women's groups in India on insurance products, and Accion International's collaboration with ABN Amro on microfinance. Brugmann and Prahalad (2007) view these collaborations as part of a trend towards 'co-creation' where business and NGOs or grassroots organizations create hybrid business models suited to the very different conditions for commercial and social success when dealing with poverty.

To a degree, these collaborations are about scaling up the success of NGO innovations as witnessed by the entrance of mainstream banks into the world of microfinance. However, companies such as Standard Chartered are bringing new capacities to existing sectors (e.g. raising capital for microfinance on international markets), while partnerships such as that between World Diagnostics and Ugandan NGOs allow existing networks to be used to provide new types of health service. This is not without its problems. For instance, ICICI's collaboration with women's self-help groups in India was criticized by some NGOs for undermining their wider social development goals, and there will be fundamental shifts in relationships as collaborations require NGOs to privilege task-driven partnerships with companies over ideology-driven dialogues.[33] Moreover, such partnerships are becoming a defining (and perhaps legitimating) feature of initiatives affecting the poor's access to, and control over, essential resources such as water privatization, projects associated with the Clean Development Mechanism, and now forest management in the context of voluntary emissions trading (see Snapshot 4.1). We discuss the implications of this kind of change later, but we should recognize that in stressing partnerships with large companies, we risk further marginalizing the contribution local small and medium-sized companies make, and the local partnerships they have historically been part of.

■ Discussion points

Commercial opportunities linked to poverty have attracted a great deal of attention in the business community.

- Are companies justified in saying they are benefitting the poor when they are pursuing a profit motive?
- Do you agree with Prahalad that the poor benefit as much from being seen as consumers as from becoming producers?
- What advantages do microfinance organizations have compared to conventional banks?

Assessing the business response

The previous discussion of business acting as a development agent provides a framework of the different types of interaction (i.e. based on cause, solution, and victimhood). What it does not reveal is: (a) the conditions under which business will actively manage its relationship with poverty, and (b) the effectiveness of its taking on a development role. It is this we turn to now.

Features of managing poverty

The business-poverty relationship can be the focus of different spheres of business activity, such as core business operations, social investment and philanthropy, as well as policy dialogue and advocacy.[34] As we have also seen, the actions taken may assume a variety of forms. In some instances, for example, when creating or destroying jobs, or choosing where to locate factories, business clearly impacts economic and social development, but does so as a development tool, not as a development agent consciously

Box 4.1 **The three conditions of business' engagement in poverty**

Condition	Examples
Condition 1: Business is more likely to act when poverty is associated with an identifiable risk to a company or industry, including risks to reputation, to the availability of commodities, to production, etc. This condition accounts for genuine innovations with respect to supply chain governance, and responsibility towards producing communities. It also accounts for some of the links created between companies and development organizations.	FWF, ETI, Worldwide Responsible Apparel Production, FLA, CAFE Practices, FSC, Cadbury's Cocoa Partnership.
Condition 2: Business is more likely to act when poverty offers a favourable ROI. This accounts for services to underserved markets, new market opportunities for the poor, and in some cases a reengineering of the benefits of trade in favour of the poor. Initiatives that seek to deliver what might be thought of as a social return on investment (SROI) in addition to ROI can position the poor as producer or consumer.	Fairtrade, microfinance, enterprises such as Freeplay, M-Pesa, or the Shakti Project, and Merrill Lynch's investment in Ulu Masen.
Condition 3: Business is more likely to act when poverty is associated with inefficiency. This accounts for initiatives to combat corruption, enhance the poor's productive capacity, increase health and safety standards, invest in education, and improve living environments.	Extraction Industry Transparency Initiative, investment in AIDS-prevention by firms such SABMiller and L'Oreal, and the education programmes of companies such as Anglo American and Cisco Systems.

negotiating its relationship with poverty. Under what conditions might companies act as development agents?

The examples in the previous section suggest that there are three basic conditions that dictate under what circumstances business can take on the development agent role. These are set out in Box 4.1.

Any of the initiatives undertaken by business as a development agent mentioned in this chapter can be explained by appeal to one or other of those three conditions. Likewise, dimensions to development that lie outside the scope of these conditions are unlikely to be addressed by business overtly. For example, redistributive elements such as corporate taxation, though part of debates about development economics, are not normally incorporated into normative debates about the responsibilities of business. Neither is there any thorough consideration of power and conflict, even though some of the areas where business affects development are historically the sites of dispute and tension (e.g. relations between buyers and small contract farmers or outgrowers). The gender dimensions to poverty are frequently ignored, and this is part of a general pattern of preferencing where the individual good is preferred to the communal, financial wealth is favoured over non-financial, and issues such as class, ethnicity, sexuality, and other determinants of privilege are discounted or isolated from their wider context. It is not that these dimensions are absent from debates about development: indeed, it is their importance to development theory that makes their absence from corporate responsibility in the development context so noticeable. These and other types of exclusion will be more apparent when we look at the impact of corporate responsibility (see Chapter 12).

■ Discussion points

Risk, profitability, and inefficiency are the conditions that underpin any business investments as a development agent.

- Can you imagine a situation where business would make such an investment even though these conditions were not met?
- What sorts of inefficiency in developing countries are significant for business?
- What issues in developing countries will business tackle in 2020 that they are not addressing today?

Business' impact on development

Despite the many examples of business seeking to act as a development agent, there remains criticism that not enough is being done. Even though companies are acting voluntarily, there is a case to be made that companies are renegotiating their social and environmental responsibilities in ways that meet the requirements of commercial competitiveness rather than societal good. Certainly the three conditions of business acting as a development agent set out in the previous section are all rooted in business self-interest. It is evidence of this kind of shift (e.g. in relation to pensions, labour relations, and taxation) that make some people fearful of companies acting as development agents because ultimately they might pick and choose what constitutes societal good and co-opt the development process. Private sector involvement can be seen as part of a process of neo-constitutionalism whereby those involved in managing the global economy see their rights being secured in law, but are increasingly isolated from popular scrutiny.[35]

There is certainly evidence that business interacts with development in particular ways, and reason to be concerned that it constricts the meaning of development itself.[36] As the business-poverty framework shows it is something that can lead companies to rethink their relationships, but does not fundamentally alter them. Moreover, elements of the business response (e.g. the adaptation of conventional management tools and concepts for development purposes; the depoliticization of economic opportunity; the reduction of complex social, cultural, and economic factors to technical problems) are ones that are characteristic of contemporary development itself.[37] Therefore, it may be harder to argue that business co-opts development than to make the case that business as a development agent mirrors the established norms of the predominant development discourse.

Rather than examining business' role as development agent as subversive either to business or development, we have concentrated on the possibilities and limitations of business' current and likely contribution. In much of the mainstream literature on business and development there is a tendency to stress the generic strengths of private enterprise to explain the significance of business' role in development (e.g. client-focus; ability to raise capital; specific skills, tools and competencies). However, the role any single company or industry can play is greatly affected by the type of relationship it has with poverty (e.g. victim or cause), whether offensive or defensive strategies are pursued, and the location and context (e.g. whether or not there is a functioning civil society and state regulatory capacity). Too often, in making the case for business to act as a development agent, advocates overlook the context-specific variables and complexities that can ultimately influence outcomes in a given situation as much as flaws in execution can.

Yet even such contextual variables are of secondary importance to the three conditions that predicate any corporate engagement in development, i.e. the association of poverty with risk, opportunity, and inefficiency. The examples of business responses in this chapter demonstrate that at least one of these conditions needs to be met for companies to act as development agents. However, knowledge of how the conditions influence development is far from complete, and to date success has been measured in terms of the instrumental benefit for companies, not the developmental benefit for communities. While the poor may participate, they do not have the means to hold others to account for the outcomes. Similarly, while a positive association between poverty and ROI can stimulate companies to deliver a SROI, there can be a tension between developmental outcomes and commercial imperatives, evident, for example, in how the demand for certified timber has been met largely by sourcing from developed nations rather than developing ones, and concerns that the expansion of fairtrade is weakening the relationships between producers, buyers, and consumers. The emphasis on the financial success, and the limited information on the social impacts, of initiatives of this kind suggest that developmental consequences can be lost or overlooked once ROI attracts more attention than SROI.

Recognizing these conditions is an important step in understanding the parameters of possibility for business as a development agent, and in particular what dimensions of poverty are likely to be included or excluded. However, we should not treat these parameters as static, and it may be too early to pass judgment on what is possible given instances such as the recent change in emphasis from simply expecting suppliers to comply with standards, to major brands working with supplier management and workers to increase local capacity, including creating spaces in oppressive regimes where workers can organize and collaborate. This offers the promise of a more effective way of dealing with reputational issues arising from allegations of exploitation.

At the same time, certain aspects of social development that complement the interests of business are being normalized, and this could explain why they appear less likely to be critiqued. These include, for instance, flexible labour markets in contrast to the emphasis on secure employment in previous eras, private ownership of natural resources, and the free flow of capital. While it is hard to claim that business' role in development exacerbates such trends in a significant way, there are issues of legitimization and delegitimization that need to be addressed. Corporate responsibility plays an important role in framing our understanding of poverty and development. For example, modern management rationalism has been incorporated into the way poverty is understood and approached. Similarly, there are examples where a term such as empowerment has come to be associated with a business quality such as entrepreneurship, thereby imbuing business behaviour with a new moral creditworthiness.[38] This is problematic morally if notions of good come to be reassessed using commercial criteria,[39] but also from a technical developmental perspective where a distinction has to be drawn between very different types of entrepreneurs, some of whom play an essential role in growth and innovation that is conducive to poverty reduction, while others create few jobs and have little security.

Nonetheless, there are examples of issues that are developmentally important being accommodated even though this means challenging conventional business wisdom as we have seen with the accommodation of practices with their roots in fairtrade. As Kolk and Van Tulder (2006) show in the context of voluntary standards, a variety of pressures contribute to what is ultimately legitimized or ignored, and often what emerges is a 'sector conditioned morality' that reflects a minimum level of expectation from civil society on the one hand, and a ceiling level acceptable to an industry on the other.

The experience of corporate responsibility and business as a development agent suggests that development ends can best be served when there is genuine collaboration whereby different sectors pursue shared or complementary poverty objectives. This conclusion can be challenged on the grounds that it relies on evidence about large companies, and says nothing about the smaller firms and informal sector that is such an important feature of developing economies. It also disregards changes associated with the new influx of foreign direct investment from countries such as China and India, and the different types of relationship that may emerge as a result, just as it ignores the role large domestic companies played in the development of countries such as Singapore, Taiwan, and South Korea. However, even if consideration of these dimensions to business in developing economies revealed very different features of managing the relationship with society, a significant part of the business community would still be looking to employ collaborative models.

Nevertheless, based on the current pattern of corporate engagement in development, there are reasons to think increasingly sophisticated models of partnership will be appealing (see Chapter 9). However, a stumbling block could be companies' unwillingness to be accountable for development objectives in any rigorous way. A test of how far this can be overcome may be the recent wave of socially-oriented entrepreneurs claiming a blend of social and commercial vision (see Chapter 11). If these find viable ways to demonstrate social returns, they may influence other companies that recognize a role as development agent, but limit their accountability to internal rationalization.

CASE STUDY 4

Poverty as a business opportunity: M-Pesa

Mobile telephony is having a huge impact in Africa where the relatively cheap infrastructure is helping bridge the gap caused by poor transport and communications infrastructure. In Kenya, for example, one in three adults carries a mobile phone, and in five years the number of mobiles in Kenya has grown from one million to 6.5 million, compared to 300,000 landlines. One driver of the boom is the large population of economic migrants eager to stay in touch with their home communities. Migrant workers are a main source of income in many rural areas, but one challenge is how to remit money home given the lack of banks, and unsafe roads.

Vodafone is the world's second largest wireless phone services carrier with more than 200 million customers, and sales of $50 billion. Although most of its business is in Europe, it has interests in companies worldwide including Safaricom in Kenya, and is increasingly looking to penetrate developing markets. In Africa, there are only 16 mobile phones for every 100 people, compared to Europe where there is more than one phone per head. Recognition of this market potential, and the unique contribution mobile phones could play in meeting consumer needs led to the introduction of M-PESA.

At first glance, there is nothing spectacular about M-PESA. For the user, it is simply an extra line on their mobile phone menu that says 'Send Money'. The subscriber goes to a shop, adds funds to their phone account, and then sends them to friends, family, or anyone else with a mobile. The recipient goes to a similar shop, shows the code on the mobile and some ID, and collects the money.

Yet in Kenya where bank accounts and plastic money are scarce, and carrying cash on journeys can leave you prey to robbers, the M-PESA money transfer system is a genuine innovation. It is not the brainchild of the conventional banking system, but an entirely new product, developed by Vodafone and Safaricom, part-funded by the British government's Department for International Development (DFID), and piloted with the help of Kenyan microfinance institution, Faulu.

M-Pesa was launched commercially in March 2007 after a two year trial period, and Safaricom CEO, Michael Joseph, says there are over two million active users. *'We also know that it channels over Kenyan Shillings (KSh) 100 million in a day. . . . I see it getting to three or four million customers very soon.'*

According to M-PESA pioneer, Nick Hughes, the idea came about at the 2002 World Summit on Sustainable Development in a conversation with someone from DFID about what Vodafone could do to address the Millennium Development Goals. One area where he thought Vodafone could play a role was making it easier to move money around so that entrepreneurs and others had better access to finance. Returns on investment would not be great, and it was likely that as with many ideas linked to social development, this one would lose out to others in the internal competition to allocate project funding. However, DFID ran a challenge fund offering capital to help ideas that were useful to developing countries circumvent the constraints of company product development processes. With the government offering 50 per cent matching funding, what would otherwise have been seen as a low yield, low priority project, started to look like an interesting idea. However, making the idea a reality presented a variety of challenges ranging from new software to the systems and capabilities of Safaricom, introducing the product to Safaricom's staff and distributors, and working with Faulu savings groups to on product testing.

None of these hurdles has proved insurmountable, and overcoming them may have put M-PESA in a stronger position in the long run because the internal support and external relations are that much stronger than before. Soon after its launch, M-PESA was being talked about as a serious competitor to existing money transfer agencies, and Safaricom has started an aggressive campaign to extend the number of subscribers by partnering with established financial institutions such as Equity Bank and Post Bank.

An unintended consequence of M-PESA is how it has spawned new enterprises. M-PESA is no longer just about sending money: the brand has grown organically, taking on a life of its own. Account-holders now deposit money in their virtual accounts, and withdraw it at dealers all over the country whenever they want. Long distance traders put money in their accounts before coming to Nairobi, and take it out when they arrive in the city. Long-distance travellers use their accounts like travellers' cheques, and some contractors even pay workers through their M-PESA accounts. The service is being expanded beyond Kenya. Vodafone is running a pilot project in Afghanistan, and its subsidiary Vodacom was due to launch M-PESA to its 4.1 million subscribers in Tanzania in April 2008. Safaricom has also joined forces with a mobile phone service operator in Uganda to expand the service there.

(Sources: Hughes & Lonie 2007; Akumu 2008; original research)

Questions

1 M-PESA was part-funded by the British government which saw its potential to contribute to its goals of poverty alleviation.

  a How does M-PESA contribute towards the Millennium Development Goals?

  b Is M-PESA an example of business acting as a development agent?

  c Do you think expansion of M-PESA will depend on continuing government support?

2 M-PESA is a product aimed at poor and marginalized consumers.

  a Is it a good example of a company identifying commercial opportunities at the 'bottom of the pyramid'?

  b Is it a financially viable business model?

  c What impacts has it had on poor consumers?

3 M-PESA's funding model allowed it to compete for internal resources.

  a Do you think the service's success will have a significant impact on either Vodafone or Safaricom in the future?

  b How might their behavior change?

  c How might Safaricom build on this success as it attempts to expand its services in East Africa?

SUMMARY

When we examine the role of business as a development agent today, what we are witnessing is part of a constantly shifting debate about business' contribution to society that plays out differently according to place, time, and culture, but is ultimately about how the norms and values of capitalism, as embodied in the modern enterprise, can be accommodated, harnessed, and utilized for societal good. The framework of business' interactions with poverty used in this chapter shows that, even if a company focuses on its financial mission, there can be good reasons to consciously manage the relationship with society. Consequently, there are companies that are mindful of poverty, and showing a degree of innovation in how they respond. But they have a narrow perspective on what to be accountable for and to whom, and the incentives to be more rigorous about this are lacking. At present, the conditions under which business engages in poverty alleviation are ones rooted in self-interest, even if responses differ depending on what is meant by that term. What are often called countervailing agents have made some progress in expanding this definition of self-interest, but these government and non-government actors have had more success in getting companies to commit to development objectives than they have in holding them to account for delivering on them. By clarifying how business relates to poverty, and under what conditions it chooses to act as a development agent, it might be easier to hold companies to account, and make it in their interests to be more accountable. Without this accountability there is likely to be a randomness and unpredictability to business' interpretation of its responsibilities, leaving open the possibility that for all of the justification for business to be a development agent, it will remain a development maverick.

FURTHER READING

Take your learning further: Online Resource Centre **www.oxfordtextbooks.co.uk/orc/blowfield_ murray2e/**

Visit the Online Resource Centre which accompanies this book to enrich your understanding of this chapter.

Students: explore web links and further reading suggestions. Keep up to date with the latest developments by undertaking web exercises.

Lecturers: you will find additional case studies, including one on the topic of Merrill Lynch/Bank of America—investing to conserve Indonesia's forests, for use in class or assessment. Show your students trailers from films related to Corporate Responsibility, and use images from the book in your PowerPoint slides.

VISIT THE WEBSITE
for links to useful sources of further information

- Clay, J, 2005, *Exploring the Links Between International Business and Poverty Reduction: A Case Study of Unilever in Indonesia*, Oxfam, Oxford.
  Innovative study of how a multinational company affects the economy of a country.
- Easterly, WR, 2006, *The White Man's Burden: Why the West's Efforts to Aid the Rest Have Done So Much Ill and So Little Good*, Oxford University Press, Oxford.
  Provocative arguments for replacing development aid with greater business involvement as a development agent.

● Prahalad, CK & Hart, SL, 2002, 'The fortune at the bottom of the pyramid,' *Strategy & Business*, no. 26, pp 2–14.

The initial exposition of an idea of business and poverty that has captured the imagination of people around the world.

● Utting, P & Marques, JC (eds), 2009, *Corporate Social responsibility and Regulatory Governance: Towards Inclusive Development?* Palgrave MacMillan, New York.

Collection of essays highlighting some of the more troublesome aspects of business' role in development.

● WBCSD 2007, *Doing Business With the World : the New Role of Corporate Leadership in Global Development*, World Business Council for Sustainable Development, Geneva.

Examples of the business case for involvement in development.

● Wilson, C, 2006, *Make Poverty Business: Increase Profits and Reduce Risks by Engaging With the Poor*, Greenleaf, Sheffield.

Instrumental arguments for why business should engage in international development.

ENDNOTES

[1] This chapter draws heavily on Blowfield, ME, 2009, 'Business, Corporate Responsibility, and Poverty' in Utting & Marques, 2009.

[2] See, e.g. Fig, 2007; Newell and Muro, 2006; Robins, 2007; Glover, 2007.

[3] Clay, 2005; Kapstein, 2008.

[4] Levy and Newell, 2002; Blowfield, 2005.

[5] Newell and Frynas, 2007.

[6] Ireland and Pillay, 2009.

[7] Utting, 2007.

[8] Bond, 2006.

[9] Kolk and Van Tulder, 2006.

[10] Kolk and Van Tulder, 2006.

[11] Kolk and Van Tulder, 2006.

[12] Chang, 2002.

[13] Raynolds et al., 2004.

[14] Graham and Woods, 2006.

[15] Chan and Siu, 2007.

[16] Pearson, 2007.

[17] Blowfield, 2004.

[18] Pearson, 2007.

[19] Jenkins, 2005.

[20] Macdonald, 2007.

[21] Fig, 2007

[22] Graham and Woods, 2006.

[23] Macdonald, 2007.

[24] Raynolds et al., 2004.

[25] Bond, 2006.

[26] O'Rourke and Williamson, 1999.

[27] Leigh Taylor, 2005.

[28] Prahalad and Hart, 2002; Prahalad, 2005; Hart, 2005; Hammond et al., 2007.

[29] Hammond et al., 2007; Karnani, 2007.

[30] Karnani, 2007.

[31] See, e.g. contributions to Rangan, 2007.

[32] Contrast with Karnani, 2007.

[33] Brugmann and Prahalad, 2007.

[34] Brainard, 2006.

[35] Sum, 2009.

[36] Blowfield, 2005.

[37] Ferguson, 1990.

[38] Rajak, 2006.

[39] Blowfield and Dolan, 2008.

5

Globalization and corporate responsibility

Chapter overview

In this chapter, we explore the importance of globalization for corporate responsibility, and how it accounts for some of the ways corporate responsibility has evolved. In particular, we will:

- discuss different meanings of globalization;

- identify the main areas in which globalization has had an impact;

- discuss the ways in which globalization has altered trade, production, and investment;

- consider how globalization influences governance and the implications of this for corporate responsibility;

- explore corporate responsibility as a business response to the challenges of globalization, identifying what it addresses and examining why some feel it is inadequate;

- examine stakeholder partnerships as a response to the aspects of globalization.

Main topics

■ Key terms

Globalization

Deterritorialization

Liberal economics

Global governance

Civil society

International development

Self-regulation

Stakeholder partnerships

■ Online resources

- Suggested additional material on business and globalization

- Teaching notes on chapter case study

- Additional case study on partnerships between football teams and development organizations

- Links to other web-based resources

Globalization and corporate responsibility

In Chapter 2, we saw how the relationship of business with society has altered during different historical periods. Now we are in a new era—globalization—which is bringing changes that are as momentous as those of the Industrial Revolution. Writers such as Wood et al. (2006), Pedersen and Huniche (2006), and Crane and Matten (2004) tie corporate responsibility to the social, political, and environmental challenges of globalization. In fact, to some degree, its success may influence the direction of globalization overall.[1] This is because globalization is associated, on the one hand, with a limited set of global governance mechanisms and weakened national governments, and on the other, with unprecedented private sector wealth, power, and impact. Corporate responsibility has thus become an important means for addressing what Stiglitz (2002) sees as the fundamental problem with contemporary globalization—a system of global governance without global government.

In this chapter, we examine the implications of globalization for corporate responsibility, and how that accounts for particular aspects of corporate responsibility such as stakeholder partnerships. But to put that in context, we need first to reflect on the meaning of globalization itself.

The meaning of 'globalization'

We touched on different meanings of globalization in Chapter 2, in particular the distinction between globalization as an economic construct, and as a social condition called deterritorialization. To clarify this more it can help to think of ice cream. Growing up in the UK, we remember summers consuming Walls ice creams, and it was a shock to go to France and Spain to find that there were brands called Miko and Frigo, with very different ideas about what an ice cream should be. Travel to far-off Indonesia and one did not find any ice cream brands, only locally produced, garishly coloured lollies, sold from homemade insulated boxes. Today, Walls, Miko, and Frigo are all part of Unilever; they all market identically tasting, identically packaged Magnums and Cornettos; the products are developed at a single Unilever laboratory, and a shop in Toronto will sell the same products as the teams of bicycle-riding sellers in Indonesian villages.

These changes are emblematic not of the power of brands so much as what some theorists believe constitutes a fundamental change in our social conditions, particularly:

1 new or intensified social networks, leading to the creation of new social orders that transcend traditional political, cultural, economic, and geographical boundaries;

2 stretched and expanded social relations, activities, and interdependencies, leading to the emergence of powerful organizations that are not linked to a specific place (e.g. global corporations, international non-government organizations, and international crime syndicates and terrorists);

3 intensified and accelerated interaction between these networks and organizations, so that what happens in one area can be shaped by events anywhere in the world;

4 a growing consciousness of our interconnectedness and interdependence, so that people do not simply observe globalization—it is something that is shaping who we are and how we act in the world.[2]

Texting friends in Thailand, engaging with the blogosphere, commercial transactions with people we never meet are all manifestations of this shift. Snapshot 5.1 shows the consequences of these four phenomena and how they have at once allowed an industry to prosper, but subjected it to unprecedented public scrutiny. It also shows some of the ways in which globalization is interpreted as both beneficial and damaging. It is to the merits and criticisms of globalization that we now turn.

Globalization—a tale of the glass half full

Few would deny that globalization is problematic. Even its supporters refer to the unavoidable pain involved and the need to have faith that it is ultimately for the good. Some

SNAPSHOT 5.1

Globalization and Kenya's rose growing industry

Non-existent before 1990, the Kenya cut flower industry is now one of that country's major economic success stories, exporting over $100 million of produce to Europe annually. It is also portrayed as an example of the success and failure of globalization: an industry that has captured significant export earnings, and introduced new technologies and investment to one of the world's poorest nations, but an industry that is blamed for damaging the environment, exploiting women, endangering workers, and damaging local communities.

In part, the industry grew out of Washington Consensus policy reforms that made it easier to invest in Kenya and export to Europe. The industry is also, however, a result of technological innovations that accelerated the impact of these policies. The removal of barriers to trade and investment created the opportunity for European entrepreneurs to establish flower farms around Lake Nayvasha to serve the European market. But equally, getting freshly cut flowers to European supermarkets was only made possible by improvements in transport and storage technology, and by a downward trend in transportation costs.

The same industry is, however, also an example of what has been called the 'dark side' of globalization. Environmental experts claim that the water levels of Lake Nayvasha have gone down and that local towns suffer water shortages. There are questions about the environmental cost of air freighting flowers from one continent to another. The influx of migrant workers has taxed the infrastructure of local towns, while on-farm accommodation is sometimes overcrowded and unsanitary. Wages are low by European standards, and the mostly casual workforce can work long hours during peak periods, such as in the run-up to Valentine's Day, and then be left without employment when demand slackens off.

Complaints about the industry have attracted attention from the European media, international NGOs and unions, development agencies, and, not least, the major retailers that have made Kenya Europe's number one source of imported flowers. The industry has adopted a code of labour and environmental practice, and has collaborated with European-based companies, NGOs, and trade unions on a two-year programme to improve working conditions. Despite being an economic success story, by 2005, the industry was being widely portrayed (in the title of one television documentary) as *Costing the Earth*.

(Sources: ETI, 2005b; Dolan and Opondo, 2005; O'Reilly, 2005)

Quick Questions

1 Do you think that the initial arguments that any such impacts were more than outweighed by the jobs created, the export earnings, the technology transfer, and other economic benefits are valid?

2 Do you feel that Kenya's producers were justified in seeing European protests as protectionism?

3 Should retailers have the right to set social and environmental standards for their suppliers?

of that good we experience today. Since 1990, the volume of international trade has increased enormously (for example, averaging 6 per cent annual growth for manufacturing). This has created jobs in many countries, allowed new industries to grow, encouraged the transfer of technology, increased the flow of capital, and, for the well-educated at least, has allowed people to pursue opportunities across the world. It has also meant that, because of international competitiveness, prices have remained stable or have fallen, and this has been an important factor behind low inflation in advanced economies.

Moreover, growth has not been confined to the major industrialized countries, as shown by the phenomenal expansion of the Chinese and Indian economies. And while China and India account for a disproportionate amount of foreign direct investment, other developing countries have entered the global economy as suppliers of everything from flip flops to flowers and, increasingly, as consumer markets themselves. What is good for business is meant to be good for society as a whole, and many have benefited from new opportunities, new technology, and the cultural shifts that phenomena such as urbanization have brought. Whether because of class, educational opportunity, or entrepreneurship, many people have seen their life expectations expand by virtue of the new types of skilled employment that have been created. The most fortunate have been able to pursue opportunities in stable, prosperous economies as multinational companies increasingly embark on a global war for talent.

Economists and politicians agree that in a capitalist or free enterprise system, economic growth is essential to long-term prosperity, and international free trade is held to be vital for sustainable growth and equity. Therefore, for many policymakers and politicians, globalization is nothing short of essential for global prosperity, demanding the removal of government-imposed trade and investment barriers, increased integration of markets across national boundaries, and the spread of market-oriented policies around the world.[3] These elements were characteristics of the first era of liberal globalization that started in the nineteenth century, the end of which is blamed on a revival of government controls and the closing down of economic interdependence, which ultimately ushered in decades of conflict and instability in the twentieth century. For Martin Wolf, the significance of liberal globalization is not only that it fosters economic growth: *'Liberalism is . . . far more than a purely economic creed. It is the bedrock of democracy at home and peaceful relations abroad.'*[4] As Friedman (2005) has observed, no two countries with McDonald's franchises have ever gone to war.

Wolf's belief, therefore, goes further than those who say globalization is simply about economics. In the traditions of Adam Smith and Hayek, he treats the rights to freedom and property, democratic government, the rule of law, and a supportive values system as being as important as liberalizing markets. Although individual elements may develop at different speeds, ultimately this is the full package that globalization both depends upon and promises. The benefits of globalization, therefore, are not simply economic growth, but the particular cultural, political, and ethical model associated with the liberal democracies of Europe, North America, and other 'Western' societies. All of this leads Wolf to conclude that, for all of globalization's shortcomings, *'the world needs more globalization, not less'.*[5]

Globalization—a tale of the glass half empty

Economic globalization has not been an unmitigated success, and corporate responsibility is, to some degree, a response to the excesses of globalization. However, it is also one of the ways that companies and others have used to navigate the new terrain associated with globalization that is not necessarily good or bad, but simply different from preceding eras. We look at two areas of globalization criticism, as follows:

1 wealth, poverty, and equity;

2 universalization of norms, values, and culture.

Wealth, poverty, and equity

In 2002, Joseph Stiglitz provided a wake-up call to those who felt that criticism of globalization was misguided. It was one thing for what Wolf labels *'antiglobalization.com'* to protest about injustice, poverty, and environmental degradation; it was quite another when a one-time chief economist of the World Bank appeared to be joining their ranks. Yet Stiglitz's conclusion was that, for millions, globalization is a failure: *'Many have actually been made worse off, as they have seen their jobs destroyed and their lives become more insecure.'*[6]

He argues that the policies that have created the conditions for overseas companies to set up factories, or source from suppliers in countries that hitherto had adopted policies of protectionism and import substitution, have led to the promotion of market solutions to the challenges of welfare and equity. Hardt and Negri (2000), for example argue that globalization needs to be understood as a *'grid of power'*, informed by the ways in which capitalism copes with the overproduction, high labour costs, and devaluation that blocks the capitalist process once markets become saturated. For Stiglitz (2002), however, the issue is not the intractable logic of capitalism, but the way in which globalization is implemented and how rich countries use their power to their advantage in institutions such as the World Bank, the International Monetary Fund, and the World Trade Organization. He counters those opposed to government intervention and restrictions on the free market, arguing that countries that have benefited most from globalization are those, such as China and India, in which governments have challenged the notion of self-regulating markets and taken charge of their own destiny.

However, globalization affects all countries, not just emerging economies. In developed economies once major industries such as steel have shrunk, if not vanished, and the number of manufacturing jobs has declined. The offshoring of certain types of blue-collar job is now being followed by that of white-collar jobs, such as data processing, computer programming, and research and development. There is public anxiety as to whether new jobs—and especially well-paying jobs—will be created in their place.[7] As predicted by early globalization theorists such as Beck et al. (1994), the nature of employment is changing. Repeatedly, surveys in the richest countries point to longer working days, stress, job insecurity, and difficulties in balancing working lives with personal lives as causes of public concern. As important as traditional divisions between skilled and unskilled, white collar and blue collar, are the distinctions between those of classes in secure employment and underclasses, such as illegal migrants and 'guest workers', without secure employment. This is not to say, however, that being a migrant is itself a disadvantage: on the contrary, according to Bauman (1998), mobility is a coveted value, because it allows people to follow opportunities.

Universalization of norms, values, and culture

Globalization is often portrayed in terms of how it affects society and culture, and, in particular, how some see it as spreading the values, ethics, and institutions of the West. MacLean (1999) argues that a key feature of globalization that distinguishes it from its historical antecedents is that it fosters, legitimizes, and universalizes a transcending form of knowledge, especially in respect to political, economic, ethical, and social ideas. For Wolf (2004), this is one of its benefits; for Klein (1999), it is one of its dangers. Whatever stance one takes, the idea that globalization alters the world in this way is a powerful one.

There are many empirical studies of how particular industries and companies have affected local populations, especially those of indigenous peoples who, by definition, live in non-capitalist societies. Logging, mining, oil and gas drilling and pipelines, and industrial agriculture have all been in the spotlight for the ways in which they affect indigenous people's land, livelihoods, and lifestyles.[8] The impact is not necessarily as simple as appropriating resources or putting people out of work. It can also involve changes in basic social institutions so that, for example, communal land becomes privately owned, or diverse economic livelihoods are replaced with daily waged labour.[9]

Such examples can be seen as evidence of more fundamental assertions of power. In addition to understanding how organizations and individuals operate in the new networks and alliances that globalization is producing, various authors have argued that we need to understand the underlying biases that favour particular norms and values,[10] and how the technologies and techniques that we use to analyze, control, and regulate globalization extend or limit the possibilities for change as much as the actions of any actor.

One of the reasons for considering partnerships in the context of globalization later in this chapter is because of what they reveal about this distinction between overt actors and underlying agency has a significant impact on corporate responsibility, and help to explain some of its successes and failures. It also helps to explain why corporate responsibility is sometimes accused of spreading particular values, or of failing to accommodate others' world views.[11] In terms of understanding the meaning of globalization, it alerts us to the fact that even seemingly neutral views can be charged with norms, values, and

---

■ Discussion points

Liberal globalization theorists, such as Wolf and Henderson, take umbrage with companies and others that support corporate responsibility.

- What are the main reasons for their hostility?
- Do you think there are shifts within corporate responsibility thinking that address their concerns?
- Referring to examples such as Unilever's work with Oxfam in Indonesia and theorists such as Stiglitz and Porritt, how would you refute Wolf and Henderson's arguments to a business audience?

meanings that legitimate and advance specific interests. Indeed, building on Gramsci's political theory, Levy and Newell (2005) argue that the moral and intellectual leadership role exhibited by business in areas such as corporate responsibility is a contemporary example of how, throughout history, powerful forces rule through consensus and hegemony.

Influence of globalization on business

Business is often portrayed as a beneficiary of globalization, but there is truth, falsehood, and myth in such a belief. Under globalization, many of the norms and values suited to private enterprise have been given preferential status, but commerce has prospered under all manner of different political and economic regimes: to say business benefits from globalization is no more or less true than to say enterprise flourished under mercantile capitalism or protectionism. However, the nature of business undoubtedly has changed in ways that have special significance for corporate responsibility.

Global capital, production, and trade

For business, the most important outcome of globalization has been the enormous increases in international trade and investment. In the last half of the twentieth century, the value of world trade soared from $57 billion to $6 trillion. This has gone hand in glove with the liberalization of financial transactions, whereby a combination of techno-logical advances and policies to remove credit controls, deregulate interest rates, and privatize banking has created much greater investment opportunities. Today, global busi-ness-to-business transactions are worth about $6 trillion and the world's financial mar-kets are becoming more like networks in cyberspace that can relay billions of trades almost instantaneously.[12] This does not mean what happens globally is divorced from the local. The consequence of over-zealous selling of mortgages to poor Americans— while in some ways promoted as a socially beneficial act—ricocheted around the world, and in turn exposed corruption and incompetence from Bear Sterns to BayernLB to Dubai's Sovereign Wealth Fund. Perhaps more important in the long term, the unprece-dentedly high levels of household and corporate debt in developed economies are only affordable because of emerging economies' willingness to buy it, marking a historic shift from when developed economies bailed out poorer countries during economic crises, to a new era—not imagined by supporters of the Washington Consensus (see Snapshot 5.1)—when weak economies come to the aid of stronger ones.[13]

Speculative investment has increased due to the ease of conducting fast, low-cost transactions. Global investment has also led to industry consolidation and increased foreign ownership, not least of formerly state-owned companies. Indeed, globalization challenges the very idea of an American or European company given how shares are owned around the world. What unites many globalization sceptics is what is viewed as an unhealthy growth in corporate power and alarm at facts such as that a third of world trade occurs between multinational corporations, or that five companies control the global market for consumer durables.[14] At times, the growing presence of multinationals has been highly contentious, as the case of the utilities sector demonstrates (see Snapshot 5.2). It has also provoked fears about security, the global power balance, and other national imperatives. The flood of foreign direct investment from China into Africa to acquire natural resource rights, the buying spree by Middle East equity funds (and subsequent sell-off), and 'foreign ownership' of strategic assets from ports to power plants have all generated controversy.

Yet this is just a continuation of a trend started by freeing up trade and capital flows which created the conditions necessary for shifting certain aspects of production to new locations. As countries, such as Malaysia, Indonesia, and, later, China, removed barriers to foreign investment, companies from developed economies rushed to them, either to invest directly or to source from new vendors. Today, we take for granted that goods and services, from training shoes to banking, can be delivered from around the world, but it is important not to overstate the degree to which poorer countries have succeeded in attracting capital and accessing markets.[15] For all of the focus on multinational firms in India and China, the bulk of investment remains within developed economies and there are still significant barriers in some industries for developing countries to access wealthy markets.[16] Moreover, investment in developing countries is often centred on export processing zones (EPZs) offering financial incentives to investors, and even labour and environmental regulations and enforcement policies which are different to those that are available elsewhere in the country.

Claims about the wealth of corporations being on a par with that of many governments may be exaggerated,[17] and corporate responsibility is full of examples demonstrating that wealth and power are not always synonymous. Nonetheless, the behaviour of multinational companies on a global stage is an important part of corporate responsibility's story and, as we examine later in the chapter ('Corporate responsibility as a response to globalization', p 117), set important parameters for what corporate responsibility addresses and how.

The changing nature of governance and enforcement

Mention of the different, often more lenient, regulatory regimes enjoyed by companies in EPZs is an example of how globalization is connected to changes in how society is governed. In part, this is because liberal globalization depends on the slew of policy changes described earlier. At the same time, deterritorialization creates a new space that cannot be readily governed by existing governance structures, such as national governments, or even the international mechanisms housed within the United Nations. For example, a national government can legislate on toxic emissions, but once those emissions affect the global commons, a multinational solution is required.

There are a few long-established institutions with an international regulatory mandate—notably the International Labour Organization (ILO), which, since the end of World War I, has brought national governments, the business community, and international trade unions together to set and enforce international labour standards. There are also national laws applying to actions overseas, such as the US Alien Tort Claims Act 1789, which has been used to hold US companies to account for human rights violations around the world. More noticeable since the 1970s, however, has been a trend away from seeing government as the sole, or even primary, solution to both regulation and social welfare.

This trend may have reached its peak on 11 September 2001,[18] and in banking in particular light-touch regulation is now being criticized by politicians, investors, and the public alike. But for anyone born before the 1970s, the changes in the roles and expectations of government have already been enormous. They continue to be at the heart of debates about how society responds to globalization and attitudes towards corporate responsibility worldwide.[19]

There are four main interpretations of what has happened.

1 National government has seen its power eroded by globalization

As a condition of joining the global market, national governments surrender much of their power to create policy autonomously and poor countries, in particular, have had policies forced upon them. Some of those policies have undermined state sovereignty, not only in areas of macroeconomic policy, but also in areas such as taxation, social welfare, and human development. Even in rich countries, governments not only no longer try and control exchange rates, but they are also afraid to raise corporate taxes or to raise the minimum wage, for fear of driving business overseas.

2 There is a governance vacuum at the global level

There is no clear responsibility or accountability for issues such as human rights and poverty, for which the forces of economic globalization may have unacceptable consequences that cannot be resolved by market forces. Equally, there are new challenges, such as the management of the global commons, that cannot be solved through conventional governance mechanisms. As Bell puts it: '*The nation-state is becoming too small for the big problems of life, and too big for the small problems of life.*'[20]

3 Government has deliberately chosen where and where not to exert influence

There are many examples in which national governments have exerted influence on the governance of globalization. For example, the World Trade Organization is a direct result of national government negotiation and agreement, and has been criticized for being too influenced by the interests of the wealthiest economies (e.g. its slowness in tackling agriculture subsidies).[21] As Braithwaite and Drahos (2000) observe, what we are witnessing may not be deregulation but '*re-regulation*', with state rollback in some areas, such as capital and trade, and a strengthening of regulation to protect other rights. Migration is another issue relating to which governments have been accused of hypocrisy, because, while they have removed barriers to trade and investment, they have put up barriers to allowing most people to pursue job opportunities through international migration.

4 Governments still maintain power

As Ward (2003) emphasizes, it is important not to dismiss the regulatory role of government. National laws, such as the US Foreign Corrupt Practices Act 1977 and Alien Tort Claims Act 1789, can affect the behaviour of multinational companies around the world. Bilateral trade agreements, for example, are one way in which the poor in developing nations can benefit from global trade and, in some instances, these agreements have created favourable environments for corporate responsibility.[22]

■ Key concept: New models of international governance—the World Trade Organization

Establishment of the World Trade Organization in 1995 was one of the most important steps in creating a new model of international governance. Part international negotiating forum, part court of arbitration, it has the power to affect trade rules and to resolve disputes, and its role is to focus on trade. Globalization sceptics point out that, while globalization raises issues about social and environmental justice, the one major international body to come out of globalization so far is an organization that focused entirely on liberalizing trade. But the WTO's defenders argue that it is not, and should not be, a world court and point, for example, to the International Labour Organization as the competent body for addressing labour rights issues.

(Source: Jones & Pollit, 2004)

Whatever one's interpretation of governance in this era of globalization, one noticeable change is the prominence of non-government actors in governance processes. While it would be flying in the face of history to deny the influence owners and managers of capital or public protest have had on government over time, nonetheless new forms of governance are emerging. There is a growing element of self-regulation by business and, in particular, of business being used by government as the initial enforcer (e.g. in the UK, supermarkets are liable for enforcing food safety standards in their supply chains). There is also widespread outsourcing of the policing of business behaviour, building on approaches originating in financial auditing, and quasi-independent bodies, notably the International Organization for Standardization (ISO), have had a significant impact on environmental management and are developing systems for corporate responsibility more broadly.

Civil society organizations are increasingly involved in both 'street regulation', through campaigns, watchdog activities, and 'naming and shaming' of particular companies, and

---

■ Discussion points

Corporate responsibility has been variously described as a 'response' to globalization and as its 'reflection'.

- What distinction is being made here?
- Do companies' policies and programmes appear to reflect one of these views more than the other?
- Selecting the ideological framework of a particular political party, how would you make the case that corporate responsibility complements its policy objectives?

participation in new regulatory systems, such as international standards and multi-stakeholder partnerships.[23] These different views of public governance are all relevant to the relationship between notions of corporate responsibility and globalization, and the changing nature of governance is especially important in the corporate responsibility context, as we discuss in the next section.

Corporate responsibility as a response to globalization

Understanding the phenomenon of globalization is a necessary part of comprehending the context within which contemporary corporate responsibility has emerged. Ruggie (2003) treats it as a manifestation of Polanyi's notion of the embedded economy (see Chapter 2): an attempt to contain and share the social adjustment costs that open markets inevitably produce. Criticisms of business—and of big business, in particular—as reaping the benefits of globalization without taking responsibility for its negative consequences have become an important driver of contemporary corporate responsibility as a whole. Moreover, specific initiatives, such as codes of labour practice or participation in the environmental agenda that first emerged out of the 1992 Rio Earth Summit, address the perceived mismatch of regulatory scope and actual economic structure that is a consequence of expanding global trade.

This does not mean corporate responsibility is a comprehensive response to business-society issues related to globalization. For example, tax avoidance by companies, though legal, arguably deprives countries of resources that could be used to tackle environmental, social and governance issues, yet is overlooked in corporate responsibility practice and much of the theory. Equally, it does not mean that the issues corporate responsibility addresses are necessarily the consequences of globalization. For example, slavery, deforestation, child labour, and over-fishing all took place before globalization. In some cases (e.g. slavery), it may not even be the case that what is happening is worse than that which occurred in the past.[24] But globalization exaggerates and exacerbates by making things quicker, larger, and more visible than before, and this has increased the pressure on companies to act responsibly. For some, corporate responsibility is about making the benefits of globalization accessible to more people, either by limiting

---

■ Discussion points

If we compare the issues raised in the sections on globalization as 'A tale of a glass half empty' (p 110) and on 'Corporate responsibility as a response to globalization' (p 117), there are clearly gaps between the consequences of globalization and the concerns of corporate responsibility.

• What are the main aspects of globalization that corporate responsibility does not address?

• What are the reasons for these gaps?

• Which of these gaps will corporate responsibility attempt to bridge in the future and why?

the need for government intervention,[25] or by making new resources available for human development. It can also be seen as a reflection of the interdependence of government and business, under which the former looks to the latter to create wealth in order to retain power, while the latter looks to the former to develop human capital and maintain stability.[26] What is more, reflecting the general widespread growth in self-regulation and voluntary agreements by business, corporate responsibility can be regarded as an element of a new system of global governance that sits alongside the democratic model of national government that is promoted by the most powerful countries.[27]

How corporate responsibility addresses the challenges of globalization

Some of contemporary corporate responsibility's earliest initiatives were related to globalization. The Rio Earth Summit, for example, brought together different sectors of society to address global environmental challenges. It succeeded in sending the message that business could and should act, and indirectly encouraged business and environmental groups to work together on initiatives such as sustainable forest management. It also lit a flame in the oil industry that influenced Shell's early corporate responsibility reporting and eventually led to BP rebranding itself as Beyond Petroleum, as its then CEO, John Browne, began to speak out on the importance of business addressing greenhouse gases and other threats to the environment.[28]

In a different way, early initiatives intended to rethink the nature of working lives were a response to the ways in which globalization had influenced the workplace. Business in the Community in the UK was started as a response to urban decay and industrial decline during the 1980s, and the lack of government action. The Prince of Wales Business Leaders' Forum was a tentative step to encourage UK business executives to think about their role in the world. At that stage, these organizations were still firmly rooted in traditions of giving back to communities through, for instance, philanthropy, community investment, and volunteering.

At the same time, the fairtrade movement was establishing itself as a way of dealing with what were seen as inequitable trading relations with poor producers in developing countries. Trade union and NGO campaigns raised public awareness about labour conditions in the apparel and sporting goods industries, which had been early movers in globalizing production. This, in turn, led to a number of companies, primarily in the UK and USA, adopting codes of labour practice and partnering with civil society organizations to implement them. This interest spilled over into parts of agriculture, which was already becoming more global, and which, in Europe, was increasingly interested in improved environmental management and product safety.

Other industries that were, perhaps, more removed from globalization were nonetheless feeling the consequences of rapid information exchange and the power of civil society alliances. Mining companies in Papua, or oil companies in Burma, came under the spotlight because of allegations about human rights, environmental damage, and corruption. Such criticisms, in turn, raised questions about the funding of major private sector projects, such as the Chad–Cameroon oil pipeline; public and private sector finance bodies, such as the International Finance Corporation, and Citigroup began to pay more attention to non-financial aspects of their investments. This eventually led, in 2003, to the Equator Principles—a framework promoting environmental and social responsibility in project financing.

In 1999, the UN announced its Global Compact to bring companies together with UN agencies, labour organizations, and civil society, to promote responsible corporate practices and to help business be part of the solution to the challenges of globalization. It has paid particular attention to business in developing countries, and the private sector's role in meeting the aforementioned Millennium Development Goals (see Chapter 4). The World Economic Forum's Centre for Public–Private Partnership has also stressed that meeting these goals cannot be done by governments, business, or civil society alone. Its mission highlights that, in addition to business' role in upholding and advancing principles on human rights, labour, environmental, and anti-corruption practices in countries with weak regulatory capacity, business competencies can improve the effectiveness of development programmes (e.g. technology development, providing essential goods and services, and managing large-scale operations).

In Chapter 4, we offer various examples of corporate responsibility as a response to poverty in developing countries. Several of these are partnerships between organizations and groups reflecting the belief that poverty, global governance, imbalances in power, and other features linked to globalization are best met through collaboration. We turn to this now.

Partnerships

One consequence of economic globalization and the changed nature of governance is that it has created the space where business impacts upon and is influenced by a more geographically dispersed, perhaps more numerous body of stakeholders than hitherto. The exact nature of stakeholder is something we explore in Chapter 9, but in terms of globalization, it is not just that business has to manage stakeholders which is important: partnering with stakeholders has become a significant element of business' relationship with wider society.

Following Preston and Post (1975), these partnerships are often described in terms of sectors—business, government, and civil society—each with discernible interests. For instance, government departments, such as the UK Department for International Development, the US State Department, and the Swedish International Development Agency, have all funded corporate responsibility in various ways, and local governments—particularly in the wake of the Rio Earth Summit—have been among the most aggressive champions of voluntary approaches to improving environmental management. Equally, companies praised for their corporate responsibility policies, such as United Utilities and Lloyds TSB Scotland, acknowledge that their programmes have often been a response to meeting government requirements, such as providing services for poor consumers. Similarly, civil society organisations such as CARE, Save the Children, and Conservation International are all involved in partnership with business.

These sectoral categorisations are problematic to a degree even though they are widely used. For example, civil society organization is an immensely broad term. It covers lobbying groups such as Greenpeace and implementation groups such as Habitat for Humanity. It lumps together the ideologically very different Oxfam and National Rifle Association. It can sometimes mask the difference between democratic membership organisations such as trade unions and charities with relatively limited accountability to the public who donate to them. Equally, the term business can imply a degree of homogeneity that in reality is absent. A company is made up of numerous internal stakeholders: executives, directors, senior managers, middle managers, the workforce to name just some. These all have their own interests and goals, but in day to day coverage of companies these distinctions can get lost or corrupted: witness for instance remarks such as 'the Royal Mail is in dispute with workers' when it might be more accurate to say that the management and workforce are in dispute.

Nonetheless, partnerships between stakeholders are often described in sectoral terms, and there are many examples to point to. Kofi Annan, seventh UN Secretary-General, for example, recognized the potential of this approach to corporate responsibility when, at the World Economic Forum in 1999, he invited business to partner with government in upholding international human rights. Not only did this lead to the creation of the UN Global Compact (see Case Study 5); it also implicitly recognized the limits of trying to uphold international human rights conventions without the willing participation of companies. WWF, the international environmental NGO, has long been an advocate of partnerships involving business thereby utilizing international markets to help to catalyze change for the benefit of the environment (e.g. the Forest Stewardship Council, the Marine Stewardship Council, and the Roundtable on Sustainable Palm Oil).

Civil society has been eagerly embraced in contemporary corporate responsibility, although it can be difficult to identify precisely what the concept means. 'Civil society' has historically referred to private interests that are distinct from those of the state. Today, even if the exact meaning is more ambiguous, the term refers to uncoerced collective action, based on shared interests, purposes, and values, by institutions that are distinct from those of the state and the market.[29] The organizations that fall into this category are often powerful in terms of influence, knowledge and not least finance. As Parkin (2001) points out in her celebration of NGOs in the democratic process, NGOs worldwide have a GDP of $1.1 trillion.

■ Discussion points

Managers often want to see the financial value of partnerships.

- Is it possible to demonstrate how a partnership contributes to the bottom line?
- What are the most convincing non-financial arguments for partnerships?
- As the director of a NGO, how would you demonstrate the financial added value of a partnership to a South African mineral company?

Reasons for partnership

'Partnership' has become a very popular word in Western democracies, reflecting the belief that different sectors of society share responsibility for delivering societal goods. In theory, any arrangement between separate organizations to achieve defined ends qualifies as a partnership, but those such as public–private sector partnerships—justified largely on financial grounds—are well outside what the term means in a corporate responsibility context. Many corporate responsibility partnerships involve a company and another entity, but some are more complex than this, involving multiple organizations from different sectors. There is no single reason for this trend in favour of partnerships, but they are frequently portrayed as a way of addressing challenges arising out of globalization. Various claims are made: that they are crucial to competitiveness in a global economy; that they define the rules and boundaries of that economy; that they offer new ways of holding companies to account; that they provide companies with access to new markets and ideas; that they lead to the creation of win–win situations, in which all stakeholders see added value.[29] From a business perspective, partnerships provide managers with unconventional mechanisms for seeing their situation anew, and for rediagnosing situations and opportunities in ways that challenge preconceived ideas and habits.[30] Depending on the industry and type of company involved, they can help companies to secure their licence to operate, to maintain relations with local and global communities, to prevent and resolve disputes, and to manage the impacts of investment and disinvestment in particular locations.[31]

The aims of partnerships range from the broad and grand, to the narrow and specific. For example, the 2002 World Summit on Sustainable Development, which is attributed with stimulating various partnerships between government and civil society, placed business at the centre of international efforts to reduce poverty. In contrast, a partnership might be formed between airport authorities, local government, local community groups, and environmental NGOs, with the specific purpose of negotiating a runway extension. Equally, partnerships involve different levels of participation and involvement, ranging from a company promising to report on social and environmental performance to stakeholders, or to fund a specific project, to civil society, business, and government groups collaborating together to achieve certain ends. It is not that one type of partnership is necessarily better than another—the question is what is fit for purpose—but it must be recognized that there are different types, each with implications for goals, design, and implementation (see Box 5.1)

The typology in Box 5.1 can be applied to different industries. For example, the Fair Labour Association, a multi-stakeholder partnership aimed at improving labour conditions in supply chains, is a shared responsibility partnership. Likewise, when Nike found that it could not buy sufficient quantities of organic cotton it created a different form of share responsibility partnership by partnering with 55 other businesses to create the Organic Cotton Exchange, a non-profit organization committed to building a global organic cotton industry.[32]

Partnerships can have very different objectives, and sometimes—as in conflict situations[33]—the very act of partnering can be a worthwhile outcome because it fosters trust

Box 5.1 Different types of partnership

1 Knowledge sharing
Long-term voluntary agreements between stakeholders to share information about the company's activities (e.g. feasibility studies, proposals, and evaluations).

2 Dialogue
Medium-term voluntary agreement that key stakeholders will consult with each other on specified activities, such as preparing regional plans, developing environmental standards, and deciding on reporting requirements.

3 Informed consent
Voluntary agreement by each party not to take action without the prior consent of others.

4 Contractual
Medium-term agreement between certain stakeholders to provide specified services to others in the partnership.

5 Shared work plans
Medium-term voluntary agreement between stakeholders to carry out separate, defined tasks in pursuit of common goals.

6 Shared responsibility
Long-term agreement between stakeholders to share responsibility for implementing tasks and to be responsible to each other for their delivery.

and mutual understanding between disparate groups. Svendesen and Laberge (2005) argue that most partnerships are formed because companies have to engage with stakeholders in order to comply with regulations, to solve operational problems, or to respond to public pressure for greater accountability. However, it is a mistake for companies to think partnerships are closed systems where relations with stakeholders can be controlled in order to meet organizational goals. As discussed in Chapter 9, the idea that companies can manage stakeholders in a conventional sense is debatable, and there are many partnerships that are best thought of as stakeholder networks, initially convened by a company to tackle challenges that it cannot address on its own, but, once established they take on a life of their own that cannot be controlled by a single organization and are inherently dynamic, unpredictable, and evolving, capable of delivering different

---

■ **Discussion points**

Throughout this book, we give examples of partnerships that have been set up for various reasons. There are many more examples we have not mentioned.

- Which partnerships do you think are the most important and why?
- Can you identify examples for each of the six types of partnership (see Box 5.1)?
- Is 'partnership' an overused or underused word in corporate responsibility?

outcomes for different members (see Box 5.2). As Warner and Sullivan describe it, in the context of the mining, oil, and gas industry:

> Tri-sector partnerships are, in essence, a new form of strategic alliance ... [A] voluntary collaboration to promote sustainable development based on the most efficient allocation of complementary resources across business, civil society and government.
>
> *(2003, p 17)*

Box 5.2 Partnership outcomes for different stakeholders—examples from mining

Outcomes for business	
Enhanced licence to operate, because communities affected by operations will be satisfied that the business unit is responsive to their concerns	Availability of new social capital for the business
Reduced community dependency on the business unit (e.g. owing to empowerment of communities to manage their own development)	Becoming 'company of choice' in the eyes of governmental authorizing agencies and removing political objections to future ventures
Basis for resolving local disputes that might delay financial approval or operations	Reduced risk to marketing, sales, and share price associated with negative image of social and environmental performance
Outcomes for local communities	
Additional resources for community development	Ensuring that those impacted by operations have an equal or greater level of welfare, income, subsistence, and security
Fairer settlement/compensation for community assets	Access to the technology, finance, and markets that are necessary for new assets, and skill sets that can be transformed into sustainable livelihoods
Improved infrastructure and capacity to manage it	
Outcomes for the public sector	
Agreed revenue distribution mechanisms before commencing operations	Increased legitimacy with local populations
More equitable distribution of revenues across government, and between government and communities	Exposure to new ways of working and international good practice
Enhanced tax and skills base	Empowerment of local communities

(Adapted from Warner & Sullivan, 2003)

Partnerships and globalization

Five different cases can be made for promoting partnering:

1 It is a better way of doing business.

2 It is a new way of regulating business.

3 It is an alternative way of harnessing the power and resources of business, and of redistributing benefits.

4 It is a more effective way of dealing with the realities of global governance.

5 It is an entirely new way of thinking about business.

In each case, the promise of partnership resonates with the challenges of globalization. For instance, we have discussed the changing nature of governance, and partnerships that can harness the respective competencies of different sectors domestically and internationally might provide an effective alternative approach to regulation. We have seen too that business has unique competencies and resources, and partnerships provide a way of leveraging these for the public good, not least in developing countries. The acquisition of TXU by two major private equity firms using a partnership with environmental NGOs, or Unilever's partnership with local women's organizations and microfinance groups for its Shakti programme are just two examples of how new business models are linked to partnering.

However, we should be cautious about uncritical faith in the actual benefits partnerships deliver. Caplan (2003) claims that the literature on partnerships too often promotes the idea that they are, by their very nature, harmonious and built on trust, common vision, and voluntary commitment. He argues that there are various myths and half-truths behind this belief. First, multi-sector partnerships, in his first-hand experience, are rarely built on a common vision, because stakeholders have different reference points and, if they focus too much on what they have in common, their aspirations get diluted or masked. The partnership then ends up with a mission statement for which nobody feels ownership. He points out that stakeholders can appear to share values when what is actually happening is that they are using the same words to mean different things. For example, for a company, 'sustainability' has some relationship to cost recovery; for the public sector, it means something that is technically sound that can sustain itself in the future; for a development NGO, it is to do with empowerment and giving communities a voice.

Second, while trust is a much-vaunted element of partnerships, it might be more accurate to say that individuals within the partnership build a mutual respect for that which people and organizations can offer. Trust is most likely when organizations can choose with whom to partner, but this rarely happens and most partners are thrust upon each other. Consequently, more important than trust can be creating an understanding of what the various partners can and cannot do. Indeed, more significant than genuine trust can be knowing partners well enough to predict how they will behave within the partnership.

Increasingly, the lessons of partnership seem to be that it is not a panacea to corporate responsibility challenges arising from globalization, and that organizations need to enter into them with their eyes open to both the strengths and the weaknesses. There are many views on why partnerships are important and how to engage in them, and perhaps insufficient information on what is appropriate in different situations. But, overall, there is little argument about the importance attached to partnerships as part of corporate responsibility's arsenal.

SNAPSHOT 5.2

Water—privatizing basic rights or giving access to basic needs?

Water is essential to life, yet the amount of accessible water per person worldwide is falling. This is why water is a global issue, with the private sector at its centre. Over 150 years after John Snow discovered the link between water and cholera, 1.1 billion people are still without access to clean water, 2.4 billion lack proper sanitary provision, and a slum dweller in Nairobi or Accra pays more per litre of water than a resident of Manhattan or Geneva.

The global water crisis is more about management than true scarcity. The current supply of fresh water is a small percentage of our planet's total water, yet it would be more than enough for the world population's current needs if it were more evenly distributed. Unfortunately, that is not the case. According to the UN Environmental Programme, demand for water will soon exceed availability by 56 per cent and two-thirds of the world's population will face water stress. Major investments in infrastructure and management are needed to amend this problem: challenges that the private sector would seem well suited to tackle.

Yet private sector interventions have met considerable resistance in some regions. Privatization of water utilities in Europe encouraged organizations, such as the World Bank, to promote private sector involvement to reach 2.4 billion new consumers by 2015 in order to meet the Millennium Development Goals. The major water companies were, however, accused of privatizing water sources, and have repeatedly been under the media spotlight for cutting off poor consumers and favouring rich customers. In Bolivia, Argentina, and the Philippines, major utilities companies terminated government contracts.

At the heart of the protests is that, for many, water is not simply a human need, but a human right. Some feel that by calling water a 'need', it opens the door to privatization and provision on a for-profit basis, whereas declaring water to be a 'right' might be used to prevent companies from buying up water sources. There are some signs that a middle ground may be reached and that the private sector should be considered neither panacea nor pariah. Talking to fellow business leaders, George Kuper, President of the Council of Great Lakes Industry, said business had a key role to play in making water accessible, but that it had no need to own the resource.

(Sources: FAO, 2003; Gleick, 1999; UN, 2003)

Quick questions

1 Is the distinction between water as a human need and a human right valid?

2 What are the implications of this distinction for business?

3 Is it accurate to see access to water as a 'management problem', as politicians and business leaders have tended to?

Unmet challenges

Corporate responsibility faces three main criticisms about how it addresses the challenges and impacts of globalization. The first of these—not least from within the business community itself—is that business can, and should, do more to find new solutions to meet the challenges that globalization presents. There is general consensus that governments cannot meet these challenges alone: hence the formation of alliances with non-state actors, such as the private sector, is essential.[34]

This criticism takes different forms: for example, it underpins the calls for action from Business Action for Africa and WEF's Centre for Public–Private Partnership. It takes a different shape in the concept that Wood et al. (2006) call '*global business citizenship*', which seeks to develop a new framework for corporate responsibility within which its boundaries are not prescribed by the competitive pressures of globalization. And it appears again in authors, such as Hart (2005), who recognize business as part of the solution to creating a sustainable environment, but push it to go beyond the business case-related thinking of the triple bottom line. What is common to all of them, however, is the acceptance of business as a crucial actor, not simply because it does harm, but because it has unique resources, scope, and competencies that need to be harnessed for society's good. As Wettstein (2005) notes, if multinational companies are as powerful as they are portrayed, perhaps they should not be allowed to stay out of political debate or to ignore global problems, but rather should be thought of as quasi-governmental institutions with an inherent responsibility for global well-being.

The second criticism is more accusatory. It acknowledges that business has tried to address society's concerns through certification schemes, adoption of global framework agreements, standard setting and monitoring, and dialogues with other sectors and its critics, but deems all of these approaches to voluntary regulation inadequate. Utting's (2005b) analysis concludes that too many companies have not participated; there has been limited penetration of corporate responsibility ideas across the corporate structure; compliance procedures are often weak; initiatives, such as codes of conduct, are often top-down and technocratic, and while focusing on particular named issues, they do not examine the impact of corporate responsibility, especially in developing countries. There are some signs of change,[35] but Reich (2007) concludes that, ultimately, corporate responsibility demonstrates the limitations of self-regulation and the need for government to assert its regulatory role, or, as Utting argues, a more robust approach to '*articulated regulation*', under which different regulatory approaches and agents would come together in ways that are complementary, mutually reinforcing, and synergistic.

The final criticism of corporate responsibility as a response to globalization builds on these debates about self-regulation and centres on corporate responsibility's capacity to alter perceptions of corporate self-interest. It holds that many of globalization's shortcomings are exacerbated, or at least overlooked, by companies pursuing their narrow self-interest. For example, lay-offs and plant closures make sense in terms of global competitiveness, but can be devastating for individuals and communities. Indeed, as Visser (2006) has argued in an African context, accepted corporate responsibility frameworks, such as Carroll's pyramid (see Chapter 2), can appear simplistic and static when applied in developing countries, and may not recognize that conflicts and contradictions should be anticipated as the norm, rather than treated as the shocking exception.

One strand of this critique holds that companies do not try to understand the consequences of their behaviour and focus only on those issues that they feel will affect their reputation, or that will serve their self-interest in other ways (e.g. investing in maintaining a healthy, educated workforce and protecting their image).[36] There are indications that companies committed to corporate responsibility are becoming more sensitive to these issues. The collaboration between Unilever and Oxfam to examine ways the behaviour of a multinational affects poverty in Indonesia is an example of how partnerships are beginning to wrestle with the complexity of international development.[37] A critical dimension to this in future will be how far companies can align around a corporate responsibility sensibility so that they are not, for example, claiming improved environmental practices, while at the same time aggressively marketing high-risk products to ill-educated consumers,[38] or not promoting better labour conditions, while using just-in-time contracting that can exacerbate labour exploitation.

The second strand of the same critique argues that aspects of trading and other contractual relationships are inherently unfair and biased towards the interests of the most powerful companies, but mainstream corporate responsibility has done little to address this. For example, as Oxfam's Make Trade Fair campaign asks, to what extent will corporate responsibility push for fairness in trading relations, both between countries and within specific supply chains?[39] And as Jenkins (2005) has noted, there are many areas that might be important for long-term development in which business seems to be silent or hostile (e.g. corporate taxation and tort reform), and corporate responsibility has done little to influence corporate investment in countries with the least foreign direct investment.

Finally, it is argued that the mindset and tools of corporate responsibility are so deeply embedded in the normative frameworks of business that corporate responsibility theory and practice ends up taking for granted, reproducing, and legitimizing, rather than providing an alternative to, the values and priorities associated with free enterprise. We saw earlier how some believe that globalization universalizes certain values; it has been argued that corporate responsibility is one way in which this is done, not only by what is included or excluded from standards of acceptable social and environmental

---

■ Discussion points

Since the 1990s, worries about the global environment have been an important driver of corporate responsibility, although some believe that social issues are now more prominent.

- What environmental challenges are most clearly associated with globalization?
- To what extent can, and should, business seek to tackle the major global environmental challenges?
- Over 15 years after the Rio Earth Summit, what are the main overall achievements of the environmental initiatives in which business has been involved?

performance, but by the way in which those tools are used.[40] Current approaches, such as ethical sourcing, have been criticized for ignoring the priorities of workers, and failing to consider the broader impacts of initiatives on other producers and neighbouring communities;[41] as case studies from Newell (2005) and Fig (2005) have shown, initiatives driven from the bottom up run the risk of being ignored or discounted by corporate responsibility. Such case studies reveal how important voices are missing from corporate responsibility partnerships and other initiatives that claim to engage with stakeholders, but often end up doing so on a selective basis.

CASE STUDY 5

The United Nations Global Compact

Partnerships aimed at helping business to meet the challenges of upholding their responsibilities in developing countries have come to the fore in recent years.[42] The United Nations Global Compact is an example of this, established in 2000 as a direct result of the call of the then UN Secretary-General, Kofi Annan, for business leaders to partner with UN agencies, and for civil society to support universal environmental and social principles. The partnership is a response to the neglect of social and environmental protections in the promotion of economic globalization, and is based on the premise that the longevity of globalization and the international economic order depends as much on such protections as it does on free markets and economic inclusivity.

The Compact was never intended to resolve all of global capitalism's deficiencies, but rather to lay a foundation of shared values, as embodied in various UN conventions and declarations, and to attempt to harness the skills and resources of the private sector to uphold those values.

> The ultimate measure of success for the initiative is the degree to which it promotes concrete and sustained action by its varied participants, especially the private sector, in alignment with broad UN objectives, the [Compact's] principles, and the international Millennium Development Goals. It does not substitute for effective action by governments, nor does it present a regulatory framework or code of conduct for companies. Rather the Global Compact is conceived as a value-based platform designed to promote institutional learning with few formalities and no rigid bureaucratic structures.
>
> (Kell & Levin, 2003, p 152)

Central to the Compact's work are its ten Principles (see Box 5.3), which mirror the commitments of UN member States under the Universal Declaration of Human Rights, the 1992 Rio Declaration on the Environment and Development, the 1998 ILO Fundamental Principles and Rights at Work, and the 2003 Convention against Corruption. Companies that sign up to the Compact make a clear statement of support for the Principles, signed by the CEO and endorsed by the board, and they agree to report publicly on progress towards meeting commitment. From this stem the Compact's three stated goals:

1 To build consensus and inspire recognition of social and environmental concerns in the global marketplace, especially around problematic areas.

2 To develop a learning bank of corporate best practices, and to integrate the Compact's ten principles into business strategies and operations.

3 To generate concrete, sustained implementation of the Millennium Development Goals.

Partnering is an important way of achieving these, and activities include: (a) learning forums to analyse case studies and examples of good practice; (b) global policy dialogues on the challenges of globalization; (c) multi-stakeholder collaborative development projects to further the Millennium Development Goals; and (d) supporting the creation of new national networks. An important part of the Compact has been local networks that serve as forums within which companies can exchange experiences in a particular region.

The Compact now has 7,700 members in 130 countries, a rapid rise that includes commitments from over 20 per cent of the world's 500 largest companies, although with underrepresentation of US companies, partly because they fear litigation based on any alleged failure to comply with the Principles and partly because they see limited value in being associated with a UN initiative. Companies that do not meet their commitments can be held to account through the Compact's integrity process, but as of 2009 over 20 per cent of members were considered inactive or not communicating progress, compared to barely four per cent judged as notable.

(Sources: **www.unglobalcompact.org**; Williams, 2004; Kell and Levin, 2003; McIntosh et al., 2004)

Questions

For the Compact to be successful, it needs to be a credible partnership tackling important issues.

1 How well aligned are the ten principles to the main issues business is being asked to address globally by governments, and civil society?

2 What are the advantages and disadvantages of striving for a large but less active membership compared to a small but very active one?

3 What can the Compact do to encourage more active involvement from companies?

Box 5.3 **The ten principles of the Global Compact**

Businesses should . . .
1 support and respect the protection of internationally proclaimed human rights within their sphere of influence.

2 ensure that their own operations are not complicit in human rights abuses.

3 uphold the freedom of association and the effective recognition of the right to collective bargaining.

4 uphold the elimination of all forms of forced and compulsory labour.

5 uphold the effective abolition of child labour.

6 eliminate discrimination in respect of employment and occupation.

7 support a precautionary approach to environmental challenges.

8 undertake initiatives to promote greater environmental responsibility.

9 encourage the development and diffusion of environmentally friendly technologies.

10 work against corruption in all its forms, including extortion and bribery.

(Source: **www.unglobalcompact.org**)

SUMMARY

Globalization is a specific historical era that is redefining the role of business in the world. The human and environmental consequences of globalization are causing us to rethink corporate responsibility. Yet there are competing definitions of globalization and these, in turn, affect what we think the responsibilities of business are, and how we believe companies should approach them.

There are various definitions of globalization that variously emphasize its economic and wider social characteristics. The meaning that we give to 'globalization' affects how we look at its impacts. For some, these impacts are synonymous with 'liberalism', whether we mean by that the benefits of free trade, comparative advantage, and enlightened self-interest, or the exploitation of workers, social inequality, and the externalization of industry's ecological costs. Others may not deny these impacts, but instead highlight that what is distinctive about globalization is how it affects social networks, generates new types of organization, and creates the need for new approaches to governance. These different views are highly evident in debates about corporate responsibility. Some treat it as either a hindrance or a palliative to economic liberalization; others see it as related to the new organizations and alliances that globalization has spawned, and as part of the response to the challenges of global governance.

FURTHER READING

VISIT THE WEBSITE for links to useful sources of further information

Take your learning further: Online Resource Centre **www.oxfordtextbooks.co.uk/orc/blowfield_murray2e/**

Visit the Online Resource Centre which accompanies this book to enrich your understanding of this chapter.

Students: explore web links and further reading suggestions. Keep up to date with the latest developments by undertaking web exercises.

Lecturers: you will find additional case studies, including one on the topic of Tree huggers at the gates—KKR's partnership with environmental organizations to buy coal power stations (expanded from first edition Chapter 14), for use in class or assessment. Show your students trailers from films related to Corporate Responsibility, and use images from the book in your PowerPoint slides.

- Narlikar, A, 2005, *The World Trade Organization: A Very Short Introduction*, Oxford: Oxford University Press.
  Useful handbook for understanding what the WTO is and is not.

- Porritt, J, 2005, *Capitalism: As if the World Matters*, London: Earthscan.
  An alternative view of capitalism's future from an important sustainability thinker and activist.

- Steger, MB, 2003, *Globalization: A Very Short Introduction*, Oxford: Oxford University Press.
  Accessible overview of theories of globalization.

- Stiglitz, JE, 2005, *Fair Trade For All: How Trade Can Promote Development*, Oxford: Oxford University Press.
  Influential economist's view on the shortcomings of liberal economic globalization.

- Warner, M and Sullivan, R (eds), 2003, *Putting Partnerships to Work*, Sheffield: Greenleaf Publishing.
  Informative introduction to the various aspects of implementing partnerships, with a particular focus on oil, gas, and mining.

- Wolf, M, 2004, *Why Globalization Works*, New Haven, CT: Yale University Press.
  Feisty response to globalization's critics.

ENDNOTES

[1] See, e.g. Demirag, 2005; Blowfield, 2005a.

[2] Steger, 2003.

[3] Henderson, 2001; Lindsey, 2002.

[4] Wolf, 2004, p 36.

[5] Wolf, 2004, p 320.

[6] Stiglitz, 2002, p 248.

[7] Johnston, 2003; Johnson, 2004.

[8] Caufield, 1996.

[9] See, e.g. Blowfield, 2004.

[10] For example, Germain, 1999; MacLean, 1999; Levy and Newell, 2005, build on theories of power from writers such as Lukes, Gramsci, and Foucault to examine how exertions of power are not necessarily overt or attributable to recognizable actors.

[11] Blowfield and Frynas, 2005.

[12] Steger, 2003; Waters, 2001.

[13] According to IMF data, household debt in the USA in 2009 was over 90 percent, in the UK it was nearly 120 percent, and in the Eurozone it was over 60 per cent. Corporate debt for the same countries was 80 per cent, 120 per cent and 100 per cent respectively. In the seven richest economies, government debt guarantees (sovereign debt) are nearly 120 per cent, the same as the period immediately after the Second World War.

[14] Bendell, 2004a.

[15] World Bank, 2005.

[16] Wolf, 2004.

[17] This is Wolf's position: he says that corporate wealth has been exaggerated by dubious arithmetic. The merits of different claims about the power and influence of multinational companies is examined in Chandler and Mazlish, 2005.

[18] Ring et al., 2005.

[19] McMurtry, 2002.

[20] Cited in Waters, 2001, p 123.

[21] See, e.g. Stiglitz, 2002; Wolf, 2004; Oxfam, 2005.

[22] Elliott and Freeman, 2003. Abrami, 2003, discusses the US–Cambodia bilateral textile agreement, which was lauded for increasing market access to the USA to improvements in workers' rights.

[23] Utting, 2005b.

[24] For an overview of modern slavery, see Bales, 2004.

[25] Block and Barnett, 2005.

[26] Stopford et al., 1991.

[27] Blowfield, 2005a.

[28] Browne, 2004.

[29] See, e.g. articles in the journal, *Partnership Matters*, issues 1–3.

[30] Sabapathy et al., undated.

[31] Warner and Sullivan, 2003.

[32] Svendsen and Laberge, 2005.

[33] Davy 2003b

[34] See, e.g. Nelson, 1996; Pedersen, 2005; Fox and Prescott, 2004.

[35] See, e.g. UN, 2005; World Bank, 2005.

[36] See, e.g. the shift from policing suppliers to engaging suppliers and workers in labour monitoring (CCC, 2005a; ETI, 2005a).

[37] Maitland, 2005.

[38] Clay, 2005.

[39] Christian Aid, 2004, and Utting, 2005b, provide examples of this kind of non-alignment.

[40] Materials on Make Trade Fair are available at www.oxfam.org.

[41] Blowfield, 2004.

[42] DFID, 2002.

Part 2

Managing and implementing corporate responsibility

6

How corporate responsibility is managed

Chapter overview

In this chapter, we begin to examine the way in which corporate responsibility is being managed within companies, and whether or not there is a business case. In particular, we will:

- discuss the different goals that companies are trying to achieve;

- identify the types and levels of corporate responsibility that companies exhibit;

- examine the shared lessons and common elements of corporate responsibility management;

- look at how corporate responsibility is managed inside companies;

- explore evidence of a business case for corporate responsibility.

Main topics

■ Key terms

Change management

Defensive corporate responsibility

Integrated business strategy

Offensive corporate responsibility

Business case

Leadership

■ Online resources

- Teaching notes on the chapter case study

- Exercises and discussion topics for students

- Suggestions for additional materials on corporate responsibility management

- Links to other web-based resources

Understanding what companies want from corporate responsibility

Corporate responsibility management is typically described in terms of organizational change and transformation, and therefore distinguishes between:

1 the purpose and results (the why and the what);

2 the principles and processes (the how);

3 leadership (the who).

The next sections broadly follow these distinctions and, therefore, we begin with a discussion of the way in which companies decide whether to adopt corporate responsibility. The exception would be companies founded with the specific goal of achieving social or environmental outcomes, and which are discussed in Chapter 11 under 'Social Entrepreneurship'.

The most basic questions that any company thinking about corporate responsibility must answer are as follows.

1 What is our purpose in doing this—i.e. what Holliday et al. (2002) call the *corporate magnetic north*?
2 What do we need to do to achieve it?

The wide range of definitions, approaches, and issues related to corporate responsibility mean that these basic questions do not necessarily have simple answers (see Chapter 1). Should a company focus on things that affect its financial bottom line? If so, what exactly are those things? Threats to the company's reputation; risks to the supply of materials; attempts to undermine the share price; harm to the company's ability to recruit or retain top quality personnel; acts that expose the firm to costly lawsuits: all of these can affect financial performance and require that significant attention be given to corporate responsibility. But should the company define its corporate responsibility more in terms of addressing social issues, such as access to education, support for the arts, or reducing inequality? Must it try to do both and, if so, is there a point at which the company's social mission overwhelms the conventional business purpose?

Immediately, we see what one study of corporate responsibility approaches concludes is the distinction between operational responsibilities and citizenship responsibilities.[1] Companies are not limited to focusing on one set of responsibilities to the exclusion of the other, but the resource implications of any decision mean that even the largest corporation has to choose what to prioritize. Yet the same study also makes clear that it is not only the company that decides what responsibilities to act upon. Consumers, for example, have their own priorities and may reward or punish a company in the marketplace if its values do not concord with their own. For the reasons spelled out in Chapter 5 and elsewhere, the contemporary capitalist has to make sense of a cacophony of voices that have little, if any, acknowledged interest in business' wants or needs,

Defining the company's corporate responsibility purpose is further complicated by the fact that perceptions of responsibility differ from country to country.[2] For example, in Germany, it is a priority that companies provide secure employment; in South Africa, it is a priority that companies improve health, education, and other elements of social welfare; in Australia, the emphasis is on environmental protection. These priorities shift and often reflect recent local crises, so that in Argentina, for example, the main expectation that people have of business is job creation, because of the unemployment and financial loss caused by the recent economic collapse. In China, the main expectation is for safe, high-quality products, because of recent incidents of fire and serious injury caused by shoddy electrical goods. In countries characterized by a strong, legally explicit framework defining the social contract that business operates within (e.g. Sweden, Japan, Australia), corporate responsibility issues look quite different to ones built on a laissez faire economy (e.g. Australia, USA, UK). Considerable effort has gone into identifying national distinctions about corporate responsibility,[3] and these are particularly valid when thinking about national or regional companies. What is less explored, however, is whether multinational companies reproduce the social contract from their place of origin. On the admittedly limited evidence available, it seems that while some attention is paid to the national setting, the frameworks used by MNCs to manage corporate responsibility are imported, meaning that while different corporate responsibility issues might get attention, there is an orthodoxy in how they are managed. Furthermore, that orthodoxy reproduces many of the features of laissez faire economics, even when the company concerned originates from one with different socio-political conditions (e.g. IKEA, VW, Toyota).

Other factors and actors also influence the purpose of corporate responsibility. For example, the European Commission has defined corporate responsibility in a way that is intended to reflect what it calls the unique European social model, under which employers and other stakeholders, such as trade unions, function together to shape society and the economy. Reflecting the ideal that companies should not focus solely on profit, but also on the welfare of the workforce, consumers, and the environment, the model sets out the purpose of corporate responsibility in terms of the benefits to workers, customers, communities, and wider society. Acknowledging the importance of different types of company across Europe, it requires that corporate responsibility be relevant to small and medium-sized enterprises. Reflecting the need to establish European competitive advantage in the global economy, it also requires that corporate responsibility find ways of demonstrating that responsible business attracts investment and builds a skilled workforce.[4]

Similarly, an industry or a multi-industry collaboration can influence a company's corporate responsibility purpose. For example, the US Business Roundtable's SEE Change initiative, comprising companies such as Alcoa, Coca Cola, Dow Chemicals, and Xerox, aims to combine the traditional business goals of higher profits and lower costs with strong corporate commitments to environmental stewardship. Not only does the initiative suggest areas in which member companies should take action (e.g. eco-efficiency and demonstrating the business impacts of sustainable investment), it also goes some way to defining how corporate responsibility is to be managed by, for example, requiring companies to report their progress against individually determined timelines and goals.

The increase in the range of organizations, individuals, and sectors of society that seek to influence business behaviour is one trend that needs to be understood in terms of thinking about a company's corporate responsibility purpose; how companies consider other trends is also an influencing factor. For example, what significance does the company attach to changing patterns of demand for (and often shrinking supplies of) natural resources, or the challenge of demographic change (see Chapters 4 and 12)? Is the threat of climate change so great that it overwhelms other aspects of the business-society relationship? How will the growing number of tangible and intangible financial factors that might affect the way business is valued and its success measured influence the way in which the company is managed, and in what it invests? Or does the company need to respond to the growing role of international institutions, and the continued acceleration in the speed of policy and behavioural change caused by the global media?[5] Each of these trends has relevance for corporate responsibility, whether in terms of the need to change energy use, or to invest in new building technology because of the natural resource situation, or the financial case for investing in innovative technologies to solve social problems, or the challenges of participating in new models of global governance.

Basic distinctions in corporate responsibility purpose

Given this array of issues, are there common frameworks to help understand a company's corporate responsibility purpose? One way of thinking about what the company aims to achieve through corporate responsibility management is to distinguish between what Kramer and Kania (2006) call 'defensive' and 'offensive' corporate responsibility. In their view, most companies view corporate responsibility in terms of vulnerability, i.e. as an external risk that needs to be managed with minimal investment. Thus, for example, a non-government organization will raise an issue and the company will seek to find the least costly way to defuse attention, through actions such as lobbying, public relations, and advertising. The defensive approach can also be used, to maintain the company's reputation and to avoid legal liabilities, and is generally employed when companies are seeking to resolve problems of their own making.

In contrast, the offensive approach can involve companies offering themselves as the solution even if they had no part in creating the problem. It requires companies to exploit their full capabilities to find and implement solutions, and requires the company to do four key things.

1 Pick the right issue—one that is important, timely, and that leverages the company's core competencies.

2 Establish concrete goals and report on progress, both inside the company and externally.

3 Deploy the company's key assets in addressing the issue, including, for example, its products and services, the relevant skills of its employees, industry expertise, and its infrastructure.

4 Work in partnership with other sectors.

BP is a widely cited example of a company deciding to adopt an offensive approach, because the company chose the single issue of global warming, confronted it squarely before others in its industry did so, publicly announced quantitative targets and deadlines, and provided objectively verified reports of its progress.

As Nike's approach to corporate responsibility demonstrates, defensive and offensive approaches are not mutually exclusive, but the two bring different results. For example, a defensive approach allows the company to make short-term gains when it has to respond to specific charges (e.g. child labour in supplier factories), but the gains flatten out as the company meets its critics' expectations. Meanwhile, a company might see little tangible benefit from initial social investments, but, as these become more focused, they can have a significant impact in differentiating the company from its peers.[6] Put simply, as Kramer and Kania conclude:

> offensive [corporate responsibility] can distinguish a company's reputation but cannot protect it; defensive [corporate responsibility] can protect a reputation but cannot distinguish it.

(2006, p 25)

This is an instrumental framework that presents a business rationale for acting, but does not provide much guidance on the intrinsic value of those actions. In contrast, Martin (2002) distinguishes between acts that are instrumental because they maintain or enhance shareholder value, and those that are done for their own sake, which are therefore regarded as having an intrinsic value. In what he calls the '*virtue matrix*', he divides instrumental acts between those that are done because they conform to norms and customs, and those that are necessitated by legal compliance. He divides intrinsically valuable acts between those that create social and shareholder value, and those that benefit society, but not shareholders. This distinction between instrumental and intrinsic value brings us back to the discussion of corporate responsibility's meaning in Chapter 1 (and the debates about impact in Chapters 13 and 14). Is a company's purpose less admirable if the business rationale is strong or vice versa as some business ethicists maintain? Is a strong business case a signal that a company will remain committed to delivering extra-financial outcomes? What is an acceptable balance between return on investment and social return on investment? People may have strong opinions about which are the right set of questions to ask, but in today's business world each is a valid way to think about purpose, and decisions are highly subjective.

Advocates of corporate responsibility as management reform largely favour the more innovative, forward-looking agendas implicit in the concepts of intrinsic value and offensive corporate responsibility. These people see corporate responsibility, to paraphrase Paul Tebo of DuPont, as the right to operate and grow, because products that make lives better and reach more people equate with expanded markets and new customers.[7] But for many companies, as we will see, the instrumental/defensive approach to corporate responsibility better defines what they want to achieve. Moreover, Waddock (2007) has argued that the defensive–offensive distinction is not comprehensive enough. She accepts that corporate responsibility can be a defensive response to crises and scandals, or a way in which to harness the power of business to meet societal needs. But she adds a third distinction, under which the company's corporate responsibility purpose is to respond to concerns in society that arise from the very success of the company's strategy. This arises when public expectations about business' behaviour are neither the result of particular abuses, such as forced labour or oil spills, nor linked to demands that companies fill societal needs. Rather, the expectations (or criticisms) are directly related to the consequences of business implementing a system within which success is equated with:

1 continual growth and expansion;
2 a focus on efficiency and externalizing costs wherever possible;
3 corporate control or influence over resources, markets, customer preferences, and employees.

In other words, whether it be outrage at the bonuses paid by Goldman Sachs or disquiet amongst independent booksellers at the competing low cost, volunteer-based business model of Oxfam bookshops,[8] success creates a set of expectations that do not comfortably fit within the two approach model, but which, as noted earlier, clearly inform public perceptions of responsibility, such as fair competition, job security, workforce prosperity, and aspects of environmental stewardship.

Stages of corporate responsibility

Several theorists use the analogy of a journey when explaining how companies define, and then develop, their corporate responsibility goals. This is a convenient way of exploring why companies' policies, processes, and programmes change, and also of discussing to what companies should aspire. The idea of responsibility as a journey was used by Post and Altman (1992) to describe the evolution of environmental management, and is the subject of numerous case studies of corporate transformation that set out the steps and missteps taken by individual companies.[9] Clarkson (1995), building on others, developed the RDAP framework that separates the 'Reactive', 'Defensive', 'Accommodative', and 'Proactive' stages of corporate responsibility. Zadek (2000) identified four types of corporate responsibility (defence of reputation, cost–benefit orientation, the strategic business case, and the 'new economy' case, in which corporate responsibility is seen as part of new approaches to learning, innovation, and risk management). He has developed this idea to analyze the experience of Nike in moving from being what he calls a '*stubborn resister*' to the idea it was responsible for the consequences of its products, into what he regards as an active citizen and what Nike itself describes as a stage at which sustainability is a core attribute of Nike product innovation.[10]

Mirvis and Googins (2006) warn that there is no single developmental pathway, but believe that there is a natural progression. Their model builds on ideas of behavioural psychology and posits that companies, like individuals, exhibit distinct patterns of behaviour at different stages of development, their activities becoming more complex and sophisticated as they mature. We can tell the level of maturity by the company's actions in seven areas of management (see Figure 6.1):

1 How corporate responsibility is defined and the comprehensiveness of the definition (what they call the '*citizenship concept*');

2 The purpose of the company's corporate responsibility ('*strategic intent*');

3 The support given by company managers ('*leadership*');

4 The day-to-day management of corporate responsibility within the firm ('*structure*');

5 Responses to social, environmental, and other relevant issues ('*issues management*');

6 Managing the relationship with key constituencies within and outside the company ('*stakeholder relationships*');

7 Openness, transparency, and disclosure about different aspects of corporate responsibility performance ('*transparency*').

Thus, for instance, a company at the '*elementary*' stage might define corporate responsibility in terms of the creation of profits and jobs, and payment of corporate taxes (its citizenship concept), it might see its corporate responsibility purpose as complying with the law (strategic intent), and it might adopt a defensive approach to issues management.

		Stages				
		Stage 1 Elementary	Stage 2 Engaged	Stage 3 Innovative	Stage 4 Integrated	Stage 5 Transforming
Dimensions	Citizenship concept	Jobs; profits; taxes	Philanthropy; environment protection	Stakeholder management	Sustainability/ triple bottom line	Change the game
	Strategic intent	Legal compliance	Maintain licence to operate	Make business case	Integration of value and values	Create new markets/social change
	Leadership	Minimal	Supportive	On top of the issues	Ahead of the curve	Visionary
	Structure	Marginal	Functional ownership	Cross-functional coordination	Organizational alignment	Integrated into mainstream
	Issues management	Defensive	Reactive	Responsive	Proactive	Defines the issues
	Stakeholder relationships	Unilateral	Interactive	Mutual influence	Alliances and partnerships	Multi-organizational
	Transparency	Enough to protect flanks	Public relations	Public reporting	Assurance	Full disclosure

Figure 6.1 **Stages of corporate responsibility**
Source: Adapted from Mirvis and Googins (2006)

By contrast, a company at the '*engaged*' stage might in addition conceptualize corporate responsibility in terms of philanthropy or environmental protection, see its purpose as maintaining a licence to operate, and begin to develop policies that allow it to predict what issues it will need to manage. Meanwhile, a company at the '*integrated*' stage might be thinking in terms of the triple bottom line, be using corporate responsibility as a way to inform its product development, and have in place management systems that allow it to predict societal trends (see Figure 6.1).

Both Zadek, and Mirvis and Googins agree that companies have yet to reach the most developed stage of corporate responsibility (what they respectively call the '*new economy*' and '*transforming*' stages). As the overview of corporate responsibility's critics in Chapter 13 shows, there are good reasons for doubting whether companies, especially large corporations, can ever have the kind of game-changing purpose envisioned for them. In reality, the stages are not distinct silos, and individual companies may find themselves exhibiting features of one stage in some areas and features of another stage in others. Furthermore, their models' focus on evolution also ignores the impact of major external events such as climate change which in certain industries at least appears to require hitherto underdeveloped companies to leapfrog to advanced evolutionary stages. None-theless, as a whole, the stages provide a framework for understanding the different purposes that companies are pursuing. Equally, as we consider in the next section, they reveal some of the key dimensions to corporate responsibility management.

■ **Discussion points**

Corporate responsibility is often presented as an evolutionary journey.

- Does it help managers to think of corporate responsibility in this way?
- Are the criteria used to measure progression adequate and appropriate?
- What companies would you put at Mirvis and Googins' Stages 3 and 4, and which would you say have reached or are approaching Stage 5?

Qualities of good corporate responsibility management

Following the three critical areas of organizational change mentioned earlier, we move now from the company's purpose in managing corporate responsibility to a discussion of its implementation (the 'how'). There are an increasing number of books about how to manage corporate responsibility, aimed largely at existing managers. Peters' *Waltzing with the Raptors* (1999) was one of the first of these, promising a practical roadmap to protecting a company's reputation and, since then, further titles have concentrated on particular advantages of corporate responsibility (e.g. risk management, the business case, enhanced strategy), and/or the needs of particular business functions (e.g. corporate responsibility for PR professionals; marketing).

A glance at the contents of these books reveals the central elements of corporate responsibility management today. For example, the *Guide to Best Practices in Corporate Social Responsibility*,[11] a book targeted at mid-level PR managers, features chapters on communicating corporate responsibility, building an integrated corporate responsibility strategy, demonstrating its value to senior management, working with stakeholders, managing crises, corporate responsibility reporting, and measuring corporate responsibility performance. Such books reveal a managerial orthodoxy that embraces much of corporate responsibility today, and is reflected in various assessments of best practice.[12] This orthodoxy comprises:

1 particular tools and approaches—the ingredients of good corporate responsibility management;

2 advice on execution—the qualities of that management.

We discuss these two dimensions below and also take a more in-depth look at some of the ingredients in coming chapters.

One of the things that distinguishes corporate responsibility today from that of the past is that it is becoming an identifiable area of management expertise. As we discuss later in this chapter, in 'Structuring the corporate responsibility function' (p 146), this expertise is housed in a variety of organizational structures, but there is also a large amount of general advice that is presented as best practice, which draws on analysis of diverse corporate experiences and case studies. This ranges from identifying broad areas to which the company should pay attention (e.g. integrating strategies into the corporate culture; adhering to declared values and standards; communicating what the company is doing, including both achievements and challenges),[13] to more specific steps. Some of the most common advice that can be offered to a company once its purpose is clear is set out in Box 6.1.

Much of this advice relates to the initial stages of adopting corporate responsibility and, as, we discuss in Chapter 9 in relation to stakeholder engagement, for example, some aspects of corporate responsibility management ultimately involve many layers of skill and complexity. This is also true of making the business case for corporate responsibility, which some consultants and theorists stress needs to be established as early as possible within the company (see The Business Case for Corporate Responsibility, p 151). However, returning to our earlier discussion about instrumental and intrinsic value, Hemingway and Maclagan (2004) argue that the commercial imperative is only part of effective corporate responsibility management and that it should also be linked to the personal values of individual managers. They point out that individual discretion allows personnel to introduce their values into corporate responsibility policies, whether

---

Box 6.1 **Common advice on introducing corporate responsibility into management**

- Get started—don't take too long before getting under way with the first activities.
- Pay attention to terminology—for example, a term such as 'sustainable growth' may have more resonance with company managers than 'sustainability', 'sustainable development', or 'social responsibility', because the latter terms can be interpreted as discarding the idea of economic growth with which managers are most familiar.
- Be frank and transparent—this is the best way to get staff attention and winning their attention makes it easier to change the corporate ethos.
- Instil a company ethic of education and learning around issues of responsibility.
- Find useful partners and corporate responsibility champions across the company.
- Get to know the communities within which the company exists, including understanding its norms, values, cultures, traditions, and, of course, applicable laws.
- Establish dialogues and debates with stakeholders from different sectors and sections of society, and make these transparent and honest, not least in terms of agreeing realistic expectations.
- Form 'smart partnerships' with stakeholders to achieve genuine corporate responsibility goals, rather than only public relations imperatives.
- Measure and account for what the company does in areas of corporate responsibility.
- Report to the public and key constituencies on what the company is doing and make these reports accessible to all who have an interest.

(Adapted from CCC, 2005a; Olsen, 2004; Holliday et al., 2002; SustainAbility/UNEP, 2001; Peters, 1999)

through officially sanctioned actions, the unintended consequences of an individual resolving a problem by drawing on personal beliefs, or an individual's entrepreneurship in bringing values into the workplace.

Leaders—or, perhaps more accurately, 'initiators' or what Pinchot (1985) calls 'intrapreneurs'—can come from almost any part of the company and a key ingredient is what Arnold and Hartman (2003) call *moral imagination*. For example, at BAT, some of the early enthusiasm for corporate responsibility is said to have come from middle managers in corporate affairs, while at The Body Shop and Timberland, it stemmed from the moral imagination of CEOs from the outset. Regardless of how it begins, however, there comes a stage at which senior management needs to give legitimacy to the corporate responsibility agenda, so that it gets valued across the company. Part of this legitimization is the creation of relevant systems to develop policies, processes, indicators, and targets, so that the full range of corporate responsibility-related activities are managed. Companies such as Anglo American and the ICT firms involved in the Global e-Sustainability Initiative (GeSI) have made a point of sharing their learning in such areas.[14]

In corporate responsibility literature, there is much more discussion of the aims of these systems (e.g. that they be inclusive, responsive, and engaged with stakeholders),[15] than there is of what they look like in practice. We examine the structuring of the corporate responsibility function in more detail in the next section, but it is typical for systems to evolve and change as the company becomes more familiar with corporate responsibility as a management area. Part of this is the creation of corporate responsibility capacity, and comparative research of company practices shows that systems can include capacity building both within the company (e.g. to understand corporate responsibility issues, or to engage with stakeholders) and among stakeholders themselves, so that they can interact more effectively with firms.[16] For example, through its Leadership Development initiative, 3M has taken the idea of ethics programmes a step further than many companies by having executives give examples of where opportunities for business advantage did not concord with the company's values, and then debating and undertaking role play based on how others would react in that situation. Companies, such as Levi Strauss and Nike, are investing in building the capacity of suppliers to manage their human resources more effectively, so as to avert the need for abusive labour practices, and others such as Tesco are training their buyers so that procurement practices do not exacerbate such problems.[17]

However, any single idea of how to manage corporate responsibility reflects received wisdom; they should not be treated as infallible truth. Research with managers from several leading companies has shown that following received wisdom can assist the corporate responsibility effort, but can, at the same time, lay potential traps.[18] For example, making the business case can help to explain why a company should take corporate responsibility seriously and legitimate the topic inside the business—but managers' experiences also show that it can cause companies or individuals to promise more than they can actually deliver or demonstrate, given the available data. In the long run, this makes it more difficult to make a compelling non-financial case. Moreover, the business case tends to be demonstrated using lagging indicators that only explain what happened in the past and do not necessarily help in deciding about future investments.

Structuring the corporate responsibility function

One area in which more detailed information about the actual management of corporate responsibility is starting to emerge is the structuring of corporate responsibility management within companies. Some of this information takes the form of consultancy advice to individual firms and is not in the public domain, but what is available (both officially and unofficially) provides a reasonably detailed picture of actual corporate responsibility management practice.

A relatively early management guide on this topic identified what it considered nine essential steps for designing a corporate responsibility structure,[19] as follows.

1 Understanding the drivers of corporate responsibility within the firm;

2 Identifying the key corporate responsibility issues;

3 Identifying and evaluating stakeholders;

4 Identifying functions within the company that support corporate responsibility efforts;

5 Analysing company systems, culture, and impending changes;

6 Evaluating structural options;

7 Developing a staff plan;

8 Creating a structure for cross-functional interaction;

9 Assessing the process and framework for budget and resource allocation.

At first glance, this can appear to be an unwieldy list of actions, but the steps can be divided between four main areas of activity:

1 understanding the drivers (Step 1);

2 mapping what is already happening inside and outside the company (Steps 2, 3, and 4);

3 coming to grips with existing systems (Step 5);

4 designing a specific corporate responsibility management structure (Steps 6, 7, 8, and 9).

Nobody knows how often this type of methodical approach is followed in real life, but it does highlight aspects of corporate responsibility structuring that have engendered debate within companies. These include the importance, or otherwise, of cross-functional interaction within the firm, decisions about resource allocation, staffing the corporate responsibility function, and, perhaps most significantly, deciding what is the most appropriate structure for a specific company. What has emerged is an array of structures. For example, at Pfizer, there is a long-standing tradition of the full board of directors making major decisions rather than specific committees and, as a result, while some firms have brought specialists in at the non-executive director level, the company has sought to diversify the full board with corporate responsibility expertise. Another approach is to place formal responsibility for corporate responsibility issues in the hands of existing executives: for example, at Novartis, the heads of legal affairs and human resources have formal responsibility for corporate responsibility issues inside the executive committee. Corporate responsibility can also be placed in other parts of the organization: at IBM, it comes under the executive vice president for innovation and technology; at Groupe Danone, the head of sustainable development and social responsibility reports to the company general secretary; at Telefónica, a standalone department was created, reporting to the head of corporate communications.

A 2005 survey of 254 managers and directors, who saw corporate responsibility as part of their role, found they had 23 job titles.[20] Another survey of 580 company structures worldwide found that, in 30 per cent of cases, corporate responsibility was managed by an existing department, such as communications or HR, without staff who have corporate responsibility as their primary function.[21] Ten per cent of companies had set up nondepartmental working committees to manage corporate responsibility and 4 per cent had outsourced corporate responsibility activities to an external consultancy. In the majority of companies (56 per cent), however, there were designated corporate responsibility personnel of some kind. The majority of these were either part of a standalone corporate responsibility department or team in the corporate centre (22 per cent), or part of another department, such as corporate communications (24 per cent). The remaining companies had several teams dispersed across the organization, either as standalone entities (9 per cent), or as part of a number of different departments (10 per cent).

These statistics tell us something about how far companies have moved towards the kind of idealized structure and systems that are depicted as corporate responsibility best practice. The fact that only 10 per cent of companies have dedicated corporate responsibility managers in the regions or business lines suggests that there is a long way to go before the ideal of embedding corporate responsibility into business operations is realized. This is in marked contrast to the areas of knowledge management and quality management, in which specialists are less likely to be located in the corporate centre and more likely to be found in teams dispersed across the business.

But before one puts too negative an interpretation on this situation, it must be asked how perfect is the idealized structure to begin with. Sutcliffe (2005) argues, based on interviews with managers and external commentators, that the right location for the corporate responsibility function depends on the company, the nature of its industry, and its internal culture. For example, at Marks and Spencer, there was a strong belief that corporate responsibility needed to be housed with corporate governance, because of its control over the board's sub-committees. But this view changed when the head of corporate responsibility came to believe that a process-driven approach of the kind associated with governance was less effective than the ability to communicate with different stakeholders and, consequently, corporate responsibility was housed in corporate affairs.

There are strong arguments for structuring corporate responsibility in different ways. Some argue that it needs to be at the locus of internal power, so that corporate responsibility factors influence business decisions (e.g. housing it where prices and deadlines are negotiated with suppliers rather than in public affairs). Some believe it should be at the nodes where key business areas connect, so as to build cross-functional influence. There is a widely felt sentiment that as important as a knowledge of corporate responsibility is an understanding of what affects company performance (e.g. operations, investors, sourcing) and, related to that, there is a desire among many external commentators that corporate responsibility issues be dealt with in the operational functions to which they belong (e.g. employee issues to be addressed by HR; sourcing issues by buying; customer issues by sales and marketing). As already noted, however, this kind of integrated corporate responsibility function is a long way from being realized in most firms.

Alongside the question of where to situate the corporate responsibility function lies that of how to resource it. Early movers in the field, such as The Body Shop, tended to establish separate, well-resourced corporate responsibility departments that were a statement of serious commitment. Now, it is less certain how large a corporate responsibility department should be, or even if there should be such a thing. In a company such as GlaxoSmithKline, a small team is said to have made significant progress, because it gained the attention and commitment of multiple departments, encouraging them to deploy their own resources and to incorporate corporate responsibility into their own practices. In other companies, such as Gap Inc, relatively large teams have been created because of the challenges faced in managing global supply chains, and procurement is an increasingly important aspect of corporate responsibility management private and public sector organizations.[22] Moreover, none of these structures are static as the demonstrated by the evolution of corporate responsibility at Marks and Spencer described in this chapter's case study.

■ Discussion points

The structure of corporate responsibility functions is often seen as an indication of how serious a company is about realizing its corporate responsibility vision.

- Do you think structure is an important indicator of a company's attitude to corporate responsibility?
- What ways of structuring corporate responsibility do you think will be most effective?
- How would you structure the corporate responsibility function in a sports shoe or apparel company?

Corporate responsibility as strategy

Underlying questions about how to locate the corporate responsibility function is the issue of an integrated strategy that makes corporate responsibility part of the corporate DNA.[23]

As early as 1973, Andrews recognized that:

> the overriding master problem ... impeding the further progress of corporate responsibility is the difficulty of making credible and effective, throughout a large organization, the social component of a corporate strategy ...

(p 57)

There is now widespread agreement with Andrews' subsequent point that a company's social policy should be as much a function of strategic planning as is its choice of products and marketing, or its establishment of profit and growth objectives. Indeed, numerous authors have explored corporate responsibility from the perspective of conventional management disciplines such as marketing and organizational behaviour.[24] As already noted, there is a widely held belief among corporate responsibility thinkers that companies should develop management approaches that establish corporate responsibility as a core driver of business performance, thereby fully aligning it with the firm's strategic operations.

This kind of belief is reflected in the definitions of the more evolved forms of corporate responsibility that we described earlier ('Stages of corporate responsibility', p 141), but there is often frustration among theorists that current corporate responsibility scorecards, standards, reports, and other widely used management tools fail to support strategic alignment or planning.[25] Subsequently, there is a stark contrast between conventional business management excellence and corporate responsibility management excellence. The former involves building a strategy that creates competitive advantage and then reinforcing that strategy with high-quality operational processes that lead to best quality and productivity. By contrast, corporate responsibility often creates programmes to tackle specific issues, and then puts in place systems to enforce and sustain what it considers to be ethical practices, finally producing a report reviewing its commitments and practices. In other words, there is a strong tendency to define excellence as the production of a report about programmes and systems, begging the question: is there any other area of business management in which this would be considered acceptable, let alone 'excellent'?

By contrast, the strategic integration of corporate responsibility means that corporate responsibility is seen as a business driver. It involves corporate responsibility creating value within the company and the company creating value for wider society. An example of this type of integration is when GE began to see spiralling health costs and difficulties in accessing health care both as social problems and a business opportunity. It responded by investing in products that were tailored to the needs of specific markets around the world, instead of focusing purely on the best technology accessible only to the wealthy.[26] Moreover, as the quote in Snapshot 6.1 shows, serving emerging markets through this kind of approach has become central to the company's strategy for growth.

The GE case is an example of a strategy for offensive corporate responsibility, but strategic integration can also be applied to more defensive objectives. For example, it is already common for companies to use corporate responsibility as part of a strategy to protect their reputations, as was the case when leading IT companies, such as IBM, HP, and Dell, established the Electronics Industry Code of Conduct as a common approach to monitoring the corporate responsibility issues in their suppliers' operations. Similarly, Fedex is applying integrated thinking in its collaboration with the Alliance for Environmental Innovation, which aims to develop trucks that are 50 per cent more fuel-efficient and less harmful to the environment than those it currently operates.

The examples above might imply that integrating corporate responsibility into business strategy is another way of making the business case for improved social and environmental performance. But true integration requires that there be processes to ensure that corporate responsibility imperatives are considered on their own merits in strategic planning, regardless of the financial implications. What proponents of integration claim is that the distinction between business imperative and responsibility imperative will become irrelevant, pointing for comparison to quality management, for which poor quality came to be seen as symptomatic of unproductive systems, just as waste, emissions, and environmental impacts are seen today. In this way, corporate responsibility ceases to be a contained entity, and becomes an inseparable part of a larger complex and changing system that, as Van Tulder (2006) says, needs to influence different levels (at which it will take different forms) and functions such as marketing, quality control, financial management, and research and development.

■ Discussion points

Integration of corporate responsibility into mainstream business strategy is a widely touted ambition among both theorists and practitioners.

- What arguments might managers make to persuade a company of the advantages of the integration of corporate responsibility?
- If integration does not happen more widely than at present, how will this affect future developments in corporate responsibility?
- What examples are there of companies successfully integrating corporate responsibility into business management decisions?

SNAPSHOT 6.1

General Electric—integrating corporate responsibility as a business driver

Edison once said, '*Vision without execution is hallucination*'. Yet much of the information on managing corporate responsibility deals with aims, expectations, and general principles, and not with the detail of its implementation. Part of what is missing is the connection between the why, the what, and the how of transformation management, i.e. the rationale, the expected results, and the way in which these will be achieved.

GE, founded by Edison, and which owns businesses in industries as diverse as aviation, film and television, transportation, energy, and healthcare, is trying to make this connection. In developing its 'ecomagination' initiative, managers consulted across the company and with what were sometimes hostile external groups, and came up with a list of social and environmental issues in relation to which it could employ its assets to bring about change. They then created a business plan that committed company resources to, set output targets for, and not least promised to double company revenues to $2,000 million by 2010 by developing products offering environmental advantage to customers. They promised to double the spend on clean technology research and development to $1,500 million, and the same kind of integration is depicted in the company's 2005 *Citizenship Report* (p 42):

> In 2004, GE's revenues from the developing world reached $21 billion, a 37 % increase. We now expect to get as much as 60% of our future revenue growth from emerging markets

including China, Russia, Eastern Europe, India, and the Middle East. In these markets, GE can provide much-needed infrastructure. We will deliver vital systems for water, power, healthcare, and transportation to improve the quality of life and access to opportunity in these countries ... By providing critical infrastructure needs, GE has the opportunity to lay a foundation for sustainable growth.

(Stewart & Immelt, 2006; GE, 2005)

Quick Questions

Under long-time CEO Jack Welch, GE was widely admired by investors, but repeatedly criticized for its environmental performance.

1 What evidence is there that GE has acted on the ecomagination promise of putting corporate responsibility issues at the core of business strategy?

2 Are the reasons that GE gives for integrating corporate responsibility convincing from a shareholder's perspective?

3 What is the business case for ecomagination?

The business case for corporate responsibility

Launching Creating Shared Value, what Nestlé calls its business response to nutrition, water, and rural development challenges, Chairman Peter Brabeck-Letmathe said, 'The financial crisis ... revealed once more a basic business axiom: if you fail to work on behalf of public interest and take short cuts that put the public at risk, you will also fail your shareholders.'[27]

Pick up any book on corporate responsibility, browse the session themes of conferences, or look at companies' social or environmental reports, and you will soon discern how important the business case has become to contemporary corporate responsibility. For business managers, government officials, academics, consultants, to name but a few, making the business case has become the Holy Grail. There is a simple reason for this: demonstrating a positive correlation between corporate responsibility and business performance is seen as giving social and environmental issues legitimacy in the world of mainstream business. In this way, it greatly increases the likelihood that corporate responsibility practices will be adopted. Consequently, information, such as that 91 per cent of executives believe that corporate responsibility creates shareholder value, or that 80 per cent say that non-financial indicators are essential to characterize future financial performance, is widely cited as proof positive of corporate responsibility's importance, not as the nice thing to do, but as part of good management practice.[28]

Making the business case has grown in importance as the focus of corporate responsibility has moved from philanthropy and generally giving a proportion of revenues back to society, to the function of corporate responsibility in core business activities, and the role of business in tackling major societal challenges.[29] Showing how corporate responsibility relates to business performance is intended to help managers to understand why they should be paying attention and to what they should be attending. It is also meant to help companies to explain the importance of social and environmental performance to investors, and vice versa. Meanwhile, away from the company-specific level, it provides a basis for corporate responsibility's advocates to demonstrate to mainstream management theorists and economists that corporate responsibility can add to shareholder value, or at least will not damage it.[30]

There are, then, good reasons why the business case has become so important to corporate responsibility. But the gravitas that it has accrued gives rise to further questions: what evidence is there of a business case, and how does its presence or absence affect corporate responsibility now and in the future? Neither question is easy to answer and there is good reason to consider what the consequences are for corporate responsibility if the business case continues to be brought to the fore. But we will begin with some examples.

Examples of the benefits to business

When BP met its target of reducing greenhouse gas emissions at twice the rate specified in the Kyoto Protocol nine years ahead of schedule, the reductions were the equivalent of 9.6 million tonnes and the company achieved operational savings of $250 million. Dow Chemical estimates that if it could make its water filtration technologies available to the 1.2 billion poorest people, it could generate $300 million in sales. DuPont saved $2 billion by reducing energy consumption and is on track to generate 25 per cent of its revenue using renewable resources by 2010. When 3M pre-empted new government regulations by abandoning the use of solvent-based coatings in favour of water-soluble ones, it benefited commercially from having an early mover advantage, and operationally from reductions in downtime, product loss, and waste related to the new technology. Staving off regulation and repairing a severely damaged reputation were key motivations for financial institutions to set up the Equator Principles to combat corruption in overseas projects.[31] Gap Inc has found that purchasing decisions that negatively impact working conditions also undermine quality, on-time delivery, and cost.[32] Wal-Mart favours suppliers that share its commitment to less packaging, and the use of recycled and non-toxic materials, while major DIY and furniture stories, such as Home Depot, Ikea, and B&Q, have made sourcing from sustainably managed resources part of their buying policy.

Different industries; different countries; different dimensions of corporate responsibility: all suggesting that a link can be made between social and environmental performance, and business performance. According to the investment group, Innovest, 85 per cent of studies show a positive correlation between environmental governance and financial performance.[33] According to UK-based telecommunications company BT, the benefits of corporate responsibility to a company's reputation, and the money that can be saved through efficient environmental planning and the identification of new market opportunities, *'often amount to a convincing financial reason for why business should engage with such issues'*.[34] According to one former executive, strategies built around the triple bottom line can yield a 46 per cent increase in profit over five years, fully costed.[35]

Meanings of the 'business case'

Examples such as those above have generated considerable excitement about the business case, but they also highlight some of the problems in making that case. The case is more than just shareholder value or return on investment: it can equally be the indirect benefits of creating a favourable business environment (e.g. maintaining reputation, innovation, licence to operate). It is not immediately clear which dimensions of corporate responsibility have the strongest or weakest links to business performance. It is also not always apparent what type of relationship exists between corporate responsibility and business performance, i.e. whether the one causes the other and under what circumstances.

Preston and O'Bannon (1997) divide the business case into three types of relationship:

1 that within which corporate responsibility relates to financial performance;

2 that within which financial performance relates to corporate responsibility;

3 that within which corporate responsibility and financial performance are synergistic.

In all three types, the relationship can be positive, neutral, or negative, so that according to Friedman (1962), for example, there is a negative relationship between corporate responsibility and financial performance, because the former misuses company assets (see Chapter 1). According to Cornell and Shapiro (1987), there is a positive relationship, because meeting the needs of stakeholders other than shareholders enhances financial performance. Case studies and other analyses exist for each type of relationship: for example, Waddock and Graves (1997) study how the strength of performance affects the amount that a company invests in corporate responsibility.

To make sense of the business performance–corporate responsibility relationship, we need to know what each term refers to. There are many different definitions available,[36] but Boxes 6.2 and 6.3 offer a generic set of possibilities applicable to a variety of industries.

The application of these measures is affected by several variables. First, each audience requires information to meet its specific needs. For example, business managers may want information that will help to convince their superiors or colleagues, while shareholders will want to know if corporate responsibility pays; governments will want information that will test if corporate responsibility is a viable basis for delivering social and environmental benefits.[37]

Second, the business case differs from industry to industry. For a mining company, such as Placer Dome, corporate responsibility might result in preferred access in future gold-mining projects, whereas for Royal Ahold, the supermarket company, it might help the company to relate better to consumers in fiercely competitive mature markets.[38]

Third, the business case partly depends on how corporate responsibility is viewed within a company and on how developed that company's approach to corporate responsibility is. For example, in the late 1990s, a company such as Premier Oil would have seen corporate responsibility as a way to offset criticism for its investment in Burma, while BP or Shell, despite being in the same industry, were thinking less about reputation and more about how corporate responsibility related to their long-term strategies.[39]

Box 6.2 Dimensions of corporate responsibility

1 the influence of *ethics, values, and principles* on a company's actions, as evident, for example, in business principles, decisions, and legal actions;

2 a company's *accountability and transparency* for its corporate responsibility performance, as evident, for example, in its reporting and management systems;

3 a company's overall commitment and performance in social, economic, and environmental areas (i.e. the *triple bottom line*);

4 a company's record on *eco-efficiency*, evident, for example, in its minimization of adverse environmental impacts associated with product processes;

5 the *environmental product focus* of a company, as seen, for example, in its redesign of products to reduce their environmental impact (e.g. cradle-to-grave product stewardship);

6 the use of a company's resources to support the *social and economic development* of communities;

7 a company's respect for, and protection of, *human rights*;

8 efforts by a company to foster a high-quality *work environment*, including health and safety issues, but also those such as work–life balance;

9 involvement of the company's *business stakeholders* (e.g. suppliers, partners, contractors, shareholders) in implementing its corporate responsibility strategy;

10 the quantity and quality of a company's engagement with *external stakeholders* (e.g. civil society organizations, government) in relation to corporate responsibility.[40]

Box 6.3 Measures of business performance

1 **Shareholder value**
   Changes in a company's stock price and dividend.

2 **Revenue**
   Changes in a company's revenues due to pricing, market share, new markets, etc.

3 **Operational efficiency**
   A company's cost-effectiveness in turning inputs into productive outputs.

4 **Access to capital**
   A company's access to equity and debt capital.

5 **Customer attraction**
   A company's ability to attract and retain customers.

6 **Brand value and reputation**
   The value assigned to a company and its brands due to their reputation.

7 **Human capital**
   The knowledge and skills of a company's employees, resulting from the ability to attract, develop, and retain a workforce.

8 **Risk management**
   Exposure of a company's assets to short- and long-term risks.

9 **Innovation**
   A company's ability to maintain its competitive advantage through better products, services, and business models.

10 **Licence to operate**
   A company's ability to maintain a level of acceptance among its stakeholders that allows it to operate effectively.

Finally, studies of the business case tend to overlook how the local, national, or regional contexts affect the business case.[41] For example, there might be quite different arguments to be made for eco-efficiency in a country with a tough regulatory regime and a strong utilities infrastructure, compared with that in a country in which environmental regulations are weak, but the cost of energy or clean water is relatively high. Just as corporate responsibility can look different from country to country (see Chapter 5), so, too, can the business case.

■ Discussion points

One reason for making the business case is that it helps to make corporate responsibility more comprehensible to senior executives and operational managers.

- Choose a particular company or industry with which you are familiar. How would you go about making the business case to the executive team?
- Is there a distinct financial performance case? What do you think are the strongest and weakest areas of that case?
- Pick a company you know that is working on corporate responsibility. Apply conventional marketing and entrepreneurship analysis tools such as Mullins' seven domains (2006) or Chan's value curves (2005) to understand the business case for one of its products addressing social or environmental issues.

SNAPSHOT 6.2

Catalytic converters—Governments creating the business case

The business case is not simply a question of economics; it also depends on the environment within which business operates. Some of the technologies we take for granted originally became viable because of government actions. The catalytic converter is an excellent example of how legislation created a market for an environmental product, and of how major automotive manufacturers overcame their resistance and worked with suppliers to reduce vehicle emissions, even as vehicle use grew.

The market for catalytic converters was a direct consequence of vehicle emissions controls introduced in 1970, notably, amendments to the US Federal Clean Air Act 1963 and the Californian Zero Emission Vehicle Mandate. The legislation was passed even though the technology to achieve the targets they set out was barely proven and not commercialized, and the automakers lobbied aggressively that it would harm their industry. But the strong stance of the Californian government and of the newly established US Environmental Protection Agency (EPA) forced automakers to enter into forward commitment procurement agreements with potential catalytic converter suppliers, towards working together to develop the technology that would meet demands for a 90 per cent reduction in carbon dioxide and nitrous oxide.

Engine modifications alone would have been unlikely to meet these much tougher standards, however, and so a real commercial opportunity emerged for companies such as Johnson Matthey, which had relevant experience from working with other industries, to work with the automakers. These companies were encouraged by the EPA's insistence that vehicle manu-facturers prove they were making a determined effort to meet the targets and, in 1972, EPA held the first of several public hearings to assess progress. Despite the automakers' initial reluctance, catalytic converters have become the norm and emissions from cars are now lower than they were in the 1960s, despite the increase in total car mileage. In terms of government action, the key learnings are that government is able to motivate private industry to deliver better technol-ogy for environmental gain at no particular cost to the public purse over the long term.

(Source: **www.managementtoday.co.uk; www.environmental-expert.com**—accessed 20 March 2007)

Quick Questions

1 What were the main government actions that encouraged automakers to adopt catalytic converters?

2 Why do you think automakers were resistant?

3 Are there other examples in which government has created a new market in this way?

Evidence of a business case

In 2001, SustainAbility, the consultancy company, in association with the UN Environ-mental Programme, reviewed multiple reports, case studies, and academic analyses per-taining to the business case for sustainable development, and issued a report that remains one of the only attempts to correlate specific dimensions of corporate responsibility with measures of business performance. A similar study (that additionally involved the International Finance Corporation) focused on emerging markets and was published in 2002.[42] Subsequent studies, such as the IMD management school's work on the business case for sustainability, have added new insights, but also show that the key findings from 2001 and 2002 remain valid. In addition, the business case has been made central to claims for the efficacy of corporate responsibility by influential management thinkers (e.g. Porter & Kramer 2002, 2006).

Using a matrix based on the themes in Boxes 6.1 and 6.2, we can see how the SustainAbility reports identify 21 areas in which there is strong evidence that corporate responsibility positively affects business performance (see Figure 6.2).[43] The most demon-strable contribution is in the area of eco-efficiency, in which changes in the use of raw materials, recycling and reuse, reductions in emissions, and other new practices have had tangible benefits in terms of shareholder value, operational efficiency, access to capi-tal, reputation, risk management, and innovation. Eco-efficiency has become so prevalent in industries such as chemicals, energy, and electrical goods that it could be seen as noth-ing more than rational profit maximization, i.e. common sense management practice. But it is relatively recently that pollution has come to be seen not as the inevitable by-product of economic prosperity, but as a form of economic waste,[44] and this change has occurred because of, not despite, the kind of transformation associated with corporate responsibility (see also Chapter 3).

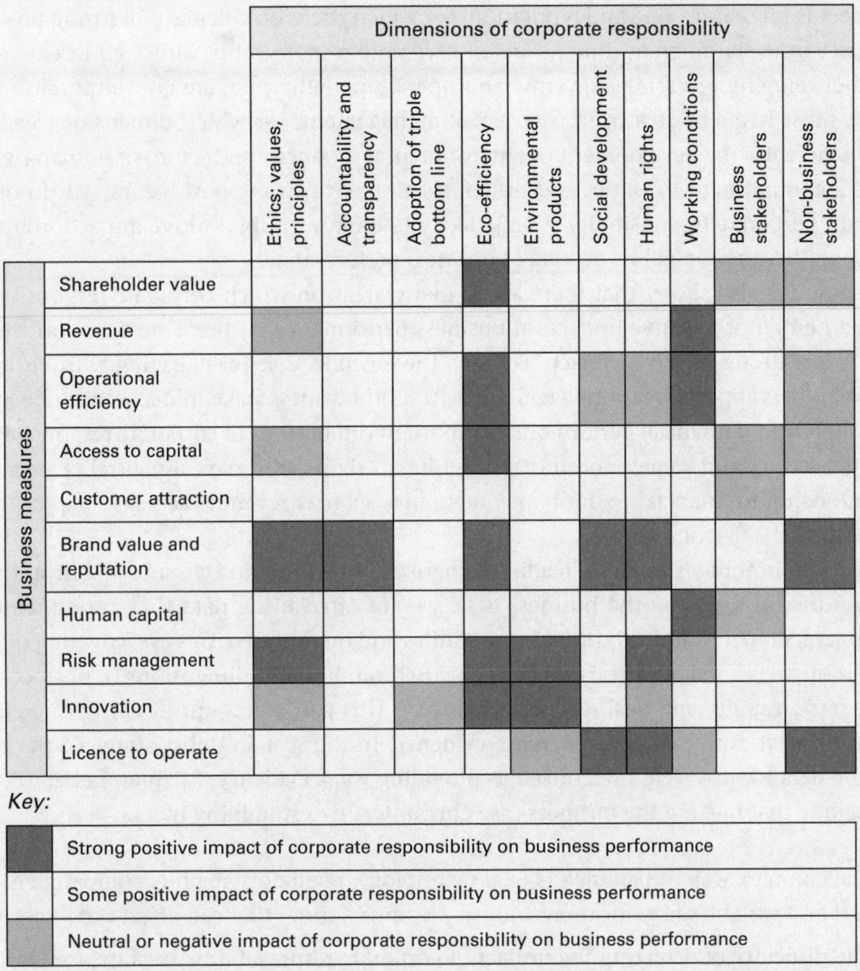

Figure 6.2 Sustainability matrix

Business measures \ Dimensions of corporate responsibility	Ethics; values, principles	Accountability and transparency	Adoption of triple bottom line	Eco-efficiency	Environmental products	Social development	Human rights	Working conditions	Business stakeholders	Non-business stakeholders
Shareholder value				■					░	
Revenue	░							■		
Operational efficiency				■		▨	▨			
Access to capital	░								▨	▨
Customer attraction										
Brand value and reputation	■	■		■		■	■	■		
Human capital								■		
Risk management	■				■		■			
Innovation	▨		▨	■	■		▨			
Licence to operate						▨	▨			■

Key:

■	Strong positive impact of corporate responsibility on business performance
▨	Some positive impact of corporate responsibility on business performance
░	Neutral or negative impact of corporate responsibility on business performance

Figure 6.2 Sustainability matrix
Sources: SustainAbility, IFC & Ethos, I. 2002, Developing Value: the business case for sustainability in emerging markets, London.
SustainAbility & UNEP 2002, Trust us: the global reporters 2002 survey of corporate sustainability reporting, SustainAbility and United Nations Environment Programme, London.
SustainAbility & UNEP 2001, Business case buried treasure : uncovering the business case for corporate sustainability, SustainAbility/United Nations Environment Programme.

There is also strong evidence that other dimensions of corporate responsibility are linked to better business performance, including: protection of human rights; high quality working conditions; relationships with external stakeholders; transparency and accountability around corporate responsibility performance. What also stands out is that, whereas eco-efficiency delivers a wide variety of benefits, these other dimensions affect a much narrower selection of business performance measures. By far the greatest impact is on brand value and reputation, for which there is evidence of a strong positive impact from six different dimensions of corporate responsibility, although in emerging and developing economies revenue and operational efficiency are also important. The next most frequent area of impact is risk management, for which dimensions such as eco-efficiency, the development of environmental products, protection of human rights, and a commitment to values and principles all have a strong positive impact. In other words, corporate responsibility is most likely to have a strong positive impact on intangible, rather than tangible, aspects of business performance.

Figure 6.2 also shows that there are as many areas on which corporate responsibility has a neutral or negative impact on business performance, as there are those on which there is a strong positive impact. Notably, the business case for engaging with business stakeholders appears weak and engaging with non-business stakeholders cannot be justified in terms of financial performance. Important dimensions of corporate responsibility, such as ethics and values, and protecting human rights, also have a neutral or negative relationship to financial performance measures, such as revenue, access to capital, and operational efficiency.

As SustainAbility's analysis readily recognizes, however, and as subsequent authors underline, in assessing the business case, we are often using data that are difficult to compare, drawn from a mixture of case studies and quantitative surveys, covering different industries and countries, and often focused on different dimensions of both corporate responsibility and business performance.[45] This partly accounts for why there is so little of what can be considered 'hard' evidence. In the SustainAbility study, 65 per cent of the data sources were categorized as providing weak evidence. Salzmann et al. (2005) conclude that making the business case encounters two stumbling blocks:

1 the complex web of parameters (e.g. technology, regulatory regime, company visibility) and variables (e.g. location, industry, country, time) that can affect outcomes;
2 the difficulty of detecting the impact of corporate responsibility, because, except in a small number of areas—notably, eco-efficiency and brand reputation—it tends to be marginal to business practice for most companies and industries.

As Margolis and Walsh (2003) conclude, in their extensive study of corporate social performance, there is little evidence to suggest that paying attention to societal impact damages shareholder value (although companies should not expect to be handsomely rewarded [Margolis et al., 2008]). Some argue that, given how little evidence there of damage to profitability, we should not be asking '*Does corporate responsibility pay?*', but rather '*Under what conditions does corporate responsibility pay?*'[46] This might mean explaining the specific conditions within a company or industry, but, more broadly, it might mean asking under what market conditions companies will maximize total value by taking account of stakeholder expectations.[47] In relation to the former issue, there are very few studies of how the business case drives corporate responsibility management and most research concentrates on how corporate responsibility affects business success. Regarding the latter, the relationship between corporate responsibility and the four conditions of perfect competition (i.e. a large number of buyers and sellers, complete information, homogeneity of products, and free entry and exit to and from the market), while alluded to by both advocates and critics of corporate responsibility,[48] has not been studied in depth.

It is a weakness in current business case literature that ways in which corporate responsibility might damage business performance are not properly explored. Corporate responsibility's critics like to make the case that it is anti-growth and that it therefore deprives people of the benefits of economic growth that, for example, have raised living standards in successful economies. There is no evidence that corporate responsibility is inherently anti-growth: on the contrary, some advocates of sustainable development say that serious economic growth is needed if we are to meet the needs of current and future generations, and some companies clearly see that addressing social and environmental issues in the future will provide growth opportunities.[49] But some companies, such as low-cost air carriers, would clearly suffer under tougher environmental norms, because air travel results in significantly higher greenhouse gas emissions than does travel by rail or sea.[50] Similarly, despite the instances of increased wages having been offset by productivity gains, it is counter-intuitive (and it therefore demands further examination) that increased labour costs due to corporate responsibility will never affect company growth.

As important, though, is that most current studies are unidirectional, focusing on how corporate responsibility affects business performance and ignoring the ways in which business performance may impact on corporate responsibility. Few companies, for example, have followed Patagonia's lead in disclosing the pros and cons of its products' social and environmental footprint, and providing the kind of information consumers would require one to make informed decisions about the performance-responsibility relationship.[51] This leaves unanswered questions such as to what extent does successful pursuit of revenue growth have a positive or negative effect on human rights or environmental management? As is explored further later in the text, in relation to criticisms of corporate responsibility (see Chapter 13), the implicit primacy given to the benefits for business is one of the concerns of some observers.

Not surprisingly, therefore, the evidence we have on the business case treats corporate responsibility as an instrumental benefit that can be divided into three types.[52]

1 Corporate responsibility as a means of avoiding financial loss (e.g. by defending a company's reputation).

2 Corporate responsibility as a driver of tangible financial gains (e.g. by improving the quality of the workforce, by driving product innovation).

3 Corporate responsibility as an integral element of the company's strategic approach to long-term business performance (e.g. by prompting a move away from dependence on non-renewable natural resources).[53]

Referring back to Martin's Virtues Matrix (p 140), some believe that a fourth type of business case is emerging, within which corporate responsibility is intrinsic to how companies learn, innovate, and manage risk in ever more dynamic and complex business environments (see Chapter 14). There is, however, limited evidence of a direct correlation between corporate responsibility and financial performance. In one study, News International had the worst corporate responsibility performance, but the best share price, while The Body Shop's good corporate responsibility reputation did not protect its share price when it suffered from poor management and may even have made it more susceptible to public criticism when it was exposed for making false claims about helping developing country suppliers.[54] Furthermore, the quest for a business case could hide the fact that other factors are at least as influential on corporate responsibility management decisions. For example, it has been argued that the widespread adoption of corporate responsibility reporting (see Chapter 12) is because of the readily recognizable analogies it has with financial reporting rather than demonstrable instrumental benefits.[55] Nonetheless, some companies, such as Monsanto, have suffered financially partly because of corporate responsibility failings, while others, such as Shell, have used corporate responsibility to rebuild a damaged image.[56] Perhaps the difficulty again lies in how the problem is framed and, rather than trying to demonstrate that corporate responsibility is a predictor or guarantee of certain outcomes, we should view it, for example, as an approach to strategy and management practice.[57]

■ Discussion points

Eco-efficiency is the main area in which a strong business case has been made, while reputation management is an important aspect of business performance.

- Can the success of eco-efficiency be attributed to corporate responsibility, or is it a case of rational profit maximization?
- In which industries do you think reputation is the main management driver of corporate responsibility?
- How would you make the case that corporate responsibility promises benefits to risk management?

CASE STUDY 6

Marks and Spencer's Plan A

Marks & Spencer was founded in 1884 in Leeds, England. A long-time fixture of British and Irish high streets, it has over 750 stores around the world and is the 43rd largest retailer. Its UK stories have 35,000 product lines and 75,000 employees, serving 21 million customers weekly. Ninety-nine per cent of its products are own-brand, sourced from 2,000 independently owned factories, and 20,000 farms that between them employ over a million workers.

Stuart Rose, Chair and former CEO, acknowledges that sustainability 'will shape everything about the way we do business.' This was not an overnight decision, but the result of a long journey. In 2000, M&S was experimenting with various ways to restore its company's reputation amongst consumers, investors, and the media after a chain of marketing and reputation failures.

Corporate responsibility was not high on the company's must-do list, and few onlookers would have noticed the recruitment of a new environmental manager as Group Finance Director Alison Reid's assistant with responsibility for the environment. But Reid, a long-time M&S employee, knew that the environment was becoming an issue for retailing, and had an inkling it would be a problem the company would need to address.

The new recruit, Mike Barry, had no line manager, and recalls the first two years as being like 'a guerrilla war.' Working alongside two existing heads of technology, it became apparent the company was out of touch with what was happening in its supply chains or amongst its consumers. It found itself caught out by scandals involving genetically modified foods and pesticide residues, and although there was no question of illegality, M&S found it hard to defend itself in the court of public opinion.

But the company's financial position was perilous, and although the need for change was apparent, radical action was out of the question. Instead, in keeping with the spirit of a guerrilla war, a number of low profile or off-the-radar actions were taken such as building internal alliances amongst people in the company with shared corporate responsibility concerns. Small initiatives were discovered across the company, and people from across the company were corralled in a common sense of purpose: something made possible because the new alliance involved people with an intimate knowledge of the firm and its suppliers. At the same time, M&S began to build external alliances with organizations such as Greenpeace, Friends of the Earth, and WWF.

A formal Head of Corporate Social Responsibility position was created overseeing two environmental specialists and two philanthropy specialists. But corporate responsibility did not save the company when results went from bad to worse in 2003. Profits which had exceeded £1 billion in 1998 were down to £145 million. However, against a bleak backdrop, corporate responsibility provided some of the few highlights with M&S winning awards in areas such as reducing pesticides and sustainable timber. When the company became embroiled in a hostile takeover bid in 2004, news that M&S had been chosen as the most responsible company in Britain was met with applause at a shareholder meeting.

In 2006, the company launched its Behind the Label campaign to inform consumers about the way M&S sources its products, a response to data showing that a third of shoppers had put clothes back on the rails amid concerns about their origins, and one in five had avoided food items because of concerns about sourcing and processing. In-store publicity and newspaper adverts talked about M&S's commitment to fairtrade and non-GM food, as well as moves to cut salt and fat in foods, promote sustainability, recycle packaging, and protect animal welfare. Publicly, Behind the Label was treated as a toe in the water: 'We'll see how it goes,' said Stuart Rose to the BBC, 'Let's test the market.' But inside the company any sense of smugness disappeared when Rose told the corporate responsibility team Behind the Label was already 'old news.' As Barry recalls it, Rose told the team they would be out of a job if in three months' time they were still doing Behind the Label: it was time to move on.

That was the spur for Plan A. The alliance of guerrillas that had come together in 2001 had become more formalized, commissioned by the CEO, and containing the directors of technology and communications, and the head of marketing. But the members were essentially the same, and they brainstormed about the social and environmental dimensions to M&S's operations, and what the company could do to have a positive impact. They eventually decided on 100 priority items based on the company's impact, estimates of the cost of taking action, and an assessment of what the competition was doing about these issues. In many instances, nobody knew what the solution would look like, but insiders felt that the risk taking culture they saw as part of the retail culture meant it was more important to know what needed to be done than to know if it could be done.

The 100 priorities became the 100 commitments contained in what was called Plan A, launched in January 2007 to enormous media and public attention. In part this was because in addition to full page adverts and in-store promotion, but it also mattered that Stuart Rose was willing to tell the Plan A story to anyone who would listen: that M&S was committed to becoming 'The greenest—genuinely the greenest—retailer in the UK by 2012.' Timing also played its part, as Rose himself stressed: 'No one had announced a big initiative up until then, and we wanted to be the first. ... I'm not going to deny, if you get it right, [being first gives] you a competitive advantage.' Two days after Plan A's launch, a competitor announced its climate change strategy. It received muted applause, along with criticism for not being up to Plan A.

There 100 commitments are divided under the five pillars of Plan A. Each has targets to which M&S is willing to be accountable, and each year it reveals its progress. Together M&S managers believe the pillars cover what the retail industry needs to cover at this time. Says Barry, '[Competitors] will have to take the same pillars and try to better our performance. But the 100 targets are already challenging enough: going beyond them right now would be commercial suicide.'

Responsibility for Plan A is now split between two teams: one under the Director of Communications and CSR focused on policy and responsible for engagement, strategic direction, problem-solving, and communications support; the other comprising successful M&S line mangers focused on delivery, and responsible for project management, integration, and making the business case (see Figure 6.3). Together, the two teams are tasked with making sure Plan A is

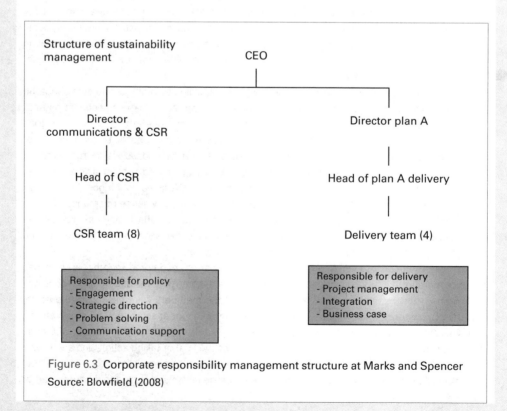

Figure 6.3 Corporate responsibility management structure at Marks and Spencer
Source: Blowfield (2008)

implemented throughout the business lines: not by the team members themselves, but as part of everyday operations so that it is treated not as a sustainability strategy, but as a business plan, part of a five pronged business strategy that also includes building the M&S brand, international expansion, internet expansion, etc.

(Sources: Mesure, 2007; Rose, 2007; Vernon, 2007; **www.marksandspencer.com**; author interviews)

Questions

1 M&S provides insight into how corporate responsibility evolves within a company.

    a What are the major differences in the M&S approach now compared to 2000?

    b Why did Rose feel it essential to move beyond Behind the Label?

    c What does the Plan A management structure indicate about M&S's commitment to embedding corporate responsibility in the company?

2 Plan A has been described as setting the bar on corporate responsibility for retailing.

    a What evidence is there that Plan A is more than a PR exercise?

    b Are there responsibility issues in retailing that Plan A does not address?

    c What evidence is there of a business case for Plan A?

3 Plan A ends in 2012, and M&S is now looking at what to do next.

    a What are the key management lessons to learn from implementing Plan A?

    b How do you think M&S's commitments are likely to change after 2012?

    c How do you think sustainability issues could make retailing look different in 2020 compared to today?

SUMMARY

Managing corporate responsibility in companies is a form of change management, and like other types of corporate transformation, corporate responsibility management activity is divided between: identifying the purpose and intended results; establishing the principles and processes to achieve the end goal; and allocating responsibility for its execution.

Companies find themselves at different stages of corporate responsibility that affect what the company wants to achieve and how to go about it. There are important distinctions to be made between defensive approaches to corporate responsibility, which are focused on reducing risks, protecting the company's reputation, and ensuring that it stays within the law, and offensive approaches, which employ corporate assets in finding solutions to societal problems. These approaches can be broken down further into evolutionary levels of responsibility, beginning with a focus on creating jobs, paying taxes, and abiding by the law, and eventually reaching a stage at which values are clearly at the heart of business decisions, the company is transparent about what it is doing, not doing, and hoping to do, and sees part of its role as standing out as a leader in tackling societal issues.

The further one gets from starting to implement corporate responsibility, the more difficult it becomes to state hard and fast rules for execution. While there is a consensus that good practice involves elements such consulting internally and externally to decide the purpose, engaging with those upon whom the company impacts or by whom it is influenced as part of the management process, and communicating what the company is trying to achieve and the progress it is making, structuring the management function, building awareness and capacity, and deciding what actions to take will vary according to the company's culture, its industry, the regions it operates in, and the resources available. Another set of challenges emerges when companies take responsibility for the behaviour of their suppliers and others in their value chains, requiring the development of additional management styles and approaches, as companies committed to corporate responsibility seek out ways of improving others' performance, not least by exerting their own power as customers.

FURTHER READING

**VISIT THE
WEBSITE**
for links to useful
sources of further
information

Take your learning further: Online Resource Centre **www.oxfordtextbooks.co.uk/orc/blowfield_
murray2e/**

Visit the Online Resource Centre which accompanies this book to enrich your understanding of this chapter.

Students: explore web links and further reading suggestions. Keep up to date with the latest developments by undertaking web exercises.

Lecturers: you will find additional case studies, for use in class or assessment. Show your students trailers from films related to Corporate Responsibility, and use images from the book in your PowerPoint slides.

- Ethical Trading Initiative, 2006, *Ethical Trade: A Comprehensive Guide for Companies*, 2nd edn, London: Ethical Trading Initiative.

  Manager-oriented handbook on the different facets of monitoring labour practices in global supply chains.

- Hennigfeld, J, Pohl, M and Tolhurst, N (eds), 2006, *The ICCA Handbook on Corporate Social Responsibility*, Chichester: John Wiley and Sons.

  Collection of papers on the meaning and management of corporate responsibility, targeted at corporate managers.

- Holliday, CO, Schmidheiny, S, Watts, P, 2002, *Walking the Talk: The Business Case for Sustainable Development*, Sheffield: Greenleaf Publishing.

  Influential argument by European executives emphasizing the importance of sustainable development to business success.

- Werther, WB and Chandler, D, 2010, *Strategic Corporate Social Responsibility: Stakeholders in a Global Environment*, 2nd edn, Thousand Oaks, CA: Sage.

  Aspects of the business case for stakeholder engagement and other corporate responsibility management practices.

- Zadek, S, 2004, 'The path to corporate responsibility (best practice)', *Harvard Business Review*, 82(12), pp 125–33.

  Evolutionary model of corporate responsibility, based on the experience of Nike.

ENDNOTES

[1] Maitland, 2006.

[2] For a detailed comparison of country differences in Europe, see www.csreurope.org/pages/en/a_guide_to_csr_in_europe_2009.html, accessed 14 February 2010.

[3] E.g. Visser and Tolhurst, 2010.

[4] European Commission, 2002.

[5] PWC, 2006.

[6] Cited in Kramer and Kania, 2006.

[7] Holliday et al., 2002, p 27.

[8] Quinn, 2009; Hale, 2009.

[9] See, e.g. Schwartz and Gibb, 1999; Holliday et al., 2002, pp 142–9; Jackson and Nelson, 2004; Werther and Chandler, 2006.

[10] Zadek, 2004; www.nike.com/nikebiz—accessed August 1 2006.

[11] *PR News*, 2006.

[12] Ethical Performance, 2008

[13] PWC, 2006.

[14] See for instance www.angloamerican.co.uk/aa/development/approach/ and www.gesi.org

[15] BSR, 2002.

[16] CCC, 2005a.

[17] CCC, 2005a.

[18] CCC, 2005b.

[19] BSR, 2002.

[20] CCC, 2005c.

[21] Melcrum, 2005.

[22] Harwood and Humby, 2007 and 2008.

[23] PWC, 2006.

[24] Jahdi and Acikdilli, 2009; Bowd et al., 2006; Weybrecht, 2009.

[25] This section draws on Holliday et al., 2002; Olsen, 2004; Werther and Chandler, 2006. The authors are also very grateful to Steve Rochlin at AccountAbility for his ideas on this topic.

[26] Stewart and Immelt, 2006.

[27] Email announcing launch of Creating Shared Value, sent from webmaster@nestle.com, 27 April 2009.

[28] *Ethical Corporation* and Nima Hunter Inc, 2003.

[29] See, e.g. Pinkse and Kolk, 2009, pp 79–85, on the business case for disclosing information relevant to climate change.

[30] See, e.g. Hawkins, 2006.

[31] Healy, 2008.

[32] Vogel, 2005; www.ford.com/sustainability; Fitzpatrick, 2004; www.corporatewatch.org; ETI, undated; Porter and Van der Linde, 1995.

[33] Innovest and Environment Agency, 2004.

[34] www.bt.co.uk—accessed 25 August 2005.

[35] Willard, 2002.

[36] See, e.g., Margolis and Walsh, 2003; Salzmann et al., 2005; Schuler and Cording, 2006.

[37] Zadek, 2000.

[38] Zadek, 2000.

[39] Zadek, 2000.

[40] Based on categories in Zadek, 2000; SustainAbility and UNEP, 2001; Zadek et al., 2003.

[41] Salzmann et al., 2005.

[42] SustainAbility and UNEP, 2002. The 2002 study uses a somewhat simplified matrix, so that direct comparisons of categories with the 2001 study are not always possible. The term 'business measures' has been changed to 'business success factors', and the number examined reduced to six from ten. The areas of sustainability and corporate responsibility have been reduced from ten to seven, with 'Ethics, values, and principles', 'Human rights', and 'Working conditions' being removed. Some other areas have been reworded without appearing to change the meaning.

[43] See SustainAbility and UNEP, 2002, p 31 for specific figures on developing economies.

[44] Porter and Van der Linde, 1995.

[45] Margolis and Walsh, 2003; Barnett and Salomon, 2006; Salzmann et al, 2005.

[46] Zadek et al., 2005; Amalric and Hauser, 2005.

[47] Amalric and Hauser, 2005.

[48] See, e.g., Holliday et al., 2002; Henderson, 2001.

[50] Holliday et al., 2002.

[51] Zadek et al., 2005.

[52] Zadek et al., 2003.

[53] Zadek, 2000.

[54] Zadek, 2000; Hopkins, 2003.

[55] Etzion et al, 2009.

[56] ABI, 2001.

[57] Zadek et al., 2005.

7

The place of corporate responsibility in the corporate governance framework

Chapter overview

Following the global financial meltdown in 2008/9, calls for better governance and greater responsibility were heard in equal measure from governments, policymakers, the media, and the public. In this chapter, we explore the connection between governance and responsibility by tracing the development of corporate governance frameworks as they evolved, prompted, in no small way, by previous scandals.

Traditional approaches to corporate governance always place the shareholder, as the 'owner' of the business, at the centre of the accountability relationship, and protection of investment as the primary goal. We examine this model and consider thereafter, how and whether it might be adapted to offer greater levels of accountability to a wider group of stakeholders. In particular, we will:

- examine what is meant by 'corporate governance';

- explore the theories of corporate governance;

- consider the 'drivers' of corporate governance;

- trace the development of the UK corporate governance framework;

- examine international developments in corporate governance.

Main topics

■ **Key terms**

Accountability

Auditing

Stakeholder engagement

Corporate governance framework

Corporate malfeasance

■ **Online resources**

• Suggested additional information on corporate governance worldwide

• Discussion topics for students

• Case studies and exercises on corporate governance

• Links to other web-based resources

What is 'corporate governance'?

In Chapter 2, we discussed the reasons for the move away from proprietor-run businesses to the limited company form of enterprise. We noted that this practice became the favoured route as businesses became larger and greater capital was required than could be easily raised by an individual or even in a partnership. The issuing of shares made it possible to reach a much wider investment community and therefore easier to raise larger amounts of money.

In turn however, the investor, whether an individual or an institution such as a bank or a pension fund, will expect that their funds are handled with care and invested in such a way that, in due course, they will receive a return on their investment. But how do they know what managers are going to do with their cash? What structures are there in place to ensure that managers do not invest in risky projects, or simply squander the investors' money on a lavish expense-account lifestyle? Above all, in the context of corporate responsibility, how does corporate governance relate to the behaviour of companies and serve to encourage, restrict, or otherwise shape their relationship with wider society? In a corporate world in which optimum profit is the measure of success and reward, is there room for any notion of social responsibility?

In this chapter, corporate governance will be examined from the perspective of both the shareholders and their *agents* (i.e. company directors and managers). How frameworks of corporate governance have developed will be contrasted with the continuing scandal of corporate collapse and fraud. The role of the auditor will be examined, to see if there is more that the audit process can contribute to good corporate governance in the face of persistent criticism from some quarters.

■ Key concept

Corporate Governance: 'deals with the ways in which suppliers of finance to corporations assure themselves of getting a return on their investment'.

(Source: Shleifer and Vishney 1997)

Our primary focus is on governance as it applies to listed companies and we have especially highlighted the situation in the UK. We have made this choice because the Anglo-Saxon notion of the firm, with the primacy it grants to investors and the role of capital markets, while not universal, has come to epitomize the efficiency and hazard of the modern company. It is also the case that the UK model of governance structures has been replicated in many other countries. We shall, however, examine international guidelines, developed to aid countries seeking to bring their own systems in line with international norms.

Theories of corporate governance

Although there are exceptions, most large companies are not run by their legal owners; rather, they are run on behalf of the owners by a board of directors and by a management structure that is intended to best serve the interests of the owners. Definitions of corporate governance invariably reflect this owner–agent relationship, and focus on issues of control and accountability in this context.

Agency theory articulates some of the conflicts of interest that must exist between an agent and owner if agents are predisposed to act in a self-interested manner. It is easy to imagine how this might manifest itself in actual situations in which a manager might pursue policies that owners may not consider to be in their best interests. What, then, can shareholders do to ensure that managers return some of the profits and manage their investments carefully?

One frequently-quoted definition of corporate governance states simply that it '*deals with the ways in which suppliers of finance to corporations assure themselves of getting a return on their investment'.*[1] This very narrow definition predicates a huge volume of research in the field of accounting and finance, and is vigorously defended when criticism is made that, for example, it omits the interests of all other stakeholder groups.[2] This shareholder emphasis is shared in many other influential definitions and discussions. The OECD, for example, broadens the scope slightly, but still maintains a strong shareholder focus:

> A good corporate governance regime helps to assure that corporations use their capital efficiently … (and) … to ensure that corporations take into account the interests of a wide range of constituencies, as well as of the communities within which they operate, and that their boards are accountable to the company and the shareholders.
>
> *(OECD, 1999)*

Although some theorists argue that it is enough to recognize and manage stakeholder groups, others believe that companies need to be accountable to them even though they may have no financial interest in the firm. Stakeholder accountability is highly contentious and its position in corporate responsibility is contested, but to understand how it has won a place in the development of governance structures, we need to consider the events that have brought calls for changes in corporate governance during the last two decades.

■ Discussion points

Directors of companies owe certain fiduciary duties to the owners of the companies.

- How far should a 'duty of care' include social and environmental responsibilities?
- What steps can directors take to demonstrate that they are taking their fiduciary duties seriously in respect of ethical issues?
- Referring to such work as that of Kent Greenfield (2006) and Corporation 2020, what key features would you want to see in an alternative governance framework?

The 'drivers' of corporate governance reform

Over the last 20 years, a number of interconnecting events have combined to keep up pressure for changes in the way in which corporations are managed and regulated. To understand how some of these changes have come about, it is useful, first, to consider the changing nature of corporate activity in the last few decades—in particular, corporate ownership and the seeming rise in malfeasance.

Changing ownership structure

The size and scope of companies has obviously increased over this period, often by merger and acquisition but additionally, the mix of ownership has altered. The Office for

National Statistics (ONS) has a detailed analysis of classes of owners of equity in UK-listed companies dating back to 1963. The statistics are now updated bi-annually, and in the table below (see Box 7.1), we have reproduced the figures for 1963 alongside more up to date figures including the most recent set available, from 2008, as this edition goes to press. If we examine the figures over that period, we can see clearly a number of trends. Firstly, there is a significant shift to foreign ownership. From a modest 7 per cent in 1963 there was a gentle upward trend until 1990, when the figure was still only 11.8 per cent, but in the 1990s foreign ownership almost trebled to 32.4 per cent, and by 2008 stood at 41.5 per cent. If this trend continues at the present rate, soon over 50 per cent of UK listed companies will be foreign owned. Public sector share ownership rose from 0.1 per cent in 2000 to 1.1 per cent in 2008, possibly a result of the reduction in interest rates which followed the banking crisis in the autumn of 2008. However, perhaps the most interesting trend, is the decline in individual share ownership which more than halved between 1963 and 1990, from 54 per cent to 20.3 per cent and has halved again since, to just 10.2 per cent. It may be that individuals find it easier to buy more convenient investment products from banks and other institutions, rather than be bothered with dealing in equities.

Box 7.1 Summary of share ownership in the UK 1963–2008

Category of Investor	1963	1990	2000	2004	2008
Rest of the world	7.0	11.8	32.4	32.6	41.5
Insurance companies	10.0	20.4	21.0	17.2	13.4
Pension funds	6.4	31.7	17.7	15.7	12.8
Individuals	54.0	20.3	16.0	14.1	10.2
Unit trusts	1.3	6.1	1.7	1.9	1.8
Investment trusts	0.0	1.6	2.1	3.3	1.9
Financial institutions	11.3	1.1	4.6	10.7	10.0
Charities	2.1	2.3	1.4	1.1	0.8
Non-financial institutions	5.1	3.8	1.5	0.6	3.0
Public sector	1.5	2.0	0.0	0.1	1.1
Banks	1.3	0.7	1.4	2.7	3.5

(Source: The Office for National Statistics; **www.statistics.gov.uk/StatBase/Product.asp?vlnk=930**)

These changes in share ownership have a number of implications for the governance of companies. Firstly, it is not always clear who the beneficial owner is, and therefore transparency in regard to ownership of shares may be obfuscated for any number of reasons, most of which have governance implications. Secondly, we might assume that foreign owners may not be as keen as UK owners to curb activities seen as damaging to the UK perhaps in terms of social or environmental stewardship. It may also be that foreign owners may not be as aware as UK nationals of the potential role for shareholders in governance structures.

Corporate collapse and malfeasance

While it is true to say that there is a long history of corporate failure going back at least as far as the South Sea Bubble of 1718, the events in the latter part of the twentieth century brought sustained calls for increased regulation of companies to protect investors. In the UK in the 1980s, there were a number of high-profile collapses, culminating with the scandals involving media tycoon Robert Maxwell (see Snapshot 7.1), and the Bank of Credit and Commerce International (BCCI; see ORC). which had revealed systematic failure in governance, and the use of dubious accounting techniques aimed at hiding liabilities, amplifying assets, and massaging profits' (Mitchell et al., 1991, Mitchell & Sikka, 2005, Sikka et al., 2007). Following the death of Robert Maxwell in November 1991, it soon became clear that similar issues were to be the focus of further damaging publicity for the financial regulators and the corporate governance framework.

SNAPSHOT 7.1

The legacy of Robert Maxwell

After an eventful military career during WW2 Robert Maxwell became involved in the business of scientific publishing and later founded Pergamon Press, starting an empire that had the Maxwell Communication Company (MCC) and Mirror Group Newspapers (MGN). By the time of his death, Maxwell had additionally built up a myriad of some 400 subsidiary companies owned by a Gibraltar trust company, and another 400 by a Charitable Foundation registered in Lichtenstein. The flow of funds between these companies—what became known as the 'public' and the 'private' sides of the business—was at the heart of the governance issue. Despite warning signs, Maxwell continued to form companies and move assets (usually cash) between the public and private sides, depending on where it was needed most.

Following the purchase of MGN, he embarked on a series of business ventures which plunged him into such massive debt that, by 1991, it was beginning to attract the attention of the financial press, and was being financed by massive movements of cash between companies and on day-to-day currency dealings.

It was only after his death that the full story began to unravel and the recriminations began. Failures were identified in the abilities of the existing regulatory bodies to draw connections between all of Maxwell's various companies and in the abilities of the regulators to instigate investigations. Non-executive directors were also accused of failing to inform the boards of those cash transfers about which they knew. The pension fund trustees were blamed for inaction, the stock exchange was blamed for failing to supervise the conduct of his listed companies, and the Serious Fraud Office was blamed for failing to start an investigation until pressured by a Swiss bank. In addition, each company had received a clean audit report from its auditors.

(Sources: Bower, 1988; 1996; Clarke, 1993; HMSO, 1971)

Quick questions

1 Would the separation of CEO and Chairman roles prevented this scandal?

2 Would following the Combined Code have prevented this?

3 Could the intervention of institutional investors have prevented this?

The development of the UK corporate governance framework

The Cadbury Committee became, in fact, only the first of a series of committees that have examined and reported on aspects of corporate governance over the last 20 years and it is now part of an ongoing process that seems set to evolve and continue into the future. What follows is a summary of the steps taken on the initiative of a variety of agencies, each with a sometimes specific, and at other times overlapping, interest in particular aspects of governance. The early initiatives were responses to specific 'shocks' to the financial systems, but later on in the process, there appears to have been a much more coordinated approach to the codes of conduct that were developed, and this trend continues.

The Cadbury Report (1992)

In response to the grave concerns about the general sinking confidence in financial reporting, auditing, and corporate governance, the Financial Reporting Council (FRC), the London Stock Exchange (LSE), and the Consultative Committee of Accountancy Bodies (CCAB) convened a committee to consider '*the financial aspects of corporate governance*'. The committee met under the chairmanship of Sir Adrian Cadbury. It met in May 1991 and was charged to consider:

> aspects of corporate governance ... the way in which boards set financial policy and oversee its implementation, including the use of financial controls, and the processes whereby they report on the activities and progress of the company to the shareholders.
>
> *(Cadbury, 1992, p 13)*

It took the form of a 'code of conduct' for companies. It recommended that company boardrooms be constituted in such a way that they would feature appropriate sub-committees dealing with matters of remuneration, audit, and nomination, with independent non-executive directors and, more crucially, a separation in the roles and functions of the CEO and the chairman. At the time, there was some debate about whether to make the recommendations compulsory but, in a trend that continues today, companies were eventually asked to comply with the recommendations in a voluntary way. Indeed, the Cadbury Report is widely regarded as the pioneer of the voluntary approach that has become the model for other internationally recognized governance codes.[3]

In the following five years new committees were formed in response to continuing criticism of corporate behaviour. The Greenbury Report (1995) looked into the salaries of directors, who were being labelled 'fat cats'. The recommendation, again voluntary, was that the remuneration committee should comprise non-executive directors, who would report annually on policy and disclose full details of the remuneration packages of the directors. Since the Greenbury Report, a feature of the company annual report has been the detailed level of disclosure on all aspects of directors' remuneration, with valuation of such items as stock options and pension contributions. This was followed by the Hampel Report (1998) which looked at how such voluntary codes were being implemented. A number of companies had decided not to implement the Cadbury recommendations for various reasons and, once again, the behaviour of corporate boards choosing this course of action came in for criticism.

This theme is discussed further below, when all of the codes of governance are analysed through the lens of corporate responsibility, but other recommendations that had far-reaching implications were that, first, there should be increased dialogue between companies and their institutional investors, and, second, that institutional investors should consider using their votes to influence company policy wherever possible. At the same time as Hampel was reporting, an initiative of the LSE aiming to consolidate the three previous codes was published. The Combined Code (1998), as its name suggests, tabulates the recommendations of the three previous committees in terms of the responsibilities of companies, on the one hand, and institutional investors, on the other. All of the issues of remuneration, audit, shareholder relations, etc., are covered. It is appended to the Listing Rules of the London Stock Exchange—now the Listing Rules of the Financial Services Authority (FSA).[4] The 'comply or explain' principle of reporting, first mentioned by Cadbury, was reinforced in the Combined Code, which laid down, in unusually prescriptive form, the requirement to report any deviation from the code.[5] A year later, The Turnbull Committee was convened by the ICAEW to give guidance specifically on issues of internal control that were highlighted in the Combined Code as being of particular importance. The subsequent report first outlined existing procedures, then made recommendations for improving internal control systems.

All of this activity led the 1990s to be referred to by commentators, such as Charkham (2005), as 'the decade of corporate governance'. Yet despite this concerted effort on the part of interested parties, from the stock exchanges to the accountancy profession, to improve systems and thus avoid further criticism, corporate scandals continued. The fall of Barings Bank in 1995 had sent further shock waves through the financial world, but it was the collapse of Enron and Worldcom in the USA that, again, led to calls for further attention. The once-dormant proposal of two US legislators became the most far-reaching (and hastily passed) piece of governance legislation—the Sarbanes–Oxley Act 2002. It was felt that that the role being played by non-executive directors was not robust enough in terms of ensuring good practice and governance. Additionally, further criticism was levelled at the accountancy profession for what appeared to be a continuing inability to uncover signals of underlying corporate distress or malfeasance. This led to a flurry of activity to try, once again, to develop systems of governance that would be sufficient to prevent further scandals.

Three more committees sat in the UK before a revised Combined Code was published in 2003. The first of these committees was the result of the UK government wishing to extend the remit of its Company Law Review and an acknowledgement of the globalization of financial markets. It was probably the first time that the collapse of a company in one country precipitated such a wide-ranging enquiry in another. The subsequent report of the Higgs Committee (2003) dealt with the responsibilities of non-executive directors, with recommendations that '*at least half the board*' should be made up of non-executive directors and that they should be paid at a rate commensurate with the additional responsibility. At the same time as the Higgs Committee was sitting, the government asked the FRC to consider the particular role of audit committees within the governance framework and the relationship that they should have with the company's external auditor.

The committee, under Sir Robert Smith, reported in January 2003 and had a number of specific points to address, mostly to do with the role of the audit committee within the overall board structure. The Smith Report reinforced the belief that accounting firms needed to be careful in deciding which services to offer to a company if they were also conducting its audit. For many, this recommendation did not go far enough, because pressure for more fundamental reforms to the audit industry was resisted.

In 2003, the DTI commissioned a further report into 'the Recruitment of Non-Executive Directors. This Report was in answer to a call made in the Higgs Report that the recruitment and composition of the boards of non-executive directors should be subject of a separate examination. The Dean of the London Business School, Laura D'Andrea Tyson chaired the committee. The Tyson (2003) Report called for greater diversity but fell short of the idea that lists of qualified individuals should be compiled, from which non-executives could be drawn. Once again, the report was in an advisory capacity, and was given little notice. It seemed to call for a similar approach to a US initiative to recruit more women to the boardroom, but seems not to have captured the imagination this side of the Atlantic.

The Combined Code 2003, (Revised 2008)

The 1998 Combined Code was revised, to take account of the various recommendations, and published in July 2003. Companies were expected to implement its recommendations for financial years beginning after November 2003. The Code is now to be reviewed and updated on a regular basis, and a revised Code was published in 2007, with the next revision scheduled to take effect from 2011. The Code is based on the notion that all companies *should* wish to be governed in 'the best interests of shareholders', and that good governance 'should facilitate efficient, effective and entrepreneurial management that can deliver shareholder value over the longer term' (Combined Code, 2008, p 1). In its preamble, the rationale for the Code is explained with an emphasis that it 'is not a rigid set of rules', rather a 'guide to good practice', where it is expected that companies will comply 'wholly or substantially' with its provisions. Significantly, however, for listed companies on the London Stock Exchange, Listing Rules require companies to describe in their annual reports their corporate governance from two points of view, 'the first dealing generally with their adherence to the Code's main principles, and the second dealing specifically with non-compliance with any of the Code's provisions' (Combined Code, 2008, p 1). What this means is that a listed company is expected to comply with the Code unless it takes the explicit stance of non-compliance, in which case it must explain the reasons to shareholders. This doctrine of 'comply or explain' is now central to the nature of the non-regulatory stance taken towards corporate governance in the UK.

■ Discussion points

Codes of corporate governance have developed to include supervision of audit procedures.

- How effective can an audit committee be in supervising the audit procedure within a major corporation?
- Can part-time non-executive directors ever be adequately effective?
- Using the example of a FTSE 100 company, how would you modify the workings of the audit committee to incorporate corporate responsibility issues?

International developments in corporate governance

It will come as little surprise that over the last decade there has been a convergence of international codes to mirror the needs of companies which are increasingly operating across boundaries, and in many different corporate formations. The accounting bodies developed International Financial Reporting Standards (IFRSs), and an examination of some of the international corporate governance guidelines suggests a similar trend. Eastern European countries which previously conformed to Soviet accounting rules, first established their own 'Accounting Acts' but as time passes so the influence of IFRSs grows, and homogenization of corporate governance rules seems also to be the trend. However, insofar as it is expected that companies will observe the somewhat prescriptive nature of the IFRSs; all corporate governance codes are explicitly 'guidelines'. Indeed, in the preamble to the *OECD Principles of Corporate Governance*, it states:

> The Principles are non-binding and do not aim at detailed prescriptions for national legislation. Rather, they seek to identify objectives and suggest various means for achieving them. Their purpose is to serve as a reference point.

(p 13)

In keeping with the discussions we have had on the development of UK guidelines, so the OECD principles are concerned with 'transparent and efficient markets', 'protecting and facilitating the exercise of shareholder rights', 'timely and accurate disclosure', etc. It does, however, explicitly recognize the rights of stakeholders when they have been 'established by law or through mutual agreements', and

> encourage active co-operation between corporations and stakeholders in creating wealth, jobs, and the sustainability of financially sound enterprises

(p 21)

In 2009, the ICGN revised its *Global Corporate Governance Principles* with a view that they should be of 'general application around the world, irrespective of legislative background or listing rules'.[6] The ICGN is a global membership organisation comprising, in the main, institutional investors who clearly have an interest in good governance. Their Principles whilst in essence espousing similar approaches to corporate governance as the other codes we have described, also provide additional practical help and direction to those wanting to implement best practice.

As emerging economies seek to develop capital markets to encourage inward investment and joint venture arrangements, so corporate governance structures increasingly come under examination. In countries like China, where there is also a conflict between the traditional command economy model and the new free-market approach, transition to that model is problematic, and many institutional obstacles still exist.

■ Discussion points

Corporate governance frameworks are not drawn up with corporate responsibility as a guiding structure.

- How would they differ if corporate responsibility were to become a major consideration?
- What changes would need to be made to the legal framework to incorporate corporate responsibility issues?
- What examples can you find from around the world (historical and contemporary) of legislative attempts to incorporate corporate responsibility into governance frameworks?

Commentary on governance codes from a corporate responsibility perspective

It is clear that corporate collapses are not only of concern to government, professional bodies, investors, and the public at large, but that various agencies have worked in a coordinated way to try to refine mechanisms of governance and to try to minimize the probability of future crises. The language of governance has changed, as is evident, for example, in the Hampel Report's acknowledgement of stakeholder interests. At the same time, the language of governance has been adopted by corporate responsibility, notably the widespread use of terms such as 'accountability' and 'transparency' in corporate responsibility reports, as guiding features of the required procedures.

■ **Discussion points**

A number of governance initiatives offer companies the opportunity to adopt voluntarily certain standards of conduct.

* Can voluntary codes ever be effective?

* Can a case be made for regulation?

* From the perspective of a financial journalist ten years from now, write an article about the effect that the EU Accounts Modernization Directive or the UK Companies Act will have had on the way in which companies are governed.

SNAPSHOT 7.2

Company Law Reform—the Companies Act 2006

For many who had campaigned for wider changes in company law reform the early signs were encouraging, but on publication there was criticism that social and environmental responsibilities had been relegated to no more than 'a consideration'. Parts of the Act are reproduced below:

s. 172 Duty to promote the success of the company

(1) A director of a company must act in the way he considers, in good faith, would be most likely to promote the success of the company for the benefit of its members as a whole, and in doing so have regard (amongst other matters) to—

* the need to foster the company's business relationships with suppliers, customers and others,

* the impact of the company's operations on the community and the environment.

We can note here that the directors owe a duty 'to promote the success of the company' for the benefit of 'its members' (shareholders) and 'have regard' to the company's impact in social and environmental terms. However, a closer examination of s. 417 of the Act, which deals with the Directors Report: Business Review, reveals that in the case of quoted companies the following applies:

(5) In the case of a quoted company the business review must, to the extent necessary for an understanding of the development, performance or position of the company's business, include information about—

* environmental matters (including the impact of the company's business on the environment),

* social and community issues, including information about any policies of the company in relation to those matters and the effectiveness of those policies. . .

(Source: **www.statutelaw.gov.uk/**)

Quick questions

1 How does company law relate to corporate governance structures, and which has precedence?

2 What steps should a company take to demonstrate compliance with s. 172 of the Companies Act 2006?

3 Where can a company find guidance or a framework which would help it to comply with the provisions of s. 417 of the Act?

'Meaningful stakeholder engagement'

As discussion of stakeholder management in Chapter 9 shows engaging with stakeholders is an important part of how corporate responsibility is managed—but there is an enormous difference between taking the views of shareholders into consideration and being accountable to them in any meaningful way. Writers on the subject of corporate governance, who are prepared to acknowledge the challenges that corporate responsibility poses to the traditional view of corporate governance still fall short, in most cases, from suggesting that the corporate governance agenda should change, Charkham (2005) talks about being accountable to shareholders and *'taking into account'* the views of stakeholders. Even Kiernan (2005), when calling for *'dramatic changes in the thought process and actions of company directors, executives, and institutional investors'* (p 216), focuses on the *'business case'* for altering course, based on assessments of balance sheet, operational, capital cost, and other *'risks'*.

Companies with strong corporate responsibility reputations are by no means immune to charges of abusing governance processes, and, while organizations such as CERES and Corporation 2020 have demonstrated the link between corporate governance and corporate responsibility, for the most part, the gaps between what many stakeholders would consider good governance and the priorities of mainstream corporate responsibility practice ultimately pose a threat to the credibility of corporate responsibility as a concept.

■ Discussion points

Most codes of corporate governance stress the importance of shareholders over other stakeholders.

• What groups of stakeholders might have particular interests in issues of corporate governance?

• What is the difference between stakeholder engagement and stakeholder management?

• Imagining that you are an activist shareholder: how would you argue for greater stakeholder representation in the company's governance structures?

CASE STUDY 7

The CORE Coalition

The Corporate Responsibility (CORE) Coalition strives to improve UK companies' impacts on people and the environment. The Corporate Responsibility (CORE) Coalition has over 130 members including representatives from ethical businesses, womens' groups, religious groups, unions, academics and environment, development and human rights groups. The Corporate Responsibility (CORE) Coalition's work is lead by a steering group of Amnesty International UK, Action Aid, Friends of the Earth, TraidCraft, War on Want and WWF (GB). The Corporate Responsibility (CORE) Coalition's members believe that in order to improve how UK companies behave, there is a need for:

1 greater transparency of business operations;

2 better accountability of businesses for their impacts on people and the environment;

3 improved access to justice for victims of harmful corporate conduct.

They campaign for stronger regulation on corporate governance and company law reform. Present activities include:

1 UK Commission for Business, Human Rights & The Environment

The UK is a key player in the global economy and UK based companies can have a positive impact in terms of reducing poverty overseas. However, some UK companies have been involved in human rights abuses and/or significant environmental damage through their overseas operations. Currently there is a lack of both authoritative guidance for companies to avoid such negative impacts, as well as for solutions and accountability when such breaches occur. This void creates greater risk for people, the environment, and businesses—as well as the UK's reputation as a whole. Better systems need to be introduced to ensure all UK companies respect human rights and protect the environment when operating abroad.

CORE proposes the establishment of a new body in the UK to help guide UK companies towards best practice when operating overseas and prevent harmful impacts to people and the environment. The Commission could also help resolve disputes between companies and those affected by the companies' activities, promoting solutions when harm had been done. This body would have the effect of reducing violations of environmental and human rights standards related to UK companies' operations abroad, and help those companies improve their corporate conduct globally.

Key objectives of a UK Commission for Business, Human Rights and The Environment:

• provide redress for overseas victims of human rights abuses involving UK companies

• promote appropriate environmental and human rights standards for UK companies operating overseas and promulgate best practice

• work with other human rights commissions and relevant bodies to share learning and build their collective capacity to strengthen the effectiveness of redress in developing countries

2 The Companies Act 2006

The Corporate Responsibility (CORE) Coalition were instrumental in securing changes to company law, helping to improve the impacts of UK companies on people and the environment. The

Corporate Responsibility (CORE) Coalition helped ensure that The Companies Act (2006) now means that:

- company directors must consider the environmental and social impacts of their decisions
- the largest public companies have to annually report on their environmental and social impacts.

However, these requirements only require the company to consider environmental and social issues it considers are material. The Corporate Responsibility (CORE) Coalition believes these obligations would be much more effective if further changes were made.

(Source: original research; **www.corporate-responsibility.org/recent-news/**)

Questions

1 Company Law has traditionally been the preserve of policymakers and parliamentarians, yet active lobbying by NGOs like CORE seems to have influenced policy in this case.

    a What role should NGOs have in role in shaping company law reform?

    b What other NGOs are concerned with changes to company regulation and governance?

    c How might NGOs collaborate more effectively to achieve specific reforms?

2 Company Law decrees the minimum reporting requirements by companies.

    a Where do corporate governance rules fit with Company Law?

    b Why is The Combined Code not Law?

    c What sanctions can be taken against companies which do not comply with The Combined Code?

3 The CORE coalition is campaigning for a UK Commission for Business, Human Rights and the Environment.

    a What are the main areas where companies are criticised on Human Rights issues?

    b What other issues might be covered by such a commission?

    c What would the likely outcomes of such a commission be?

SUMMARY

Increasingly, corporate governance is being linked with concepts of corporate responsibility. In this chapter, we have seen how a framework of corporate governance has developed in the wake of some spectacular corporate failures, which have focused attention on the way in which companies are run both internally and in relation to external auditors. We have noted how, in the discharge of 'accountability', the relationship between the board and the shareholder is enshrined within corporate governance codes, and how writers on the subject support this, almost without question.

This has caused those who see corporate responsibility as the ethical driver of corporate governance mechanisms to call for more rigorous control of the audit firms, which seem easily to escape accountability in cases of corporate collapse. The case studies highlight both these issues and the initiatives that have been made by various organizations on a voluntary basis to improve the way in which companies approach governance issues. As time goes on, it seems likely that more questions will be posed in the arena of corporate governance around ethically based issues that, at present, continue to remain unresolved by the conventional approaches to the subject.

FURTHER READING

VISIT THE WEBSITE
for links to useful sources of further information

Take your learning further: Online Resource Centre **www.oxfordtextbooks.co.uk/orc/blowfield_murray2e/**

Visit the Online Resource Centre which accompanies this book to enrich your understanding of this chapter.

Students: explore web links and further reading suggestions. Keep up to date with the latest developments by undertaking web exercises.

Lecturers: you will find additional case studies, including one on the topic of BCCI—Lessons learnt? (from first edition Chapter 8), for use in class or assessment. Show your students trailers from films related to Corporate Responsibility, and use images from the book in your PowerPoint slides.

- Charkham, J, 2005, *Keeping Better Company*, Oxford: Oxford University Press.
  Comparison of governance strategies in five different countries.
- Combined Code 2008, *The Combined Code on Corporate Governance*, London: Financial Reporting Council.
- Dallas, G (ed), 2005, *Governance and Risk: An Analytical Handbook for Investors, Managers, Directors and Stakeholders*, New York, NY: McGraw Hill.
  Analysis of the problems of governance from multiple perspectives.
- Mallin, CA, 2009, *Corporate Governance*, New York, NY: Oxford University Press.
  Internationally focused textbook on corporate governance.
- Sikka, P, Haslam, C, Kyriacou, O and Agrizzw, D, 2007, *Professionalizing Claims and the State of UK Professional Accounting Education: Some Evidence*, Accounting Education, 16 (1), pp 3–21.
- Solomon, J, 2010, *Corporate Governance and Accountability*, Chichester: John Wiley and Sons.
  Latest edition of an overview of governance and accountability issues.

ENDNOTES

[1] Shleifer and Vishney, 1997.

[2] See, e.g. Jensen, 2001. Sternberg, 2009

[3] Jones and Pollitt, 2004.

[4] This change took effect on 1 May 2000, because criticism had also been levelled at the system of supervision within the financial services sector.

[5] Combined Code, 1998.

[6] www.icgn.org/.

8

Social accounting

Chapter overview

Financial Reporting is acknowledged to be central to the corporate function. There are many reasons for this, not least, the statutory requirement in most countries for directors to report to their shareholders. However, over the last 30 years or so, an increasing proportion of companies in most countries have chosen to report non-financial information, including information about their position on corporate responsibility, sustainability, and latterly, on climate change. We noted in the last chapter, when considering the rational for corporate governance structures, that the prime requirement of management is to maximise returns for shareholders, yet this activity seems, potentially at least, to be at odds with that objective. In this chapter, we look at how, and why, companies report their corporate responsibility activities to external stakeholder groups. We examine how the corporate responsibility reports of today have developed, considering the conventional financial reporting process and contrasting it with the views of social accounting researchers. We discuss the difference between corporate social responsibility and corporate social reporting. In particular, we will:

- discuss the key role of accounting in understanding corporate responsibility;

- examine what is meant by 'social accounting';

- trace the emergence of corporate social reporting and social accounting research;

- examine the upsurge in social reporting that began in the 1990s;

- assess the relationship between conventional financial reporting and social reporting;

- examine the link between social reporting and sustainability/sustainable development;

- examine the role of 'third-party verification statements'.

Main topics

■ **Key terms**

Reporting awards

Social accounting

Social reporting

Third-party verification statements

■ **Online resources**

• Suggested additional information on social and environmental reporting

• Discussion topics for students

• Company and industry case studies

• Links to other web-based resources

Understanding corporate responsibility by examining corporate social reports

It is easy to be confused about what is understood when the terms 'corporate social responsibility' and 'corporate social reporting' are referred to, especially when the abbreviation CSR is used, and when the context is not immediately apparent. It is important to be clear when reading commentaries, especially in academic journals, exactly which term is being discussed. Essentially, corporate social reporting relates to the disclosures companies make with regard to their non-financial activities. It is part of the overall corporate reporting process, usually seen as the way companies discharge accountability to shareholders and other stakeholders. In the early years of social reporting, environmental, community, product, and employee issues, the traditional non-financial matters upon which certain companies reported, were normally included as a section in the

Annual Report. Indeed, early research into links between the social performance of a company and its financial performance used a database of social disclosures compiled by Ernst & Ernst (now Ernst & Young) to plot possible associations.[1] So whilst corporate responsibility reporting is often viewed as an emerging activity, born out of comparatively recent concerns for issues of environmental degradation or social injustice, literature on corporate social reporting reveals that companies have been engaged in the reporting of their non-financial activities for a considerable time. Such reporting, however, was traditionally examined as part of the accounting, or financial reporting, function and, although overlooked by some, has been of interest to a sub-set of accounting researchers for some 30 or more years.

Many authors writing about corporate responsibility neglect to make the connection between their subject and the crucial role that social reporting plays in the field. Whether it relates to the decision to adopt corporate responsibility strategies, or to how a company subsequently reports its activities, social reporting plays a crucial role for a number of reasons and it might be useful to explain how this comes about.

■ Key concepts: Social Accounting

Accounting for non-financial aspects of a company's performance; extending accountability to a wider range of stakeholders within society.

It is important to bear in mind that conventional definitions of accounting emphasise that its purpose is to provide financial information that should be useful for decision makers. This is the starting point for most academic courses in accounting, and throughout their training accountants are directed to concentrate their focus on 'the entity'; the business for which they are preparing the accounts. This means that accounting information tends to be built on data of relevance only to that entity, ignoring external events if they do not explicitly affect the entity.

Financial accounting and reporting is, essentially, for external stakeholders. Reports of past activity and measures of historic performance are produced both as a legal obligation, and as an exercise of accountability to the owners of the business: the shareholders. They are produced using accounting conventions, policies, and standards that have developed over time and which are referred to as the Generally Accepted Accounting Principles (GAAP). Recent developments in the internationalization of accounting standards are aimed at bringing consistency across national boundaries as companies adopt global perspectives in their operations. These are the results against which analysts' forecasts are measured, and against which anticipated company performance is compared and management competence assessed, in terms of market performance.

Traditionally, these measures of performance have focused exclusively on financial issues. Implicitly, as discussed elsewhere in the book, profit maximization is the goal against which performance is assessed and the only items that are applied to this equation are those to which, in the past, accountants have ascribed this privileged status. Thus, measures of profit omit to take account of by-products of commercial activity for which others have to pay, such as pollution, emissions, road use, etc.—issues that economists refer to as 'externalities' and issues that, in an effort to increase profitability, actually benefit from being maximized. In the past, it has been suggested that the reason why externalities have never been included in financial statements is to do with difficulties in measuring them, in financial terms, but if it is possible to assess the value of depreciation, intangible assets, and financial derivatives, this argument seems difficult to sustain. It is more that taking note of externalities is seen as an obstacle to commercial activity, affecting profits and competitiveness. We will return to discuss this issue further when we look at the meaning of 'social accounting'.

What we examine here is the external reporting function—a concept that is familiar to anyone who has researched corporate activity—and what we go on to look at now is how traditional financial accounting and reporting is contrasted with the approach taken in social accounting and reporting.

There are also two additional aspects of accounting that deserve comment. First, accounting provides the accepted language of business, a language that even non-accountants are keen to adopt to instil elements of what are perceived as essential components of strategic arguments in a business framework. This language and the underlying notions that drive corporate activity, such as year-on-year growth and market positioning, shape the context of corporate activity and help to explain both the power of accounting within corporate activity, and how easily thereby it might act against longer term initiatives that have been designed to take account of sets of more responsible objectives.

Second, there is an implicit assumption about the nature of accounting that is shared by the public as well as by many accountants, i.e. that it is a 'neutral' or 'objective' activity. We have already explained that accounting is subject to GAAP, rules, and conventions that have been agreed by particular interest groups. Accountants thereafter apply their subjective judgements to the application of such principles—judgements that are values-based, and which often have social and environmental consequences that do not appear in subsequent financial statements. A number of studies have examined the complicity of accounting in such issues as environmental pollution and foreign exploitation,[2] plant closures,[3] and social conflict.[4] The perceived partisan nature of accounting informs a more critical approach that motivates much of the research output in such journals as *Critical Perspectives on Accounting, Accounting, Organizations and Society*, and the *Accounting, Auditing and Accountability Journal*. It can also be said that it is in this context that social accounting acts as a critique of conventional accounting practices.

■ Discussion points

Corporate reporting is traditionally associated with the accounting function.

- Why might it be appropriate for accountants to have a role in compiling corporate responsibility reports that, at face value, seem to have little to do with accounting?
- Which other department within the structure of a company might take on this role?
- What role does measurement play in compiling social reports?

SNAPSHOT 8.1

Social accounting at Traidcraft plc

The company was established in 1979 as a Christian response to poverty, and is both a trading company and a development charity, based on building lasting relationships with producers, and in supporting people to trade out of poverty and working to bring about trade justice. Having published its first independently audited report in 1993, the methodological approach that Traidcraft developed with the New Economics Foundation has been adopted and adapted by many larger organizations.

Traidcraft state that 'social accounting is an important way of demonstrating the wider impacts that an organisation has. Traidcraft's social accounts attempt to show both what we are achieving and what our various stakeholders think about the way we work with them.' The Traidcraft Social Accounts for 2008/9 contain some of the most detailed reports about their activities of any company, stretching to some 186 pages. The Trustees of the Charitable Foundation were then invited to review and comment on the accounts. Among the comments made, the Trustees noted that 'although (they) were happy with the clarity and disclosure within the accounts, (they) felt there was still scope for further benchmarking and context setting to allow better assessment of the achievements reported. They added that, 'Although Trustees accepted that some aspects of Traidcraft's impact are difficult to measure, benchmarking and better indicators needs to be in place where at all possible. For example, it would be helpful if we were able to show how many people were affected by different aspects of Traidcraft's work.'

This demonstrates the evolving nature of social accounts compared to traditional financial accounts, and how a critical view from outside the organisation can help fashion future plans.

(Source: Adapted from **www.traidcraft.co.uk**)

Quick Questions

1 Why is it important to be clear about who the stakeholders are?

2 Why is it essential to measure performance against indicators?

3 In Traidcraft's case, what additional information do the social accounts give that might help strengthen the business?

The nature of social reporting

We have already explained that financial reporting is traditionally understood as the reporting of the financial results of a company's past activities to external stakeholders. The requirement for such reports is now part of company law in most countries, but, as in the UK and USA, the requirements almost invariably cover only the financial activities, and commonly call for the Directors' Report, the profit and loss account and balance sheet to be reported to the members of the company. These reports are often augmented by various other requirements of GAAP but, with the exception of a few European countries, all of these requirements—either by law or quasi-law—relate to financial aspects of performance. Reporting of the non-financial aspects of a company's performance is largely voluntary.[5] It is the nature of this form of reporting that has attracted the interest of a growing sub-set of accounting researchers since the genesis of social accounting.

But before we look back at the emergence of social reporting, we should be clear about what it means. The social accounting project in the UK dates back to the mid-1980s and one of the earliest definitions of corporate social reporting, which still stands up today, states that it is:

> the process of communicating the social and environmental effects of the organisations' economic actions to particular interest groups within society, and society at large. As such, it involves extending the accountability of organisations (particularly companies) beyond the traditional role of providing a financial account to the owners of capital, in particular, shareholders. Such an extension is predicated upon the assumption that companies do have wider responsibilities than to simply make money for their shareholders.

(Gray et al., 1987)[6]

Immediately, this definition challenges the taken-for-granted objectives of financial reporting which are to discharge accountability to the members of the company—the shareholders. In this sense, social accounting research may be regarded as critical of mainstream accounting practice, and researchers have long called for reforms to company law and corporate governance frameworks.

What is immediately obvious from the statement of Gray et al., and unavoidable in any subsequent discussion, is the debate about what is meant by 'accountability'. We examined this issue in the previous chapter in the context of corporate governance, but it might be useful to consider, at this stage, how 'accountability' can be interpreted differently by different constituents, and how, within its meaning, there is an implicit relationship of unequal power between the person or body requiring an account and that which is giving the account. This unequal power relationship is evident in the use of phrases such as being *'called to account'*, or being asked to *'account for one's actions'*. Of course, the word 'account' is not always related to finance, but, in the corporate context, it invariably has this financial emphasis, and the power relationship here lies in the requirement laid down in law and in the custom for the directors of a company (the agents) to supply (financial) accounts to the owners (principals).[7] The same legal obligation to be called to account for responsibilities that go beyond the financial, however, is largely absent from the corporate responsibility sphere, and any such reporting is undertaken largely as a voluntary act, and it is this aspect which is the focus of much social accounting research. Social accounting theorists both challenge the primacy of the shareholder group and recognize an explicit obligation for companies to be accountable to wider society.

In the context of this book, the connection between a company's social performance and social reporting is obvious. In many ways, social reporting is the first insight into the social performance of the company, and, certainly, it is the easiest way in which a company can explain its approach and operationalization of its corporate responsibility strategy to interested parties external to the company. Indeed, in research studies, social disclosures have frequently been used as a proxy for social performance.[8] However, the information a company reports will largely depend on how it defines its activities in terms of corporate responsibility, and activities upon which it chooses *not* to report is often as significant as the activities on which it does report. Indeed, many studies looking into the reporting activities of corporations comment on the way in which some companies appear to 'cherry pick' the activities on which they can report favourably, while ignoring those issues towards which criticism may be directed. Equally, many companies report on various issues that come within a broad corporate responsibility remit, while failing to address major issues at the core of the business activity. So, an energy company may stress how it promotes its staff development to improve leadership qualities in its employees, but may not detail how it aims to tackle the challenges of climate change.

■ Discussion points

In attempting to assess a company's commitment to a corporate responsibility, the volume and content of company disclosures play an important part.

- To what extent can a company's social performance be judged from the various reports it publishes throughout the year?
- What other sources of evidence may found?
- How much notice should we take of those NGO reports that are often critical of company activity?

The emergence of corporate social reporting

Before discussing these issues in further detail, it is useful to consider how social reporting developed and to understand that it is far from a recent phenomenon. For example, research in the 1980s demonstrates that some US and Australian companies were reporting on social issues before World War I.[9] Likewise, in the European context, a similar pattern was observed in the early days of Shell.[10] These studies suggest that company managers have always been concerned to some degree with considering non-financial issues that are relevant.

Hogner (1982) suggests that US Steel's disclosures were motivated by the need to respond to perceived societal pressures of the period. But it was, perhaps, as societal awareness of environmental issues grew in the 1960s, and as concerns over corporate behaviour were prompted by various company collapses and scandals in the 1970s, that companies responded by including more non-financial information in their annual reports. It was also in the 1970s that, in different countries, new laws required companies to report on aspects of performance relating to, inter alia, employment practices, pollution expenditure, and the like.[11]

There was also interest in the subject among the UK accounting profession and, in 1975, the publication of *The Corporate Report* represented a radical rethink of the role of reporting to external stakeholders.[12] It emphasized how the traditional role of the annual report could be made more relevant by the inclusion of social and environmental information. In the USA, the American Institute of Certified Public Accountants entered the debate, offering guidance on the measurement of social performance in a 1977 publication,[13] and the atmosphere was one of examining the role of reporting, in general, and the purpose of reports, in particular. The traditional reason that companies report an account of their activities is for the benefit of the 'users' of accounts. This would normally be thought to be the shareholders, but, in the case of social reporting, traditional theory (i.e. that this information is useful for the purpose of decision making) does not seem to stand up.

As interesting as its emergence in the 1970s might have been, however, so too was the decline in social reporting in the 1980s and its subsequent re-emergence in the 1990s. The decline is largely attributed to the political shifts in the USA and UK that came with the respective elections of Reagan and Thatcher, and the renewed focus on market economics. *The Corporate Report* largely failed to bring about any major changes and disappeared from the accounting agenda until memories of its recommendations were stirred, in the 1990s, with the initiatives pioneered by such organizations as the Institute of Social and Ethical Accountability, the Council on Economic Priorities, and the World Business Council for Sustainable Development.[14]

The upsurge in social reporting since the early 1990s

Despite the varying pattern of corporate reporting of social and environmental issues, a very clear upward trend in social reporting began to emerge in the 1990s and this can be readily observed from the triennial surveys conducted by the accountancy firm KPMG. Apart from minor changes in corporate governance recommendations, a number of factors began to influence change within companies. These included action at a number of levels, from initiatives within professions and industries, to UN and EU initiatives, all encouraging greater detail in the reporting of social and environmental issues.

For example, the UNEP/SustainAbility 'Engaging Stakeholders' programme was launched in 1994. It served to raise awareness among companies, initially, of environmental reporting and it continues to stress the business case for wider reporting. The programme has clearly encouraged participation by widely publicizing the results of the survey and the benefits of participation. The series of surveys continues to the present, and the latest report saw Standard & Poors join the research team and the report taking on even more of a market orientation.[15] The European Union Eco-Management and Audit Scheme also promoted the introduction and reporting of environmental management systems, following the introduction of BS 7750 in 1992 and, thereafter, the ISO 14000 series.

At a national level, the UK government's DEFRA/DTI Environmental Reporting Guidelines were published in 2001, and France has followed Denmark, Norway, Sweden, and Holland in introducing mandatory reporting requirements, although the focus here continues to display a financial emphasis. At a business-to-business level, the International Chamber of Commerce published its *Business Charter for Sustainable Development* in 1991, featuring a 16-point guide to environmental reporting. In 1995, the World

Business Council for Sustainable Development (WBCSD) was established, through a merger of the Business Council for Sustainable Development and the World Industry Council for the Environment, the two organizations that responded on behalf of business to the challenges arising from the Rio Summit in 1992. The WBCSD maintains an influential voice for business and boasts a membership comprising major corporations worldwide.[16]

Around the same time, various industries began to look at how environmental issues affected the perceptions of activities within their sectors. A good example of this is the initiative by the European Chemical Industry Council (CEFIC). Founded in 1972, it has, over the years, expanded and developed its approaches to various aspects of concern within the industry. It is now closely allied to the International Council of Chemical Associations and, in 2006, the ICCA launched its Responsible Care Global Charter, a development of CEFIC's Responsible Care Programme's reporting guidelines.

At the level of the professions, the *Fédération des Experts Compatibles Européens* (FEE)—the coordinating organization for the European accounting professions—has been involved in developing reporting guidelines and making representation to the European Parliament on connected issues. In the UK, the initiative taken by the ACCA in 1991 in establishing the Environmental Reporting Awards has done much to encourage and improve social reporting over the years (see below). The ACCA not only runs award schemes in the UK, but in several other countries around the world.[17]

Each of these initiatives, or a combination of more than one, served to increase the incidence and volume of environmental reporting. In the early stages of this development, the reports bore little resemblance to the best reports we see today. In general, reporting on environmental issues comprised a section in the annual report and was largely qualitative in nature. Even when the first standalone reports began to appear, they seemed to be, as Owen (2003) suggested, *'rather crude exercises in public relations'*.

■ **Discussion points**

There is strong evidence from recent surveys that an increasing number of companies are reporting on social and environmental issues.

- What theories can you suggest that might help to explain this trend?
- What theories lie behind the notion that statements should be independently verified by third parties?
- Given that there are no statutory standards against which to audit third-party verification statements, how is it possible to compare their value between companies?

Trends in social reporting

Two other trends emerged in the 1990s that, to some extent, still continue today. First, there was the separation of the 'environmental' from the 'social'. Whereas the reports in the 1970s had, in many ways, a shared focus, the trend in the 1990s was to separate the two and to place a greater emphasis on the environmental aspects of company performance. This is significant because corporate responsibility, as a field, is not concerned solely with issues of environmental management: indeed, at the core of the Brundtland definition of sustainability (see Chapter 3) is the notion of social justice. Second, criticism started to be levelled at companies for failing to embed social and environmental policies into the strategy and 'real' purpose of the business (see Chapter 6).

We can conjecture over the reasons for both trends. In the case of the environmental focus, it is worth remembering that there had been a spate of very significant environmental disasters in the mid- and late-1980s, including, for example, Bhopal in 1984, Chernobyl in 1986, Piper Alpha in 1988, and the *Exxon Valdez* disaster in 1989. For obvious reasons, media coverage of these events was concentrated and prolonged, and the events themselves led to many changes in the way in which companies operated and reported. Indeed, each of these events had a lasting impact within their respective industries that is felt even today. Therefore, it is probably unsurprising that companies opted for more of an environmental focus in their activities and reports. In many ways, if this conclusion is correct, it also explains why the strategy may be easily criticized as an 'add-on', because, at least initially, that is what it was. It would have been a reaction, most likely of companies within the affected industry sectors, to how they perceived they should act.

Research into social reporting

Although there is evidence of companies reporting non-financial aspects of their businesses going back over a hundred years, a genuine body of research only really began to emerge in the 1970s.[18] During the period 1970–1980, this mainly consisted of empirical (statistical) studies that, while focusing on some aspects of social and environmental information, still had a clear instrumental rationale aimed at discovering the usefulness of this information to investors.[19] Some discursive work began to appear towards the end of the 1970s,[20] however, and these works widened the debate to include more philosophical issues, with the phrase 'social responsibility' appearing in many studies.[21]

Research gained momentum from the mid-1980s, at which time a number of authors, principally in the UK and Australia, began to explore the social dimensions of corporate activity. Influential journals, sympathetic to this subject matter, were also founded in this period: *Critical Perspectives on Accounting* (established 1990), *Accounting, Auditing and Accountability Journal* (1988), *Journal of Accounting and Public Policy* (1982), joined *Accounting, Organizations and Society* (1975) to provide a wide forum through which to engage academics and broaden the terms of the debate.

These works presaged the increase in social reporting of the early 1990s, and heralded a social and environmental accounting project that has continued, and grown in strength, scope, and reach, ever since. Indeed, from modest beginnings, with only a handful of researchers worldwide, social and environmental accounting research is now conducted by hundreds of researchers in many countries and features in many international accounting conferences, as well as having a number of its own dedicated conferences, each year.[22]

Such evidence as there is from research studies looking at the value that investors place on such information is no more than suggestive of 'possible' relevance to investment decisions.[23] Indeed, despite the huge amount of research in the late 1970s and early 1980s into the link between social performance and financial performance, no clear evidence emerged to explain the increasing incidence of social reporting. It prompted one author to suggest that the research was based on *'data in search of a theory'*.[24]

Theories of social reporting

Researchers responded to Ullmann's (1985) call for new theories to be explored to explain the phenomena and a number of studies followed. Roberts (1992) discussed stakeholder theory in an empirical context and, subsequently, Gray et al. (1996), prompted also by evidence in increasing volumes of social disclosure, reviewed theories of disclosure that might explain the phenomena. Traditional theories of disclosure aimed at informing market participants were largely discounted and alternative theories focusing on political economy were considered. One of the theories identified has since become one of the most discussed in the literature: 'legitimacy theory'. The notion of a company existing only with the sanction of society, with connotations of a 'public interest' element to its continued existence may have seemed somewhat fanciful but the events surrounding Enron and the collapse of Arthur Andersen, one of the world's largest and, at the time, most respected firms of accountants, demonstrated that it is, indeed, possible to lose the licence to operate if one's actions are seen to go beyond what society deems acceptable. That companies might choose a strategy to support or enhance their legitimacy in these terms is something that has formed a strand of research since 1990. Indeed, many researchers suggest that rather than exercising the discharge of accountability in reporting their social activities, they are actually engaged in a process of legitimation of their operations. Legitimacy theory suggests that company disclosures may be a reaction to the perception that companies have of how they are viewed by different stakeholder groups within society. The company, therefore, needs to disclose details about its activities to achieve this objective and to reassure society about its activities. Lindblom[25] sparked a long-running debate on legitimacy theory by positing four alternative strategies which might be employed by companies when deciding whether and why to publish. She suggests that companies may seek to 'align activities with expectations', 'educate and inform', 'change perceptions', or 'alter expectations'. We may surmise that each and all of these strategies are connected with the way the company wishes to communicate with stakeholders, and that they *may* also be connected to its actual performance.

A related theory relating to disclosure strategy concerns the manner in which a company manages its reputation. There is an increasing literature on reputation management and the risks attaching to events which can damage it.[26] The relationship between social disclosure and social performance is critical if we are to do anything but discount social reports as some form of public relations exercise. Unless we are able to align reports with performance we are always likely to be left with this dilemma.

Conventional financial reporting and social reporting

The major difference between conventional financial reporting and social reporting hinges on the approach taken to the use of the information reported upon. Traditionally, financial reports contain both aggregated data, which may conceal much of the underlying activity, and analyses that focus on very narrow performance measures. We can only imagine the range of activity that is represented by the income statements of BP or Wal-Mart and, in looking at the earning per share figure or other performance ratios, no consideration is given to the wider implications of the range of activities that led to the derivation of that measure. Indeed, in the application of many accounting techniques, little concern is given to any factors outside the concern of the entity, and ratios of liquidity, profitability, and solvency, for example, are often used only to compare performance against historic or other data. The same figures are also often used to compare performance of one company against another (this type of comparison is frequently requested in degree and professional accounting courses dealing with 'financial statement analysis'). Equally, what Chua (1986) calls 'mainstream accounting research' tends to have a similar narrow focus, and, regularly, research questions focus around issues of market efficiency and the usefulness of certain categories of information to investors. It is little wonder, therefore, that the bigger picture is often overlooked in an effort to examine the minutiae of procedure or practice.

On the other hand, social reporting, at a theoretical level, is concerned with how commercial activity links into other social systems and presents an alternative ontological approach to how one views the role of corporations. 'Systems theory', explained in more detail in Gray et al. (1996), is an approach that is 'designed to reverse the tendency in scientific thought towards reductionist reasoning'. Systems theory has its origins in the natural sciences and can be explained as follows.

- An attempt to study a part without understanding the whole from which the part comes (reductionism) was bound to lead to misunderstandings. The part can only be understood in its context.
- Understanding tends to be directed by and limited to one's own discipline. Natural phenomena are complex and cannot be successfully studied by artificially bounded modes of thought.

(Gray et al., 1996, p 13)

The essence of systems thinking demands that we think about all of our activities in the context of how they affect other systems, with what Birkin (2000) calls, 'an ontology of interconnected events'. If the relevance to social reporting emerges from this logic then, in relation to sustainability issues, which are explained in detail in Chapter 3, it is highly persuasive.

> ### ■ Key concept: External Verification Statement
>
> An opinion regarding the quality and verifiability of the social reports. Unlike financial audits, which are carried out by registered auditors following comprehensive auditing standards, external verification statements on social reports have no such authority.

Reporting issues for corporate management

From the management perspective, there are a number of problems in making the decision to disclose non-financial information. First, who is the intended audience? Traditionally, corporate reports are released for the benefit of the analyst/investor group. That constituency is relatively homogenous and easy to define, their needs have been the focus of investor relations departments and boardroom discussions for decades, and their needs are backed by numerous research studies. The audience for reports on social, environmental, and sustainability issues is, however, much more diverse. These users do not form a homogenous group and, indeed, may have widely diverging interests. Equally, their desire for information may not always have the company's best interest in mind. Indeed, it is easy to make an argument that few investors take any interest in the non-financial aspects of corporate activity, except if it impinges on issues of risk or governance. Certainly, there is little evidence from research that investors are swayed by social and environmental disclosures. Thus, management must form an opinion on the purpose and scope of the report, and this may pose many challenges.

It is relatively straightforward to make statements along the lines of '*within this company we make every effort to maintain the highest standards of social and environmental practice*'. Indeed, statements such as this peppered annual reports throughout the late 1990s, as companies became aware that they were expected to address additional non-financial issues, but were unsure how to position themselves in that regard. What is more difficult to do is to explain how any particular programme is to be rolled out and the effect that it might have on profit figures. At that point, conflict will almost inevitably arise within organizations and one can see the kind of compromises that are reached by examining such reports, many of which fill the list of criticisms of awards judges (see Snapshot 8.2).

If one looks at it from the outside the company, the picture is entirely different. As a member of society, concerned about aspects of corporate activity that affect you, we may view the issue as one of accountability. Companies and policymakers often talk about 'transparency', yet on close examination, it is sometimes difficult to uncover the level of detail that we require in order to be satisfied on any particular issue. On the other hand, how does the company know the level of detail that any single individual or group might want? These issues reveal that company management involved in the reporting process are better placed to report effectively if they have knowledge of the theories and functions of social reporting to be able to effectively position the company in terms of its corporate responsibility profile and reputation management.

The role of third-party verification statements

We have discussed the fact that continuing research has found that increasing numbers of companies are now reporting on social and environmental performance. We also note that, in judging the 2006 ACCA awards for Sustainability Reporting, criticisms were made of the quality of third-party assurance statements. Despite acknowledging that external assurance has become widespread, the judges were concerned about the language and tenor of many of the reports, which appeared to be:

> often written for the company's directors/senior management. Some assurance statements do not include or refer to any recommendation for improvement ... and so offer no insight into how the assurance process is helping an organisation to improve its reporting and performance.
>
> *(ACCA, 2006)*

SNAPSHOT 8.2

Report of the Judges—ACCA UK Awards for Sustainability Reporting

The Association of Chartered Certified Accountants (ACCA) founded the Environmental Reporting Awards in 1991 to give recognition to the organizations that were reporting on environmental issues. Over the years, the criteria have expanded and the awards are now made for Sustainability Reporting, and are also replicated in several countries around the world.

Following the announcement of the winners, the judges give feedback to participants, aimed at offering guidance for subsequent reports. While acknowledging the high standard of reporting by many companies the following comments, taken from the Report of the Judges, 2008, suggest that there is still room for improvement, for example, by reporting on opportunities as well as risks, and reporting on 'the bigger picture'.

'Many reporters are still not reporting on the 'bigger picture' of sustainable development and how the organization fits into it. Disclosures tend to focus on the company's own operations, products and performance rather than the wider social and environmental systems within which it operates.

Organizations should in particular be demonstrating in their report that they are addressing the issue of how they are going to 'reinvent themselves'. Judges felt that although significant improvements have been made to reporting over the last twenty years, organisations were not yet disclosing how ... resource depletion is featuring in their business plan and strategy.'

(Source: ACCA, 2008)

Questions

Despite a huge upsurge in the volume of reporting over the last few years, various aspects of reporting practice continue to invite criticism.

1 Is there a case for statutory standards to cover sustainability reporting, in the same way as there is for financial reporting?

2 If a voluntary approach is to continue, how might companies be persuaded to take note of the criticisms above?

3 What is the value of such an award scheme?

In view of the fact that these reports are designed to be targeted at external stakeholder groups, with the intention of giving assurance to that audience of the intentions and future actions of the company in order to build trust, it is useful to consider the reasons why companies might wish to consider using third parties to offer assurance.

The trend towards external verification

We know that the initial choice of whether or not to report at all is made by the company, as part of a strategy by the management and motivated for any number of reasons. It is a largely voluntary act and may have much to do with the activity of competitors, perceptions of stakeholder expectation, or other strategies to obtain *'managerial advantage'*.[27] As companies embrace a global perspective, many will view both the mandatory requirements of some countries and the recommendations under the Global Reporting Initiative sustainability reporting guidelines, which make specific reference to verification, as an opportunity to review and to implement external assurance practices. The trend has been observed to be growing steadily and, in its most recent international survey, KPMG (2008) found that the number of companies in the Global 250 with a formal assurance statement had increased to 40 per cent (from 30 per cent in 2005); for the top 100 national companies, it had increased to 39 per cent (from 33 per cent). The overriding motivation is probably to build trust between company management and external stakeholders over the implementation and maintenance of corporate responsibility strategies. In an ideal world, the verification process should achieve this and reassure the relevant audience, thereby adding value for the company.

This motivation is, however, easily contrasted with the theoretical purpose of such accounts—the idea that with transparency comes accountability. There is a real concern, expressed by a number of researchers, that the upsurge in reporting is part of a process whereby the accountability agenda is 'captured' by corporate management, who react to calls for greater accountability and transparency by artefacts, aimed at taking control of the agenda, and at taking equal control of the nature and extent of the information reported upon.[28] The idea that such reports only contain information that management wants released adds to criticisms that reports lack completeness and credibility.[29] This notion continues to motivate social accounting researchers to examine the verification process, and to press for the imposition of strict and robust assurance processes.[30]

The KPMG (2008) Report devotes a full chapter to the question of assurance statements, (not too surprisingly it notes that 'major accountancy organizations are still leading the corporate responsibility reporting assurance field' (p 55)), and identifies the highest use of assurance 'still …to be in sectors with known impacts and high media attention' (p 61). It notes that companies with consumers also provide assurance statements, and that while for large retail chains and supermarkets the incidence is low at present, it is expected that this sector will show an increase over time, as they make ever wider claims about product safety, packaging, and supply-chain issues.

When asked to identify the 'drivers' to seeking assurance statements, companies responded in almost equal measure that they were motivated by the hope of: (a) improving the quality of reported information; (b) reinforcing credibility; and (c) improving the reporting process. In only 2 per cent of responses was there a local requirement for assurance, reinforcing the essentially voluntary nature of this process.

■ Discussion points

Awards for producing high-quality social reports have attracted participation from some of the world's best-known companies.

- Can you suggest reasons why companies should want to subject themselves to this level of scrutiny and so run the risk of criticism?
- Why do so many criticisms from the judges recur year after year?
- What makes it difficult for companies to address the judges' criticisms and what can be done about it?

CASE STUDY 8

BT PLC's sustainability reporting

BT PLC is a global telecommunications company employing in excess of 35,000 in 50 countries. It has always positioned itself as a leader in Corporate Responsibility, and it has always enjoyed a high reputation for its social reports, confirmed in 2007 and 2008, by receiving the top accolade in the ACCA Sustainability Reporting Awards. In presenting the award, Rachel Jackson, head of Social and Environmental Issues, for the ACCA, said, 'It is becoming ever more apparent that sustainability must be integral to business strategy and we are glad to see organizations are recognizing this. The diverse range of companies honoured at the awards demonstrates how important it is for organizations to make this commitment to transparent and ethical reporting, regardless of the size or type of industry they operate in'.

Chris Tuppen, BT's Chief Sustainability Officer responded, 'We are delighted to receive the ACCA sustainability reporting award for our 2008 report. We want to continue to improve the coverage of the key material issues in our reporting. This is why we have placed greater emphasis on the opportunities that sustainability brings. We think the biggest potential in the future for us to make a positive difference lies through our products and services.'

In their 2009 Sustainability Report, BT state:

Our goal is to transform our business in ways that benefit BT, our customers, society and the environment. In doing so, we are committed to maintaining responsible business practices and further integrating corporate responsibility into our business processes.

The company then details its approach to responsible business in core areas which each affect several stakeholder groups, in particular, with regard to:

- Investing in future technologies
- Supply chain
- Human rights

- Product stewardship
- Privacy and data protection.

Despite facing a recession over the last two years BT have a clear position on their stance to Corporate Responsibility:

In a time of economic uncertainty, responsible business practices are more important than ever. Employees and customers alike are becoming increasingly aware of the ethical issues surrounding business. Suppliers, partners and potential customers are becoming just as likely to ask to see your environmental policy as they are your pricelist. At BT, we also find that it saves us money. Over the five years to March 31, 2009, the economic benefits of our environmental programmes were worth more than £400 million. And it reduces the risks we face. To protect our reputation, for example, we ask our suppliers to meet or exceed standards in areas including human rights and protection of the environment.

We set our first carbon reduction target back in 1992, well before other companies became aware of the problem and decided to act. By taking leadership on sustainability, we have added value to our business as well as delivering benefits to society and to the wider environment.

(Source: **www.bt.com**. Reproduced with kind permission of BT PLC.)

Questions

1 BT has consistently received accolades for its social reports

    a What features of their reporting practice put BT ahead of its rivals?

    b To what extent does BT use targets to monitor emissions reductions?

    c What does BT identify as an ICT company's major contribution to 'sustainable economic growth', and how does it go about this task?

2 Social Reports are often used by researchers as a proxy for actual social performance.

    a What indicators can we use from a BT's social reports, to measure its actual social performance?

    b What are the two elements of BT's 'sustainable economic growth' programme?

    c How has BT improved the quality of its summary documents from the previous report?

3 BT operates in 50 countries around the world, including some with poor records on human rights issues?

    a What human rights issues would impinge on a global communications company?

    b How can a multinational company influence policy in a developing country?

    c How effectively does BT cover human rights issues in its reports?

SUMMARY

In this chapter, we have examined how companies report to audiences outside the company. This, we discovered, encompasses a complex series of issues that pose some serious challenges for management, especially if the process is designed to be more than an exercise in corporate communication, marketing, or public relations. This process developed through extending the financial reporting function and, until relatively recently, the annual report was the usual medium through which such disclosures were made.

This posed a number of problems for companies as it became clear that stakeholder groups were scrutinizing the information contained in these social and environmental accounts with different intentions than those of the traditional audience of annual reports, i.e. the shareholder. Academics also began scrutinizing these social disclosures, offering varying levels of critique and, as the reporting medium moved to the internet, so pressure groups were now using the same medium to counter some of the claims made in corporate releases. Even when companies enter reporting award schemes, they rarely emerge without criticism.

There are various reasons for the dramatic increase in the incidence and volume of social reporting, and a large number of contributory factors, a combination of which is most likely to offer explanation. But with this increase has come criticism from certain quarters that the reports are more akin to public relations initiatives. Indeed, as the incidence and volume of corporate responsibility reports has increased, so criticism of corporate behaviour does not seem to have abated, not least because the material is accused of being incomplete or inadequate, as attested to by successive judging panels of environmental and similar awards.

Accounting plays an important part in this process of improving the credibility of corporate responsibility performance. Accounting for an activity is the essence of discharging accountability to the appropriate body. Impacts and effects need to be measured in order to gauge accurately whether particular strategies are worthwhile and effective. The design and implementation of appropriate information systems and reporting structures play an essential part of this process. There are, therefore, strong arguments to be made that accountants become aware of the social, environmental, and sustainability issues that are challenging the 'business as usual' approach. These professionals will then be better placed to devise accounting systems that can capture non-financial activity in a more meaningful way. Equally, there are new forms of accounting that might be developed, looking to measure different things to those that are traditionally associated with accounting systems.

What this chapter sets out to demonstrate is that accounting plays a central role in the corporate responsibility process and has the potential to play an even greater role. Social, environmental, corporate responsibility, and sustainability reports have emerged from the financial reporting function within companies. But, whereas financial reporting procedures are highly regulated and controlled, there seems no appetite to impose such controls on non-financial reporting. If that situation continues, despite continued criticism over the format and content of such reports, then these reports will continue to require careful analysis and critical judgement.

FURTHER READING

Take your learning further: Online Resource Centre **www.oxfordtextbooks.co.uk/orc/blowfield_ murray2e/**

Visit the Online Resource Centre which accompanies this book to enrich your understanding of this chapter.

VISIT THE WEBSITE
for links to useful sources of further information

Students: explore web links and further reading suggestions. Keep up to date with the latest developments by undertaking web exercises.

Lecturers: you will find additional case studies, including one on the topic of Stakeholder accountability—challenging the primacy of shareholders (from first edition Chapter 8), for use in class or assessment. Show your students trailers from films related to Corporate Responsibility, and use images from the book in your PowerPoint slides.

- Bebbington, J, Larrinaga, C and Moneva, JM 2008, Corporate Social Reporting and Reputation Risk Management, *Accounting, Auditing and Accountability Journal*, 21(3), pp 337–61.

Exploration of theories of social disclosure

- Friedman, A and Miles, S, 2001, Socially Responsible Investment and Corporate Social and Environmental Reporting in the UK: An Exploratory Study, *British Accounting Review*, 33(4), pp 523–548.
  Introduction to environmental reporting.
- Gray, RH, Owen, D and Adams, C, 1996, *Accounting and Accountability: Changes and Challenges in Corporate Social and Environmental Reporting*, London: Prentice Hall.
  Making the case for social and environmental reporting.
- Gray, RH, 2006b, 'Social, environmental and sustainability reporting and organisational value creation? Whose value? Whose creation?', *Accounting, Auditing and Accountability Journal*, 19(6), pp 793–819.
  Revisiting and updating the debate on reporting on the social and environmental dimensions of business.
- Hasseldine, J, Salama, AI and Toms, JS, 2005, Quantity Versus Quality: The Impact of Environmental Disclosures on the Reputations of UK PLCs, *British Accounting Review*, 37(2).
  Evaluation of reporting's impact.
- Gray, RH, Dillard, J and Spence, C, 2009, Social Accounting as If the World Matters: Towards Absurdia and a New Postalgia, *Public Management Review*, 11(5).
  Discussing Social Accounting in the context of a sustainable world.

ENDNOTES

[1] Ernst and Ernst 1976 et seq., *Social Responsibility Disclosure*, Cleveland, Ohio: Ernst & Ernst.

[2] Tinker, 1985.

[3] Berry et al., 1985.

[4] Lehman, 1992.

[5] Changing corporate governance guidelines have increased the amount of recommended disclosure, categorized as social disclosure, relating to the remuneration of directors, following the Cadbury and Greenbury Reports in the mid-1990s. (See Chapter 7.)

[6] For a more recent discussion on the definition, see Gray et al., 1996.

[7] This 'agency' relationship lies at the heart of modern corporate activity and is further explored in Chapter 9.

[8] There are a number of examples in which disclosure is used when no other measure of performance is available: see, e.g., Belkaoui, 1976; Ingram, 1978; Mahapatra, 1984; Freedman and Ullman, 1986; Belkaoui and Karpic, 1989.

[9] Lewis et al.,1984; Hogner, 1982; Guthrie and Parker, 1989.

[10] Unerman, 2003.

[11] Gray, 2002b.

[12] ASSC, 1975.

[13] AICPA, 1977.

[14] Deegan, 2002.

[15] UNEP/SustainAbility/Standard&Poors, 2006.

[16] It also has an extensive website covering issues of climate change, international development, ecosystems, and the business role. There is a section on projects in progress and there are a large number of case studies for reference. See www.wbcsd.org.

[17] For a full list of awards schemes around the world, see www.enviroreporting.com.

[18] See Mathews, 1996, for a detailed discussion of the development of social accounting research in different time periods.

[19] See, e.g. Bowman, 1973; Bowman and Haire, 1976; Belkaoui, 1976.

[20] See, e.g. Estes, 1975; Estes, 1976a; Ramanathan, 1976.

[21] See, e.g. Jacoby, 1973; Browne and Haas, 1974; Feldberg, 1974; Beresford, 1975; Parket and Eilbert, 1975; Estes, 1976b.

[22] The Centre for Social and Environmental Accounting Research (CSEAR) at the University of St Andrews boast membership in excess of 300 people from over thirty countries and holds an annual conference for researchers each September; see www.st-andrews.ac.uk.

[23] Bowman, 1973; Chenall and Juchau, 1977; Ingram, 1978; Goodwin et al., 1996; Chan and Milne, 1999; Milne and Chan, 1999; Friedman and Miles, 2001.

[24] Ullmann, 1985.

[25] Lindblom, 1994.

[26] Friedman and Miles, 2001, Toms, 2002, Hasseldine et al., 2005.

[27] Owen et al., 2000.

[28] See, e.g., Owen et al., 2000; O'Dwyer and Owen, 2005.

[29] Dando and Swift, 2003; Adams, 2004; Adams and Evans, 2004.

[30] O'Dwyer and Owen, 2005.

9

Stakeholder management and engagement

Chapter overview

In this chapter, we explore the significance of stakeholders, and how they relate to the way in which corporate responsibility is perceived and managed through partnerships, alliances, and voluntary standards. In particular, we will:

- examine stakeholders as a managerial concept;

- identify the different types of stakeholder and difficulties with the 'stakeholder' construct;

- explore the role of stakeholders in defining and implementing voluntary codes of corporate responsibility practice and standards;

- review experiences of stakeholder management.

Main topics

■ **Key terms**

Stakeholder

Code of conduct

Partnership

Voluntary standard

Engagement

Developing countries

■ **Online resources**

- Suggested additional materials on real-life partnerships

- Additional case study of multi-stakeholder engagement

- Further discussion and materials on the challenges of implementing voluntary standards

- Links to other web-based resources

Meaning and origins of stakeholder

The theme of this chapter is stakeholders: what they are, how they can be managed, how they influence the management of the company, and the validity of the very concept. We have raised the idea of stakeholders in Chapter 5 when we discuss the partnerships companies are creating with stakeholders as a feature of the business-society relationship that has come to the fore during the current era of globalization. As we touched on then, partnerships are not always straightforward affairs, and one of the reasons for this is the complexity of the stakeholder concept. Prominent CEOs such as IBM's Sam Palmisano have called the shift in business from shareholder companies to stakeholder companies as a defining element of the modern corporation,[1] but there is plenty of disagreement about what this implies in terms of definition, management practice, and consequences.

It might seem obvious but while the term stakeholder has gained popularity fairly recently, companies have always had stakeholders of one kind or another. There have always been investors, employees, business customers, consumers, and local communities that are affected by and have an influence on the organization called the company. They can be subdivided so that, for instance, employees comprise managers, supervisors,

> ### ■ Key concept: Stakeholder
>
> A stakeholder is any person or organization affected by or with the power to influence a company's decisions and actions. Because of the company's impact or their influence, stakeholders are deemed to have a stake in the company. In the shareholder theory of the firm which began to dominate the Anglo-Saxon debate about business' purpose in the 1960s, the outcome that executives are accountable for is shareholder value. Stakeholder theory of the firm offers an alternative to this by making it explicit that the firm has material and/or moral reasons to consider its relationship with more than just investors. In countries such as Austria, stakeholder participation in corporate governance is enshrined in law, but elsewhere such as the USA and Australia it is a voluntary aspect of management that is being accepted as at worst prudent and better still performance enhancing.

skilled workers, labourers, and so on, all with their own vested interests. Indeed, although a lot of corporate responsibility literature uses the term company to refer to an homogenous entity (reflecting common practice in the mass media and day to day parlance), companies often need to be understood as the locus of multiple, frequently competing contracts between individuals and their alliances. There is a long history of viewing companies in this way, but it is no longer commonplace. In fact, critics of stakeholder theory might argue that replacing unsympathetic terms such as worker-management relations with the seemingly more neutral, inclusive 'stakeholder' is a victory for normative modern management theory. We will return to the ideational nature of stakeholder theory later, but first it is worth considering, if stakeholders have always been part of the business landscape, why we need a special term now, and why that term has gained particular popularity in corporate responsibility literature.

In Chapter 5, we talk about contemporary corporate responsibility practice as the product of a particular socio-political discourse: one where companies are responding to certain features of globalization such as the changing nature of governance and the multi-tiered values framework that shapes expectations of business. Stakeholder, in part, has gained its prominence because of such changes. A company might legally have a primary duty to its shareholders, and senior managers might feel more comfortable exercising that responsibility than a more loosely defined one to society, but examples throughout this book demonstrate how companies are affected in a material sense by a range of organizations, individuals, and alliances built around common interests that typically position the company's behaviour as something they want to influence. Equally, there have been numerous examples of how the company affects others such as workers in supplier factories, consumers reliant on product safety for their well-being, communities dependent on a company for employment creation, former employees living off of company pensions, and so on. Into an already tangled web, rising concern about sustainable development (see Chapter 3) has added non-human stakeholders such as the natural environment, the global commons, and climate.

As awareness of the social and political consequences of globalization rose from the 1970s onwards, stakeholder as an analytical construct became widely used, for example in the influential work of Giddens (1991, 1994) and Ackerman (1999). The term had been used in business literature since the 1930s[2] as a way of distinguishing between the main groups towards which companies have different kinds of duty: in particular, shareholders, customers, consumers, and employees. In 1984, however, Freeman's *Strategic Management: A Stakeholder Approach* presented stakeholders as something more extensive, complex, and nuanced than this. What is more, they were not simply to be viewed as a convenient taxonomic device: for Freeman, managing stakeholders effectively was essential to the very survival and prosperity of the enterprise. In what he calls '*radical externalism*', Freeman proposes that managers pay attention to stakeholders as a matter of course by adopting integrative strategic management processes.

In light of the very significant impact that Freeman's book has had on management theory, there are two points to note. First, as Walsh (2005) observes, Freeman wrote at a time when business was seen as weak and '*on the ropes*'. As discussed in Chapters 2 and 5, stagflation was undermining major capitalist economies; US business, in particular, was under threat from Japanese competitors; there were unprecedented levels of mergers and acquisitions; companies were increasingly targets of consumer and environmentalist advocacy. Ironically, given how stakeholder engagement is today portrayed by some as a way of harnessing or reducing the power of corporations, the business world that Freeman sought to help was something fragile and troubled.

Second, in contrast with some later authors, Freeman is not positing stakeholder theory as an attack on the shareholder-centric theory of the firm that is central to liberal economics. On the contrary, he adopts a very instrumental approach to stakeholder theory, under which companies choose who their stakeholders are, based on the potential of those stakeholders to jeopardize the firm's survival. This is an important point to note because, subsequently, others have presented the shareholder and stakeholder theories of the firm as something mutually opposed. But as Walsh notes, Freeman only raises this possibility right at the end of his book when he asks (and leaves unanswered):

Can the notion that managers bear a fiduciary relationship to stockholders ... be replaced by a concept of management whereby they must act in the interests of the stakeholders of the organization?

(Freeman, 1984, cited in Walsh, 2005, p 249)

Freeman is not alone in subsuming stakeholder management to the purpose of wealth creation,[3] but his work is widely cited by those who have a quite different view of stakeholder engagement. Rather than sets of discrete, typically bilateral, relationships upon which the company chooses to embark with stakeholder groups, more recent stakeholder theory treats the firm as an organism that is embedded in a complex web of relationships, and requires the company to see these other organisms not as objects of managerial action, as was often the case hitherto, but as subjects with their own objectives and purposes. The stakeholder management model therefore involves the company being aware of, and responsive to, the demands of its constituents, including employees, customers, investors, suppliers, and local communities. In contrast with Freeman, an important consequence of this is that shareholders are no longer regarded as the most important constituents and shareholder value is not the sole criterion for assessing the company's performance.

This pluralist notion of the company's responsibilities clearly runs counter to the liberal economic model of the firm, which postulates that business contributes to the public good by pursuing its narrow economic goals and, hence, that managers should concentrate on maximizing the market value of their companies. It is predicated on the belief that, in real life, the distinction between economic and social ends is seldom as clear as liberal economists pretend, because economic decisions have social consequences and vice versa, and the very idea of separate social and economic worlds is seen by some as mistaken.[4] Although perhaps not what Freeman intended, the stakeholder model has become the dominant framework for seeing companies as integrated in, rather than separated from, the rest of society.

■ Discussion points

Stakeholder has become a common term in corporate and government parlance.

- What is attractive about the term?
- Is Freeman right to emphasize the importance of knowing one's stakeholders?
- Think of a company: who are its stakeholders?

Management or engagement?

According to Andriof et al. (2002), today's stakeholder thinking concerns the interactive, mutually engaged, and responsive relationships that '*establish the very context of doing business, and create the groundwork for transparency and accountability*' (p 29). From this perspective, Freeman's stakeholder management is one that is too business-centric, but one reason that managers have accepted the stakeholder concept may be that it complements management thinking. In Chapters 1 and 2, we discuss the difficulty of defining what business' responsibilities are, and often managers are faced with sets of issues that beg the questions, '*What am I responsible for?*' and '*To whom am I responsible?*' For managers who have been trained to manage processes such as marketing, production, or finance, it can be easier to understand responsibility in the context of such functional disciplines and, therefore, responsibilities to defined constituencies may have more resonance than long, seemingly ad hoc, lists of normative social and environmental issues.[5]

In other words, for stakeholder theorists at least, the value of an issue for a manager derives from the fact that a stakeholder has legitimized it. As Rasche and Esser (2006) point out, this is in line with social theorist Habermas' notion of discourse ethics, wherein ethical norms are justified not by reference to a priori principles, but because all members of society can reach a consensus around them. In contrast with ethicists such as Mill, Kant, Nozick, or Rawls, who offer universal ethical principles (see Chapter 2), Habermas claims that ethical norms can vary according to differences in context. Thus, what is ethical in one situation can change, provided that it is tested and justified through a context-specific discourse involving members of society. Moreover, although the norms can change, what must remain constant and universal are the rules under which the discourse itself is carried out.

Corporate responsibility theory offers a great deal of advice on how to conduct a consistent, robust, and credible discourse with stakeholders (see Box 9.1). The AA1000 Series, for example, is, in some ways, an attempt to spell out the universal rules for reaching an ethical consensus through stakeholder participation, comprising four main elements that are underpinned by the principle of stakeholder engagement: (a) company commitment to social and ethical accounting, auditing, and reporting, with stakeholders playing a key role; (b) defining and accounting for the company's actions through stakeholder consultation that identifies issues relating to social and ethical performance, the scope of the social audit, relevant indicators, and the collection and analyses of information; (c) preparation of a corporate responsibility report to be audited by an external group, and subjected to external feedback; and (d) embedding social accountability systems into mainstream management practice.[6]

But there are a number of problems involved in applying stakeholder theory in everyday management. First, it can be difficult to identify who stakeholders are. At the broadest level, they are individuals, groups, or entities (including, some would argue, the natural environment) that claim rights or interests in a company and in its past, present, and future activities. To narrow this down, Freeman (1984) drew a distinction between 'primary' and 'secondary' stakeholders. Primary stakeholders are those without whose participation a company cannot survive (e.g. investors, employees, suppliers, customers, and the governments and communities that provide infrastructure and markets). Secondary stakeholders are those that influence the company or are affected by it, but who are not essential to its survival, although they may be able to help or harm the company (e.g. the media, terrorists). The manager's duty, therefore, is to create sufficient

---

Box 9.1 **Commonly cited phases and factors in engaging with stakeholders**

Phases of managing stakeholder dialogue

1 Selection of stakeholders
2 Stakeholder dialogue
3 Interpretation of information from dialogue
4 Decisions about company actions
5 Response to the dialogue through activities

Key factors in acting on stakeholder dialogue

1 Awareness that an issue exists
2 Commitment to prioritize and resource an issue
3 Capacity/availability of resources to tackle an issue
4 Consensus amongst the company and its stakeholders over the issues and relevance of stakeholder dialogue in general

---

(Sources: Adapted from Pedersen, 2006; Andriof et al., 2002)

wealth, value, or satisfaction for primary stakeholders to ensure that they remain part of the stakeholder system. He may pay attention to secondary stakeholders as well, but there may often be circumstances under which the interests of primary stakeholders are pursued at the expense of those that are secondary (e.g. taking a money-losing product sold to poor communities off the market).

Stakeholders include groups with quite different expectations. One common distinction made is that between those who are influenced by the company's actions and those who have an interest in what the company does. In order to understand the nature of a particular stakeholder and to assess what priority to give its expectations, managers are often advised to make judgements about which they have significant or insignificant degrees of interest, and about those with whom the company has high or low degrees of influence (see Figure 9.1). This type of approach, however, does little to help managers to make decisions based on a stakeholder's moral claim and has led to a situation in which companies are accused of responding to stakeholders with the loudest voices or most power, rather than to those with the greatest need or strongest entitlement. Phillips (2003) criticizes stakeholder theory for failing to distinguish between, and prioritize, stakeholders based on a moral rather than a business obligation. For Goodpaster (2002), stakeholder analysis is incomplete if it does not weigh the significance of the identified options for the different stakeholder groups and make a normative judgement that integrates this information into a decision. As Gibson (2000) argues, if we do not accept this ethical dimension to the notion of stakeholder, the term itself becomes meaningless, its use limited to a form of shorthand for referring to a, possibly ad hoc, group of individuals.

Partly because of this, Freeman abandoned the primary–secondary stakeholder distinction, although it remains widely used by corporate responsibility practitioners. One outcome he saw was that stakeholders were being treated as the means to corporate

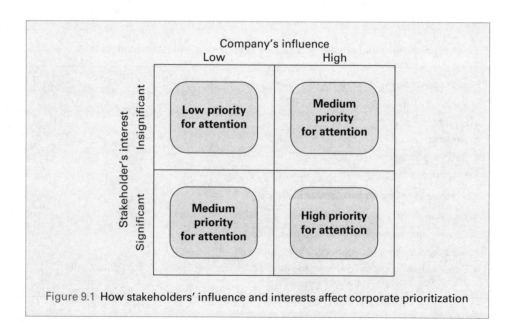

Figure 9.1 **How stakeholders' influence and interests affect corporate prioritization**

ends, rather than as entities whose interests should be served by the company.[7] This is certainly evident in much of what is called 'stakeholder engagement' today, in which consultation and dialogue is carried out with the aim of gathering important input and ideas, anticipating and managing conflicts, improving decision making, building consensus among diverse views, and strengthening the company's relationships and reputation. There can be a strong business case for stakeholder engagement, including reduced costs, opening new markets, and protecting the company against activism. But this leaves companies open to criticism that they are picking and choosing who to call a stakeholder, and hence whom to listen to, and some managers feel that they are under pressure to respond to some stakeholders rather than others, based on who corporate headquarters regards as important rather than who the company affects.[8]

These tensions are highlighted in some of the examples of partnership discussed in Chapter 5, but it is worth reiterating that there is an important distinction to be made between the promise of the stakeholder model, as described by some corporate responsibility theorists, and the way in which it is actually being used by companies at the present time. In theory, stakeholder dialogue, engagement, and participation are at the heart of a more democratic form of corporate accountability. As a leading advocate of a stakeholder approach to corporate responsibility describes it:

> Corporate accountability, especially when based on stakeholder engagement ... is all about learning and change: learning about the organization itself, about those who have a relationship with it, and learning about its place in the larger scheme of things.

> *(AccountAbility, 2002, p 5)*

In practice, the stakeholder model is more typically applied so that a company can manage its stakeholders in the sense of influence and control. This is not to say that stakeholders are taken advantage of, or experience no benefit from this approach: at the very least, companies that participate in extensive stakeholder dialogue have become more sensitized and sensitive to stakeholder concerns. But it is also becoming clear that, if the stakeholder model is to become part of a new way of managing the business–society relationship, companies will need to give up some of their power and influence in order to become accountable to, rather than simply in discussion with, the wider stakeholder community.[9] One arena of corporate responsibility management where this would need to be evident is in the partnerships between a company and other organizations. We

---

■ **Discussion points**

The list of a company's stakeholders is potentially enormous.

- Is the distinction between primary and secondary stakeholders valid and useful?
- What are the strengths and weaknesses of using stakeholders to decide the responsibilities of a company?
- Should companies be accountable to stakeholders?

e discussed these in general in Chapter 5; now we turn to the particular type of nership created through voluntary corporate responsibility standards.

Corporate responsibility standards

Stakeholder partnerships are frequently presented as an approach to corporate responsibility well-suited to companies wrestling with the challenges of globalization. Advocates often cite them as a way to hold companies to account in an era when the limits of traditional governance structures are being tested (see Chapter 5). This is taken a step further in the idea of voluntary multi-stakeholder standards or codes of practice. Voluntary standards are a particular approach to managing business' effects on stakeholders. We begin by discussing this approach in general, but will then highlight in particular the stakeholder dimension to it.

Features of standards

Standards, guidelines, and codes of conduct or practice are largely synonymous terms for an important tool in the management of corporate responsibility. The terms might be interchangeable, but there are many types and to say that a company has adopted a standard says little, in itself, about the performance, policies, or strategies of that company. Over half of the 200 largest companies have business codes of some fashion, yet there are enormous differences between businesses in terms of what aspects of corporate behaviour are covered and the extent to which they influence what the company does.[10] Paine et al. (2005) have tried to make sense of this by identifying eight principles that cover the statements, commitments, and requirements found in business codes (see Box 9.2).

Box 9.2 **Underlying principles of business codes**

---

1 Fiduciary principle—aspects of a code that define the responsibilities of directors and management to the company and its investors.

2 Property principle—concerning respect for the property rights and assets of the company and its competitors.

3 Reliability principle—concerning the honouring of commitments.

4 Transparency principle—concerning the conduct of business in a truthful and open manner.

5 Dignity principle—concerning respect for people's dignity, including health and safety, human rights, freedom from coercion, and human development.

6 Fairness principle—aspects to do with engaging in free and fair competition.

7 Citizenship principle—aspects requiring the company to act as a responsible citizen of the community, including legal compliance, environmental responsibility, and non-involvement in politics.

8 Responsiveness principle—aspects requiring the company to be responsive to parties with legitimate claims and concerns about its activities.

(Sources: Adapted from Paine et al., 2005; Carroll & Buckholtz, 2006; and Rasche, 2010).

These show that the codes go beyond much of what is included in corporate responsibility today. Many of contemporary corporate responsibility's issues fall under their principles of 'dignity' (e.g. labour rights, workplace health and safety), 'citizenship' (e.g. environmental management, community involvement), and 'responsiveness' (e.g. stakeholder engagement). As is evident in the discussion of corporate responsibility in the global value chain (see Chapter 5), there are some who would like corporate responsibility to do more to address the principles of transparency and fairness (e.g. treating suppliers fairly and ensuring fair competition). There are also those in the business community who argue that it is hypocritical for companies to talk about corporate responsibility if they disregard the principles of property and reliability.

Broad business codes can provide a context for managing corporate responsibility, as is the case, for example, with Johnson & Johnson's statement of principles (see Box 9.3). For the most part, however, modern corporate responsibility has more narrowly defined concerns. In their compendium of codes, Cragg and McKague (2003) identify seven main issues covered by corporate responsibility standards:

1 the natural environment;

2 labour;

3 corporate governance;

4 money laundering;

Box 9.3 **Johnson and Johnson's credo**

We believe our first responsibility is to the doctors, nurses and patients, to mothers and fathers and others who use our products and services. In meeting their needs everything we do must be of high quality. We must constantly strive to reduce our costs in order to maintain reasonable prices. Customers' orders must be serviced promptly and accurately. Our suppliers and distributors must have an opportunity to make a fair profit.

We are responsible to our employees, the men and women who work with us throughout the world. Everyone must be considered as an individual. We must respect their dignity and recognize their merit. They must have a sense of security in their jobs. Compensation must be fair and adequate, and working conditions clean, orderly and safe. We must be mindful of ways to help our employees fulfil their family responsibilities. Employees must feel free to make suggestions and complaints. There must be equal opportunity for employment, development and advancement for those qualified. We must provide competent management, and their actions must be just and ethical.

We are responsible to the communities in which we live and work and to the world community as well. We must be good citizens, support good works and charities and bear our fair share of taxes. We must encourage civic improvements and better health and education. We must maintain in good order the property we are privileged to use, protecting the environment and natural resources.

Our final responsibility is to our stockholders. Business must make a sound profit. We must experiment with new ideas. Research must be carried on, innovative programs developed and mistakes paid for. New equipment must be purchased, new facilities provided and new products launched. Reserves must be created to provide for adverse times. When we operate according to these principles, the stockholders should realize a fair return.

(Source: **www.jnj.com/connect/about-jnj/?flash=true**—accessed 20 January 2010)

5 bribery and corruption;

6 human rights;

7 corporate responsibility reporting principles (see Box 9.4).

In some instances, these issues are addressed in individual company standards which, despite sometimes involving a degree of stakeholder consultation, fall short of what

Box 9.4 Examples of corporate responsibility standards

Issue covered	Examples of standards
Environmental	CERES principles ISO14000 environmental management series Kyoto Protocol
Labour	Fair Labor Association workplace code of conduct ETI base code International Confederation of Free Trade Unions basic code of labour conduct
Corporate governance	OECD principles of corporate governance Principles for corporate governance in the Commonwealth Toronto Stock Exchange guidelines for improved corporate governance
Money laundering	Wolfsberg anti-money laundering principles Basel Committee on banking supervision
Bribery and corruption	OECD convention combating bribery of foreign public officials in international business transactions International Chamber of Commerce rules of conduct to combat extortion and bribery Extractive Industry Transparency Initiative
Human rights	Amnesty International human rights principles for companies UN draft norms on the responsibilities of transnational corporations and other business enterprises with regard to human rights Voluntary principles on security and human rights
Corporate reporting	AA1000 series Global Reporting Initiative guidelines on social, economic and environmental reporting
Comprehensive	UN Global Compact principles OECD guidelines for multinational enterprises ISO 26000 corporate responsibility standard

might be considered a stakeholder partnership. However, they can also form part of comprehensive industry-specific or general business standards, such as the Forest Stewardship Council's principles of sustainable forest management and the Equator Principles for the financial industry.

The distinctions between standards have become important as interest has grown in assessing the effectiveness of so-called 'voluntary' standards.[11] Particular attention has been paid to the way in which standards are developed, as a determinant of their robustness, effectiveness, and credibility, and the following types are common.

1 Company standards developed within a company for its own use, perhaps with some external consultation, and with reference to relevant international norms and standards (e.g. on human rights, emissions, or corruption).

2 Company standards built on consultation with relevant stakeholders and making explicit reference to international standards.

3 Industry standards developed by a peer group of companies, perhaps with external consultation, and with differing degrees of reference to international norms and standards.

4 Multi-stakeholder standards developed for an industry, or a wider range of companies, built on a consensus among business, non-government, and trade union organizations.

5 Independent standards made available to an industry, or wider range of companies, but developed by non-business groups, such as trade unions and NGOs.

6 Framework agreements between a company and trade unions.

Some argue that standards developed by companies, separately or with their peers, are more likely to reflect the concerns of Northern consumers than the full breadth of social or environmental issues relevant to a company, and that standards developed independently of business are more comprehensive.[12] Kolk et al. (1999) claim that certain types of standard are likely to have a greater impact than others: for example, that those developed by international organizations, such as the Organisation for Economic Co-operation and Development and the International Labour Organization, or those developed by civil society organizations, such as the Clean Clothes Campaign and Social Accountability International, will be more rigorous than those developed by individual companies or industries, such as Levi Strauss, Nike, and the Apparel Industry Partnership. There is, however, less difference in content between company standards and independent ones today than there was a few years ago and Sethi (2003) argues that company standards can be more effective, provided that they are subject to external scrutiny (see below).

Ranganathan (1998) says that a standard should meet the '3 Cs' used in financial auditing; that is, they must be:

1 *comprehensive*, or complete enough to cover the issues that are most pertinent or material to be the company;

2 *comparable*, to allow inter-company assessment of performance;

3 *credible* enough to allow business and other stakeholders to trust their integrity and to use them in making informed judgements.

This last requirement is also sometimes called 'materiality'. Various additional characteristics of a credible standard have been identified, as follows.[13]

1 Content that is relevant to the industry, but not simply a reflection of the most publicized problems.

2 Clarity and conciseness in terms of language, style, and format.

3 Explicit reference made to relevant international standards and conventions.

4 Inclusivity, requiring the participation of all key stakeholders who have a legitimate interest in what the standard is measuring.

5 Continual improvement of the criteria against which performance is assessed.

6 A commitment regarding to whom the results of any assessment will be disclosed.

7 Suitability of the standard for implementation, including setting out indicators that are measurable and trackable over time.

8 Availability of the standard in the main languages of the locations within which it will be used.

■ Discussion points

Stakeholder standards are often portrayed as the most robust way of implementing voluntary regulation.

- What roles do you think stakeholders can play in implementing standards?
- Should stakeholders ignore the law when deciding standards?
- How can it be ensured that all stakeholder voices are heard?

Multi-stakeholder standards

There are many standards, and a common complaint heard from managers is that they are required to comply with too many standards, many of which address the same issues. Initiatives such as JOINT (the Joint Initiative on Corporate Accountability and Workers' Rights) involving several voluntary labour standard organizations, and Global Social Compliance comprising companies looking to harmonize the implementation of labour and environmental standards, are attempts to address this concern, but it remains an issue, especially amongst suppliers of Western retailers and brands, some of which have received up to 40 audits in a month. Only a relatively small number of standards can show extensive stakeholder participation in their development, implementation, and

SNAPSHOT 9.1

The Global Reporting Initiative guidelines

The Global Reporting Initiative (GRI) guidelines serve as a framework for reporting on social, economic, and environmental performance. Launched in 2000, they are now in their third iteration based on input from thousands of people in many parts of the world. They are neither a performance standard nor a management system, although they can be useful to the development of both. Their primary purpose is to provide a common benchmark to encourage companies to communicate what actions they are taking to improve non-financial performance, the outcomes of these actions, and the future strategies for improving performance.

The guidelines, which are freely available at **www.globalreporting.org**, represent what GRI has identified as the most relevant reporting content. There are also supplements for industries, such as mining and banking, and technical protocols on specific indicators, such as child labour and energy. Companies can choose whether to produce reports '*in accordance with*' or more loosely '*with reference to*' the guidelines, and 90 per cent of those that cite the guidelines choose the latter. This figure may change as GRI introduces more levels of reporting, but questions about how many and how fast new levels should be introduced are indicative of a wider issue that GRI faces in balancing prescription and flexibility.

Despite any shortcomings, proponents say that the guidelines have provided the signposts that have led many companies away from producing reports consisting of, what critics call, photos of happy, smiling children and not much else, to those that at least begin to recognize the array of social, economic, and environmental issues with which the company is involved. Furthermore, by retaining the support of business and non-business constituencies while undertaking two major revisions, the guidelines have become a testing ground for global stakeholder engagement.

(Sources: GRI, 2002; Baker, 2002; Leipziger, 2003; **www.globalreporting.org**)

Quick Questions

The GRI guidelines are intended to provide a common framework for company reporting on sustainability issues.

1 Why is this kind of common framework necessary?

2 Why has the GRI focused on guidelines rather than on a certifiable standard?

3 What are the strengths and weaknesses of this kind of approach?

accountability. But even those that can have their distinct characteristics as the following three examples show:

SA8000—the independent code[14]

In 1998, the Council on Economic Priorities (now Social Accountability International, or 'SAI') created SA8000, with advice from representatives of business, trade unions, and NGOs. It is a verifiable standard, focusing on labour rights and worker welfare, and intended to be applicable to any industry and in any country. It combines elements of ILO labour conventions with ISO management systems, and has been revised and extended, to include more detailed provisions for specific industries such as agriculture.

SAI and its panel of companies, civil society organizations, and academics certify companies that comply with its provisions. This means that conditions in their facilities have been verified by independent, accredited SA8000 auditors, and that the auditors' findings have been ratified by SAI.

SA8000 is different from many standards in that it has both performance and process elements, prescribing not only the labour criteria with which a company must comply, but also acceptable systems for embedding the standard into daily management practice. Over 1,000 facilities in 55 countries have been certified to date. A bone of contention is that these facilities bear the cost of auditing, even though certification is typically a buyer's requirement. But this is not fundamentally different from other costs relating to management systems such as ISO certification.

Forest Stewardship Council—a stakeholder-owned standard[15]

The Forest Stewardship Council (FSC) was first mooted as an idea in 1990 in response to the failure of traditional approaches to arrest the decline of the world's forest resources. The organization, which is managed by a secretariat and overseen by a partnership comprising business, indigenous rights organizations, community groups, and environmental NGOs, acts as custodian to a certification standard that sets out key principles and criteria of forest stewardship. The standard provides a basis for assessing if a forest is being responsibly managed in relation to silviculture practices, environmental impact, working conditions, workers' and community rights, and indigenous people's rights. Certification of a forest involves a fairly extensive four-stage auditing process, including pre-assessments, field visits, peer review, and ratification. A certificate is valid for five years, although there may be interim inspections.

A feature of FSC is that it is not only a standard, but also a partnership. As an organization, it draws support from a wide membership base around the world. Moreover, its governance structure is designed to limit the influence of any single member, or category of member. The FSC board features representatives of those with a commercial interest, those with an environmental interest, and those with a social interest in forests, and these groups all have a say in major decisions at the general assembly. This structure is an interesting example of global democracy in action and, although it has been criticized for being slow and unwieldy, the FSC standard is widely regarded as the benchmark for forest certification.

The Equator Principles—an industry-wide stakeholder code[16]

The Equator Principles stipulate how financial institutions should consider environmental and social issues in their project finance operations. The signatories are primarily European and North American banks, and the standard clearly reflects reputational concerns about their portfolios of lending to developing countries. These arise from the potentially high risk of adverse social and environmental impacts that are attached to the infrastructure, energy, extractive, and other projects financed in this way (e.g. relocation, ecological damage, impact on communities). The Principles commit banks to formulating environmental and social policies and processes against which individual projects can be assessed for compliance. Their provisions are based on the social and environmental policies and procedures of the International Finance Corporation, which, among other things, require banks to screen proposed projects according to their potential social and environmental impacts. The outcome of the screening process, in turn, triggers a range of follow-up activities, and the most dangerous projects are subjected to more rigorous assessment, public consultation, and information disclosure requirements.

While signatory banks agree to adopt these policies and procedures, implementation is left up to the individual bank and, in contrast with FSC or SA8000, there is no requirement that companies independently verify how they are implementing the standard. Indeed, the Principles explicitly state that they are a benchmark for use in the development of each member company's policies. There is, however, an implicit assumption that, by involving large project finance banks, the Principles will create an environment within which good social and environmental policies are the norm, and will encourage industry-wide improvements. The standard is too new to say whether this will happen and, at present, success is being measured in terms of the number and size of the signatory companies, with about forty banks signing up to the most recent revision of the Principles in 2006.

Stakeholder consensus: deviance and uniformity

A promise of stakeholder engagement is that it will allow companies to better understand and respond to the expectations of society. Standards are a way to establish a widely applicable benchmark for measuring corporate responsibilities, but one should be careful not to overestimate the feasibility or desirability of universal norms and practices. It is possible to portray the stakeholder role in applying standards as a mere embellishment on the uniformity and standardization found in conventional quality or financial management. But the additionality of stakeholder engagement is if it helps meet the specific challenges of non-conventional performance management. An example of this is the defining and securing of good performance in diverse locations. Cannon (1994) identifies five types of community in which business might have a role to play to ameliorate the effect of economic downturns. The first is high-stress environments, in which the community has endured a long period of economic disadvantage, and has consequently suffered economically and psychologically. The second is structurally disadvantaged areas, such as remote islands or towns, which have lost their physical competitive advantage, as, for example, happened in Liverpool when UK trade shifted from having a transatlantic, to a more European, focus. Another type is the crisis zone, within which a dominant company or industry in a region collapses, as has happened with the automotive industry in the UK's Midlands. A different type of community is that of the transitional area, within which the important industries for the local economy are changing, as has happened in the German Ruhr. Finally, there are communities in which powerhouse industries that have been the catalyst for local growth (e.g. California's software industry) find themselves buffeted by competition from elsewhere and have to adjust accordingly.

Hamann et al. (2005) have pointed out, in the South African context, that corporate responsibility needs to take into account five realities specific to that country. First, there is the historical legacy of poverty and inequality that is reflected today in the 55 per cent of the population living in poverty, in over 30 per cent unemployment, in chronic housing and sanitation shortages, and in high HIV prevalence. Second, corporate responsibility needs to recognize, and be rigorous enough to combat, the distrust of certain companies and industries arising from their complicity in exploitation and the apartheid regime. Third, there are established traditions of corporate responsibility in South Africa, particularly community social investment, and now black economic empowerment, through which black entrepreneurship is being encouraged. Fourth, the struggle against apartheid and the consequent emphasis put on legislation to ensure social justice, fundamental human rights, and democracy, mean that government has a crucial role to play in corporate responsibility. Finally, small and medium-sized companies in the formal and informal sectors make up 95 per cent of South African business and their role, capacity, and needs are all relevant for corporate responsibility.

These issues are not only pertinent to South Africa, or even Africa more widely. The particular issues that are high on the African corporate responsibility agenda may not be identical to those of other regions (see Box 9.5), but, more significantly, they are often different to, or at least more nuanced than, the corporate responsibility agendas that many multinational companies think of as globally relevant. Often these agendas are built on what Western-based multinationals and more significantly what Western-oriented stakeholders think should be the priorities of Africa or elsewhere. Thus, for example, Western stakeholder priorities for Africa might be to combat corruption, improve governance and transparency, and improve infrastructure, while local priorities might be to improve the terms of trading, create good jobs, and transfer technology. Such issues may not be mutually exclusive, but it can be questioned how far corporate responsibility can progress if both sets of priorities are not recognized, and there remain serious questions about the effectiveness of stakeholder participation in getting multinationals in particular to tackle local priorities. As Rajak's work on corporate responsibility in the mining industry shows (2006), companies may not deliberately seek to rule out local priorities, but their decisions about what to support have the effect of legitimizing or delegitimizing particular issues.

Different perspectives on what corporate responsibility's priorities are have also been noted in Latin America, where advocates in the West may focus on rainforest conservation and biodiversity, while local people may be more concerned about poverty, poor education, bad housing, and scarce healthcare.[17] According to Schmidheiny:

> the key [corporate responsibility] challenges for these regions ... have to do not so much with the number of companies talking about [corporate responsibility], but with creating a home-grown, meaningful form of [corporate responsibility] that addresses local issues and improves society, while also strengthening government's capacity.

(2006, p 22)

■ Discussion points

The responsibilities of companies can vary according to location and circumstance.

- Why do some stakeholders misunderstand local priorities?
- Is it useful for a company to have a universal vision of its responsibilities of the kind developed by Johnson & Johnson (see Box 9.3)?
- What are the difficulties companies face in recognizing regional differences?

Box 9.5 Comparison of social and environmental issues across selected countries and regions

Country/region	Social and environmental issue
European Union	Decoupling growth from consumption Sustaining welfare, health, and labour standards in a global economy Clean air and emissions trading Marine environment and fisheries
USA	Energy security, including renewed calls for nuclear power Climate change policy Public health accessibility Social security Corporate governance
Latin America	Rich–poor divide Basic environmental management Good public governance and fighting corruption Infrastructure Competitiveness and security of small farmers
Africa	Good public governance and fighting corruption Terms of trading Infrastructure Conflict Managerial capacity
Japan	Nuclear power Air pollution Exploitation of offshore fisheries and foreign tropical forests Urban environment Foreign workers

(Sources: PWC, 2006; Ethical Corporation, 2006)

SNAPSHOT 9.2

The European Alliance for Corporate Social Responsibility

In 2006, the European Commission announced that it would embrace corporate responsibility as a voluntary approach to help business to develop the skills for effective relationships with stakeholders, for mainstreaming corporate responsibility in the minds of business leaders and in business processes, and to provide companies with effective tools for internal analysis and evaluation. In the words of Günter Verheugen, European Commissioner:

> There will be no monitoring, no benchmarking, no naming and shaming, no reporting requirements. [Corporate responsibility] is completely voluntary. We will never have a framework for [corporate responsibility] because it is a philosophy, a concept.

The involvement of the Commission dated back to several years, and had largely been welcomed because, depending on one's point of view, there was unease about what corporate responsibility meant and where its limits lay, and also about the lack of a government role in issues that hitherto had largely been the purview of elected parliaments. A 2001 Green Paper stirred up controversy, however, because it was seen to use corporate responsibility as a springboard for new regulations, rather than to create the conditions for the vigorous free market entrepreneurship that some saw as essential to Europe's prosperity.

The Green Paper was shelved, but in 2006, the Commission announced the European Alliance for Corporate Social Responsibility, which it describes as a multi-stakeholder partnership to help business to engage in corporate responsibility without putting any new regulatory burdens upon it. Vladimir Špilda, European Commissioner, declared corporate responsibility *'a business opportunity'*; Ethical Performance called the Alliance *'a ragbag of measures dressed up as strategy'* that effectively ended the EU dream of becoming a pole of corporate responsibility excellence.

What it certainly left unresolved was whether corporate responsibility could fulfil what some saw as its most important role in the European context: to help to reconfigure the balance between institutions that, together, make up society; something the German government's Sustainability Council had identified as essential. Equally, the emphasis on voluntary soon seemed at odds with existing European legislation. France's 2001 *Loi relative aux nouvelles régulations économiques* (Law on New Economic Regulations) already required companies to report on social and environmental performance, and the EU Accounts Modernisation Directive of 2003 makes specific mention of non-financial performance.

(Sources: Habisch et al., 2005; *Ethical Performance*, 2006d; Špilda, 2006)

Quick Questions

The European Commission has tried to carve out a European vision of corporate responsibility, based on the Union's historical values and the role that it sees business playing in a cohesive society in future.

1 Is government right to get involved in corporate responsibility in a facilitating, rather than a regulatory, way?

2 Would a regulatory approach do more to maintain European social values in the face of global competition?

3 Is it realistic for Europe to have its own vision of social welfare in the twenty-first century?

Government and governance

As Visser et al. (2006) point out, what makes corporate responsibility important in the context of any developing country is that it embodies many of the dilemmas that business faces in trying to be responsible, sustainable, and ethical. For example, it raises questions about when local traditions take precedence over international standards, about how far a company's responsibilities extend in providing public services, and about when business' involvement in local governance enhances a weak governance infrastructure and when it constitutes an unhealthy intrusion into the political process. This last question reflects a wider theme that marks out discussions about corporate responsibility in developing economies, i.e. the role of government. While the European Union, for example, has chosen to emphasize corporate responsibility as a voluntary approach that places no extra legislative burden on business (see Case Study 9), the role of government and the links between corporate responsibility and regulation are central to debates in developing nations. There are various explanations for this. For example, in China, the government has defined corporate responsibility in terms of its own priority of ensuring social stability and uses the term to mean government regulation.[18] In parts of Latin America, Asia, and Africa, an important element of the corporate responsibility agenda concerns fighting corruption and improving public governance, and therefore includes activities to build government capacity and the rule of law. Companies also do not want to be saddled with an unsustainable burden of providing public goods, and would therefore prefer to partner with government and others. In general, it seems to come down to the fact that the business community is reasonably satisfied that, in countries with developed economies and democracies, government is able to maintain social stability; it is more concerned that business will be over-regulated. In developing economies, however, especially those in which governments are either weak or dictatorial, the business community is more concerned about the rule of law, and the creation of social stability and a favourable business environment, and therefore under-, rather than over-, regulation is the issue.

None of this is to pretend that some companies have not, over the years, thrived in oppressive regimes, or that companies are not prepared to do business in countries, such as Burma and China, that are openly resistant to Western ideals of public governance. But there is evidence that companies operating in such countries at times use corporate responsibility not simply as a substitute for good public governance, but as a way of introducing good governance norms, in the hope that they will shape public institutions in the future.[19] This, in turn, reflects a belief that if ever there was a business case for taking advantage of unstable, oppressive political conditions, for multinational companies and industries in a global economy these conditions represent an undesirable risk—one that, if it cannot be avoided entirely (e.g. because of the physical location of natural resources, or the competitive advantage of low-waged labour), must be reduced, and corporate responsibility offers a means of achieving that end.

These are compelling arguments, especially if one believes that Western prosperity is a consequence of democracy as much as of capitalism. It is also worth noting that, in countries such as Morocco, governments have used corporate responsibility as a framework within which to promote a renewed commitment to better labour practices, controlling child labour, and new legislation to combat corruption, and to improve workplace rights of women and the disabled, and the rights of trade unions. Indeed, seeing this as a way of complying with trade agreements and attracting businesses in competition with lower waged competitors, the government has made corporate responsibility part of its strategy to win foreign investment.

Yet many still resent or resist corporate responsibility and see it as an outsiders' imposition. This is not simply a case of the status quo resisting reform. Developing countries can be victims of the subsidies and protections that the USA, European, and other countries give to industries such as agriculture and defence; policies that, in turn, are related to poverty and lack of economic opportunity. Moreover, poverty and exploitation are seen by some as the hallmark of colonial and post-war entrepreneurs, and this sudden conversion to responsibility is seen as hypocrisy, at best, and commercial gamesmanship, at worst.[20] As multinationals headquartered in countries such as India, China, Brazil, and Mexico gain prominence, and foreign direct investment from such countries grows (see Chapter 4), so speculation has mounted that this will undermine Western multinationals' efforts to raise standards. Such views reflect a somewhat rose-tinted view of Western corporate behaviour in developing countries over the years, and may at times be inflected with racial prejudice. At the very least, such assumptions need more sophisticated analysis than they have received to date. In countries such as India, where some conglomerates date back to the nineteenth century, there is resentment of the implication that they are irresponsible, or have not built a relationship with the society. Tata, for example, has established various institutes that invest in social and environmental innovation, and has a long tradition of giving back to communities. In 1998, it formalized the Tata Code of Conduct, which includes areas such as involvement with communities, ethical conduct for company officers, and a commitment not to support any political party or political activity. This, in turn, is backed up with whistle-blower protections, and sanctions such as demotion and dismissal for anyone breaching the code.

One response to disquiet at the imposition of corporate responsibility from overseas has been the creation of local corporate responsibility organizations. While many individual companies have started to produce corporate responsibility reports, these are often aimed at overseas audiences, not least the US or European stock markets, on which

---

■ Discussion points

Stakeholder participation has been described as more inclusive than the conventional government system.

- Is stakeholder participation democratic?
- Is the role of companies in tackling governance issues in developing and developed economies different?
- Will companies headquartered in emerging economies have different ideas of responsibility to their Western counterparts?

some of these companies are now listed. Corporate responsibility organizations, however, have more flexibility in terms of developing a locally relevant corporate responsibility agenda, and they include the South-Africa-based African Institute for Corporate Citizenship, the EMPRESA network of corporate responsibility organizations in 16 Latin American countries, and the Chinese Association for Corporate Social Responsibility was established in 2006 by foreign and domestic companies.

CASE STUDY 9

Are independent stakeholders an asset or a hazard?—Mattel Inc

Toymaker Mattel Corp. agreed Friday to pay $2.3 million in civil penalties for violating a federal lead paint ban that resulted in the recall of millions of its Barbie, Dora and other popular-branded toys in 2007.

The Consumer Product Safety Commission said the fine against the No. 1 toymaker and its Fisher-Price pre-school division was the highest ever for the agency's regulated product violations and the third largest in its history.

Thus read CNN's story on 5 June 2009 about a civil action against Mattel Inc which had sold Chinese-made toys in the USA that contained lead paint. Behind the story of the fine, the damage to brand reputation, and the unwanted attention of consumer groups was the story of a company that had adopted a unique approach to engaging stakeholders in monitoring its social and environmental performance.

Large companies are increasingly requiring suppliers to adopt 'voluntary' social and environmental standards as a condition of doing business. Mattel Inc announced its global manufacturing principles in 1997. Alongside the principles was a commitment to developing a worldwide independent auditing and monitoring system—the first time such a commitment had been made in relation to a company standard. The manufacturing principles would apply to every facility manufacturing the company's products and, in line with labour standards such as SA8000, included provisions on wages, working hours, child labour, forced labour, discrimination, freedom of association, and working conditions. But the principles went beyond the concerns of labour standards to include legal and ethical business practices, product safety and quality, the environment, and import and export laws. They also required that suppliers take specific actions to ensure effective evaluation and monitoring of their facilities, and spelled out the consequences of non-compliance.

To make the principles effective, Mattel established the Mattel Independent Monitoring Council for Global Manufacturing Principles (MIMCO), a group of external monitors comprising three academics. MIMCO was responsible for regular audits, and had access to all facilities, workers, and supervisors, as well as to payroll and financial records, at plants of Mattel and its primary suppliers. After an initial pre-audit visit to all factories in Asia and Mexico, MIMCO established a three-year audit cycle, based on plant ownership and importance to Mattel's supply chain. An internal audit team now does the bulk of the auditing, but MIMCO (now integrated into the Sethi International Center for Corporate Accountability [ICCA]) conducts verification audits of a random sample of plants using its own audit protocols. The company has published findings in company-wide and country-specific vendor reports, and these include responses to the problems disclosed in Mattel's supply base in 2007. Jon Entine of the American Enterprise

Institute, wrote that prior to these incidents, *'anyone knowledgeable about corporate responsibility would have nominated Mattel as the ethical gold standard among toy manufacturers.'* Business professor, Prakash Sethi, ICCA's president, said, *'I was as surprised as anyone about the lead paint crisis, but probably no more so than Mattel.'*

Yet events raised questions about Mattel's monitoring model, and the ICCA itself. Although there were numerous news stories leading with the information that ICCA was an independent auditor, key people at ICCA had been involved in establishing the system, and the small organization could be accused of being far too commercially dependent on its Mattel contract. Similarly, Mattel's previous claims that its model was more robust than other stakeholder models now came into doubt, and observers began to look at other reasons for the company wanting to have a less inclusive stakeholder initiative.

(Sources: Kavlianz, 2009; Entine and Miller, 2007; Sethi, 2003)

Questions

1 Mattel has been widely touted as a model of supply chain monitoring in the corporate responsibility context.

    a Does the discovery of lead paint in its products by regulators rather than its own auditors undermine those claims?

    b What could Mattel have done differently to prevent this situation arising?

    c Is ICCA a representative stakeholder organization?

2 Some initiatives involve a wider array of stakeholders in monitoring their suppliers' non-financial performance.

    a Which of these multi-stakeholder initiatives are you aware of?

    b What are the different types of stakeholder that belong to such initiatives?

    c Do you think multi-stakeholder initiatives would have benefitted Mattel in this case?

3 Mattel is one of many companies that have tried to identify their impact on stakeholders.

    a Which are the main stakeholders Mattel has an impact upon?

    b Are these different from the ones that influence the company?

    c What problems might Mattel face in engaging with suppliers' workers, and how could it overcome these?

SUMMARY

The notions of stakeholder, and the evolution of stakeholder management and engagement are pivotal in contemporary corporate responsibility practice. While stakeholder management theory regards stakeholders as entities to recognized but ultimately controlled, stakeholder engagement views companies as parts of complex, interdependent webs, within which many groups claim a stake (i.e. a right) in the company by virtue of the impact that the company has on them, or their power to influence the company in some way. Voluntary standards, codes of conduct, and guidelines are one concrete outcome of stakeholder engagement. There are, however, many examples of standards being designed and implemented without any real stakeholder engagement, and some advocates of stakeholder management, such as Phillips et al. (2003), believe that normative instruments such as standards run counter to the emphasis of stakeholder theory on continual dialogue and responsiveness.

There are many kinds of standard and a variety of institutional arrangements for developing them. It is in the area of implementation that stakeholder engagement is widely seen as good practice, although, in reality, many companies remain reluctant about how far to go in involving others in what are seen as management decisions. Nonetheless, the stakeholder model has clearly affected the way in which many companies see the world and their role within it, and there is widespread acceptance that, in addition to any responsibility to shareholders, there are also responsibilities to employees, consumers, customers and suppliers, and communities. The location from which a company is engaging with stakeholders has a significant effect on how these processes are managed. In fact, one of the features of corporate responsibility that distinguishes it from many other areas of management, such as quality control, is that good practice can vary by country or region. And herein lies the challenge of managing corporate responsibility: not only the balancing of the expectations and values of diverse, often globally dispersed, stakeholders, and the demonstration of one's accomplishments in concrete terms, but also the accommodation of the fact that these expectations and values are subject to continual change.

FURTHER READING

Take your learning further: Online Resource Centre **www.oxfordtextbooks.co.uk/orc/blowfield_murray2e/**

Visit the Online Resource Centre which accompanies this book to enrich your understanding of this chapter.

Students: explore web links and further reading suggestions. Keep up to date with the latest developments by undertaking web exercises.

Lecturers: you will find additional case studies, including one on the topic of the Ethical Trading Initiative—a multi-stakeholder approach to implementing labour standards, for use in class or assessment. Show your students trailers from films related to Corporate Responsibility, and use images from the book in your PowerPoint slides.

VISIT THE WEBSITE for links to useful sources of further information

- Andriof, J, Waddock, S, Husted, B and Rahman, SS, 2002, *Unfolding Stakeholder Thinking Vol. 1: Theory, Responsibility and Engagement*, Sheffield: Greenleaf.
  Introduction to stakeholder engagement from the perspective of advocates.

- Freeman, RE, 1984, *Strategic Management: A Stakeholder Approach*, Boston: Pitman.
  Seminal work setting out the rationale behind stakeholder management.

- Jensen, MC, 2002, 'Value maximization, stakeholder theory, and the corporate objective function', *Business Ethics Quarterly*, vol 12, pp 235–256.
  Arguments against companies being accountable to stakeholders.

- O'Rourke, D, 2006, 'Multi-stakeholder regulation: privatizing or socializing global labor standards?', *World Development*, vol. 34, no. 5, pp 899–918.

  Empirically informed analysis of the achievements, failures, and challenges of multi-stakeholder standards.

- Phillips, R, Freeman, RE and Wicks, AC, 2003, 'What stakeholder theory is not', *Business Ethics Quarterly*, vol. 13, no. 4, pp 479–502.

  Review of stakeholder management's strengths and engagement's limitations.

- Rasche, A, 2010, 'The limits of corporate responsibility standards', *Business Ethics: A European Review*, vol. 19, no. 3, pp. 280–291.

  An up to date review of what standards have achieved.

- Zakhem, AJ, Palmer, DE and Stoll, ML eds. 2007, *Stakeholder theory: essential readings in ethical leadership and management*, Amherst, N.Y: Prometheus Books.

  Comprehensive reader on how stakeholder theory relates to corporate responsibility management.

ENDNOTES

[1] Blowfield and Googins, 2007.

[2] Preston and Sapienza, 1990.

[3] See, e.g., Post et al., 2002; Phillips, 2003.

[4] See, e.g., the discussion of the work of Karl Polanyi in Chapter 2.

[5] Clarkson, 1995.

[6] Leipziger, 2003; AccountAbility, 2006.

[7] Evan and Freeman, 1988.

[8] CCC, 2005a.

[9] CCC, 2005a; Rasche and Esser, 2006.

[10] Kaptein, 2004.

[11] Utting & Marques 2010.

[12] See, e.g. Varley et al., 1998; Kolk et al., 1999; Seyfang, 1999; Ascoly et al., 2001.

[13] See, e.g., MacGillivray and Zadek, 1995; ISEA, 1999; Leipziger, 2003; Mamic, 2004.

[14] Leipziger, 2001.

[15] Bartley, 2003.

[16] Wright and Rwabizambuga, 2006.

[17] Svendsen and Laberge, 2005.

[18] CCC, 2005c. Mitchell et al., 2003, seem to agree with this: out of six benefits that they cite in their case study, four are given as intangible, i.e. with no assigned monetary value.

[19] Sabapathy et al., undated.

[20] Svendsen and Laberge, 2005.

Socially responsible investment[1]

Chapter overview

In this chapter, we examine socially responsible investment (SRI). We outline the origins and development of SRI, and address the impact that these investment strategies can have. In particular, we will:

- review the evolution of socially responsible investment;

- describe the main approaches used in SRI decision-making;

- examine the performance of SRI funds;

- provide an overview of the international market for SRI and its development in different regional contexts;

- examine emerging trends in SRI.

Main topics

■ **Key terms**

Socially responsible investment (SRI)

Negative screening

Positive screening

Sustainable investing

Engagement

Cleantech

Venture capital

■ **Online resources**

• Additional materials for use with the chapter's Snapshots and Case Study

• More discussion topics for students

• Suggestions for materials on SRI

• Links to SRI resources

The origins and development of socially responsible investment

In Chapter 7, we addressed the place of corporate responsibility in the corporate governance framework and how companies shape their relationships with a wider society. That discussion included consideration of the structures that are in place to ensure that managers do not invest in risky projects. This chapter looks at the structures in place to ensure that investors—individual investors, institutional investors, and fund managers—consider carefully the social, environmental, and ethical consequences of their investments. This kind of investment is known as 'socially responsible investment' (SRI). Yet, as we will see, SRI encompasses different styles of investment decisions and investor behaviour such as 'ethical investing', 'values-based investing', 'cleantech investing', 'impact investing', 'sustainable investing', and simply 'responsible investing' (see Box 10.1). These

Box 10.1 Different styles of socially responsible investment

Style	Overview
Negative screening—ethical	Avoiding companies/industries on moral grounds
Negative screening—environmental or social	Avoiding companies/industries because of their social or environmental practices
Norms-based screening	Avoiding companies because of non-compliance with international standards
Positive screening	Active inclusion of companies because of social and environmental factors
Extra-financial best in class	Active inclusion of companies that lead their sectors in social/environmental performance
Financially-weighted best in class	Active inclusion of companies that outperform their sector peers on financially material social/environmental criteria
Community investing	Allocating capital directly to enterprises and projects based on their societal contributions
Sustainability themes	Selecting companies on the basis of sustainability factors (e.g. renewable energy)
Blended value investing	Active allocation based on a blend of financial and social/environmental return on investment
Engagement	Dialogue between investors and company management to improve management of environmental, social and governance issues
Shareholder activism	Using shareholder rights to pressure companies to change environmental, social and governance practices
Integrated analysis	Active inclusion of environmental and social factors within conventional fund management

(Adapted from Krosinsky, 2008; Lydenberg, 2005; Sparkes, 2002)

styles share a degree of overlap, but are not semantic synonyms: in fact, the points of differentiation can be hotly contested. However, what they share is the incorporation of extra-financial factors into investment decision-making. This includes all manner of asset classes (although listed equity predominates), and applies to all regions. It also has relevance along the investment chain—asset owner, consultant, asset manager, investment researcher, asset—and each of these stages are potential points of breakthrough or blockage depending on the levels of awareness, incentive, requirements, and opportunities on offer.

> ■ **Key concept: Performance**
>
> Performance is a major aspect of an investment decision. But what is the real meaning of performance? The word 'performance' comes from the English 'to perform' which itself comes from the French '*parformer*'. The real meaning of performance is, therefore, achievement. And the achievement of an investment cannot only depend on return and risk. This would be a very limited approach. The investor has to think about a third dimension: the meaning.
>
> (Source: Xavier de Bayser of Integral Development Asset Management cited in Bellagio Forum for Sustainable Development and Eurosif, 2006, p 11)

We begin by setting out the historical development of SRI and the evolving interests of investors. Pre and post-investment strategies regarding publicly traded companies and funds are addressed, including the screening methods that are used in assessing a company's products, services, or business practices. We examine how investors are contributing to social and environmental impact through their investment activities and, subsequently, how the role of fund managers is evolving. The provision of alternative investment opportunities is also discussed, including social and environmental venture capital. We look at different geographies and, in relation to the international SRI marketplace, at the investment options that address the unique social, environmental, and economic factors of those regions.

The origins of ethical investment

The principles of socially responsible investing are rooted in the Judaeo-Christian and Islamic traditions, which embrace peace and avoid business practices designed to harm fellow human beings. In the USA, the Religious Society of Friends (also known as the Quakers) is credited with planting the seeds of modern SRI as early as the seventeenth century, by following strategies that adhered to their principles of non-violence and human equality. Early Methodist stock market investment strategies purposely avoided companies that were involved with alcohol or gambling and this, in essence, created some of the first 'screens' or frameworks under which investors could evaluate business practices.

Some churches and charities with sufficient capital were able to persuade individual financial institutions to establish ethical funds, eliminating those companies that were engaging in business practices they perceived as unethical. It was, however, not until the mid-1960s that retail funds were available to private investors: the first such fund being established in Sweden in 1965. The Vietnam War marked another milestone in SRI, when certain investors started screening their investments to identify companies that supported the war: in 1971, the Pax World Fund was launched in the USA, which responded to the demand for investment options that excluded companies benefiting from that war.

In the 1980s, concerns grew among investors about supporting businesses with operations in South Africa, thereby supporting apartheid and the poor treatment of employees. Stocks were removed from portfolios, based mainly on ethical or non-financial reasons, and a divestiture movement in South Africa by US corporations emerged. While the public statement was also significant, there is also some evidence that institutional shareholdings increased when companies divested.[2] Attention also shifted to domestic business practices, including the use of child labour.

As discussed in Chapter 7, awareness of corporate conduct and responsibility grew during the 1980s and 1990s. In 1983, the Ethical Investment Research Service (EIRIS) was established, providing research on company activities and, subsequently, informing the development and analysis of more investment vehicles for both institutional and private investors. The first UK ethical fund—the Friends Provident Stewardship Unit Trust—was set up in 1984, while the US Social Investment Forum conducted the first industry-wide survey and identified $40 billion of assets managed under SRI principles. Funds addressing concerns about the environment were also established, including the Merlin Ecology Fund (renamed the Jupiter Ecology Fund).

In the early 2000s, the end of the equities boom plus a series of major corporate failures linked to egregious governance practices made pension funds in particular aware of the need to behave as real owners of companies, and to take a longer-term view of investing (see Chapter 7). Consequently, traditionally conservative pension funds began to be innovators in integrating social, environmental and governance issues into decision-making. In 2001, FTSE launched the FTSE4Good family of social indices, which will be discussed later in this chapter (see 'Fund indices', p 238). This sent a strong signal to investors that SRI was indeed becoming mainstream.

Since 2003, SRI funds and other offerings have emerged to meet the needs and interests of most investors with offerings in large-cap funds, US domestic equity index funds, international funds, and small-cap offerings. In 2005, the first socially screened Exchange-Traded Funds (ETFs) were launched. New funds are being developed continually and in 2004, having seen the success of Islamic banks in the Middle East and Indonesia, HSBC launched its Amanah Pension Fund, a fund that was designed to comply with Shari'ah law, obeying special rules according to, and avoiding certain investments that are contrary to, Islamic teaching.

At the political level, 2000 signalled the mainstreaming of SRI in Europe, and the beginning of a more international and coordinated approach towards the disclosure of social, environmental, and ethical practices. The EU heads of state agreed to the Lisbon Agenda, in which corporate social responsibility and measures promoting sustainability were core to achieving the agenda's goal of 3 per cent average economic growth and the creation of 20 million jobs by 2010. The first Global Reporting Initiative (GRI) Sustainability Guidelines were also released, setting out a framework for reporting (see Chapter 8).

In 2001, the European Sustainable and Responsible Investment Forum (Eurosif) was launched with the support of national European social investment forums and the European Commission. Also in the UK, the Myners Review of Institutional Investment published its final report, a short list of non-mandatory principles for investment decision making that applied to all pension funds and institutional investors. In the same way as the Cadbury Code addressed corporate governance (see Chapter 7), the Myners

Review addressed investment, helping to set a new standard advocating shareholder activism.[3] In 2002, at the World Summit on Sustainable Development in Johannesburg, the 'London Principles' were announced to address how the financial sector, specifically, could contribute to sustainable development (see Box 10.2). Also that year, a second version of the GRI Guidelines was published.

Large-scale global SRI initiatives have continued. In 2004, Kofi Annan, then Secretary-General of the United Nations, issued *Who Cares Wins*, drafted in conjunction with several leading international financial institutions, outlining roles and responsibilities for different groups, including cooperation, working towards the goals of better investment markets, and working towards more sustainable societies. In 2006, the UN Global Compact and United Nations Environment Programme's Finance Initiative (UNEP-FI) coordinated the creation of the Principles for Responsible Investment (see Box 10.3). Initially, 20 mainstream investors worth $2 trillion signed on to the agreement. Within one year, as of June 2007, assets quadrupled to $8 trillion and the number of signatories grew to 183, mostly from Europe and Asia, and is now $20 trillion.[4]

The G8 declaration from the 2007 meeting in Germany highlighted investment decisions, transparency, and sustainable development.[5] The latest iteration of the GRI—called the G3—has been toted as a standard for performance analysis, although the investor-driven Climate Disclosure Project may be more influential. It must, however, be remembered that all of these initiatives, including GRI and the Global Compact, are non-binding and voluntary. And while there has arguably been significant progress made in the last decade, it can be argued that more is needed—raising further questions about what it

Box 10.2 The 'London Principles' on the financial sector's role in sustainable development

Economic prosperity

Principle 1 Provide access to finance and risk management products for investment, innovation, and the most efficient use of existing assets.

Principle 2 Promote transparency and high standards of corporate governance in themselves, and in the activities being financed.

Environmental protection

Principle 3 Reflect the cost of environmental and social risks in the pricing of financial and risk management products.

Principle 4 Exercise equity ownership to promote efficient and sustainable asset use, and risk management.

Principle 5 Provide access to finance for the development of environmentally beneficial technologies.

Social development

Principle 6 Exercise equity ownership to promote high standards of corporate social responsibility by the activities being financed.

Principle 7 Provide access to market finance and risk management products to businesses in disadvantaged communities and developing economies.

(Source: Adapted from **www.environmental-finance.com**)

Box 10.3 UN Principles for Responsible Investment

1 We will incorporate ESG (environmental, social, and corporate governance) issues into investment analysis and decision-making processes.

2 We will be active owners and incorporate ESG issues into our ownership policies and practices.

3 We will seek appropriate disclosure on ESG issues by the entities in which we invest.

4 We will promote acceptance and implementation of the Principles within the investment industry.

5 We will work together to enhance our effectiveness in implementing the Principles.

6 We will each report on our activities and progress towards implementing the Principles.

(Source: **www.unpri.org**)

would take, or if indeed it is possible, for SRI to become the investment norm. The answer to these questions will be taken up in later sections of the chapter.

Sustainable investing

In the evolution of SRI, one can discern a shift from concerns about tainted money (i.e. capital allocated to unethical or socially and environmentally harmful businesses) to finding ways of deploying capital to address major societal challenges. The most noticeable of these in recent years has been the growth of cleantech investment focused on renewable, alternative energy and other technologies suited to the demands of a low carbon economy; but issues such as sustainable forestry, water, and natural resource conservation have also attracted investors' attention. Important figures within the SRI field are pushing to redefine SRI as 'sustainable investing' (or to preserve the original abbreviation, 'sustainable and responsible investing').

Sustainable investing recognizes the social, environmental and governance goals of SRI generally, but stresses the need for patterns of finance and investment focused on long-term value creation, sustaining natural as well as financial assets, and a needs-based orientation to financial innovation that would serve the poor. Underlying sustainable investing are two claims: one, that fully incorporating long-term social and environmental trends will deliver superior risk-adjusted returns; two, that global sustainability of the kind discussed in Chapter 3 requires the mobilization and recasting of the world capital markets. For some it is entirely distinct from SRI,[6] because while ethically motivated investors' behaviour is affected by the societal consequences of business, sustainable investment is built on the premise that sustainably managed enterprises are better able to add value over the long term. The former is highly subjective (i.e. what values are given priority), and taken to its logical conclusion could be an argument for business as usual if one felt (as many do) that 'the business of business is business' was a strong moral position. Values-derived SRI may be profoundly attractive to some for ethical reasons, but it is not underpinned by an encompassing financial discipline or universal logic.[7] Moreover, it is often defensive: the avoidance of certain companies and industries as if to demonstrate that—in defiance of modern portfolio theory—it is possible to build efficient investment portfolios despite excluding parts of the investment universe.

In contrast, it is argued, sustainable investing positively seeks to invest in companies with practices and policies aligned with sustainability goals, not because of ideological reasons, but because the best investments are companies that adhere to long-term drivers of performance, i.e. companies that exhibit superior sustainability. This is a powerful argument (although its persuasiveness hinges in part on an investor's beliefs), and one that gains force from (a) the uncertainty about conventional financial analysis and innovation that is the fall out from the 2008–2009 financial crisis, and (b) the apparent flood of investment opportunities emerging from addressing climate change (e.g. alternative energy, energy reduction, low carbon construction, geoengineering). However, as we return to later, there is a need for caution, both because of the interpretation and reliability of the historical data produced to support the thesis that sustainable investing outperforms conventional investment, and because the analytical and predictive tools needed to deal with sustainability are only in their infancy. Without a stronger basis for accounting for the past, and for predicting the future, extrapolating too much from a narrow range of companies and industries associated with tackling climate change could be as mistaken as the over-investment SRI fund managers made in IT and health stocks in the late 1990s when their funds slumped and underperformed the market.

■ Discussion points

This chapter reviews the chronology and spread of SRI initiatives throughout the world, particularly since the 1980s.

- What has driven consumer demand for responsible investment offerings and what are likely drivers for the next decade?
- What are some of the various pre-investment and post-investment SRI strategies?
- What are some of the initiatives that have helped to encourage the international expansion of SRI?

Types of SRI analysis and practice

Box 10.1 summarizes the types of SRI strategies, the main ones of which we review in this section. Screening is the longest established strategy. Religious groups have long limited their investment universe by avoiding industries and activities that offend their moral principles. Screening is a pre-investment stage question that asks if a company is engaging in business practices that support or go against the investor's social, ethical, or environmental principles. Individual and institutional investors take different approaches to answering this question, and to determining which companies are therefore 'socially responsible'. Here, we review the different types of screen that are used, and introduce some of the funds and fund indices that employ screens.

Negative screening

'Negative' screening eliminates from an investment portfolio companies that are engaging in what are perceived to be negative business or environmental practices. In a survey of 201 socially screened funds in the USA, the Social Investment Forum (SIF) found that tobacco is the most commonly applied social screen, affecting more than 88 per cent of the total assets in the socially screened fund universe. Alcohol affects 75 per cent and gambling affects roughly 23 per cent.[8] Other negative screens include weapons, pornography, nuclear energy, poor employment practices, the manufacture of hazardous or ozone-depleting substances, genetic engineering, and animal testing.

The potential risk associated with negative screening is the possibility of biasing the geographic or sector allocation of the investment portfolio. As noted earlier, screened SRI funds appeared to outperform conventional ones in the late 1990s but this was because they were overexposed to IT and health stocks which subsequently dropped in value at the turn of the decade. Equally, anti-ethically screened funds such as the Vice Fund (VICEX) have outperformed the S&P 500 for significant periods, but are now struggling to return to their 2005 value following the latest major financial crisis. We discuss performance later in this chapter, but one needs to be cautious about leaping to conclusions on screened fund performance.

'Norms-based' screening is a variation on negative screening, requiring monitoring corporate compliance with internationally accepted norms, such as the Millennium Development Goals, the International Labour Organization core conventions, or the UN Global Compact.[9] Like other negative screening it is used to eliminate specific risks to the portfolio, and to communicate with the general public and corporate members on the ethics of the organization. Because the screen itself makes an ethical statement, it might also be used to guard the reputation of the investor.

Positive screening

Unlike negative screening, a particular industry is not excluded from positively screened portfolios. Rather, 'positive' screening is the selection of investments that perform best against corporate governance, social, environmental, or ethical criteria, and which support sustainability. Positive screening is associated with a 'triple bottom line' investment approach, ensuring that a company performs well according to financial, social, and environmental criteria. 'Best-in-class' screening is one such strategy, which selects the best performing companies within a given sector of investments, while 'pioneer' screening chooses the best-performing company against one specific criterion.

Examples of positive screens might include: improvement of health and safety conditions; integration of environmental criteria into the purchasing process; prevention of corruption; elimination of child labour; promotion of social and economic development.[10] Such screens have the advantage of encouraging companies to improve extra-financial performance irrespective of their industry, but they can be problematic. There is the challenge of how to measure performance in a robust, replicable manner, and professional organizations such as the Certified Financial Analysts Institute are only starting to find ways to incorporate this into their certification and career development programmes. More fundamentally, there is the question of whether such screens result in significantly different investment portfolios. Benson et al. (2006) found that SRI mutual funds were virtually no different to mainstream ones, reinforcing Hawken's (2004) conclusion that SRI fund managers were no less likely than conventional ones to put financial returns ahead of trying to combat social injustice or environmental degradation.

In practice, funds may offer a mix of positive and negative screens, BankInvest Global Emerging Markets SRI, an emerging market equity fund, was one of the pioneers. Its negative screen excludes companies that have continuing violations of human rights, the environment, and labour rights, and those that derive more than 10 per cent of turnover from war material, alcoholic beverages, gambling, tobacco, or three per cent from pornography. The positive screen rewards the best and fast movers, and companies that have a high score in supporting human rights, labour standards, the environment, and corporate governance. The first investor in this fund was Mistra, the foundation for strategic environmental research, that is based in Sweden and which manages its assets in a socially responsible way. Some 80 per cent of its capital of SEK3.6bn is invested on the basis of environmental and ethical criteria.

■ Discussion points

SRI strategies require consideration of ethical, moral, environmental, social, and governance issues.

- How would you go about identifying SRI investment opportunities?
- What are some initiatives that try to ensure that companies are disclosing their social or environmental business practices, so that investors can make an accurate assessment?
- What do investors expect from their SRI investments and how might their expectations differ from those of traditional investments?

Fund indices

One way of addressing the need for reliable performance measurement is the use of specialist fund indices. Three of the major SRI indices are KLD's Domini 400, the Dow Jones Sustainability Group Indexes, and the FTSE4Good Index, which is produced jointly by the *Financial Times* and the London Stock Exchange. Each of the indices uses a different weighting system for financial and non-financial performance.

In May 1990, the Domini 400 Social Index (DSI) was launched by Amy Domini, Peter Kinder, Steve Lydenberg, and Lloyd Kurtz. The index removed 200 of the 500 stocks in the S&P 500[11] through the application of social screens and then added another hundred stocks to balance out the new index by sector. The goal of the index was to set a benchmark for SRI fund managers, similar to the S&P 500, but subject to social and environmental screens. Today, approximately 250 DSI companies are S&P 500 companies, a hundred are non-S&P 500, and 50 others are chosen for their 'exemplary' records of environmental, social, and corporate governance practices.

The Dow Jones Sustainability Indexes (DJSI) were established in 1999 as the first indices to track sustainability-driven companies on a global basis. They were launched together by the Dow Jones Indexes, STOXX Limited (a European index provider) and SAM Group (a pioneer in SRI). There are over $8 billion assets in DJSI-based investment vehicles. The DJSI uses a rules-based methodology and focuses on best-in-class companies. Assessment criteria include corporate governance, risk and crisis management, codes of conduct (including anti-corruption), labour practices, human capital development, sustainability and project finance (for banks), climate strategy (including eco-efficiency and protection of biodiversity), and emerging markets strategy.[12]

The FTSE4Good Index was launched in July 2001 and is derived from the FTSE Global Equity Index Series as an initiative of FTSE, in association with EIRIS and the United Nations Children's Fund (UNICEF). Today, there are two series: a benchmark index and a tradable index. The initial screening process looks at the starting universe—FTSE All-Share Index; FTSE Developed Europe Index; FTSE US Index; FTSE Developed Index—and screens against tobacco producers, companies providing parts, services, or manufacturing for whole nuclear weapon systems, weapons manufacturers, and owners or operators of nuclear power stations that mine or produce uranium. Positive screens are applied on the subsets of companies, corresponding with each of the original indices, to include companies that are working towards environmental sustainability, have positive relations with stakeholders, and uphold and support universal human rights. The inclusion criteria *originate from globally recognized codes of conduct such as the UN Global Compact and the Universal Declaration of Human Rights*.[13] Since 2004, FTSE4Good has launched a series of regional indexes including ones for Japan, Australia, the USA, South Africa, and emerging economies. New climate change criteria were introduced in 2007, and it also operates an index of European environmental leaders.

New indices and initiatives

While the KLD's Domini 400, DJSI, and FTSE4Good remain the flagship indices, other initiatives have emerged to address newer dimensions of the SRI market. In 2003, Dutch asset management company Kempen Capital Management and SNS Asset Management launched Europe's first SRI smaller companies index. USA-based Kenmar has a SRI hedge fund of funds. SRI indices are also spreading to emerging markets, with the Johannesburg Stock Exchange SRI Index (South Africa), and the OWW Responsibility Malaysia SRI Index, which applies criteria to the FTSE Bursa 100 Index to determine if the companies are deemed socially responsible. One of the six groups of criteria in the Malaysian index is community, including Rakyat policies based on Islamic banking principles and Halal accreditation.

Brazil's Stock Exchange, BOVESPA, took the concept one step further by creating a 'social stock exchange' (SSE), replicating the stock market environment for non-profit organizations.[14] SSEs have also been established in Kenya and South Africa where SASIX (South African Social Investment Exchange) was launched in June 2006 with the support of the Johannesburg Stock Exchange. The Rockefeller Foundation is exploring the possibility of creating a SSE in the UK. The current focus in Brazil is on educational projects that benefit children between the ages of seven and 25 who live in poor communities.[15] Education specialists recommend the best NGO projects to the board of BOVESPA, which then approves a list to become the portfolio of projects presented to investors by BOVESPA and its 120 brokerage firms. Individuals or organizations can buy 'social shares' in the projects, which are transferred entirely to the listed organizations without commissions, fees, or deductions. As of 2008, almost $5.5 million had been raised for 71 NGOs listed on the SSE.[16]

SSEs are intended to solve the liquidity problem facing investors wanting to allocate capital in social enterprises or societally beneficial projects, but concerned about exiting the investment. The concept of a 'social stock exchange' is, however, arguably too alien for most investors. When the idea of SSE was presented to other exchanges in Latin America and Europe, it was met with resistance by those who think SRI is anathema to shareholder interests.

Engagement

While one set of questions posed by SRI investors arise at the pre-investment stage, another set arises at the post-investment stage: is the company *continuing* to engage in socially responsible business practices? Engagement is the process by means of which investors become involved with the business to influence its activities, behaviours, and operations. This section discusses some of these engagement strategies, including shareholder activism, proxy voting, policy statements, and engaging at different levels.

Engagement occurs in response to the company's approach to corporate responsibility, or to a change in ethical and social practices. Other issues that might be cause for concern include the company's overall performance, internal controls, compliance, or general business practices, and responsible investors may raise these matters. Both private and institutional investors may raise the issues, although, typically, it is fund managers that play the largest role in the process. Chatterji and Levine (2006) argue that fund managers are in a position to play an important role in reforming performance metrics of socially responsible funds, enabling firms better to monitor social responsibility and manage shareholder value.

Shareholder activism

Shareholder activism includes activities that are undertaken in the belief that investors and shareholders can work together with management to change course and to improve financial performance over time. These activities can be conducted privately or publicly. Private methods might include letters to other shareholders, or to company management, to raise concerns. Institutional investors might raise issues during their routine meetings with company managers, or communicate their concerns to other investors to build pressure on the company; they might even join forces with other like-minded investors to take subsequent public actions. Public mechanisms for shareholder advocacy include raising questions during annual general meetings, or calling an extraordinary general meeting to propose shareholder resolutions. Investors might also issue press statements, or arrange briefings to make their reservations known to the wider international community of investors.

The mix of public and private facets to shareholder activism means it is difficult to quantify. There are examples such as the nuns who threatened a shareholder resolution at a GE AGM about pollution of the Hudson River where activists have affected corporate behaviour. There are also famous individual and institutional activists such as CalPERS the pension fund, Robert Monks and John Bogle who have fought for more shareholder power, not least in the arena of governance (see Chapter 7). But overall, given the primacy allocated to shareholders by law, company owners have not had the huge influence on extra-financial issues that one might have expected. Even companies with a strong stance on particular social or environmental issues may lack a clear responsible investment policy, although there are signs that this is changing in some markets (e.g. 80 per cent of UK pension funds in one survey now have such a policy[17]). Moreover, public sector pension funds such as CalPERS, the Norwegian Sovereign Wealth Fund, and the Korean National Pension Fund have formed the P8 Group with a focus on getting pension funds to exert leadership in the shift to a low carbon economy.

Proxy voting

To understand the relative paucity of shareholder activism, one only needs to look at proxy voting. At a company's annual general meeting, shareholders are given the opportunity to vote on a number of issues on the agenda. Following major corporate scandals such as Enron, Parmalat, and Royal Ahold, more shareholders are beginning to understand the importance and relevance of their voting and active participation. Usually, proxy voting applies to issues of corporate governance and, by voting against the mandatory approval of annual accounts and reports, investors register their protest against company practices. Leading SRI issues that are likely to be the focus of attention include climate change, environmental reporting, sustainability, global labour standards, the HIV/AIDS pandemic, corporate political contributions, and equal employment opportunity.

Voting practices vary from country to country, and Box 10.4 highlights some of the international resources and guidelines available. The Institutional Shareholders' Committee (ISC) Statement of Principles recommends that 'Institutional shareholders and/ or agents should vote all shares held directly on behalf of clients wherever practicable to do so'. It further recommends that institutional shareholders should:

> not automatically support the Board; if they have been unable to reach a satisfactory outcome through active dialogue then they will register an abstention or vote against the resolution. In both instances it is good practice to inform the company in advance of their intention and the reasons why.

(IMA, 2005, p 20)

Box 10.4 **Resources on voting guidelines**

Organization	Code
Commissie Tabaksblat (Tabaksblat Commission—The Netherlands)	Concept Code on Corporate Governance (*Concept-Code voor Corporate Governance*)
International Corporate Governance Network (ICGN)	Global Share Voting Principles
Mouvement des Entreprises de France (MEDEF—France)	Bouton Report (*Rapport Bouton*), *Promoting Better Governance in Listed Companies*
National Association of Pensions Funds (NAPF—UK)	Corporate Governance Policy and Voting Guidelines for Investment Companies
Organisation for Economic Co-operation and Development (OECD)	Guide for Multinational Enterprises
Swiss Stock Exchange (SWX—Switzerland)	SWX Code

Quarterly reporting to clients is standard; at which point the fund managers could also report how they voted and any shareholder resolutions. More and more, voting details are made available on fund websites, which could list resolutions, issues, and companies for any given period.

However, a study by Shearman and Sterling (2005) of the largest 100 US publicly traded companies found that nearly one third did not include any shareholder proposals in their proxy statements during the 2005 proxy season. The study did find, though, an increase in shareholder proposals supporting the removal of supermajority voting provisions in its proxy statement and for majority voting in director elections, and a more recent study of UK pension funds found 90 per cent of those with a SRI policy exercised their voting rights.[18]

■ **Discussion points**

Please review the preceding section on 'Engagement'.

- As a private investor, what are some of the ways in which you might make others aware of your concerns about a company's SRI practices?
- As a fund manager, how might you communicate to the company your concerns about its business practices?
- What are some of the ways in which you think international investors might better coordinate on their engagement efforts, either as institutional members or as members of organizations such as the UN Global Compact?

SNAPSHOT 10.1

CalPERS in Japan: shareholder activism to change corporate governance

CalPERS, or the California Public Employees' Retirements System, provides pensions to nearly 1.5 million active and retired teachers in California. Its fund managers are cited as having revolutionized corporate governance in the USA in the 1980s and 1990s. It was one of the first foreign pension funds to invest in Japan and, in 1992, owned $3.7 billion in Japanese equities. There were three stages to CalPERS' activities in Japan:

1 pursuing activities on its own, voting proxies, using the media, and meeting with company officials;

2 working together with other institutional investors and domestic groups that also wanted to change Japanese corporate governance;

3 withdrawing from large-scale activism and moving towards '*firm-specific efforts based on relational investing*' (p 6).

Between 1988 and 1990, CalPERS voted proxies in ways similar to other foreign investors and then wanted to replicate its US proxy voting practices in Japan. CalPERS was particularly concerned with barriers to takeovers and the absence of independent directors, each of which CalPERS had grappled with in the USA. Dividend levels were also an issue of concern and CalPERS wanted so see more cash go to shareholders. Not wanting to be accused of greed or insensitivity to Japanese norms, however, the company was careful to vote against inadequate dividends as well as against excessive dividends.

But proxy voting proved to be an ineffectual way of inducing governance change in Japan and, beginning in the mid-1990s, CalPERS instead applied more 'general principles' of corporate governance. It also engaged in a public relations campaign, championing the virtues of foreign investors. By 1996, it had $5.6 billion invested in Japanese equities. It also found allies, who shared the CalPERS vision, to engage in its second phase of activism, including local partners, and a small group of Japanese businessmen and academics that added legitimacy.

(Sources: Jacoby, 2007; www.calpers.com; Sterngold, 1993)

Questions

1 How do financial institutions diffuse the US model of corporate governance?

2 What was it about the local Japanese context that brought about a change in strategy?

3 What are the advantages and disadvantages of adopting a partnership strategy to foster change?

Other SRI approaches

One does not need to invest in publicly listed companies to engage in SRI, or indeed trade in stocks (cf. SRI property portfolios). There are a variety of other SRI options, including venture philanthropy, social and environmental venture capital, community investment, and microcredit.

Venture philanthropy

'Venture philanthropy' refers to the application of the venture capital model, principles of entrepreneurial business, and the deployment of private equity to charities and other social purpose organizations. On the heels of the technology boom over the last two decades and the economic success of innovative technology entrepreneurs, there is a broad range of initiatives applying the strategies of venture capital within the social sector. Rather than expect a financial return, venture philanthropists are looking for 'social returns' from the project in receipt of the investment. They recognize that capital is necessary for growth and to cover cash flow difficulties, but can be difficult for social purpose organizations to access. Grant makers or banks may be unwilling finance in these situations, creating a space where venture philanthropy alone or co-investing with grant-making trusts offers solutions.

The term venture philanthropy is not new (it was used by John D Rockefeller III as early as 1969), but its use and its definition are evolving and spreading internationally, embodying the following:

1 a long-term investment in organizations;

2 a partnership between the donor and the recipient (usually a charitable or non-profit organization);

3 provision of finance;

4 provision of expertise, skills, and/or resources that add value to the development of the organization and/or entrepreneur (which often includes access to the venture philanthropist's network of partners, who might be able to provide services such as accounting, marketing, or strategic consulting);

5 a view towards maximizing a 'social return on investment', or the bottom-line leaning, towards outcome-based solutions to the underlying problem;

6 a focus on accountability, because venture philanthropists hope to understand the cause of the social problem in order to develop effective solutions;

7 an exit strategy, making the organization self-sustaining and financially independent after a few years of support.

Much has been written about the pioneering venture philanthropy organizations, largely based in the USA, which embraced these principles to support local, social innovation (e.g. Venture Philanthropy Partners, REDF—creator of the 'Social Return on Investment' Index—Accumen Fund, and Social Venture Partners to name but a few). In the last few years, these principles have been embraced by philanthropists throughout the world to drive social innovation in both industrialized and developing countries, including traditional foundations (e.g. Rockefeller), newer foundations (e.g. Bill and Melinda Gates, Google.org), and individuals charting their own course in the social sector (e.g. the USA's Pierre Omidyar and South Africa's Mark Shuttleworth).

What is called the 'blended value approach' to investing has also been attractive to foundations looking to align the guidelines set in their programmes with their investment strategies. Typically, 95 per cent of a foundation's resources are used to generat this is called the asset 'corpus' and normally leaves 5 per cent to support payouts, a istration costs, and grant-making activities. But if the asset corpus is invested only to mize financial return (sometimes without any consideration to the make-up c portfolio), only 5 per cent of the resources are driving 100 per cent of the social mission of the foundation. An idea put forward by some scholars and foundations is that, if the 95 per cent of the foundation's resources could be used to maximize the financial, social, and environmental impacts—i.e. the 'blended value' approach—the benefits generated by the investments could be exponentially greater than the impact of grants alone.

Environmental venture capital

Concern about sustainability and in particular the transformation to a low carbon economy as a response to climate change (see Chapter 3) has created a significant demand for capital in areas such as alternative energy, geoengineering, and green buildings. One aspect of this is 'environmental venture capital', or 'cleantech' which looks at investment opportunities in entrepreneurial, environmental projects and companies that will reap financial, social, and environmental rewards for the investors. Opportunities for these investments include sustainable energy technologies, such as renewable energy, transportation, and distributed generation of power. The size of some of these initiatives means that much of the capital will have to be raised from conventional financial markets and from government-backed bonds. Certainly, some of the immediate investment needs such as nuclear power and an energy distribution system matched to the specifics of alternative energy are not suited to venture capital. Nonetheless, in 2009 venture investors put $5.6 billion into cleantech startups based in North America, Europe, China and India, and although this was down about 33 per cent on 2008 this was due to global economic decline rather than loss of faith in the technology. Furthermore, green technology is an important part of the recent economic stimulus packages in some countries. For example, the USA, and South Korea, the European Union, and China have allocated 81 per cent, 59 per cent, and 31 per cent of their respective economic stimulus packages to green investment ($31 billion, $23 billion, and $221 billion).[19]

Emerging economies such as China, India, and South Africa are fossil fuel-dependent nations, and need to take actions to safeguard a reliable stream of fossil fuels, to identify alternative sources of energy, and to pursue greater energy efficiency through technology and innovation. China has already taken significant steps in this regards, although the challenge is enormous (see Case Study 10). India has not attracted the same amount of international scrutiny, but in many ways faces equal challenges, and by some accounts lags far behind where it should be on environmental issues.[20] South Africa, which obtains 95 per cent of its electricity from coal fired power stations, faces significant difficulties in transitioning to low carbon energy without jeopardizing political stability and economic growth.

There are a multitude of renewable projects presently active in the USA and in Europe. Germany has been a leader in developing wind power, with some German states sourcing more than 1,800 megawatts of their power from wind. To date, solar and wind power have attracted the most investment dollars, while other experimental technologies are being tested, such as biomass—producing electrical power from agricultural crops—and photovoltaics—producing electricity from sunlight.

Cleantech investors expect both high environmental and financial returns. Fluctuations in oil prices, global concerns about water supplies, and an attention to fossil-fuel dependency have inspired both technological innovation and entrepreneurs looking to build enterprises to address the environmental challenges. Cleantech investors are supporting this new wave of innovation. There is, however, also evidence of caution, because investment dollars deployed in cleantech have fluctuated and decreased at times, owing to the high risk involved with the development of new technology.

SNAPSHOT 10.2

CANOPUS Foundation—european venture philanthropy

The CANOPUS Foundation, based in Freiburg, Germany:

> promotes private *social investment* and *social enterprise* in order to fight poverty and environmental degradation, and provides business development assistance for social entrepreneurs in developing countries working in the field of clean energy technologies.

It invests only in non-profit organizations that operate in the field of clean energy technologies.

CANOPUS, like many other European venture philanthropy funds, provides several non-financial services in addition to its giving of grants. A recent study from the Skoll Centre of Entrepreneurship[21] found that many such funds deliver support through both their board members and through partnerships. At CANOPUS, business development is built into every project activity. In-house project managers (which are not all fully-paid staff) undertake site visits, field trips, and conduct reports. In addition to its in-house resources, CANOPUS works with people within its network of cities and local governments to identify those active in sustainable development who are on site, willing, and able to act as consultants. Specific services are provided through CANOPUS partners who have provided pro bono services to the foundation, including business plan evaluation, accounting, and writing year-end balance sheets for the portfolio organizations. Fundraising support is also provided to the entrepreneurs. The Foundation is prepared to receive calls, or to go a step further and take part in a meeting with the entrepreneur to speak in support of the project. CANOPUS is also said to be a useful partner in helping the entrepreneur to understand clean energy markets, supply and demand, and to get margins at the lowest price.

(Sources: Interview with CANOPUS Foundation; John, 2007)

Questions

1 Which aspects of the partnership do you feel are most beneficial to the social and/or environmental entrepreneur—funding, business services, strategic advice, etc.?

2 Why does the CANOPUS Foundation refer to itself as a venture philanthropy organization rather than as an environmental venture capitalist or cleantech investor?

3 How might the needs of a social entrepreneur differ from those of a business entrepreneur?

Community development investment funds

Community development investing is defined by the Social Investment Forum as:

> financing that generates resources and opportunities for economically disadvantaged people in urban and rural communities that are under-served by traditional financial institutions.
>
> *(SIF, 2001, p 6)*

Community development investment funds deploy equity and equity-like investments into small businesses in geographic areas that are traditionally overlooked by traditional venture capital and private equity funds. Typically, the businesses are located in disadvantaged communities, which will increase the entrepreneurial capacity of the area and create jobs, and results in what is termed 'high social impact'. Other development investment funds pool together investors, such as banks, corporations, insurers, foundations, and public pension funds, to provide support that can enable to provision of affordable housing, education, community centres, and small businesses.

Microcredit

'Microcredit' is the making of very small loans (or 'microloans') to individuals. The fundamental idea is to make money available to the poor, based on terms and conditions that are appropriate and reasonable. The concept emerged out of initiatives in the 1970s by organizations, such as Accion International and the Grameen Bank, which wanted to provide economic opportunity to poor people looking to start small businesses. Traditional banks were not interested in making small loans to what were considered 'the unbankable' (i.e. people without collateral), so a system of community banking was set up, under which small informal groups (called 'solidarity groups' within the Grameen Bank) were formed. Their collateral was the social networks these savers and borrowers formed so that loans were effectively guaranteed by a combination of peer pressure and social cohesion. Women's groups in particular proved successful, and loan repayment far exceeded the normal percentage in traditional banking.

We discuss aspects of microcredit (also called microfinance) elsewhere (Chapters 4 and 12). It has spread rapidly, and not only in developing economies. Originally, the brainchild of NGOs, it is now offered by mainstream banks such As Deutsche Bank and Standard Chartered. However, it is not an unalloyed success. A little money can support the development of a one-person business or the beginnings of a small shop, for example, but scaling up the business to the next level is not always easy when further financial support is needed. If one looks at a country such as Bangladesh where microcredit is the main form of banking, the signs that it has lifted people out of poverty (e.g. growth in incomes or GDP) are not obvious. This may be due to the entrenched nature of poverty, and microcredit could be as much a strategy for survival as a means of growth. But while the largest bank in Bangladesh is now the microcredit NGO, BRAAC, the impact of microcredit on the poor is only starting to be measured systematically (see

Chapter 13). In the drive to scale up microcredit, there is evidence from around the world that the solidarity group based model has been increasingly bypassed in favour of direct loans to borrowers. Interest rates are also often very high compared to other formal moneylending. This may make the lending organizations more viable but it raises questions about the social impact and how microcredit is ultimately different from traditional banks other than the size of their loans.

■ Discussion points

Most screening techniques are not limited to one screen (e.g. the exclusion of tobacco industries), but consider a variety of factors.

- Pick one of the SRI indices discussed in this chapter and explain its selection criteria.
- If you were to apply an Islamic screen to this SRI index, what companies would you remove and why?
- Pick one of the companies on your screened list and look at recent proxies and/or shareholder resolutions filed. Discuss reasons why corporate governance actions might have been taken.

SRI performance

Although there is a philanthropic type of SRI, most investors want to see a reasonable financial as well as social or environmental return on their investment, and many want to know how SRI performs compared to traditional full universe funds. A company may engage in socially, ethically, and environmentally sound business practice, but the financial performance, or potential for return on investment, is undoubtedly an important factor driving the investment decision. As Statman (2000) found, socially responsible investors do not want to sacrifice return for social responsibility. To a degree, this is because of the way some SRI funds have been promoted, promising that they can outperform the mainstream indices in defiance of conventional investor wisdom that screening out part of the investment universe puts investors at a disadvantage.

SRI index performance

One way to compare SRI performance with mainstream investment vehicles is to look at the various indices available. In an analysis of 29 SRI indices (not investment funds), Schröder (2005) found that they did not exhibit a different risk-adjusted return to that of conventional benchmarks. In other words, there was no significant difference in SRI and conventional index performance. Schröder did note, however, that many SRI indices have a higher risk relative to the benchmarks.

A closer look at the performance of the KLD DS400, DJSI, and the FTSE4Good indices provides a clearer picture of the overall performance of the SRI industry in comparison with overall market performance. Comparing the performance of the KLD's DS400 Index to the S&P 500 (as of May 2007, i.e. prior to the financial crisis), the former outperformed the latter since its inception in 1990 (12.28 per cent compared with 11.71 per cent). Annualized returns over a ten-year period were equal, with 7.78 per cent returns. Looking at the five-year, three-year, and one-year periods, however, the picture looks slightly different, showing an underperforming DS400 Index. Equally, analyses of the FTSE4Good indices, conducted over different time periods, found that investors would not necessarily be worse off by investing in a fund that tracks the FTSE4Good index. An important factor to consider is the risk of the market sectors and individual stocks that are included in the index.

Krosinsky's (2008) comparison of different types of SRI with mainstream indices suggests that there is a difference in performance between general SRI funds (values-based ethical investing) and sustainable investing (see Figure 10.1). The former underperform or at best are comparable to mainstream indices depending on what time horizon one uses; the latter outperform the mainstream irrespective of the time period being compared. A study of 90 ethical funds over 10 years in the UK concluded that annual returns were 0.1 per cent less than the FTSE All Share Index.[19] However, sustainable investing funds have not only outperformed ethical investing ones, but also even the best of the mainstream indices (18.7 per cent versus 17 per cent for 2002–2007). The most recent analysis, covering the 2008 Western stock market crash, shows that sustainable investing funds lost slightly less of their value in 2008, produced net positive returns over the 2003–2008 period (compared to a net loss on the mainstream indices), and outperformed mainstream indices in the first half of 2009. (see Figure 10.2)

SRI fund performance

There are an estimated $50 trillion of managed assets worldwide, and just under $7 trillion of these are affected by some form of social screening and shareholder advocacy.[20] For some advocates of SRI, the fact that SRI index performance is broadly comparable to mainstream indices, and in some circumstances offers superior performance, it is a mystery why investors are not more keen. Several academic studies that have compared the performance of ethical and non-ethical funds have found no difference in financial performance,[21] and a review of 16 academic and broker studies concluded that there was a positive correlation between fund performance and attention to extra-financial issues in 38 per cent of cases, and a neutral correlation in 44 per cent.[22]

Accompanying the success stories, however, is continuing criticism of SRI funds. While there are some funds with five-year returns of 50 or 60 per cent, the shorter term returns for one year might only be 3 per cent or lower.[23] SRI advocates are keen to emphasize the importance of time horizons in evaluating fund performance and investment strategies. In part, this is because the high turnover of stocks in mainstream funds is blamed for

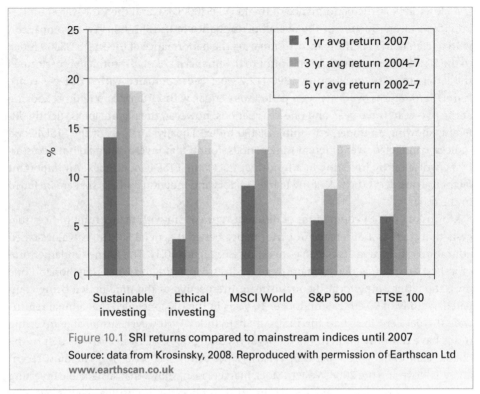

Figure 10.1 SRI returns compared to mainstream indices until 2007
Source: data from Krosinsky, 2008. Reproduced with permission of Earthscan Ltd
www.earthscan.co.uk

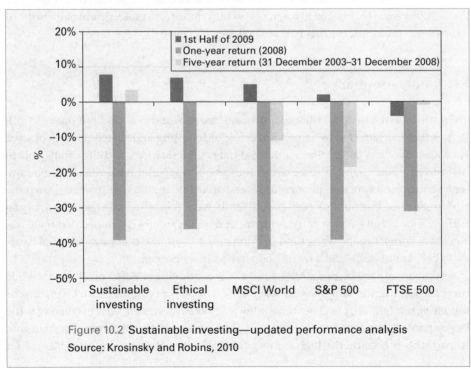

Figure 10.2 Sustainable investing—updated performance analysis
Source: Krosinsky and Robins, 2010

investors' disinterest in extra-financial dimensions of business performance, and the disconnect between corporations and their owners. But there is also evidence that sustainable investing funds, for example, that have a low turnover (i.e. their portfolios change every three to five years) exhibit stronger performance.[24] However, one needs to be cautious about the period one is considering. For example, a comparison in late 2007 of the Winslow Green Growth Fund (WGGF), a Morningstar five-star rated fund with an aggressive growth policy focused on small growth companies that have a positive or neutral environmental impact, with Berskhire Hathaway (BRK-A), investment sage Warren Buffett's holding company, would have found that the latter grew by 100 per cent in the preceding five years, but the sustainable investing fund grew by 200 per cent.[25] However, from 2008 onwards, BRK-A consistently outperformed WGGF: as of April 2010 it had delivered roughly 90 per cent growth on 2003, compared to WGGF's approximately 60 per cent.

There is an inherent bias in some SRI funds towards particular sectors such as stocks, and the overall volatility of such stocks over a particular period, although some argue that this should be considered another way of diversifying one's overall portfolio. Relative size is another problem when looking at the figures used to portray SRI's success. Although growth rates in percentage terms can be large, the actual amount invested in SRI funds is small when compared, for example, to that invested in hedge funds,[26] and the impact of applying the current SRI strategies on a grander scale would almost certainly affect the value of those assets. Additionally, SRI screening of some kind is being applied beyond the relatively small universe of SRI retail funds, making it increasingly difficult to calculate the exact size of the SRI market.

A further factor is uncertainty about the utility of SRI analysis as a forecasting tool, and the absence of, or analysts' unfamiliarity with, tools to analyze performance. Much of what we know about corporate responsibility is about what has happened and why, and therefore falls within the explicative concerns of accounting. Analysis, in contrast, is predictive, so that, for instance, financial analysis—no matter how imperfectly—allows one to forecast future flows in order to obtain the net present value. In the case of sustainable investing, for example, an analyst would want to integrate environmental, social, and governance factors into financial valuation tools, but while as we have seen throughout this book there are plenty of ideas about how such factors are material to companies, their incorporation into areas such as risk analysis is not yet commonplace.[27]

Market growth

Throughout the 2000s, the growth of the SRI investment universe has outstripped that of the wider investment market. There is increasing interest in India and China (see Case Study 10), and as described earlier Brazil and South Africa were innovators in establishing social stock exchanges. Nonetheless, the main interest has been in developed economies. Australia has experienced enormous growth, going from practically zero in 2003 to $16.49 billion in 2007. A quarter of Australian managed funds now subscribe to the UN

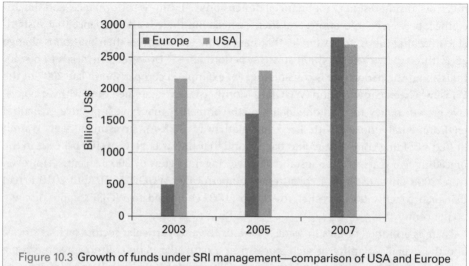

Figure 10.3 Growth of funds under SRI management—comparison of USA and Europe
Source: data from Robins, 2008. Reproduced with permission of Earthscan Ltd
www.earthscan.co.uk

Principles for Responsible Investment.[28] Similarly, SRI funds under management in Canada grew from under $49 billion in 2003 to $472.62 billion by the end of 2007. However, the largest markets are the USA and Europe (see Figure 10.3). In 2005, over 9 per cent of the $24.4 trillion tracked in Nelson's Information's Directory of Investment Managers, were involved in socially responsible investing, equivalent to nearly one out of every ten dollars under professional management in the USA. Mutual funds have been the fastest growing segment of SRI. Between 1995 and 2005, there was a 15-fold increase in assets in SRI mutual funds: $1.5 trillion in assets were in socially screened separate accounts, managed for individual clients ($17.3 billion) and institutional client accounts ($1.49 trillion). This represents 3 per cent of the $5,716.1 billion that is held in separately managed accounts identified by Money Management Institute.[29] Shareholder advocacy has also become increasingly important. In 2005, institutional investors that filed, or co-filed, resolutions on environmental or social issues controlled nearly $703 billion in assets. Assets in community investing institutions, managed on behalf of institutions and individuals, accounted for $19.6 billion.

The European SRI market has overtaken the USA to some degree (see Figure 10.3), although there is disagreement about what assets are included. For example, some use the classification 'broad' SRI (including positive and negative screens, engagement by fund managers, and the inclusion by asset managers of corporate governance and social, ethical, or environmental risk into financial analysis),[30] which is a broader definition than that used by SRI investment research company, EIRIS, for instance. The assets managed under 'broad' SRI can appear large, but it raises the question of how broad is 'broad'? If, for example, companies are screened for little more than pornography or eco-efficiency (one that is largely an illegal activity; the other, a proven business efficiency), SRI may be nothing more than efficient fund management, spurring doubts about the extent to which some of the figures on SRI are useful.

There are a number of developments behind this growth, some of which shed light on the potential of similar trends happening in other markets. One influence was the change in attitude amongst pension funds following the failure of companies such as Enron in the early 2000s (p 233). Coincidentally or consequently a group of sustainable investing practitioners emerged (e.g. fund managers and rating agencies) who in turn instigated catalytic initiatives such as the establishing of analytics firms Innovest Strategic Value Advisers, Trucost, and Vigeo. Ethical research organizations such as KLD and EIRIS emerged, and alongside agencies initially focused on corporate governance such as PIRC have evolved to include corporate responsibility and sustainability analysis. In other words, in understanding the growth of a market, it is important to look at the enabling infrastructure, and not just the allocation of capital.

Trends in SRI

Whether one is looking at fears about global warming, the opportunities presented by the shift to a low carbon economy, the governance lessons from the financial crisis, or the increased interest in products and services for the poor, some long-established concerns of SRI are now higher on political and business agendas than ever before. This is not only creating an environment in which SRI can flourish; it is causing governments and investors to take a closer look at ideas from the SRI world. For example, socially responsible bonds or bond funds have provided an investment vehicle for SRI investors, offering a comparatively low-risk alternative, particularly for endowments and institutional investors looking for safe investment strategies with guarantees. Green bonds for environmental projects have been issued by the US government since 2004, the European Investment Bank issues 'Climate Awareness Bonds' and the Malaysian government issues bonds for reforestation.

The financial crisis has drawn attention to a long-running concern of the SRI community, the importance of investment for the long-term, and the importance of investors acting as genuine owners rather than rent-seekers. Renewed interest in the idea of a Tobin Tax to limit speculation reflects another well-established concern amongst SRI advocates. As noted earlier, the two main premises behind sustainable investing are that incorporating long-term sustainability-related trends will offer superior risk-adjusted growth, and there needs to be a recasting of the world's capital markets. The first of these is in many ways contingent upon the second, and while some have criticized sustainable investing advocates for appearing to say that nothing can be achieved unless everything is changed, there is a far greater appetite for reform than there was just a few years ago.

However, the question remains as to whether the environment for long-term growth upon which much of SRI's superior performance seems to hinge can be created without further major financial, social or environmental shocks. While segments of SRI, not least offshoot sustainable investing, are booming, the consistent institutional and legal framework necessary to mobilize capital and bring convergence between SRI issues and financial analysis is scarcely happening. SRI might seem large, but set against the size of the world's capital markets or indeed the scale of transformation some say is necessary to meet the world's social and environmental challenges it barely casts a shadow.

Moreover, this is unlikely to change if the social and environmental costs of business are not internalized. Furthermore, for all the debate about regulation, and the undeniable fact that at a national level banking is an extremely highly regulated industry, it remains that finance enjoys a privileged status; free, for instance, of the kind of regulation applied to many other sectors. Thus, while pharmaceutical companies will spend years getting regulatory approval for new drugs, financial institutions plough ahead with newer and ever more complex products such as derivatives without any accountability or oversight.

■ **Discussion points**

In the light of what we have discussed about SRI's origins and future trends, consider the following.

- What new initiatives are likely to emerge or develop between now and 2015?
- Please describe and comment on the Global Reporting Initiative. What are its merits and limitations?
- Which leading social issues are likely to gain attention in your country in relation to corporate governance and why?

CASE STUDY 10

China—SRI's rising star or nemesis?

For many years, SRI funds avoided China and took companies to task for labour standards, human rights, lack of transparency, and environmental conditions in that country. While many multinationals argued that avoiding China would be disastrous to their competitiveness, or that transferring best practice from around the world to an isolated autocracy would open new opportunities for democracy, SRI proponents said that foreign investment would inevitably support and legitimize an unacceptable, exploitative form of capitalism.

At first glance, China's emergence as the most-polluting nation in 2007 seemed to reinforce the SRI position. Its greenhouse gas emissions exceed those of the USA, 700 million of its people (about half of its population) lack access to safe drinking water, it is home to 16 of the 20 most polluted cities in the world, and 68 per cent of its power comes from coal. Yet, while human rights and democratization have provoked enervation amongst Chinese politicians, the threats of environmental catastrophe have spurred innovation. Since the mid-2000s, there has been a raft of policy and administrative initiatives such as the Eleventh Five Year Plan for Energy Development (2006–2010), the 2006 Renewable Energy Law, the 2008 amendments to the Energy Conservation Law, and the strengthening of the Ministry of Environmental Protection. The government has promised to reduce the nation's energy consumption as a proportion of GDP by 20 per cent through energy efficiency and new technologies. Stretch targets have been set for increase in renewable energy have been enshrined in law (see table at the Online Resource Centre), and by 2020 it is expected that renewables will make up 16 per cent of total primary energy, and 20 per cent of electric power capacity.

The investment opportunities implicit in this redirection of energy policy in what should be one of the world's largest and fastest growing economies has attracted attention from conventional investment funds, but also from SRI ones which have been pioneers of cleantech investing. Some predict that reaching China's renewable energy targets will require investments of $174 billion until 2020, and already venture capital inflows are booming (e.g. $420 million in 2006 with an average deal size of $16.2 million).

China is also home to leading renewable energy companies such as solar panel maker Jiangsu Shunda, and is the largest producer of wind turbines. Thinking about the low carbon economy is also leading to other innovations such as BYD Auto, producer of electric cars. Its leading green companies such as Goldwind, Shoto, and LDK Solar are listed on foreign exchanges, and the initial public offerings have been profitable.

None of this is to say that there are not any challenges. The growth in solar power is threatened by the dependence on imported silicon for which Chinese firms are paying a premium, and biodiesel distribution has not yet been incorporated into the main petrol station networks. The profitability of wind power is still dependent on the sale of carbon credits, without which electricity is up to twice the price of that from coal-fired power plants. Moreover, most of the wind power is generated far from the major urban areas making transmission costly or otherwise unfeasible. A combination of these factors means that many Chinese firms face rising costs and shrinking profit margins on top of an unstable demand: a fact reflected in the share price of companies such as Solarfun Power, JA Solar, and China Sunergy which have failed to achieve the NASDAQ average since late 2009.

Nonetheless, many SRI funds see China's environmental markets as the ideal opportunity to support positive change in this huge economy. The Taida Environmental Index is the country's first social responsibility index, and Chinese institutions have started to create SRI funds such as the Sustainable Growth Equity Fund, and the green private equity fund ZheShang Nuohai Low Carbon Fund. Organizations promoting SRI have emerged such as the Association of Sustainable and Responsible Investment in Asia (ASrIA). Calvert, a leading SRI house in the USA, was amongst the first partners in the highly profitable, cleantech focused China Environment Fund. For some SRI investors such as CalPERS the appeal of environmental investment has meant reversing previous boycott-China policies, and led them to wrestle with compromises about the potentially enormous environmental impacts, and their principles on human rights and democratic values. Following the argument made by many multinationals, SRI advocates say that the infrastructure for change is being put in place (e.g. an emerging corporate responsibility culture, and new SRI vehicles), and that one cannot bring about change without being active in the country. Their expectation is that a vibrant and indigenous SRI industry will be created, expanding beyond cleantech to other corporate responsibility issues.

(Sources: Guo, 2009; Cheung, 2008; **www.chinacsr.com**)

Questions

1 SRI investors have long been reluctant to invest in China.

    a What are their main objections to investing in China?

    b Do their more recent changes in investment policy reflect an ethical or a business argument?

    c What are the dangers of a narrow focus on environmental industries?

2 China's environmental challenges have attracted SRI investors' attention.

    a Why are companies and the government in China interested in the environment?

    b What investment opportunities are arising as a result of these challenges?

    c Can SRI offer anything to environmental investment that mainstream investors cannot?

3 'Buyer beware' is an adage often applied to doing business in China.

    a What investment infrastructure needs to be in place to establish a viable indigenous SRI industry?

    b What might be the role of foreign SRI organizations in establishing SRI in China?

    c What are the advantages for Chinese companies of attracting stable, long-term investors of the kind identified with SRI?

SUMMARY

In this chapter, we have looked at the development of socially responsible investment, and at its appeal to investors as a way in which to maximize financial, social, and environmental returns in the long term. We have looked at both pre-investment and post-investment strategies used to identify SRI opportunities—namely, screening and engagement. In reviewing the comparative performance of SRI vehicles to traditional ones, we learned that, on the whole, there is no evidence that SRI indices or funds underperform, and that some SRI-related strategies offer better returns, particularly if one takes a longer term perspective.

While there are those who think that SRI and traditional investment are diametrically opposed, it can be argued that we are in the midst of a convergence. Cleantech, for example, is at the intersection—appealing to both conventional investors and SRI investors. This convergence may continue as reporting mechanisms become more transparent, analytical methods become more sophisticated, established SRI issues become of increasing concern to companies and investors, and SRI offerings continue to grow. But this is not to predict that SRI will radically transform the investment world, and the importance of SRI needs to be considered in the context of the other business, governance, and investment trends that are discussed elsewhere in this book.

FURTHER READING

**VISIT THE
WEBSITE**
for links to useful
sources of further
information

Take your learning further: Online Resource Centre **www.oxfordtextbooks.co.uk/orc/blowfield_
murray2e/**

Visit the Online Resource Centre which accompanies this book to enrich your understanding of this chapter.

Students: explore web links and further reading suggestions. Keep up to date with the latest developments by undertaking web exercises.

Lecturers: you will find additional case studies, including one on the topic of Caterpillar versus the Church – investors give corporate responsibility muscle (from first edition Chapter 13), for use in class or assessment. Show your students trailers from films related to Corporate Responsibility, and use images from the book in your PowerPoint slides.

- Bogle, JC, 2009, *Enough: True Measures of Money, Business, and Life*, John Wiley & Sons, Hoboken, N.J.

  Mutual funds pioneer's overview of why financial markets have failed, and what needs to be done to make them fit for their human purpose.

- Chatterji, A and Levine, D, 2006, Breaking down the wall of codes: evaluating non-financial performance measurement, *California Management Review*, 48(2), pp 29–51.

  Informative discussion of approaches to measuring non-financial performance and the current state of play.

- Krosinsky, C and Robins, N (eds), 2008, *Sustainable Investing: The Art of Long-Term Performance*, Earthscan, London.

  Prominent professionals from the sustainable investment world examine the case for sustainable investing, and how it differs from SRI.

- Lydenberg, SD, 2005, *Corporations and the Public Interest: Guiding the Invisible Hand*, Berrett-Koehler Publishers, San Francisco.

  Co-founder of SRI pioneer KLD examines the role of business, and the role of investors in fostering companies that serve the public interest.

- Sparkes, R, 2002, *Socially Responsible Investment: A Global Revolution*, John Wiley & Sons, New York.

  Important introduction to SRI by an early and influential practitioner.

ENDNOTES

[1] This chapter draws heavily on the work of Nick Robins and Cary Krosinsky, and we are especially grateful to Nick for his comments. The first edition version of this chapter was written by Kimberly Ochs. All errors and opinions are the authors' own.

[2] Teoh et al., 1995.

[3] More detailed information can be found online at **www.hm-treasury.gov.uk**.

[4] Odell, 2007.

[5] Keefe, 2007.

[6] Krosinsky and Robins, 2008.

[7] GRI, 2007.

[8] SIF, 2006, pp 6–7.

[9] More information can be found about the Millennium Development Goals online at **www.un.org/millenniumgoals** and the ILO core conventions at **www.labourstart.org/rights**.

[10] See extensive lists available at **www.eufosif.org**.

[11] The Standard and Poor's 500 is an index of 500 large-cap companies and is often used as a baseline for comparison. Stocks are chosen using S&P's methodology. Detailed guidelines can be found at **www.indices.standardandpoors.com**.

[12] See www.sustainability-index.com for a summary of indices and screening criteria.

[13] www.ftse4good.com.

[14] See www.bovespasocial.org.br.

[15] Grecco, 2007, p 131.

[16] www.newsweek.com/id/139436, accessed 21 April 2010.

[17] UKSIF, 2009.

[18] UKSIF, 2009.

[19] Cobb et al., 2005; Collison et al., 2007.

[20] Reddy, 2008.

[21] John, 2007.

[22] Jewson Associates, 2008.

[23] Monitor, 2009.

[24] See, e.g., Kreander et al., 2002; 2005; Gregory et al., 1997; Bauer et al., 2002.

[25] UNEP FI, 2007.

[26] See historical data on Ave Maria Catholic Values fund, or Calvert Large Cap Growth, as examples of this.

[27] Krosinsky, 2008.

[28] Krosinsky, 2008.

[29] Total money in SRI Funds 2005 = £6.1bn; total money in hedge funds 2006 = $1.786 trillion. Based on figures from EIRIS and HedgeFund.net.

[30] Lucas-Leclin and Hahal, 2008.

[31] Figures in this section from Robins, 2008.

[32] SIF, 2006, p 11.

[33] Eurosif, 2006.

Corporate responsibility in smaller enterprises

Chapter overview

In this chapter, we look at corporate responsibility as an aspect of business theory and management practice as it applies to small and medium-sized enterprises. As part of this, we include the field of Social Entrepreneurship. In particular, we will:

- discuss what is unique about SMEs in the corporate responsibility context;

- explore the distinctions between SMEs, and how these affect their behaviour;

- consider corporate responsibility as an area of opportunity and competitive advantage for SMEs;

- examine how corporate responsibility is being managed in practice;

- discuss those small and medium sized enterprises that are categorized as social entrepreneurs.

Main topics

■ Key terms

Small and medium-sized enterprises

Supply chains

Social enterprise

Lifestyle enterprises

Corporate social opportunity

■ Online resources

- Additional case studies of social enterprise

- Teaching notes

- Exercises and discussion topics for students

- Suggestions for additional materials on SMEs

- Links to other web-based resources

The small business 'problem'

For a long time in corporate responsibility literature smaller businesses were considered either irrelevant or problematic. Normative corporate responsibility theory was typically portrayed as something universal with application to all companies, irrespective of their size.[1] Corporate responsibility practice was depicted as something that could be fairly easily transferred from multinational enterprises to smaller companies.[2] However, as the notion of corporate responsibility as a managerial construct gained hold, its application to smaller businesses—not least in developing countries—began to receive more attention.[3] There was increasing recognition that contemporary ideas of corporate responsibility needed special consideration in the small business context, whether because they were seen as irresponsible, or at risk for failing to meet corporate responsibility performance standards.

The role of smaller businesses, particularly entrepreneurs, earned further attention with the rise of new business concepts focused on societal outcomes such as the bottom of the pyramid (see Chapter 4) and social entrepreneurship (see page 279). Smaller business was no longer just seen as irrelevant or problematic; it was increasingly talked about as having unique contributions to make. Today, there is a significant body of research and innovation built around the theme of corporate responsibility and smaller businesses. This ranges from the types of business involved, to the quantity and quality of corporate responsibility-related activity, the business case, and what constitutes best practice.[4]

In this chapter, we focus primarily on smaller businesses that for the most part would not see themselves as having an overt societal mission. We will leave until later in this chapter discussion of social enterprise, and those organizations that treat social and environmental outcomes as at least as important as financial results.

The meaning and significance of smaller business

Smaller businesses are typically lumped together under the abbreviation SME—small and medium-sized enterprise. The meaning of SME is explained in the Key Concept box which highlights how firms in this sector are defined primarily by number of workers, size of turnover, and ownership. Although relatively small individually, collectively SMEs are the largest employers worldwide and comprise the vast majority of businesses

---

■ Key concepts: Small and medium-sized enterprise

SMEs may account for 50–60 per cent of employment worldwide. In countries such as Russia and Kenya they are the major job creators, and even in more developed capitalist economies such as the UK they account for nearly half of all jobs. In the European Union, a SME has less than 250 workers, an annual turnover of less than €40 million (or a balance sheet not exceeding €27 million), and is an independent enterprise where no more than 25 per cent of capital or voting rights belong to larger enterprises. The World Bank separates out small and medium enterprises, classifying small enterprises as those with 10–50 workers, total assets of $100,000–$3 million, and total sales of $100,000–$3 million. It further defines micro-enterprises as those with less than ten workers, assets of less than $100,000, and annual sales of less than $100,000.

However, as authors such as Jenkins (2006) and Burns (2001) point out, there are many less quantifiable characteristics of SMEs such as less formal management structures, the role of individual personality, and difficulties in diversifying risk. Furthermore, it can be misleading to treat SMEs as homogenous because factors such as industry, ownership, location, and position in supply chain can all significantly affect how a SME behaves. It is also misleading to treat SMEs as marginal to economic life. In economies such as Italy and Ghana they have always been major sources of employment, and now, with shifting patterns of work in economies such as northern Europe and the USA, the SME sector has grown broader and more complex than ever before.[5]

(90 per cent by some measurements). Moreover, they cannot be defined by quantitative measures alone. As a sector, SMEs exhibit management features that mark them out from larger businesses (e.g. the influence of the entrepreneur/founder/leader; greater informality in management practices; narrower strategic vision; weak capacity to influence the wider business environment), but it is also a mistake to treat such businesses as homogenous. For example, despite being grouped into the same sector, the owner of rickshaws rented out to forty drivers in Jogjakarta, Indonesia, is likely to have little in common with a software engineering start-up in Iceland even if the number of workers is about the same. Indeed, SMEs often appear to be defined as much by what they are not (i.e. they are not multinational enterprises) as what they share in common.

One reason SMEs are not homogenous is that they represent different types of entrepreneurship. Much of the excitement about the potential of SMEs in a corporate responsibility context stems from the fact that all innovators start small, and that is true of sustainability innovation and green entrepreneurs. However, these entrepreneurs are a specific type, called variously 'opportunity entrepreneurs' and 'gazelles'.[6] They are often the serial entrepreneurs who derive enormous satisfaction from establishing new businesses, and whom it is hoped will be attracted by the opportunities found in tackling major societal challenges. Thus, it could be Stephan Schmidheiny, who got out of asbestos, bought Swatch, and now runs the triple bottom-line conglomerate, GrupoNuevo; or it could be Robert Matthams, the young entrepreneur behind Shiply.com which offers solutions to empty running by haulage firms.

The opportunities that are arising connected with mega trends such as demographic change and global warming (see Chapter 14) are already being seized on by such people. It has been argued that they are far more likely to be receptive to ideas and practices associated with corporate responsibility, and should therefore get preferential treatment in the allocation of resources (e.g. government funding to foster corporate responsibility).[7] Even if their products do not have a societal orientation, they will have a growth orientation that provides an added incentive to be aware of their social and environmental footprint, increases the importance of a robust and more complex approach to stakeholder management, and opens the door to new sources of capital (e.g. venture philanthropy). Innocent, the drinks company, and LoveFilm.com the DVD rental firm are examples of this type of 'gazelle'.

However, when we talk about corporate responsibility and SMEs, the gazelles are only one part of the conversation. There are 25 million SMEs in Europe, and most of them are 'lifestyle' businesses, run by people who have chosen to work for themselves or have been left little choice given the changing nature of employment in wealthier economies. They have little desire or indeed potential to grow, and they may regard running a SME not as an exciting springboard to business success, but more as a trade-off between factors such as independence, income, employment, and other lifestyle-related decisions.[8] Most of them serve local markets. They may be heavily engaged in their local communities, and have particular passions such as education or conservation, but they are likely to be unaware of or suspicious of terms such as corporate responsibility and sustainability. When Napoleon described England as a nation of small shopkeepers, he was talking about a nation of lifestyle SMEs. Often it is a lifestyle chosen by immigrants who may lack the education and social networks to enter other strands of economic life, and therefore includes people such as Iranian refugee, Kazem Ariaiwand, who owns the Red Polar Bear, the world's most northerly kebab van on Spitsbergen, Sweden; German émigré Frederick Drumpf who ran the Arctic Restaurant serving gold prospectors in late nineteenth century Canada and was to be grandfather of Donald Trump; and the Bell family from Scotland whose Canadian farm housed the first workshop of telephone inventor Alexander Graham Bell.

Lifestyle SMEs have a different relationship to corporate responsibility than the gazelles as we will discuss. On the one hand, there is a perception that they have poor employment practices akin to Charles Dickens' portrayal of 'Bleak House'.[9] On the other hand, they may feel they have a closer bond with workers and local communities, and treat formal corporate responsibility requirements on issues from freedom of association to child labour to pesticide management as unwarranted interference. Ghana's small commercial pineapple growers, for instance, have identified a list of areas that could be considered part of corporate responsibility practice (e.g. skill transfer, strengthening property claims, job creation, stimulating local economies, investing in local infrastructure) but which are not recognized in the corporate responsibility requirements of their overseas buyers.[10]

As part of a shift in ideas of economic development assistance, fostering of entrepreneurship in developing economies has gained increasing attention.[11] There is a tendency in this context to mix up gazelle and lifestyle SMEs, and as important to overlook the specific features of what have been called 'necessity entrepreneurs', i.e. small operations (often in the informal economy) where own-account enterprise is the option of last resort, and where the opportunities and incomes are typically worse than in formal employment.[12] Examples include the small female market traders in Nairobi, food hawkers in Jakarta, and the laid-off Detroit car worker who is trying to run his own machine shop. This type of SME presents yet different challenges in a corporate responsibility context: the owners may see the venture as a temporary occupation until something better comes along; there will be little capital to invest in anything that does not show an immediate return; and the very existence of such entrepreneurs may cause tension with local authorities and residents. Moreover, insofar as these enterprises are recognized in a corporate responsibility context, they are more likely to be described as potential recipients of acts of responsibility from larger operations (e.g. preferential contracts, donations) than as actors in their own right.

■ Discussion points

People have very different motivations for setting up SMEs.

- Why might 'gazelles' be more interested in corporate responsibility than others?
- Why did necessity entrepreneurs increase in number in North America and Europe in 2008–2009?
- Are SMEs from ethnic minorities likely to have different notions of responsibility than others?

Local, national, and regional differences between SMEs

In addition to the above, there are other differentiators of SMEs relevant in a corporate responsibility context. We have mentioned that immigrants are an important part of the lifestyle SME group. In developed economies these have a particular importance in poorer communities because they often provide a range of services where other businesses are reluctant to go.[13] Interestingly, these are often more growth-oriented than other lifestyle SMEs, notably once the business has been passed on to second or later generations. They are major employers amongst ethnic minorities, and often have a high local multiplier effect as their customers, owners, and workers typically live within a small radius of the business. Furthermore, depending on the ethnic group concerned, there can be a high degree of female ownership of the businesses (e.g. 75 per cent of African and Caribbean businesses in the UK are owned or co-owned by women).[14] Indeed, no matter what sort of SME we are talking about, we should not overlook the importance of women in this sector, whether it be the female traders who are the backbone of West Africa's fish trade, the women's savings groups that were behind the growth of microfinance in Bangladesh, or waste trader Zhang Yin, the richest woman in China.

Figure 11.1 shows the types of social impact these businesses have, although one needs to be careful not to exaggerate their role in tackling issues such as economic regeneration and social exclusion.[15] In some ways, the close association such businesses have with local communities is both a strength and a weakness in terms of responsibility. The need to build a strong licence to operate is an important driver of responsible behaviour, but it also means that what constitutes responsibility will be locally determined. Thus, for example, the relationship SMEs in Tuscany build involving trade unions, local authorities, and other established stakeholders, is quite different to those SMEs in Uzbekistan seek to create where 'responsibility' is to a degree defined by Islamic norms of philanthropy and tithing.[16] Equally, these relationships are affected by the socio-political context. For example, while much attention has been paid to the role of multinationals such as oil

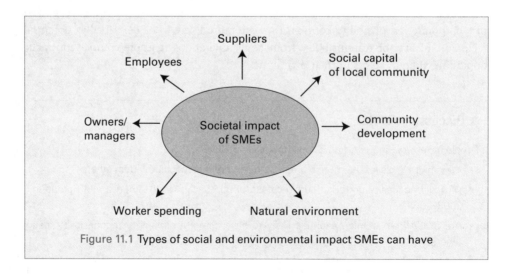

Figure 11.1 Types of social and environmental impact SMEs can have

companies in regional conflicts, SMEs can also be a flashpoint. Race riots that periodically erupt in Indonesia are often focused on Chinese-owned SMEs because they are an easy target for unrest. In Nigeria, markets have been flashpoints for ethnic conflict, although conversely they can serve as spaces to bring together conflicting groups. The example of SMEs in Russia (see Snapshot 11.1) highlights the significance of political context.

SNAPSHOT 11.1

SMEs in Russia—unique challenges and common ground

Many of the private enterprises that have arisen in Russia since the end of communism are SMEs. Their situation is interesting in that they have emerged out of an economy that did not recognize private enterprise, and now exist in one where there is enormous suspicion of business. In the 1990s, American economist Jeffrey Sachs and others encouraged 'shock therapy' to the Russian system that not only left many in greater poverty than before, but through the USA-funded Russian Privatization Center, positioned the private sector as the main engine of economic reform. But instead of allowing a million SME stars to shine, the largest part of the new economic pie seemed to go to a new class of private sector oligarchs including Lisin (steel), Prokhorov (mining), and Abramovich (oil). The way these people acquired and managed their resources as well as their close relationship to the state has led many locally to feel big business is detrimental to Russia's interests, and caused others to wonder how business' legitimacy can be improved.

Putin, Russia's current Prime Minister and former President, has initiated efforts to reassure the public that business will be mindful of general welfare, and this has been a driver behind the government's promotion of corporate responsibility, including requirements about corporate responsibility policies and transparency. This has been accepted by many larger companies as the quid pro quo for protecting their assets and independent management. However, SMEs do not have this kind of relationship with the state, and moreover often do not want to be seen as aligned to government. Their concerns are corruption, insecure property rights, arbitrary law enforcement, and bureaucratic inconsistencies.

Thus, there are two tiers of corporate responsibility in Russia: one involving the largest companies concerned about their international reputation and the success of initial public offerings, and the other SMEs worried about local socio-political conditions and often resentful of the state. The former are often eager to be involved in international initiatives such as the UN Global Compact, but although the Compact advertises advice to SMEs on its Russian website, there is little mention of the issues smaller businesses want to see addressed, or how to go about tackling them.

(Sources: original research; **www.undp.ru**; Avtonomov, 2006; Tsalikis & Seaton, 2008)

Quick Questions

In Russia, corporate responsibility is treated as irrelevant by most SMEs.

1 What issues should corporate responsibility practice include to make it of interest to SMEs?

2 Why are SMEs reluctant to be involved in state-backed initiatives?

3 How could the Global Compact's SME guidelines be improved in a Russian context? (downloaded from **www.unglobalcompact.org/docs/news_events/8.1/Operational_guide_ME.pdf**)

SMEs as society members

It is widely held that SMEs often practice corporate responsibility without knowing it. This is because if they are visible members of local communities, they need to build a strong licence to operate, whether that be through sponsorship of local sports teams, charitable donations, or involvement in community activities. Moreover, as they typically lack the influence over local authorities and other local leaders that bigger companies have, individually or collectively they need to find alternative ways to remain effective. For example, the Rotary and Lyons Clubs found around the world are primarily made up of smaller entrepreneurs, and as well as networking are used as a means of contributing funds to the local community.

Historically, the need to maintain a licence to operate stems from the particular role entrepreneurs such as traders have played in society. Those engaged in trade were often treated with suspicion by local communities concerned about profiteering, and at the same time were relied upon to get the best deal for local products traded with outsiders.[17] It is no coincidence that groups who came to dominate trade were often immigrants or other types of outsider, sometimes differentiated by religion: these were already stigmatized to some degree, and being a trader did not lower their status in the way it might for indigenous citizens.

Whether it be Arabs in coastal Java, Chinese in Malaysia, or Lebanese in West Africa, suspicion of traders has led them to invest heavily in their own and their adopted communities, often in very visible, prestige projects from temples to schools. Some of this suspicion can be explained sociologically, but other perceptions have more to do with business reality. Employment conditions in SMEs are often considered poor, characterized by long hours, low wages, poor working conditions, and few protections. Women working in sweatshop conditions be it in London or Manila are emblematic of SME exploitation. Some of the criticism of labour rights in the production of popular apparel is about the conditions amongst second and third tier suppliers who are often SMEs. Indeed, to strangers there can appear to be a contradiction between the desire of certain SMEs to retain a respectable external face, and their internal neglect.

Not all SMEs can be tarnished with the same brush, and poor working conditions are much less prevalent than they once were in some parts of the world, not least because of greater regulatory oversight and the need to attract good employees.[18] A small hardware store may not be able to compete with the big box stores on price, for instance, but if it has knowledgeable staff it can be a more attractive consumer destination. In industries from tourism to coffee bars, the quality of staff can be essential in wooing customers away from large companies. All of this amounts to a concern with stakeholder management and engagement (see Chapter 9), even if it is done informally and unconsciously. In fact, when SMEs have been approached about corporate responsibility, owners frequently feel that in terms of both issues and approaches, much of what is discussed is what SMEs have historically engaged in.[19]

Box 11.1 **SME objections to corporate responsibility**

- It is too costly (e.g. the cost of verifying performance)
- Outsiders mistakenly think corporate responsibility strategies from big companies can simply be scaled down for SMEs
- There aren't any real business benefits
- It takes up too many financial and human resources
- There are more immediate concerns to deal with to survive
- SMEs don't have the expertise to manage corporate responsibility
- SMEs typically don't seek external help until late in the day
- It is yet another way customers can exert power over SMEs

(Sources: Jenkins, 2009; Grayson & Dodd, 2007; Quayle 2003)

SME perspectives on corporate responsibility

Confronted directly with the question, 'Should SMEs do corporate responsibility?', the response is often negative. Some typical answers are captured in Box 11.1, and the SME attitudes can be summarized as too hard, too expensive, irrelevant, and unwarranted. Some of these attitudes hardened in the rush to formalize corporate responsibility management practices in the late 1990s, especially in the supply chains of large companies, when SMEs came to be treated as 'little big companies' where practices simply needed scaling down to be effective.[20] As already noted, SMEs are not homogenous, and even if they were they still exhibit quite different managerial, operational, and ownership features to large listed firms.[21] These features tended to be overlooked early on, not least in developing countries where listed firms felt most at risk from the possibility of poor social and environmental performance by SMEs. For example, in Kenya and Zimbabwe, major supermarkets, in collaboration with NGOs and trade unions, sent delegations to get SME suppliers to adopt labour codes of practice. This often came across as heavy-handed, especially early on, and was worsened by the seeming lack of coordination between technical staff responsible for the codes of conduct, and supermarket buyers who continued to focus solely on price, quality, and delivery times.[22] In one instance, a supplier in Kenya had its contract terminated despite investing heavily in meeting supermarket J Sainsbury's ethical standards (Dolan & Humphrey, 2004). Such examples reinforced existing tensions in supply chains, and hardened SME attitudes to corporate responsibility which was seen by some as yet another way for large firms to exert control over their suppliers.

Another reason SMEs have viewed corporate responsibility negatively is that terms such as corporate social responsibility and sustainability appear vague, too broad, and not especially business-related. When the terms are explained or substituted for others, SME managers may start to see managing the business-society relationship not so much as a cost burden but a source of competitive advantage[23] (see Box 11.2). Furthermore, it

Box 11.2 Reasons for SMEs to adopt corporate responsibility management practices

- SMEs often already 'doing' corporate responsibility even if they don't know it
- Social and environmental performance already a common part of supply chain management requirements
- Provides SMEs a way to attract and retain good quality personnel
- Young people often seem attracted to values-driven organizations
- The modern, networked economy attaches a premium on reputation and relationships, and corporate responsibility is a way of contributing to this
- Early adoption of corporate responsibility issues helps SMEs anticipate future legislation
- A growing number of 'lohas' consumers (lifestyles of health and sustainability)
- Corporate responsibility can be a business opportunity to create new platforms for competitiveness

(Sources: Morsing & Perrini, 2009; Grayson & Dodd, 2007)

has started to be recognized that many SMEs are already 'doing corporate responsibility'; that it is a natural part of running a successful business to engage with local communities, manage stakeholders, create a good working environment, preserve local natural resources. If this is so, it begs the question whether rather than see SMEs at fault, one should revisit the question 'Should SMEs do corporate responsibility?' Jenkins (2009) argues that it is the corporate responsibility debate that is the problem because it fails to engage SMEs. But this remark in itself treats corporate responsibility as a fixed management approach, and not as a sphere of business concern where the theory (what are the responsibilities of business?) and management practice (how are those responsibilities managed?) are continually evolving as part of the shifting nature of business' role in society.

One can argue with some of the reasons proposed for SMEs to take corporate responsibility seriously (see Box 11.2). Some such as attracting good personnel, anticipating legislation, and the growth in 'lohas' are the same reasons given why large companies should 'adopt corporate responsibility.' Others seem vague or dubious: for instance, are young people more value-driven than in the past, or is it a feature of youth that values play a particular part in decision-making, and if so for how long will values be an advantage to the SME? Equally, how generalizable is the evidence that a premium is being put on relationships and reputation, particularly given the global spread of the debate about SMEs, and the continuing promiscuity of producer-buyer relations at the second and third tier of global supply chains?

The idea that corporate responsibility can be a business opportunity may also seem inexact, but it is one that has attracted considerable attention. Grayson and Hodges (2004) refer to it as 'corporate social opportunity' by which they mean the willingness to look for innovation in non-traditional areas such as those that form part of the contemporary corporate responsibility agenda. Comparative case studies of European SMEs suggest that many smaller firms are well-placed to take advantage of these opportunities, even if it is a field requiring much more investment.[24]

Box 11.3 SME vantage points on corporate responsibility

Your outlook on corporate responsibility depends where you sit in the universe of SMEs. Three types of SME viewpoint stand out:

First, there is the 'responsibility innovator' most often seen in social enterprises, and amongst entrepreneurs who regard for profit and not-for-profit private sector mechanisms as an important way of achieving social and environmental benefits. But these innovators are also behind for-profit companies that are trying to balance social, financial and environmental outcomes, building on the concept of the triple bottom-line (Chapter 3). A recent manifestation of this in the USA is B Corporation (where B stands for beneficial), a set of companies that are certified for their social and environmental performance, but it would also include companies such as Seventh Generation, technology firm Linden Lab, and craft seller Etsy.[25]

Second, there are 'supply chain victims'; SMEs that are pressured into adopting certain social and environmental standards as a requirement of doing business with large customers such as retailers. While for some the word 'victim' may describe an early, passing disgruntlement that evaporates when the relationship with the customer improves, there are still examples of SMEs that feel their customers' commitment to corporate responsibility brings little tangible benefit.[26]

Third, there are the 'unconscious agents'; SMEs that in order to maintain their licence to operate, or because of the values of the owner or manager, are already engaging in activities that help manage the company's relationship with society, and are not intended to have a direct impact on the financial bottom-line. This accounts for much of the corporate responsibility activity associated with SMEs, but is typically considered informal.

■ **Discussion points**

Corporate responsibility is often portrayed as a burden on SMEs.

- Which do you think are the strongest and weakest reasons for SMEs to take corporate responsibility seriously?

- What are some examples of corporate social opportunity that could be attractive to SMEs?

- Are some SMEs right to see corporate responsibility as an extension of supply chain bullying by larger companies?

Responsibility issues for SMEs

SMEs, as mentioned earlier, often practice aspects of corporate responsibility management without recognizing it. Given that many SMEs recruit locally, and produce, buy and sell locally, it would be hard for them to escape the consequences of poor stakeholder engagement. In Tuscany, for instance, SMEs exist within sophisticated networks involving trade unions, competitors, and local authorities as well as the public, without which they could not operate effectively.[27] In developing economies, the creation of stakeholder partnerships is reckoned by some to be a key element in gaining competitive advantage.[28] Philanthropy and involvement in community development are long-established traditions for many SMEs, reflecting the pragmatic reasoning behind maintaining a licence to operate, or the values-based orientation of a SME owner/manager.

The relatively greater influence an owner's values can have in SME behaviour compared to other types of business has been widely held up as a unique advantage such companies can have.[29] Because the company is seen as an extension of the owner's sense of self, and because s/he has more control over how to distribute the benefits of the enterprise amongst stakeholders, there may be greater opportunity to use the company as an instrument for realizing personal virtue. However, we should not get carried away with this viewpoint as for various reasons (e.g. inadequate regulatory oversight, struggle for financial survival, lack of transparency, indifference), SMEs may have poor employment practices, inadequate health and safety provisions, and so on. This is evident, for instance, in slave labour on cocoa farms, employer lobbying against maternity and paternity rights in Europe, and the various instances of workers trapped inside blazing sweatshops with locked fire doors. While it may well be true that attention to working conditions is essential to SMEs in skill-intensive sectors where there is a battle for good employees, it would be counterintuitive to expect the same degree of care to be valued as central to business survival in labour-intensive sectors where there is significant unemployment. Moreover, in the latter case, a SME might have an active external-facing programme to secure its reputation amongst the community, while exploiting its workforce with impunity. For example, in Uzbekistan, as already noted SMEs abide by religious norms about charity and other matters that enhance their public reputation, but they do not proscribe workplace discrimination and unequal employment opportunities.[30]

Again, it is difficult to generalize about SMEs, even if there is a tendency so to do in some corporate responsibility literature. However, there are other features of employment in SMEs that deserve attention. SMEs can offer opportunities to people who would find it difficult to work in larger companies. This could be because of their educational background, their race or ethnicity, their gender, the need to balance household and income generating activities, or accommodating physical or mental disorders. While in the worst instance, SMEs' willingness to be an employer of last resort for disadvantaged people can lead to exploitation, in societies where there is sufficient impetus to control abuses a SME's flexibility can benefit those who might otherwise be low down in the employability pecking order.

SNAPSHOT 11.2

Zippos—a responsible circus?

Zippos is a small travelling circus, founded in 1986. It has an international staff of 70, including its owner Martin Burton. It tours Britain from February to November every year, taking the Big Top, the acts, their equipment, and the performing horses and budgerigars from town to town each week.

Circuses may embody family entertainment, but they are also controversial. The word circus conjures up images of poorly treated lions, elephants and other wild animals. It also brings to mind unsafe facilities, diesel-belching trucks, and unhygienic food. Consequently, over the years, circuses have attracted unwanted attention from local authorities, immigration officials, and animal rights campaigners.

One of the first things one sees at a Zippos show is the red lorries, each with 'fueled by chip fat' written on the side. The chip fat comes from the food vans at the circus, next to the entrance to the Big Top. The audience is shown to their seats by people in red tunics who a few minutes later turn out to be the high-wire or wheel of death stars. Like many SMEs, 'and other jobs as required' is a standard part of everyone's contract of employment. Even the owner appears as one of the clowns.

He is also one of the initiators of the circus industry's code of conduct on animal welfare, and was a pioneer of circuses without wild animals. However, this has not stopped Zippos being the target for animal rights protests or local authority bans, and its one time artistic director, David Hibling, gave evidence in favour of Mary Chipperfield who was found guilty of twelve counts of animal cruelty training animals for other circuses.

According to Burton, much of his time is taken up with filling out risk assessments as the industry is held to ever higher health and safety standards. But he is also aware that a good reputation is essential to his company's future, and on the Zippos website there is a page devoted to the various causes it supports, as well as a section on the circus academy that the company has established to train future generations of circus performers.

(Sources: www.news.bbc.co.uk/1/hi/uk/259098.stm, accessed 7 April 2010; www.business.timesonline.co.uk/tol/business/career_and_jobs/article3707452.ece, accessed 7 April 2010; www.oxfordmail.co.uk/news/5198052.Big_Top_boss_opposes_plan_for_animal_ban/, accessed 7 April 2010)

Quick Questions

Zippos Circus is an unusual but in many ways very typical example of a SME.

1 Does Zippos have a corporate responsibility strategy?

2 What are the drivers behind Zippos' attention to corporate responsibility?

3 Which of these drivers are typical of SMEs, and which ones are specific to this company?

SMEs and corporate responsibility management

Introducing corporate responsibility to a SME

There are some who hold that SMEs are by their very nature more responsible than other types of company because of aspects such as their close relationship to communities, long-term family ownership of the enterprise, paternalism towards workers, and less pressure to maximize shareholder value.[31] If this were always true, then it would be relatively straightforward to enhance management performance to improve social and environmental outcomes. To a degree this is what has been tried in initiatives such as People and Profit in Denmark where 12,000 SME personnel were trained to understand corporate responsibility as a way of enhancing competitiveness. However, as the earlier comparison of gazelles and lifestyle enterprises makes clear, not all SMEs are equally responsive to corporate responsibility ideas, from which we can infer that something more sophisticated is required to engage and then enhance the impacts from SMEs.

Grayson and Dodd (2007) highlight five factors that can affect SME receptiveness toward corporate responsibility ideas:

- Using acceptable, understandable terminology: A term such as corporare social responsibility could have a very different impact than one such as sustainable enterprise or good citizen.

- Targeting: Given the sheer number of SMEs and the fact that some are likely to be more receptive to ideas of corporate responsibility than others, prioritising which companies are involved in awareness raising and capacity building initiatives seems crucial.

- The messenger: Support for improving SME corporate responsibility management may have to come from government, but this does not mean that the public sector is best placed to deliver the message. There is evidence that anything that makes corporate responsibility issues seem part of a political agenda generates indifference or even hostility, and that organizations known and respected by SMEs such as chambers of commerce and trade associations are better conduits.

- An evolutionary journey: In Chapter 6 we explore the idea that corporate responsibility management is an evolutionary journey, and this is as true of SMEs as other companies. Because of the diverse nature of SMEs and the effect this has on the company's orientation towards or away from corporate responsibility management, the journey may actually be more complex, but comprehending that 'corporate responsibility' is not a state to achieve but a definitional construct and managerial process is essential to understand direction and progress.

- Think of SMEs as people: Following the theory that SMEs are different in character as well as size from larger companies, some argue that they exhibit more 'human' traits. For example, while larger firms value orderliness, formal systems, planning/strategy, and accountability, SMEs might be as comfortable with informality, intuitiveness, and trust. Recognition of such characteristics would in turn affect how SMEs were introduced to corporate responsibility as a concept.

Managing corporate responsibility

Despite the arguments why corporate responsibility means something different in the SME sector, the advice to SME on corporate responsibility management has much in common with that to other types of company. The Danish People and Profit programme mentioned previously is one of the most extensive attempts to reach out to SME managers. Its practical guide to corporate responsibility management, however, comprehensive though it is in terms of the aspects of management, shares similarities with ones targeted at multinational companies.[32] (The guide can be downloaded at **www.csrgov. dk/sw51121.asp**) This is true of the broad areas of suggested managerial activity (see Figure 11.2), and also the more detailed advice on areas from communication to innovation to customer relations. For example, on environmental management the guide recommends ISO 14001 environmental management system or the EU Eco-management and Audit Scheme (EMAS) as a basis for a systematic approach to planning, implementation, and reporting. It provides a checklist for assessing current performance, and advises the use of a think-plan-do-check model of continual improvement. Such advice may be practical for a Danish SME, but despite the numerous claims made that SMEs are not scaled down versions of large companies, the advice offered is not significantly different to what might be given to any business.

The same comments are true of guidance about adopting the UN Global Compact, and involvement in poverty alleviation.[33] This would not matter but for the evidence that SMEs are unwilling to manage social and environmental issues because of their specific managerial circumstances and constraints.[34] Even in the area of innovation, highlighted already as an aspect of particular interest to SMEs (or at least the growth oriented gazelles), the models proposed rely heavily on conventional consultancy and academic models of innovation (e.g. the Doblin Group; Mullins & Komisar, 2009). If other constraints are not overwhelming, this may not be a bad thing in that framing corporate responsibility issues within established management models could improve their acceptability, but the limits on transferability of such models set out throughout this chapter do beg questions that current literature does not seem able to answer.

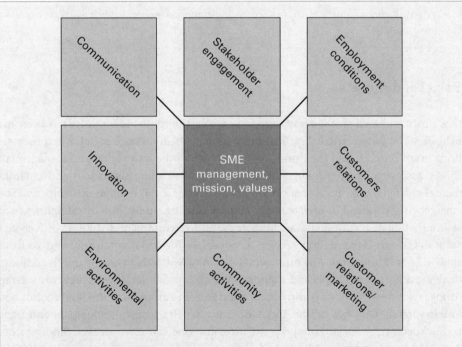

Figure 11.2 Areas of SME management where corporate responsibility issues are relevant

Source: Adapted from People and Profit, 2007

Exceptions to this are work on social enterprises (p 274) and the attention given to the SME dimension to certain aspects of mainstream corporate responsibility management approaches such as stakeholder engagement (Jenkins, 2005; Spence et al. 2003), the distinction between formal and informal aspects of management in SMEs (Russo & Tencati, 2009), and supply chain management, although in the latter case most guidance is aimed at multinationals and how to deal with SME suppliers (ETI, 2006; DCCA, 2008; Pedersen, 2009) and the difficulties that can arise (Tencati et al., 2008). We are left, therefore, with the sense that although there are unique responsibility dimensions that SMEs should pay attention to, an array of areas where SMEs are already active, and good reasons for some SMEs to consider corporate responsibility issues as part of their competitive advantage, nonetheless the specifics of corporate responsibility as a distinct element of SME management are not well understood.

■ Discussion points

SMEs are frequently described as having unique characteristics that affect their attitude to corporate responsibility issues.

- Given the above characteristics, why do you think a comprehensive body of distinct management approaches has yet to emerge?
- Why have SMEs in supply chains received more attention than most others?
- What role can government play in encouraging corporate responsibility management practices in SMEs?

Social enterprise

One of the most vibrant areas of corporate responsibility in recent years has been the field of social entrepreneurship. An international phenomenon, social enterprises are being established around the world, applying much of the innovation and management theory associated with entrepreneurship in general to addressing social and environmental challenges. Business schools are now teaching social entrepreneurship, and the emergence of this field of private sector activity is being studied too by disciplines such as international development, anthropology, and environmental studies. Universities such as Oxford, Harvard, and Alberta have centres for social enterprise, and you can study it in institutes from Argentina and Belgium to Switzerland and Spain. In addition, there are a host of networks and support organizations for social entrepreneurs such as Ashoka (worldwide), NESsT (Latin America and Eastern Europe), and the Skoll Foundation (international). One can call on specialist consultancies such as Bridgespan, and trade bodies such as the Social Enterprise Alliance, and one can one can seek funding from dedicated sources such as EVPA and the Acumen Fund.

By some measures, start-up rates and employment growth in social enterprises is outstripping that in conventional commercial enterprises, and they are having an impact on significant numbers of people: for example, Grameen Bank has 2.4 million micro-credit customers in Bangladesh and Afghanistan, while the Bangladesh Rural Advancement Committee is the country's second largest employer after the government.[35] The size of these organizations raises questions about what is meant by social enterprise, and certainly why it is part of a chapter on SMEs. For some, size is not a determining factor, and therefore GE's ecomagination initiative (Chapter 6) or the retail company Wholefoods deserve the label social entrepreneurship as much as Fairtrade's web of small producers or Andrew Mawson's Bromley-by-Bow Centre, a focal centre for enterprise in one London community.[36] By blurring the definitions of social enterprise, advocates are able to make major claims about its impact. For example, classifying all not-for-profit organizations as social enterprises allows proponents to claim the sector is worth over a trillion dollars; and subsuming the long-standing credit union sector within social enterprise enables the claim that 25 per cent of the USA population is affected by social enterprise.[37] As noted in other chapters, there is a tendency in certain areas of corporate responsibility for advocates of a particular approach or idea to use self-serving data, but it can lead to the conclusion that almost any business activity that feasibly has a positive social or environmental outcome is worthy of the mantle 'social enterprise', or that any socially or environmentally oriented activity is an enterprise. In other words, it can become harder to identify what is not a social enterprise than what one is.

Meanings of social enterprise

Definition

From the outset, 'social entrepreneurship' has been used to embrace a wide range of entrepreneurial activity. A collection of 14 academic articles on social enterprise used 10 different definitions of the term, including basic disagreements about whether it applied to individual entrepreneurs or to organizations; whether trade and financial objectives were an essential element, or if it were as likely to be found in public and non-profit sectors as the private sector; and whether the defining characteristics are the goals and outcomes (e.g. tackling social problems) or the process (e.g. employing ideas of innovation to create new social value).[38]

In a field where practitioners and theorists can often appear intoxicated by the excitement of their endeavours, it is not surprising that many define social enterprise in terms of its ambition and intent. The entrepreneurs are called 'disruptive change agents' and 'sectoral iconoclasts', and their enterprises are described as 'social justice in motion' and world changers.[39] As a social entrepreneur explains:

> the real measure of social entrepreneurship should be 'direct action that generates a paradigm shift in the way a societal need is met.' What such people do, in effect, is to identify and attack an 'unsatisfactory equilibrium.' Their endeavors are transformative, not palliative, with the power to catalyze and shape the future.
>
> *(Elkington & Hartigan, 2008, p 6)*

In what remains an important introduction to the field, Dees (1998) sets out a continuum of social entrepreneurship organizations defined by the way they are funded. On one side are organizations with a social or environmental mission that are run by and largely funded by volunteers; at the other end are socially-oriented ventures conducted within commercial private sector organizations. In between, lie an array of not-for-profit and for-profit enterprises that variously are funded through grants, capital investments, and revenues. As Leadbeater (1997) points out, these enterprises can be found in the public, private, and civil sectors, and one thing that marks them out is how the competencies associated with one sector are transferred to another. For example, a public sector social enterprise may be marked out by its adoption of business skills to pursue its social and environmental remit; businesses may choose social or environmental returns/outcomes ahead of financial ones; and NGOs may adopt entrepreneurial solutions.

With this in mind, social entrepreneurship could be defined as the innovative use of combinations of resources to build organizations and practices that yield and sustain social and environmental benefits.[40] However, this would still leave us with a large range of only tangentially related initiatives, some of which we have discussed in other chapters (e.g. ecomagination, M-Pesa, and Wholefoods).[41] It would also draw us into a discussion of the roles of government and third sector welfare provision, both of which largely fall outside of the scope of this book. Therefore, Haugh's (2006) definition is broad enough yet not too inclusive to act as a working definition of social enterprise in this chapter (see Key Concept). It needs to be expanded to explicitly include environmental benefits, but it does emphasize the importance of business-led solutions in pursuit of social (and environmental) outcomes. While some would contest this as too narrow, it fits the purposes of this chapter, and also chimes with an important strand of business-focused (though not necessarily for-profit) social enterprise.[42]

■ Key concept: Social enterprise

Social enterprise is a collective term for a range of organizations that trade for a social purpose. They adopt one of a variety of different legal formats but have in common the principles of pursuing business-led solutions to achieve social aims, and the reinvestment of surplus for community benefit. Their objectives focus on socially desired, nonfinancial goals and their outcomes are the nonfinancial measures of the implied demand for and supply of services'

(Source: Haugh, 2006, p 183)

Social and environmental mission and process

Haugh's definition also helps highlight that even if social enterprises are run at a profit, this is not their primary purpose. For many, what is special about social enterprise is the primacy attached to the social or environmental mission. This means identifying and addressing an unmet need or value creation opportunity. For example, La Fageda in Spain was established to provide meaningful work for the mentally ill, shifting them from producing ashtrays and trinkets to being the core personnel in a dairy business; the Population and Community Development Association in Thailand exists to tackle over-population as a cause of poverty, and does this by funding its birth control programmes from its social business ventures. In such enterprises, financial returns are not an indicator of business performance: rather, they are a means to a nonfinancial end where what matters is social or environmental impact.

However, measuring this performance is not straightforward, especially as the goods and services produced may be only one form of social enterprise output. For example, in some social ventures, creating employment, engaging community members, empowering individuals, attracting government services, and achieving the social integration of marginalized people may be more significant benefits than the actual delivery of tangible products such as potable water, schools, or trading opportunities: a lesson learned from international development (see Chapter 4). These process benefits are widely accepted as being essential to the kinds of sustainable transformational social change that social enterprise aspires to achieve, but they can be difficult to measure and to realize, especially compared to more concrete but perhaps short-term outcomes such as a wage, a playground, or a surgery. The case study of Fairtrade in Chapter 12 highlights this, and in-depth studies of the impact of social enterprise such as Lyon and Moberg (2010) show the complexity of understanding benefits.

Therefore, one finds some who consider social enterprise primarily in terms of the field of social endeavor (e.g. poverty alleviation, health care, education, community development, advocacy), and others who concentrate more on the operational features of the enterprise (e.g. decision-making not based on capital ownership, beneficiaries of the venture are participants not just recipients, limitations on profit distribution, social goals). Neither of these is mutually exclusive, but they might be reflected in the workings of the enterprise. For example, social enterprises are often closely identified with their founders, and the strengths of such single-minded visionaries (e.g. their self-assurance, their emotion, their 'insane ambition' (Elkington & Hartigan, 2008)) can create institutional weaknesses (e.g. unwillingness to delegate or build organizational capacity, reluctance to recognize criticism or fault, inability to think strategically or objectively), and these in turn can prove a barrier to achieving goals such as genuine empowerment, democratization, and indeed the scaling up of the enterprise.

A further feature is the context within which social enterprises develop. If a social need were being met adequately by other means (e.g. state welfare services), arguably social enterprises would be redundant, and some of the criticisms of social entrepreneurship focus on the extent too which they represent an ideologically motivated privatization of public services, rather than a genuine innovation.[43] Emerson (2003) stresses that social entrepreneurs typically work in dysfunctional markets where there might be high transaction costs, a lack of innovation, or no credible information on performance. Enterprises working at what has come to be called the bottom of the pyramid[44] (see Chapter 4) are amongst those working in underserved markets, but the rationale of initiatives such as Hindu Lever's Shakti is to generate a profit by serving poor markets. By contrast, social enterprises are more concerned with the social impact of working in areas of market failure. Moreover, there are examples of 'critical social entrepreneurship' (Nicholls, 2008) that challenge existing institutional structures and aim to build alternatives, and there is a historical continuity between the Rochdale cooperative movement in nineteenth century England, and Fairtrade cooperatives set up to counter price monopsony in certain commodity chains.

Examples

There are examples of what might be categorized as social entrepreneurship throughout this book, including Vodafone's M-Pesa (see Case Study 4), Merrill Lynch's investment in Ulu Masen (see Chapter 4), Fynsa (see Case Study 11), and Fairtrade (see Case Study 12). Another example of the many that have been written about is Witness, a non-profit enterprise that helps human rights activists and others film human rights abuses. It began by giving cameras to victims and witnesses of abuses, and was funded by the Reebok Human Rights Foundation. It then progressed to build better technical and tactical (i.e. advocacy) capabilities, and is now operating in about sixty countries, serving as a watching eye on public and private sector abuses.

Despite Witness' radical social goals, it is a fairly conventional social organization, relying on grants in the same way as most non-government organizations have done since the 1960s. Freeplay Foundation is somewhat different. It was born out of Freeplay Energy, a producer of wind-up radios and other electronic devices. Its main markets are North America and Europe where emergency workers, outdoor enthusiasts, and emergency response teams use the company's torches, radios, generators, and medical instruments. However, profits are used to subsidize the supply of the same robust products to poor nations through the Freeplay Foundation. Thus, Freeplay represents a hybrid of for-profit and non-profit elements, and the founders are keen to emphasize that the company and the foundation are not senior and junior partners in the enterprise, but the foundation simply represents a more effective way of having a social impact.

This was the situation until 2008 when—a year after winning *Time* magazine's Heroes of the Environment award—Freeplay Energy was bought out by Narang Group following financial difficulties.[45] The new owners severed links with the Foundation, and the hybrid model ceased. The Foundation continues, and receives funding mostly from philanthropists in the USA, but it is now having to rethink its model of revenue generation, service delivery, and overall strategy.

Recycla Chile deals with electronics in a different way: it tackles end of product life-cycle issues to do with computers, televisions, mobile phones, and other electronic goods. Recycla recognized 'e-waste' as a business opportunity, and employs ex-convicts to dismantle appliances and prepare the parts for export. However, income is reinvested in Recycla's greater social mission, to raise awareness of the need to recycle e-waste, and to create a legislative framework to support this. Within four years, the social enterprise was profitable, and it is now the preferred recycling outlet for many companies.

These examples demonstrate quite different funding and business models. The degree of long-term viability of each example is debatable as is its scalability, although scale and replication are not defining characteristics of social enterprise. What they have in common is that they seek to serve dysfunctional or underserved markets through innovative ideas, and give primacy to their social/environmental impacts.

Why now?

One effect of the wide variety of definitions of social enterprise is that the term can be applied to all manner of historical examples including the Quaker-family enterprises of Victorian capitalism, the gilded age philanthropy of Andrew Carnegie (see Chapter 1), and the Rochdale cooperative movement. Yet, placing contemporary social entrepreneurship in a long historical tradition goes against some of the claims that it is a new and unique response to a particular set of events and circumstances. For example, it has been portrayed as a response to the market dysfunctions associated with global poverty (see Chapter 4), leveraging the overall rise in global wealth, the spread of capitalist democracies, and the rising crises in health and the environment, income inequality, and inefficient public service delivery.[46] It also complements the 'third way' political paradigm that seeks to balance the free market bias of conventional democratic right-wing parties, and the state-control bias of their left-wing opponents. The third way, which has dominated much European and North American political policy since the early 1990s, treats economic development as an apolitical good that can be achieved through technological development, education, and competitive mechanisms. Entrepreneurship and social inclusion are important parts of this narrative, and social enterprise is often seen as uniquely placed to bridge them.

Social enterprise can also be portrayed as part of a more overt political paradigm where the values of the free market are transferred to arenas that hitherto were the sphere of the public sector. Thus, not only are social entrepreneurs filling roles that in previous decades' government agencies were the duty of government (even if the entrepreneurs often remain dependent on government funding), the frameworks and language of business come to dominate the poverty alleviation and environmental management discourse. For example, the poor are considered 'dynamic', the 'solutions' to poverty are to be found in 'entrepreneurship' and 'innovation', and even sustainability of the planet is described in terms of natural 'capital.'

As discussed in Chapters 4 and 14, an aspect of corporate responsibility that needs consideration is the extent to which it causes us to translate social and environmental issues into the norms and metaphors of business. However, it is misleading to think of a golden age when government was the sole purveyor of social goods. In some countries during a particular period as the result of particular social and political upheavals, the state took on a role unprecedented in history. But whether it be mosques and churches, mutual societies and cooperatives, or guilds and masons, there has long been a private social sector that has often been at least as active as government in spawning innovative solutions to meet social and environmental needs.

One new feature of contemporary social enterprise, however, is the widening sources of funding. Our earlier example of Witness shows how conventional grant giving remains important, and Orlando Rincón Bonilla, the Colombian social entrepreneur, is similar in many ways to Carnegie and Rowntree, wealthy businessmen who decided to spend their wealth on tackling social needs. But, as explored further as part of socially responsible investing (see Chapter 10), alternative and increasingly sophisticated capital markets focused on social entrepreneurs are emerging. There are mentor organizations such as

UnLtd that provide incremental seed capital as well as advice; there are networks that bring together angel investors and social entrepreneurs; and there are market brokers such as Investing for Good linking investors interested in a blend of social and financial returns on investment with social enterprises. This latter group is focused on what is variously called impact investing, programme related investing, or blended value investing.[47] These investments inhabit a space between philanthropy (where no financial return is expected) and pure financial investments (where social/environmental considerations are only a factor in so far as they affect profit maximization). The impact investing market is estimated to reach $500 billion by 2020.[48]

Impact

Much of the analysis about the impact of corporate responsibility in Chapter 12 is applicable to the particular field of social enterprise. In general terms, there are a large number of case studies that show social entrepreneurship in action, but these tend to be written by advocates of the field and consequently the cases themselves are weak on objectivity and rigour, and highlight successes rather than the inevitable large number of failures that are typical of entrepreneurship generally.[49] Systematic impact assessment is still at an early stage, even in well-established areas of social entrepreneurship such as fairtrade and microfinance. Moreover, there is a growing body of analysis (again often reliant on individual case studies) that challenges the effectiveness of social entrepreneurship.[50]

It seems likely that a more rigorous approach to understanding impact will be an inevitable consequence of the impact investing market where investors (perhaps unlike philanthropists) will be more concerned with evidence of social returns on investment. Yet, even if a significant number of social enterprises prosper and have a distinctively strong impact in dysfunctional markets, there may be limits on the change they can bring about. Muhammad Yunus, founder of the Grameen Group of social enterprises, says that the *'future of the world lies in the hands of market-based social entrepreneurs. The more we can move in the direction of business, the better off we are— in the sense that we are free.'*[51] There are echoes in his words of the Hungarian school of business thinkers and economists such as Hayek and Mises (see Chapter 2) who interpreted free markets as an escape from dictatorial governments, but there is also an assumption that entrepreneurship is an abundant quality that simply needs to be harnessed. However, most entrepreneurs are 'necessity entrepreneurs' of the kind discussed on p 263 rather than the 'gazelles' that advocates of social entrepreneurship idealize. As one social entrepreneur puts it, *'One does not decide to be an entrepreneur. One is an entrepreneur [from birth].'*[52] If this is true, then social entrepreneurs may never be sufficient in number to make a significant impact on the social and environmental challenges of the twenty-first century. But if what is meant are the hordes of necessity entrepreneurs who would rather not be entrepreneurs at all, then it seems unlikely the innovation hoped for from social enterprises will ever be realized.

CASE STUDY 11

Fynsa Bouquets—small enterprise in South Africa

There are two noticeable features about the Agulhas Plain in South Africa. It is home to some of the richest biodiversity on the African continent. It also has an unemployment rate of about 80 per cent. Fynsa is a small enterprise in the region that, working with a local conservation NGO, identified the potential to sustainably harvest fynbos flowers for bouquets in order to create employment and protect the biodiversity-rich habitat.

Fynsa reckoned its main outlet would be the European fresh flower market which is always hungry for new ideas, and where several leading retailers incorporate sustainability in their business strategies. However, it would not be enough for Fynsa to have a good idea or even a good product: a retailer's appetite for a responsibly harvested product was only the start. To meet the demands of European retailers, it needed to be able to deliver a consistently high quality product at the right time and in the right quantities, while also being mindful of the need to continually innovate and develop.

Fynsa understood they needed assistance to succeed. The Shell Foundation, a NGO assisting new enterprises in developing economies, funded the post of a full-time business manager, training, and the purchase of equipment. Shell Foundation also facilitated contact with retailer Marks and Spencer which in turn ensured its buyers, technologists and senior managers invested time into developing the product and overcoming various product and supply chain issues. The retailer also worked with Fynsa to make sure it understood and could meet standards on quality, efficiency, and product development. Meanwhile, the NGO that had helped set up Fynsa worked with local authorities and other NGOs to establish a sustainable harvesting code of practice, trained over 90 fynbos harvesters, and worked with Fynsa to establish acceptable worker facilities, social policies and systems.

According to Shell Foundation director Kurt Hoffman, 'It is possible simultaneously to eradicate poverty in retailer supply-chains and make a profit. This is crucial because without the profit element, ethical-sourcing is just meaningless PR-greenwash.' However, with so much external assistance, there was always a risk that Fynsa would become a puppet for others' benevolence rather than a viable business in its own right. This placed a burden on Fynsa's manager to build worker confidence in the responsibility-based business model, to establish key strategic relationships locally and internationally, and to develop the product so that new bouquets could be launched at higher price points.

A year and a half after Fynsa's Cape Flora bouquets were launched, a million bouquets had been sold in Europe, and were available in 350 stores. The company employs 135 people in an area of high unemployment, and protects and restores 30,000 hectares of fynbos meadows. Its success has spawned new businesses such as Better Trading, a company specializing in building links between responsible SMEs and retailers. As then Marks and Spencer sustainable development manager Katie Stafford, said, 'This partnership isn't about trying to put products on shelves that nobody really wants but are doing some good. To create sustainable, long-term change we look for those businesses that have really got a chance of commercially succeeding, but they need a helping hand to get there.'

(Sources: Shell Foundation, undated; **www.shellfoundation.org**; **www1.givengain.com**)

Questions

1 Fynsa is a small enterprise that was established with particular social and environmental objectives in mind.

    a What are the main social and environmental issues Fynsa addresses?

    b How replicable is the Fynsa model?

    c Is Fynsa a gazelle, a lifestyle, or a necessity enterprise?

2 The business opportunity benefits corporate responsibility offers SMEs are often highlighted.

    a If you were pitching corporate responsibility as a concept to a SME, what aspects of the Fynsa experience would you emphasize?

    b Which aspects of Fynsa might not resonate with other SMEs?

    c Is the Fynsa model relevant to developed economies?

3 Large companies are often accused of misusing their power over their suppliers.

    a What are examples of how large companies abuse their relationship with SMEs?

    b Why do retailers appear to have collaborated with Fynsa?

    c What are the advantages for larger companies if they collaborate with SMEs on corporate responsibility issues?

SUMMARY

Small and medium-sized enterprises have often been overlooked in discussions of corporate responsibility. For a long time they were either viewed as smaller versions of larger companies, or as a threat to large companies because of their perceived poor social and environmental standards in global supply chains. Nowadays, SMEs are more likely to be considered as worthy of special attention. Not just in terms of size, they are fundamentally different to other types of business (e.g. their close relationship to local communities; the resource constraints; their style of management; their different measures of success).

However, it is misleading to think that SMEs are more naturally responsible or indeed irresponsible than other firms. The SME sector is not homogenous and a SME's attitude towards corporate responsibility is affected by its attitude to growth, the values and goals of the owner/manager, and the reasons why the company was established in the first place. There are SMEs that were established in part to achieve social and/or environmental goals, and for small firms keen on growth 'corporate social opportunity' can help identify profitable openings. However, most SMEs are better seen as 'lifestyle enterprises' or indeed 'necessity enterprises' where the reason for establishing the business is because of personal preference or lack of other choices. For these types of SME, corporate responsibility is less immediately attractive, and is typically greeted as a burden. Yet often such SMEs are practising corporate responsibility of a kind in order to maintain their licence to operate in their communities, or to achieve business objectives such as attracting and retaining staff.

The difficulty in these instances is that corporate responsibility practices can be too selective (e.g. an emphasis on charitable giving but a failure to attend to working conditions), or they may be ignored (e.g. when a large customer imposes its own standards on SME suppliers irrespective of what they are already doing). For many SMEs, corporate responsibility management is seen as an additional bureaucratic burden or another instance of large companies exerting power over small ones. However, there are examples of companies in the supply chain working together to achieve common corporate responsibility objectives that have demonstrable business benefits. There is also growing private and public sector investment in improving SME corporate responsibility management. What is still missing, though, is a detailed understanding of corporate responsibility management practice as something distinct from the approaches adopted in larger firms.

FURTHER READING

Take your learning further: Online Resource Centre **www.oxfordtextbooks.co.uk/orc/blowfield_ murray2e/**

VISIT THE WEBSITE
for links to useful sources of further information

Visit the Online Resource Centre which accompanies this book to enrich your understanding of this chapter.

Students: explore web links and further reading suggestions. Keep up to date with the latest developments by undertaking web exercises.

Lecturers: you will find additional case studies, including one on the topic of Freeplay Foundation—a social enterprise partnership between business and NGO, for use in class or assessment. Show your students trailers from films related to Corporate Responsibility, and use images from the book in your PowerPoint slides.

- *Business Ethics: a European Review,* 2009, special edition on SMEs, vol 18, no. 1
  Series of articles on different aspects of corporate responsibility amongst SMEs including contributions from important thinkers in the field.

- Elkington, J and Hartigan, P, 2008, *The Power of Unreasonable People: How Social Entrepreneurs Create Markets that Change the World*, Harvard Business School Press, Boston.
  Wide range of examples of social entrepreneurship assembled and discussed by two strong advocates in the field.

- Grayson, D and Hodges, A, 2004, *Corporate Social Opportunity!: 7 Steps to Make Corporate Social Responsibility Work For Your Business*, Greenleaf, Sheffield.
  Arguments for why companies that seek social and environmental outcomes can gain competitive advantage.

- Jenkins, H, 2009, 'A 'business opportunity' model of corporate social responsibility for small-and medium-sized enterprises', *Business Ethics: A European Review*, 18(1), pp 21–36.
  Theoretical framework for understanding when SMEs are most and least likely to overtly address corporate responsibility issues.

- Jones, O and Tilley, F, 2003, *Competitive Advantage in SMEs: Organising for Innovation and Change*, John Wiley & Sons, Chichester.
  A study of how SMEs can best respond to innovation opportunities, including the opportunities in tackling social and environmental challenges.

- Southern, A, 2009, *Enterprise and Deprivation: Small Business, Social Exclusion and Sustainable Communities*, Routledge, London.
  A collection of contributions exploring the complex role SMEs play in tackling social exclusion and building sustainable communities.

ENDNOTES

[1] E.g. Carroll, 1999; Crane and Matten, 2004.

[2] E.g. Bennett et al., 1999; Hennigfeld et al., 2006.

[3] E.g. NRET, 1999; Lyon, 2003.

[4] See for instance Pedersen, 2009; Spence, 2007; Jamali, 2009.

[5] Sources: Burns, 2001; UNIDO, 2002; Jenkins, 2006.

[6] Patricof and Sunderland, 2006; Grayson and Dodd, 2007.

[7] Grayson and Dodd, 2007.

[8] Jenkins, 2008; Grayson and Dodd, 2007.

[9] Jenkins, 2006.

[10] Blowfield, 2010.

[11] Wilson, 2006; Brainard, 2006; Nelson, 2007.

[12] Patricof and Sunderland, 2006.

[13] Lyon and Bertotti, 2007.

[14] Lyon pers comm, March 2010.

[15] Southern, 2009.

[16] Battaglia et al., 2010; Stevens et al., 2008.

[17] Evers and Schrader, 1994.

[18] Jenkins, 2006.

[19] Jenkins, 2006; Perrini et al., 2007; Jamali et al., 2010.

[20] Tilley, 2000.

[21] See instance.g. Goffee and Scase, 1995; Spence and Rutherfoord, 2000.

[22] Blowfield, 2010.

[23] Oswald and Tilley, 2003.

[24] Jenkins, 2009; Murillo and Lozano, 2006.

[25] See also Hollender and Breen, 2010.

[26] Tencati et al., 2008; Ballinger, 2010.

[27] Battaglia et al., 2010.

[28] Nelson, 2007.

[29] E.g. Hammann et al., 2009; Jenkins, 2006; Enderle, 2004.

[30] Stevens et al., 2008.

[31] Murillo and Lozano, 2006; Grayson and Dodd, 2007; Morsing and Perrini, 2009.

[32] Compare People and Profit, 2007 with Hennigfeld, 2006 and PR News, 2006.

[33] Respectively UNDP, 2009 available at www.csrgov.dk/sw51121.asp; Brainard, 2006; Wilson, 2006.

[34] Thankappan et al. 2004; Lyon and Vickers, 2009.

[35] See Nicholls 2008, p 3.

[36] Elkington & Hartigan, 2008; Mawson, 2008.

[37] Salamon, 2003; Smallbone et al., 2001 cited in Nicholls, 2008, p 3.

[38] See the contributions collected in Mair et al., 2006.

[39] Nicholls, 2008; Bornstein, 2007; Mawson, 2008.

[40] Mair and Naboa, 2006.

[41] Kanter 1999 provides an overview of social innovation in major companies, and Weiser et al., 2006 offers numerous examples.

[42] Dees et al., 2002;Drayton, 2002.

[43] Leadbeater, 2004.

[44] Prahalad & Hart 2002, Prahalad 2005, Hart 2005, Hammond et al. 2007.

[45] The company's debt reached over $13 million on less than $8 million of revenue, apparently due to problems in assimilating an acquisition made in 2006.

[46] Nicholls, 2008.

[47] See for instance Emerson, 2003; Nicholls, 2010.

[48] Monitor, 2009.

[49] For examples of cases see Elkington and Hartigan, 2008; Mawson, 2008; Hollender, 2010.

[50] E.g. Edwards, 2010; Lyon and Moberg, 2010.

[51] Elkington and Hartigan, 2008, p 17.

[52] Ibid. p 22.

Part 3

Impact, critics, and future of corporate responsibility

12

The impact of corporate responsibility

Chapter overview

In this chapter, we examine the impact that the practice of corporate responsibility has had. In particular, we will:

- consider the importance of understanding impact;

- look at the ways we learn about impact and the ways it is assessed;

- establish a framework for understanding the different dimensions to impact;

- provide an overview of the impact of corporate responsibility to date;

- discuss the challenges of assessing impact.

Main topics

■ **Key terms**

Impact

Non financial performance

Corporate Responsibility reports

Ratings indices

Corporate Responsibility awards

■ **Online resources**

- Exercises and discussion topics for students

- Additional case study on the impact of Wal-Mart's environmental programmes

- Links to other web-based resources

- Teaching notes for the chapter case study

Understanding impact

What does corporate responsibility do? Does it help to make the earth more sustainable? Does it restore trust in corporations? Does it reduce poverty? Uphold international human rights? Reduce corporate malfeasance? Increase business profitability? Lessen corruption and improve public governance? End illegal activity such as smuggling and human trafficking?

These are some of the areas in which, as we have already seen, corporate responsibility is intended to have an impact. In this chapter, we look at the evidence to support these claims. In business or any area of life, understanding the impact is essential for making decisions, justifying courses of action, and recognizing the point at which we stand on particular journeys. In the corporate responsibility context, impact is essential if corporate responsibility is to defy its critics and move from being a 'feel-good thing' to being recognized as a 'good thing'. Whether one looks at the theoretical work on corporate social performance in the 1970s and 1980s, or at that on social accountability since the 1990s, the importance of measurement is apparent. Yet, given the emphasis put on '*if you want it to count, count it*', or the rooting of important corporate responsibility tools and methods in financial accounting, it is surprising how patchy attempts to measure corporate responsibility have been and that we do not know more about corporate responsibility management's overall impact.

Corporate responsibility embraces big goals, such as contributing to sustainable economic development, improving the lives of workers and their communities, and accelerating progress towards the Millennium Development Goals. Moreover, these contributions are often linked to conventional ones of corporate growth and profitability. Part of this chapter is concerned with finding out what evidence there is to show how far corporate responsibility has met these goals and, as importantly, the extent to which the evidence itself is being gathered. As we will see, the information is fragmented and, to make sense of it, we offer a framework that clarifies the different types of impact about which we do know something ('A framework for understanding impact', p 296). We use this framework in an overview of the current state of play in 'Different dimensions of the impact of corporate responsibility' (p 296), and conclude the chapter with a section discussing 'The challenges of determining impact' (p 313) and what might happen in the future.

The meaning of 'impact'

In its most general sense, 'impact' refers to outcomes associated with particular actions. Although this is too simple a definition, it draws attention, first, to the importance of outcomes (cf. outputs) and, second, to the significance of causality. As examples in this chapter reveal, discussion of impact often confuses 'outputs' for 'outcomes'. But although the two words overlap in some contexts, the former is narrower in meaning, referring to the specific actions that are needed to achieve a larger result, whereas the latter is the larger result itself. (For example, degrees are an *output* of university that have the *outcome* of creating a better educated population.) Thus, in the corporate responsibility context, a corporate responsibility report is an output, not an outcome, if our aim is to enable business to manage its relationship with society better.

Demonstrating a causal relationship between inputs, outputs, and outcomes is, however, far from straightforward. A company might be clear about what it wants to achieve (e.g. to remove child labour from its supply chain), but even if this happens, can it be sure that the outcome was the result of its own actions rather than, for example,

---

■ Discussion points

Some people claim that, when we talk about corporate responsibility's 'impact', what we are actually referring to are its 'actions' or 'outputs'.

- What are examples of the distinction between 'actions' and 'outputs', and 'outcomes' and 'impacts'?
- What is the significance of thinking in terms of actions rather than outcomes?
- Taking a real company's corporate responsibility report as the basis, how would you modify it to focus on outcomes?

a concerted enforcement effort by the police? Roche (1999) argues that one should not place too much emphasis on causality, defining impact assessment as *'the systematic analysis of lasting or significant changes—*positive or negative, *intended or unintended—in people's lives brought about by an action or series of actions'* (emphasis added). This definition also highlights how, for many, impact refers to the outcomes for people, although as we shall see, the beneficiary of corporate responsibility may also be a company or a particular stakeholder group.

How we learn about impact and the limits of our knowledge

There are three readily available sources of information relating to the impact of corporate responsibility: corporate responsibility reports (including social, environmental, and sustainability reports); ratings of companies such as FTSE4Good, the Ethibel Sustainability Index, the KLD Indexes, ARESE social ratings, and the Dow Jones Sustainability Indexes; case studies of companies undertaken by companies, corporate responsibility organizations, and others.

There are also case studies of companies and industries that are undertaken by a variety of organizations monitoring corporate behaviour (e.g. CorpWatch, Christian Aid, *Stichting Onderzoek Multinationale Ondernemingen*, or 'SOMO'—the Centre for Research on Multinational Corporations). These have been very influential in the overall development of corporate responsibility and, in important ways, have set out benchmarks against which the corporate responsibility practices of firms can be assessed. There are reports documenting the progress of companies within particular partnerships, such as the annual reports on compliance with labour standards by the Ethical Trading Initiative or the Fair Labor Association. There are also publicly available reports about the certification of particular resources in accordance with the criteria of bodies such as the Marine Stewardship Council, or, in some cases, of facilities such as those adopting the ISO 14000 series (although often the information most pertinent for assessing the impact of these is considered proprietary and not in the public domain).

In addition, there are what can be called 'trend-tracking' reports, focused on particular aspects of corporate responsibility (see Box 12.1). There has been a well-documented rise in the number of corporate responsibility reports and, according to the KPMG 2008 *International Survey of Corporate Responsibility Reporting*, 80 per cent of the 250 largest public companies in the world were issuing reports, containing a mix of environmental, social and governance (ESG) information. The framework of the report, and how that is used over a number of years, is an important factor in showing impact. 75 per cent of the companies in the KPMG survey used the Global Reporting Initiative Sustainability Reporting Guidelines described in Chapter 8. Various company reports also refer to the UN Global Compact, the International Labour Organization's core labour standards, the UN Declaration on Human Rights, the Kyoto Protocol, and other agreements that, while not binding on business, are often used in defining corporate responsibility performance. As we shall discuss later, a significant

Box 12.1 Surveys and reports on corporate responsibility performance

- *Business in the Community's* Corporate Responsibility Index
- *State of Corporate Citizenship*—a biennial annual report highlighting trends and corporate attitudes to corporate responsibility among US companies.
- *Business Ethics'* 100 Best Corporate Citizens list.
- *Covalence's* Ethical Ranking—a reputation index of the largest market capitalizations in the Dow Jones Index, based on their contributions to human development.
- *Business Week/Climate Group's* Climate Change Rankings—multinational companies by their total reduction of greenhouse gases.
- *Sustainability Reporting Survey* (Germany)—an overview of company reporting.
- Fortune 100 *Accountability Rating*—scoring Global 100 companies on how seriously their future decisions will consider non-financial matters.
- *GMI's* Corporate Governance Ratings—3,200 global companies.
- Transparency International's *Global Corruption Barometer*—public opinion of corporations.
- World Economic Forum's biannual *Trust Poll*.

area of impact is how corporate responsibility's success has impacted its own behaviour ('The impact of corporate responsibility on itself', p 312) and the adoption of common standards that facilitate comparison between companies is an important aspect of this.

The limitations of the information

Before we look at the types of impact that the above sources of information reveal, it is worth noting some of the comments that have been made, particularly about reports, ratings, and case studies. The 2008 KPMG survey noted that industries with the greatest environmental impact have the highest levels of reporting (e.g. 80 per cent of electronics and computers, utilities, automotive, and oil and gas companies produce reports), although there has been a rapid rise in the financial sector, which is not considered to be an industry with a heavy environmental footprint. The range of topics is increasing so that, now, about two-thirds of reports have sections on corporate governance and 85 per cent mention climate change. Nonetheless, certain issues are seldom reported upon, such as economic impacts (25 per cent of reports), and, in general, environmental impacts are better reported on than social ones. Furthermore, while 40 per cent of reports base their content on GRI guidelines, only 21 per cent employ stakeholder consultation to identify the issues that the reporting company should be addressing.

The use of particular standards—even if well regarded—tells us only so much about impact. As Clark (2005) shows, corporate responsibility is being undermined by such practices as the falsification of records and the training of workers in how to respond to auditor questioning. The UK consultancy firm, Impactt Ltd, says that 95 per cent of factories it visits in China probably falsify records and that managers can buy software to help with this. In response, some have called for stronger independent assurance and, in 2005, 30 per cent of reports were independently assured in some way, mostly by the large accounting firms, even though there are question about the objectivity of such organizations (see Chapter 8). As the 2002 *Trust Us* report[1] points out, however, there are big questions about how far such companies have restored public trust in their own integrity, although there is evidence that competition between firms and the need for credibility has improved the market for standards.[2]

As discussed in Chapter 8, the Association of Chartered Certified Accountants, which runs sustainability reporting award programmes in different parts of the world, has identified recurring weaknesses in company reports. These are summarized in Box 12.2, but those that particularly stand out are the lack of systemic ecological footprint analysis of the company's impact, the lack of comprehensive maps of stakeholders, and the lack of information on the key impacts that the company's operations and products, or services, have on society and the natural environment.[3]

Ratings, in as much as they derive data from corporate reports, will reflect the above limitations to some degree. The situation is also confused by the heterogeneous methods they use. Schafer (2005) distinguishes between ratings systems that are economically oriented (i.e. those that focus on the economic impact of ethical, environmental, and social criteria on the company) and those that are normatively oriented, within which evaluation criteria are dominated by what he calls 'ethical'

Box 12.2 **Strong and weak areas of corporate responsibility reports**

Strengths	Weaknesses
• Comprehensibility; appropriateness of report length.	• Little evidence of coherent and collective management of sustainable development strategy and any issues arising from it.
• Identification of key social, environmental and economic impacts and business issues as a basis for credible reporting.	• Lack of a clear and credible articulation of the meaning of sustainable development, consideration of the implications of its pursuit, and any tensions that emerge.
• Explanation of the process behind decisions on key impacts and issues for the business and report indicators.	• Lack of description of risk identification and management processes, including disclosure of actual risks identified and opportunities resulting from them.
• Identification of key stakeholders, including rationale for their selection.	
• Explanation of the governance structure in place to manage sustainability performance (e.g. existence of named board director).	• Identification of, and accounting for, social and environmental externalities is rare.
	• Need for more demonstration that sustainability is integrated into core business strategy.
	• Few reports provide description of how incentives for staff and managers are linked to sustainability performance and achievements of targets.

(Source: Summarized from ACCA, 2008)

motivations. Among the economically oriented systems (which he says predominate), there are four groups:

1 risk assessment approaches (how the company deals with its social or environmental risks);

2 efficiency models (how management strategies relate to sustainability, on the assumption that sustainability offers competitive advantage);

3 industries of the future (identifying the above-average growth companies inside what are considered to be the hot sectors of tomorrow);

4 best-practice corporate responsibility management (identifying companies with the best approaches to corporate responsibility management).

For Margolis and Walsh (2003), this focus on the economic consequences for the company is a basic weakness in our understanding. Echoing some of what we have discussed regarding the business case (see Chapter 6), they say '*if corporate responses to social misery are evaluated only in terms of their instrumental benefits for the firm and its shareholders, we never learn about their impact on society*'.[4] Indeed, they argue that the emphasis on instrumental benefits is so great that there is little attempt to examine when it is permissible or necessary to act on other stakeholders' interests if they are not consistent with those of shareholders.

Recent work on impact by the United Nations Development Programme (focusing on developing countries), and the Overseas Development Institute (focusing on tourism) have stressed the instrumental benefits of corporate responsibility, and the World Business Council for Sustainable Development's impact assessment framework begins by stating it was '*built by business for business and thus, begins with the business perspective.*'[5] The consequences of an economic orientation in reporting and ratings will become apparent when we look, in the next section, at what we do and do not know about the actual impact of corporate responsibility. Moreover, we should not be surprised at this orientation, given the degree to which corporate responsibility has sought legitimacy by rooting important elements of its methods and approaches in the norms and instruments of financial management, accounting, and managerial efficiency.

Finally, we need to note the limitations of case studies as a way in which to assess impact. These have proved important in terms of drawing attention to particular issues and examples of company behaviour. The most well known are probably those of civil society organizations, such as the Clean Clothes Campaign's case study of an Indonesian factory producing for Fila, or SOMO's 2005 investigation of labour rights violations in computer factories. There are also interesting examples commissioned by companies, such as Impactt Ltd's (2005) study of overtime in Chinese factories. But by their very nature, case studies tend to use differing methodologies and a meta-analysis of findings is all but impossible. Moreover, as Elliott and Freeman (2003) note, the organizations that produce many of the case studies typically only need to understand the situation on the ground in order to start a campaign; from that point on, the main dynamics happen away from the site of the problem, i.e. through the media, company responses, consumer reaction, and government action.

A framework for understanding impact

If we think about the possible answers to the question posed at the start of this chapter—
'*What does corporate responsibility do?*'—it is readily apparent that 'impact' has a different
meaning if we are talking, for example, about helping to make the earth more sustainable than if we are referring to reducing corporate malfeasance, or to improving business
profitability. What is recognized as impact also differs if one is looking at instrumental or
normative dimensions of performance.

To help to make sense of these different dimensions, we offer a framework that captures the different ways in which impact is being interpreted. It is based on what others
have written about the impact of corporate responsibility and measuring corporate social
performance,[6] and also the different aspects of impact included in a selection of award-
winning corporate responsibility reports.[7] What emerges are five dimensions on which
corporate responsibility practice is held to have an impact.

1 The social, environmental, and governance 'big picture'
   This refers to large social and environmental issues, including global warming, human
   rights, economic growth, and poverty reduction.

2 Instrumental benefits
   This covers the connection between financial performance, and ESG performance,
   including the impact of making the business case for corporate responsibility.

3 Business attitudes, awareness, and practices
   These refer to the impact that corporate responsibility is having on the way in which
   companies think about non-financial aspects of business operations and the way that
   they operate.

4 Non-business stakeholders
   This refers to the impact of corporate responsibility on other stakeholders, including
   the critics who advocate for greater ESG responsibility.

5 The impact of corporate responsibility on itself
   This area covers the way in which corporate responsibility's evolution and growth has
   affected how we think about and practise corporate responsibility today.

We use this framework throughout the following section.

Different dimensions of the impact of corporate responsibility

The impact of corporate responsibility on the 'big picture'

One only has to think of the US\$ 65 billion Bernie Madoff scandal, the sub-prime lend-
ing origins of the 2008 financial meltdown, or the Montara oil spill in the Timor Sea
to realize that business remains a highly problematic element of society. It would be very
unrealistic to expect corporate responsibility to eradicate the abuses and excesses
that have always dogged human economic activity. Moreover, one would need an

unprecedented belief in industry self-regulation to think that corporate responsi
initiatives could have a fundamental impact on financing given the disparity th
between the uniquely high level of regulation applied to banks nationally in the larg
economies and the absence of regulation at a global level (see Chapter 10). Nonetheless,
increasingly corporate responsibility is being linked to many of the biggest challenges
around the world. These include how we:

1 respond to climate change;

2 address the consequences of globalization;

3 increase the effectiveness of internal corporate governance;

4 uphold international human rights;

5 increase justice and equity, especially in the poorest countries;

6 fight corruption and poor governance;

7 achieve stable and sustainable economic growth.

Although some corporate responsibility initiatives have been framed in terms of these
big picture issues, it is impossible to show attributable impact at this level. Instead, we
can only understand pieces of the mosaic. The GRI Sustainability Reporting Guidelines,
the ISO 26000 draft international standard on corporate responsibility, and various other
internationally used standards are attempts to break these overarching goals down into
addressable pieces.

In this section, we examine what is known about the impact of corporate responsibility on some of these issues. Areas such as corruption are inherently unsuited to measurement of external outcomes, at least in the short term, and have largely been viewed in
terms of changes in business attitudes and practices (see 'Impact and the business case',
p 302). Therefore, we will look at the broad areas of environmental, social, and economic
impact.

Environmental impact

Environmental management has been central to corporate responsibility thinking since
the 1980s and it is not surprising that we know more about the impact of corporate
responsibility in this area compared with others. The term embraces such aspects as
natural resource management, waste management, recycling, marketing of green products, and pollution prevention and control. There are a number of well-developed initiatives that can demonstrate their impact over a period of several years. For example, in
1995, the Forest Stewardship Council had certified less than 5 million hectares of responsibly managed forest, but that figure had grown to over 125 million by 2010.[8]

Many companies, such as Diageo, Procter and Gamble, and Unilever, have successfully
reduced their water use. For example, Unilever has lowered its own worldwide usage by
54 per cent over 10 years and has extended this by working with its suppliers so that, for
example, tomato growers have reduced their consumption by half.[9] Unilever is often
cited as a leader in terms of environmental reporting and other areas of impact are
also worth noting. Before selling on its Birds Eye brand, the company estimated by 2006

it would source 60 per cent of the fish it sold within Europe from sustainably managed fish stocks; it has increased its paper-based packaging to 83 per cent in Europe; it has reduced diesel fuel usage for transportation; it has lowered carbon dioxide emissions from its manufacturing operations by 25 per cent since 1995. It demonstrates year-on-year reductions in units per tonne of production in what it recognizes as seven key areas of eco-efficiency, including energy, hazardous waste, and improvements in the management of ozone depleting gases.

In some instances, companies' management of the environment is basically in compliance with national laws. Therefore, it can be difficult to conclude what is an impact of corporate responsibility and what is the result of government regulation. In fact, unlike social impacts, most environmental information seems to concern developed, rather than developing, economies, even though government regulation in the latter seems likely to be weaker.[10] In the USA, however, where federal government was not at the forefront on environmental issues such as global warming, companies, such as DuPont, Procter and Gamble, and Coke, adopted targets for reducing greenhouse gas emissions that broadly reflect the spirit of the Kyoto Protocol.

BP, the second largest oil and gas sector company, positioned itself at the forefront of thinking about how business can contribute to sustainability when, in 1996, it became the first energy firm to withdraw from the Global Climate Change Coalition, which challenged scientific arguments for climate change. It said it would reduce its greenhouse gas emissions at twice the rate specified in the Kyoto Protocol and met those targets nine years ahead of schedule, reducing emissions by the equivalent of 9.6 million tonnes and bringing operational savings of $250 million.[11] Wal-Mart has now positioned itself in a similar leadership position on the environmental impacts of retail supply chains, achieving for instance a 25 per cent reduction in waste in the first three years of its sustainability programme, and committed to a 20 per cent improvement in the energy efficiency of its buildings by 2012.[12] Public investment in variations of what Barrack Obama calls the Green New Deal will lead to more scrutiny of the impact of corporate environmental actions, and the importance attached to taking environmental issues seriously is evident in companies such as Johnson and Johnson, Pacific Gas and Electric, and Exelon withdrawing from the US Chamber of Commerce because of the latter's policy on climate change.

Figures on individual company performance in important areas of environmental management are available for most major companies in oil and gas, automotive, utilities, and other industries with high levels of environmental impact. But commentaries on ratings and reporting continue to emphasize that too many companies have not identified what their key sustainability issues are, or how they most affect the environment.[13] The information available is synthesized by ratings organizations, but there has been little attempt to assess the overall impact of corporate responsibility on key areas of environmental management. Furthermore, the data highlight trends (e.g. the year-on-year percentage change in a particular performance area), but do little to show what is the 'right' number, such as the level of carbon dioxide emissions that is ultimately acceptable, or the amount of water usage needed to maintain a certain ecosystem. Indeed, companies have tended to shy away from this type of claim. Failure to gauge systemic impact will become a more important issue as certain approaches are accepted as best practice, something that is already evident in the questions being posed about carbon trading.[14]

■ **Discussion points**

Companies seem to have made most progress in demonstrating their environmental impact.

- How far do you think the experience with environmental impact is a forerunner for what we will see with social and economic impact? What do you think are the possible differences?

- What are the weaknesses in our understanding of environmental impact at present?

- What is the most important thing that a company can do to have a positive impact on public trust in its environmental performance?

Social impact

Social impact includes such issues as human rights, working conditions, labour rights, the impact on indigenous peoples, and the impact on local communities. As already noted, this is a more recent development than that of environmental management and, not surprisingly, there are fewer data on impact. But the different ways that companies have a social impact are also less well understood, and certainly less comprehensively reported on. In an industry such as horticulture, for example, extended production times, piece work, short-term contracts, and job insecurity have all come to be seen as necessary for competitiveness, and insofar as these are poorly addressed, corporate responsibility protections can appear as a shield for deflecting attention from the most profound social impacts.

Although companies such as Anglo American with its Socio-Economic Assessment Toolbox (SEAT) have been lauded for developing tools designed to fully understand the their social impact, overall there has been a focus on particular aspects with the adoption of labour standards in supply chains becoming a significant component of corporate responsibility. Vogel's (2005) comprehensive review of the literature concluded that there had been little systematic analysis of the impact on workers and their families, but a study of 800 suppliers in 51 countries concluded that, if monitoring of labour conditions were to be accompanied by other interventions (e.g. improved factory management), there would be significant improvements for workers.[15] A multi-country empirical study of the impact of monitoring a voluntary labour standard endorsed by major companies in the UK showed that conditions in some places had improved (especially with regards to health and safety, and child labour), but there had been little effect on wages or freedom of association, and some improvements had even left workers worse off (e.g. a decline in take-home pay due to reduced working hours).[16] However, Nelson et al.'s (2007) comparison of South African wine producers and Kenyan cut flower producers that compared firms adopting voluntary labour codes of practice and those that had not shows working conditions and standards of living were higher amongst workers in the former than the latter. The apparel industry, in particular, has made significant advances in driving out child labour and the ILO says that child labour fell by 11 per cent during 2000–2004. There is also evidence, however, that removing children from an export-oriented factory can be a mixed benefit if other opportunities are worse, or if opportunities for education decrease. In fact, the net impact can be that Western consumers have their demand for goods produced by adult labour fulfilled, but that there is no change in the numbers of working children.[17]

Exploring labour conditions in Indonesia, Harrison and Scorse (2004) conclude that codes of labour conduct, together with anti-sweatshop campaigns, were responsible for increasing wages in export-oriented factories during the 1990s and, moreover, that this was achieved without lessening employment opportunities. This finding is interesting, because of the large dataset with which they had to work, but smaller studies can also be insightful. For example, data from 142 southern Chinese factories audited by Verité in 2002–2003 revealed excessive overtime in 93 per cent of cases, supporting the findings of Impactt Ltd that compliance-focused auditing of labour conditions has had little impact on improving working hours. As ETI remarked in its 2003–2004 report, improved compliance with codes is not necessarily a sign of sustained improvements in labour practice and may only mean that suppliers are becoming better at passing audits. A glance at the most recent ETI report bears this out, stressing as it does the importance of worker training and capacity building amongst suppliers in order for codes of conduct to be effective.[18]

This is probably truer for some aspects of social performance than it is for others. For example, although there may be little sign that workers are getting true living wages because of corporate responsibility, Vogel (2005) concludes that there are attributable signs of improvements in working conditions, and ETI's annual reports consistently show that the majority of non-compliances detected and addressed relate to workplace health and safety. Although this has been derided for being a simple target in terms of the greater corporate responsibility challenge, when one considers that, in 2005 in China, based only on official figures, there were a quarter of a million workplace accidents and over 126,000 deaths,[19] advances in working conditions are a significant achievement.

But companies are frequently not making data about social impact available. According to Ruggie et al. (2006), only one company—BP—has made public the findings of a human rights impact assessment. Likewise, companies may admit to the need for public reporting on all material aspects of their performance, but this does not mean that they are consistently reporting on the benefits of programmes with potentially significant social impact, such as those in the pharmaceutical industry to combat HIV/AIDS in poor countries.[20] This reinforces the impression noted earlier that many companies are not systematically identifying key issues.

The picture is not necessarily clearer when one examines niche areas of corporate responsibility with explicit social objectives. A series of case studies comparing the social impact of fairtrade, organic farming, and forest certification projects found that they increased livelihood opportunities and income levels for many participants, and provided access to new markets, and the opportunity to develop human and social capital.[21] The studies also showed, however, that certain groups of people can be excluded, projects can have negative impacts on those not participating in them, and, ultimately, that the most significant long-term determinants of success are factors that are not normally considered to be part of corporate responsibility, such as building the capacity to run a business, overcoming trade barriers, and lowering entry barriers to new markets. Similar findings emerged from a 2009 meta-analysis of fairtrade case studies (Nelson & Pound, 2009).[22]

The insights offered by case studies, such as those available on Rio Tinto's website, suggest that individual company programmes are having positive impacts for local communities. However, in areas such as human rights and security, the consequences for local communities of voluntary principles and other corporate responsibility approaches will always be difficult to measure, while the outcomes of actions such as investing or disinvesting, which may even be a consequence of corporate responsibility policies, are not normally being addressed. Moreover, as Rajak's (2008) study of corporate responsibility amongst mining communities reveals, companies may redefine what they mean by corporate responsibility and hence what they consider to be legitimate impacts.

Economic impact

The distinction between social and economic impact is to some degree artificial: after all, what is the economy if it is not part of society, and hence a social institution? Polanyi (1944) argued that a well-functioning society is one where economic activity aligns with society's, and Ruggie (2003) believes that embedding the economy in this way is something companies and governments should strive for, not least through corporate responsibility. Nonetheless, corporate responsibility practice and theory still often makes a distinction between the social and the economic.[23] There are case studies that seek to test models for defining the meaning of economic impact,[24] and companies such as Unilever and SAB Miller have commissioned studies to examine the economic impact of their operations.[25] Mining companies such as Anglo American and Rio Tinto have also now begun to examine the economic impacts of their investments in local communities.[26]

Mainstream companies tend to think of economic impact as the consequences of the conduct of their normal business operations. In contrast, there are alternative business models where the rationale for the operation itself is that it is an effective means for contributing to the social good. Amongst the most well-known examples of this are fairtrade and microfinance as well as a large number of organizations that fall under the social entrepreneurship umbrella (see Chapter 11). Such enterprises are looking further afield than before to raise capital, and new investor interest in knowing about impact has led to the creation of impact analysis tools such as GOODadviser. Nonetheless, social and environmentally focused enterprises are still at the experimental stage of impact assessment. A 2006 overview of microfinance found that, to the extent the impact was known, the poor benefited, but to a limited extent.[27] Awareness that social goals are not being managed has led to the belated creation of the Imp-Act Consortium to promote social performance measurement in the microfinance community.

The situation is similar with the equally well-established approach called fairtrade. Fairtrade is often held up as a clear example of the kind of economic impact corporate responsibility has brought, particularly relating to the economic condition of producers in poor countries. In impact assessments, a number of proxies for economic benefit for such producers are used. These include the growth in the volume of fairtrade produce, the increase in the number of producer groups, sales outlets, and importing organizations, and the ability of fairtrade to maintain a floor price that is equivalent to the cost of production.[28] For example, the fairtrade price for coffee in 2003 was $1.26 per pound compared with $0.82 per pound on the world market. As the fairtrade company, Traidcraft, recognizes, however, sales volume and market growth are not necessarily synonymous with the benefit brought to poor producers, and, in its award-winning social accounts, it looks at the value of purchases, the sales of goods from developing countries, and the per centage of cost of sales spent in developing countries' volume of sales, revealing, for example, that not only have sales of products from developing countries increased, but that the money spent there has risen from £2 million in 2001 to £3.4 million in 2005.

Case studies of producer groups around the world show that the fairtrade price for farmers can be significantly higher than that available on conventional markets. For example, a study of seven cooperatives found that the price to farmers was twice the world price and three times that which was paid by local traders, while in Ethiopia, fairtrade producers get 70 per cent of the export price compared with 30 per cent for coffee sold on conventional markets.[29] And even when fairtrade only results in modest increases in per capita incomes, this can be the difference between destitution and survival.[30] However, as Ronchi (2002) acknowledges, overall information on the actual impact that fairtrade has on individual producers is scarce and the International Federation of Alternative Trade admits that there is neither a comprehensive collection of data about fairtrade producers, nor a clear methodology about how to quantify the impact of fairtrade.[31] Furthermore, the main case study in this chapter draws out some of the difficulties of measuring fairtrade's impact, and how actual impact on the intended beneficiaries can be overlooked (see Case Study 12). Filling this kind of information gap will be a challenge for corporate responsibility more widely in the coming years.

■ Discussion points

Economic impact is something that has started to appear in some corporate responsibility reports.

- What distinguishes 'economic impact' from financial performance?
- What are the ways in which a company has an economic impact?
- Using the Unilever–Oxfam study of impact in Indonesia as a basis (Clay, 2005), how would you develop this into a framework for understanding economic impact in another industry?

Impact and the business case

The majority of impact studies since the 1970s have concentrated on corporate responsibility's relationship with financial performance, and major studies conclude there is not a strong correlation between doing well financially and doing good for society.[32] But making the business case for corporate responsibility has remained relevant (see Chapter 6), setting corporate responsibility apart from other areas of management[33] even though the rationale for expecting investments in corporate responsibility demonstrably to create shareholder value when other business investments are not held to the same standard is certainly questionable.

But making the business case for corporate responsibility has remained relevant (see Chapter 6), and is highlighted as an important aspect of corporate responsibility reporting by the ACCA and other European bodies involved in social accounting. The emphasis on the business case sets corporate responsibility apart from other areas of management[34] even though the rationale for expecting investments in corporate responsibility demonstrably to create shareholder value when other business investments are not held to the same standard is certainly questionable.

This is not the result of any conspiracy by the anti-corporate responsibility groupings. In fact it as much as anything a result of developments within corporate responsibility. The socially responsible investment movement, in order to distinguish itself from the conventional investment world, has sought to establish a link between wealth creation and the way in which companies address social and environmental issues. SRI performance is discussed in Chapter 10, but overall it is hard to conclude that many firms have been rewarded or punished by investors for their social/environmental performance.[35]

There are other ways of examining corporate responsibility's outcomes from a business case perspective, as we explore in Chapter 6. There is a fair amount of anecdotal evidence that employees and prospective applicants value corporate responsibility and a company's overall image, although there has not yet been a definitive analysis of this. At times, it gets personal and there is some evidence that employees of companies such as Nike and Dow decided to change attitudes inside their companies after too many taunts about their companies' reputations made over the barbeque grill.[36]

The financial return on corporate responsibility can also be seen, to some degree, in its impact on consumer behaviour. Smith (2003a) argues that corporate responsibility has helped companies to avert boycotts of brands and has increased consumer loyalty. We have already mentioned the emergence of corporate responsibility labelling, such as FSC, Rugmark, and Fairtrade, and reputation surveys such as Covalence's EthicalQuote.com demonstrate how companies such as Marks and Spencer can gain global reputation advantages through successful corporate responsibility initiatives.

As described in Chapter 6, the strongest link between financial and non-financial performance is probably the impact of corporate responsibility on environmental management. The often-significant improvements in eco-efficiency environmental management that we cited earlier are largely attributed to their neutral or positive impact on the financial bottom line. Company reports provide a wealth of case study material in this area, although, as noted earlier, many companies are not rigorous when it comes to identifying the most material issues for their business and it can therefore be hard to conclude if they are addressing genuine priorities, or simply those that are the most financially advantageous. Wal-Mart is one company that has tried to identify its major environmental impact and develop actions to tangibly reduce them; in the process making considerable savings from waste reduction, less energy consumption, and more efficient management processes. Furthermore, Wal-Mart has had a considerable impact on its supply chain, forcing suppliers to rethink their environmental practices as a condition of continued business.

There is a question as to whether this same kind of positive financial link can be made for areas of social performance. There are numerous individual cases in which companies have stressed that there is money to be made from tackling social needs (e.g. from Vodafone targeting of the migrant remittance market, valued at $270 billion, to Innocent's growth to become a £80 million business in ethical smoothies, now part-owned by Coca-Cola).[37] Vogel (2008) says there are noteworthy examples of US-based companies with a good reputation for corporate responsibility that have fared poorly in leveraging this for improving financial performance (e.g. Starbucks, Gap, Timberland). Collinson has developed and tested a methodology for assessing the business costs of ethical supply chain management, and some consultancy firms, such as Cost Benefit Systems, have product offerings that claim to demonstrate the return on investment of corporate responsibility activities.[38] In general, however, this remains an unexplored area.

While most companies emphasize the financial–ethical win–win outcomes brought by corporate responsibility, Cooperative Financial Services in the UK is exceptional in that it reports on the business opportunities foregone as a result of applying its ethical principles. Although this is widely admired, it might also only be possible because of the organization's cooperative status, and a publicly held company might face legal action if it appeared to be breaking its fiduciary obligations by disclosing this type of business decision.

■ Discussion points

Margolis and Walsh (2003) say that, because companies are so focused on understanding the instrumental benefits, they may never tackle some of the key impacts they have on society.

- Do you think this argument is valid?
- Give examples in which society in general might want a company to have an impact, although there may not be a clear business case.
- Under what conditions do you think companies will take action if there is not a business case?

Impact on business attitudes, awareness, and practices

A very important part of the impact of corporate responsibility in recent years has been the way in which it has affected business thinking and practice. Wood (2000) expressed surprise at how quickly corporate responsibility practice had caught up with theory, and Kanter (2009) provides examples supporting her argument that managing social good is now key to future business success. We have already noted the large percentage of the

SNAPSHOT 12.1

The impact of ethical trading on workers

In 2002, the Ethical Trading Initiative commissioned a three-year, three country impact assessment study that is one of the first in-depth empirical studies of how voluntary labour codes affect the lives of workers and their communities. The findings on the impact of the codes at the worker level were mixed as can be seen from the comparison of work places in three countries (see Table 12.1).

Table 12.1 **Summary of impacts by ETI Base Code principle at Country Study supply sites**

Base Code principle	South Africa (6 worksites)		Vietnam (6 worksites)		India (6 worksites)	
	Management	Workers	Mgmt	Wkrs	Mgmt	Wkrs
Freedom of employment	None	None	None	None	None	None
Freedom of association	None	None	None	Minor	None	None
Health and safety	Minor	Minor	Major	Major	Major	Major
Child labour	Minor*	Minor*	Minor*	Minor	Minor	None
Living wage	Minor	None	Minor	Minor	Minor	Minor
Working hours	None	None	Major	Major*	Minor	Minor*
Discrimination	Minor	None	Minor	Minor	Minor	None
Regular employment	None	None	Minor	None	Minor	Minor
Harsh treatment	Minor	None	None	None	Minor	Minor

*An asterisk marks impacts that were considered negative by some respondents

(Source: Adapted from Barrientos & Smith, 2007)

The table shows the mix of outcomes. For instance, reductions in working hours, or the introduction of health and safety precautions at over half the sites constitutes a major change, whereas the introduction of age documentation, or the correct payment of annual leave observed at a few sites is a minor change. In some instances, seemingly positive impacts were viewed as negative by at least some workers (e.g. because a reduction in working hours resulted in a decrease in take home pay).

Overall, the assessment shows ETI has brought demonstrable impacts, notably under the provisions on health and safety, and on legal employment entitlements such as the minimum wage, working hours, and deductions for employment benefits such as health insurance and pensions. At most workplaces, workers' physical and social well-being has been enhanced through health and safety improvements, and reductions in working hours. Other improvements may have occurred prior to the study: for instance, the assessment did not discover any child labour. Some improvements were limited to certain types of worker, so that for example there was evidence of improvement in the treatment of permanent and regular workers, but contract labour was still poorly treated in most countries.

However, there were other areas where the impact was either mixed or unclear. For example, ETI has not led to a substantial increase in income in terms of guaranteeing a living wage, and there are workplaces where use of an ETI-based code of conduct has led to a reduction in working hours and resultant decrease in take home pay (although this is not necessarily considered a negative outcome if there are other benefits such as more leisure time). ETI has also not had an impact on underlying patterns of employment related to gender, ethnicity, caste, and religion, although there is evidence of a connection to certain changes in relation to discrimination in some locations (e.g. employment benefits to women, access to training and promotion). There is an emergent awareness in ETI that these and other apparently intractable issues ultimately depend on achieving a balance between company power over suppliers, and empowerment of workers to have greater control over their lives. Hence, it is not enough to enforce codes: instead, there is a parallel need to help build the capacity of workers and other local agents to implement a sustainable system of monitoring, enforcement, and remediation.

(Sources: Barrientos & Smith 2007; Barrientos & Smith 2006; Blowfield, 2007)

Quick Questions

1 What are the most important impacts of ETI?

2 What are the major areas of disappointment?

3 How can ETI improve its impact in the future?

Global Fortune 250 companies reporting on corporate responsibility, and in some countries this growth is also evident amongst small and medium companies.[39]

Although there may be many companies that have still to commit to corporate responsibility, and the uptake is stronger in certain sectors and types of firm (e.g. export-oriented companies, or those with a high public profile),[40] there has been a significant change in awareness and behaviour. It was hard to imagine, as short as five years ago, a company declaring a five-year plan addressing health, working conditions, climate change, waste, and sustainable raw materials, yet this is what UK-based retailer Marks and Spencer did, in 2007, in its Plan A programme. Few major multinational companies with extensive supply chains would now deny that they have a responsibility for the social and environmental performance within those chains—a marked change to the situation in the early 1990s. Not only have they introduced standards for their vendors in areas as diverse as resource management, good agricultural practice, bribery and corruption, human rights, and labour practices, but these have also evolved over time, both in terms of their content and overall implementation. For example, despite predictions that a large number of labour standards might lead to contentious issues being omitted,[41] in reality, competition has largely mitigated against weak standards and to a degree disingenuous monitoring.[42] A similar trend has been observed in the field of forest management standards. Although there is some evidence that companies pick and choose which standard to join based on how stringent or lax it is perceived to be,[43] standards as a form of industry self-regulation have largely been welcomed by non-commercial stakeholders, with examples including the Kimberly Process Certification Scheme (diamonds), the World Gold Council, and the Responsible Jewellery Council. Furthermore, companies that do not participate in credible voluntary standards for their industry can attract criticism in their own right as has happened to Littlewoods, BHS and Topshop which have refused to join initiatives backed by other major UK retailers, and to Boots which left the Ethical Trading Initiative after it was bought up by the private equity firm, KKR.

The successful use of particular corporate responsibility approaches in one industry appears to encourage other industries to become engaged. For example, the model for managing palm oil developed by the Roundtable on Sustainable Palm Oil has been replicated in the Roundtable on Sustainable Soy Association and the Better Sugarcane Initiative. Early thinking that corporate responsibility would somehow be part of individual firms' comparative advantage has largely been displaced by a belief in the greater potential of shared learning and joint initiatives. Thus, for example, leading organizations behind international labour codes of conduct—such as the Workers' Rights Consortium, Social Accountability International, the Fair Wear Foundation, and the Clean Clothes Campaign—are collaborating in the Joint Initiative on Corporate Accountability and Workers' Rights to develop common guidelines on aspects of monitoring and implementing the provisions of voluntary codes of labour practice. The Equator Principles for managing social and environmental dimensions of project financing in developing countries are the result of a partnership between a range of major financial institutions. There are also a growing number of examples of global framework agreements between international unions and multinational companies.

It is not only that the number of corporate responsibility initiatives has grown; there are also clear signs of learning, both in terms of how to implement corporate responsibility and what issues can, or should, be considered. The Ethical Trading Initiative is an interesting example of how a corporate responsibility initiative can influence companies and change their practices in different ways. ETI's impact on workers is not straightforward (see Snapshot 12.2), but ETI can also claim to have had the following types of impact on company behaviour:

1 improving the knowledge of its member organizations and others about how to monitor labour conditions among suppliers;

2 improving knowledge about what to monitor and what the elements are of the chains (e.g. that there are homeworkers and smallholder farmers, as well as large factories and commercial farms, who are parts of the supply chain);

3 raising member companies' awareness of labour rights issues;

4 influencing legislation (e.g. ETI played an important role in the UK Gangmasters (Licensing) Act 2004);

5 increasing the overall level of monitoring of overseas' suppliers;

6 building the capacity of companies and others to implement voluntary labour standards.

Furthermore, there are measurable outcomes in support of some of the above claims, such as changes in buyer behaviour as they integrate labour rights into their business practices, examples of terminating business relations with persistently non-compliant suppliers, increased ability to identify non-compliance in factories, and the integration of labour standards into supplier contracts.

Public commitments to future actions within a certain timeframe are another indication of changing behaviour. While ExxonMobil is said to emit a world-leading 146 million tonnes of carbon dioxide a year, BP set itself the target of reducing emissions in the late 1990s, and is now almost twice as efficient, emitting 261 tonnes of CO2 per US$ 1 million in sales compared to ExxonMobil's 436 tonnes. In 2007, Toyota committed itself to reducing its emissions by 20 per cent by 2010, and spends nearly 14 per cent of annual capital investment on sustainable options such as alternative fuels and new technologies. Wal-Mart spends notably less (about 3 per cent of capital expenditure), but its public commitment could have a significant impact on the behaviour of consumers and suppliers.[44]

Examples of how corporate responsibility has affected attitudes and behaviour are to be found throughout this book, even if the recent safety scandals affecting BP and Toyota show that positive change in one area may not be repeated in another. What we want to emphasize here is that this is an important element of corporate responsibility's impact. Overall, corporate responsibility has increased awareness of, and has spawned initiatives to address, issues as diverse as corruption, international development, labour rights, global warming, human rights, environmental management, and sustainable resourcing. It has raised the profile of long-established concerns, such as workplace health and safety, diversity, and discrimination, especially in suppliers' facilities. It has turned these issues into ones of legitimate business interest, even if it has not always found effective ways of addressing them (or, as importantly, has not yet been able to demonstrate its effectiveness). Its impact has been recognized in countries such as China, where corporate responsibility has become something of a buzzword.[45] In recent years, the appearance in corporate responsibility discussions of corporate taxation, company valuation, responsibilities to women, the role of small producers, the place of local suppliers and small retailers, the terms of trading, and other topics has shown that new issues continue to be recognized, even if it is less clear if and how they can be addressed from within a corporate responsibility framework.

It is important, however, to also acknowledge the limits of this impact. Some companies are clearly very responsive; others are less so and some, hardly at all. Despite corporate responsibility reporting becoming the norm amongst major companies, the geographical spread is inconsistent, and as noted FTSE4Good has expressed concern about the lack of uptake in the USA, other than by its leading multinational companies. The relationship between corporate responsibility as management practice in medium-sized firms remains problematic (see Chapter 11). Equally, most social and environmental standards apply to export-oriented production and the impact of corporate responsibility on the behaviour of producers for domestic markets (the majority) is unknown. Moreover, it might remain difficult to implement standards effectively, even in export sectors, because auditing capacity is not keeping up with demand[46] and its quality has been criticized, not least by companies.[47]

Companies that are well-ranked in corporate responsibility awards, may be open to criticism for particular aspects of their performance. For example, the Royal Mail, an organization with serious labour relations problems, was a finalist in the 2009 Business in the Community awards for excellence; Fortis NV, Royal Bank of Scotland, Citigroup, and HBOS were all listed as 'sustainability leaders' in 2007, and were either out of business or dependent on government bail-outs a year later.[48] Such examples raise big questions about analysis of corporate responsibility information, and the usefulness of the data companies provide. Many companies do not make available the information that would help others to assess the degree and effectiveness of their commitment. Similarly, belonging to a partnership means very little if the quality and nature of that partnership is unclear. There is some evidence that partnerships with members from different sectors of society are associated with stronger corporate responsibility performance, compared with those that only involve business, although the latter are still more effective than when companies work on their own. As Chapter 5 explores in more detail, however, it is still uncertain what constitutes a successful partnership and how this can be evaluated.

A standard such as the AA1000 Stakeholder Engagement Standard goes some way towards assessing the process of effectively implementing corporate responsibility, although it has been criticized for not taking power relations seriously. Methodologies used by some of the ratings indices also seek to value the degree to which corporate responsibility is embedded into companies, a question that was also central to a 2007 European study of 200 organizations that concluded managers were tied to a fairly conservative view of corporate responsibility, focusing on avoiding negative impacts rather than opportunities to have a positive impact.[49]

Overall, therefore, although there have been changes in company behaviour, we are still a long way from understanding, or being able to compare, the relative effectiveness of companies' different approaches. Perhaps this is nowhere more evident than in the

---

■ Discussion points

One area of corporate responsibility in which there appears to have been significant changes is in terms of management awareness and attitude.

- Is it valid to regard these changes as indicators that corporate responsibility is bringing about wider changes?

- Is it more important to understand this type of change in the context of some companies than that of others?

- How would you set about measuring and communicating this type of change to external stakeholders?

SNAPSHOT 12.2

Levi's and China

Levi Strauss, producer of Levi's jeans and Dockers, sources much of its product from China. In that, it is no different from numerous other global clothing brands such as GAP, Abercrombie & Fitch, or Ralph Lauren. But Levi's relationship with China is more complicated than most, and highlights many of the tensions between competitiveness and responsibility.

In the early 1990s, Levi's was one of several companies exploring the possibility of sourcing from China's emergent garment sector. Low cost labour, favourable tax and excise regimes, and reliable infrastructure were amongst the attractions. But politically China was a closed country; a single party state with a poor record on human rights. On issues from freedom of speech to the death penalty to forced pregnancy testing of workers, Chinese practices seemed to jar with Levi's commitment to being a values-centred business. It had a big manufacturing base in the USA where its factories were held to be amongst the best employers in their sector, but the tariffs that helped make domestic production competitive were being phased out.

Levi's went into China hesitantly, making it clear that it expected all suppliers to abide by its Global Sourcing Guidelines that set out how workers should be treated. But by 1993, it was clear that 'pervasive human rights abuses' were taking place, and the company decided to phase out most of its operations. The move was heralded as a victory for values-driven business, but in the following years Levi's looked less of a leader than an isolated figure as its competitors poured ever more investment into China.

In 1998, Levi Strauss announced it would be expanding output in China once again. Company President, Peter Jacobi, said '*Levi Strauss is not in the human rights business*', adding, '*It is clear to us that the environment is getting better there.*' The question in labour activists minds, however was whether he meant the human rights environment, or the consumer market as Levi's found itself losing out to Lee and Esprit in the battle to win the hearts of China's new middle class.

PS: Levi Strauss closed its last USA factory in 2002.

(Sources: Beaver, 1995; Landler, 1998; Colwell, 2002)

Quick Questions

1 What does Levi's decision tell us about corporate responsibility's impact?

2 Would keeping production in the USA be more 'responsible'?

3 Should companies be in the 'human rights business'?

extent success in non-financial performance is a feature of individual performance reviews. Fifty FTSE 100 companies now use a non-financial measure in their annual bonus schemes, but none of them uses more than one measure, and only seven per cent factors such measures into long-term incentive plans.[50]

Impact on other stakeholders

A further way to look at the impact of corporate responsibility is to look at its outcomes for others in society. For example, we mentioned earlier the growing number of framework agreements between international trade unions and multinational companies that, at least indirectly, seem to relate to a rising awareness of corporate responsibility. Furthermore, after years of declining union strength, particularly in developed economies, union recognition agreements are part of the criteria used in ratings indices such as FTSE4Good.

There is mixed evidence about the impact that corporate responsibility has had on consumers, with some citing evidence of consumers' willingness to pay higher prices for improved working conditions, while others suggest that attributes unrelated to corporate responsibility, such as customer satisfaction and financial performance, ultimately have more influence on a company's reputation.[51] Environmental and health issues have affected branding, even if there are differences of opinion about what an 'ethical brand' is. A positive relationship between corporate responsibility and purchasing decisions might be expected, but measuring the related benefits seems difficult and a company's reputation can vary greatly from country to country (see Box 12.3). Moreover, when consumers become suspicious about the benefits of ethical consumption, they may change their behaviour as seems to have happened with the hitherto high-flying sales of organic foods in the UK which fell 5 per cent in 2008–2009.[52]

Corporate responsibility has an impact on the investment community, as evidenced by the growth in socially responsible investment (see Chapter 10), and the appointment of ESG specialists by banks such as UBS. It has also had some success in persuading students to think more critically about the role of business, rather than simply to criticize companies. For example, NetImpact claims a 15,000 strong network of members, primarily MBA and graduate students seeking to use the power of business to improve the world, and it will be interesting to see if this less aggressive approach will prove more sustainable than, for example, the Workers Rights Consortium, which, despite having used college campuses to affect corporate behaviour, has struggled to maintain more

Box 12.3 **Country variations in ratings of brand reputation**

France	UK
1 Danone	1 Co-op
2 adidas	2 Body Shop
3 Nike	3 Marks and Spencer
4 Nestlé	4 Traidcraft
5 Renault	5 Cafedirect and Ecover
Germany	**USA**
1 adidas	1 Nike
2 Nike	2 PepsiCo
3 Puma	3 Procter and Gamble
4 BMW	4 Prudential Insurance
5 Demeter	5 Sony Playstation

(Sources: Grande, 2007; Werther & Chandler, 2006)

than a handful of its 140 college chapters.[53] Business-oriented web-based resources such as GreenBiz, and less structured, web-based networks, such as the 1300-member CSR Chicks listserv, have also become ways in which corporate responsibility both influences people and is sustained.

The impact of corporate responsibility can also be seen in aspects of government. The UK briefly had a minister for corporate responsibility, and corporate responsibility has been recognized in legislation in both France and the UK. In Brazil, the government officials who have played a big role in that country's relatively effective approach to slowing deforestation often came out of the FSC organization there. Corporate responsibility's impact is felt in the EU Accounts Modernisation Directive, which requires that directors' reports contain a business review including information that is material to the well-being of the environment, communities, and employees.

The impact of corporate responsibility on itself

Over the past few years, there have been significant changes in how we conceive of, and conduct, corporate responsibility and, in any discussion of impact, we should not ignore how the experience of addressing corporate responsibility has affected the evolution of corporate responsibility itself. Earlier, we mentioned an expansion in the range of issues that fall within the, at least theoretical, purview of corporate responsibility. By comparing the initial GRI Guidelines with its two subsequent iterations in 2002 and 2006, we can see how the range of criteria for reporting on sustainability has been extended, the indicators used in measurement have become more sophisticated, and the advice on using the guidelines has expanded (e.g. the guidance on sustainability reporting for small and medium-sized enterprises). Similarly, the AA1000 series relating to stakeholder engagement has been through several modifications since its launch in 1999, incorporating the experiences of its users and others.

Moreover, the experience of one initiative affects others. For example, national social and environment standards, such as those of the Wine Industry Ethical Trade Association in South Africa or of the Agricultural Ethics Assurance Association of Zimbabwe, have been strongly influenced by European initiatives. It is interesting to note how what were once contentious issues have been adopted, even to the point of being considered corporate responsibility best practice. There were concerns that codes of labour practice would be more likely to address issues that damaged a company's reputation (e.g. child labour, health and safety) than those that were opposed by management (e.g. freedom of association, collective bargaining), but while some rights have proved easier to address than others, in general, the most credible and influential initiatives have proved to be those that set the bar relatively high. This has remained the case even when companies have collaborated to reduce the costs of implementing standards such as the Global Social Compliance Programme involving Migros, Ikea, Tesco, and others. Even issues that were once regarded as leading edge or contentious, have started to filter into the mainstream. For example, advocates of more local involvement and capacity building in implementing social and environmental standards have seen some of their demands begin to be accommodated, as have groups wanting attention paid to the specific conditions of homeworkers.

This is not to say that there is a virtuous race to the top. Some projects seeking to extend the boundaries of corporate responsibility such as the Sigma Project in the UK to benchmark sustainability have failed despite their close links to other corporate responsibility actors and initiatives. The Race to the Top project, coordinated by the International Institute for Environment and Development, brought together NGOs, trade unions, and UK retailers to track what supermarkets are doing to promote a greener and fairer food system, but ended in 2003.[54] Beyond the UK, the Global Alliance for Workers and Communities, established by major US companies and NGOs to help empower workers, also withered away after failing to win long-term support.

The challenges of determining impact

The picture that emerges is that measuring corporate responsibility's impact is as difficult today as it was in the past. There are three main reasons for this, each of which we examine in this section:

1 the practical challenges of assessing impact;
2 the problem of what to measure;
3 the question of in whose interests it is to understand impact.

There are three main sources for information on impact: ratings indices; corporate reports; case studies of individual companies, industries, or locations. These are self-referential to a large degree in that, for example, in compiling ratings, researchers will use corporate reports and case studies, in addition to other sources of information, while the report may allude to the company's rating as a performance indicator. A fundamental difficulty is that the basic data needed to assess impact are often lacking, because, for example, the company has not properly identified its key issues, or has not reported on them in a clear and consistent fashion. But ratings indices can exacerbate this problem by the a priori assumption that they make about outcomes and causal relations. For example, they assume that the outcome of a blend of stakeholder participation and rigorous social or environmental standards will be better working conditions, sustainable fisheries, etc. Consequently, what is measured is more likely to be the criteria of the standard and indicators for the partnership, rather than an attempt to examine the contribution that such a combination makes towards those bigger goals.

Mattingly and Berman (2006) argue that some ratings indices make incorrect assumptions about associations between different types of social action and that, because they do not properly recognize the context within which actions take place, they end up rewarding actions that appear to be proactive, but which are not especially laudable (e.g. those that are easily solved problems or easily achieved targets). In doing so, they overlook those that may appear weak or reactive, but which are actually impressive if the context is understood (e.g. becoming a pioneer in tackling hazardous waste in an otherwise unresponsive industry).

Ratings indices continue to evolve and some of the above limitations may be overcome. For example, the Enhanced Analytics Initiative seeks to redress some of the current information gaps by encouraging quality, long-term research, which considers material extra-financial issues that can be used by sell-side analysts. In 2006, the Center for Sustainable Innovation in Vermont, USA, launched Social Footprint to assess the degree to which corporate responsibility contributes to true sustainability. Trucost Ltd, a London financial research firm, has also launched TrueVa (True Valuation) to measure companies' overall value added by subtracting from the firm's operating surplus not only its costs of capital, but also the environmental damages that it imposes elsewhere in the economy.

Ratings indices and other attempts to synthesize company performance are nonetheless hampered by a strong dependency on case studies, including those from companies, in media stories, and in academic or other reports. There is a tendency for organizations to choose the case study that best tells the story they want to communicate, but even in instances in which that is not true, taken together, case studies do not have the consistency of approach to constitute a systematic body of evidence, or, if taken individually, may not have the necessary depth from which to draw wider conclusions. This is starting to change as impact assessments about particular corporate responsibility approaches and initiatives begin to appear. Two early assessments by business and academics observed that increased incomes alone did not prove that people were better off, and that harder to measure, factors, such as terms of trade and building strong local institutions, were important. Equally, standards did not adequately capture local people's concerns and priorities.[55] Moreover, even if researchers know what information to gather, there are challenges in obtaining it, either because of the risk of false documents and of respondents who are reluctant to talk honestly or openly, or because of the sheer size of company operations.[56] And when the data are reliable, it can still be difficult to demonstrate whether an action or outcome is the result of corporate responsibility, or of some other event, such as changes in local laws or improved enforcement.[57]

An alternative approach would be to assign a monetary value to particular outcomes such as generating income for the poor. For example, a dollar paid to someone earning just two dollars a day can be predicted to have far greater impact than the same amount paid to someone earning US$100 a day. Therefore, one could assign extra value to the dollar paid to the poor person, for example three dollars. Consequently, US$ 1 million paid to genuinely poor people could be calculated as having a social worth of US$ 3 million. Such figures could be included in income statements in annual reports which would then include in addition to total revenues, total costs, and net income, the value of external benefits, the external costs of greenhouse gas emissions, etc. While this would undoubtedly be controversial, it highlights the importance of issues raised in Chapter 8 about how we account for corporate responsibility.

Another challenge is how to measure and assess the effectiveness of initiatives that are intended to encourage learning about how to tackle large issues, rather than to have a direct, demonstrable impact on those issues themselves. For example, the UN Global Compact highlights how about half of its signatory companies have changed their policies to reflect the Compact's principles and the high level of managers' recognition of the Compact's role as a catalyst for change (see Chapter 5). But relatively few companies have participated in the Compact's learning forums, raising questions about whether participation in the network is responsible for these outcomes.[58]

Ultimately, it could be that companies are producing the wrong kind of data: focusing on outputs and activities when stakeholders want information on outcomes.[59] Yet, the type of information that is required depends on knowing who is really interested in corporate responsibility's impact. It is quite possible to argue that it is not in the self-interest of certain stakeholder groups, with a significant influence on corporate responsibility, to gain a more sophisticated understanding of the impact of corporate responsibility practice. Groups such as worker or environmental activists have particular short-term aims when collecting data and may not be motivated to monitor a particular company over the longer term.[60] Professional monitors, on the other hand, have an interest in building a long-term relationship with a company, but are subject to confidentiality agreements and other restraints on how their data are used. Companies, in turn, may have an interest in selecting what they disclose and to whom, especially when reporting is voluntary, or the resource implications of proving a company's impact on societal issues may be too great.[61] Whether from companies or multi-stakeholder partnerships, what is disclosed to the public is often a synthesis of a larger, more complex, picture that, according to some, too often requires the public to trust the reporters without providing adequate justification for this trust.[62] Arguably, unless there is a change in how investors value companies, real non-instrumental impact in the sense Margolis and Walsh (2003) intended is not in the interests of the most influential groups that are engaged in corporate responsibility. That kind of impact may only matter to corporate responsibility's stated beneficiaries, whether these are the poor, the natural environment, the victims of human rights abuses, or future generations. Yet the outcomes of corporate responsibility for this type of stakeholder have still not been thoroughly demonstrated and it remains an open question whether others are prepared to invest in providing this type of information.

CASE STUDY 12

Can corporate responsibility guarantee an impact?—Fairtrade

'Fairtrade guarantees a better deal for third world producers.' That is the promise made of products—coffee, tea, flowers, bananas, cocoa, etc.—that are certified as fairtrade. So confident are fairtrade advocates of the benefits to poor farmers and workers in developing countries that some claim, '*[companies] can meet some corporate responsibility targets just by changing their coffee.*' However, neither individual fairtrade organizations such as Cafédirect nor umbrella organizations such as the Fairtrade Foundation systematically monitor the impact on beneficiaries. Consequently, much of what we know about the impact comes from case studies which are notoriously difficult to compare because of the different methodologies used. A 2009 review of 33 case studies, the majority from coffee growing, found that the majority of farmers earned higher returns and had more stable incomes because of fairtrade, but in other areas such as local democracy and labour rights the evidence was less compelling.

Part of the problem according to the above review is that most case studies provide a snapshot in time, and there are few instances of impact being monitored over a long period of time. An exception is a recent two year study of smallholder tea farmers in Kenya. Tea is good example of where fairtrade should help developing country producers. The tea trade in the West is controlled by seven multinationals companies, and in the UK, the third largest tea importer in the world, the top three packers currently enjoy a 60 per cent share of the tea market. The power of these companies puts pressure on producer countries to cut costs while improving quality to remain competitive. Smallholders, who are affected by poor infrastructure (electricity, roads and water) and resource constraints (land and capital), face declining prices while wage workers on tea estates face low wages, employment insecurity, and long working hours.

There are various ways fairtrade seeks to redress this situation, but three of the most important are through better farmgate prices, fostering democratic producer-run institutions, and helping marginalized producers to become more secure. More specifically, to gain fairtrade certification farmers must receive a price that is at least equal to the cost of sustainable production, and farmer organizations must also receive a premium from buyers to be reinvested for the benefit of the community. Equally, the organizations should be democratic and transparent, and not discriminate against any individual or social group. In other words, fairtrade's 'better deal' for producers is predicated on better wages, democracy, and inclusion.

Amongst the Kenya smallholders, there is doubt about the reality of this better deal. During the first three years smallholders sold to fairtrade buyers, there was no price guarantee. When a floor price was introduced in 2008, it was well below the actual market price the farmers were receiving, and there is fear that if they demanded more buyers would switch to other fairtrade farmers in Rwanda and South India where the floor price is much lower.

Nonetheless, the farmer organizations are receiving a separate social premium that has been used for projects such as schools, roads, and dispensaries. Over 80 per cent of smallholders acknowledge the contribution fairtrade has made, although farmers seem to be happier with the choice of projects than farm labourers. This raises questions about the democratic process within the farmer organizations. There are several democratic bodies that have been set up, but participation is low, and there is evidence that local power relations have a significant influence on decisions. The challenge of creating effective democratic organizations is apparent if one looks at women in the tea growing community. Women are responsible for much of the on-farm labour, but account for less than 20 per cent of the 12,000 registered farmers because they are far less likely to own land. Only land-owners receive the tea registration number that allows them to vote in the main fairtrade bodies. As a result, the majority of people who produce the tea are excluded from the fairtrade democracy.

The fairtrade movement is starting to recognize that there are important gaps in what is known about impact, and believes *a new 'wave' of formal, strategic impact studies and participatory monitoring and evaluation is now underway.* As a recent Fairtrade Foundation press release concluded,

There is an inherent tension faced by fairtrade of using simple and positive messaging to inform consumers about fairtrade whilst recognising and being transparent about the complexities involved in any development intervention. There is no easy solution but furthering understanding of how fairtrade has an impact in different contexts based on the perspectives of farmers and workers is a critical first step along the way.

(Blowfield & Dolan, 2010; Bounds, 2009; Nelson & Pound, 2009)

Questions

1 Fairtrade is perhaps the most well-known example of social entrepreneurship.

   a Is fairtrade right to claim it guarantees a better deal for producers?

   b Has the fairtrade movement paid enough attention to the outcomes for producers?

   c Why has it paid more attention to instrumental indicators such as market growth and consumer interest?

2 Measuring fairtrade's impact on producers is likely to be costly and time-consuming.

   a How important is it to demonstrate the benefits for producers?

   b What might be some more affordable, effective ways to assess impact than multi-year studies?

   c What are the risks of not being able to demonstrate impact?

3 Companies such as Cadbury and Starbuck's have committed to putting fairtrade certified commodities into important product lines.

   a What impact are these companies hoping to have?

   b Are they at risk from the current situation regarding impact?

   c Will they have a positive or negative long-term impact on fairtrade?

SUMMARY

Many claims are made about how managing corporate responsibility can help business to have a positive impact through its social, environmental, and economic performance. The reality is, however, that the data to demonstrate such impact are lacking, and, moreover, that collecting and collating such data does not appear to be a priority. This is not to deny the numerous case studies of companies addressing important issues, or the efforts of ratings, surveys, and company reports to demonstrate the efficacy of what companies are doing. But there are deficiencies in each of these sources of information.

There are many levels and categories of impact. Most of what we know about relates to the instrumental benefits of corporate responsibility, i.e. how it affects the financial bottom line. This can be considered a sign of progress, in that it creates a link between good business management and corporate responsibility, but it can also be a cause for concern if it precludes companies from considering actions for which the business case is weak.

Also, much of what we know relates more to activities than it does to outcomes. For example, companies may have environmental policies in place, or may be committed to international standards on corruption, but the actual outcome of these actions is often not known. This is less true of environmental issues than it is of those that are social or economic, and the growing sophistication of some companies' environmental management and reporting is a possible harbinger of the future of corporate responsibility more broadly. Even here, however, there is no clear consensus about what acceptable levels of performance look like, or about how to measure impact beyond the level of the individual company.

It remains an open question as to how the current partial understanding of impact will affect corporate responsibility in the future. Critics are using the lack of information to conclude that corporate responsibility is an inadequate response to tackling the social, governance, and environmental consequences of modern business. There is pressure within corporate responsibility for companies to become more rigorous in terms of what they manage and the targets they set themselves. Ultimately, what we know about impact will depend on the demand for information and the current situation suggests that the various stakeholders are only beginning to understand what it is they need to know.

FURTHER READING

**VISIT THE
WEBSITE**
for links to useful
sources of further
information

Take your learning further: Online Resource Centre **www.oxfordtextbooks.co.uk/orc/blowfield_
murray2e/**

Visit the Online Resource Centre which accompanies this book to enrich your understanding of this chapter.

Students: explore web links and further reading suggestions. Keep up to date with the latest developments by undertaking web exercises.

Lecturers: you will find additional case studies, including one on the topic of the Forest Stewardship Council – the impact of new governance partnerships, for use in class or assessment. Show your students trailers from films related to Corporate Responsibility, and use images from the book in your PowerPoint slides.

- Barrientos, S, 2007, *Do Workers Benefit From Ethical Trade? Assessing Codes of Labour Practice in Global Production Systems*, London: Third World Foundation for Social and Economic Studies.
  Detailed case study of the impact of ethical trade, highlighting the possibilities and difficulties of assessing impact.

- Heal, GM, 2008, *When Principles Pay: Corporate Social Responsibility and the Bottom Line*, New York: Columbia Business School.
  Chapter 11 sets out the challenges and some of the alternatives for measuring corporate responsibility's impact.

- Henriques, A, 2010, *Corporate Impact: Measuring and Managing Your Social Impact*, London: Earthscan.
  An exploration of the different ways to measure a company's extra-financial impact.

- KPMG, 2008, *KPMG International Survey of Corporate Responsibility Reporting 2008*.
  An overview of companies reporting on corporate responsibility, and insights into the strengths and weaknesses of their reports.

- Macdonald, K and Marshall, S, 2010, *Fair Trade, Corporate Accountability and Beyond : Experiments in Globalizing Justice*, Ashgate, Farnham.
  Contributions by academics, activists, and corporate responsibility professionals looking at the impact approaches to corporate responsibility management have had around the world.

- Margolis, JD and Walsh, JP, 2003, 'Misery loves companies: rethinking social initiatives by business', *Administrative Science Quarterly*, 48(2), pp 268–305.
  Widely cited study of impact from a corporate social performance perspective.

- McWilliams, A and Siegel, D, 2000, 'Corporate social responsibility and financial performance: correlation or misspecification?', *Strategic Management Journal*, 21(5), pp 603–9.
  Useful discussion of approaches to understanding the impact of corporate responsibility.

- Vogel, D, 2005, *The Market for Virtue: The Potential and Limits of Corporate Social Responsibility*, Washington, DC: Brookings Institution Press.

  Detailed critique of corporate responsibility's effectiveness as a response to social and environmental challenges.

ENDNOTES

[1] SustainAbility and UNEP, 2002.

[2] See, e.g., Elliott and Freeman, 2003, on improved labour standards and monitoring.

[3] See also Chapter 8. The 2007 ACCA awards also reflect these broad criticisms. Information can be obtained from www.accaglobal.com.

[4] Margolis and Walsh, 2003, p 282.

[5] www.wbcsd.org/templates/TemplateWBCSD5/layout.asp?type=p&MenuId=MTU3Mw, accessed 19 November 2009.

[6] There is a distinction between corporate social performance and corporate responsibility. CSP is an ex post measurement of past performance (e.g. assessing if there is a relationship between social impact and corporate reputation), whereas corporate responsibility can be ex ante.

[7] The main sources for understanding the impact and measurement of corporate responsibility and corporate social performance were Sethi, 1975; Anshen, 1980; Wartick and Cochran, 1985; Margolis and Walsh, 2003; the discussion in Birch, 2003. The company corporate responsibility reports used included the Anglo American 2005 Report, Unilever 2005 Environmental Report, Cooperative Financial Services Report 2005, and Traidcraft Report 2005.

[8] Forest Stewardship Council statistics published at www.fsccertified-forests.org/facts-figures.html—accessed 29 June 2010.

[9] Unilever, 2005.

[10] Vogel, 2005, pp 110–11.

[11] Vogel, 2005, p 126.

[12] www.walmartfacts.com/reports/2006/sustainability/companyPerformance.html, accessed 18 November 2009.

[13] Michael Blowfield, personal observation, 15 November 2000.

[14] See, e.g. the BBC news broadcast 13 March 2007 headlined 'BA green scheme fails to take off'.

[15] Locke et al., 2006.

[16] Barrientos and Smith, 2007.

[17] Elliott and Freeman, 2003.

[18] ETI, 2009.

[19] Phylmar Group, 2006.

[20] Abbott Laboratories, 2005; www.gsk.com—accessed 15 May 2006.

[21] Vogel, 2005, p 102.

[22] NRET, 1999.

[23] See BSR, 2005; KPMG, 2005.

[24] www.economicfootprint.org offers economic impact reports for the agriculture, mining, pharmaceutical, and financial services sectors.

[25] See Clay 2005, BER 2008, Kapstein 2008.

[26] Rio Tinto case studies, and its framework for understanding linkages between its investment in communities and their development, can be found at www.riotinto.com.

[27] The Economist 2006.

[28] See, e.g. Raynolds et al., 2004; IFAT, 2006; Nicholls and Opal, 2005.

[29] Raynolds et al., 2004; Vogel, 2005.

[30] Vogel, 2008.

[31] IFAT, 2006, p 6.

[32] Margolis and Walsh, 2003; McWilliams and Siegel, 2000.

[33] Vogel, 2005.

[34] UNEP FI & Mercer, 2007.

[35] Vogel, 2005, p 73.

[36] Vogel, 2005, p 59.

[37] UK government data at www.financialdeepening.org—accessed 5 June 2007; www. innocent-drinks.co.uk—accessed 5 June 2007.

[38] Collinson, 2001; Collinson and Leon, 2000.

[39] CCC, 2005c.

[40] Vogel, 2005.

[41] Varley et al., 1998.

[42] Eliott and Freeman, 2003, p 63.

[43] Lenox and Nash, 2003.

[44] Figures taken from Uren 2007.

[45] McGregor, 2007.

[46] Ascoly and Zeldenrust, 2003.

[47] ETI, 2006.

[48] Sources: www.bitc.org.uk, accessed 24 November 2009; SAM-PWC 2008.

[49] Insead et al., 2007

[50] Source: www.lapfforum.org, accessed 30 March 2008.

[51] Compare, e.g., Brown, 2004; Elliott and Freeman, 2003, with Vogel, 2005.

[52] Industry data cited in Skapkinker, 2009.

[53] Kauffman and Chedekel, 2004.

[54] Information on Sigma is accessible at www.projectsigma.com—accessed 21 March 2006. Information on Race to the Top, including an analysis of why it failed, is accessible at www. racetothetop.org—accessed 21 March 2006.

[55] DFID, 2002.

[56] DFID, 2002; ETI, 2004.

[57] ETI, 2004; Vogel, 2005; Barrientos and Smith, 2007.

[58] Vogel, 2005, pp 157–8.

[59] Mattingly and Berman, 2006; Mitnick, 2000.

[60] Elliott and Freeman, 2003

[61] Weiser and Rochlin, 2004.

[62] Sustainability and UNEP, 2002.

13

Criticisms of corporate responsibility

Chapter overview

In this chapter, we focus on the most fundamental criticisms of corporate responsibility. In particular, we will:

- discuss why some see corporate responsibility as being anti-business or anti-free markets;

- examine how some regard corporate responsibility as being too pro-business;

- explore why corporate responsibility has been criticized for failing to deal with major areas of the interaction of business with society;

- discuss why some feel that corporate responsibility needs to become more rigorous and tougher in its approach.

Main topics

■ **Key terms**

Civil society organizations

Corporate accountability

Liberal economics

Self-regulation

■ **Online resources**

- Links to additional material on critiques of corporate responsibility

- Additional snapshots of real-world corporate responsibility criticisms

- Examples of companies under fire for corporate responsibility shortfalls

- Links to other web-based resources

Introducing critiques of corporate responsibility

If corporate responsibility came to prominence due to criticisms of business behaviour, in recent years, it has itself become the object of criticism. To a degree, this reflects the extent to which ideas of corporate responsibility have influenced business thinking, public debate, and public policy in some parts of the world: after all, nobody criticizes what is irrelevant. We raise some of those criticisms in other chapters (e.g. in Chapter 1, difficulties in defining corporate responsibility; in Chapters 7, 8, and 9, the many challenges of implementing corporate responsibility).

These criticisms are part of an often-lively debate within the field about how to carry out corporate responsibility in ways that are efficient, effective, and best able to satisfy the needs of business while recognizing the concerns of other stakeholders. They are largely technical or instrumental in nature, focusing more on 'how to do it' than on 'what it means' and 'why to do it'. For a few, this focus in itself has been the subject of criticism, because it turns corporate responsibility into a pursuit of technical excellence and ignores (or stifles discussion of) more fundamental questions about what the responsibilities of business to twenty-first-century society are.[1] This situation is changing and a scan through mainstream corporate responsibility media such as *Ethical Corporation*, *CSRWire*, and *Ethical Performance* shows that such topics are becoming more widely discussed. But it is debatable how effective new discussions of what constitutes responsibility will be and how desirable they are.

Corporate responsibility theorists and practitioners have raised each of these questions over the past few years. Doubts about effectiveness stem from a sense that the parameters of corporate responsibility have already been set, not least through the ways in which different issues and ideas are assessed and, ultimately, included or excluded. In Chapter 6, we discussed at length the importance of the business case and how this influences corporate responsibility. We also showed how certain tools, techniques, and approaches have come to be regarded as best practice in the ways in which corporate responsibility is managed and implemented: new areas of responsibility are more likely to be accepted if they can be tackled using such established methods.

Doubts about the desirability of extending the realm of corporate responsibility to include a potentially endless array of new issues and expectations stem from a fear that companies will find the demands placed on them overwhelming, and will become more resistant to change. This itself derives from the experiences of academic corporate responsibility theory. As discussed in Chapter 2, there is a rich history of academic debate about what the nature of the corporation's responsibilities should be. But as we also saw, there was frustration, in the past, that academic debate was having little impact on the corporate world and, therefore, there is now a strong desire not to jeopardize the current enthusiasm among companies for addressing corporate responsibility concerns, even if these concerns are not as broad or their address as thorough as some might have liked.

The urge of some to want to 'protect' corporate responsibility as a discipline for fear of stymieing progress ignores the fact that allegations regarding the negative effects of business behaviour continue to emerge from civil society organizations, academics, and legal actions. Most of the criticisms of corporate responsibility discussed so far emanate from within the loose community of corporate responsibility theorists and practitioners. In the rest of this chapter, we want to concentrate on voices that are external to that community: those who, for the most part, either reject corporate responsibility, or are waiting for a different approach before they condone it. We have divided their criticisms into four types of accusation.

1 *'Corporate responsibility stifles the primary purpose of business and, ultimately, hampers the functioning of free markets.'*

2 *'Corporate responsibility favours the interests of business over the legitimate concerns, demands, and expectations of wider society.'*

3 *'Corporate responsibility is too narrow in its focus and does nothing to address the key aspects of the business–society relationship today.'*

4 *'Corporate responsibility is failing to achieve its objectives and needs to adopt new approaches if it is to succeed.'*

Before exploring these, it is worth noting that each strand of criticism relates back to the theoretical perspectives outlined in Chapters 1 and 2. The argument that corporate responsibility stifles the primary purpose of business is rooted in liberal economics, whereas the view that it favours the interests of business is a development of the long-standing critique of free enterprise externalizing its costs onto wider society. Similarly, arguments that corporate responsibility is too narrow are part of a wider debate about the role of business in society and contrast with criticisms, rooted in management science, that new approaches are required if corporate responsibility is to succeed.

■ Discussion points

The criticisms of corporate responsibility in this chapter are primarily external ones, i.e. those from outside the world of academics, practitioners, and companies that promote corporate responsibility as a legitimate area of business management. Yet we know from other chapters that there have been internal critiques of corporate responsibility.

- What are the main differences between the internal and external critiques of corporate responsibility?

- To which of the external criticisms should companies respond? Are these the same as those to which they are *likely* to respond?

- Examine the external criticisms made of Berkshire Hathaway's investment in Chinese companies operating in Darfur, Sudan, and Warren Buffet's response, and explain which is strongest, and why.

'Corporate responsibility is anti-business'

On 20 January 2005, *The Economist* published a series of articles that presented corporate responsibility as a threat to the effective functioning of capitalism and free markets, and hence to global prosperity. On the one hand, the articles were a sign that corporate responsibility had come of age, and had entered mainstream business and economic debate; on the other, they offered a sharp rebuke to corporate executives, whom the magazine regarded as being too weak in the face of public criticism and as ignoring their fiduciary duty to shareholders by paying too much attention to the demands of others.

Reflecting a wider sense of anger and unease at the growth of corporate responsibility, the articles' core argument was as follows. The standard of living in Western industrial democracies is higher today than ever before and is at a level that would have been unimaginable 200 years ago: '*In the West today the poor live better lives than all but the nobility enjoyed throughout the course of modern history before capitalism.*'[2] This is largely due to the success of free enterprise, yet we have entered an age in which capitalism is deplored, suspected, and feared by a broad cross-section of society, even by some business leaders. This anti-capitalist sentiment stems from beliefs that profit has nothing to do with the public good, and that the pursuit of profit drives companies to put crippling burdens on society and the environment. These beliefs have given rise to corporate responsibility as a check on business behaviour. Yet they are ill founded, because they see profit as an unfortunate necessity that can be controlled and muzzled, whereas it is, in fact, the engine that allows business to make its phenomenal contributions to the public good and restrictions on profit or wealth creation—especially those that come from civil society rather than from governments—will be more harmful than anything else to society.

The articles repeatedly present corporate responsibility as a victory for the concerns of NGOs over the traditional priorities of business. But it is not simply that the public is failing to acknowledge the positive role that business plays that is *The Economist*'s concern: it is also that the uptake of corporate responsibility by mainstream companies might have a serious effect on business' ability to fulfill its role within the capitalist system. An example of this is that corporate responsibility distracts public company management from its primary purpose of serving the interests of shareholders. This echoes the views of Friedman (1962) and Jensen (1986), both of whom have argued that corporate responsibility negatively affects company agents' abilities to maximize profits for investors (see Chapter 7). *The Economist* fully accepts that managers must be ethical and that much needs to be done in this area. But it says that they should never lose sight of the fact they are employees, not owners, and that it is unethical to put the owners' assets to any use other than maximizing long-term value. Ideas such as the triple bottom line (see Chapter 1) distract management from this goal and, by making companies accountable on multiple fronts, threaten to make them accountable for nothing, because they offer no measurable test of business success.

The articles make clear that none of this is to argue in favour of corporate *irresponsibility*. On the contrary, there is need for governance reform and, *The Economist* says (although without offering any evidence), '*broken corporate governance and CSR are close relations. You often see them together*'.[3] In this, however, as in other areas of corporate reform, the articles stress that it is the role of government to regulate business. As one of the articles says, '*getting the most out of capitalism requires public intervention of various kinds, and a lot of it: taxes, public spending, regulation . . .*'.[4]

It is important to note that these remarks distinguish *The Economist*'s position from some free-market critics of corporate responsibility who would want much less government intervention in business. They argue that it is a priori almost impossible to identify what interventions cause growth[5] while empirically it is highly apparent that economic success is associated with free trade and deregulation,[6] Whereas *The Economist* claims that intervention is essential, but is the preserve of government, not the wider universe of stakeholders. There are two reasons for this: first, when managers have to pay attention to too many stakeholder groups they get distracted. It might be good business practice to take account of multiple stakeholders (see Chapter 9), but that is quite different to being held accountable to them. And even if, as in Germany, companies are legally required to have non-shareholders on the board, *The Economist* argues that owner interests should always be the primary concern.

The second reason given is that corporate responsibility is unnecessary because in a well-functioning free market the marketplace provides consumers with a forum in which to express their opinions about companies (e.g. by not buying their goods, or by not working for them if they disagree with their policies).

It is ironic that *The Economist's* articles were not criticized by the kind of free market purists who Chang (2008) calls 'bad samaritans' because of their strict adherence to a narrow capitalist orthodoxy. Indeed, it is ironic too that such purists have been slow to embrace voluntary corporate responsibility as an answer to managing the business-society relationship in a deregulated environment, in a world where younger generations through Facebook and similar online resources can redefine what constitutes a business issue.[7]

Instead, pro-business critics of corporate responsibility have more often focused their attention on business' overt critics, arguing that corporate responsibility is an anti-corporate strategy.[8] The website *CSRWatch*, for example, with the tagline 'Your eye on the anti-business movement', posted information on a range of anti-corporate criticisms. However, it is indicative of corporate responsibility's acceptance in once critical quarters that *CSRWatch* is no longer online, and more significantly still that in January 2008 *The Economist* itself ran a special feature recognizing the merits of corporate responsibility.

SNAPSHOT 13.1

The Church takes on Caterpillar over Palestine—giving corporate responsibility muscle

The world's largest construction machinery company, Caterpillar, is a strong advocate of a values-based approach to corporate responsibility and has a worldwide code of business conduct that states that '*our success should also contribute to the quality of life and the prosperity of communities*'. This commitment was challenged in 2004, following claims by a UN Special Rapporteur that the company's equipment is being used to deny Palestinians the right to food by destroying their farmlands. Critics such as War on Want, a NGO, argue that the company sold equipment to the US government knowing that it would be sold on for use in military operations. Some NGOs and watchdog groups have denied this, and the company has retorted that it has neither the capacity, nor the legal right to determine how its equipment is used once it has been sold.

For both sides, this has become a test of the ability of corporate responsibility to guide companies in ethical decision making. The Synod of the Church of England voted to recommend selling the church's shares in the firm. This decision generated criticism of the Church of England itself: whether it was using a stance on corporate responsibility to attack Israeli national policy and whether disinvestment was more effective than using the church's holdings to engage with the company. The church's Ethical Investment Advisory Group advised against selling Caterpillar stock and instead began what it called a '*progressive dialogue*' with the company. The company, meanwhile, said it did not sell machinery to Israel, and found itself caught in the crossfire of a campaign targeting the policies of the US and Israeli governments.

The Caterpillar case remains controversial, with some arguing that it proves the effectiveness of corporate responsibility approaches, such as a voluntary code of conduct and stakeholder dialogue, and others saying that corporate responsibility has allowed the company to deny any culpability for human rights violations caused by its products. It is also possible to argue that the case is not ultimately about the role of the company, but shows how the public profile of multinational firms makes them a leveraging point in campaigning about wider geopolitical issues.

(Sources: War on Want, 2005; *Ethical Performance*, 2006a; UN Commission on Human Rights report on economic, social and cultural rights, January 2005, online at **www.ohchr.org**—accessed 30 June 2006; Caterpillar code of conduct, online at **www.cat.com**—accessed 18 July 2006)

Questions

The church's Ethical Investment Advisory Group says that disinvestment would be too strong at this stage, but that it is looking for change as a result of progressive engagement.

1 What changes do you think Caterpillar might make that would convince its critics that corporate responsibility can make a meaningful difference to company policies?

2 Is the company right to say that it cannot be held responsible for the end use of its products?

3 Is the company right to choose not to sell to the military in certain countries?

■ Discussion points

A criticism made by liberal economists is that corporate responsibility hinders company financial performance and poses an obstacle to economic growth.

- What evidence do such economists need to present to substantiate this claim?

- In your experience, is there evidence to support *The Economist*'s claim that '*broken corporate governance and CSR are close relations*'?

- What evidence can corporate responsibility advocates offer to show that it improves company management and makes companies more reliable engines of economic growth?

'Corporate responsibility is pro-business'

Most current criticism of corporate responsibility begins from the position that business is in various ways damaging to the social good, and that neither the theory nor practice developed under the corporate responsibility umbrella has remediated this situation. Critics argue that a key element of corporate responsibility should be to realign business with the values of society and to optimize its contribution, but that companies will not return to their original purpose without reform of the legislative and economic environment surrounding private companies.

This is a broad school of criticism, ranging from those who believe corporate responsibility is not up to the task of reforming business,[9] to those who regard corporate responsibility as a weak countervailing force,[10] to those who see business interests as being opposed to societal ones.[11] Some highlight the role ownership plays in determining a company's impact, arguing that there is nothing inherent in the legal definition of a company that stops it from having a social purpose, and Kelly (2001) and others point to examples of privately held companies that have just that. But, it is argued, once a company is publicly owned, its purpose can only be to maximize profits. This means that no matter how well intentioned corporate responsibility practice might be, it ultimately will not serve the common good. Arguments such as those described earlier that business serves the common good by creating wealth and goods are refuted with examples of companies that have rigged prices, deceived regulators, caused environmental damage, produced harmful products, and otherwise acted in ways that were intended to create shareholder value (and management rewards) at the expense of public well-being. Moreover, some argue, the larger and more powerful some companies become owing to the opportunities of economic globalization, the greater the risk is that the public good will be jeopardized by what Bakan (2004) calls the '*pathological pursuit of profit*'.

It is worth noting that some pro-business thinkers would agree that some of the corporate actions set out above are unethical, and that companies and the public would benefit from better governance, and from greater transparency and disclosure. They might also agree that what is required is better regulation of business, but what they mean by this is only regulations that improve market efficiency. This is in marked contrast to those who are sceptical of business' purpose, who tend to want to see regulation that limits both markets and companies. What both tacitly agree upon, however, is that corporate responsibility is not the best way in which to put right the wrongs of corporate behaviour.

One reason for this is that corporate responsibility is simply too weak for the task at hand. A company such as Unilever, for example, might put in place policies of social and environmental responsibility, but some blame its demand for palm oil for deforestation. Similarly, British Airways might have corporate responsibility policies, but it is part of an industry that is accused of externalizing its enormous environmental costs. This criticism focuses on corporate responsibility as a voluntary approach, something that is already tainted because self-regulation is seen as the corollary of diminished government capacity or unwillingness to regulate private enterprise, and becomes more damaged by examples of how companies have allegedly used voluntary initiatives to dilute their responsibilities to others. An oft-cited example of this is how companies have become signatories to the UN Global Compact—an action that requires them to uphold the Compact's ten responsibility Principles—and yet, according to critics, many such signatories continue to violate UN Principles, knowing that, until very recently, the Compact was without a disciplinary, or even a complaints, mechanism in relation to these transgressions (see Chapter 9). There are many other examples, such as the 2005 Amnesty International report on how the agreement about the Chad–Cameroon oil pipeline—held up as a model of corporate responsibility practice—actually created disincentives for the governments involved to protect human rights by making such rights the responsibility of the private sector, or a study of how voluntary labour standards have failed workers in Vietnam.[12]

As we will discuss later, such examples are, for some, evidence that corporate responsibility needs to be implemented more effectively; for others, they reveal the fallacy of trying to achieve justice without confronting power. Unless this is recognized, critics claim, then engagement with business through corporate responsibility initiatives or similar means leads to co-option by business and fosters an illusion that issues, such as global poverty, can be addressed while continuing to do business as usual.[13] The most obvious recent test of corporate responsibility in practice was the financial crisis of 2008–2009, and especially the role of banks. This is the topic of Case Study 14, but the failure of corporate responsibility theory to predict, explain, or resolve the crisis, and the accusations made about banks such as Citigroup and Barclays which have award-winning corporate responsibility programmes, have provided ample ammunition for critics of contemporary corporate responsibility.

Again, there is an irony here: those who see corporate responsibility as anti-business regard it as an imposition of activist agendas onto corporations, while those who see it as pro-business regard it as a co-option and dilution of those agendas by corporate interests. In both cases, corporate responsibility is being criticized for failing to meet particular sets of expectations, yet given the centrality of business in most of the modern world, these expectations embrace all aspects of human welfare and values. As Broad (2002) and others describe, the array of expectations from those who oppose the behaviour of large corporations is diverse and far more sophisticated than is typically portrayed in the media, and in articles such as those of *The Economist* discussed earlier. Consequently, the issues that corporate responsibility is accused of not addressing are equally diverse. For some, it is corporate responsibility's failure to tackle what are seen as aspects of corporate behaviour that pose a threat to the functioning of society and democracy that is at issue. This includes corporate lobbying of government, the avoidance of corporation taxation in developing countries and elsewhere, and the consequences for business and wider society of privatization and liberalization. Others highlight the behaviour of particular companies and industries, such as marketing and smuggling in the tobacco industry, the impact of supermarkets on small farmers, and the conditions of workers in computer manufacturing.[14] And then again, there are goods and services that at one stage are lauded for their social benefits (e.g. sub-prime lending to facilitate house buying for the poor), and end up being derided for being exploitative. As an early pioneer of private equity argues, this now widely criticzed financial instrument began with the purpose of freeing up business for the good of workers and investors.[15]

There are a vast number of reports and briefings on these and similar issues, and as we will see in the next section not everyone sees corporate responsibility as being powerless to address them. In fact, a criticism of corporate responsibility sometimes heard from within the corporate responsibility community is that it has stimulated rather than appeased civil society organizations' demands. This is probably a misplaced sentiment, which assumes that there are a finite number of issues in which companies have a role in addressing, or that winning the support of such organizations will end their criticisms of corporate behaviour. Perhaps more significant is to note that, for some, the fact that corporate responsibility does not tackle certain issues is a sign of its inherent weakness, while, for others, it is part of the process of mapping out future challenges and directions.

Some who regard corporate responsibility as inherently weak are not opposed to business, per se, as is evident from their support for fairtrade and other alternative trading companies, and particularly for ethically oriented firms, such as nosweatapparel.com. Some also support the new agendas for engaging with companies. But none of this detracts from the repeated call for government intervention and legislative frameworks that prescribe business activity.

Mitchell (2001, 2005) says that corporate responsibility can only succeed if there is a well-developed conceptualization of corporate law that exposes human responsibility and accountability. Arguing that companies are nothing but their individual members, he suggests that the law, companies, and markets need to be structured so as to encourage responsible behaviour and to discourage the irresponsible. He highlights that corporate responsibility has come to the fore at the same time as executive pay has spiralled, corporate governance reforms have too often been about making it easier to conduct mergers and acquisitions, and shareholders—not least, institutional investors—have pressured companies into producing quicker and higher returns. Thus, we see two distinct trends happening: one called 'corporate responsibility', under which companies are reconsidering their duties to society, and the other wherein what critics see as irresponsible behaviour is increasingly considered to be acceptable business practice. Corporate responsibility is not only blamed for failing to mitigate the latter, but also for helping to foster it by putting a gloss on corporate reputations.

A frequently cited example of how corporate responsibility has been hijacked in this way is that of the tobacco industry (see Snapshot 14.1). For some critics, there are industries, such as tobacco, arms, and gambling, that can never be responsible because of the very nature of their products and we have already seen how this principle has informed the responsible investment movement (see Chapter 10). There are also those who regard particular companies as egregiously irresponsible, and see it as proof positive of the coercion and co-option by business' interests of corporate responsibility when companies such as Nestlé—long-criticized for its marketing of infant milk formula in poor countries—are accepted into high-profile corporate responsibility initiatives such as the UN Global Compact.

A central question here is whether business is best influenced by engagement (e.g. through stakeholder partnerships) or by confrontation. We have discussed this at length in Chapter 10 and there are many civil society organizations, such as Oxfam and WWF, that engage with companies while keeping up a critique of business in society. For some observers, however, the crucial point is not who takes part in the process of engagement, but rather the norms and conventions that dictate that process, and thereby its possible outcomes. Much of corporate responsibility theory treats the participation or exclusion of particular agents as indicative of corporate responsibility's efficacy (e.g. Kolk et al., 1999). But it is possible to argue that the very nature of business as an element of the capitalist economy excludes certain values and ideals (e.g. Banerjee & Prassad, 2008; Blowfield, 2005). This raises questions about how particular social systems influence responsibility, and the parameters of what can be achieved by business within the capitalist system. As Wilmott and Alvesson (2002) argue in the wider context of organizational theory, the primacy given to prediction and control in all walks of organizational life not only makes it difficult to introduce ideas that don't directly relate to organizational effectiveness, it also reinforces the notion of knowledge as something value-free and empirically derived. What some critics of contemporary corporate responsibility would like to see is business adopting values beyond those justified by an instrumental logic. Therefore, the participation of some of business' harshest critics in a corporate responsibility partnership should not be seen as a sign of success, because the discourse (i.e. the language, mechanisms, tools, agendas, etc.) that governs it has already been settled and, moreover, is that which favours business' interests. Thus, for example, what can be dealt with or not in a corporate responsibility initiative, the priority given to an issue in terms of time, expertise and other resources, the array of possible solutions, and even the very language that is used to discuss the issues are all ultimately a reflection of what benefits or causes no harm to business. Moreover, this is something of which the participants themselves may be unaware, because, as Lukes (1974) has noted, '*the most effective and insidious use of power is to prevent . . . conflict arising in the first place*' (p 23).

The questions of power—who holds it, what form it takes, how it is exhibited, and what it allows or precludes—are an implicit underlying theme in many of the current critiques of corporate responsibility and those that are likely to occupy debates about the field in the coming years.[16] In fact, the essential criticism set out in this section is that corporate responsibility (both theory and management practice) is not able to confront corporate power and that alternative approaches are therefore required. Thus, for example, while corporate responsibility has gone some way to challenging both management and neoliberal orthodoxy, it is ultimately an example of how business secures the conditions for the ongoing and long-term accumulation of wealth and power, albeit in more socially and environmentally sensitive ways.[17] The critiques outlined in the following sections, however, draw a different conclusion: one under which power can be addressed and dominant institutions reformed, even if this has not been achieved as yet.

■ Discussion points

In the influential corporate responsibility book, *Walking the Talk*, Holliday et al. (2002) argue that sustainability is best achieved through open, competitive international markets that promote human progress by encouraging efficiency and innovation.

- Does this claim support or counter the arguments of critics who regard corporate responsibility as being too favourable to business?
- What alternatives to market-based solutions are these critics advocating?
- Are such alternatives plausible in today's world?

SNAPSHOT 13.2

Tobacco—can bad industries produce responsible companies?

For some corporate responsibility critics, nothing speaks more loudly to its pro-business agenda than the fact that some tobacco firms have positioned themselves as socially responsible. How, they ask, can companies that deliberately hid the addictive nature of nicotine from the public's knowledge be responsible? How can companies that have aggressively marketed their harmful products to the young be responsible? How can companies that knowingly produce something that will kill its consumers in any way claim to be responsible?

Since the 1950s, the industry has continuously been in the crosshairs of governments, consumers, and of course lawyers, but it was only in the 1990s, when state governments alleged that companies had long known about the addictive risk of nicotine and had not only lied about this in public enquiries, but had artificially boosted the nicotine content of cigarettes, that the industry finally agreed to multi-billion-dollar settlements. The settlements were held up as a victory for consumers—but to investors, at least, they were also seen as a victory for the industry and tobacco company stock prices rose.

They also prompted companies to think about corporate responsibility as an approach to managing their societal relations. BAT's endowment to the University of Nottingham to establish the International Centre for Corporate Responsibility prompted protests both on and off campus, and those who seem to embrace companies' commitment to behaving more responsibly, such as the Dow Jones Sustainability Group Index, have themselves been criticized.

Moreover, critics claim the way in which tobacco companies operate highlights the essential weaknesses of the corporate responsibility approach. For example, the World Health Organization has accused the industry of opportunism by making self-regulation on issues such as marketing to children part of their corporate responsibility programmes, thereby hoping to avoid legislation. Similarly, tobacco companies have been accused of working closely with PR firms simultaneously to promote corporate responsibility and to undermine scientific findings about the effects of smoking. But the industry points to the effectiveness of its anti-smoking campaigns on youth consumption. It highlights that smoking is a fact of life and that it is better to have a responsible industry, than the one dominated by organized crime that might emerge from prohibition. And they argue that the industry will make most progress when critics engage with it rather than when they attempt to isolate it.

(Sources: WHOTF Initiative, 2008; National Conference of State Legislatures, **www.ncsl.orgs**—accessed 4 July 2006; Palazzo & Richter, 2005)

Questions

Tobacco is one of a small group of industries the products of which knowingly cause human death or suffering.

1 What are other examples of such industries, and can they ever be considered responsible?

2 What do companies in these industries stand to gain from self-regulation?

3 Are the tobacco industry's critics right to refuse to engage as stakeholders with tobacco companies?

'The scope of corporate responsibility is too narrow'

We have seen that corporate responsibility is criticized for not addressing what are seen as important areas of corporate behaviour and that, to a degree, those who are supportive of, and sceptical about, the role of business share this view. We have also seen that critics in both camps regard corporate responsibility as not being suited to addressing these larger issues and see government as the proper institution in many cases. This overlooks the fact that, for the time being at least, effective regulatory mechanisms do not exist in many areas of global business activity. Indeed, as pointed out in earlier chapters, corporate responsibility is, at least partly, a response to the limited power of national governments in a global economic system.

Consequently, there are some critics who regard corporate responsibility as desirable, but who feel that the range of issues it currently addresses is too narrow. We have already mentioned corporate lobbying, tax avoidance, and how practices in specific industries to do with marketing, smuggling, and sourcing are said to affect society adversely, especially in poor countries. Some point out that the CEO of Wal-Mart earns more in three hours than a US worker on minimum wage does in a year,[18] and that therefore not only fair wages, but also broader policies concerning wealth distribution should be part of the corporate responsibility agenda. Indeed, employment generally needs to be tackled more comprehensively than at present. For example, corporate responsibility practice does not typically require companies to address the social costs of moving their production to another location, even though the consequences of such actions can be highly beneficial for the company and potentially devastating for the communities left behind. Also, given the worldwide trend for more flexible labour arrangements that are said to aid company competitiveness, but make employment less secure than it has been in the past, corporate responsibility is challenged to address the nature of the employment contract by, for example, giving workers stronger protections. There is a strong national/regional dimension to this because even in countries where there is limited employment protection, the consequences of redundancy are very different: for example, in the USA (with weak welfare provisions) compared to Denmark dismissed workers can claim state benefits for up to four years. Flexibilization of the workforce is accused of having particular impacts on women, but gender issues are only starting to enter mainstream corporate responsibility.[19] Moreover, while corporate responsibility has had a significant impact on the way in which companies think about labour conditions in developing countries, issues that are central to labour relations in many developed economies, such as gay and disabled rights, have not been part of the mainstream corporate responsibility debate in places such as China, India, and Latin America.

Outside the workplace, there are expectations that corporate responsibility should do much more to ensure that a company's corporate responsibility policies are not at odds with its policies in other areas. Home Depot, the American DIY chain, has attracted praise from environmental groups because of its timber sourcing policies and, as well as being a major corporate philanthropist, it moved early to provide help to communities affected by the Katrina hurricane in 2005. Yet, in marked contrast to its response to civil society organizations, the company garnered a poor reputation for listening to shareholders, exemplified by then-CEO Robert Nardelli's refusal not only to answer questions properly at the company's annual meeting, but also even to allow the board to attend the meeting.[20]

Equally, companies that have established strong corporate responsibility credentials are criticized for abandoning, or for failing to build on, these when they face a crisis. Enron is a widely cited example of a company that had a strong corporate responsibility reputation that did not reveal, but rather masked, the corruption and malfeasance that eventually brought the company down. But tarring corporate responsibility with the

Enron brush is probably unfair, given how that company's officers deceived so many institutions. A more illuminating example is Merck, the pharmaceutical company, which had long been held up to be a model of business ethics. That tradition appeared to help the company when, in September 2004, it responded to concerns about its pain reliever, Vioxx, by withdrawing it from sale—at least in the USA. It has since been alleged on numerous occasions, however, that, from 2000 on, the company vigorously sought out researchers and physicians who would endorse the drug, and tried to intimidate and stifle those who criticized it.[21]

Another area in which companies have been criticized for inconsistency between their corporate responsibility policies and their business practices is in their terms of trading and the way in which some companies use their power in the marketplace to drive out small businesses, or to force producers to adopt management practices that, ultimately, exploit workers, communities, and the natural environment. Just-in-time purchasing practices and promiscuous sourcing in search of low costs are examples from the apparel industry of how retailers and major brands are said to exploit their supply chains. These are issues that have started to register in mainstream corporate responsibility, and Tesco, for example, has started to train its buyers in understanding responsibility issues.[22] Yet Tesco is an example of the mixed messages a company can send out: training buyers, supporting research on sustainable consumption, and initiating programmes on carbon labeling, for instance, but also getting embroiled in arguments over animal cruelty, and the stifling of press freedom by using its wealth and questionable litigation.[23]

There are many more examples of aspects of business that critics say corporate responsibility could be addressing, but which it is not. But a list of issues does nothing to explain why some things have been included and others not. For some corporate responsibility theorists, as touched on in Chapter 2, this is a test of how the nature of business' role in society is defined and hence what we mean by 'corporate citizenship'.[24] A 2005 collection of critical essays from different academic disciplines reveals a number of ways of understanding this inclusion and exclusion.[25] At one level, companies are said to choose the limits of their actions. In some cases, they regard corporate responsibility as being fairly low down in terms of corporate objectives, allocated too few resources, and benefiting from little push to have the issues taken up by other agents (e.g. by government service agencies). In fact, it is claimed that corporate responsibility can be used to prevent alternative political, economic, and social solutions from being developed— something that has been observed in Nigeria, and also in South Africa, where, critics argue, corporate responsibility has had more to do with helping to erase memories of business' role in apartheid than in seriously tackling today's societal challenges.

Critics argue that corporate responsibility is more likely to include contentious issues if companies are under pressure from governments and civil society, and therefore that we should not view effective corporate responsibility as voluntary. But some take this further and argue that the limits of corporate responsibility may have already been reached. Not only may corporate responsibility be partially to blame for drawing attention away from certain traditional expectations about the role of business (e.g. payment of taxes to fund public policy initiatives), but many of the issues and conflicts that it is now being asked to address are, ultimately, the result of global economic and political systems that cannot be tackled at the company, industry, or other levels at which most corporate responsibility initiatives operate.

Implicit in such criticisms, there are questionable assumptions about the effectiveness and willingness of even liberal democratic governments to act in the public interest, and especially their acceptance of the need to be accountable and transparent.[26] There is also a tendency to blur the ways business engages with society, failing to distinguish, for instance, between companies as citizens, as governors of citizenship, and as the providers of arenas where stakeholders can interact.[27] Often, those who are most skeptical criticize companies' track-record on being citizens, and are fearful of the power they can exert as governors (e.g. influencing government and civil society agendas).

■ Discussion points

A recurring criticism is that corporate responsibility has yet to deliver on its promises and therefore has not proved strong enough to deal with important aspects of the business–society relationship.

- What are the most important areas in which corporate responsibility needs to demonstrate progress in order to win public support?

- How would you structure an effective complaints procedure for use in relation to a voluntary set of principles?

- Is imposing informal sanctions on business through actions such as 'naming and shaming' more likely to influence business behaviour than inter-company learning and peer pressure?

'Corporate responsibility fails to achieve its goals'

For those who see corporate responsibility as a whitewash, greenwash, or bluewash, the fact that corporate responsibility fails to deliver on its promises is no surprise. On numerous email listservs and blogs, corporate responsibility is dismissed as a kind of Faustian pact between business, NGOs, and government that weakens more effective policies. Such criticisms have been levelled at the UK's Business in the Community, which has spoken out against the need for government regulation of corporate responsibility, and been criticized for giving its Platinum Performance award to a bank accused of having '*a culture of ruthlessness and lies*.'[28]

It is often these types of organization, as much as companies, which are the focus of critics who claim that corporate responsibility has not lived up to people's expectations. They are blamed for focusing too much on corporate responsibility's successes and failing to consider its real impact. Bennett and Burley (2005) point out that only 3 per cent of multinational companies report on their social and environmental performance, and little over 2 per cent have signed up for the UN Global Compact: '*In what realm of life other than the strange world of* [corporate responsibility] *would a 2–3 per cent take-up rate be considered to be a success?*'

Moreover, some say that being a signatory to the Global Compact has little effect on corporate behaviour. As already noted, the Compact only agreed a complaints procedure to deal with allegations that signatory companies were breaching its Principles in late 2005. Now, companies that do not respond to complaints can be removed from the signatory list, barred from Compact activities, and forbidden to use its logo. Almost immediately, *Corpwatch*, the NGO, lodged complaints against six firms, and *Globalcompactcritics. net* is a conduit for complaints against the Compact. But the longer term question is how the Compact's small staff will make this system work among 2,500 participating companies, especially once the independently developed Global Compact Plus research tool begins to be used to assess and rank company performance.[29]

One criticism of the Global Compact is that the high profile granted to a voluntary initiative detracts from broader UN attempts to regulate business behaviour. For example, critics point to the way in which the Compact rose to prominence at the same time as the UN Commission on Human Rights was backtracking on its draft Norms on the Responsibilities of Transnational Companies and Other Business Enterprises with regard to Human Rights, following pressure from business and the US government. Since then, John Ruggie, a respected Harvard academic with UN and corporate responsibility experience, has been brought in to assess whether the UN should develop binding norms on human rights for multinational companies and made clear at the outset that he felt the current system of global rule making was imbalanced in favour of markets rather than human rights. His interim conclusion was that the norms so far were too difficult to monitor and enforce, and *'too engulfed by their doctrinal excesses'*.[30] But, in a subsequent report, he was optimistic that voluntary human rights initiatives would become the basis for binding standards and that it would be in business' interests to lobby government for stronger regulations.

Some find it bizarre that the UN sees business as a protector of civil rights, and such criticisms are indicative of wider concerns about what can be achieved through voluntary corporate responsibility. According to Doane (2005), what she refers to as 'CSR' is built on four myths (see Box 13.1). These are a retort to some of the arguments put forward by corporate responsibility thinkers, such as Zadek's work on the competitive advantage of nations and the many people who have written about the business case. Doane stresses the contradiction between short-term financial returns and long-term societal contributions. This echoes *The Economist's* view that business serves the public good only when companies focus on 'long-term profitability'. What *The Economist* leaves unexplained is that, as discussed in Chapter 12, in recent years, there has been a strong trend in major capital markets towards short-term investment, even among institutional investors, and this is something that is well understood by corporate responsibility theorists. Although some of the challenges of corporate responsibility probably derive, in part, from investor short-termism, it is misleading either to argue that corporate responsibility theory disregards this problem, or to imply that executives feel free to manage companies with a long-term view.[31]

Similarly, it is disingenuous to claim that any worthwhile actions carried out under the banner of corporate responsibility are simply acts of good management. There are elements of good management practice today that were once unknown or unacceptable

Box 13.1 **The four myths of corporate responsibility**

Myth	Reality
The market can deliver short-term financial returns and long-term societal benefits.	This assumes that shareholders are investors with an interest in the company's long-term success; today's investor is more accurately considered an 'extractor', i.e. driven by short-term profit seeking.
Ethical consumers will drive change.	In reality, consumers shop in their own narrow financial self-interest and are much more sensitive to price than they are to ethical considerations.
Companies will compete in a 'race to the top' over ethics.	Although companies may present themselves as socially responsible, there are many areas in which they deliberately pursue acts of social irresponsibility.
In the global economy, countries will compete to have the best ethical practices.	In reality, voluntary standards in developing nations have brought mixed results and competition for foreign investment has led such countries to weaken their insistence on strong labour or environmental standards.

(Source: Adapted from Doane, 2005)

(e.g. systems for reducing water and energy usage, policies on bribery and corruption) and which might not have entered into the mainstream but for corporate responsibility initiatives. Nonetheless, as we have seen in Chapter 12, there is surprisingly little information on the impact of corporate responsibility that can be used to defend it against criticisms that it is not achieving its goals.

Utting (2005b) makes clear that there has been demonstrable progress in corporate responsibility, although in some areas more than others. For example, as mentioned in Chapter 12, it has had more effect on workplace health than on equal pay, job security, and abusive disciplinary practices. More importantly, however, while corporate responsibility has been successful in increasing the array of issues that companies agree it is legitimate for them to address, the procedures to implement standards often remain weak. He points to the examples of the Global Compact and the Global Reporting Initiative, which tend to rely on dialogue and shared learning between participating companies and other stakeholder groups, rather than on monitoring performance and compliance. He also criticizes current approaches for being too top-down, exclusionary, and technocratic, assigning a minimal role to local organizations. This situation is exacerbated, because corporate responsibility tends to categorize people and social formations in ways that are misleading, if not damaging, in certain societies and cultures.[32]

Certainly, some corporate responsibility initiatives reflect a belief that companies will improve their performance by learning from peers, and this has become the basis for the Global Leadership Network and the London Benchmarking Group. Whether this approach is more effective than others is unproven, but it is one that many companies find acceptable, even if, to outsiders, it raises questions about the degree to which business decides by itself what issues to tackle and what constitutes acceptable perform-ance. Equally, it is criticized as a way in which companies can control the speed of progress, allowing them to put the emphasis on process rather than on measurable out-comes in relation to major social and environmental issues.

Frustration with the slow progress of corporate responsibility led a group of interna-tional NGOs, including WWF, Oxfam, Friends of the Earth, and Amnesty International, to refuse to participate in the UK government's 'draft international strategy for CSR'. They claimed that the strategy lacked direction and coherence, and that it inadequately analysed the mismatch between company behaviour and society's expectations.[33] As if to confirm the NGOs' scepticism, development of the strategy fizzled out—although this might be used as an argument against government involvement as much as it might be as evidence of the slowness of corporate responsibility.

SustainAbility, one of the organizations that also refused to participate, has more recently argued that a reason why corporate responsibility is not achieving its goals is that it has focused on the social and environmental aspects of the triple bottom line, largely overlooking the economic aspect. While fair trade, fair pricing, and fair wages are addressed to some degree, critics argue that there is a need for a broader economic agenda that includes the accountability of companies, the affordability of products, diversity, and equity.[34]

BSR and AccountAbility, two other organizations that are closely associated with cor-porate responsibility, have developed a framework for including these kinds of economic responsibilities.[35] Studies of Unilever's economic impact in Indonesia and South Africa provide similar insights, as does other industry-specific work on tourism.[36] This is part of a wider trend, promoted from both inside and outside corporate responsibility, to expand its scope. Indeed, it is one of the achievements of contemporary corporate responsibility that it has reinvigorated thinking about what society should expect from companies, even if the irony is that it is now criticized for failing to answer some of the questions it has provoked.

For some critics, the answer to these questions is to be found in moving from corporate responsibility to what has been named 'corporate accountability'.[37] The often top-down, exclusionary nature of corporate responsibility noted earlier leaves it open to criticisms that it has been dominated by organizations with limited accountability to external agents, who have taken it upon themselves to set out how companies should balance the rights of business with its voluntary responsibilities. Corporate accountability offers the different promise of balancing companies' rights with a more robust set of obligations for which companies will be held to account. Thus, it is argued, the goals of corporate respon-sibility will only be delivered if, for example, officers of public companies are required to report on their social and environmental impacts, to consult with communities that will be affected by their companies' actions, and to take negative impacts into account in deci-sion making. Equally, legal liability of company directors might be extended to include breaches of social and environmental laws, and the right of redress should be guaranteed for citizens and communities that have been affected by company activities.

Although the ideas of corporate accountability advocates are anathema to some who see the very promise of corporate responsibility as being a way of removing business' regulatory burden, it does highlight a dynamic that promises to inform developments within corporate responsibility over the coming years. This will be a debate, important to both private sector and public policy, over what aspects of the business–society relationship can be addressed by actions rooted in self-regulation, societal pressure, and business self-interest, and what aspects demand formal government intervention, whether through legislation or public sector management of social development. It is apparent from some of the views described in this chapter that some clearly favour one approach over the other, but, as is evident from our discussion of impact in Chapter 12, the information does not yet exist to decide what balance of approaches will be optimal.

■ Discussion points

Among Doane's (2005) four myths of corporate responsibility are claims that companies and countries will compete to improve their ethical performance.

- What do you think would dissuade companies from competing with each other on improving their social and environmental performance?

- Are these reasons different to those that might dissuade countries from setting higher social and environmental standards?

- Are corporate responsibility's critics right to argue that governments, rather than companies, must set these higher standards?

CASE STUDY 13

Can corporate responsibility be blamed for a financial crisis?

Bernie Madoff: sentenced to 130 years' imprisonment for a $64 billion plus financial fraud, 2009. Dick Fuld: the final Chair and CEO of financial services firm, Lehman Brothers, which became the largest corporate bankruptcy in US history, 2008. Allen Stanford: international financier facing charges of an $8 billion securities fraud, 2009. Fred Goodwin: CEO of Royal Bank of Scotland, once the fifth largest bank in the world, who saw the bank bailed out by government and eventually nationalized, 2009. And to this list we can add Fortis, Landbanski, Anglo Irish, Roskilde, IKB, Shinsei and many more financial institutions that were variously hit by and blamed for the international financial crisis of 2008–2009.

  Some financial institutions with a strong record of corporate responsibility practice seem to have survived the crisis relatively well: for instance, Cooperative Financial Services, Standard Chartered, and Audur Capital. But institutions like Citigroup, Bank of America, and UBS, all previously acclaimed for their corporate responsibility initiatives, were all embroiled in major controversies during the crisis. Moreover, notions of responsibility seem to have played no part in the ensuing allocation of government bail-outs or the rapid, frequently engineered acquisitions. Goldman Sachs, which received $31 billion in US government support, was accused of being '*a great vampire squid wrapped around the face of humanity, relentlessly jamming its blood funnel into anything that smells like money*.' Having announced it would pay nearly half of that sum in employee bonuses, its CEO. Lloyd Blankfein, claimed bankers are '*doing God's work*' when they raise the capital companies need to grow: '*We have a social purpose*,' he says. And vice-chair, Brian Griffiths, rammed the point home saying people should '*tolerate the inequality as a way to achieve greater prosperity for all*.'

Why, then, despite the resurgence of interest in corporate responsibility since the late 1990s, was such a conventional financial crisis allowed to happen? What does it tell us about corporate responsibility today? One perspective is that business cannot be allowed to self-regulate, and as importantly should be reined in from interfering with regulatory governance. In major economies, banking had lobbied for less restraints on their behaviour and for light-touch regulation. In some ways, Goldman Sachs and similar institutions' success was the creation of influential networks that penetrated into public policy. In what amounted to 'regulatory capture', they were able to outsmart civil servants and politicians, creating an environment where ill-comprehended and ultimately damaging financial instruments became desirable. While this was taking place, companies such as Citigroup and ABN Amro, burnished their reputations by establishing the Equator Principles and supporting other responsible finance initiatives such as the United Nations Principles for Responsible Investment. In hindsight, critics say these acts were a smokescreen.

A second perspective is that this was a wake up call to corporate responsibility thinkers. Perhaps too much attention was being paid to a relatively narrow aspect of investment—i.e. the universe of listed companies—and not enough to banking behaviour (from governance to product offerings). The knowledge of corporate responsibility champions in the financial industry came into question: were these people at the core of the industry? Did they have any real clout? Why were there so few people like David Pitt-Watson of Hermes with a history of running funds, and why did concerned industry leaders such as Stephen Green and John Bogle have little impact on corporate responsibility thinking?

A third perspective is that, even if much of the heavy-lifting to do with financial sector reform is driven by government, corporate responsibility ideas will have an important role. The Tobin Tax, which some theorists have discussed in a corporate responsibility framework, is being seriously considered as part of the reform package. Banking bonuses might be something that self-regulation can address. Understanding the social and environmental impact of investments is an area where corporate responsibility practice is starting to develop. Corporate governance is getting more attention as a specific aspect of corporate responsibility.

Whatever perspective one adopts, the banking crisis raises fundamental questions about how society manages corporate behaviour. Corporate responsibility may not have predicted the crisis, but neither did government regulators despite the fact that banking is probably the most tightly regulated industry, with banks in major markets having to submit daily balance sheets. A different way to look at the issue is to consider how much can be achieved through banks addressing problems of which they are a part unless some of the experiences and ideas of contemporary corporate responsibility are recognized. Complaints that if one country over-regulates the industry, the main players will migrate elsewhere strike to the heart of the global governance challenge which is central to corporate responsibility. The sense of injustice that bailed out banks damaged their investors and were spared the consequences is something that might be remediated through genuine stakeholder dialogues as well as political intervention. Even if the largest questions such as whether banks that are too big to fail are also too big to exist may not be addressed through the kind of approaches associated with contemporary corporate responsibility, but does this mean theory and practice have nothing to offer?

(Sources: Taibbi, 2009; Hopkins, 2009; Arlidge, 2009; Barrera, 2000)

Questions

1 The case study points to different perspectives on banks and corporate responsibility.

    a Is it more responsible to allow banks to fail than to bail them out?

    b What aspects of banking did corporate responsibility theorists overlook before the crisis?

    c What aspects should they prioritize now?

2 Many argue that the financial crisis is indicative of contemporary corporate responsibility's weaknesses.

    a What are the main arguments for relying on a regulatory governance solution to banking reform?

    b Are there areas where a non-regulatory approach might be more effective?

    c What do the weaknesses of self-regulation and regulatory governance reveal about the challenges of global governance?

3 Bankers' bonuses have become a lightning rod during the financial crisis.

    a What are the arguments for considering bankers' bonuses a corporate responsibility issue?

    b What are the arguments against this?

    c Should bailed-out banks be allowed to pay bonuses?

SUMMARY

Corporate responsibility has come in for increasing criticism, especially from outside the field, perhaps as a reflection of its growing influence on business life. The criticisms fall into four main areas: (a) that corporate responsibility is a specific agenda imposed on business by civil society organizations that damages profitability and, therefore, business' ability to generate wealth for society; (b) that ideas of corporate responsibility is now dominated by business, which is able to shape the agenda in its own narrow interests; (c) that the current concerns within corporate responsibility are too narrow and leave out many of the key issues for which the public expects business to take responsibility; and (d) that corporate responsibility practice, to date, has failed to achieve its goals, and needs to be more rigorous and innovative in the future.

The stance taken on these issues is often informed by individuals' responses to two questions: what is the purpose of business, and what kind of societal issues can corporate policies rooted in self-regulation, public pressure, and business self-interest adequately address? If one thinks that the primary purpose of business is to make a profit, then corporate responsibility will be criticized if it does not support that end. But if one thinks that the purpose is its social function (e.g. producing useful, affordable goods), then corporate responsibility will be assessed on a different set of criteria. Similarly, those who see legislation as a barrier to competitiveness will look at corporate responsibility in terms of its capacity to remove the regulatory burden, while those who are suspicious of market-based self-regulation will want to know whether corporate responsibility is as rigorous and effective as are government interventions.

In consequence, there is neither a dominant critique of corporate responsibility, nor even a common definition of what is meant by the term. But the points raised are often insightful, thought-provoking, and deserving of proper consideration, regardless of whether they are accepted or not.

FURTHER READING

VISIT THE WEBSITE
for links to useful sources of further information

Take your learning further: Online Resource Centre **www.oxfordtextbooks.co.uk/orc/blowfield_murray2e/**

Visit the Online Resource Centre which accompanies this book to enrich your understanding of this chapter.

Students: explore web links and further reading suggestions. Keep up to date with the latest developments by undertaking web exercises.

Lecturers: you will find additional case studies, including one on the topic of Nike—the evolution of responsibility in a multinational business, for use in class or assessment. Show your students trailers from films related to Corporate Responsibility, and use images from the book in your PowerPoint slides.

- Doane, D, 2005, 'The myth of CSR: the problem with assuming that companies can do well while also doing good is that markets don't really work that way', *Stanford Social Innovation Review*, Fall, pp 23–9.
  Examination of the shortcomings of corporate responsibility as a means of managing business' impacts on society.

- *The Economist*, 2005a, 'The ethics of business: good corporate citizens, and wise governments, should be wary of CSR', *The Economist*, 20 January, online at **www.economist.com**.

- *The Economist*, 2005b, 'The good company: the movement for corporate social responsibility has won the battle for ideas', *The Economist*, 20 January, online at **www.economist.com**.

- *The Economist*, 2005c, 'The world according to CSR', *The Economist*, 20 January, online at **www.economist.com**.

- *The Economist*, 2005d, 'The union of concerned executives: CSR as practised means many different things', *The Economist*, 20 January, online at **www.economist.com**.
  Collection of articles from a special edition of The Economist, critiquing corporate responsibility from a liberal economics perspective. However, see also the very different articles on corporate responsibility in the January 17 2008 edition.

- Mitchell, LE, 2001, *Corporate Irresponsibility: America's Newest Export*, New Haven, CT, Yale University Press.
  Interesting discussion of why the nature of the modern corporation and its legal status make companies inherently irresponsible.

- Moon, J, Crane, A and Matten, D, 2008, *Corporations and Citizenship*, Cambridge, Cambridge University Press.
  A detailed discussion of differing notions of citizenship, the distinct roles business plays as a citizen, and what these reveal about the shortcomings of corporate responsibility.

- Utting, P and Marques, JC, 2010, *Corporate Social Responsibility and Regulatory Governance: Towards Inclusive Development?* Basingstoke, Palgrave Macmillan.

  A collection of articles exploring different aspects of how ideas of corporate responsibility relate to regulatory governance, with a particular focus on developing and emerging economies.

ENDNOTES

[1] See, e.g. Blowfield, 2005a; Levy and Newell, 2002; Strathern, 2000.

[2] *The Economist*, 2005c.

[3] *The Economist*, 2005a.

[4] *The Economist*, 2005b.

[5] Harberger, 2003.

[6] Friedman, 2000.

[7] Ethical Performance, 2007.

[8] Manheim, 2004.

[9] E.g. Reich, 2007.

[10] E.g. Ballinger, 2010.

[11] Ballinger, 2010.

[12] Bakan, 2004.

[13] Monbiot, 2005.

[14] Friends of the Earth, 2005, and WWF and SustainAbility, 2005, address lobbying; Christian Aid, 2005, examines corporate taxation; WDM et al., 2005, examines privatization and liberalization; Christian Aid et al., 2005, is a study of the tobacco company, BAT; Action Aid, 2005a; 2005b, are studies of the retail, food, and agriculture industries' impact on small farmers in developing countries; CAFOD, 2005, examines working conditions in the computer industry. An up-to-date source of similar reports is **www.corporate-responsibility.org**.

[15] Brooke and Penrice, 2009.

[16] Power in the corporate responsibility context is a central theme in Bendell, 2004a; Blowfield, 2005b; Newell, 2005.

[17] Utting, 2005b; Rajak, 2006.

[18] Data from **www.issproxy.com**—accessed 20 June 2006.

[19] Radin and Werhane, 2003, discuss changing employment contracts; Grosser and Moon, 2005, and Barrientos et al., 2001, discuss gender dimensions to corporate responsibility.

[20] Nocera, 2006.

[21] Ginsberg, 2005; Prakash, 2006.

[22] Pamela Robinson, pers. comm.

[23] For a newspaper perspective on this litigation see Rusbridger, 2009.

[24] See, e.g. Moon et al., 2005; Wood et al., 2006.

[25] Frynas, 2005, and Fig, 2005, provide case studies of corporate responsibility in Africa; Nielsen, 2005, and Newell, 2005, provide insights into power in Bangladesh and India; Lund-Thomsen, 2005, and Jenkins, 2005, explore the wider context corporate responsibility operates within and its consequences.

[26] E.g. Brooke, 2010.

[27] Crane et al., 2008.

[28] Murphy, 2007.

[29] *Ethical Performance*, 2005a; 2005b.

[30] *Ethical Performance*, 2005d; 2006b.

[31] Blowfield and Googins, 2007.

[32] Dunn, 2004; Tharoor, 2001.

[33] *Ethical Performance*, 2004.

[34] Elkington and Lee, 2006.

[35] Available at www.economicfootprint.org.

[36] Unilever publishes various economic development studies at www.unilever.co.uk/sustainabil-ity/casestudies/economic-development/ (accessed 30 March 2010), although the South Africa study is no longer available on the website. Information on the economic development of tourism can be found at www.odi.org.uk/programmes/tourism/ and www.icrtourism.org/.

[37] See Utting, 2005b; Bennett and Burley, 2005; Doane, 2005.

14

The future of corporate responsibility

Chapter overview

In this chapter, we focus on the current trends in corporate responsibility and consider in what directions the field is moving. In particular, we will:

- examine the major trends that will affect what is meant by 'corporate responsibility' over the coming years;

- explore aspects of contemporary corporate responsibility that may be refined or enhanced;

- discuss evolving types of approach to corporate responsibility;

- reflect on what corporate responsibility reveals about the changing role of business in twenty-first-century society.

Main topics

■ Key terms

Capital markets

Social and environmental trends

Corporate governance

Business in society

Demographic change

Sustainable consumption and

production

■ Online resources

- • Additional resources on new trends in companies

- • Exercises and discussion topics for students

- • Teaching ideas on the future of corporate responsibility

- • Links to other web-based resources

Where is corporate responsibility heading?

'The world cries out for repair,' declare Margolis and Walsh starting their 2003 overview of companies' social initiatives. They recognize the increasing pressure that companies are under to provide solutions to social and environmental problems, even as they pursue seemingly competing financial demands, not least because, despite their limitations, in the current era of economic globalization they may be the entities of last resort for achieving all manner of societal objectives.

For some, this is an exciting agenda in which business will increasingly become a conscious and accountable agent in delivering non-financial outcomes. Our discussion of Social Enterprise (see Chapters 4 and 11) demonstrates how a new field has emerged that defines the corporate purpose in terms of societal outcomes. Yet there are many who would argue that what cries out for repair is capitalism itself. Corporate responsibility's relatively minor role in addressing the first major economic crisis of the twenty-first century is discussed in Chapter 13, but events such as financial meltdown, recession, and geopolitical shifts all serve as a reminder that, to paraphrase Marx, companies may make their own choices, but they do so in circumstances not of their own choosing. Faced with an array of mega-trends such as decarbonization (see Chapter 3), demographic growth (see Chapter 4), and the emergence of new economic powerhouses (see Chapter 5), companies find themselves operating in new circumstances that present challenges both in terms of what their responsibilities are, and how they can be managed. To return to the definition of corporate responsibility used throughout this book: it is about what the responsibilities of companies are, how they are negotiated and defined, and how they are managed. In other words, there are theoretical and management practice dimensions. As we look at corporate responsibility's future, both of these spheres are relevant.

In 2005, Allen White set out three scenarios for corporate responsibility in the year 2015. Now that we are halfway between those dates, they provide an interesting vantage point for viewing yesterday and tomorrow.

1 In Scenario 1, which White calls *'fad and fade'*, he imagines a severe economic downturn that causes companies and governments to concentrate on basic economic survival and recovery, and to discard any thoughts of making corporate responsibility integral to corporate strategy, management, and governance. Companies will still face corporate responsibility challenges, such as transparency, labour standards, human rights, and climate change, but government mandates and regulation, rather than business innovation, will drive their responses.

2 Under Scenario 2 (*'embed and integrate'*), calls for a business case for corporate responsibility have disappeared, because the benefits have already been persuasively demonstrated. Companies of all sizes and types of ownership accept corporate responsibility as the norm and not only adhere to international standards on good governance, labour practices, and environmental stewardship, but have melded their moral and ethical commitment to corporate responsibility into all facets of their business. In contrast with the fad-and-fade scenario, corporate responsibility is seen as an integral part of corporate management that will be resilient to economic conditions.

3 Scenario 3 (*'transition and transformation'*) describes a wholly different approach, under which frustration with the types of programme discussed in other chapters spurs the formation of a coalition of civil society, labour, and business, pushing for *'corporate redesign'*. For White, this transformation marks an ending of the narrow focus on short-term shareholder value and its replacement with a stakeholder model of the company, within which employees, communities, suppliers, and shareholders are all considered as 'investors' with the right to participate in the firm's governance and to benefit from its surplus.

Parts of the world have clearly experienced the kind of downturn envisaged in Scenario 1 in the late 2000s, but it does not seem to have marked the demise of corporate responsibility Allen speculated upon. The economic recession may have prevented some companies from adopting certain practices, and to cut back in some areas, but there has not been a large forsaking of investment. This is partly because companies from Marks and Spencer to Jones Lang LaSalle to Thomson Reuters are well along the path to embedding and integration (Scenario 2), and corporate responsibility is part of the way they do business. It is also because, although not to the degree some had hoped, in important jurisdictions such as the European Union companies are required to report on social, environmental, and governance factors material to the firm.

A further reason is that corporate responsibility management has often been implemented without increasing the company's headcount. Predictions that corporate responsibility would require new specialists have come true only to a limited extent. This may differ from country to country, and where corporate responsibility is new as an area of management practice, or where companies are moving beyond philanthropy, the human resource requirements will vary just as it did in the early days at companies such as Rio Tinto, KPMG, and Google.

A final reason is that companies better understand how issues such as demographic change and sustainable development are significant determinants of the environment in which business will be done in the coming years, and corporate responsibility provides useful tools and insights for managing these challenges. A small example of this is that climate change was flagged as a major issue for future corporate responsibility management in the first edition of this book, and in the second has become one of the main mega-trends affecting the field (see Chapter 3). Likewise, other mega-trends such as developing country poverty have become part of mainstream corporate responsibility (see Chapter 4). Indeed, a weakness of White's scenarios is that, aside from economic downturn, they overlook the wider context within which corporate responsibility evolves. They assume that it is business that decides what it will do, when in reality it is continually renegotiating its relationship with wider society. Therefore, in considering the future, we structure our discussion both in terms of management practice (White's scenarios), and shifts in the business-society relationship that in turn are affected by mega-trends (see Figure 14.1).

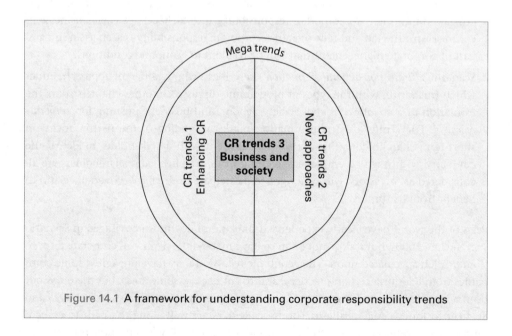

Figure 14.1 **A framework for understanding corporate responsibility trends**

Mega-trends affecting corporate responsibility

Climate change

By far the most noticeable global issue affecting corporate responsibility has been climate change. Although there has been a resurgence in climate change denial, and there remains a significant amount of public debate about the science, many companies are treating it as a serious business issue. We discuss this in detail in Chapter 3, but it is worth remembering that if the consensus of the large part of the international science community is correct, greenhouse gas emissions will need to be reduced by 80–90 per cent by 2050 if we are to avert *'dangerous climate change'*.[1] To achieve this equitably, the largest emitters such as the USA would have to reduce their emissions from 25 tons per person to about five tons; countries such as Germany, South Africa, and Japan would have to halve their emissions; and while China could raise its emissions slightly, the question remains how it could meet the expectations of an increasingly wealthy population while achieving a low carbon economy.

This would be challenging enough with a static global population, but by 2050 the population is likely to reach 9.1 billion, compared with 2.5 billion in 1950. Eight billion of these will be living in the poorest countries, within which illiteracy and malnutrition hamper human development. Therefore, while we discuss climate change, the geo-political shift in economic power, and poverty in other chapters, we need to highlight a further mega-trend, demographic change.

Demographic change

Climate change would be challenging enough with a static global population, but by 2050 the population is likely to reach 9.1 billion, compared with 2.5 billion in 1950. Eight billion of these will be living in the poorest countries, within which illiteracy and malnutrition hamper human development. The field of corporate responsibility may provide a framework within which business is able to help to resolve climate change challenges. But there is also a risk that climate change will swamp the corporate responsibility agenda and draw attention away from other major societal changes affecting business' relationship with society. Demographic change is an example of this that highlights some of the complexities of business' involvement in tackling sustainability.

The world's population has expanded enormously since 1950, but this growth has been unevenly spread in terms of age or location (see Box 14.1). Although the total population is predicted to level off at 9.1 billion by 2050, 95 per cent of growth will be in poorer countries, while that of wealthier nations is expected to remain fairly stable at 1.2 billion. Demographic change will pose all sorts of challenges for companies, including migration (from poor countries to rich, and from rural to urban areas), wealth flows (transfer of remittances from migrant workers to families around the world), health care (as the number and proportion of elderly in developed economies and also in emerging ones, such as China and India, continue to grow), social welfare provision (due to the

Box 14.1 **World demographics at a glance**

- Total population has risen from 2.5 billion in 1950 to 6.5 billion today.
- Seventy-six million new inhabitants are added each year because births outnumber deaths by more than 2:1.
- Nearly half of the world's population is under the age of 25.
- Population in the least developed countries will triple by 2050 and will change little (it may even decline) in more developed regions.
- Emerging economies, such as China and India, have increasingly large proportions of elderly people (31 per cent and 21 per cent by 2050, respectively).

changing ratio of economically active and inactive people), competition for natural resources (from energy to land to water), and pressure on ecosystems (owing to increased demands for housing, waste disposal, food, etc.).

The upshot of these changes is not known for sure. Malthus' idea that population growth hinders development persists, but some argue that rapid population growth promotes economic prosperity by adding human capital and increasing market size. Perhaps the dominant view today is that population size and growth, in isolation from other factors, have little impact on economic performance. But this perspective ignores a critical variable: the way in which a population is distributed across different age groups and how this affects development. For example, a high proportion of young or old dependants can limit economic growth, because of the resources devoted to their care (especially by women). Countries with more working-age people can experience higher growth, because of the higher earnings and savings levels, and less spending on dependants, creating a 'demographic dividend' that developing countries might enjoy just as the US baby boomers did after World War II.[2]

Global geo-political change

A third trend we are currently witnessing is a fundamental shift in geo-political power that is recognized within the corporate responsibility context, although at times is misrepresented. In Chapter 4 we highlight how the relationship between business and poverty in developing countries is an important element of corporate responsibility practice. However, in many ways this reflects a historical tradition where many have argued it is the duty of the rich world to help the poor. This has been the premise behind government to government aid as well as the work of many international NGOs. In addition to this, as we have mentioned (see Chapter 5) there is a tension between corporate responsibility as a means through which values are universalized, and corporate responsibility as something that is constructed and affected by localized cultural and political conditions. This has inspired an interesting body of theoretical work, as well as inter-country studies of corporate responsibility.

However, as became evident in the financial crises of the late 2000s, the rich but heavily indebted developed economies that have been seen as leaders in corporate responsibility, are now very reliant on loans from emerging economies.[3] In contrast with previous crises in the developed world, emerging economies did not overall suffer a marked downturn. With corporate debt exceeding 100 per cent of GDP in the Eurozone and household debt over 90 per cent in the USA (in the UK it is 100 and over 110 per cent respectively), it is emerging market governments and sovereign wealth funds that have prevented economic meltdown. In the seven largest economies, sovereign debt is running at almost 120 per cent of GDP, a figure last seen in the aftermath of the Second World War. This is only sustainable because emerging economies such as China and Malaysia (and other countries notably Japan and Germany) are willing to use their reserves to buy sovereign debt. How long that willingness will remain is unknown, but the consequences of this shift in dependency are likely to be lasting and profound.

■ Discussion points

Demographic change is likely to be a significant influence on what is considered to be corporate responsibility in the coming years.

- What are the ways in which demographic change might affect business in wealthy democracies?

- What are the scenarios for business in 2050, resulting from demographic change in China, Brazil, or India?

- What can business do to ensure that developing economies better enjoy their 'demographic dividend'?

Embedding and integrating corporate responsibility

What are likely to be the responses within corporate responsibility to the above megatrends? Based on what is already happening and what is being talked about, there are two readily discernible types of change occurring. One is the emergence of 'New types of approach' to corporate responsibility (p 358); the other is the enhancement and refinement of some of the well-established responses, and it is to these that we first turn.

The professionalization of corporate responsibility

Perhaps the broadest refinement is likely to be the growing professionalization of corporate responsibility. Among other factors, this is an inevitable outcome of some of the wider trends in corporate governance that we have already noted. Internally, the increased focus on non-financial dimensions of governance generally means that boards want to know that extra-financial risk is being managed effectively and that many companies are emphasizing the internal reporting of such data. Cross-functional teams are being created to manage non-financial risk and compliance agendas, and, as noted in other chapters, new management and reporting systems are being developed to address corporate responsibility risks (e.g. the ethical and environmental management systems used in Nike and Adidas' supply chains).

This is part of a trend for internal audit functions to extend their scope of work beyond the financial into areas such as health, safety and the environment, and responsible supply chain management. There are already many consultancy and certification businesses meeting the demand for outsourcing in these areas. To envisage how this will grow, one needs only to imagine the likely demand for metrics and reporting systems with which to track progress in companies with major commitments to corporate responsibility. For example, Hewlett Packard is one of several companies that discloses its supplier factories, encouraging labour organizations and others to verify conditions. Patagonia provides detailed information on the footprint of its products to help consumers make informed decisions. Companies committed to integrated reporting (i.e. producing joint reports on financial, environmental and social performance) such as Timberland and BASF now offer quite sophisticated online resources to help users assess their performance.

The more that these metrics become material to companies, the more impetus there will be for greater professionalization of corporate responsibility. This professionalization will happen in different areas of business. For example, corporate responsibility is likely to become a specific managerial competency, with prospective managers increasingly exposed to the field as an aspect of management practice; corporate responsibility professionals will undergo continual development; managers, in general, will need to be aware of the issues. Professionalization is also likely to lead professional service firms to build the capacity of accountants, lawyers, and others so that they can offer corporate responsibility services to companies. Equally, if corporate responsibility becomes of more importance to the investment community, analysts, fund managers, trustees, and others will need to meet new standards of professional competence (see Box 14.2).

Beyond ethical sourcing

One driver of professionalization is concern that current services are of insufficient quality. For example, a 2006 report by the US National Labor Committee pointed to numerous labour rights abuses in audited factories and member companies of the

Box 14.2 Initiatives aimed at professionalizing corporate responsibility—examples

- Fifty FTSE100 companies have had their non-financial reports externally verified, ten of which verifications have been performed by one of the Big Four accountancy firms.
- The Prince of Wales's Accounting for Sustainability project is helping organizations to measure more effectively the environmental and social costs of their actions.
- PricewaterhouseCoopers and Ernst & Young are among the sponsors of the AA1000 sustainability assurance standard, which has a professional qualification element.
- The International Federation of Accountants (IFA) has issued standards on non-financial assurance engagements.
- The Institute of Chartered Accountants in England and Wales (ICAEW) has started to analyse sustainability from an accountancy perspective.

Ethical Trading Initiative have been highly critical of the auditing of labour conditions.[4] Such auditing is a key feature of corporate responsibility management in global supply chains, and its poor quality has been cited as an indicator of the dysfunctional relationship between brand owners and their suppliers. Companies such as Levi Strauss and Gap have tried to move away from a situation in which they felt they were policing suppliers through auditing, towards one that was intended to build the capacity of managers and workers. But, even if the auditing were perfect, auditors alone would not improve social or environmental performance. As Utting (2005a) points out, there are about 70,000 multinational companies with 700,000 affiliates, served by innumerable millions of smaller companies. Yet no more than 5,000 companies produce corporate responsibility reports, about 700 firms use the Global Reporting Initiative's Guidelines, and a similar number have adopted SA8000. Even the most widely used certification scheme, ISO14001 on environmental management, has been applied in just over 90,000 facilities worldwide.

More ambitious still are efforts to think not only of single issues within the chain, but about what constitutes a sustainable supply chain as a whole, including social, economic, and environmental dimensions. The Sustainable Agriculture Initiative Platform, backed by companies such as Danone, Nestlé, and Unilever, is an example of this, although it is concerned primarily with the environmental aspects of agricultural production. Ongoing work by companies such Cadbury-Schweppes, as well as initiatives such as the Roundtable on Sustainable Palm Oil, are applying a larger lens that includes issues such as working conditions, land rights, and terms of trading.

Adopting international standards

The desire to use standards in supply chains more effectively is part of a wider debate in corporate responsibility about international standards. For example, in Boston in July 2006, at a meeting of representatives from corporate responsibility organizations such as the International Business Leaders Forum, AccountAbility, Business for Social Responsibility, and the Center for Corporate Citizenship, a United Nations representative proposed that the UN Global Compact and the Global Reporting Initiative's Guidelines be established as global frameworks around which corporate responsibility organizations might align their activities.[5] For some, this is seen as essential for corporate responsibility to reach critical mass and to obtain a broad political legitimacy: without it, it is feared that the corporate responsibility movement will disintegrate into specialized niches and an incoherent array of commercial applications.

A similar sentiment lies behind other collaborative initiatives, such as Jo-In, under which some of the most prominent ethical sourcing organizations are sharing learning on how to implement voluntary codes of labour practice. Although not made explicit, such collaboration is also an attempt to address complaints by companies that there are simply too many codes and that, if different standards were to be recognized as equivalent, this would reduce the cost of auditing and win more acceptance from suppliers.

There are legitimate concerns that, if those who support corporate responsibility cannot decide meaningful parameters with regards to the meaning and implementation of corporate responsibility, then the so-called movement will fragment. At the same time, it is equally appropriate to be concerned about who is most likely to influence any ultimate consensus and whether what emerges is a genuine agreement, or more the result of coercion. If we look again at the idea of using UNGC and GRI as the basis of a global framework, we see that the organizations involved in this discussion are corporate-funded in some way, whereas a major criticism of corporate responsibility discussed in Chapter 13 is that corporate influence is already undermining its legitimacy.[6] Hence, while alignment around particular definitions and approaches might be desirable, any trend in this direction will ultimately only be sustained if there is an accompanying consensus about what society expects from business (see 'The role of business in society', p 361).

Making corporate responsibility more inclusive

One of the challenges in creating a global vision of corporate responsibility is that norms and values are strongly influenced by cultural factors (see Chapter 5). Moreover, current corporate responsibility practices have been criticized for overlooking, or excluding, the priorities of particular social groups. For example, mirroring the male bias of which business is often accused, codes of labour practice have been criticized for favouring the interests of male workers and ignoring the needs of women.[7] Similarly, some argue that corporate responsibility practice can only be effective when it accommodates the cultural perspectives of the locations in which it is being implemented, while it has also been proposed that non-Western value systems, such as those practised in labour-intensive Indian organizations, are better suited to achieving positive outcomes.[8]

Awareness of the exclusiveness exhibited in some areas of corporate responsibility has been recognized for a number of years and is one of the insights provided by work in developing countries (see Chapter 4). But it is far from certain whether there will be a trend towards tackling the issue in any concerted way over the coming years. On the contrary, there may be a stronger trend towards seeing those who do not fit readily within the company's vision of what constitutes a legitimate stakeholder as hostile adversaries—something that may be inadvertently reinforced by the tools that companies use to manage corporate responsibility.[9]

Responsible consumers

One area of corporate responsibility that is already starting to receive more attention from companies is that of 'product' responsibility. There are different facets to this. In the area of corporate philanthropy, pharmaceutical companies and others are taking product donations more seriously in terms of ensuring that the products are useful and well used. Rather than designing a product and then ensuring that it is made responsibly, companies from Nike, to GE, to Boots, are using external inputs from the outset to think through the meaning of a responsible product—something that is being given a further push by legislation on product life cycle responsibilities (e.g. the EU Waste Electrical and Electronic

Equipment Directive). Media and entertainment corporations, such as Time-Warner, are starting to put in place policies relating to how they portray others' products (e.g. the use of cigarettes in films) and, as the discussion of Social Enterprise shows (see Chapter 11), there is increasing thought going into the responsibility of companies to make products available to the poor.

Uniting each of these examples is a new sense of the company's responsibility towards consumers. This, in turn, reflects a renewed interest to engage the consumer in corporate responsibility and an awareness that one of the constraints faced by companies in advancing a corporate responsibility agenda is consumer ignorance, or indifference. January 2006 saw the high-profile launch of Product Red, a global 'brand' under which major companies, such as American Express, Motorola, and Giorgio Armani, launched product lines, some of the profits of which would go towards fighting HIV/AIDS in Africa.

Devinney et al. (2006), however, say that any belief that consumers are ready to make purchasing decisions based on ethical criteria is not borne out to any significant degree in practice. They point to a marked difference between consumer opinions and purchasing behaviour that suggests that morals stop at the wallet. If, as many corporate responsibility managers seem to believe, the adoption of corporate responsibility as an element of mainstream management practice depends on consumers making decisions based less on price and more on an awareness of what lies behind the price, then, over the coming years, we might see a variety of initiatives put in place.

■ Discussion points

Embedding corporate responsibility into mainstream management practice is considered by many to be essential.

- Why are international standards important to integrating corporate responsibility?
- What are the main weaknesses with ethical sourcing at present?
- Why is corporate responsibility sometimes called exclusive?

Engaging financial institutions

The growth of socially responsible investment has been heralded as one of the successes of corporate responsibility (see Chapter 10), but to put that in perspective, the amount invested in SRI funds is less than one 1 per cent of that invested in hedge funds.[10] It is not surprising, therefore, that many see the future development of corporate responsibility as closely linked to trends in the mainstream financial community. Hope for rapid advances were dashed by the collapse, bailing out, and subsequent destruction of reputation experienced by investment banks (see 'Corporate governance' p 362), but it is notable that despite these upheavals the investment community continues to engage in corporate responsibility. Institutions hit by scandal such as UBS and Merrill Lynch (now part of Bank of America), have continued to have senior personnel focusing on sustainability, and Goldman Sachs has continued to promote its Environmental Policy Framework as a way of linking capital to sustainability.

The figures tend to be presented in ways that suit advocates' beliefs, but there is significant money available for investing on environmental issues. Green stimulus packages that have been part of public economic growth spending are estimated to be $221 billion in China, $112 billion in the USA, and $31 billion in South Korea.[11] Green venture capital is well established, especially in the USA, Proven venture firms, such as Kleiner Perkins Caufield and Byers, which has created a $100 million fund for green technology companies, are investing heavily in clean and green innovators. Attracted by trends such as rapid growth in renewable energy and green building materials, roughly 10 per cent of North American venture capital now goes into green technologies, while more than £660 million has been invested in European clean technology since 2001.[12]

Corporate responsibility issues are highly unlikely to be addressed adequately without the engagement of financial markets—but markets only respond when a price is attached to an issue. This has happened with carbon trading, for which London has established itself as the global centre, while New York or Chicago are emerging as competitors as the USA considers national emissions reduction targets.[13] Despite the European carbon market's problems in 2006, over 1 billion tonnes of carbon dioxide were traded in Europe alone, at a value of more than £12 billion. Blue-chip investment houses have been major investors: Goldman Sachs took a 10 per cent stake in London-listed carbon trader Climate Exchange and Morgan Stanley has promised to invest $3 billion in carbon trading by 2012.[14] But there is little sign that markets will be formed for other issues and limited debate about whether markets for other important issues, such as poverty, could ever be created.

Financial firms, such as Henderson Global Investment, have broadened the abbreviation 'SRI' (see Chapter 10) to mean 'sustainable and responsible investment' and focus on what they consider to be the technologies of the future. Along with initiatives that we have noted in other chapters, such as the emergence of specialist indices from within the conventional investment world (e.g. FTSE4Good and the Dow Jones Sustainability Indexes), these are examples of how corporate responsibility is starting to be integrated into mainstream analysis. In Germany, for example, investors and analysts are demanding increasingly sophisticated information on sector-specific sustainable development key performance indicators.[15] But overall, the investment community is ill equipped to judge the significance of sustainable development actions, because it remains focused on assessing financial data and management quality, and the sums of money saved through, for example, eco-efficiency, although large, may not be large enough to attract analysts' attention. Most investors see their role as based on price, rather than on the kind of adding value that some feel is achieved by relationship investing and other long-term relationships.[16]

To a degree, progress will depend on distinguishing what Lydenberg (2005) calls '*investable*' issues that are material to a company, but not yet factored into the share price (i.e. *mispricing*) from those that are '*non-investable*', for which engagement with investors is unlikely to have any effect. An important theme in future corporate responsibility debates will be how to tackle non-investable issues. Much will depend on the success of the initiatives noted elsewhere in this book in increasing the interest of mainstream analysts (e.g. the Marathon Club, the London Accord, the Enhanced Analytics Initiative, and the United Nations' Principles for Responsible Investing—see Snapshot 14.1).

SNAPSHOT 14.1

UN Principles for Responsible Investment

The United Nations' Principles for Responsible Investment (PRI) is one of several initiatives aiming to persuade investors to think of matters other than the financial bottom line when placing their money. Its backers are investors responsible for 10 per cent of global capital (or more than $4,000 billion of assets), including Dresdner, Citigroup, Goldman Sachs, and UBS. By signing up to the PRI, these investors commit to integrating environmental, social, and governance (ESG) issues into conventional investment analysis, to being active, responsible owners by promoting good corporate practice in these areas, and to reporting transparently on what actions have been taken in this area.

What marks out the PRI is that its supporters are major global institutions that are not known for putting their name to frivolous or marginal initiatives. The initiative's principles make explicit that ESG issues, or extra-financial risks, have an effect on the long-term performance of companies. They mark a step towards learning about measuring companies in ways that do not necessarily fit into the normal accounting framework and, ultimately, towards identifying long-term investment drivers.

(Sources: Scott, 2006; **www.unpri.org**—accessed 1 April 2010; **www.greenbiz.com**—accessed 1 April 2010)

Questions

The PRI has been welcomed as a step towards getting the international investment community to focus on long-term drivers of company value.

1 What is the significance of the PRI?

2 Are its principles genuine ones for responsible investment?

3 How will the PRI influence the development of corporate responsibility?

■ Discussion points

Throughout this book, we have looked at the criticisms, strengths, and limitations of corporate responsibility.

- Considering what has been discussed in earlier chapters, which of the trends in this chapter are likely to be most significant?
- Which are those that are likely to be least significant?
- Are there trends that have not been identified?

Transition and transformation

A new kind of business case

The business case for corporate responsibility is discussed in Chapter 6, but the limitations identified there have led some to argue for a different type of case that essentially requires people to look at companies differently. Although the liberal economic critique of corporate responsibility discussed in Chapter 13 argues that corporate responsibility constitutes harmful meddling with the efficiency of free markets, the alternative business case presents corporate responsibility as a way to address market imperfections and failures. As some liberal economists would agree, efficient resource allocation depends on markets yielding prices that reflect true social costs; when they fail to do so, such as when polluters do not have to pay the cost of pollution, then the invisible hand can lead one in the wrong direction.[17] Therefore, instead of seeing corporate responsibility as an assault on free markets, it can be argued that it will ultimately make markets, or at least companies, more efficient.

This argument takes three different, if sometimes overlapping, forms. One is that, although there may not be a causal relationship between corporate responsibility and business performance, there can be a correlation between the quality of a company's technical systems and processes, and its corporate responsibility practices, and good social and environmental performance can be achieved by companies that perform well financially.[18] If the most important factor with regards to profitability, growth, and future earnings is good management, then corporate responsibility may be an indicator of a well-managed company.

The second argument emerges, in part, from the above observation and, more generally, from a belief that there is a need for alternative measures of company performance. For example, some maintain that the current methods for assessing a company's value and performance are flawed because, among other reasons, they do not adequately value the kinds of intangible assets to which corporate responsibility adds value (e.g. reputation, licence to operate). Moreover, conventional methods are poor at predicting long-term business performance, because sell-side analysts, in particular, are primarily concerned with short-term financial performance. A repeated claim made about corporate responsibility is that its true value to business will become apparent once companies focus more on long-term performance, because responsible and sustainable products and strategies are those that are most profitable in the long run.[19] Indeed, according to Goldman Sachs, which has launched an Environmental and Social Index, 60 per cent of company value is determined by long-term returns and corporate responsibility issues will affect share prices if they come to be seen as affecting those returns. For this to happen, however, proponents claim that there need to be significant changes in the way in which capital markets function, in the types of accounting system used (e.g. the adoption of full cost accounting of the kind developed at Glasgow University's Centre for Social and Environmental Accounting), and the other means by which business performance is measured.

There are a number of corporate responsibility thinkers who argue that the strongest element of the business case is the important part that corporate responsibility will play in the successful companies of the future. The growth strategies of the past are portrayed as increasingly less effective, creating a need for new ways to grow. In this scenario, aspects of corporate responsibility are proposed as part of that change, requiring that corporate responsibility be accepted as part of core business strategy (see Chapter 6).[20] Thus, rather than asking how a dimension, such as human rights or eco-efficiency, affects access to capital, the business case hinges more on treating corporate responsibility as a critical link in innovation and learning, or as part of new, more sophisticated approaches to risk management.

This kind of thinking moves us a long way from trying to attach a monetary value to corporate responsibility activities. The alternative business case is already being reflected in the ways in which some large companies are approaching, or at least talking about, corporate responsibility. For example, a group of companies within the World Business Council for Sustainable Development, an early pioneer of eco-efficiency, has tried (in their words) to reunite the interests of business and society by restating the purpose of business as follows: '[The] *fundamental purpose of business is to provide continually improving goods and services for increasing numbers of people at prices they can afford.*'[21] The group holds that tomorrow's leading companies will be those providing goods and services in ways that address major societal challenges, such as poverty, climate change, depletion of natural resources, globalization, and demographic shifts. This is not a major reinterpretation of the role of business and signatory companies claim most firms benefit society simply by doing business. But two distinctions separate the group's perspective from those who advocate that 'business is the only business of business'. First, the signatory companies state that, while substantial and sustainable action by business to address pressing societal needs has to be profitable, shareholder value is not an end in itself, but a measure of how successfully companies deliver value to society. Second, the group emphasizes the importance of taking a long-term perspective on company performance and thereby echoes what was noted earlier about the ways in which capital market short-termism undermines the business case. They stress that the purpose of any sustainable company has to be more than generating short-term value for shareholders; yet '*simply by adding the word long-term to shareholder value, we embrace everything necessary for the survival and success of the company*'.[22]

As already noted, any claim that the business case for corporate responsibility can only be made by changing the rules of the game may not strengthen the credibility of corporate responsibility, at least in the short run, because it clearly implies that, in order to make a business case, we first need to redefine the purpose of business. It can also be argued, however, that one of the contributions of corporate responsibility is to stimulate thinking about such fundamental issues. As Van Tulder (2006) notes, corporate responsibility will need to distance itself from simplistic debates about profit maximization if it is to be more than a fad. He holds that, whether it is Prahalad (2005) arguing for societal issues, such as poverty, to be integrated into company strategies, or Handy advocating for a new type of company scorecard that includes contributions to society and the environment, or de Geus and his belief that companies need to harmonize their values with those of society to survive societal turbulence, leading business theorists have consistently set out the rationale for a different kind of business case. But he also maintains that this is not a business case for corporate responsibility in the way that notion is typically conceptualized; rather, it is a business rationale for approaching the interface between business and society more efficiently, equitably, and effectively: what he terms '*societal interface management*'. Citing Mintzberg, he argues that companies are social institutions, the existence of which is justified only in so far as they succeed in serving society, in contrast with human beings, for example, who have an inherent right to be. This is a very different perspective to those that underpinned initial thinking about 'doing well by doing good' and the benefits of eco-efficiency, but building (or rebuilding) a societal case for business, rather than what can sometimes appear to be the business case for society, is, for some theorists and also executives, the kind of change that has to occur for the long-term prosperity of global society.[23]

Sustainable consumption and production

Another way of considering transformation is the new type of approaches that have entered the corporate responsibility sphere. Social Enterprise (see Chapter 11) and some of poverty-focused initiatives (see Chapter 4) are examples of such approaches. Another that is starting to gain attention is described below.

For sustainable development theorists, one of the key challenges of the coming decades is how to decouple certain types of growth—particularly those associated with harmful emissions and unsustainable energy use—from prosperity. This has especially come to the fore as the demands that fast-growing economies, such as India and China, will put on natural resources become apparent, and it has been estimated that for the consumption and production patterns of Canada or the UK to be adopted worldwide would require resources equivalent to those of three earths—to adopt those of the USA would require those of five.[24]

'Sustainable consumption and production' (SCP) embraces an array of approaches that are aimed at addressing this problem. It refers to the challenge of achieving continuous economic and social progress that respects the limits of the earth's ecosystems, and meets the needs and aspirations of everyone for a better quality of life, both now and for future generations. SCP requires better alignment between consumption, the natural resources needed for production, and the ecological sinks available to absorb waste.[25] Organisation for Economic Co-operation and Development (OECD) governments have been committed for decades to ensuring that the prices people pay reflect the full social and environmental costs involved, and European governments are committed to SCP through the 2000 Lisbon Agenda. Historically, however, governments have been weak and inconsistent in promoting SCP, for fear that consumers would have to pay higher prices. Moreover, concerns regarding relative national competitiveness have consistently trumped those about sustainable development.

Various principles have emerged for tackling SCP, and centres such as the Tesco-funded Sustainable Consumption Institute are being established to focus on these issues. But, as we have seen with other areas of corporate responsibility, the wider business environment does not always encourage companies to take sustainability-based decisions and may even create disincentives. Moreover, at present, the place of SCP initiatives in the context of corporate responsibility is still uncertain. On the one hand, the core issue—how growth can be achieved while realizing a drastic per capita reduction in the use of resources—is one that is central to corporate responsibility; on the other, much of the current interest has come from government and there is a sense that only government can break the kind of 'I will if you will' impasse that is preventing more business action in this area. But governments, too, are constrained by not wanting to take action unilaterally for fear that this would sacrifice competitive advantage, while those who view corporate responsibility as voluntary, rather than mandatory, may feel uncomfortable with government-driven SCP for ideological reasons.

■ Discussion points

Companies often depend on the behaviour of consumers, investors and customers to determine how responsible they can be.

- Why is an emphasis on short-term performance seen by some as incompatible with corporate responsibility?
- Should companies drive changes in consumer behaviour?
- Why do you think an early report on sustainable consumption and production was called 'I will if you will'?

The role of business in society

Today, one does not need to venture far from the mainstream of corporate thinking to hear questions being raised about the effects and efficacy of capitalism. Stephen Green, current chair and former CEO of HSBC, had a best-selling book on the value of values and sustainability in business (2009); John Bogle, founder of the Vanguard Group with $1 trillion in assets, has railed against Wall Street's greed (2009). Along with recent books by George Soros (2009), and business thinkers such as Warren Bennis (2009) and Rosabeth Moss Kanter (2009), they are part of group of respected individuals from the business status quo who are asking what were hitherto considered radical questions.

What is the role of business?

The roles business plays vary over time (see Chapters 2 and 5), and because of the major shifts that global society is undergoing, the historical roles assigned to business and government are widely held to be outdated. Corporate responsibility practice has had a mixed record in recent years of offering solutions to major aspects of the business-society relationship: providing a range of initiatives on sustainability, poverty, human rights, and climate change, but unprepared for tackling the mis-selling, greed, and deceit that was behind the 2008 financial crisis. Insofar as corporate responsibility is interpreted as an approach to business self-regulation, it is not surprising that it is treated with scepticism by people disenchanted with ideas such as light touch regulation.

The financial crisis also exposed numerous instances of corporate irresponsibility, often in countries with the worst recessions. In addition to instances of corruption such as Bernard Madoff's investment fraud in the USA, and the bribery scandal surrounding Siemens' top management in Greece, there have been various instances where the line between managerial incompetence and abuse has been blurred. Companies with strong corporate responsibility reputations were still exposed by the debt default of Dubai World in 2009, and in hindsight Citigroup's commitment to corporate responsibility could be interpreted as a way of masking its fundamental management problems.

Such examples show the influence business can exert over government and the dangers of not getting the regulatory balance right. Robert Monks, corporate governance thinker, has said that, given the level of distrust about business' influence over government policy, the starting point should be: *'What is the responsibility of the 'good company' with respect to government?'* His prescriptions that companies disclose relevant information, exercise restraint in trying to influence government, and obey the law are less ambitious than some would want from a comprehensive corporate responsibility agenda, but nonetheless are, in many respects, a significant departure from what is currently on offer.

■ Discussion points

Charles Handy (2002) has asked the question 'What's a business for?'

- Is the role of business different today than it was 50 years ago?
- How would you answer Monks' question about the good company's responsibility towards government?
- What is a business for in the twenty-first century?

Corporate governance

There has been enormous clamour for tougher regulation of financial institutions since 2008, and these may still lead to tighter control of investment banking, not least in the light of the Valukas report into the Lehman's Brothers collapse and other enquiries.[26] Although corporate responsibility theorists can claim little credit in predicting the financial crisis, there is likely to be considerable interplay between new governance ideas and corporate responsibility more generally. The trend towards greater transparency, for example, complements demands that environmental and social issues be incorporated into corporate governance. As noted in other chapters, aspects of sustainable development have also found their way (with mixed results) onto governance reform initiatives, such as the UK Company Law Review. In Europe, reporting on aspects of sustainability will increase as a result of the EU Accounts Modernization Directive, which requires that directors' reports contain a business review that includes information about

environmental matters, employees, and social and community issues, including information on relevant policies and their effectiveness. This is reflected, for example, in the
UK Companies Act 2006, which, for publicly listed companies, requires directors to
report on non-financial issues to the extent that is necessary for an understanding of the
business (see Chapter 7).

Central to such initiatives is a debate about the duties of corporate officers to those
other than shareholders and the idea of enlightened shareholder value. Some legislation
regarding directors' liabilities has been strengthened (e.g. the UK Corporate Manslaughter
Bill), and recent decisions by the UK and EU courts mean that it is not only in the USA
that companies can be held liable for their social and environmental actions abroad.
New regulations have also been introduced, relating to sustainability issues. For example,
the EU's Pollution Prevention and Control Directive raises the bar on controlling industrial pollution across Europe, and its Waste Electrical and Electronic Equipment Directive
deals with end-of-life issues for electronic products, which will influence the behaviour
of both manufacturers and retailers.

The attention given to the responsibilities of business has increased further since the
introduction of the 2007 UK Climate Change Bill, the first attempt to set legally binding
targets on greenhouse gas emissions. But it is not legislation alone that is causing companies to act: codes of business practice that include aspects of corporate responsibility
can serve to forestall legislation, but equally to meet requirements that companies demonstrate they have a strong control environment. Basel II (the revised international capital framework), for example, requires major financial institutions to show that they have
key risk measuring and monitoring systems and controls in place.

Most large companies now have codes, or sets of principles, that span wide areas of
non-financial performance and are underpinned by a framework of policies. Such codes
can also help companies to deal with the ethical responsibilities and liabilities that stem
from such legislation as the US Sarbanes–Oxley Act 2002, the UK bribery and corruption
law, the US Foreign Corrupt Practices Act 1977, and the UK Enterprise Act 2002.

The role of capital markets

The sub-prime mortgage bubble that led to the first major twenty-first century recession
brought to the fore some of the structural issues that some believe make capital markets
incompatible with responsible corporations. As the global market for capital expands
and the costs of trading tumble, investors—even institutional investors—are focused on
increasingly shorter time horizons.[27] Furthermore, the logic that owners of public companies are in a strong position to effect change has been challenged by the emergence
of private equity firms as an alternative source of capital. Companies engaged in corporate responsibility, such as Georgia Pacific, Littlewoods, and Aramark, have all become
privately held, removing them from many of the non-mandatory drivers associated
with improved social and environmental performance (e.g. public reporting). This is
not to say that publicly held companies are more likely to address corporate responsibility issues than are those that are privately held: Dunkin' Donuts, for example, is owned
by a private equity firm, but has gone further than most in mainstreaming fairtrade

coffee; Cargill, one of the largest family owned companies in the world, is nonetheless under pressure from retailers to adopt ethical sourcing policies. Indeed, in some cases, it may be that, removed from the pressure to meet quarterly earnings targets, some privately held companies may be better placed to take a longer-term perspective than if they were publicly listed. Nonetheless, most large companies are publicly held and many large private companies, such as Levi Strauss, continue to look to the same capital markets to some degree.

Hence, there is a dichotomy that lies at the heart of corporate responsibility's future development: on the one hand, there are many corporate responsibility theorists and practitioners, both inside and outside the business community, who believe that companies that ignore the business–society perspective are putting their long-term prosperity in jeopardy; on the other hand, the short-term culture of the capital markets is affecting, and effectively putting damaging constraints on, how companies address societal issues. If the former viewpoint is true, then short-termism is damaging shareholder, as well as stakeholder, value, but this is going unnoticed. Whether this perspective is accurate or not is, at present, more a matter of supposition than demonstrable fact, but the reaction of the capital markets will have a major influence on future trends in corporate responsibility. This is true of the investment community's own decisions, as is already evident, for example, in the way in which climate change is starting to be factored into financial analysis. But it is also true in terms of the way in which the investment community affects the decisions of others. For example, it affects the advice that executives follow so that even a company with a strong corporate responsibility track record might find itself under pressure to make decisions that would undermine its reputation, in the name of optimization and efficiency.

SNAPSHOT 14.2

Tree-huggers at the gate—private equity and NGOs collaboration over coal-fired power

Kohlberg Kravis Roberts' 1989 acquisition of RJR Nabisco became infamous as an example of hard-headed, shareholder value-driven capitalism in Burrough and Helyar's *Barbarians at the Gate* (1990). Two decades on and KKR's record-breaking private equity deal to purchase the energy utility, TXU, has made headlines for different reasons.

TXU had been under attack from environmental groups because of its plans to build 11 old technology, coal-fired power plants in Texas. The plans became bogged down in a swamp of public outcry, political manoeuvring, and litigation. In what some are holding up as a landmark collaboration between private equity and environmental activists, two environmental NGOs, the Natural Resources Defence Council and Environmental Defense, negotiated a deal whereby, in return for their backing the purchase, KKR agreed to suspend developments of eight of the power plants, pilot a 'clean coal' plant, cut greenhouse gas emissions, invest in alternative energy, and back government climate change legislation.

For the NGOs involved, it is another example of how to collaborate with business to achieve environmental objectives, although this, in turn, has led to criticism from other environmental groups that the KKR–NGO agreement contained too many loopholes. For KKR, the support of these multi-million-dollar NGOs reduces the risk that the purchase might otherwise represent and, it hopes, will strengthen TXU's licence to operate. It also signifies a new development in private equity strategy, under which firms bet on the profits to be made from social and political change.

(Sources: Paulden, 2009; *The Economist*, 2007; Smith & Carlton, 2007)

Questions

The purchase of TXU is one of the first examples in which corporate responsibility issues and partnership with NGOs have overtly played a part in a private equity firm's investment decisions.

1 Although it is portrayed as a 'win–win agreement' between KKR and the NGOs, what do you think were the advantages for the former?

2 What do you think were the risks and potential disadvantages for the NGOs?

3 Do you think this will be a one-off example, or will it extend to other industries?

The power of multinationals

It is not true that corporate responsibility is only an issue for the world's largest companies (see Chapter 11), but the power of major corporations and how their responsibilities are negotiated and enacted are likely to influence any debate about corporate responsibility as management practice. The power of supermarkets, for example, reflects a wider concern about the power of large companies. Some critics of globalization have turned their attention away from trade legislation, and more towards anti-trust and anti-monopoly activism. For example, there is concern that we inhabit a world dominated by global oligopolies that not only have enormous purchasing power, but are also exercising great political power. Consumers have benefited historically from anti-trust laws that present price gouging, but companies such as Wal-Mart and Tesco are today being accused of having such power, even over multinational suppliers such as Procter and Gamble, or Rubbermaid, that they can set prices almost at will. They are also suspected of using this muscle to intimidate local governments and to drive through planning applications for new stores, irrespective of local community sentiment. And, of course, this same kind of power can be used against workers, as when McKinsey and Co helped Wal-Mart to prepare a memo on how to cut back employee benefits even though these were already among the lowest in the US retail industry.

The issue of corporate power applies to any industry, not only to that of retail. Suspicion is especially strong in relation to the lobbying of government on legislation, procurement, and spending. Corporate responsibility itself has been a target for lobbyists. For example, the Confederation of British Industry lobbied to have sections of the Company Law Reform Bill altered to limit company accountability to stakeholders and has been accused, more generally, of influencing the government's sustainable development policies. From a different perspective, WWF and SustainAbility (2005) compared corporate responsibility commitments and corporate lobbying activities, and found that, although many companies included discussion of lobbying in corporate responsibility reports, they were reluctant to lobby actively to improve social and environmental frameworks.

One area in which companies have been accused of using their power in ways that might harm the common good is taxation. Worldwide, there has been a trend to cut back corporate taxation, partly based on the argument that this will stimulate growth and generate more total revenues for government programmes. The Tax Justice Network and the Publish What You Pay Campaign are examples of civil society responses to the suspicion that companies are not paying their fair share, and even that corporate responsibility is window dressing that is intended to divert attention away from the tax evasion strategies of multinationals. Greider (2006) proposes that corporate taxation could be refashioned, so that tax liabilities might be reduced for those that adhere to higher social or environmental standards. Parts of the accountancy profession argue, however, that there is insufficient understanding of the true scale of business' taxes and PricewaterhouseCoopers, for example, has proposed a new framework for reporting a company's total tax contribution, i.e. all of the direct and indirect tax that business pays into the economy.

Transforming the corporate purpose

In previous chapters, we have alluded to the ways in which consideration of corporate responsibility relates to debates about new forms of accountability and new ways of valuing the company, and how these, in turn, reflect a resurgence of interest in rethinking the purpose of business. This interest is manifesting itself in different arenas across the spectrum, from theory, to practice (see Box 14.3).[28]

It is as yet hard to detect a widespread appetite for pushing through this kind of radical rethinking of business' purpose and a recurring question in this book is to what extent the ambitions of some regarding corporate responsibility can be realized without such reform. Nonetheless, we should not ignore the possibility that society is at the threshold of major change. This is certainly the belief of some who see the future of business as closely intertwined with climate change and who hold that this will—in contrast with models of gradual, linear change in the past—precipitate dramatic, unpredictable,

Box 14.3 **Principles of the redesigned corporation**

1 The purpose of the corporation is to harness private interests in the service of the public good.

2 Corporations shall accrue fair profits for shareholders, but not at the expense of the legitimate interests of other stakeholders.

3 Corporations shall operate sustainably to meet the needs of the present generation, without compromising the ability of future generations to meet theirs.

4 Corporations shall distribute their wealth equitably among those who contribute to its creation.

5 Corporations shall be governed in a manner that is participatory, transparent, ethical, and accountable.

6 Corporate rights shall not supersede or weaken the rights of natural persons to govern themselves.

(Source: White, 2005)

non-linear change. If non-linear theory is true, it could fundamentally affect the way in which we approach the world, causing policymakers and corporate managers to base their assumptions not on the expectations of gradual, predictable growth that justify a focus on efficiency and optimization, but rather on the new realities of unpredictability and vulnerability that, in turn, will make areas such as resilience, sufficiency, and complexity the new focuses of management. In such an environment of upheaval, the future directions within corporate responsibility would be hugely influenced by how useful the discipline proved itself to be, in relation to the innovative approaches to management practice, technology, and policy that would be required.

Among the criticisms of corporate responsibility is that it only tinkers at the edges of these major societal issues and trends, and has so far lacked the rigour (of theory and practice) to address the most important dimensions of the business–society relationship. With reference to climate change, for example, some of the most demonstrable changes in business practice in recent years relate to eco-efficiency, but these are minor variations to the established models of business that do little to tackle what some argue are the fundamental questions about capitalism's role in ensuring the sustainability of the earth's carrying capacity. Indeed, it can be argued that the question at the heart of corporate responsibility and its different forms that will surface over the coming years is whether capitalism itself is sustainable. For those who conclude that it is, corporate responsibility may be the discipline that allows them to consider if, and what, changes are needed to the capitalist model; for those who conclude that it is not, it remains to be seen if the frameworks and models within the corporate responsibility umbrella prove to be useful, obstructive, or irrelevant to the new paradigm.

CASE STUDY 14

Google—global struggles and responsibilities

'Don't be evil.' These are the opening words of Google's code of conduct. Founded in 1998, the company behind the world's most used internet search engine has revenues of over US$ 23 billion. It employs nearly 20,000 people, only 250 of whom are at corporate HQ in Mountain View, California.

Google has joined Hoover as one of the few brands that have become a verb. But as a premier citizen in cyberspace, Google faces unique responsibility challenges. First, there is the conventional problem of market dominance: Google has the world's most used search engine that is the backbone of the advertising business that generate most of the firm's revenue. In this sense, Google shares the same issues that in previous eras faced Standard Oil, De Beers, and the British East India Company. At the same time, Google's rise has been portrayed as way of undermining the dominance of another Information Technology giant, Microsoft, and its public acceptance as a brand is evident in places from the blogosphere to Simpson's cartoons.

Google added to its kudos in some quarters by its stand on information access in China. Since 2005, Google and the Chinese government have tussled over the data Google's search engine provides. The government has demanded that links it has censored such as the 1989 Tiananmen Square protest should not appear on Google, and moreover that Google should hand over information about the sites alleged dissidents are visiting. Early on Google seemed to comply, but in 2009 it threatened to pull out of the Chinese market after largescale attempts to hack into messages on the company's Gmail service, and to steal proprietary code. The hacking was particularly sensitive because in 2006, Yahoo! Had handed over personal data from a Chinese journalist who ended up serving a prison sentence. The US government was increasingly insistent that US companies needed to think about the human rights aspects of their businesses.

Google's stand in China brought protests from the Chinese government, but was well-received in many other parts of the world which saw the company making a stand for freedom of expression despite the business costs. However, some said Google was simply looking for a way out of the Chinese market where it had been second-bested by local competitor, Baidu. Some speculated that it was a way of deflecting attention from other Google problems. Its Street View service, photographing entire neighbourhoods and making them available on the web, had been criticized as an aid to burglars. The publishing of email accounts on its Buzz social networking service had become the latest in a line of concerns about the amount of information Google collects and that gets used. The company was also being criticized for its tax avoidance policies which, for instance, saw earnings shifted from its British to its Irish subsidiary.

A further example of concerns about Google's hold over data is Google Book Search (GBS). At first sight, GBS is another useful innovation: Google has digitized over ten million books, giving it the potential to become the largest library in the world. Some of these are copyrighted and in print, so GBS would make them available in digital formats and act as little more than a printer. Some are copyrighted and out of print, often with unidentified rightsholders. Under a proposed settlement, authors would have to opt out rather than opt in to deals with GBS. Google's aim is to become the largest player in digital publishing, raising concerns about pricing, and also the use of data obtained about book users.

Google has sought an agreement about the ownership and use of data in a New York district court. Given that the case has worldwide ramifications for access to information, the fact it is being tried in a minor court has itself raised suspicions. The French and German governments have asked that the settlement Google proposes be rejected in its entirety, condemning the proposed settlement for sanctioning the 'uncontrolled, autocratic concentration of power in a single corporate entity.'

At present, a decision is still pending on GBS, and Google is still negotiating over its position in China.

(Sources: Waters, 2010; Wines, 2010; Darnton, 2009; Watts, 2009)

Questions

1 Google aspires to provide a new model of business.

    a What are the features of Google's code of conduct, and are they distinct?—see **investor.google.com/conduct.html**.

    b What are the challenges for a cyberspace-based company compared, for example, to a conventional retailer or publishing company?

    c What are the drivers of Google's emphasis on responsibility?

2 Google has developed a strong reputation as a responsible company, but has also been criticized.

    a What do you think Google is doing that marks it out as a responsible company?

    b What aspects of the company raise questions about the ethos of Don't Be Evil?

    c What should the company do in future to be a corporate responsibility pace-setter?

3 In this chapter, we have set out various future trends and directions in corporate responsibility.

    a What does the case of Google tell us about the role of business in society?

    b What significant contributions is the Google Foundation making to social entrepreneurship and sustainability?—see google.org

    c What aspects of Google's business have the greatest impact on society and the environment? Is the company addressing these adequately?

SUMMARY

There are many elements to the corporate responsibility universe, as we have seen throughout this book. The indications are that this firmament will grow larger in the coming years for two reasons: first, there are pressing social and environmental issues that represent genuine challenges for both sustainability and global justice; second, there is an increasing expectation from different sectors of society that business will help to meet those challenges.

The future course of corporate responsibility will, to a large extent, be determined by how business' obligations to involve itself in major societal issues, such as climate change, demographic change, and global poverty, are defined and realized. No single institution will dictate how business responds: rather, as with other areas of corporate responsibility, the trends that emerge will be decided in various arenas of conflict, contestation, and collaboration. The growing power of multinational enterprise will be a significant factor, in terms of the resources and influence that major corporations possess, and the way in which they act as a pole star for both public protest and aspiration. Moreover, struggles within the corporate world—not least the role of private equity funds as owners of what were hitherto publicly traded companies—will affect how ideas of corporate responsibility evolve.

Government responses both to the mega-trends affecting global society and to the changing form of the corporation will also significantly influence what happens in the name of corporate responsibility. In some areas, such as that of flexible labour markets, it would appear that many governments are comfortable encouraging voluntary approaches and relaxing regulations; in other areas, however, notably that of climate change, some governments appear reluctant to rely on non-mandatory solutions. Given this situation, defining corporate responsibility in terms of voluntary actions seems likely to be increasingly less useful. This does not mean that non-mandatory approaches will be unimportant, and there are various ways in which corporate responsibility as management practice may be refined and enhanced over the coming years. Equally, there are strong signs of new types of approach gaining prominence, some of which (e.g. social entrepreneurship) will constitute free market responses to societal needs and others (e.g. sustainable consumption and production) that are likely to require significant government intervention.

One of the major trends around corporate responsibility will, however, be less to do with management practice or government intervention, and more about the way in which we consider the role of business itself. Many of the current criticisms of corporate responsibility relate to how the prerogatives of the modern corporation determine its societal role. For some, this severely limits what business can do and, in important instances, causes business to act in ways that are counter to the overall societal good. This will remain the case, it is argued, until the corporate purpose is altered to reflect the rights, duties, and obligations of business as a citizen. There is by no means a consensus that such a radical shift should happen: some argue that this kind of philosophical reflection will divert attention away from the strength of current approaches as pragmatic management responses; others, that society should resist the notion of legal entities such as companies being thought of as citizens.

In terms of corporate responsibility as a discipline, there is no right or wrong answer to this type of debate. (Indeed, the weakness of recent corporate responsibility debates may be that thinkers have been too willing to champion either theory or practice as if they are mutually opposed, and their inability to consider reflexively what underlies this division.) Whether we are thinking about the chartered trading companies of the eighteenth and nineteenth centuries, the corporate philanthropists that emerged during the Industrial Revolution, the European cooperative movement, the place of international companies in twentieth-century banana republics, the sense of social obligation that is central to some of the most successful examples of business in Japan, South Korea, and Germany, or the denial of responsibility to anyone other than shareholders that dictated much of corporate strategy in the 1980s and 1990s, we are constantly reminded that, regardless of what we choose to call it, the role of business in society is fundamental both to business and to the world at large. This will not change, regardless of what names we choose to assign to the pantheon of issues, practices, and hypotheses that have relevance to the business–society relationship. Future trends in corporate responsibility will not be determined by names, but by the discourse that evolves around the role of business and the relevance of corporate responsibility as a discipline, as a profession, as an antagonist, as a protagonist, or as a commentator in relation to that discourse.

FURTHER READING

VISIT THE WEBSITE for links to useful sources of further information

Take your learning further: Online Resource Centre **www.oxfordtextbooks.co.uk/orc/blowfield_murray2e/**

Visit the Online Resource Centre which accompanies this book to enrich your understanding of this chapter.

Students: explore web links and further reading suggestions. Keep up to date with the latest developments by undertaking web exercises.

Lecturers: you will find additional case studies, including one on the topic of Blended investing—new approaches to balancing financial and social returns on, for use in class or assessment. Show your students trailers from films related to Corporate Responsibility, and use images from the book in your PowerPoint slides.

- Accenture and UN Global Compact, 2010, *A New Era of Sustainability*, New York, Accenture and UN Global Compact.
  800 plus CEOs give their impressions of what sustainability means to their business.

- Green, S. 2009, *Good Value: Reflections on Money, Morality and an Uncertain World*, Allen Lane, London.

  HSBC boss reflects on the role of business and the importance of responsibility.

- Greenfield, K, 2006, *The Failure of Corporate Law: Fundamental Flaws and Progressive Possibilities*, Chicago, IL: University of Chicago Press.

  Arguments for a radical overhaul of company law.

- Henriques, A, 2007, *Corporate Truth: The Limits to Transparency*, London: Earthscan.

  An exploration of the limits of transparency in the contemporary corporate world and arguments about how far to push the boundaries.

- Hollender, J and Breen, B, 2010, *The Responsibility Revolution: How the Next Generation of Businesses Will Win*, San Francisco: Jossey-Bass.

  Popular corporate responsibility entrepreneur provides admittedly USA-biased insights into trends in innovation, social entrepreneurship, and investment.

ENDNOTES

[1] International Panel on Climate Change fourth assessment, online at **www.ipcc.ch**.

[2] Bloom and Canning, 2006.

[3] This analysis draws heavily on the series of lectures on the global financial crisis and developing countries by Valpy FiztGerald at Queen Elizabeth House, Oxford, May 2010.

[4] ETI, 2007.

[5] Bradley Googins, personal communication, 14 August 2006.

[6] Among the organizations receiving corporate funding to a significant degree are the International Business Leaders Forum, Accountability, Business for Social Responsibility, the Center for Corporate Citizenship, the Conference Board, the World Economic Forum, Harvard Kennedy School of Government, and Sustainability.

[7] Barrientos and Smith, 2007.

[8] Pio, 2005.

[9] See, e.g. Hughes and Demetrious, 2006; Blowfield, 2004.

[10] Total money in SRI funds 2005 = £6.1bn; total money in hedge funds 2006 = $1.786 trillion. Based on figures from **www.eiris.org and HedgeFund.net**—accessed 19 March 2007.

[11] HSBC estimates presented by Nick Robins, London Business School, 27 February 2009.

[12] McCarthy, 2006.

[13] McCarthy, 2006; Gascoigne, 2007.

[14] See also Chapter 11.

[15] **www.altenergystocks.com**—accessed 21 January 2007.

[16] Hesse, 2006.

[17] Lydenberg, 2005.

[18] Bahgwati, cited in Holliday et al., 2002, p 17.

[19] Benjamin Heineman in *Wall Street Journal*, 2005; Weiser and Zadek, 2000.

[20] Forum for the Future, 2006.

[21] Holliday et al., 2002.

[22] WBCSD, 2006.

[23] WBCSD, 2006, p 9.

[24] See, e.g. Dyllick and Hockerts, 2002, on the need to move beyond eco-efficiency to 'socio-efficiency' and to factor not only efficiency, but also effectiveness, into social and environmental performance; see also the quotes from executives on the dangers to capitalism of not considering the role of business, cited in Blowfield and Googins, 2007.

[25] Wackernagel et al., 1996.

[26] CPI, 2007.

[27] See www.lehmanreport.jenner.com/—accessed 29 June 2010.

[28] Bogle, 2005.

[29] See, e.g. contributions to *Business and Society*; alternative constructs of the corporation on the Corporation 2020 website; the work of authors such as Plender, 2003, and Greenfield, 2006.

■ APPENDIX

Corporate responsibility information resources

Here are some of the most well-known newsletters, magazines, and web resources offering regular news, analysis, and thinking on corporate responsibility. We have provided dedicated web links where these are available, but you should note that some of these online resources are available only by subscription.

Readers should also check the occasional coverage of corporate responsibility issues in management journals (such as the *Harvard Business Review*), development and economics journals (such as the *Third World Quarterly* and *International Affairs*), and the mainstream media (such as the *Financial Times* and *The Economist*).

Accountability Forum   Practitioner-oriented journal, focusing on accountability for sustainable development; published by Greenleaf Publishing.

Brooklyn Bridge-TBLI Group e-newsletter   Comprising articles and features on the triple bottom line and sustainability; online at www.tbli.org/index-newsletter.html.

Business and Human Rights Resource Center   Web-based resource with links to coverage of discrimination, environment, poverty and development, labour, access to medicines, health and safety, security, and trade; online at www.business-humanrights.org.

Business and Society   Academic journal, focusing on social issues and ethics, and their impact and influence on organizations; published by Sage and sponsored by the International Association for Business and Society; online at www.bas.sagepub.com.

Business Ethics   Quarterly academic journal debating issues of business ethics; published by Blackwell Publishing.

Business Ethics Magazine   Magazine of Corporate Responsibility Officers, a professional association; online at www.business-ethics.com.

Business Ethics Quarterly   Academic journal bringing different disciplinary perspectives to bear on the general subject of the application of ethics to the international business community; published by the Society for Business Ethics.

CasePlace   Collection of corporate responsibility-related case studies; online at www.caseplace.org.

The Chronicle of Philanthropy   Newspaper focusing on corporate philanthropy; online at www.philanthropy.com.

Chronos   E-learning tutorial on the business case for sustainable development; online at www.sdchronos2.org.

Corporate Citizenship Briefing Magazine for corporate responsibility news and analysis; published by Corporate Citizenship Company; online at **www.ccbriefing.co.uk**.

Corporate Governance Academic journal, focusing on international business and society; published by Emerald.

CorporateRegister.com Online collection of corporate responsibility reports; online at **www.corporateregister.com**.

Corpwatch.com Online information resource monitoring corporate behaviour and malfeasance; online at **www.corpwatch.com**.

Critical Perspectives on International Business Academic journal, presenting social science perspectives on international business and society; published by Emerald.

CSR and government British government website devoted to CSR information; online at **www.societyandbusiness.gov.uk**.

CSR Asia Online resource offering information on corporate responsibility in Asia; online at **www.csr-asia.com**.

CSRWatch Web-based media service offering criticisms of corporate responsibility; online at **www.csrwatch.com**.

CSRWire Web-based resource featuring corporate responsibility news and press releases from publicly traded corporations; online at **www.csrwire.com**.

E-Business Ethics.com Online resource offering information on business ethics, corporate citizenship, and organizational compliance; hosted by Colorado State University; online at **www.e-businessethics.com**.

Eldis Information gateway to web-based resources on globalization and international development, including special section on corporate responsibility; online at **www.eldis.org**.

Ethical Corporation Monthly magazine featuring corporate responsibility news and analysis in both print and online versions; free email newsletter also available; online at **www.ethicalcorp.com**.

Ethical Performance Monthly newsletter on corporate responsibility and socially responsible investment; online at **www.ethicalperformance.com**.

ETHICOMP Journal Journal on computer ethics and social responsibility, connected to the ETHICOMP conference series; online at **www.ccsr.cse.dmu.ac.uk/journal/home.html**.

Faith in Business Quarterly Journal relating Christian faith and values to the business world; published by the Ridley Hall Foundation and Industrial Christian Fellowship; online at **www.fibq.org**.

Global Corruption Report Annual report focusing on the consequences of corruption; published by Transparency International; online at **www.transparency.org/publications/gcr**.

Governancefocus.com   Web-based resource offering information on worldwide corporate and board governance issues; online at www.governancefocus.com.

GreenBiz.com   Free web-based resource for companies seeking information on environmental business practices; online at www.greenbiz.com.

Green Money Journal   Newsletter offering resources and contacts for environmentally and socially responsible investing; online at www.greenmoneyjournal.com.

Greener Management International   Management journal focusing on strategic environmental and sustainability issues; published by Greenleaf Publishing.

ID21   Online information service featuring links to research on globalization and international development, plus a series of issues Insights papers; online at www.id21.org.

Journal of Business Ethics   Academic journal, covering ethical issues related to business; published by Kluwer Academic Publishers.

Journal of Corporate Citizenship   Quarterly academic journal dedicated to corporate responsibility; published by Greenleaf Publishing.

New Academy Review   Now defunct quarterly journal that addressed strategic and policy issues related to corporate responsibility; online at www.new-academy-review.com.

Oneworld.net   Web-based community and resource focusing on globalization and development; online at www.oneworld.net.

Origo Cross-Sector News   News service focusing on the intersection between business and social innovation; online at www.origonews.com.

SD Gateway   Online resource offering information from members of the Sustainable Development Communications Network; online at www.sdgateway.net.

SocialFunds.com   Web-based resource for individual socially responsible investors; online at www.socialfunds.com.

Socially Responsible Investing Compass   Online resource featuring all existing green and ethical retail funds and indices in Europe; online at www.sricompass.org.

Society and Business Review   Practitioner-oriented journal, aiming to assist businesses in enhancing their commitment to societal purposes; published by Emerald.

Stanford Social Innovation Review   Journal focusing on strategies for non-profit organizations, foundations, and socially responsible businesses; online at www.ssireview.org.

SustainableBusiness.com   Online resource offering information and links for environmentally oriented businesses; hosted by Green Dream Jobs, a sustainable business jobs service; online at www.sustainablebusiness.com.

■ GLOSSARY

accountability   The obligation to render an account of one's actions.

auditing   The evaluation of an organization in order to establish the validity and reliability of information about that organization. Social auditing relates to the validity and reliability of information about a company's social performance (e.g. its impact on local communities, its relationship with stakeholders); environmental auditing relates to its performance in relation to the environment (e.g. emissions, waste management).

best-in-class screening   An approach to positive screening in socially responsible investment that involves selecting the best within a given sector of investments, based on certain criteria.

bottom of the pyramid   (also known as base of the pyramid) The potential commercial market provided by the six billion people who live on less than two US dollars a day. Developed by CK Prahalad and Stuart Hart, American business theorists, the concept regards poor people as a seriously underserved market that might be the engine of the next wave of global trade and economic prosperity. Examples include microfinance (the provision of innovative financial services to poor people in ways that help their development), Cemex's affordable housing programme, and Hindustan Lever's marketing of iodized salt to rural communities. Bottom of the pyramid is one of the most discussed areas of social entrepreneurship.

bribery   The giving of favour to influence another's action. (*See* corruption.)

Brundtland Commission   (formally, the World Commission on Environment and Development) Convened in 1983 by the United Nations and widely known by the name of its chair, Gro Harlem Brundtland, the Commission proved to be a highly influential enquiry into environmental deterioration and the challenge of sustainable development. Its definition of sustainable development—development that meets the needs of the present without compromising the ability of future generations to meet their own needs—is frequently cited in discussions about the role of business in sustainability.

business and society   An area of academic enquiry (normally undertaken by social scientists), concerning the relationship between business and wider society. Long established, with its own journals and professional association, the themes of business and society have recently been more widely acknowledged by corporate responsibility scholars and practitioners. The consultancy firm McKinsey and Co is among those offering services that will help companies to understand business and society issues.

business ethics   Typically regarded as a strand of applied ethics, focusing on the ethical issues facing a company and its officers. The US branch of the field, in particular, is primarily concerned with helping individuals to navigate the ethical dilemmas that arise in a commercial context. There is, to a degree, an alternative European approach that is more concerned with the role of business in society, and with the ethical duties and obligations that arise from this. Some would argue that corporate responsibility is a subset of business ethics.

capitalism   An economic system under which the means of production are privately owned, and the price of inputs and outputs are determined by markets within which people engage on a free and voluntary basis, and within which goods and services are sold with a view to making a profit. Adam Smith, the eighteenth-century philosopher, was the first to describe comprehensively the free market capitalist system in his books *The Theory of Moral Sentiments* and *The Wealth of Nations*. He recognized that an economic system could not be treated as something separate from society, and hence had implications for the way we live. Issues relating to the moral dimensions of capitalism—such as the responsibilities, duties, and obligations of business—in many ways underlie corporate responsibility.

capital markets   The financial markets on which long-term debt and equity securities are traded. The role of these markets in influencing corporate behaviour is an area of debate within corporate responsibility.

change management   (also known as transformation management) A systematic approach to managing change within an organization that includes adapting to, controlling, and effecting change. Within management practice, corporate responsibility is often described from a change management perspective.

civil regulation   A theory positing that companies are not only regulated by government, but increasingly by the norms and actions of civil society that control a business' licence to operate. This is most evident in the role that civil society organizations play in affecting company behaviour irrespective of legal requirements. In the 1990s, for example, trade unions and non-government organizations were able to pressurize Nike into paying attention to working conditions in its supply chain, despite there having been no government pressure to do so.

civil society   Historically, the term has meant private interests that are distinct from those of the state, but in the corporate responsibility context, it tends to refer more specifically to the uncoerced collective action around shared interests, purposes, and values of institutions that are distinct from those of the state and the market (e.g. civil society organizations).

civil society organizations (CSOs)   Non-government, non-business organizations with a social function. CSOs include non-government organizations and free trade unions, and are an important constituency both in influencing corporate behaviour (civil regulation) and in conducting partnerships.

climate change   Significant change in measures of climate, such as temperature, or precipitation, that last for an extended period (i.e. decades or longer). These changes can be the result of natural factors and processes, such as alterations in ocean circulation, or of human activity, such as deforestation and burning fossil fuels. (*See also* global warming.)

code of conduct/practice   A set of principles, typically with accompanying criteria, that set out a company's commitment to maintaining a standard in a specific area of its operations. Corporate responsibility codes set standards regarding the natural environment, labour, corporate governance, money laundering, bribery and corruption, human rights, and corporate responsibility reporting principles. While codes may make mention of legal requirements (e.g. minimum wage, toxic emissions), they are themselves voluntary in nature.

corporate accountability   A company's moral or legal obligation to account for its actions and performance to its stakeholders. In the corporate responsibility context, it is also often discussed in terms of the capacity of those stakeholders to influence company actions.

corporate citizenship   At times used synonymously with corporate responsibility, CSR, etc., but (in the USA, in particular) can specifically refer to discretionary initiatives undertaken by a company, such as employee volunteering and corporate philanthropy.

corporate governance   Conventionally refers to the system by which companies are directed and controlled for the benefit of shareholders. In some jurisdictions, the scope of benefit includes multiple stakeholders, and, in recent years, there has been renewed interest in the balance between economic and social goals, and between individual and communal goals as the object of governance, as per the 2002 Cadbury Report.

corporate governance framework   The regulatory structure, designed to safeguard investors' assets, within which the rules for the running of companies are outlined.

corporate malfeasance   Misconduct by a company or by an officer of a company.

corporate philanthropy   Proportion of corporate revenues donated for philanthropic purposes. (In the USA, the amount is typically 1 per cent.) Once associated with somewhat arbitrary donations to worthy causes, there is increasing focus on strategic philanthropy, under which donations are targeted towards areas that are synergistic with the company's interests or competencies.

corporate reporting   The act of publicly reporting on a company's performance. In the corporate responsibility context, emphasis has been placed on the publishing of social, environmental, and sustainability reports that, in some cases, form part of the company's annual report to shareholders.

corporate responsibility   An umbrella term embracing theories and practices relating to how business manages its relationship with society.

corporate social performance   The way in, and degree to, which a business organization's principles of social responsibility and related processes motivate actions on behalf of a company and deliver outcomes of societal benefit.

corporate social responsiveness   The response of companies to the demands that they address their social responsibilities. The term was introduced by scholars in the mid-1970s to denote a greater focus on corporate responsibility as an area of management practice, in contrast to more theoretical debates about the meaning of responsibility that had previously dominated academic thinking.

corruption   The misuse of power associated with a public or corporate office for the purpose of personal gain. It includes bribery, which is the giving of favour to influence another's action.

defensive corporate responsibility   Actions taken by a company or industry to protect its reputation and to reduce its risk in relation to aspects of its non-financial responsibility.

deterritorialization   The detachment of social practices from a specific place, so that the relationship between culture and geographical location is no longer paramount. The phenomenon is a consequence of the social and political processes associated with globalization.

developing country   A country with low per capita income relative to the world average. In many developing countries, incomes can be less than two US dollars a day. (*Compare* emerging economy.)

eco-efficiency   Achieving efficiencies through the reduced use of natural resources and energy, fewer harmful emissions, greater recycling and reuse, increased lifespan, and the increased use of renewable resources in the design, manufacture, and consumption/use of products.

economic globalization   (also referred to as liberal economic globalization) Increased world integration as a result of free trade, and financial, technology, and labour flows. The terms is sometimes treated as synonymous with globalization, but, strictly speaking, refers to only one feature of that phenomenon.

embedded economy   Stemming from Polanyi's argument (1944) that a feature of capitalism is the way in which the economy is treated as something separate from society ('*disembedded*'), whereas the interests of justice and prosperity are best served when the economy is interrelated with social, political, and religious institutions ('*embedded*'). Corporate responsibility (theory and practice) can be interpreted as concerned with re-embedding business so that it is more than simply an economic actor.

emerging economy   A country that, based on GDP and indicators of human development, is considered to be on a path towards being included among the wealthy/developed nations in the foreseeable future. (*Compare* developing country.)

engagement   An approach, used in responsible investment, by which investors become involved with the companies in which they invest in order to influence the activities, behaviours, and operations of those companies.

environmental auditing   The evaluation of an organization to ascertain the validity and reliability of information about that organization's claims concerning its performance in relation to the environment (e.g. emissions, waste management).

environmental ethics   Enquiry into the ethical relationship of human beings to the environment and non-human entities, and into the value and moral status of these.

environmental impact assessment   Assessment of a company or facility's environmental consequences, normally focusing on inputs and outputs within a particular geographical location.

environmental, social, governance (ESG)   Commonly used term that captures the areas of non-financial performance with which corporate responsibility management practice is often concerned.

ethical sourcing   A company's recognition of its responsibilities for the social and environmental conditions under which products are manufactured/grown within its supply chain. Typically, this involves the application of a code of practice as a condition of doing business with suppliers, although it may also involve engaging with suppliers to improve their capacity to meet that standard.

ethical theory   Theories of what is right and wrong, based on reason. (*Compare* moral theory.)

ethical trade   An umbrella term for a variety of approaches under which companies take responsibility for the conditions under which products are manufactured/grown within their supply chains. Includes ethical sourcing, fairtrade, and sourcing from sustainably managed forests and fisheries.

fairtrade   A trading partnership established as a contribution to achieving greater equity in international trade through, for example, ensuring a price paid to the producer that is greater than the cost of production, a surplus paid to the producer group (not the individual) for investing in social development activities, and a long-term relationship between producer and buyer. Originally intended to help small producers in developing countries, larger producers are now included, and, for these, the emphasis is on worker rights. Fairtrade takes different forms, but is most widely associated with the Fairtrade label, which certifies that an item has been produced and traded according to the principles set out by the Fairtrade Labelling Organizations International (FLO International).

fair wage   (also called a living wage) A wage sufficient to provide the basic needs (food, shelter, education, health care), with some discretionary income, for a worker and his or her immediate dependents within a reasonable working week (typically, not more than forty hours). It is often a provision in codes of labour practice and workers rights, although it is sometimes replaced with a minimum wage, which is a legally defined wage that should reflect a fair wage (although, in practice, it may not).

financing sustainability   An emerging facet of corporate responsibility, dealing with the interrelationship between companies' corporate responsibility objectives and the behaviour of the finance community (investors, analysts, fund managers, etc.). At its core is the perceived mismatch between the long-term nature of sustainability and the short-term orientation of much investment activity.

free trade union   A type of trade union that is able to operate without interference from employers and government.

global commons   Natural assets important to human well-being that are outside national jurisdiction (e.g. the oceans; outer space; the atmosphere).

global governance   Historically, governance has referred to the exercise of political, economic, and administrative authority in the management of the affairs of a country or other locality. Globalization and accompanying phenomena, such as deterritorialization, present particular challenges for governance, because important areas of life cannot be managed by the nation state alone. Hence, increasing concern is paid to global governance, including the governing of global commons, such as the atmosphere, and the behaviour of multinational companies. The institutions for addressing such issues are, however, still weak and incomplete for the most part, giving rise to what some see as a governance deficit. The emergence of corporate responsibility as an area of business practice can be seen as a contribution to filling that deficit by making companies pay attention to their global social and environmental performance.

globalization   A term used to refer to the increasing global connectivity, integration, and interdependence in the economic, social, technological, cultural, and political dimensions of existence. It is often used to focus on particular aspects of the phenomenon (e.g. global cultural homogenization, economic globalization, the spread of particular ideas such as democracy and free markets), but what marks it out as historically unique is the interplay of its different facets, which presents all manner of challenges for global governance, justice, and sustainability.

Global Reporting Initiative   The custodian body behind an international effort to create a common framework for the voluntary reporting of the economic, environmental, and social impact of business' and other organizations' activities. This framework is set out in the GRI Guidelines.

global warming   The average increase in atmospheric temperature near the earth's surface and in the troposphere, which can contribute to changes in global climate patterns (*see also* climate change).

government   A particular group of legitimate representatives of the state.

health and safety   (also known as occupational health and safety; workplace health and safety) The dimension of corporate responsibility relating to the health and safety of people at work. Some of the most measurable outcomes of corporate responsibility programmes have been in this area.

human rights   Basic entitlements accorded to all human beings. There are significant differences of opinion as to what these rights should be, although the most commonly mentioned ones in a corporate responsibility context concern legal, civil, and political rights, especially those set out in the Universal Declaration of Human Rights.

human rights impact assessment   An assessment of the human rights dimensions of a company's operations, including, for example, issues of the rights of indigenous peoples, intimidation of local communities by company security forces, and the fundamental rights of workers in the workplace.

Industrial Revolution   The historical period, lasting throughout most of the nineteenth century, during which the economies of the USA and many European nations shifted from an agricultural to a manufacturing base, with an accompanying strengthening of the capitalist economic system.

integrated business strategy In a corporate responsibility context, 'integration' refers to the embedding of corporate responsibility issues into mainstream business practice. The consequence of this is that corporate responsibility becomes a business driver that creates value for the company at the same time as the company creates value for wider society. (*Compare* corporate philanthropy.)

international development The policies and programmes undertaken by government and non-government agencies in developed and developing economies, with the intention of alleviating poverty and creating sustainable livelihoods for people in developing countries.

liberal economic globalization See economic globalization.

liberal economics A theory of economics that is rooted in the belief that individuals' economic actions based largely on self-interest ultimately make the greatest contribution to the common good. Some see globalization as synonymous with economic liberalism, particularly its free flow of capital, goods, services, and (more contentiously) labour with minimal government or other non-market interference.

licence to operate The right granted to a company (or other organization) to carry out its business. In the corporate responsibility context, licence to operate usually refers to the licence granted by a community or other stakeholder group, rather than by a formal regulatory authority.

limited liability Form of incorporation under which the liability of a partner or investor is limited to the value of his or her shares in the company. The introduction of this legal concept in the nineteenth century greatly affected the role of business, the nature of investment, and the notion of risk.

living wage See fair wage.

microfinance Financial model that involves making small loans available to help poor people who are denied access through conventional lending channels, typically towards their starting, or expanding, a small business.

Millennium Development Goals (MDGs) A set of eight targets (including eradicating extreme poverty and hunger, improving maternal health, and ensuring environmental sustainability) that were adopted by all countries represented in the UN General Assembly, and which are to be achieved by 2015. The targets commit countries to a particular vision of international development and are widely used as a framework for measuring development progress.

minimum wage A legally defined wage that should reflect a fair wage (although, in practice, it may not). (*See also* fair wage.)

moral theory Theories of right and wrong, based on norms and custom. (*Compare* ethical theory.)

the Natural Step An approach to sustainability that is based on four systematic principles, relating to people's capacity to meet their needs, and aspects of the interaction between humanity and the earth. Karl-Henrik Robèrt first proposed the approach in 1989, following the publication of the Report of the Brundtland Commission.

negative screening An approach to socially responsible investment that involves the excluding of certain companies based on their poor performance against corporate governance, social, environmental, or ethical criteria. (*Compare* positive screening.)

New Deal   The legislative and administrative programme, established under FD Roosevelt's administration during the 1930s, which was intended to promote economic recovery and social reform following the Great Depression. It marked the end of a period during which the theories of liberal economics had gone largely unquestioned, particularly in the USA.

non-financial performance   Aspects of business performance not normally addressed in financial reporting and auditing, including wider environmental, social, and governance indicators.

non-government organization (NGO)   A loose term distinguishing a range of organizations that are concerned with particular social and environmental objectives from profit-making organizations and government agencies. Commonly called 'non-governmental organizations', some actually perform a governmental function by way of their role in influencing the process of governing (*see also* civil regulation).

occupational health and safety   See health and safety.

offensive corporate responsibility   Policies, strategies, and programmes undertaken with the specific intention of addressing societal needs in order to gain commercial advantage. (*Compare* defensive corporate responsibility.)

partnership   A collaboration between two or more parties conducted with the intention of realizing mutually acceptable or beneficial outcomes that are greater than those which any single party could achieve. Stakeholder partnership has become an important area of corporate responsibility management practice.

performance standard   A code of conduct or similar instrument by means of which achievement is largely measured in terms of specific outcomes, such as workers being paid a fair wage, the eradication of workplace discrimination, etc. Codes of labour practice, organic standards, and good agricultural practice guidelines are examples of this type of standard. (*Compare* process standard.)

pioneer screening   An approach to positive screening in socially responsible investment that involves choosing the best-performing company against one specific criterion.

positive screening   An approach to socially responsible investment, under which companies are chosen based on their performance against corporate governance, social, environmental, or ethical criteria. Positive screening can be subdivided into best-in-class screening and pioneer screening. Conversely, SRI investors can use negative screening.

process standard   A code of conduct or similar instrument by means of which achievement is largely measured in terms of the process that an organization undergoes rather than fixed outcomes. The ISO 14000 series on environmental management and the AA1000 series are examples of this type of standard. (*Compare* performance standard.)

proxy voting   A method of voting at a company's annual general meeting on environmental, social, and governance issues.

reporting awards   Schemes offering awards for the quality of corporate reports.

reputation management   The aspect of management practice that is concerned with understanding perceptions of an organization's reputation, and the actions necessary to protect or enhance it. Reputation management has been identified as a significant driver of defensive corporate responsibility.

rights   Powers, privileges, or other entitlements that are assured by custom or law.

Rio Earth Summit   A meeting, in Rio de Janeiro in June 1992, of over a hundred heads of state, plus representatives of non-government organizations, business, and local government, which was the summit of an international discussion of environmental and development issues of the kind raised by the Brundtland Commission. It was the first time that a multi-sectoral dialogue had been conducted to address these issues, and resulted in leaders signing a number of important agreements, including the United Nations Framework Conventions on Climate Change (UNFCCC) and the Convention on Biological Diversity (CBD), the Rio Declaration on Environment and Development, and Agenda 21 (an international plan of action for achieving a more sustainable pattern of development in the twenty-first century). The meeting is highly significant in the history of contemporary corporate responsibility, because it recognized the importance of business–government–civil society cooperation in achieving sustainable development goals—something that was developed further at the 2002 World Summit on Sustainable Development.

risk management   The aspect of management practice that is concerned with understanding and acting upon the degree of risk presented to an organization by political, social, environmental, and economic factors. Risk is often seen as a driver of defensive corporate responsibility and is evident, for example, in the support of food companies for sustainable agriculture and fisheries.

screening   A strategy used in socially responsible investment. (*See also* positive screening.)

self-regulation   This refers to the practice of a company or other organization voluntarily putting constraints on what it does—e.g. through the adoption of a code of practice or adherence to voluntary guidelines—even though the constrained policy or action might be legal. Some see voluntary self-regulation as a defining feature of corporate responsibility.

shareholder activism   Actions taken by shareholders with the intention of improving corporate governance.

small and medium-sized enterprises (SMEs)   A classification of company that is normally based on number of employees (or, occasionally, on turnover). In the EU, a small enterprise employs less than 50 people and a medium one, less than 250; in the USA, the figures are higher, but still not more than 100 and 500 respectively. SMEs comprise the vast majority of businesses in the world (99 per cent in the EU) and account for the bulk of private sector employment generation.

social accounting   Accounting for the non-financial aspects of corporate reporting.

social and environmental ratings   The rating of companies for investment purposes, according to defined criteria for their social and/or environmental performance. Examples include the Domini 400 Social Index, the KLD Climate Change Index, the FTSE4Good Index series, and the Dow Jones Sustainability Indices.

social auditing   The evaluation of an organization to ascertain the validity and reliability of information about that organization's claims concerning its social performance.

social contract   The implied agreement between members of a society that defines and puts limits on the duties, responsibilities, and obligations of each member. Social contract theory is associated with the ethical theory of John Locke and underpins ideas about the company's licence to operate.

social entrepreneurship   An imprecise term used to refer to a wide range of organizations—both profit-making and non-profit—for which the primary purpose is to deliver social and/or environmental value in contrast with financial value.

social impact assessment   Assessment of the social consequences of a company or facility, normally focusing on inputs and outputs within a particular geographical location. (*Compare* environmental impact assessment and human rights impact assessment.)

socially responsible investment (SRI)   An approach to investing that considers the social, environmental, and ethical consequences of investments within the context of financial analysis.

social reporting   The reporting of the social and environmental aspects of corporate activity.

stakeholder   An entity with a stake in another organization, by virtue of the fact he, she or it is affected by, or has influence over, that organization. In corporate responsibility terms, 'stakeholder' usually refers to the stake that an individual or organization has in a company, and includes employees, local communities, shareholders, customers, and clients.

stakeholder dialogue   The convening of a discussion between a company and (all, or some of) its stakeholders.

stakeholder engagement   The managed process of interaction between a company and its stakeholders.

stakeholder management   The application of stakeholder theory to management practice. It includes stakeholder engagement, stakeholder dialogue, and stakeholder partnership.

stakeholder partnership   A partnership between a company and its stakeholders, intended to capitalize on their combined capabilities in pursuit of a particular purpose.

state   An organized political community, occupying a definite territory and governed by a sovereign government. In some corporate responsibility literature, the term 'state' is used interchangeably with government—but the terms are distinct.

strategic philanthropy   A form of corporate philanthropy, under which donations are targeted towards areas that are synergistic with the company's interests or competencies.

sustainability   Referring to those forms of human economic and cultural activity that can be conducted without long-term degradation of the resources that used. The term is often used interchangeably with sustainable development.

sustainable consumption and production   Continuous economic and social progress that respects the limits of the earth's ecosystems, and meets the needs and aspirations of everyone for a better quality of life—now, and for future generations.

sustainable development   According to the Brundtland Commission, which is the most widely known definition, this is human development to meet the needs of the present generation without compromising the ability of future generations to meet their own needs.

third-party verification statements   Statements made by third parties, verifying the content of corporate reports.

trade union   An association of workers in any trade, or allied trades, for the protection and furtherance of their interests in regard to wages, hours, and conditions of labour, and for the provision, from their common funds, of pecuniary assistance to the members during strikes, sickness, unemployment, old age, etc. There is an important distinction between free trade unions and yellow unions. (*Compare* workers' committee.)

transformation management   See change management.

triple bottom line   A framework for measuring company performance and added value, in terms of economic, social, and environmental parameters. Triple bottom line accounting is an extension of the conventional financial accounting framework to measure these additional areas of performance.

United Nations   A supranational organization founded in 1945, with the purposes of: (a) maintaining international peace and security; (b) developing friendly relations among nations; (c) cooperating in solving international economic, social, cultural, and humanitarian problems, and in promoting respect for human rights and fundamental freedoms; (d) acting as a centre through which nations can work jointly to attain those ends. It comprises member States, as well as bodies such as the General Assembly, Security Council, and the International Court of Justice, and it administers programmes to achieve its purpose through agencies such as the UN Development Programme, UN Environment Programme, and the International Labour Organization.

Universal Declaration of Human Rights   A 1948 UN Declaration—signed and ratified by most of the world's countries—that sets out a basic definition of universal human rights. The Declaration is often referred to in human rights and worker rights codes of conduct.

United Nations Global Compact   A United Nations-convened initiative to promote concrete and sustained action by business participants, to align their actions with broad UN social and environmental objectives, the Compact's ten principles, and the international Millennium Development Goals (MDGs). It aims to achieve this through: (a) learning forums to analyse case studies and examples of good practice; (b) global policy dialogues on the challenges of globalization; (c) multi-stakeholder collaborative development projects to further the MDGs; (d) support for new national networks, such as those in India and South Africa.

venture philanthropy   Application of the venture capital model of investment and the deployment of private equity to achieve social and environmental outcomes.

Washington Consensus   The set of policies that, during the 1980s and 1990s, became a condition of loans to countries from the World Bank. Countries were required to open their domestic markets to foreign competition, to limit state intervention (including income redistribution, public education, and welfare provision), and to establish policies that would promote a favourable business environment. The Consensus encouraged private foreign direct investment and encouraged countries—such as Indonesia and Mexico—to focus on export markets. Some saw it as responsible for creating the exploitive social and environmental conditions that, in turn, led to calls for greater corporate responsibility, especially in relation to multinational corporations.

welfare state   A system under which government seeks to provide an economic safety net for the general population (e.g. through unemployment, child, and disability benefits), and the opportunity for individual improvement (e.g. through health care and education). A feature of Communist Bloc countries, it also became widespread in Western Europe (especially after World War II), was mirrored in the US New Deal, and was a feature of many newly independent governments in Africa and Asia. It put a greater tax burden on business, in return for reducing the pressures on companies to take on social responsibilities. Dismantling of the welfare state was typically a condition of the Washington Consensus policies adopted by developing countries in the 1980s and 1990s.

World Commission on Environment and Development   See Brundtland Commission.

workers' committee   Sometimes treated as the equivalent of a trade union, but different, in that it brings together employees within a single company (rather than a trade). Some workers' committees are similar to yellow unions.

workplace health and safety   See health and safety.

yellow union   A type of trade union that is tightly controlled by parties other than union members.

■ BIBLIOGRAPHY

Aaronson, S.A., Reeves, J.T. & National Policy Association (U.S.) 2002, *Corporate responsibility in the global village: the role of public policy*, National Policy Association, Washington, D.C.

Abbott Laboratories 2005, *2004 Corporate citizenship report*, Abbott Laboratories, Chicago.

Abrami, R. 2003, "Worker rights and global trade: the US-Cambodia bilateral textile trade agreement", *Harvard Business School Case Study*.

ACCA 2008, *ACCA UK awards for sustainability reporting 2008: report of the judges*, Association of Chartered Certified Accountants, London.

ACCA 2005, *ACCA UK awards for sustainability reporting 2005: report of the judges*, ACCA, London.

Accountability 2006, *What assures?*, Accountability, London.

AccountAbility 2003, *Redefining Materiality: Practice and public policy for effective corporate reporting*, AccountAbility, London.

Accountability 2003, *The state of sustainability assurance*, Institue of Social and Ethical Accountability, London.

Accountability 2002, *AA1000 conversations: lessons from the early years (1999–2001)*, AccountAbility, London.

Ackerman, R.W. & Bauer, R.A. 1976, *Corporate social responsiveness: the modern dilemna [sic]*, Reston Pub. Co, Reston, Va.

Ackerman, B.A. 1980, *Social justice in the liberal state*, Yale University Press, New Haven.

Ackerman, B.A. & Alstott, A. 1999, *The stakeholder society*, Yale University Press, New Haven.

Action Aid 2005a, *Power hungry: six reasons to regulate global food corporations*, Action Aid, London.

Action Aid 2005b, *Rotten fruit*, Action Aid, London.

Adler, J. 2006, *Go-green*.

Aidt, T., Tzannatos, Z. & World Bank 2002, *Unions and collective bargaining: economic effects in a global environment*, World Bank, Washington, D.C.

Akumu, W. 2008, *M-PESA turning into a big virtual bank*, 8 April 2008 edn, Nairobi.

Alvesson, M. & Willmott, H. 2002, "Identity regulation as organizational control: producing the appropriate individual", *Journal of Management Studies*, vol. 39, no. 5, pp 619–644.

Amalric, F. & Hauser, J. 2005, "Economic drivers of corporate responsibility activities", *Journal of Corporate Citizenship*, vol. Winter 2005, no. 20, pp 27–38.

Ambachtsheer, J. 2005, *SRI: What Do Investment Managers Think?*, Mercer Investment Consulting, Toronto.

Amba-Rao, S.C. 1993, "Multinational corporate social responsibility, ethics, interactions and third world governments", *Journal of Business Ethics*, vol. 12, pp 553–572.

Amin, S. 1997, *Capitalism in the age of globalization: the management of contemporary society*, Zed Books, London; Atlantic Highlands, N.J.

Amnesty International 2005, *Contracting out of human rights: the Chad-Cameroon pipeline*.

Anderson, R.C. 1998, *Mid-course correction: toward a sustainable enterprise: The Interface model*, Peregrinzilla Press, Atlanta, Ga.

Anderson, R. 2003, 'Ethics ain't rocket science', Seattle Weekly, 6 August, online at www.seattleweekly.com.

Anderson, R. 2005, 'From CEO to cipher', Seattle Weekly, 9 March, online at www.seattleweekly.com.

Andrews, K. 1973, "Can the best corporations be made moral?", *Harvard Business Review*, pp 57–64.

Andriof, J. & McIntosh, M. 2001, *Perspectives on corporate citizenship*, Greenleaf, Sheffield.

Andriof, J., Waddock, S., Husted, B. & Rahman, S.S. 2002, *Unfolding stakeholder thinking vol. 1: theory, responsibility and engagement*, Greenleaf, Sheffield.

Andriof, J., Waddock, S.A., Husted, B. & Rahman, S.S. 2003, *Unfolding stakeholder thinking 2: relationships, communication, reporting and performance*, Greenleaf Pub., Sheffield UK.

Anshen, M. 1980, *Corporate strategies for social performance*, Macmillan, New York.

Arce, A. & Long, N. (eds) 2000, *Anthropology, development, and modernities: exploring discourses,* counter-tendencies, and violence, Routledge, London.

Arlidge, J. 2009, I'm doing God's work. Meet Mr Goldman Sachs, TimesOnline edn, London.

Arnold, D.G. & Hartman, L.P. 2003, "Moral imagination and the future of sweatshops", Business and Society Review, vol. 108, no. 4, pp 425–461.

Arnold, D.G. 2003, "Libertarian Theories of Corporation and Global Capitalism", Journal of Business Ethics, vol. 48, pp 155–173.

Ascoly, N., Oldenziel, J. & Zeldenrust, I. 2001, Overview of Recent Developments on Monitoring and Verification in the Garment and Sportswear Industry in Europe, Amsterdam.

Ascoly, N. & Zeldenrust, I. 2003, Considering complaints mechanisms, Centre for Research on Multinational Companies, Amsterdam.

Ashridge Centre for Business and Society 2005, A catalogue of CSR activities, Ashridge Centre for Business and Society, Berkhamsted.

Asmus, P. 2007, NGO engagement.

Asongu, J.J. "The History of Corporate Social Responsibility", Journal of Business and Public Policy, vol. 1, no. 2, pp 1–18.

Attfield, R. 1999, The ethics of the global environment, Purdue University Press, West Lafayette, Ind.

Attfield, R. & Wilkins, B. 1992, International justice and the third world: studies in the philosophy of development, Routledge, London New York.

Australian Government 2005, Corporate social responsibility discussion paper, Australian Government Corporations and Markets Advisory Committee, Canberra.

Avtonomov, V. 2006, "Balancing state, market and social justice: Russian experiences and lessons to learn", Journal of Business Ethics, vol. 66, no. 1, pp 3–9.

Ayres, C.E. 1946, The divine right of capital, Houghton Mifflin Company, Boston.

Bagehot, W. & Marshall, A. 1885, The postulates of English political economy, G. P. Putnam's sons, New York & London.

Baird, L., Post, J.E. & Mahon, J.F. 1990, Management: functions and responsibilities, Harper & Row, New York.

Bakan, J. 2004, The corporation: the pathological pursuit of profit and power, Free Press, New York.

Baker, M. 2002, The GRI—the will to succeed is not enough.

Baker, R.W. 2005, Capitalism's Achilles heel: dirty money and how to renew the free-market system; John Wiley & Sons, distributor, Hoboken, N.J.; Chichester.

Balch, O. 2005, CSR on the map.

Bales, K. 2004, Disposable people: new slavery in the global economy, Rev. edn, University of California Press, Berkeley.

Ballinger, J. 1992, "The new free trade heel: Nike's profits jump on the backs of Asian workers", Harper's Magazine, vol. 285, pp 46–47.

Ballinger, J. 2010, "The threat posed by 'corporate social responsibility' to trade union rights", in Fairtrade, corporate accountability and beyond, eds. K. MacDonald & S. Marshall, 1st edn, Ashgate, Farnham.

Ballinger, J. & Olsson, C. 1997, Behind the swoosh: the struggle of Indonesians making Nike shoes, Global Publications Foundation; Icda, Uppsala; Brussels.

Banerjee, S.B. 2001, "Managerial perceptions of corporate environmentalism: interpretations from industry and strategic implications for organizations", Journal of Management Studies, vol. 38, no. 4, pp 489–513.

Banerjee, S.B. & Prasad, A. 2008, "Introduction to the special issue on 'Critical reflections on management and organizations: a postcolonial perspective'", Critical Perspectives on International Business, vol. 4, no. 2/3, pp 90–98.

Bank of America "Corporate responsibility for social problems: a bibliography" in Bank of America, San Francisco, pp 4 v.

Bannock, G., Baxter, R.E. & Davis, E. 2003, Dictionary of economics, Bloomberg Press/Profile Books, Princeton, N.J.

Barmann, T.C. 2006, Glaxo settles Paxil complaint with 46 states.

Barnard, C.I. 1938, The functions of the executive, Harvard University Press, Cambridge, Mass.

Barnett, M.L. & Salomon, R.M. 2006, "Beyond dichotomy: The curvilinear relationship between social responsibility and financial performance", Strategic Management Journal, vol. 27, no. 11, pp 1101–1122.

Baron, D.P. 2002, Business and its environment, 4th edn, Prentice Hall, Upper Saddle River, N.J.

Barrera, A. 2000, "Social Principles as a Framework for Ethical Analysis (With an Application to the Tobin Tax)", Journal of Business Ethics, vol. 23, no. 4, pp 377–388.

Barrett, R. 1998, *Liberating the corporate soul: building a visionary organization*, Butterworth-Heinemann, Boston.

Barrientos, S., Dolan, C. & Tallontire, A. 2001, *Gender and Ethical Trade: a mapping of the issues in African horticulture*, Natural Resources Institute, Chatham.

Barrientos, S., Dolan, C. & Tallontire, A. 2003, "A Gendered Value Chain Approach to Codes of Conduct in African Horticulture", *World Development*, vol. 31, no. 9, pp 1511–1527.

Barry, B.M. 1989a, *Democracy, power, and justice: essays in political theory*, Clarendon Press, Oxford.

Barry, B.M. 1989b, *Theories of justice*, University of California Press, Berkeley.

Barry, N.P. 1979, *Hayek's social and economic philosophy*, Macmillan, London.

Bartley, T. 2003, "Certifying forests and factories: states, social movements, and the rise of private regulation in the apparel and forest products fields", *Politics and Society*, vol. 31, no. 3, pp 433–464.

Basu, K & Palazzo, G, 2005, An Inductive Typology of Corporate Social Responsibility, Best paper proceedings of the annual meeting of the Academy of Management Conference, Hawaii.

Batstone, D.B. 2003, *Saving the corporate soul– & (who knows?) maybe your own: eight principles for creating and preserving integrity and profitability without selling out*, Jossey-Bass, San Francisco, Calif.

Battaglia, M., Bianchi, L., Frey, M. & Iraldo, F. 2010, "An innovative model to promote CSR among SMEs operating in industrial clusters: evidence from an EU project", *Corporate Social Responsibility and Environmental Management*, vol. 9999, no. 9999.

Bauman, Z. 1998, *Globalization: the human consequences*, Columbia University Press, New York.

BBC 2005, *"Costing the earth": the Kenya flower trade*, BBC, London.

Beauchamp, T.L. & Bowie, N.E. 1983, *Ethical theory and business*, Prentice-Hall, Englewood Cliffs, N.J.

Beauchamp, T.L., Bowie, N.E. & Arnold, D. (eds) 2008, 8th edn, Pearson Education, London.

Beaver, W. 1995, "Levi's is leaving China", *Business Horizons*, vol. 38, no. 2, pp 35–40.

Beck, U., Giddens, A. & Lash, S. 1994, *Reflexive modernization: politics, tradition and aesthetics in the modern social order*, Polity Press, Cambridge.

Beck, U. 2000, *What is globalization?* Polity Press, Cambridge.

Beck, U. 1992, *Risk Society: Towards a New Modernity*, Sage Pubns.

Bellagio Forum For Sustainable Development and Eurosif 2006, PRIME Toolkit Primer for Responsible Investment Management of Endowments, Osnabrueck: Bellagio Forum for Sustainable Development.

Bendell, J. 2004a, *Barricades and boardrooms: a contemporary history of the corporate accountability movement*, United Nations Research Institute for Social Development, Geneva.

Bendell, J. 2004b, *Flags of Inconvenience? The Global Compact and the Future of the United Nations*, Nottingham.

Bendell, J. 2000, *Terms of Endearment: business, NGOs and sustainable development*, Greenleaf Publishing, Sheffield.

Bennett, C. & Burley, H. 2005, "Corporate Accountability: an NGO perspective", in *Research Handbook on Corporate Legal Responsibility*, ed. S. Tully, Edward Elgar, Cheltenham, pp 372–394.

Bennett, M., James, P. & Klinkers, L. 1999, *Sustainable measures: evaluation and reporting of environmental and social performance*, Greenleaf Publishing, Sheffield.

Bennett, M., Rikhardsson, P.M. & Schaltegger, S. 2003, *Environmental management accounting: purpose and progress*, Kluwer Academic Publishers, Dordrecht; Boston.

Bennis, W.G., Goleman, D. & O'Toole, J. 2008, *Transparency: how leaders create a culture of candor*, 1st edn, Jossey-Bass, San Francisco, CA.

Benson, K.L., Brailsford, T.J. & Humphrey, J.E. 2006, "Do socially responsible fund managers really invest differently?", *Journal of Business Ethics*, vol. 65, no. 4, pp 337–357.

Bentham, J. 1789, *An introduction to the principles of morals and legislation, etc. MS. notes [by the author]*, T. Payne & Son, Londn.

BER 2008, *The contribution of South African Breweries Limited to the South African economy*, Bureau for Economic Research, Cape Town.

Berger, F.R. 1984, *Happiness, justice, and freedom: the moral and political philosophy of John Stuart Mill*, University of California Press, Berkeley.

Berle, A.A., Means, G.C. & Columbia University. Council for Research in the Social Sciences 1932, *Modern corporation and private property*,

Commerce Clearing House, Loose leaf service division of the Corporation Trust Company, New York, Chicago.

Bernauer, T. & Caduff, L. 2004, "In Whose Interest? Pressure Group Politics, Economic Competition and Environmental Regulation", *Journal of Public Policy*, vol. 24, no. 01, pp 99–126.

Bernstein, P.L. 1996, *Against the gods: the remarkable story of risk*, John Wiley & Sons, New York.

Bhagwati, J.N. 2004, *In defense of globalization*, Oxford University Press, Oxford, New York.

Bhattacharya, C.B. & Sen, S. 2004, "Doing better at doing good: when, why, and how consumers respond to corporate social initiatives", *California Management Review*, vol. 47, no. 1, pp 9–24.

Birch, D. 2001, "Corporate citizenship: rethinking business beyond corporate social responsibility", in *Perspectives on Corporate Citizenship*, eds. G. Andriof & M. McIntosh, Greenleaf Publishing, London, pp 53–65.

Birch, D. 2003, "Corporate Social Responsibility: Some Key Theoretical Issues and Concepts for New Ways of Doing Business", *Journal of New Business Ideas and Trends*, vol. 1, no. 1, pp 1–19.

Black, E. 2001, *IBM and the Holocaust: the strategic alliance between Nazi Germany and America's most powerful corporation*, 1st edn, Crown Publishers, New York.

Black, J. 2003, *A dictionary of economics*, 2nd edn, reissue with new covers and corrections, Oxford University Press, Oxford; New York.

Bladen, V.W. 1974, *From Adam Smith to Maynard Keynes: the heritage of political economy*, University of Toronto Press, Toronto; Buffalo.

Blake, D.H., Frederick, W.C. & Myers, M.S. 1976, *Social auditing: evaluating the impact of corporate programs*, Praeger, New York.

Blanchard, K.H., O'Connor, M.J. & Ballard, J. 1997, *Managing by values*, Berrett-Koehler Publishers, San Francisco.

Block, W. & Barnett, W. 2005, "A positive programme for laissez-faire capitalism", *Journal of Corporate Citizenship*, vol. 19, pp 31–42.

Bloom, D.E. & Canning, D. 2006, 'Booms, busts, and echoes', Finance and Development, 43(3), pp 8–15.

Blowfield, M.E. 2010, "Business and poverty reduction" in *Corporate social responsibility and regulatory governance: towards inclusive

development?*, eds. P. Utting & J.C. Marques, 1st edn, Palgrave Macmillan, New York.

Blowfield, M.E. 2007, "Reasons to be cheerful? what we know about CSR's impact", *Third World Quarterly*, vol. unknown.

Blowfield, M.E. 2005a, "Corporate Social Responsibility—the failing discipline and why it matters for International Relations," *International Relations*, vol. 19, no. 2, pp 173–191.

Blowfield, M.E. 2005b, *Does society want business leadership? An overview of attitudes and thinking*, Center for Corporate Citizenship at Boston College, Chestnut Hill.

Blowfield, M.E. 2004, "Implementation Deficits of Ethical Trade Systems: lessons from the Indonesian cocoa and timber industries", *Journal of Corporate Citizenship*, no. 13, pp 77–90.

Blowfield, M.E. 2003, *Ethical Trade: the negotiation of a global ethic*, University of SussexEditor.

Blowfield, M.E. 2002, "ETI - a multi-stakeholder approach", in *Corporate Responsibility and Ethical Trade: codes of conduct in the global economy*, eds. R.O. Jenkins, R. Pearson & G. Seyfang, Earthscan, London, pp 184–195.

Blowfield, M.E. 2000a, *A guide to developing agricultural markets and agro-enterprises; fundamentals of ethical trading/sourcing in poorer countries*, World Bank, Washington DC.

Blowfield, M.E. 2000b, "Ethical Sourcing: a contribution to sustainability or a diversion?", *Sustainable Development*, no. 8, pp 191–200.

Blowfield, M.E. 1991, *Does Bo Know Nike?*, Jakarta.

Blowfield, M.E. "Will the WTO Prevent the Growth of Ethical Trade: implications of the international policy environment for ethical trade schemes", *Journal of International Development*, vol. 12, pp 571–584.

Blowfield, M.E. & Dolan, C. 2008, "Stewards of virtue: the ethical dilemma of CSR in Africa", *Development and Change*, vol. 39, no. 1, pp 1–23.

Blowfield, M. & Dolan, C. 2010, "Outsourcing governance: Fairtrade's message for C21 global governance", *Corporate Governance*, vol. 10, no. 4, pp 484–499.

Blowfield, M.E. & Frynas, J.G. 2005, "Setting new agendas: critical perspectives on Corporate Social Responsibility in the developing world", *International Affairs*, vol. 81, no. 3, pp 499.

Blowfield, M.E. & Googins, B. 2007, Step Up: A Call for Business Leadership in Society-CEOs Examine Role Of Business In The 21st Century, Chestnut Hill, MA: Center for Corporate Citizenship at Boston College.

Blowfield, M.E. & Murray, A. 2008, *Corporate responsibility: a critical introduction*, Oxford University Press, Oxford.

Blyth, M. 2002, *Great transformations: economic ideas and institutional change in the twentieth century*, Cambridge University Press, New York.

Bogle, J.C. 2009, *Enough: true measures of money, business, and life*, John Wiley & Sons, Hoboken, N.J.

Bogle, J.C. 2005, *The battle for the soul of capitalism*, Yale University Press, New Haven.

Bond, P. 2006, "Global Governance Campaigning and mdg s: from top-down to bottom-up anti-poverty work", *Third World Quarterly*, vol. 27, no. 2, pp 339–354.

Bornstein, D. 2007, *How to change the world*, Updated edn, Oxford University Press, Oxford.

Bounds, A. 2009, *Ethiopian refugees discover benefits of coffee*, 7 May 2009 edn, Financial Times, London.

Bowd, R., Bowd, L. & Harris, P. 2006, "Communicating corporate social responsibility: an exploratory case study of a major UK retail centre", *Journal of Public Affairs*, vol. 6, no. 2, pp 147.

Bowen, H.R. 1953, *Social responsibilities of the businessman*, 1st edn, Harper, New York.

Brady, K. 1984, *Ida Tarbell: portrait of a muckraker*, Seaview/Putnam, New York.

Brainard, L. 2006, *Transforming the development landscape: the role of the private sector*, Brookings Institution Press, Washington, D.C.

Braithwaite, J. 2000, *Global business regulation*, Cambridge University Press, Cambridge.

Brand, S. 1999, *The clock of the long now: time and responsibility*, 1st edn, Basic Books, New York.

Broad, R. (ed) 2002, *Global backlash: citizen initiatives for a just world economy*, Rowman & Littlefield Publishers, Lanham, Md.; Oxford.

Brontë, C. 1849, *Shirley, a tale*, Smith, Elder, London.

Brooke, H. 2010, *The silent state*, 1st edn, William Heinemann, London.

Brooke, P.A. & Penrice, D. 2009, *A vision for venture capital: realizing the promise of global venture capital and private equity*, New Ventures Press; In association with University Press of New England, Boston; Hanover.

Brower, M., Leon, W. & Union of Concerned Scientists 1999, *The consumer's guide to effective environmental choices: practical advice from the Union of Concerned Scientists*, 1st edn, Three Rivers Press, New York.

Brown, D.K. 2004, *Improving working conditions: what works and what doesn't - existing empirical evidence and historical experience*, Paper for presentation at Globalization and Labor in Developing Countries conference, Brown University edn.

Brown, T.J. & Dacin, P.A. 1997, "The company and the product: corporate associations and consumer product responses", *Journal of Marketing*, vol. 61, pp 68–84.

Brown, C.C. 1979, *Beyond the bottom line*, Macmillan, New York.

Brown, W.S., McCabe, D. & Primeaux, P. 2003, "Business Ethics in Transitional Economies: Introduction", *Journal of Business Ethics*, vol. 47, no. 4, pp 295–297.

Browne, J. 2004, "Beyond Kyoto", *Foreign Affairs*, vol. 83, no. 4, pp 20–32.

Brugmann, J. & Prahalad, C.K. 2007, "Cocreating business's new social compact", *Harvard Business Review*, no. February 2007, pp 80–90.

BSR undated, *Overview of business ethics*, Business for Social Responsibility, San Francisco.

BSR 2005, *Reporting on economic impacts*, Business for Social Responsibility, San Francisco.

BSR 2002, *Designing a CSR structure: a step-by-step guide including leadership examples and decision-making tools*, Business for Social Responsibility, San Francisco.

BT 2005, *BT social and environmental report*, BT Group.

Buchanan, A.E. 1985, *Ethics, efficiency, and the market*, Rowman & Allanheld, Totowa, N.J.

Buchanan, J.M. & Yoon, Y.J. 2002, "Globalization as framed by the two logics of trade", *The Independent Review*, vol. 6, no. 3, pp 399–405.

Buchholz, R.A., Marcus, A.A. & Post, J.E. 1992, *Managing environmental issues: a casebook*, Prentice Hall, Englewood Cliffs, N.J.

Bunting, M, 2005, "Africa's flash moment", *Guardian Weekly*, 24–30 June, p 5.

Burns, P. 2001, *Entrepreneurship and small business*, Palgrave, London.

Business Week 2005, *Social issues retailing: can Wal-Mart fit into a white hat?*

Butler, E. 1985, *Hayek, his contribution to the political and economic thought of our time*, Universe Books, New York.

Byron, N. & Arnold, M. 1998, *What Futures for the People of the Tropical Forests?* Centre for International Forestry Research, Bogor.

CAFOD 2005, *'Clean up your computer' progress report*, CAFOD, London.

Cairncross, F. 1995, *Green, Inc.: a guide to business and the environment*, Island Press, Washington, DC.

Callahan, D. 2002, *Kindred spirits: Harvard Business School's extraordinary class of 1949 and how they transformed American business*, John Wiley & Sons, Hoboken, N.J.

Cannon, T. 1994, *Corporate responsibility: a textbook on business ethics, governance, environment: roles and responsibilities*, Pitman, London.

Caplan, K. 2003, "The purist's partnership: debunking the terminology of partnerships", *Partnership Matters*, vol. 1, pp 31–35.

Carey, J. 2006, *Business on a warmer planet.*

Carnegie, A. 1889, *The gospel of wealth*, F. C. hagen & co., London.

Carney, W.J. 1998, "Limited liability", *Encyclopedia of Law and Economics*, pp 659–691.

Carroll, A.B. 1999, "Corporate social responsibility: evolution of a definitional construct", *Business & Society*, vol. 38, no. 3, pp 268.

Carroll, A.B. 2000, "A commentary and an overview of key questions on corporate social performance measurement", *Business and Society*, vol. 39, no. 4, pp 466–478.

Carroll, A.B. 1979, "A Three-dimensional Conceptual Model of Corporate Performance", *Academy of Management Review*, vol. 4, no. 4, pp 497–505.

Carroll, A.B. & Buchholtz, A.K. 2003, *Business & society: ethics and stakeholder management*, Thomson/South-Western, Mason, Ohio.

Carroll, A.B. 1977, *Managing corporate social responsibility*, Little, Brown, Boston.

Carroll, A.B. & Buchholtz, A.K. 2006, *Business & society: ethics and stakeholder management*, 6th edn, Thomson/South-Western, Mason, Ohio.

Carroll, S.J. & Gannon, M.J. 1997, *Ethical dimensions of international management*, Sage Publications, Thousand Oaks, Calif.

Carson, R., Darling, L. & Darling, L. 1962, *Silent spring*, Houghton Mifflin; Riverside Press, Boston; Cambridge, Mass.

Carswell, J. 1960, *The South Sea bubble*, Stanford University Press, Stanford, Calif.

Caufield, C. 1996, *Masters of illusion: the World Bank and the poverty of nations*, 1st edn, Henry Holt, New York.

Center For Corporate Citizenship 2005a, *Going Global: How US-Based Multinationals are Operationalizing Corporate Citizenship on a Global Platform*, Chestnut Hill, MA: Center for Corporate Citizenship at Boston College.

Center For Corporate Citizenship 2005b, *Integration: Critical Link for Corporate Citizenship*, Boston, MA: Center for Corporate Citizenship at Boston College.

Center For Corporate Citizenship 2005c, *State of Corporate Citizenship in the US: Business Perspectives in 2005*, Boston, MA: Center for Corporate Citizenship at Boston College/US Chambers of Commerce.

CECP 2006, Giving in numbers 2006, New York: Committee Encouraging Corporate Philanthropy.

CEP 1997, *SA8000*, Council on Economic Priorities, New York.

CEPAA 1999, *Guidance Document for Social Accountability 8000*, New York.

CERES undated, *CERES principles*, Colation for Environmentally Responsible Economies, Boston, MA.

CFS/CIS 2005, *Sustainability report 2004*, Cooperative Financial Services.

Chamberlain, N.W. 1973, *The limits of corporate responsibility*, Basic Books, New York.

Chan, A. & Siu, K. 2007, "Wal-Mart's CSR and labor standards in China", *International Network on Business, Development and Society workshop, September 12–14 2007.*

Chandler, A.D. & Mazlish, B. (eds) 2005, *Leviathans: multinational corporations and the new global history*, Cambridge University Press, Cambridge.

Chang, H. 2008, *Bad Samaritans: the guilty secrets of rich nations and the threat to global prosperity*, Random House Business, London.

Chang, H. 2002, *Kicking away the ladder: development strategy in historical perspective*, Anthem, London.

Chenoweth, J. & Bird, J. 2005, *The business of water and sustainable development*, Greenleaf, Sheffield.

Cheung, R. 2008, China. In Krosinsky & Robins (cited elsewhere) pp 149–164.

Christian Aid 2005, *The shirts off their backs: how tax policies fleece the poor*, Christian Aid, London.

Christian Aid 2004, *Behind the Mask: the real face of corporate social responsibility*, London.

Christian Aid 1997, *Change at the Check-out?—supermarkets and ethical business*, Christian Aid, London.

Christian Aid, ASH & Friends of the Earth *BAT in its own words*, Christian Aid, Action on Smoking and Health (ASH) and Friends of the Earth (FoE).

CIE 2003, *The Global Alliance: benefit-cost framework and application*, Canberra.

Clark, E. 2005, *Manufacturing the evidence*.

Clark, J.M. 1939, *Social control of business*, 2d edn, Whittlesey house, McGraw-Hill book company, inc, New York, London.

Clarkson, M.B.E. 1995, "A stakeholder framework for analyzing and evaluating corporate social performance", *Academy of Management Review*, vol. 20, no. 1, pp 92–117.

Clay, J. 2005, *Exploring the links between international business and poverty reduction: a case study of Unilever in Indonesia*, Oxfam, Oxford.

Coase, R. 1937, "The nature of the firm", *Economica*, no. 4, pp 386–405.

Cody, E. 2004, *Unrest stirs among Chinese factory workers*.

Coffee, J.C. 2000, "The Rise of Dispersed Ownership: The Role of Law in the Separation of Ownership and Control", *Columbia Law and Economics Working Paper*.

Cogan, D. 2004, *Corporate governance and climate change: making the connection*, CERES, Boston.

Coleman, J. 2002, "Gender, power and post-structuralism in corporate citizenship", *Journal of Corporate Citizenship*, vol. 5, pp 17–25.

Collinson, C. 2001, *The business costs of ethical supply chain management: Kenya flower industry case study*, Natural Resources Institute, Chatham.

Collinson, C. & Leon, M. 2000, *Economic Viability of Ethical Cocoa Trading in Ecuador*, Natural Resources Institute, Chatham.

Cone, M.H. 2003, "Corporate citizenship: the role of commercial organisations in an Islamic society", *Journal of Corporate Citizenship*, vol. 9.

Conference Board 2006, *Philanthropy and business: the changing agenda*, Conference Board, New York.

Cornell, B. & Shapiro, A.C. 1987, "Corporate stakeholders and corporate finance", *Financial Management*, vol. 16, no. 1, pp 5–14.

Corcoran, T, 2006, 'Just say no to NGOs', *National Post*, 1 April, online at **www.canada.com/ nationalpost**.

Courville, S. 2000, *Promoting biological diversity through sustainable certification and fair trade*, Institute for Agriculture and Trade Policy.

Cowe, R. 2002, *No scruples?: managing to be responsible in a turbulent world*, Spiro, London.

Cragg, W. & McKague, K. 2003, *Compendium of ethics codes and instruments of corporate responsibility*.

Cramer, J. 2006, *Corporate social responsibility and globalisation: an action plan for business*, Greenleaf Publishing, Sheffield.

Crane, A. & Matten, D. 2004, *Business Ethics*, Oxford University Press, Oxford.

Crane, A., Matten, D. & Moon, J. 2008, *Corporations and citizenship*, Cambridge University Press, Cambridge, UK; New York.

Crenson, M.A. & Ginsberg, B. 2002, *Downsizing democracy: how America sidelined its citizens and privatized its public*, Johns Hopkins University Press, Baltimore.

Crowther, D. & Caliyurt, K.T. 2006, *Globalisation and social responsibility*, Cambridge Scholars Press, Newcastle, U.K.

Cummins, A. 2004, "The Marine Stewardship Council: a multi-stakeholder approach to sustainable fishing", *Corporate Social Responsibility and Environmental Management*, vol. 11, pp 85–94.

Daly, H.E. 1996, *Beyond growth: the economics of sustainable development*, Beacon Press, Boston.

Darnton, R. 2009, *Google and the new digital future*, New York Review of Books, New York.

Daum, J.H. 2003, *Intangible assets and value creation*, John Wiley & Sons, Chichester.

Davies, P.W.F. 1997, *Current issues in business ethics*, Routledge, London; New York.

Davis, K. 1973, "The case for and against business assumption of social responsibilities", *Academy of Management Review*, no. 16, pp 312–322.

Davis, K. 1960, "Can business afford to ignore social responsibilities?", *California Management Review*, no. 2, pp 70–76.

Davis, P. 2006, *Time to embed the Anglo-Saxon brand of corporate responsibility*.

Davis, S.M., Lukomnik, J. & Pitt-Watson, D. 2006, *The new capitalists: how citizen investors are reshaping the corporate agenda*, Harvard Business School Press, Boston, Mass.

Davy, A. 2003a, "Companies in conflict situations: a role for partnerships?" in *Putting partnerships to work*, eds. M. Warner & R. Sullivan, Greenleaf Publishing, Sheffield, pp 220–229.

Davy, A. 2003b, "Ownership and control of outcomes" in, eds. M. Warner & R. Sullivan, Greenleaf Publishing, Sheffield, pp 210–219.

DCCA 2008, *Small suppliers in global supply chains: how multinationals can target small and medium-sized suppliers in their global supply chains*, Danish Commerce and Companies Agency in association with Hewlett Packard, Copenhagen.

de Oliveira, J.A.P. 2006, "Corporate citizenship in Latin America", *Journal of Corporate Citizenship*, vol. 21, pp 17–20.

Dees, J.G. 1998, "The Meaning of 'Social Entrepreneurship'", *Comments and suggestions contributed from the Social Entrepreneurship Funders Working Group*, 6pp.

Dees, J.G., Emerson, J. & Economy, P. 2002, *Strategic Tools for Social Entrepreneurs: Enhancing the Performance of Your Enterprising Nonprofit*, Chichester, John Wiley & Sons.

Demirag, I. 2005, *Corporate Social Responsibility, Accountability and Governance*, Greenleaf Publishing, Sheffield.

Department for Trade and Industry 2001, *Business and society: developing corporate social responsibility in the UK*, London, UK Department for Trade and Industry.

Derber, C. 1998, *Corporation nation: how corporations are taking over our lives and what we can do about it*, St. Martin's Press, New York.

DFID 2002, *The challenges of assessing the poverty impact of ethical trading: what can be learnt from fair trade initiatives and the sustainable livelihoods approach*, Department for International Development, London.

Dicken, P. 2003, *Global shift: reshaping the global economic map in the 21st century*, 4th edn, Sage Publications, London; Thousand Oaks.

DiLorenzo, T.J. 2004, *How capitalism saved America: the untold history of our country, from the Pilgrims to the present*, 1st edn, Crown Forum, New York.

Dion, M, 2001, "Corporate citizenship as an ethic of care, corporate values, codes of ethics and global governance", in *Perspectives on Corporate Citizenship*, eds. J. Andriof & M. McIntosh, Greenleaf Publishing, Sheffield, pp 118–138.

Doane, D. 2005, "The Myth of CSR: the problem with assuming that comanies can do well while also doing good is that markets don't really work that way", *Stanford Social Innovation Review*, vol. Fall 2005, pp 23–29.

Dobb, M.H. 1973, *Theories of value and distribution since Adam Smith; ideology and economic theory*, University Press, Cambridge, Eng.

Dolan, C. & Humphrey, J. 2004, "Changing governance patterns in the trade in fresh vegetables between Africa and the United Kingdom", *Environment and Planning A*, vol. 36, no. 3, pp 491–509.

Dolan, C.S. & Opondo, M. 2005, "Seeking common ground", *Journal of Corporate Citizenship*, vol. 18, pp 87–98.

Donaldson, T. 2003, "Ethics Away from Home", in *Readings and cases in international management: a cross-cultural perspective*, ed. D.C. Thomas, Sage, Thousand Oaks, Calif, pp 133–140.

Donaldson, T. 1989, *The ethics of international business*, Oxford University Press, New York.

Donaldson, T. & Dunfee, T.W. 1999, *Ties that bind: a social contracts approach to business ethics*, Harvard Business School Press, Boston, Mass.

Donaldson, T., Werhane, P.H. & Cording, M. 2002, *Ethical issues in business: a philosophical approach*, Prentice Hall, Upper Saddle River, N.J.

Donaldson, T. & Gini, A. 1996, *Case studies in business ethics*, 4th edn, Prentice Hall, Upper Saddle River, N.J.

Donaldson, T., Werhane, P.H. & Van Zandt, J. 2008, *Ethical issues in business: a philosophical approach*, 8th edn, Pearson Prentice Hall, Upper Saddle River, N.J.

Doppelt, B. 2003, *Leading change towards sustainability: a change-management guide for business, government and civil society*, Greenleaf, Sheffield.

Drayton, W. 2002, "The Citizen Sector: Becoming as Entrepreneurial and Competitive as Business", *California management review*, vol. 44, no. 3, pp 120–132.

Drucker, P.F. 1946, *Concept of the corporation*, The John Day Company, New York.

DTI 2004, *DTI international CSR strategy consultation*, British Department for Trade and Industry, London.

Du Cann, R. 1993, *The art of the advocate*, Repr. with revisions edn, Penguin Books, Harmondsworth.

Du Toit, A. 2000, *Private regulation and equitable change in the Western Cape agro-food sector*.

Durkheim, E. & Halls, W.D. 1984, *The division of labor in society*, Free Press, New York.

Dyllick, T. & Hockerts, K. 2002, "Beyond the business case for corporate sustainability", *Business Strategy and the Environment*, vol. 11, no. 2, pp 130–141.

Easterly, W.R. 2006, *The white man's burden: why the West's efforts to aid the rest have done so much ill and so little good*, Oxford University Press, Oxford.

Economist, The 2005, *The ethics of business: good corporate citizens, and wise governments, should be wary of CSR*.

Economist, The 2005, *The good company: the movement for corporate social responsibility has won the battle for ideas*.

Economist, The 2005, *Profit and the public good: companies that merely compete and prosper make society better off*, The Economist, London.

Economist, The 2005, *The union of concerned executives: CSR as practised means many different things*.

Economist, The 2005, *The world according to CSR*.

Economist, The 2004, *Two-faced capitalism*.

Economist, The 1999, *The key to industrial capitalism: limited liability*, The Economist, London.

Economy, E. 2004, *The river runs black: the environmental challenge to China's future*, Cornell University Press, Ithaca.

Edwards, M. 2010, *Small Change: Why Business Won't Save the World*, Berrett-Koehler Publishers, San Francisco.

Edwards, M., Hulme, D. & Save the Children Fund (Great Britain) 1995, *Non-governmental organisations: performance and accountability: beyond the magic bullet*, Earthscan, London.

Efstathiou, J. 2008, *Carbon trading can raise billions of dollars to save forests*, Dublin.

Ehrenreich, B. 2001, *Nickel and dimed: on (not) getting by in America*, Metropolitan Books, New York.

Elfstrom, G. 2000, "The ethical responsibilities of multinational corporations: the case of the North American aluminum companies in Jamaica", in *Ethics in international affairs*, ed. A. Valls, Rowman and Littlefield, New York, pp 185–200.

Elkington, J. 1998, *Cannibals with forks: the triple bottom line of 21st century business*, Gabriola Island, BC/Stony Creek, CT: New Society Publishers.

Elkington, J. & Lee, M. 2006, "It's the economics stupid: has the corporate responsibility movement lost sight of the big picture", *Grist Magazine*, no. May 9 2006.

Elkington, J. & Hartigan, P. 2008, *The power of unreasonable people: how social entrepreneurs create markets that change the world*, Harvard Business School Press; McGraw-Hill distributor, Boston, Mass.; London.

Elliott, K.A. & Freeman, R.B. 2003, *Can labor standards improve under globalization?* Institute for International Economics, Washington, DC.

Ellsworth, R.R. 2002, *Leading with purpose: the new corporate realities*, Stanford Business Books, Stanford.

Emerson, J. 2003, "The blended value proposition: integrating social and financial returns", *California Management Review*, vol. 45, no. 4, pp 35–51.

Enderle, G. 2004, "Global competition and corporate responsibilities of small and medium-sized enterprises", *Business Ethics A European Review*, vol. 13, no. 1, pp 50–63.

Englander, E. & Kaufman, A. 2004, "The end of managerial ideology: from corporate social responsibility to corporate social indifference", *Enterprise and Society*, vol. 5, no. 3, pp 404–450.

Entine, J. & Miller, R. 2007, *Managing brands under siege*.

Ernst & Young, KPMG, PWC & House of Mandrag Morgan 1999, *The Copenhagen charter: a management guide to stakeholder reporting*, House of Mandrag Morgan, Copenhagen.

ESRA 2004, *European sustainability reporting awards 2004: report of the judges*, European Sustainability Reporting Awards.

Estes, R.W. 1996, *Tyranny of the bottom line: why corporations make good people do bad things*, 1st edn, Berrett-Koehler Publishers; Publishers Group West distributor, San Francisco; Emeryville, CA.

Ethical Corporation 2006, *Multi-fibre agreement forum in Bangladesh*.

Ethical Corporation 2005, February 2005-last update, *The role of the big four in shaping corporate responsibility* [Homepage of Ethical Corporation], [Online]. Available: www.sustain-online.org [2005, June 20].

Ethical Corporation 2005, *Why The Economist is wrong about CSR*.

Ethical Corporation & Nima Hunter Inc. 2003, *The business of business: managing corporate social responsibility—what business leaders are saying and doing 2002–2007*, Nima Hunter Inc., London.

Ethical Performance date unknown, *French motor giant signs CSR deal with trade unions*.

Ethical Performance date unknown, *French navy makes waves with first CSR assessment*.

Ethical Performance date unknown, *Morocco embraces CSR*.

Ethical Performance 2008, *Ethical Performance Best Practice: presenting case studies of corporate social responsibility*, Ethical Performance, London.

Ethical Performance 2007, "Facebook generation puts firms in the dock", *Ethical Performance*, no. November 2007, pp 8.

Ethical Performance 2006a, *Caterpillar gets reprieve*.

Ethical Performance 2006b, *Criticisms augur end of 'flawed' human rights norms*.

Ethical Performance 2006c, *EC white paper unveils European CSR alliance*.

Ethical Performance, 2006d, "Sliding ingloriously down the pole of excellence", *Ethical Performance*, 7(11), online at **www.ethicalperformance.com**.

Ethical Performance, 2005a, 'Firms put on notice as UN Compact gets teeth', *Ethical Performance*, October, p 1.

Ethical Performance, 2005b, "The United Nations deserves some credit", *Ethical*

Ethical Performance 2005c, *Ruggie takes on delicate task of considering UN norms*.

Ethical Performance 2004, *Angry critics run boycott over 'slow' CSR progress*.

ETI undated, *Bridging the gap between commercial and ethical agendas*, Ethical Trading Initiative, London.

ETI 2009, *Marking our first decade: ETI annual review 2007–2008*, Ethical Trading Initiative.

ETI 2006, *Ethical Trade: A Comprehensive Guide for Companies*, Ethical Trading Initiative, London.

ETI 2005a, *Addressing labour practices on Kenyan flower farms: report of ETI involvement 2002–2004*, Ethical Trading Initiative, London.

ETI 2005b, *ETI smallholder guidelines*, Ethical Trading Initiative, London.

ETI 2005c, *Annual Report 2004/2005 "Driving Change"*, Ethical Trading Initiative, London.

ETI 2005d, *Managing compliance with labour codes at supplier level: a more sustainable way of improving working conditions?*, Ethical Trading Initiative, London.

ETI 2005e, *Moving production: stalling the race to the bottom*, Ethical Trading Initiative, London.

ETI 2004, *Putting ethics to work: annual report 2003/2004*, Ethical Trading Initiative, London.

ETI 2003, *Raising the stakes: annual report 2003*, Ethical Trading Initiative, London.

ETI 2001, *ETI, From Good Intentions to Good Practice: annual report 2003*, London.

ETI 1999, *Learning from Doing Review: a report on company progress in implementing ethical sourcing policies and practices*, London.

ETI 1998, *Purpose Principles Programme Membership Information*, London.

Etzion, D., Ferraro, F. & Pearson, A. 2010, "The Role of Analogy in the Institutionalization of Sustainability Reporting", *Organization Science*, no. articles in advance, pp 1–16.

Etzion, D., Ferraro, F. & Pearson, A. "The Role of Analogy in the Institutionalization of Sustainability Reporting", *Organization Science*.

European Commission 2002, *Companies face their social responsibilities in Europe and abroad*.

Evan, W.M. & Freeman, R.E. 1988, "A stakeholder theory of the modern corporation: Kantian capitalism", *Ethical Theory and Business*, vol. 3, pp 97–106.

Evans, E.J. 1983, *The forging of the modern state: early industrial Britain 1783–1870*, Longman, London.

Evers, H. & Schrader, H. 1994, *The Moral economy of trade: ethnicity and developing markets*, Routledge, London; New York.

FAO 2003, *Agriculture, food and water*, Food and Agriculture Organisation, Rome.

Farmer, R.N. & Hogue, W.D. 1985, *Corporate social responsibility*, Lexington Books, Lexington, Mass.

Felix, D. 1995, *Biography of an idea: John Maynard Keynes and The general theory of employment, interest and money*, Transaction Publishers, New Brunswick, N.J.

Ferguson, I. 12 March 2003-last update, *Corporate timelines* [Homepage of openDemocracy],

[Online]. Available: www.openDemocracy.net [2005, June 22].

Ferguson, C. 1999, *Global Social Policy Principles: human rights and social justice*, London.

Ferguson, C. 1998, *A Review of UK Company Codes of Conduct*, London.

Ferguson, J. 1990, *The anti-politics machine: "development," depoliticization, and bureaucratic power in Lesotho*, Cambridge University Press, Cambridge England; New York.

Ferguson, N. 2003, *Empire: how Britain made the modern world*, Allen Lane, London.

Fig, D. 2007, *Corporations and moral purpose: South Africa's Truth and Reconciliation Commission and business responsibility for apartheid.*

Fig, D. 2005, "Manufacturing amnesia: corporate social responsibility in South Africa", *International Affairs*, vol. 81, no. 3, pp 599–618.

FinancialWire 2006, *Faith-based institutional investors take aim at reforming Wal-Mart.*

Fitzpatrick, M. 2004, *Business Case for Sustainability: Finding a New State of Equilibrium*, Keynote address, Green Chemistry and Engineering Conference, Washington DC, June 29 2004 edn.

Foer, F. 2004, *How soccer explains the world: an unlikely theory of globalization*, HarperCollins, New York.

Foster, R.N. & Kaplan, S. 2001, *Creative destruction: why companies that are built to last underperform the market, and how to successfully transform them*, 1st edn, Currency/Doubleday, New York.

Fourie, A. & Eloff, T. 2005, "The case for collective business action to achieve systems change: exploring the contributions made by the private sector to the social, economic and political transformation process in South Africa", *Journal of Corporate Citizenship*, vol. 18, pp 39–48.

Fowler, A. 2000, "NGDOs as a moment in history: beyond aid to social entrepreneurship or civic innovation?", *Third World Quarterly*, vol. 21, no. 4, pp 637–654.

Fox Gorte, J. 2008, "Investors: a force for sustainability", in *Sustainable investing: the art of long-term performance*, eds. C. Krosinsky & N. Robins, Earthscan, London, pp 31–40.

Fox, T. & Prescott, D. 2004, *Exploring the role of development cooperation agencies in corporate responsibility*, Conference on Development cooperation and corporate social responsibility, Stockholm, 22–23 March 2004, Stockholm.

Frank, A.G. 1979, *Dependent accumulation and underdevelopment*, Monthly Review Press, New York.

Frederick, W.C. 1960, "The growing concern over business responsibility", *California Management Review*, no. 1, pp 54–61.

Frederick, W.C. 2006, *Corporation be good!: the story of corporate social responsibility*, Dog Ear Pub., Indianapolis, IN.

Frederick, W.C. 1995, *Values, nature, and culture in the American corporation*, Oxford University Press, New York.

Freeman, D. 2003, "Homeworkers in Global Supply Chains", *Greener Management International*, pp 107–118.

Freeman, R.E. 1984, *Strategic management: a stakeholder approach*, Pitman, Boston.

Freeman, R.E., Pierce, J. & Dodd, R. 2000, Environmentalism and the New Logic of Business: How Firms Can Be Profitable and Leave Our Children a Living Planet, Oxford University Press, Oxford.

French, P.A. 1984, *Collective and corporate responsibility*, Columbia University Press, New York.

Friedman, M. 1962, *Capitalism and freedom*, University of Chicago Press, Chicago.

Friedman, M. & Selden, R.T. 1975, *Capitalism and freedom: problems and prospects; proceedings of a conference in honor of Milton Friedman*, University Press of Virginia, Charlottesville.

Friedman, T.L. 2005, *The world is flat: a brief history of the globalized world in the twenty-first century*, Allen Lane, London.

Friedman, T.L. 2000, *The Lexus and the olive tree*, Rev. edn, Farrar, Straus, Giroux, New York.

Friends of the Earth 2005, *Hidden voices: the CBI, corporate lobbying and sustainability*, Friends of the Earth, London.

Frynas, J.G. 2005, "False promises: evidence from multinational oil companies", *International Affairs*, vol. 81, no. 3, pp 581–598.

FTSE4Good 2005, *Impact of new criteria and future direction: 2004–2005 report*, FTSE, London.

Fukuyama, F. 1989, "The end of history", *The National History*, no. Summer 1989, pp 1–18.

Fussler, C., Cramer, A. & van der Vegt, S. (eds) 2004, *Raising the bar: creating value with the United Nations Global Compact*, Greenleaf, Sheffield.

Gabor, A. 1999, *The capitalist philosophers: the geniuses of modern business–their lives, times, and ideas*, 1st edn, Times Business, New York.

Gabriel, Y. & Lang, T. 1995, *The unmanageable consumer: contemporary consumption and its fragmentation*, Sage Publications, London; Thousand Oaks, Calif.

Galbraith, J.K. 1972, "The emerging public corporation", *Business and Society Review*, vol. 1, pp 54–56.

Galbraith, J.K. 1967, *The new industrial state*, Houghton Mifflin, Boston.

Galbraith, J.K. 1952, *American capitalism, the concept of countervailing power*, Houghton Mifflin, Boston.

Galea, C. 2004, *Teaching business sustainability*, Greenleaf, Sheffield.

Gardner, S. 2006, *Pushing business-driven corporate citizenship*.

GE 2005, *Solving big needs: GE corporate citizenship report 2005*, General Electric, Fairfield CT.

GEE 2002, *Corporate social responsibility monitor*, GEE, London.

Geertz, C. 1963, *Peddlers and princes; social change and economic modernization in two Indonesian towns*, University of Chicago Press, Chicago.

Geisst, C.R. 2004, *Wall Street: a history: from its beginnings to the fall of Enron*, Rev. and expand edn, Oxford University Press, Oxford; New York.

Gereffi, G., Humphrey, J. & Sturgeon, T. 2005, "The governance of global value chains", *Review of International Political Economy*, vol. 12, no. 1, pp 78–104.

Gereffi, G.A. 1999 , *Commodity Chains Framework for Analyzing Global Industries*.

Germain, R.D. 1999, *Globalization and its critics: perspectives from political economy*, Macmillan/St. Martin's Press, Basingstoke.

Ghazali, B.H. & Simula, M. 1996, *Study on the Development and Formulation and Implementation of Certification Schemes for all Internationally Traded Timber and Timber Products*, International Timber Trade Organisation, Manila.

Gibson, K. 2000, "The moral basis of stakeholder theory", *Journal of Business Ethics*, no. 26, pp 245–257.

Giddens, A. & Hutton, W. 2000, *On the edge: living with global capitalism*, Jonathan Cape, London.

Giddens, A. 2000, *The third way and its critics*, Polity Press, Malden, Mass.

Giddens, A. 1994, *Beyond left and right: the future of radical politics*, Polity, Cambridge, UK.

Giddens, A. 1991, *Modernity and self-identity: self and society in the late modern age*, Stanford University Press, Stanford, Calif.

Giddens, A. 1990, *The consequences of modernity*, Stanford University Press, Stanford, Calif.

Gillon, R. & Lloyd, A. 1994, *Principles of health care ethics*, John Wiley & Sons, Chichester; New York.

Gilpin, R. & Gilpin, J.M. 1987, *The political economy of international relations*, Princeton University Press, Princeton, N.J.

Ginsberg, T, 2005, 'Threats to critics of Vioxx alleged', *Philadelphia Inquirer*, 5 June, accessed 10 June online at **www.lexis.nexis.com**.

Glasbeek, H.J. 2002, *Wealth by stealth: corporate crime, corporate law, and the perversion of democracy*, Between the Lines, Toronto.

Gleick, P.H. & Pacific Institute for Studies in Development, Environment, and Security 1999, "The world's water: the biennial report on freshwater resources".

Glover, D. 2007, "Monsanto and Smallholder Farmers: a case study in csr", *Third World Quarterly*, vol. 28, no. 4, pp 851–867.

Godfrey, A., Huane, K., Liying, L., Witchalls, B. & Yambayamba, E. 2005, "Findings from a learning partnership", *Partnership Matters*, vol. 3, pp 37–39.

Goffee, R. & Scase, R. 1995, *Corporate realities: the dynamics of large and small organisations*, Thomson Learning Emea.

Good Corporation undated, *Good corporation charter*.

Goodijk, R. 2000, "Corporate governance and workers' participation", *Corporate Governance*, vol. 8, no. 8, pp 303–310.

Goodpaster, K., E. 2002, "Stakeholder thinking: beyond paradox to practicality", in *Unfolding stakeholder thinking: theory, responsibility and engagement*, eds. J. Andriof, S.A. Waddock, B. Husted & S.S. Rahman, Greenleaf, Sheffield, pp 43–64.

Graham, D. & Woods, N. 2006, "Making corporate self-regulation effective in developing countries", *World Development*, vol. 34, no. 5, pp 868–883.

Grande, C. 2007, *Ethical consumption makes mark on branding*.

Gray, R.H., Kouhy, R. & Lavers, S. 1996, "Corporate social and environmental reporting: a review of the literature and a longitudinal study of UK disclosure", *Accounting Auditing and Accountability Journal*, vol. 8, no. 2, pp 47–77.

Gray, R.H. 1996, *Accounting & accountability: changes and challenges in corporate social and environmental reporting*, Prentice Hall, London.

Gray, R.H. 2003, *Social and environmental accounting and reporting: from ridicule to revolution? from hope to hubris?*, University of Glasgow.

Gray, R. 2001, *Accounting for the environment*, 2nd edn, SAGE Publications, London.

Grayson, D. & Dodd, T. 2007, *Small is sustainable (and beautiful!): encouraging European smaller enterprises to be sustainable*, Doughty Centre for Corporate Responsibility, Cranfield.

Grayson, D. 2004, *Corporate social opportunity!: 7 steps to make corporate social responsibility work for your business*, Greenleaf, Sheffield.

Grayson, D. and Hodges, A. 2004, Corporate Social Opportunity: Seven Steps to Make Corporate Social Responsibility Work for Your Business, Greenleaf Publishing, Sheffield.

Green, S. 2009, *Good value: reflections on money, morality and an uncertain world*, Allen Lane, London; New York.

Gregory, C.A. 1982, *Gifts and commodities*, Academic Press, London; New York.

Greider, W. 2003, *The soul of capitalism: opening paths to a moral economy*, Simon & Schuster, New York.

Greider, W. 1997, *One world, ready or not: the manic logic of global capitalism*, Simon & Schuster, New York.

GRI 2002, *Sustainability reporting guidelines*, Global Reporting Initiative, Boston.

GRI 2000, *Sustaianbility reporting guidelines on economic, environmental and social performance*, Global Reporting Initiative, Boston.

Gribben, C. & Olsen, L. 2004, *An anchor—not the answer: trends in social and sustainable development reporting*, Ashridge Centre for Business and Society, Ashridge.

Griesgraber, J.M. & Gunter, B.G. 1997, *World trade: toward a fair and free trade in the twenty-first century*, Pluto Press, London; Chicago, IL.

Griffin, J.J. & Mahon, J.F. 1997, "The Corporate Social Performance and Corporate Financial Performance Debate: Twenty-Five Years of Incomparable Research", *Business & Society*, vol. 36, no. 1, pp 5–31.

Grinspun, R. & Cameron, M.A. 1993, *The political economy of North American free trade*, St. Martin's Press, New York.

Grosser, K. & Moon, J. 2005, "Gender Mainstreaming and Corporate Social Responsibility: Reporting Workplace Issues", *Journal of Business Ethics*, vol. 62, no. 4, pp 327–340.

Gunther, M. 2008, *Merrill Lynch's carbon bet: Why a Wall Street firm wants to save a forest in Sumatra*, Online Edition edn, New York.

Guo, B. 2009, *Building a comprehensive strategy for China's environmental clean-up*, China Currents.

Habisch, A., Jonker, J., Wegner, M. & Schmidpeter, R. (eds) 2005, *Corporate social responsibility across Europe*, 1st edn, Springer, New York.

Hale, A. & Shaw, L.M. 2001, "Women workers and the promise of ethical trade in the globalised garment industry: a serious beginning?", *Antipode*, vol. 33, no. 3, pp 510–530.

Hale, B. 2009, *Oxfam is the new Tesco say angry independent bookshops being driven to the wall by charity shop's growth*, Dail Mail, London.

Hamann, R. 2003, "Kelian Equatorial Mining: mine closure", in *Putting partnerships to work*, eds. M. Warner & R. Sullivan, Greenleaf Publishing, Sheffield, pp 138–150.

Hamann, R., Agbazue, T., Kapelus, P. & Hein, A. 2005, "Universalizing corporate social responsibility? South African challenges to the international organization for standardization's new social responsibility standard", *Business and Society Review*, vol. 110, no. 1, pp 1–19.

Hamann, R., Woolman, S. & Sprague, C. 2008, *The business of sustainable development in Africa: human rights, partnerships, alternative business models*, Unisa Press; Tokyo, Japan; United Nations University Press, Pretoria, South Africa; New York.

Hammond, A.L., Kramer, W.J., Katz, R.S., Tran, J.T. & Walker, C. 2007, *The next four billion: market size and business strategy at the base of the pyramid*, International Finance Corporation/World Resources Institute, Washington DC.

Hampden-Turner, C. & Trompenaars, A. 1993, *The seven cultures of capitalism: value systems for creating wealth in the United States, Japan, Germany, France, Britain, Sweden, and the Netherlands*, 1st edn, Currency/Doubleday, New York.

Handy, C. 2002, "What's a Business For?", *Harvard business review*, vol. December 2002, pp 49–55.

Handy, C.B. 1998, *The hungry spirit: beyond capitalism: a quest for purpose in the modern world*, 1st edn, Broaday Books, New York.

Hannerz, U. 1996, *Transnational connections: culture, people, places*, Routledge, London and New York.

Hardt, M. & Negri, A. 2000, *Empire*, Harvard University Press, Cambridge, Mass.

Harrison, A. & Scorse, J. 2004, *Moving up or moving out? Anti-sweatshop activists and labor market outcomes*.

Harrison, R., Newholm, T. & Shaw, D. 2005, *The ethical consumer*, Sage, London; Thousand Oaks.

Harrison, R. 1964, *Animal machines*, Vincent Stuart, London.

Hart, S.L. 2005, Capitalism at the Crossroads: The Unlimited Business Opportunities in Solving the World's Most Difficult Problems, Upper Saddle River, NJ: Great Britain and Wharton School.

Hart, S.L. & Christensen, C.M. 2002, "The great leap: driving innovation from the base of the pyramid", *Sloan management review*, vol. 44, no. 1, pp 51–56.

Hartman, L.P., Shaw, B. & Stevenson, R. 2003, "Exploring the ethics and economics of global labor standards: a challenge to integrated social contract theory", *Business Ethics Quarterly*, vol. 13, no. 2, pp 193–220.

Harvey-Jones, J. 1988, *Making it happen: reflections on leadership*, Collins, London.

Harwood, I. & Humby, S. 2008, "Embedding corporate responsibility into supply: a snapshot of progress", *European Management Journal*, vol. 26, no. 3, pp 166–174.

Harwood, I. & Humby, S. 2007, "Embedding corporate responsibility into procurement: a force field analysis".

Haugh, H. 2006, "Social enterprise: beyond economic outcomes and individual returns", in *Social entrepreneurship*, eds. J. Mair, J. Robinson & K. Hockerts, Palgrave Macmillan, Basingstoke, pp 180–206.

Hawken, P. 2004, "Socially responsible investing. How the SRI industry has failed to respond to people who want to invest with conscience and what can be done to change it", *Natural Capital Institute*.

Hawken, P. 1993, *The ecology of commerce: a declaration of sustainability*, HarperCollins, New York, N.Y.

Hawken, P., Lovins, A.B. & Lovins, L.H. 1999, *Natural capitalism: creating the next industrial revolution*, 1st edn, Little, Brown and Co., Boston.

Headd, B. 2000, "The characteristics of small-business employees", *Monthly Labor Review*, vol. 123, no. 4.

Heal, G.M. 2008, *When principles pay: corporate social responsibility and the bottom line*, Columbia Business School Pub., New York.

Heald, M. 1970, *The social responsibilities of business, company, and community, 1900–1960*, Press of Case Western Reserve University, Cleveland.

Hebrew Union College-Jewish Institute of Religion 1980, *Ethics and corporate responsibility*, Hebrew Union College-Jewish Institute of Religion, Cincinnati, Ohio (3101 Clifton Ave., Cincinnati 45220).

Held, D. & McGrew, A.G. 2003, *The global transformations reader: an introduction to the globalization debate*, 2nd edn, Polity, Oxford.

Hemingway, C.A. & Maclagan, P.W. 2004, "Managers' personal values as drivers of corporate social responsibility", *Journal of Business Ethics*, vol. 50, no. 1, pp 33–44.

Hemp, P. & Stewart, T. 2004, 'Leading change when business is good', *Harvard Business Review*, vol. 82, no. 12, pp 61–70.

Henderson, D. & Institute of Economic Affairs 2001, *Misguided virtue: false notions of corporate social responsibility*, The Institute of Economic Affairs, London.

Henderson, D. 2004, *The Role of Business in the Modern World*, Institute of Economic Affairs, London.

Hennigfeld, J., Pohl, M., Tolhurst, N., *The ICCA handbook on corporate social responsibility*, John Wiley & Sons, Chichester, England; Hoboken, NJ.

Henriques, A. & Richardson, J.A. 2004, *The triple bottom line, does it all add up?: assessing the sustainability of business and CSR*, Earthscan, London.

Henriques, A. 2010, *Corporate impact: measuring and managing your social footprint*, Earthscan, London.

Hertz, N. 2001, *The silent takeover: global capitalism and the death of democracy*, Heinemann, London.

Hill, P. 1970, *Studies in rural capitalism in West Africa*, Cambridge University Press, London.

Hillary, R. 2000, *ISO 14001: case studies and practical experiences*, Greenleaf, Sheffield.

Hillary, R. 2000, *The risk society and beyond: critical issues for social theory*, SAGE, London.

Hinrichsen, D. & Earthscan 1987, *Our common future: a reader's guide*, Earthscan, London.

Hirst, P.Q. & Thompson, G. 1999, *Globalization in question: the international economy and the possibilities of governance*, Polity Press/Blackwell Publishers, Cambridge.

Hollender, J. 2010, *The responsibility revolution: how the next generation of businesses will win*, Jossey-Bass; John Wiley & Sons distributor, San Francisco, Calif.; Chichester.

Hollender, J. & Breen, B. 2010, *The responsibility revolution: how the next generation of businesses will win*, Jossey-Bass; John Wiley & Sons distributor, San Francisco, Calif.; Chichester.

Holliday, I. 2005, "Doing Business with Rights Violating Regimes Corporate Social Responsibility and Myanmar's Military Junta", *Journal of Business Ethics*, vol. 61, no. 4, pp 329–342.

Holliday, C.O., Schmidheiny, S., Watts, P. & World Business Council for Sustainable Development 2002, *Walking the talk: the business case for sustainable development*, Greenleaf, Sheffield.

Hoogvelt, A.M.M. 2001, *Globalization and the postcolonial world: the new political economy of development*, Johns Hopkins University Press, Baltimore, MD.

Hopkins, K. 2009, *Public must learn to tolerate the inequality of bonuses, says Goldman Sachs vice-chairman*, guardian.co.uk edn, The Guardian, London.

Hopkins, M. 2003, *The planetary bargain: corporate social responsibility matters*, Earthscan, London; Sterling, VA.

House of Commons 1999, *House of Commons Select Committee on Trade and Industry Sixth Report: ethical trading*, House of Commons, London.

Hudson, W.H. 1996, *An introduction to the philosophy of Herbert Spencer*, Routledge/Thoemmes, London.

Hughes, N. & Lonie, S. 2007, "M-PESA: mobile money for the 'unbanked' – turning cellphones into 24-hour tellers in Kenya", *Innovations*, vol. 2, no. 1–2, pp 63–81.

Humphrey, J. & Schmitz, H. 2001, "Governance in global value chains", *IDS Bulletin*, vol. 32, no. 3, pp 19–29.

Huntington, S.P. 1996, *The clash of civilizations and the remaking of world order*, Simon & Schuster, New York.

Hutton, W. 1995, *The state we're in*, Jonathan Cape, London.

Hutton, W. & Giddens, A. 2000, *Global capitalism*, New Press, New York.

IFAT 2006, *Fair trade in Europe 2005: facts and figures on Fair Trade in 25 European countries*, International Fair Trade Association.

Igalens, J. & Gond, J. 2005, "Measuring corporate social performance in France: a critical and empirical analysis of ARESE data", *Journal of Business Ethics*, no. 56, pp 131–148.

ILO 1998, *Declaration on Fundamental Principles and Rights at Work and its Follow-up*, International Labour Organisation, Geneva.

Impactt 2005, *Changing over time: tackling supply chain labour issues through business practice*, Impactt Ltd, London.

INGI Labour Working Group 1991, *Button up, button down: women workers and overtime in Indonesia's garment and textile industry*.

INGI Labour Working Group 1991, *Unjust but doing it! Nike's operations in Indonesia*.

Inglis, F. 2000, *Clifford Geertz: culture, custom, and ethics*, Polity Press, Malden, Mass.

W.H.O.T.F. Initiative, 2008, "Tobacco industry interference with tobacco control".

Innovest 2005, *Intangible value assessment: Swiss Reinsurance company*, Innovest Strategic Value Advisors, London.

Innovest & Environment Agency 2004, *Corporate environmental governance: a study into the influence of environmental governance on financial performance*, Environment Agency, London.

INSEAD, Copenhagen Business School, Universita Commerciale Luigi Bocconi & Leon Kozminski Academy 2007, *Understanding and responding to societal demands on corporate responsibility (RESPONSE)*, INSEAD; Copenhagen Business School; Universita Commerciale Luigi Bocconi; Leon Kozminski Academy, Brussels.

International Chambers of Commerce undated, *Business charter for sustainable development*.

International Development Research Centre. 1999, *Mining and the environment: case studies from the Americas*, International Development Research Centre, Ottawa, Ont.

International Institute of Tropical Agriculture & International Labour Organisation 2002, *Child labour in the cocoa sector of West Africa*, International Institute of Tropical Agriculture and International Labour Organisation, Ibadan.

Ireland, P. & Pillay, R. 2007, "Corporate Social Responsibility and the New Constitutionalism",

ISEA 1999, *Accountability 1000: overview of standard and its applications*, Institute of Social and Ethical Accountability, London.

Ite, U.E. "Multinationals and corporate social responsibility in developing countries: a case study of Nigeria ", *Corporate Social Responsibility and Environmental Management*, vol. 11, no. 1, pp 1–11.

Jackson, I.A. & Nelson, J. 2004, *Profits with principles: seven strategies for delivering value with values*, 1st edn, Currency/Doubleday, New York.

Jacoby, N.H. 1973, *Corporate power and social responsibility; a blueprint for the future*, Macmillan, New York.

Jahdi, K.S. & Acikdilli, G. 2009, "Marketing Communications and Corporate Social Responsibility (CSR): Marriage of Convenience or Shotgun Wedding?", *Journal of Business Ethics*, vol. 88, no. 1, pp 103–113.

Jamali, D., Zanhour, M. & Keshishian, T. 2009, "Peculiar strengths and relational attributes of SMEs in the context of CSR", *Journal of Business Ethics*, vol. 87, no. 3, pp 355–377.

Jamison, L. & Murdoch, H. 2004, *Taking the temperature: ethical supply chain management*, Institute of Business Ethics, London.

Jenkins, H. 2009, "A'business opportunity'model of corporate social responsibility for small-and medium-sized enterprises", *Business Ethics: A European Review*, vol. 18, no. 1, pp 21–36.

Jenkins, H. 2006, "Small business champions for corporate social responsibility", *Journal of Business Ethics*, vol. 67, no. 3, pp 241–256.

Jenkins, H. 2004, "A critique of conventional CSR theory: an SME perspective", *Journal of General Management*, vol. 29, pp 37–57.

Jenkins, R.O. 2005, "Globalization, corporate social responsibility and poverty", *International Affairs*, vol. 81, no. 3, pp 525–540.

Jenkins, R.O. 2002, "The Political Economy of Codes of Conduct", in *Corporate Responsibility and Labour Rights: codes of conduct in the global economy*, eds. R.O. Jenkins, R. Pearson & G. Seyfang, Earthscan, London, pp 13–30.

Jenkins, R.O. 2001, *Corporate Codes of Conduct: self-regulation in a global economy*, UNRISD, Geneva.

Jenkins, R.O. 1999, "The Changing Relationship between Emerging Markets and Multinational Enterprises", in *Multinational Enterprises and Emerging Markets: Managing Increasing Interdependence*, eds. P.J. Buckley & P.N. Ghauri, Pergamon.

Jenkins, R.O., Pearson, R. & Seyfang, G. 2002, *Corporate responsibility and labour rights: codes of conduct in the global economy*, Earthscan, London; Sterling, VA.

Jensen, M.C. 2002, "Value maximization, stakeholder theory, and the corporate objective function", *Business Ethics Quarterly*, vol. 12, pp 235–256.

Jensen, M.C. 2000, *A theory of the firm: governance, residual claims, and organizational forms*, Harvard University Press, Cambridge, MA.

Jensen, M.C. & Meckling, W.H. 1976, "Theory of the firm: managerial behavior, agency costs and ownership structure", *Journal of Financial Economics*, vol. 3, no. 4, pp 305–360.

Jeucken, M. 2001, *Sustainable finance and banking: the financial sector and the future of the planet*, Earthscan, London.

Jewson Associates Research report on ethical investment for Oxford University, *The costs of ethical investing*, Jewson Associates, London.

Johnson, J. 2004, "Global trends in employment, productivity and poverty", *Paper presented at the conference on Globalization and Labor in Developing Countries, Watson Institute for International Studies, Brown University, December 10–11 2004*.

Johnston, D.C. 2003, *Perfectly legal: the covert campaign to rig our tax system to benefit the super rich- and cheat everybody else*, Portfolio, New York.

Jones, O.T. 2003, *Competitive advantage in SMEs: organising for innovation and change*, John Wiley & Sons, Chichester.

Jones, O. & Tilley, F. 2003, *Competitive advantage in SMEs: organising for innovation and change*, John Wiley & Sons, Chichester.

Jones, K.A. 2004, *Who's afraid of the WTO?* Oxford University Press, Oxford; New York.

Jones, L.B. 1995, *Jesus, CEO: using ancient wisdom for visionary leadership*, Hyperion, New York.

Jonkers, J. 2005, "CSR Wonderland: navigating between movement, community and organisation", *Journal of Corporate Citizenship*, Winter 2005, pp 19–22.

Kabeer, N. 2000, *The power to choose: Bangladeshi women and labour market decisions in London and Dhaka*, VERSO, London, New York.

Kakabadse, A.P. 2006, "Management thinking: making CSR work", *Ethical Corporation*, June 20 2006, online edition.

Kamara, J. 1986, *Socially responsible investment and economic development*, Division of Research, Michigan School of Business, University of Michigan, Ann Arbor, Mich.

Kaminsky, J.S. 1995, *Corporate responsibility in the Hebrew Bible*, Sheffield Academic Press, Sheffield.

Kanter, R.M. 1999, "From spare change to real change. The social sector as beta site for business innovation", *Harvard business review*, vol. 77, no. 3, pp 122–32, 210.

Kanter, R.M. 2009, *Supercorp: how vanguard companies create innovation, profits, growth, and social good*, 1st edn, Crown Business, New York.

Kaplan, R.E.B. & Berenbeim, J.M. 2004, *Ethics programs: the role of the board: a global study*, Conference Board, New York, NY.

Kaptein, M. 2004, "Business codes of multinational firms: what do they say?", *Journal of Business Ethics*, vol. 50, pp 13–31.

Kapstein, E.B. 2008, *Measuring Unilever's economic footprint: the case of South Africa*, Unilever, London.

Karnani, A. 2007, "The Mirage of Marketing to the Bottom of the Pyramid", *California Management Review*, vol. 49, no. 4, pp 90.

Katz, J.P., Swanson, D.L. & Nelson, L.K. 1999, *Culture based expectations of corporate citizenship: a propositional framework and comparative analysis of four countries*.

Kauffman, M. & Chedekel, L. 2004, 'As colleges profit, sweatshops worsen', *Hartford Courant*, 12 December, online at **www.courant.com**.

Kavlianz, P. 2009, *Mattel fined $2.3 million over lead in toys*, www.CNNMoney.com, Atlanta.

Keefe, J.F. 2007, *From SRI to sustainable investing*, Green Money Journal, unknown.

Kell, G. & Levin, D. 2003, "The Global Compact network: an historic experiment in learning and action", *Business and Society Review*, vol. 108, no. 2, pp 151–181.

Kelly, M. 2001, *The divine right of capital: dethroning the corporate aristocracy*, Berrett-Koehler Publishers Inc, San Francisco, CA.

Kelly, P.J. 1990, *Utilitarianism and distributive justice: Jeremy Bentham and the civil law*, Clarendon Press; Oxford University Press, Oxford; New York.

Kennedy, A. 2000, *The end of shareholder value*, Orion Business, London.

Kennedy, P.M. 1987, *The rise and fall of the great powers: economic change and military conflict from 1500 to 2000*, 1st edn, Random House, New York, NY.

Khurana, R. 2007, *From higher aims to hired hands: the social transformation of American business schools and the unfulfilled promise of management as a profession*, Princeton University Press, Princeton.

Killick, N. 2003, "BP and others, Azerbaijan: conflict prevention" in *Putting partnerships to work*, eds. M. Warner & R. Sullivan, Greenleaf, Sheffield, pp 98–107.

Kim, W.C. 2005, *Blue ocean strategy: how to create uncontested market space and make the competition irrelevant*, Harvard Business School, Boston, Mass.

Klein, G.D. 1978, "Corporate social responsibility: an assessment of the enlightened self-interest model", *Academy of Management Review*, vol. 3, no. 1, pp 32–39.

Klein, N. 1999, *No logo: taking aim at the brand bullies*, Picador USA, New York.

Klein, T.A. 1977, *Social costs and benefits of business*, Prentice-Hall, Englewood Cliffs, N.J.

Knights, D. & Tinker, T. 1997, *Financial institutions and social transformations: international studies of a sector*, St. Martin's Press, New York.

Koch, K.-. 1974, *War and peace in Jalémó: the management of conflict in highland New Guinea*, Harvard University Press, Cambridge, Mass.

Kolb, R.W. 2008, *Encyclopedia of business ethics and society*, Sage Publications, Thousand Oaks.

Kolk, A. & Tulder, R.v. 2006, "Poverty alleviation as business strategy? Evaluating commitments of frontrunner Multinational Corporations", *World Development*, vol. 34, no. 5, pp 542.

Kolk, A. & Tulder, R.v. 2002, "Child labor and multinational conduct: a comparison of international business and stakeholder codes", *Journal of Business Ethics*, vol. 36, no. 3, pp 91–301.

Kolk, A., Tulder, R.v. & Welters, C. 1999, "International Codes of Conduct and Corporate Social Responsibility: can transnational corporations regulate themselves?", *Transnational Corporations*, vol. 8, no. 1, pp 143–180.

Korten, D.C. 1995, *When corporations rule the world*, Kumarian Press; Berrett-Koehler Publishers, West Hartford, Conn. San Francisco, Calif.

Korten, D.C. 1999, *The post-corporate world: life after capitalism*, Berrett-Koehler, San Francisco, CA; United Kingdom.

KPMG 2005, *KPMG international survey of Corporate Responsibility reporting 2005*, KPMG, Amsterdam.

Kramer, M. & Kania, J. 2006, "Changing the game: leading corporations switch from defense to offense in solving global problems", *Stanford Social Innovation Review*, vol. Spring 2006, pp 20–27.

Kreps, T.J. & Murphy, K.R. 1940, *Measurement of the social performance of business*, U.S.Govt.Print. Off., Washington.

Krosinsky, C. 2008, "Sustainable equity investing: the market-beating strategy", in *Sustainable investing: the art of long-term performance*, eds. C. Krosinsky & N. Robins, Earthscan, London, pp 19–30.

Krosinsky, C. & Robins, N. 2008, *Sustainable investing: the art of long-term performance*, Earthscan, London.

Krugman, P. undated, undated-last update, *Why aren't we all Keynesians yet?* [Homepage of MIT], [Online]. Available: http://web.mit.edu/krugman/www/keynes.html [2006, May 30].

Krugman, P. 1998, *The accidental theorist: and other dispatches from the dismal science*, Norton, New York.

Krumsiek, B. 2004, "Voluntary codes of conduct for multinational corporations: promises and challenges", *Business and Society Review*, vol. 109, no. 4, pp 583–593.

Kukathas, C. 1989, *Hayek and modern liberalism*, Clarendon Press; Oxford University Press, Oxford, England; New York.

Kurtenbach, E. 2005, *Chinese Sofa Factory Workers Go on Strike*, Associated Press.

Kwan, A. & Frost, S. 2002, "Made in China: rules and regulations versus codes of conduct in the toy sector", in *Corporate Responsibility and Ethical Trade: codes of conduct in the global economy*, eds. R.O. Jenkins, R. Pearson & G. Seyfang, Earthscan, London, pp 124–134.

Ladbury, S., Young, G. & Gibbons, S. 2000, *Mid-term review of the ETI: a review of the progress of the Ethical Trading Initiative for the UK Department for International Development*.

Ladkin, D. 2006, "When deontology and utilitarianism aren't enough: how Heidegger's notion of 'dwelling' might help organisational leaders resolve ethical issues", Journal of Business Ethics, vol. 65, no. 1, pp 87–98.

LaFeber, W. 2002, *Michael Jordan and the new global capitalism*, New and expand edn, W.W. Norton & Co., New York.

Laffer, A.B. & Miles, M.A. 1982, *International economics in an integrated world*, Scott, Foresman, Glenview, Ill.

Lash, S. 2002, *Critique of information*, SAGE, London.

Laszlo, C. 2003, *The sustainable company: how to create lasting value through social and environmental performance*, Island Press, Washington, DC.

Laszlo, E. 2006, *The chaos point: the world at the crossroads*, Hampton Roads Pub. Company, Inc., Charlottesville, VA.

Lawrence, A.T., Weber, J. & Post, J.E. 2005, *Business and society: stakeholders, ethics, public policy*, 11th edn, McGraw-Hill/Irwin, Boston.

Leadbeater, C. 2004, *Personalisation through participation: a new script for public services*, Demos.

Leadbeater, C. 1997, *The rise of the social entrepreneur*, Demos.

Leipziger, D. 2003, *The corporate responsibility code book*, Greenleaf, Sheffield.

Leipziger, D. 2001, *SA8000: the definitive guide to the new social standard*, Financial Times Prentice Hall, London.

Lenox, M.J. & Nash, J. 2003, "Industry self-regulation and adverse selection: a comparison across four trade association programs", *Business Strategy and the Environment*, vol. 12, no. 6, pp 343–356.

Levy, D. & Newell, P. 2002, "Business Strategy and International Environmental Governance: Toward a Neo-Gramscian Synthesis", *Global Environmental Politics*, vol. 2, no. 4, pp 84–101.

Levy, D.L. & Newell, P. 2005, *The business of global environmental governance*, MIT Press, Cambridge, Mass.

Light, A. & Smith, J.M. 1997, *Space, place, and environmental ethics*, Roman & Litterfield Publishers, Lanham.

Light, A. & Rolston, H. 2003, *Environmental ethics: an anthology*, Blackwell Pub., Malden, MA.

Lindblom, C.K. 1994, *The implications of organizational legitimacy for corporate social performance and disclosure*, Paper presented at the Critical Perspectives on Accounting Conference, New York edn.

Lindsay, J. 1975, *William Morris: his life and work*, Constable, London.

Lindsey, B. 2002, *Against the dead hand: the uncertain struggle for global capitalism*, John Wiley & Sons, New York; Chichester.

Little, W.G. 2002, *The waste fix: seizures of the sacred from Upton Sinclair to the Sopranos*, Routledge, New York.

Litvin, D.B. 2003, *Empires of profit: commerce, conquest and corporate responsibility*, Texere, New York.

Locke, R., Fei, Q. & Brause, A. 2006, *Does monitoring improve labor standards? Lessons from Nike*, MIT Sloan School of Management working paper 4612–06 edn, Cambridge.

Lodge, G.C. 2006, *A corporate solution to global poverty: how multinationals can help the poor and invigorate their own legitimacy*, Princeton University Press, Princeton, N.J.; Woodstock.

Loftus, P. 2009, *Merck Sees $80 Million Vioxx Settlement*, 3 August 2009 edn.

Logan, D. 1997, *The case for business action on family planning and AIDS prevention in Ghana*, Corporate Citizenship Company, London.

Logsdon, J.M. 2004, "Global Business Citizenship: Applications to Environmental Issues", *Business and Society Review*, vol. 109, no. 1, pp 67.

Lort-Phillips, L, 2006, "China: one country, two systems", *Corporate Citizenship Briefing*, December/January (85), online at **www.ccbriefing.co.uk**.

Lucas-Lecin, V. & Nahal, S. 2008, "Sustainability analysis", in *Sustainable investing: the art of long-term performance*, eds. C. Krosinsky & N. Robins, Earthscan, London, pp 41–56.

Lukes, S, 1974, *Power: A Radical View*, London: Macmillan.

Lund-Thomsen, P. 2005, "Corporate accountability in South Africa: the role of community mobilizing in environmental governance", vol. 81, no. 3, pp 619–634.

Lydenberg, S.D. 2005, *Corporations and the public interest: guiding the invisible hand*, 1st edn, Berrett-Koehler Publishers, San Francisco.

Lyon, F. 2003, "Community groups and livelihoods in remote rural areas of Ghana: how small-scale farmers sustain collective action", *Community Development Journal*, vol. 38, no. 4, pp 323.

Lyon, F. & Bertotti, M. 2007, "Measuring the contributions of small firms to reducing poverty and increasing social inclusion in the UK", in IAP/Information Age Pub.

Lyon, F. & Vickers, I. 2009, "Challenges of encouraging enterprise in deprived areas", in *Enterprise and deprivatoin: small business, social exclusion and sustainable communities*, ed. A. Southern, 1st edn, John Wiley & Sons, Basingstoke.

Lyon, S. & Moberg, M. (eds) 2010, *Fair trade and social justice: global ethnographies*, NYU Press, New York.

Macdonald, K. 2007, *Globalising justice within coffee supply chains? Fair Trade, Starbucks and the transformation of supply chain governance.*, Third World Foundation for Social and Economic Studies, London.

Macdonald, K. & Marshall, S.E. 2010, *Fair trade, corporate accountability and beyond: experiments in globalizing justice*, Ashgate, Farnham.

MacGillivray, A. & Zadek, S. 1995, *Accounting for change: indicators for sustainable development*, New Economics Foundation, London.

MacKenzie, D.A. 2006, *An engine, not a camera: how financial models shape markets*, MIT Press, Cambridge, Mass.

Maclean, J. 1999, "Towards a political economy of agency in contemporary international relations", in *Politics and Globalisation: knowledge, ethics and agency*, ed. M. Shaw, Routledge, London.

MacLean, J. 2000, "Philosophical Roots of Globalization and Philosohpical Roots to Globalization", in *Globalization and its Critics: perspectives from political economy*, ed. R.D. Germain, Macmillan Press, Basingstoke, pp 3–65.

Mair, J. & Noboa, E. 2006, "Social entrepreneurship: how intentions to create social venture are formed" in *Social entrepreneurship*, eds. J. Mair, J. Robinson & K. Hockerts, Palgrave Macmillan, Basingstoke, pp 121–136.

Mair, J., Robinson, J. & Hockerts, K.E. 2006, "Social entrepreneurship", in *International social entrepreneurship research conference*, eds. J. Mair, J. Robinson & K. Hockerts, Palgrave Macmillan, Basingstoke.

Maitland, A, 2005, "Big business starts to scratch the surface", *Financial Times*, 14 September, online at **www.ft.com**.

Maitland, A, 2006, "A responsible balancing act", *Financial Times*, 1 June, online at **www.ft.com**.

Mamic, I. 2004, *Implementing codes of conduct: how businesses manage social performance in global supply chains*, Greenleaf Publishing and International Labour Office, Sheffield, UK.

Mander, J. & Goldsmith, E. 1996, *The case against the global economy: and for a turn toward the local*, Sierra Club Books, San Francisco.

Manga, J.E., Mirvis, P., Rochlin, S.A. & Zecchi, K. 2005, *Integration: Critical Link for Corporate Citizenship; Strategies and Stories from Eight Companies*, Center for Corporate Citizenship, Chestnut Hill.

Manheim, J.B. 2004, *Biz-war and the out-of-power elite: the progressive-left attack on the corporation*, Lawrence Erlbaum Associates, Mahwah, N.J.; London.

Manheim, J.B. 2000, *The death of a thousand cuts: corporate campaigns and the attack on the corporation*, Lawrence Erlbaum Associates, Publishers, Mahwah, NJ.

Manne, H. & Wallich, H.C. 1972, *The Modern Corporation and Social Responsibility*, Washington DC: American Enterprise Institute for Public Policy Research.

Margolis, J.D., Elfenbein, H.A. & James, P.W. 2008, "Doing well by doing good: Don't count on it", *Harvard Business Review*, vol. 86, no. 1, pp 19.

Margolis, J.D. & Walsh, J.P. 2003, "Misery loves companies: rethinking social initiatives by business", *Administrative Science Quarterly*, vol. 48, no. 2, pp 268–305.

Margolis, J.D. & Walsh, J.P. 2001, *People and profits?: the search for a link between a company's social and financial performance*, Lawrence Erlbaum Associates, Mahwah, N.J.

Markopoulos, M. 1999, *Community Forest Enterprise and Certification in Mexico: a review of experience*, Oxford University Press, Oxford.

Markopoulos, M. 1998, *Impacts of Certification on Community Forest Enterprises: a case study of the Lomerio community forest management project, Bolivia*, London.

Marland, G., Boden, T.A. & Andres, R.J. 2003, "Global, Regional, and National CO2 Emissions." in *Trends: A Compendium of Data on Global Change* Carbon Dioxide Information Analysis Center, Oak Ridge National Laboratory, U.S. Department of Energy, Oak Ridge, Tennessee.

Marling, W.H. 2006, *How "American" is globalization?* Johns Hopkins University Press, Baltimore.

Martin, R.L. 2002, "The virtue matrix: calculating the return on corporate responsibility", *Harvard Business Review*, vol. 80, no. 3, pp 68.

Marx, K. & McLellan, D. 1972, *The Grundrisse*, Harper & Row, New York.

Marx, K., Moore, S., Aveling, E.B., Engels, F. & Besant, A.W. 1887, *Capital: a critical analysis of capitalist production*, S. Sonnenschein Lowrey & Co, London.

Marx, K. 1973, *Grundrisse. Foundations of the critique of political economy*, Vintage Books, New York.

Mason, E.S. 1960, *The corporation in modern society*, Harvard University Press, Cambridge.

Mathews, MR, 1993, *Socially Responsible Accounting*, Chapman and Hall, London.

Matten, D. & Moon, J. 2008, "'Implicit' and 'Explicit' CSR: A Conceptual Framework for a Comparative Understanding of Corporate Social Responsibility", *The Academy of Management Review (AMR)*, vol. 33, no. 2, pp 404–424.

Matten, D. & Crane, A. 2005, "Corporate citizenship: toward and extended theoretical conceptualization", *Academy of Management Review*, vol. 30, no. 1, pp 166–180.

Mattingly, J.E. & Berman, S.L. 2006, "Measurement of corporate social action: discovering taxonomy in the Kinder Lydenberg Domini ratings data", *Business and Society*, vol. 45, no. 1, pp 20–46.

Mawson, A. 2008, *The social entrepreneur: making communities work*, Atlantic, London.

Maxwell, S. 2005, *The Washington Consensus is dead! Long live the meta-narrative*, 243rd edn, Overseas Development Institute, London.

May, S., Cheney, G. & Roper, J. 2007, *The debate over corporate social responsibility*, Oxford University Press, New York; Oxford.

McCord, N. 1970, *Free trade: theory and practice from Adam Smith to Keynes*, David & Charles, Newton Abbot.

McDonough, W. & Braungart, M. 2002, *Cradle to cradle: remaking the way we make things*, 1st edn, North Point Press, New York.

McEwan, T. 2001, *Managing values and beliefs in organisations*, Financial Times Prentice Hall, Harlow.

McGee, R.W. 1994, *A trade policy for free societies: the case against protectionism*, Quorum Books, Westport, Conn.

McGreal, C. 2009, *International: US healthcare industry dispenses $380m to block key measures of Obama's reform plans: Large donations made to important politicians: Lobbyist admits firms money is morally suspect*.

McGregor, R, 2007, "China's good corporate citizens find their voice", *Financial Times*, 25 February, online at www.ft.com.

McGuire, J.W. 1963, *Business and society*, McGraw-Hill, New York.

McIntosh, M. & Thomas, R. 2000, *Global companies in the twentieth century: selected archival histories*, Routledge, London.

McIntosh, M., Waddock, S.A. & Kell, G. (eds) 2004, *Learning to talk: corporate citizenship and the development of the UN Global Compact*, Greenleaf, Sheffield.

McIntosh, A. 2002, *Soil and soul: people versus corporate power*, Aurum, London.

McIntosh, M. 2003, *Living corporate citizenship: strategic routes to socially responsible business*, Financial Times Prentice Hall, Harlow.

McIntosh, M. 2003, *Raising a ladder to the moon: the complexities of corporate social and environmental responsibility*, Palgrave Macmillan, Houndmills, Basingstoke, Hampshire; New York, N.Y.

McIntosh, M. 1998, *Corporate citizenship: successful strategies for responsible companies*, Financial Times, London.

McLean, B. & Elkind, P. 2003, *The smartest guys in the room: the amazing rise and scandalous fall of Enron*, Portfolio, New York.

McMichael, P. 2004, *Development and social change: a global perspective*, 3rd edn, Pine Forge Press, Thousand Oaks, Calif; London.

McMurtry, J. 2002, *Value wars: the Global market versus the life economy*, Pluto Press, London; Sterling, Va.

McQuaid, K. 1977, "Young, Swope and General Electric's new capitalism: a study in corporate liberalism 1920–33", *American Journal of Economics and Sociology*, vol. 36.

McWilliams, A. & Siegel, D. 2000, "Corporate social responsibility and financial performance: correlation or misspecification?", *Strategic Management Journal*, vol. 21, pp 603–609.

Meh, A. 2004, *Uneasy Partnerships and Contradictions: Corporate Social and Environmental Responsibility*, Paper presented to the 3rd Annual Global Studies Association Conference, Brandeis University, date unknown.

Melcrum 2005, *How to structure the corporate responsibility function*, Melcrum Publishing, London.

Mesure, S. 2007, *Tesco follows M&S with climate change move*, The Independent, London.

Mill, J.S. 2002, *The basic writings of John Stuart Mill*, 2002 Modern Library pbk. edn, Modern Library, New York.

Mill, J.S. 1987, *Utilitarianism*, Prometheus Books, Buffalo, N.Y.

Mirvis, P. & Googins, B.K. 2006, *Stages of corporate citizenship: a developmental framework*, Center for Corporate Citizenship at Boston College, Boston.

Mirvis, P.H. 2000, "Transformation at Shell: Commerce and Citizenship ", *Business and Society Review*, vol. 105, no. 1, pp 63.

Mitchell, J., Shankleman, J. & Warner, M. 2003, "Measuring the added value of partnerships", in *Putting partnerships to work*, eds. M. Warner & R. Sullivan, pp 191–200.

Mitchell, L.E. 2005, *Roles and incentives: the core problems of corporate social responsibility*.

Mitchell, L.E. 2001, *Corporate irresponsibility: America's newest export*, Yale University Press, New Haven.

Mitnick, B.M. 2000, "Commitment, revelation, and the testaments of belief: the metrics of measurement of corporate social performance", *Business and Society*, vol. 39, no. 4, pp 419–465.

Mittelman, J.H. 2000, *The globalization syndrome: transformation and resistance*, Princeton University Press, Princeton, N.J.

Monbiot, G, 2005, "Africa's new best friends", *Guardian Weekly*, 5 July, p 4.

Monitor 2009, *Investing for social and environmental impact*, Monitor Group, Boston.

Monks, R.A.G. & Minow, N. 1991, *Power and accountability*, HarperCollins, London.

Moody-Stuart, S.M. 2004, "The role of business in developing countries", *Business Ethics A European Review*, vol. 13, no. 1, pp 41–49.

Moon, J, Crane, A & Matten, D, 2005, "Can corporations be citizens? Corporate citizenship as a metaphor for business participation in society", *Business Ethics Quarterly*, vol. 15, no. 3, pp 427–451.

Moore, B. 1966, *Social origins of dictatorship and democracy; lord and peasant in the making of the modern world*, Beacon Press, Boston.

Moorhead, J, 2007, "Milking it", *The Guardian*, 15 May, pp 7–11.

Morris, C.W. 1999, *The social contract theorists: critical essays on Hobbes, Locke, and Rousseau*, Rowman & Littlefield, Lanham, Md.

Morsing, M. & Perrini, F. 2009, "CSR in SMEs: do SMEs matter for the CSR agenda?", *Business Ethics: A European Review*, vol. 18, no. 1, pp 1–6.

Moss, D.A. 2002, *When all else fails: government as the ultimate risk manager*, Harvard University Press, Cambridge, Mass.

Mullins, J.W. & Komisar, R. 2009, *Getting to plan B: breaking through to a better business model*, Harvard Business School Press, Boston, Mass.

Mullins, J.W. 2009, *Getting to plan B: breaking through to a better business model*, Harvard Business School Press, Boston, Mass.

Mullins, J.W. 2006, *The new business road test: what entrepreneurs and executives should do before writing a business plan*, 2nd edn, Financial Times Prentice Hall, Harlow.

Murillo, D. & Lozano, J.M. 2006, "SMEs and CSR: an approach to CSR in their own words", *Journal of Business Ethics*, vol. 67, no. 3, pp 227–240.

Murphy, D.Y. & Bendell, J. 1999, *Partners in Time? Business, NGOs and sustainable development*, Geneva.

Murphy, R. 2007, *Platinum performers must shine all the way through*, Ethical Performance, London.

Murray, A.S. 2007, *Revolt in the boardroom: the new rules of power in corporate America*, 1st edn, Collins, New York.

Murray, J. 2002, "Labour Rights/Corporate Responsibilities: the role of ILO labour standards", in *Corporate Responsibility and Labour Rights: codes of conduct in the global economy*, eds. R.O. Jenkins, R. Pearson & G. Seyfang, Earthscan, London, pp 31–42.

Nader, R. & Taylor, W. 1986, *The big boys: power and position in American business*, 1st edn, Pantheon Books, New York.

Nair, C. 2006, "Eyes wide shut: corporate citizenship in Asia", *Ethical Corporation*, vol. May 2006, pp 46–47.

Narlikar, A. 2005, *The World Trade Organization: a very short introduction*, Oxford University Press, Oxford.

Nash, L.L. & Kantrow, A.M. "Multinational corporations and economic development", in *Capitalism and equality in the Third World*, ed. P.L. Berger, Institute for Educational Affairs, Lanham.

Nelson, J. 2007, *Building linkages for competitive and responsibile entrepreneurship*, Harvard University John F Kennedy School of Government & UNIDO, Cambridge MA.

Nelson, J. 1996, *Business as partners in development: creating wealth for countries, companies and communities*, Prince of Wales Business Leaders' Forum, London.

Nelson, V. & Galvez, M. 2000, *Social impact of ethical and conventional brazil nut trading on forest-dependent people in Peru*, Natural Resources Institute, Chatham.

Nelson, V., Martin, A. & Ewert, J. 2007, "The Impacts of Codes of Practice on Worker livelihoods: empirical evidence from the South African wine and Kenyan cut flower industries", *Journal of Corporate Citizenship*, vol. 2007, no. Winter, pp 61–72.

Nelson, V. & Tallontire, A. 2002, "Assessing the benefits of ethical trade schemes in cocoa (Ecuador) and Brazil nuts (Peru) for forest-dependent people and their livelihoods", *International Forestry Review*, vol. 4, no. 2, pp 99–109.

Nelson, J. 1998, *Building Competitiveness and Communities: how world class companies are creating shareholder value and societal value*, Prince of Wales Business Leaders Forum, London.

Nelson, J. & Zadek, S. 2000, *Partnership Alchemy: new social partnerships in Europe*, The Copenhagen Centre, Copenhagen.

Newell, P. 2005, "Citizenship, accountability and community: the limitations of the CSR agenda", *International Affairs*, vol. 81, no. 3, pp 541–558.

Newell, P. & Muro, A. 2006, "Corporate social and environmental responsibility in Argentina: the evolution of an agenda", *Journal of Corporate Citizenship*, no. 24, pp 49–68.

Newman, P. & Hotchner, A.E. 2003, *Shameless exploitation in pursuit of the common good*, Nan A. Talese, New York.

Newton, A. 2005, 'Defining the art of conversation', *Ethical Corporation*, November, pp 46–7.

Nicholls, A. 2010, "The Institutionalization of Social Investment: The Interplay of Investment Logics and Investor Rationalities", *Journal of Social Entrepreneurship*, vol. 1, no. 1, pp 70–100.

Nicholls, A. 2008, *Social entrepreneurship: new models of sustainable social change*, 2nd edn, Oxford University Press, Oxford.

Nicholls, A. & Opal, C. 2005, *Fair trade: market-driven ethical consumption*, SAGE, London.

Nielsen, M.E. 2005, "Child labour in the Bangladeshi garment industry", *International Affairs*, vol. 81, no. 3, pp 559–580.

Nocera, J, 2006, "The board wore chicken suits", *New York Times*, 27 May, pp B1–B2.

Novak, M. 1982, *Spirit of democratic capitalism*, Simon and Schuster, New York.

Nozick, R. 1974, *Anarchy, state, and utopia*, Basic Books, New York.

NRET 1999, "Ethical trade and sustainable rural livelihoods", in *Sustainable rural livelihoods: what contribution can we make?*, ed. D. Carney, Department for International Development, London, pp 107–129.

Nussbaum, M.C. & Sen, A.K., 1993, *The Quality of life*, Clarendon Press/Oxford University Press, Oxford.

Osterberg, R. 1993, *Corporate renaissance: business as an adventure in human development*, Nataraj Pub, Mill Valley, CA.

O'Rourke, D. 2006, "Multi-stakeholder regulation: privatizing or socializing global labor standards?", *World Development*, vol. 34, no. 5, pp 899–918.

Okali, C. 1983, *Cocoa and kinship in Ghana: the matrilineal Akan of Ghana*, Published for the International African Institute by Kegan Paul International, London; Boston.

Olsen, L. 2004, *Making corporate responsibility work: lessons from real business*, Ashirdge Centre for Business and Society and the British Quality Forum, Ashridge.

Ong, A. 1999, *Flexible citizenship: the cultural logics of transnationality*, Duke University Press, Durham.

O'Rourke, D. 2003, "Outsourcing regulation: non-governmental systems of labor standards and monitoring ", *Policy Studies Journal*, vol. 31, no. 1, pp 1–29.

O'Rourke, K.H. & Williamson, J.G. 1999, *Globalization and history: the evolution of a nineteenth-century Atlantic economy*, MIT Press, Cambridge, Mass.

O'Rourke, K.H. 2005, *The international trading system, globalization, and history*, Edward Elgar, Cheltenham, UK; Northampton, MA.

Orr, D. 2005, *The triumph of Neo-liberalism "but will it really make poverty history? What the campaign shows is how the political landscape has altered.*

Ougaard, M. unpublished, "Instituting the power to do good? The CSR movement and global governance", *unknown*.

Oxfam 2005, *Rigged rules and double standards: trade, globalisation and poverty*, Oxfam, Oxford.

Paine, L., Deshpande, R., Margolis, J.D. & Bettcher, K.E. 2005, "Up to code: does your company's conduct meet world-class standards?", *Harvard business review*, vol. 83, no. 12, pp 122–33, 154.

Palazzo, G. & Richter, U. 2005, "CSR business as usual? The case of the tobacco industry", *Journal of Business Ethics*, vol. 61, pp 387–401.

Parker, J. 1998, *Citizenship, work, and welfare: searching for the good society*, Macmillan Press; St. Martin's Press, Houndmills, Basingstoke, Hampshire; New York.

Patricof, A. & Sunderland, J. 2006, "Venture Capital for Development", in *Transforming the Development Landscape: The Role of the Private Sector*, ed. L. Brainard, Brookings Institution, Washington DC, pp 74–84.

Paulden, P. 2009, *TXU LBO 'disaster' punishes bondholders with offer*, online edn, Bloomberg, New York.

Pava, M.L. & Krausz, J. 1995, *Corporate responsibility and financial performance: the paradox of social cost*, Quorum Books, Westport, Conn.

Pearson, R. & Seyfang, G. 2001, "New hope or false dawn?: voluntary codes of conduct, labour regulation and social policy in a globalizing world", *Global Social Policy*, vol. 1, no. 1, pp 49–78.

Pearson, R. 2007, "Beyond women workers: gendering CSR", *Third World Quarterly*, vol. 28, no. 4, pp 731–749.

Pedersen, E.R. 2009, "The many and the few: rounding up the SMEs that manage CSR in the supply chain", *Supply Chain Management: An International Journal*, vol. 14, no. 2, pp 109–116.

Pedersen, E.R. 2006, "Making corporate social responsibility (CSR) operable: how companies translate stakeholder dialogue into practice", *Business and Society Review*, vol. 111, pp 137.

Pedersen, E.R. 2005, "Guiding the invisible hand: the role of development agencies in driving corporate citizenship", *Journal of Corporate Citizenship*, vol. Winter 2005.

Pedersen, E.R. & Huniche, M. (eds) 2006, *Corporate Citizenship in Developing Countries: New Partnership Perspectives*, Copenhagen Business School Press, Copenhagen.

Peinado-Vara, E. 2006, "Corporate social responsibility in Latin America", *Journal of Corporate Citizenship*, vol. 21, pp 61–69.

Perkins, R. 2004, "Sweeter partnerships? An NGO's engagement with the sugar sector", *Partnership Matters*, vol. 2, pp 33–35.

Perrini, F., Russo, A. & Tencati, A. 2007, "CSR strategies of SMEs and large firms. Evidence from Italy", *Journal of Business Ethics*, vol. 74, no. 3, pp 285–300.

Peters, G. 1999, *Waltzing with the raptors: a practical roadmap to protecting your company's reputation*, John Wiley & Sons, New York.

Peters, T.J. 1995, *In search of excellence: lessons from America's best-run companies*, HarperCollins, London.

Phillips, R. & Caldwell, C.B. 2005, "Value chain responsibility: a farewell to arm's length", *Business and Society Review*, vol. 110, no. 4, pp 345–370.

Phillips, R., Freeman, R.E. & Wicks, A.C. 2003, "What stakeholder theory is not", *Business Ethics Quarterly*, vol. 13, no. 4, pp 479–502.

Phillips, K.P. 2002, *Wealth and democracy: a political history of the American rich*, Broadway Books, New York.

Phillips, R. 2003, *Stakeholder theory and organizational ethics*, 1st edn, Berrett-Koehler, San Francisco; Great Britain.

Phylmar Group 2006, *Phylmar ENews February 2006*.

Pilger, J. 2002, *The new rulers of the world*, Verso, London.

Pinchot, G. 1985, *Intrapreneuring: why you don't have to leave the corporation to become an entrepreneur*, 1st edn, Harper & Row, New York.

Pinkse, J. & Kolk, A. 2009, *International business and global climate change*, Routledge, London.

Plender, J. 2003, *Going off the rails: global capital and the crisis of legitimacy*, John Wiley & Sons, West Sussex, England.

Plender, J. 1997, *A stake in the future: the stakeholding solution*, Nicholas Brealey, London.

Polanyi, K. 1944, *The great transformation*, New York, Toronto, Farrar & Rinehart, inc. 1944 xiii, 1, 305 p.

Pomeranz, K. & Topik, S. 2006, *The world that trade created: society, culture, and the world economy, 1400 to present*, M.E. Sharpe, Inc., Armonk, New York.

Porritt, J. 2005, *Capitalism: as if the world matters*, Earthscan, London.

Porter, M.E. 1990, *The competitive advantage of nations*, Free Press, New York.

Porter, M.E. & Kramer, M. 2006, "Strategy and society: the link between competitive advantage and corporate social responsibility", *Harvard Business Review*, no. December 2006, pp 78–92.

Porter, M.E. & Kramer, M.R. 2002, "The Competitive Advantage of Corporate Philanthropy", *Harvard Business Review*, vol. 80, no. 12, pp 56–68.

Porter, M.E. & Linde, C.V.D. 1999, "Green and Competitive: Ending the Stalemate", *Journal of Business Administration and Policy Analysis*.

Posner, R.A. 1981, *The economics of justice*, Harvard University Press, Cambridge, Mass.

Post, J.E. & Altman, B.W. 1992, "Models of corporate greening: how corporate social policy and organizational learning inform leading-edge environmental management", *Research in Corporate Social Performance and Policy*, vol. 13, pp 3–29.

Post, J.E., Lawrence, A.T. & Weber, J. 1999, *Business and society: corporate strategy, public policy, ethics*, 9th edn, Irwin/McGraw-Hill, Boston, MA.

Post, J.E., Preston, L.E. & Sauter-Sachs, S. 2002, *Redefining the corporation: stakeholder management and organizational wealth*, Stanford Business Books, Stanford, Calif.

PR News 2006, *Guide to best practices in corporate social responsibility*, PR News, unknown.

Prahalad, C.K. 2005, The Fortune at the Bottom of the Pyramid, Upper Saddle River, NJ: Wharton School Publishing.

Prahalad, C.K. & Hart, S.L. 2002, "The fortune at the bottom of the pyramid", *Strategy + Business*, no. 26, pp 2–14.

Prakash, S. 2006, *Conflicted Safety Panel Let Vioxx Study Continue*, National Public Radio, Washington DC.

Preston, L.E. & O'Bannon, D.P. 1997, "The Corporate Social-Financial Performance Relationship: A Typology and Analysis", *Business & Society*, vol. 36, no. 4, pp 419–428.

Preston, L.E. & Sapienza, H.J. 1990, "Stakeholder management and corporate performance", *Journal of Behavioral Economics*, vol. 19, no. 4, pp 361–375.

Preston, L.E. & Post, J.E. 1975, *Private management and public policy: the principle of public responsibility*, Prentice-Hall, Englewood Cliffs, N.J.

Pruzan, P.M. undated, *From optimization to transformation—my path to the wellspring of rationality, morality and spirituality*.

Putnam, R.D. 2000, *Bowling alone: the collapse and revival of American community*, Simon & Schuster, New York.

PWBLF 1998, *Managing Partnerships: tools for managing the public sector, business and civil society as partners in development*, Prince of Wales Business Leaders Forum, London.

PWC 2006, *Corporate responsibility: strategy, management and value*, PricewaterhouseCoopers, London; New York.

Quayle, M. 2003, "A study of supply chain management practice in UK industrial SMEs", *Supply Chain Management: An International Journal*, vol. 8, no. 1, pp 79–86.

Quinn, J. 2009, *Goldman chairman admits Wall St greed*, online edn, Daily Telegraph, London.

Quinn, T.K. 1962, *Unconscious public enemies*, Citadel Press, New York.

Rachels, J. 1999, *The elements of moral philosophy*, 3rd edn, McGraw-Hill College, Boston.

Radin, T.J. & Werhane, P.H. 2003, "Employment-at-will, employee rights, and future directions for employment", *Business Ethics Quarterly*, vol. 13, no. 2, pp 113–130.

Raimbaev, A. 2009, "Corporate Social Responsibility", *Global Perspectives on Corporate Governance and CSR*, pp 187.

Rajak, D. 2008, "'Uplift and empower': The market, the gift and corporate social responsibility on South Africa's platinum belt", *Research in Economic Anthropology*, vol. 28, pp 297–324.

Rajak, D. 2006, "The gift of CSR: power and the pursuit of responsibility in the mining industry", in *Corporate Citizenship in Africa: Lessons from the Past, Paths to the Future*, eds. W. Visser, M. McIntosh & C. Middleton, Greenleaf Publishing, Sheffield.

Rand, A. 1966, *Capitalism, the unknown ideal*, New American Library, New York.

Rangan, V.K. 2007, "Business solutions for the global poor: creating social and economic value", *Conference on Global Poverty: Business Solutions and Approaches*, ed. V.K. Rangan, Jossey-Bass; John Wiley & Sons, distributor, San Francisco, Calif.; Chichester.

Rangan, V.K., Quelch, J.A. & Herrero, G. 2007, *Business solutions for the social poor: creating social and economic value*, 1st edn, Jossey-Bass, San Francisco.

Ranganathan, J. 1999, "Signs of sustainability: measuring corporate environmental and social performance" in *Sustainable measures: evaluation and reporting of environmental and social performance*, eds. M. Bennett & P. James, Greenleaf, Sheffield, pp 475–495.

Ranganathan, J. 1998, *Sustainability rulers: measuring corporate, social, environmental and social performance*, World Resources Institute, Washington DC.

Rasche, A. & Esser, D.E. 2006, "From stakeholder management to stakeholder accountability: applying Habermasian discourse ethics to accountability research", *Journal of Corporate Citizenship*, no. 65, pp 251–267.

Raufflet, E. & Mills, A.J. (eds) 2009, *The dark side: critical cases on the downside of business*, Greenleaf, Sheffield.

Rawls, J. 1971, *A theory of justice*, Belknap Press of Harvard University Press, Cambridge, Mass.

Raynolds, L.T., Murray, D. & Leigh Taylor, P. 2004, "Fair trade: building producer capacity via global networks", *Journal of International Development*, no. 16, pp 1109–1121.

Redclift, M.R. 2000, *Sustainability: life chances and livelihoods*, Routledge, London; New York.

Reddy, D. 2008, "India", in *Sustainable investing: the art of long-term performance*, eds. C. Krosinsky & N. Robins, Earthscan, London, pp 165–176.

Reddy P.L.S. 2002, "Corporate Governance-Emerging Trends". *Corporate Governance*, vol. 1, no. 1.

Reich, R.B. 2007, *Supercapitalism: the transformation of business, democracy, and everyday life*, 1st edn, Alfred A. Knopf, New York.

Rembert, T.C. 2005, "CSR in the crosshairs: a broad counter-attack against corporate reform is growing. (Could that be a sign of progress?)", *Business Ethics*, vol. Spring 2005, pp 30–35.

Ricardo, D. 1817, *On the principles of political economy, and taxation*, J. Murray, London.

Ring, P.S., Bigley, G.A., D'Aunoo, T. & Khanna, T. 2005, "Perspectives on how governments matter", *Adademy of Management Review*, vol. 30, no. 2, pp 308–320.

Robertson, R. 1992, *Globalization: Social Theory and Global Culture*, Sage Pubns.

Robins, N. 2008, "The emergence of sustainable investing" in *Sustainable investing: the art of long-term performance*, eds. C. Krosinsky & N. Robins, Earthscan, London, pp 3–17.

Robins, N. 2007, "The imperious company", *Journal of Corporate Citizenship*, no. 25, pp 31–42.

Rockoff, J. & Kendall, B. 2009, *Corporate News: Pfizer Pleads Guilty to Improper Marketing*, 3 September 2009 edn.

Roddick, A. 2000, *Business as unusual*, Thorsons, London.

Rodrik, D. 1997, *Has globalization gone too far?* Institute for International Economics, Washington, D.C.

Ronchi, L. 2002, *Impact of fair trade on producers and their organisations: a case study with Coocafe in Costa Rica*, Poverty Research Unit, University of Sussex, Falmer.

Rondinelli, D.A. 2002, "Transnational Corporations: international citizens or new sovereigns?", *Business and Society Review*, vol. 107, no. 4, pp 391–413.

Roner, L. 2005, *Seeing is believing: the Business Roundtable SEE Change initiatives on corporate sustainability*.

Rose, S. 2007, "Back in fashion: how we're reviving a British icon (Marks & Spencer)", *Harvard business review*, vol. May, no. May 2007, pp 51–57.

Rosenberg, H. 1999, *A traitor to his class: Robert A.G. Monks and the battle to change corporate America*, John Wiley & Sons, New York.

Rosenberg, J. 2000, *The Follies of globalisation theory: polemical essays*, Verso, London.

Rowledge, L.R. 1999, *Mapping the journey: case studies in strategy and action toward sustainable development*, Greenleaf, Sheffield.

Rowley, T.J. & Moldoveanu, M. 2003, "When will stakeholder groups act? An interest- and identity-based model of stakeholder group mobilization", *The Academy of Management Review*, vol. 28, no. 2, pp 204–219.

Ruggie, J.G. 2003, "Taking embedded liberalism global: the corporate connection", in *Taming Globalization: Frontiers of Governance.Polity Press, Cambridge*, eds. D. Held & M. Koenig-Archibugi, Polity Press, Cambridge.

Ruggie, J., Wright, M. & Lehr, A. 2006, *Business recognition of human rights: global patterns, regional and sectoral variations*, United Nations Human Rights Commission, Geneva.

Runciman, D. 2003, "Partnering the state", *Partnership Matters*, vol. 1, pp 12–15.

Runping, Y, 2006, "Business starts taking social responsibility seriously", *China View*, 17 May, online at **news.xinhuanet.com**.

Rusbridger, A. 2009, *A chill on 'The Guardian'*, January 15, 2009 edn, New York Review of Books, New York.

Russo, A. & Tencati, A. 2009, "Formal vs. informal CSR strategies: evidence from Italian micro, small, medium-sized, and large firms", *Journal of Business Ethics*, vol. 85, pp 339–353.

Russo, A. & Perrini, F. 2010, "Investigating Stakeholder Theory and Social Capital: CSR in Large Firms and SMEs", *Journal of Business Ethics*, vol. 91, no. 2, pp 207–221.

Sabapathy, J., Swift, T., Weiser, J. & Polycarpe, M. undated, *Innovation through partnership*, Accountability and Brody-Weiser-Burns, London.

Saha, P, 2006, "Doing ethics the Tata way", *Ethical Corporation*, June, pp 26–8.

Saha, P. 2005, 'Shopping around: a leaked company document may dampen the Christmas spirit at Asda' *Ethical Corporation*, December 2005, online edition.

SAI 1999, *Guidance Document for Social Accountability 8000*, Social Accountability International, New York.

Saith, A. 2006, "From Universal Values to Millennium Development Goals: Lost in Translation", *Development and Change*, vol. 37, no. 6, pp 1167–1199.

Salamon, L.M. 2003, *The resilient sector: the state of nonprofit America*, Brookings Institution; University Presses Marketing, distributor, Washington, D.C.; Bristol.

Salzmann, O., Ionescu-Somers, A. & Steger, U. 2005, "The Business Case for Corporate Sustainability: Literature Review and Research Options", *European Management Journal*, vol. 23, no. 1, pp 27–36.

Sampson, G.P. 2005, *The world trade organization and sustainable development*, United Nations University, Tokyo.

Sampson, G.P. 2001, *The role of the World Trade Organization in global governance*, United Nations University Press, Tokyo; New York.

SAM-PWC 2008, *Sustainability year book 2008*, Sustainable Asset Management and PriceWaterhouse Coopers, unknown.

Satre, L.J. 2005, *Chocolate on trial: slavery, politics, and the ethics of business*, 1st edn, Ohio University Press, Athens, Ohio.

Save the Children *Big business, small hands: responsible approaches to child labour*, Save the Children, London.

Scammell, M. 2000, "The Internet and Civic Engagement: The Age of the Citizen-Consumer", *Political Communication*, vol. 17, no. 4, pp 351–355.

Schafer, H. 2005, "International corporate social responsibility rating systems: conceptual outline and empirical results", *Journal of Corporate Citizenship*, no. 20, pp 107–120.

Scherer, A.G. & Palazzo, G. 2007, "Toward a Political Conception of Corporate Responsibility-Business and Society Seen from a Habermasian Perspective", *Academy of Management Review*, vol. 32, pp 1096–1120.

Schiller, B. 2006, "Turkish progress: sampling the delights of corporate responsibility", *Ethical Corporation*, June 2006, online edition.

Schirato, T. & Webb, J. 2003, *Understanding globalization*, Sage Publications, London; Thousand Oaks, Calif.

Schmidheiny, S. 2006, "A view of corporate citizenship in Latin America", *Journal of Corporate Citizenship*, vol. 21, pp 21–24.

Schmidheiny, S. 1992, *Changing course: a global business perspective on development and the environment*, MIT Press, Cambridge, Mass.

Schmidheiny, S. & World Business Council for Sustainable Development. 1996, *Financing change: the financial community, eco-efficiency, and sustainable development*, MIT Press, Cambridge, Mass.; London.

Scholte, J.A. 2000, *Globalization: a critical introduction*, St. Martin's Press, New York.

Schwartz, M.S. & Carroll, A.B. 2003, "Corporate Social Responsibility: a three domain approach", *Business Ethics Quarterly*, vol. 13, no. 4, pp 503–530.

Schwartz, P. & Gibb, B. 1999, *When good companies do bad things: responsibility and risk in an age of globalization*, John Wiley & Sons, New York.

Scott, L. 2005, *Twenty first century leadership*, Speech by Lee Scott, CEO, Wal-Mart edn.

Scrase, H., Wenban-Smith, M. & Judd, N. 1999, *Certification of Forest Products for Small Businesses: improving access—issues and options. Report for the Department for International Development*, London.

Seeger, M.W. & Ulmer, R.R. 2001, "Virtuous Responses to Organizational Crisis: Aaron Feuerstein and Milt Colt", *Journal of Business Ethics*, vol. 31, no. 4.

Seidman, G.W. 2003, "Monitoring Multinationals: Lessons from the Anti-Apartheid Era", *Politics Society*, vol. 31, pp 381–406.

Seidman, G.W., 2004, *Deflated citizenship: labor rights in a global era*. In Alison Brysk and Gershon Shafir, editors People out of place: globalization, human rights, and the citizenship gap, Routledge, New York, pp 109–129.

Sen, A.K. 2000, *Development as freedom*, Anchor books, New York.

Sethi, S.P. 1975, "Dimensions of Corporate Social Performance: An Analytical Framework", *California Management Review*, vol. 17, no. 3, pp 58–65.

Sethi, S.P. 2003, *Setting global standards: guidelines for creating codes of conduct in multinational corporations*, John Wiley & Sons, Hoboken, N.J.

Sewing, T, 2006, "Mired in the regulation debate", *Ethical Corporation*, January, pp 13–14.

Shaw, M. 2000, *Theory of the global state: globality as unfinished revolution*, Cambridge University Press, Cambridge.

Shaw, M. 1999, *Politics and globalisation: knowledge, ethics and agency*, Routledge, London; New York.

Singer, N. 2009, *Judge Orders Former Bristol-Myers Executive to Write Book*, 9 June 2009.

Skapkinker, M. 2009, *Consumers are savvy about organic food*, UK edn, Financial Times, London.

Sklair, L. 2002, *Globalization: capitalism and its alternatives*, Oxford University Press, Oxford; New York.

Skocpol, T. 2003, *Diminished democracy: from membership to management in American civic life*, University of Oklahoma Press, Norman.

Smart, J.J.C. & Williams, B.A.O. 1973, *Utilitarianism; for and against*, University Press, Cambridge, Eng.

Smith, N.C. 2003, "Corporate social responsibility: whether or how?", *California Management Review*, vol. 45, no. 14, pp 52–76.

Smith, A. 1976, *The theory of moral sentiments*, Clarendon Press, Oxford.

Smith, A. 1776, *An inquiry into the nature and causes of the wealth of nations*, Whitestone, Dublin.

Smith, A. 1759, *The theory of moral sentiments*, A. Millar, London.

Smith, C. 2009, *Mainstreaming corporate responsibility*, John Wiley & Sons, Hoboken, N.J.; Chichester.

Smith, N.C. 2003, "Corporate social responsibility: whether or how?", *California Management Review*, vol. 45, no. 14, pp 52–76.

Solomon, J. 2004, *Corporate governance and accountability*, John Wiley & Sons, Chichester.

SOMO 2005, *SOMO research finds violations in computer factories.*

Soros, G. 2008, *The new paradigm for financial markets: the credit crisis of 2008 and what it means*, 1st edn, PublicAffairs, New York.

Sorell, T, & Hendry, J. 1994, Business Ethics, Butterworth-Heinemann, Oxford.

Southern, A. 2009, *Enterprise and deprivation: small business, social exclusion and sustainable communities*, Routledge, London.

Sparkes, R. 2002, *Socially responsible investment: a global revolution*, John Wiley & Sons, New York.

Spence, L.J. 2007, "CSR and Small Business in a European Policy Context: The Five 'C's of CSR and Small Business Research Agenda 2007", *Business and Society Review*, vol. 112, no. 4, pp 533–552.

Spence, L.J. & Rutherford, R. 2001, "Social responsibility, profit maximisation and the small firm owner-manager", *Journal of Small Business and Enterprise Development*, vol. 8, no. 2, pp 126–139.

Spence, L.J., Schmidpeter, R. & Habisch, A. 2003, "Assessing social capital: small and medium sized enterprises in Germany and the UK", *Journal of Business Ethics*, vol. 47, no. 1, pp 17–29.

Spidla, V. 2006, *Corporate social responsibility: the European perspective.*

Stacey, J. 2003, "A global partnership with a mining multinational: exploring and realising the capacity for strategic biodiversity conservation", *Partnership Matters*, vol. 1, pp. 25–29.

Starbuck, W.H., 2005, "Four great conflicts of the twenty-first century", in *Leadership and management in the Twenty-First Century*, ed. C.L. Cooper, Oxford University Press, Oxford, pp 21–55

Steger, U. 2004, *The business of sustainability: building industry cases for corporate sustainability*, Palgrave Macmillan, Basingstoke.

Steger, M.B. 2003, *Globalization: a very short introduction*, Oxford University Press, Oxford; New York.

Stern, S, 2006, "Corporate responsibility and the curse of the three-letter acronym", *Financial Times*, 30 May, online at **www.ft.com**.

Stern, N.H. 2009, *A blueprint for a safer planet: how to manage climate change and create a new era of progress and prosperity*, Bodley Head, London.

Stevens, D., Kim, A., Mukhamedova, L., Mukimova, M. & Wagner, R. 2008, "How Far Can CSR Travel? Reflections on the Applicability of the Concept to SMEs in Uzbekistan", *The Ashgate Research Companion to Corporate Social Responsibility*, pp 319.

Stewart, T.A. & Immelt, J. 2006, "Growth as a process", *Harvard Business Review*, vol. June 2006, pp 60–70.

Stiglitz, J.E. 2002, *Globalization and its discontents*, W. W. Norton, New York.

Stiglitz, J.E. 2005, *Fair trade for all: how trade can promote development*, Oxford University Press, Oxford.

Stopford, J.M., Strange, S. & Henley, J.S. 1991, *Rival states, rival firms: competition for world market shares*, Cambridge University Press, Cambridge; New York.

Strange, S. 1996, *The Retreat of the state: the diffusion of power in the world economy*, Cambridge University Press, New York.

Sullivan, R. 2003, Business and Human Rights: Dilemmas and Solutions, Sheffield: Greenleaf Publishing.

Sum, N.L. 2009, "Controlling the Supply Chain through CSR: Wal-Martization in China", in *Corporate social responsibility and regulatory governance: towards inclusive development?*, eds. P. Utting & J.C. Marques, 1st edn, Palgrave Macmillan, New York.

SustainAbility, IFC & Ethos, I. 2002, *Developing Value: the business case for sustainability in emerging markets*, London.

SustainAbility & UNEP 2002, *Trust us: the global reporters 2002 survey of corporate sustainability reporting*, SustainAbility and United Nations Environment Programme, London.

SustainAbility & UNEP 2001, *Business case buried treasure: uncovering the business case for corporate sustainability*, SustainAbility/United Nations Environment Programme.

Sutcliffe, H. 2005, "Finding the CR structure that fits your organization", in *How to structure the corporate responsibility function*, ed. Melcrum, London, pp 6–10.

Svendsen, A. & Laberge, M. 2005, "Convening stakeholder networks: a new way of thinking, being and engaging", *Journal of Corporate Citizenship, Issue*, vol. 19.

Swenson, P. 1989, *Fair shares: unions, pay, and politics in Sweden and West Germany*, Cornell University Press, Ithaca.

Taibbi, M. 2009, *Inside the great American bubble machine*, Rolling Stone, San Francisco.

Tencati, A., Russo, A. & Quaglia, V. 2008, "Unintended consequences of CSR: protectionism and collateral damage in global supply chains: the case of Vietnam", *Corporate Governance*, vol. 8, no. 4, pp 518–531.

Thankappan, S., Hitchens, D. & Trainor, M. 2004, *Dichotomy between attitudes and environmental performance: a case of European SMEs*, Centre for Business Relationships, Accountability, Sustainability and Society at Cardiff University, Cardiff.

Tharoor, S. 2001, "Are Human Rights Universal?", *New Internationalist*, vol. 332, pp 34–35.

The Economist 1999, *The key to industrial capitalism: limited liability*.

Thornber, K. 2000, *Impacts of certification on forests, stakeholders and markets: case study Bainings ecoforestry project*, London, IIED.

Thornber, K. 1999, *An Overview of Global Trends in FSC Certification*, International Institute for Environment and Development, London.

Thurow, L.C. 1996, *The future of capitalism: how today's economic forces shape tomorrow's world*, 1st edn, W. Morrow, New York.

Tinker, A.M. & Lowe, E.A. "Rationale for corporate social reporting: theory, evidence from organizational research", *Journal of Business Finance and Accounting*, pp 1–15.

Tinker, T. 1985, *Paper prophets: a social critique of accounting*, Praeger, New York.

Toffler, A. 1980, *The third wave*, 1st edn, Morrow, New York.

Traidcraft 2005, *Traidcraft social accounts 2004–2005*, Traidcraft, Gateshead.

Tropenbos 1997, *Hierarchical framework for the formulation of sustainable forest management standards: principles, criteria and indicators*, Tropenbos Foundation, Leiden.

Tsalikis, J. & Seaton, B. 2008, "Consumer Perceptions of Business Ethical Behavior in Former Eastern Block Countries", *Journal of Business Ethics*, vol. 82, no. 4, pp 919–928.

Tschopp, D.J. 2005, "Corporate social responsibility: a comparison between the United States and the European Union", *Corporate social responsibility and environmental management*, vol. 12, pp 55–59.

Tsoukas, H. & Knudsen, C. 2003, *The Oxford handbook of organization theory*, Oxford University Press, USA.

Tucker, R, 2006, "The next level of corporate responsibility", *Women's Wear Daily*, 16 May, online at **www.wwd.com**.

Tulder, R.v. 2006, *International business-society management: linking corporate responsibility and globalization*, Routledge, London.

Turner, R.K. 1994, *Environmental economics: an elementary introduction*, Harvester Wheatsheaf, New York; London.

UKSIF 2009, *Responsible business: sustainable investment*, UK Social Investment Forum, London.

UN 2005, *Business UNusual*, United Nations, New York.

UN 2003, *Water for people, water for life: world water development report*, United Nations, New York.

UNDP, 2009, Global Compact—Small and medium-sized enterprises on their way towards global responsibility, New York: United Nations Development programme.

UNEP FI & Mercer 2007, *Demystifying responsible investment performance: a review of key academic and broker research on ESG factors*, UNEP Finance Initiative and Mercer, unknown.

UNEP, Accountability & Stakeholder Research Associates 2005, *Stakeholder engagement manual—from words to action: Vol. 1 the guide to practioners' perspectives on stakeholder engagement*, United Nations Environmental Programme, Accountability and Stakeholder Research Associates, New York.

UNIDO 2002, *Corporate Social Responsibility: Implications for Small and Medium Enterprises in Developing Countries*, United Nations Industrial Development Organization, Vienna.

Unilever 2005, *Environmental report 2004*, Unilever, London.

Uphoff, N.T. 1996, *Learning from Gal Oya: possibilities for participatory development and post-Newtonian social science*, IT Publications, London.

Upton, C. & Earthscan 1995, *The forest certification handbook*, Earthscan, London.

Uren, S. 2007, *Hall of shame: which companies are the worst polluters?*, Guardian Newspapers, London.

Utting, P. 2007, *CSR and equality*, Third World Foundation for Social and Economic Studies, London.

Utting, P. 2005, *Rethinking business regulation: from self-regulation to social control*, United Nations Research Institute for Social Development, Geneva.

Utting, P. & Marques, J.C. (eds) 2009, *Corporate social responsibility and regulatory governance: towards inclusive development?*, Palgrave Macmillan, New York.

Utting, P. & Zammit, A. 2006, *Beyond pragmatism: appraising UN-business partnerships*, UNRISD, Geneva.

Varley, P., Mathiasen, C., Voorhes, M. 1998, *The sweatshop quandary: corporate responsibility on the global frontier*, Investor Responsibility Research Center, Washington, DC.

Veblen, T.B. 1904, *The Theory of Business Enterprise*, pp vii. 400. Charles Scribner's Sons, New York.

Veer, v.d., J. 2007, *States should create a climate for change*.

Veitch, M. 2006, *Going green will keep firms in the pink*.

Velasco, G. 2005, "Cross-sector partnership in action: a framework for knowledge management", *Partnership Matters*, vol. 3, pp 10–14.

Verite 2004, *Excessive overtime in Chinese supplier factories: causes, impacts and recommendations for action*, Verite, Amherst Mass.

Vernon, P. 2007, *Stuart Rose is the UK's greenest grocer. His mission: to turn Marks & Spencer carbon neutral by 2012*, The Observer, London.

Vidal, J. 1997, *McLibel: burger culture on trial*, New Press, New York.

Virilio, P. 2000, *The information bomb*, Verso, New York, N.Y.

Visser, W. 2005, "Revisiting Carroll's pyramid: an African perspective", in *Corporate citizenship in developing countries*, eds. E.R. Pdersen & M. Huniche, Copenhagen Centre, Copenhagen.

Visser, W., McIntosh, M. & Middleton, C. (eds) 2006, *Corporate citizenship in Africa: lessons from the past; paths to the future*, Greenleaf Publishing, Sheffield, UK.

Visser, W., Matten, D., Pohl, M. & Tolhurst, N. eds 2007, *The A to Z of corporate social responsibility: a complete reference guide to concepts, codes and organisations*, John Wiley & Sons, Chichester.

Visser, W. & Tolhurst, N. (eds) 2010, *The world guide to CSR*, Greenleaf, Sheffield.

Vogel, D. 2008, *CSR doesn't pay*, www.Forbes.com.

Vogel, D. 2005, *The market for virtue: the potential and limits of corporate social responsibility*, Brookings Institution Press, Washington, D.C.

von Hayek, F.A. 1960, *The constitution of liberty*, University of Chicago Press, Chicago.

von Hayek, F.A. 1944, *The road to serfdom*, G. Routledge & sons, London.

Waddell, S. 2000, "New Institutions for the Practice of Corporate Citizenship: Historical, Intersectoral, and Developmental Perspectives", *Business and Society Review*, vol. 105, no. 1, pp 107.

Waddock, S. 2005, *Corporate citizenship: the dark-side paradoxes of success*.

Waddock, S. 2001, "Integrity and Mindfulness: Foundations of Corporate Citizenship", *Journal of Corporate Citizenship*, vol. 1, pp 25–37.

Waddock, S.A. & Graves, S.B. 1997, "The corporate social performance–financial performance link", *Strategic Management Journal*, vol. 18, no. 4, pp 303–319.

Waddock, S. & Bodwell, C. 2002, "From TQM to TRM: total responsibility management approaches", *Journal of Corporate Citizenship*, vol. 7, p 113.

Waddock, S.A. 2006, *Leading corporate citizens: vision, values, value-added*, 2nd edn, McGraw-Hill, Boston, Mass.

Walker, R.B.J. 1994, "Social movements/world politics", *Millennium: Journal of International Studies*, vol. 23, no. 3, pp 669–700.

Wall Street Journal 2005, *Corporate social concerns: are they good citizenship or a rip-off for investors*.

Wall, C. 2007, *Kazakh public policy and corporate social responsibility: an analysis of health care provision in an era of CSR and Kazakh nationalism*, Presented at the Conference on Business, Social Policy and Corporate Political Influence in Developing Countries, 12–13 November, 2007, Geneva, Switzerland.

Wallerstein, I.M. 1978, *The capitalist world-economy: essays*, Cambridge University Press, Cambridge Eng.; New York.

Wallerstein, I.M. 1974, *The modern world-system*, Academic Press, New York.

Walsh, J.P. 2005, "Book review essay: Taking stock of stakeholder management", *Academy of Management Review*, vol. 30, no. 2, pp 426–452.

War on Want 2005, *Caterpillar: the alternative report*, War on Want, London.

War on Want & GMB 2005, *Asda Wal-Mart: the alternative report*.

Ward, H. 2003, *Legal issues in corporate citizenship*, Interational Institute for Environment and Development, London.

Warhurst, A. & Noronha, L. 2000, *Environmental policy in mining: corporate strategy and planning for closure*, Lewis, Boca Raton.

Warner, M. 2004, "Getting started", in *Putting partnerships to work*, eds. M. Warner & R. Sullivan, Greenleaf Publishing, Sheffield, pp 166–181.

Warner, M. & Sullivan, R. 2004, *Putting partnerships to work: strategic alliances for development between government, the private sector and civil society*, Greenleaf Publishing, Sheffield.

Wartick, S.L. & Cochran, P.L., 1985, "The evolution of the corporate social performance model", *Academy of Management Review*, vol. 10, no. 4, pp 758–769.

Waters, R. 2010, *Google in fresh retreat on Buzz*, FT. com edn, Financial Times, London.

Waters, M. 2001, *Globalization*, 2nd edn, Routledge, London; New York.

Watkins, K. 1997, *Globalization and liberalization: implications for poverty, distribution and inequality*, United Nations Development, New York.

Watts, R. 2009, *Google avoids £100m UK tax*, TimesOnline edn, The Times, London.

WBCSD 2007, *Doing Business with the World: The New Role of Corporate Leadership in Global Development*, World Business Council for Sustainable Development, Geneva.

WBCSD 2006, *Doing Business with the World: The New Role of Corporate Leadership in Global Development*, World Business Council for Sustainable Development, Geneva.

WBCSD 2005, *Business for development: business solutions in support of the Millennium Development Goals*, World Business Council for Sustainable Development, Geneva.

WDM, War on Want, NUS & Friends of the Earth 2005, *2005 and sustainable development*, World Development Movement, War on Want, National Union of Students and Friends of the Earth, London.

Weber, M., Parsons, T. & Giddens, A. 1992, *The Protestant ethic and the spirit of capitalism*, Routledge, London; New York.

Weinberg, A. & Weinberg, L.S. 1961, *The muckrakers; the era in journalism that moved America to reform, the most significant magazine articles of 1902–1912*, Simon and Schuster, New York.

Weinstein, J.R. 2001, *On Adam Smith*, Wadsworth/Thompson Learning, Australia; Belmont, CA.

Weiser, J., Kahane, M., Rochlin, S. & Landis, J. 2006, *Untapped assets: Creating value in underserved markets*, Berrett-Koehler, San Francisco.

Weiser, J. & Rochlin, S. 2004, "Walking in order to run: practical challenges in measuring community and economic development", *AccountAbility Forum*, vol. 1, no. 1, pp 26–32.

Weiser, J. & Zadek, S. 2000, *Conversations with disbelievers: persuading companies to address social challenges*, BrodyWeiser, New York.

Wei-Skillern, J. 2004, "The evolution of Shell's stakeholder approach: a case study", *Business Ethics Quarterly*, vol. 14, no. 4, pp 713–728.

Weiss, L. 1998, *The myth of the powerless state*, Cornell University Press, Ithaca, NY.

Welford, R. 2004, *Corporate social responsibility in Europe, North America and Asia: 2004 survey results*, Hong Kong.

Welford, R. 1995, *Environmental Strategy and Sustainable Development: the corporate challenge for the 21st century*, Routledge, London.

Werhane, P.H. & Freeman, R.E. 1997, *The Blackwell encyclopedic dictionary of business ethics*, Blackwell, Oxford.

Werther, W.B. & Chandler, D. 2011, *Strategic corporate social responsibility: stakeholders in a global environment*, 2nd edn, SAGE Publications, Thousand Oaks.

Werther, W.B. & Chandler, D. 2006, *Strategic corporate social responsibility: stakeholders in a global environment*, SAGE Publications, Thousand Oaks.

Wettstein, F. 2005, "For causality to capability: toward a new understanding of the multinational corporation's enlarged social responsibilities", *Journal of Corporate Citizenship*, vol. 19, pp 105–117.

Weybrecht, G. 2009, *The sustainable MBA: the manager's guide to green business*, John Wiley & Sons, Hoboken, N.J.

Whalley, J. 2001, "World Trade Organization", in *International encyclopedia of the social and behavioral sciences*, eds. N.J. Smelser & P.B. Baltes, Elsevier Science, Oxford, pp 16613–16616.

White, C. 2006, "The spirit of disobedience", *Harpers*, April 2006, pp 31–40.

Wick, A. 2001, *Workers' Tool or PR Ploy? A guide to codes of international labour practice*, Friedrich-Ebert-Stiftung/SÜDWIND Institut für Ökonomie und Ökumene, Bonn.

Wiesmann, G. & Simensen, I. 2007, "German blue chips ponder switch to SE format", *Financial Times*, 12 April, pp 24.

Wijnberg, N. 2000, "Normative Stakeholder Theory and Aristotle: the link between ethics and politics", *Journal of Business Ethics*, no. 25, pp 329–342.

Willard, B. 2002, *The sustainability advantage: seven business case benefits of a triple bottom line*, New Society, Gabriola Island, B.C.

Williams, O.F. 2004, "The UN Global Compact: the challenge and the promise", *Business Ethics Quarterly*, vol. 14, no. 4, pp 755–774.

Willums, J., World Business Council for Sustainable Development, United Nations Environment Programme, Bellagio Forum for Sustainable Development & Foundation for Business and Sustainable Development. 1998, *The sustainable business challenge: a briefing for tomorrow's business leaders*, Greenleaf, Sheffield.

Wilson, C. 2006, *Make poverty business: increase profits and reduce risks by engaging with the poor*, Greenleaf, Sheffield.

Windsor, D. 2001, "Corporate citizenship: evolution and interpretation", in *Perspectives on corporate citizenship*, eds. J. Andriof & M. McIntosh, Greenleaf, Sheffield, pp 39–52.

Wines, M. 2010, *Is Google case a rights bellwether?*, International Herald Trbune, Paris.

Wohlmeyer, H. & Quendler, T. (eds) 2001, *The WTO, agriculture and sustainable development*, Greenleaf, Sheffield.

Woidtke, T., Bierman, L. & Tuggle, C. 2003, "Reining in activist funds", *Harvard Business Review*, no. March 2003.

Wolf, M. 2004, *Why globalization works*, Yale University Press, New Haven.

Wolff, J. 1991, *Robert Nozick: property, justice, and the minimal state*, Stanford University Press, Stanford, Calif.

Wood, D.J. & Logsdon, J.M. 2001, "Theorising business citizenship", in *Perspectives on Corporate Citizenship*, eds. J. Andriof & M. McIntosh, Greenleaf Publishing, Sheffield, pp 83–103.

Wood, D.J. & Logsdon, J.M. 2002, "Business Citizenship: From Individuals to Organizations", *Ethics and Entrepreneurship: The Ruffin Series*, vol. 3, pp 59–94.

Wood, D. 2000, "Theory and Integrity in business and society", *Business and Society*, vol. 39, no. 4, pp 359–378.

Wood, D.J., Logsdon, J.M., Lewellyn, P.G. & Davenport, P.G. 2006, *Global business citizenship: a transformative framework for ethics and sustainable capitalism*, M.E. Sharpe, Inc., Armonk, N.Y.

Wood, E.M. 1995, *Democracy against capitalism: renewing historical materialism*, Cambridge University Press, Cambridge.

World Bank 2006, *World development report 2006: equity and development*, World Bank; Palgrave distributor, Washington, D.C.; Basingstoke.

World Bank 2005, *World development report 2005: Better Investment Climate For Everyone*, World Bank; Palgrave distributor, Washington, D.C.; Basingstoke.

World Bank 2003, *Strengthening the implementation of corporate social responsibility in global supply chains*, The World Bank, Washington DC.

World Bank Group 2003, *Company codes of conduct and international standards: an analytical comparison vol. 1*, World Bank Group Social Responsibility Practice, Washington DC.

World Commission on Environment and Development & Brundtland, G.H. 1987, *Our common future*, Oxford University Press, Oxford.

World Economic Forum 2006, *Harnessing private sector capabilities to meet public needs: the potential of partnerships to advance progress on hunger, malaria and basic education*, World Economic Forum, Geneva.

WRI 2002, *Tomorrow's markets: global trends and their implicatins for business*, World Business Council for Sustainable Development, Washington DC.

WRI & WBCSD 2004, *The greenhouse gas protocol: a corporate accounting and reporting standard*, World Resources Institute/World Business Council on Sustainable Development.

Wright, C. & Rwabizambuga, A. 2006, "Institutional pressures, corporate reputation, and voluntary codes of conduct: an examination of the equator principles", *Business and Society Review*, vol. 111, pp 89.

Wright, T. 2007, *Indonesian proposal: Pay us not to chop down our trees*, New York.

Wright, S. & Rees, S. 2000, *Human rights and corporate responsibility*, Pluto Press.

WWF & SustainAbility 2005, *Influencing Power: reviewing the conduct and content of corporate lobbying*, WWF and Sustainability, London.

Yunus, M. 1998, *Banker to the poor: the autobiography of Muhammad Yunus, founder of the Grameen Bank*, Aurum, London.

Zadek, S. 2004, "The path to corporate responsibility", *Harvard Business Review*, vol. 82, no. 12, pp 125–133.

Zadek, S. 2002, *Third Generation Corporate Citizenship*, Foreign Policy Centre/ AccountAbility, London.

Zadek, S., Raynard, P. & Oliveira, C. 2005, *Responsible competitiveness: reshaping global markets through responsible business practices*, AccountAbility, London.

Zadek, S., Sabapathy, J., Dossing, H. & Swift, T. 2003, *Responsible competitiveness: corporate responsibility clusters in action*, AccountAbility, London.

Zadek, S. *Doing good and doing well: making the business case for corporate citizenship*, Conference Board, New York, NY.

Zadek, S. 2001, *The civil corporation: the new economy of corporate citizenship*, Earthscan Publications Ltd, London.

Zadek, S., Foreign Policy Centre & Institute of Social and Ethical AccountAbility 2001, *Third generation corporate citizenship: public policy and business in society*, The Foreign Policy Centre, London.

Zadek, S., Pruzan, P.M. & Evans, R. 1997, *Building corporate accountability: emerging practices in social and ethical accounting, auditing and reporting*, Earthscan, London.

Zakhem, A.J., Palmer, D.E. & Stoll, M.L. 2007, *Stakeholder theory: essential readings in ethical leadership and management*, Prometheus Books, Amherst, N.Y.

Zenisek, T.J. 1979, "Corporate Social Responsibility: A Conceptualization Based On Organizational Literature", *Academy of Management Review*, vol. 4, no. 3, pp 359–369.

Zimmerman, A., Matthews, R.G. & Hudson, C. 2005, *Can employers alter hiring policies to cut health costs?* Wall Street Journal, October 27 2005, online edition.

■ NAME INDEX

■ SUBJECT INDEX